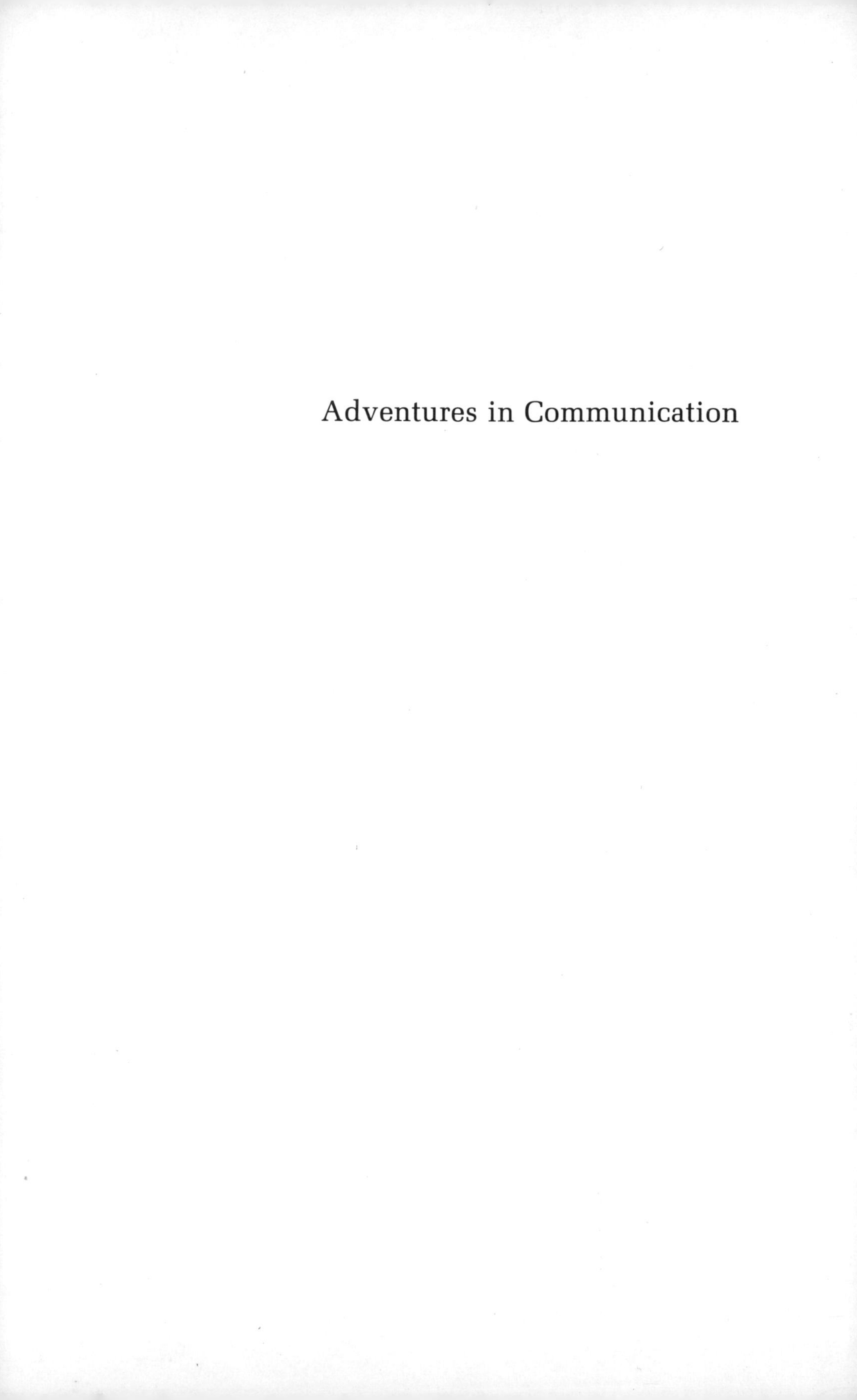

Adventures in Communication

Adventures in Communication: Language Arts Methods

James A. Smith

State University of New York
at Oswego

Allyn and Bacon, Inc. Boston

Seventh printing . . . December, 1972

470 Atlantic Avenue, Boston, Mass. 02210

Library of Congress Catalog Card Number: 78–185291

Printed in the United States of America

To my boys

MICHAEL
and
SCOTT

Contents

Preface

This is a book about creative teachers in action.

They are creative teachers because they teach differently from other teachers; they teach in *their own way*, not in the way prescribed by textbooks or dictated by manuals. Their methodology is sound; it is based on tried and proven principles of learning and child development, and they get results, but the means are different, unusual, and unique.

Because their methods are different from those of the run-of-the-mill teacher, creative teachers make each day in their classrooms an adventure, a series of new experiences for the children. They motivate children so highly to learn that each pupil finds his place as a worthwhile, contributing member of a congenial group. "Discipline" problems are minimized; creative production abounds.

These teachers function in all kinds of schools. They teach in ghetto schools among children with impoverished backgrounds of experience. They teach in the affluent suburbs, in the inner-city schools, in the periphery schools of the large cities, in small-town schools, and in central schools. They are teachers of the dull, the disadvantaged, the retarded, the handicapped, the brilliant, and the average. The one thing they all have in common is their ability to reach children and to teach them creatively.

This is also a book about communication: How it is learned, how it is developed, and how it is effectively put to use. In this book you will not find the so-called recommended "drills" of the past, the dull textbook and workbook exercises that have characterized the language arts program in the American public school for so many years. This book is based on the concept that the major difference between man and other animals is that man has a brain which is so developed that he can create language and thereby communicate. The development of this skill of communication is the greatest adventure in Man's life. Without it he cannot reason, make known his ideas, or absorb the ideas of others. Without it he cannot develop understandings, create empathy, project sympathy, acquire knowledge, or express himself to his universe.

The inability of many people in today's culture to communicate is living testimony to the fact that much of the language teaching in the public schools up to the present time has been largely ineffective. Part of this is due to the great emphasis placed on "correct" communication and the small emphasis on "effective" communication. This "correct" communication stressed in the public-school program has often consisted of spending time on written exercises, of squelching oral communication, and of preparing children for some mystic time in the future when they will need something they are learning in the present. Most of the time such instruction serves to confuse the child and results in the learning of two communication systems: one for talking and writing in school, the other for communicating outside of school. The schools have not been "telling it like it is!"

All of which leads us to the matter of relevancy. Throughout the country today, students on college campuses are telling us what it is that educators and teachers have left out of their education: relevancy! And they are not necessarily talking about relevancy in their college education. My interviews with hundreds of young college students entering teacher education have repeatedly brought out in bold type one specific concept: They are tired to death of sitting behind desks filling in meaningless blanks in insipid workbooks; of always being told what to do, and never being able to say what they think; of being told what to learn but having no part in that learning; of being the victims of a decal process that makes education a veneer rather than a sound preparation for life. These young people are now reaching the age where they are away from the pressures of home and high school, and their first chance to exercise their freedom as individuals has caused them to rebel with hostility and frustration against the system which kept them enslaved for years and makes little or no provision for each to "do his thing." The revolt is not against the college so much as it is against a long sequence of teaching and learning to which they attach no relevance.

Relevancy, individuality, and creativity: These are what this book is all about. It is about teachers who respect children enough to make their teachings relevant to them here and now, who see our greatest national resource to be the individuality within each person, and who seek to preserve that individuality through planned, creative, meaningful experiences which, in the language arts program, are truly adventures in communication. This book retells many of those adventures.

This volume is intended for two audiences: (1) the teacher-in-service who may feel a need to bring herself up to date on current research and philosophies of teaching the language arts program, and (2) the teacher-in-training who may see that teaching, although based on sound truths and principles, is, nevertheless, as exciting and rewarding as her own creative powers can make it.

Not all the material in this volume is new. In 1967, the author published a book entitled *Creative Teaching of the Language Arts in the Elementary School* as part of the Allyn and Bacon Creativity Series. This book was so well received that a more detailed and comprehensive volume was requested. Another book in that series was also well received, *Setting Conditions for Creative Teaching in the Elementary School*. The author has drawn heavily on these two volumes.

Some of my readers will dislike the use of the personal pronoun "she," which I employ throughout the book when I refer to the teacher. In many instances, I refer to a specific person and, wherever possible, use names, both male and female. In spite of the fact that I observed many creative males at work, the vast majority of the teachers with whom I worked were women, and I justify the use of "she" in referring to them simply because I had a specific person in mind and it was more comfortable writing that way.

The author is indebted to many people for new materials presented in this edition. Many of the illustrations are accounts of his own adventures with children, but many are those sent to him by teachers with whom he has worked. To these creative teachers he owes a special debt of gratitude. They are the hope of our nation.

I should also like to thank the many children who granted me permission to use their materials, my creative student teachers who were often more adventurous in their teaching than their master teachers, and the many school superintendents, teachers, and students who allowed me to work in their classrooms.

Special acknowledgement must be made to the following people who continue to fan the creative spark in children and who have supplied me with beautiful reading: Mrs. June Anderson, Norfolk Public Schools, Virginia; Mrs. Ruth Baxter, Utica, New York, Public Schools; Mr. Paul Bell, Corning, New York, Public Schools; Mrs. Jane Bilbrech, Solvay, New York, Public Schools; Miss Joan Bogman, La Mesa Spring Valley School District; Miss Dorothy Brown, West Genesee, New York, School System; Miss Nancy McCaffrey, Smith Road School, North Syracuse, New York; Miss Amelia Carpenter, Liverpool, New York, Central Schools; Dr. William Forte, Norfolk Public Schools, Virginia; Miss Joanne Helmer, Westmoreland Road School, Whitesboro, New York; Miss Margaret Kalette, Franklin School, Syracuse, New York; Miss Judy Lefler, Interlaken, New York, Public Schools; Miss Jean McCormick, Ithaca, New York, Public Schools; Mrs. Lillian Moyer, Camillus, New York, Public Schools; Mrs. Andrew Nevin, Manlius, New York, Elementary School; Miss Marion Raymer, Columbus School, Utica, New York; Miss Patricia Ryan, Camillus, New York, Central Schools; Mrs. Evelyn Shaffer, Buffalo, New York; Miss Elizabeth Schneiders, Woodland School, East Detroit, Michigan; Miss Kay Ward, Hinkley Road

School, New Hartford, New York; Mrs. Norma Wambold, Ovid, New York, Public Schools; Miss Marilyn A. Roehm, Sayville, Long Island; Miss Jocelyn Weissman and Miss Linda Rauscher, student teachers in the Westmoreland Road School, Whitesboro, New York.

I must also express special gratitude to Miss Carol Jo Darby and Miss Patricia Smith, and to their students at the MacNamara School in Baldwinsville, New York, for their unique contributions. Teachers and students in our campus school have given me invaluable help, and I must especially thank Mrs. Helen Benjamin, Mr. Robert Schaffer, Miss Hazel Hewitt, Mrs. Dorothy Clark, Miss Debby Osborne (student teacher), and Mr. Dudley Morgan (student teacher) for their valued assistance and creative enthusiasm.

Last, but of great importance, I wish to thank Mrs. Nancy Osborne for her poem about life, which opens this book. She has been a creative and gratifying student.

JAMES A. SMITH

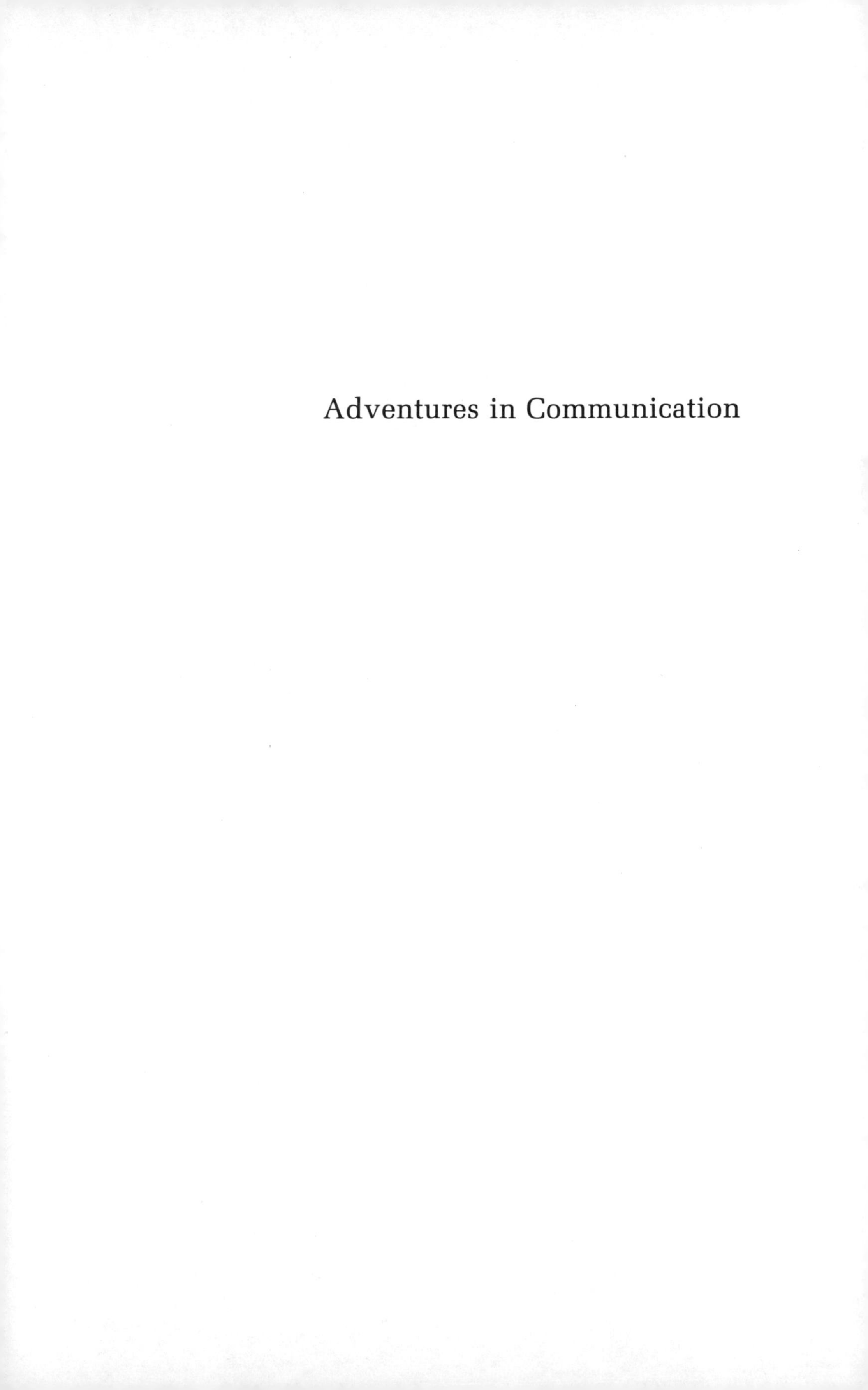

Adventures in Communication

Figure 1 *Freddie had a bowl of popcorn. His teacher said, "You may not eat the last few kernels until you write about it."* Freddie wrote:

I ate a bowl of popcorn
Buttery with salt just right,
Golden and white and fluffy
Each kernel curled and light.
I thought I was full of popcorn.
All kernels were gone but three.
But, I can't wait to eat them
To smell them is torturing me!

1

The Adventure of Life

A Poem

When I was six I painted a picture.
I drew life as I saw it, through new, shining eyes.
I believed that I had drawn life as it really was.

And then you moved your easel near me,
Your painting was different
And I felt threatened.

I reached over and deliberately added designs
of my own making to your picture,
so certain that my way was best.

I thought you would see how good I was
but instead you cried and
said you wanted to do it by yourself.

And I tried to erase my design from your paper
but it only smudged and turned purple
and, laughing, we both began again with fresh paper.

—Nancy Osborne

This poem was written by one of my college students. It sets the tone and character of this book. In essence, it says that we cannot live in isolation from each other—even in creative endeavor, for life means rubbing elbows, sharing feelings, passions, ideas, knowledge. Man, above all animals, has been endowed with the gift of speech so he can better share his ideas and emotions.

"And then you moved your easel near me." We shared an idea—we were threatened by each other—but "laughing, we both began again with fresh paper."

Relevant communication experiences are the essence of the adventure we call life.

A Psychodelic Light Party: A Relevant Adventure in Communication

I recently had a beautiful and unusual experience: I attended a Psychodelic Light Party in a middle school. It was presented by fifty children who worked with a team of teachers.

Jonathan brought a flashing color light to school. It could be attached to a stereo phonograph set, and the vibrations caused the colors to change and flash. The children were enthralled with the flashing light and experimented with all types of music, ranging from Strauss waltzes to rock-and-roll recordings.

The team of instructors working with these children included a science teacher, an art teacher, a language arts consultant, and a home economics teacher. They decided to capitalize on the children's interest in the colored lights. Other teachers offered support, but this core of instructors met together to do the planning; to set objectives for developing the unit; to select experience; and to record the behavior changes they expected to effect.

As soon as a tentative outline was developed and some basic plans had been established, the children were brought into the act. Their ideas were sought and incorporated into the unit.

Some of the activities in which the group engaged as a result of this planning were the following: They made a visit to a neighboring Niagara-Mohawk plant, they conducted reading research on the history of light and the use of light in staging theatrical productions, they tried out various dramatics, experimented in painting, and visited a light show. In addition, they became interested in music and sought out poems inspired by light, especially sunlight and moonlight. They engaged in studies of the rate of light travel, of the planets and stars in relation to light, of the function of ultraviolet light and how it can be used, and of the manner in which infrared light is used to cook foods.

The Psychodelic Light Party was the culminating activity for the unit. It was obvious that the children were excited about their learnings and that they had accumulated incredible amounts of knowledge from their studies. But, above all, each student had been encouraged to grow individually and creatively. Each child had, for instance, chosen a committee on which to work for the party, and each committee had brainstormed ideas for its part of the show.

The party was held in a large classroom—two classrooms really, with the sliding doors between the two opened.

One committee had stretched white wrapping paper from floor to ceiling across one end of the room. Jonathan, very interested in ways that light might be used, had consulted the industrial arts teacher and had learned how to pull and twist pieces of Scotch tape over a slab of glass in such a way that he created tension spots on the tape. When this was placed on an overhead projector and a revolving disk was added to the lens, the tension spots broke down into color and the revolving disk made them flow and move across the white paper. The entire front of the room was alive with the flowing colors. The rest of the room was dark. A Simon and Garfunkel record was played, and the seven boys and girls of this particular committee were dancing behind the paper so that only their shadows moved about on the flowing colors, creating an astonishing effect.

I entered the room through a tunnel made from large cardboard boxes split open at the bottom and shaped to make a dome. The children had worked for a weird color effect. The sides and top of the tunnel were painted with imaginative and original sea animals which glowed as a concealed black light flashed on and off. To add to the unusual effect, long pieces of yarn, dipped in glow paint, were suspended from the ceiling and gently slapped the face of each person who entered the tunnel.

Once one emerged from the tunnel, the living wall of color was the first thing to confront the eye, with the music playing and the children dancing, their bodies in silhouette on the sea of flowing color.

On one side of the room, a committee had stretched white paper from floor to ceiling and had splattered colored paint over it. Behind the paper, children moved their hands, over which were draped miniature blinking Christmas tree lights in a multitude of colors. The effect was that of hundreds of fireflies blinking about the wall.

On the other side of the room, another committee had set up a large screen and an overhead projector light filled it. The guests at the party were invited to make interesting moving color effects on the screen by experimenting with the materials that the committee had collected.

Some children dropped vegetable dye onto a pyrex cake plate with water in it, which was set on top of the overhead projector. The effect on the screen was that of a red spot appearing on a white wall, then gradually spreading, followed by a green, then a blue, and then a yellow spot, all reaching toward each other. A slight shaking of the cake plate made the colors on the screen move faster and run closer together.

Pieces of ground glass shaken around in the cake pan also produced beautiful effects on the screen. Chunks of colored plastic made other unusual effects.

Cut-glass dishes, especially in color, were rotated on the projector and sunbursts appeared on the screen.

Each table in the classroom had been covered with white wrapping paper. At the beginning of the party, each group was to make its table top into a finger paint, a spatter paint, or a tempera paint design.

Mobiles, made prior to the party, floated from the ceiling.

As part of the entertainment, one group sang and danced behind the colored wall to an original song (soul music) which they had composed.

Each group, previous to the party, had experimented with making slides. At the party the groups shared what they had done. Group one had taken exposed film and had cleared it with chemicals. They had then drawn with flo-pens directly on the clear film to produce a series of slides quite like modern painting with bold splashes of color. To accompany the showing of the slides, they played a recording by Herb Alpert with exploding brass accompaniment—very dramatic! Group two had also worked with film that was overexposed. But they wet their film, and then with nails, tweezers, and other pointed objects, scratched the chemicals from the film in tiny patterns allowing the light to pass through and be reflected on the screen. They, too, used musical accompaniment when showing their slides. Some of the slides were colored, because one of the boys discovered that he could mark on the shiny side with a flo-pen and make the white light any color.

Group three had been instructed by the science teacher on how to make photographic slides, and they had made a series of slides around their town showing the places that were highly colorful: the flower beds in the park, the bright fire hydrants, the lake rolling in, colored sailboats on the lake, children in bright garments playing in the snow. This group found suitable snatches of music to fit each picture, made a choral poem to go with the sequence of pictures, and combined them on a tape. The result was a stunning effect!

Group four had also worked with film, but they had drawn directly on the film with flo-pens, and the colors danced and pranced on the screen with honky-tonk piano music playing in the background.

Group five had charge of the refreshments. They created their own punch: Hawaiian punch, ginger ale, eggs, and whipped cream—beaten until it was frothy and poured over ice. This committee baked cupcakes and put frosting in tubes borrowed from the Home Ec room. Every child had to decorate his own cupcake by squeezing the colors from the tubes onto it.

The Refreshment Committee had made the napkins: Some were round, some triangular, and they were decorated with bright-colored crayons. Even the cups were special—transparent with psychodelic stickers on the outside.

An unusual party indeed. Later I saw the books of stories and poems these children had written about their experiences with light and color. I have selected a few here, chosen from among hundreds.

What Is Gray?

Gray is dreariness; gray is coldness,
Gray is rain drizzling on a cloudy day,
It is gloominess, too.
Gray is all hope gone, and despair in its place.
But, it can also be beautiful;
A soft, warm being
Entirely different in its own special way.
Gray can be soft and quiet,
Or rough and violent,
It is gray that hides the ships away
Sitting quietly in the bay.
Gray separates the feelings of joy and sadness.
That is gray.

—Roberta Witt

Blue

Blue is the bluebirds in a tree
And the sky above.
Swift is the river that flows free
Blue—it's the color I love!

—Joann

Blue

The sky is blue
When the weather is clear,
Just like your eyes,
When you are near!

—Gary

As part of the unit, one teacher had introduced cinquain poetry. The children were to describe some object colorfully. Wendy wrote about flowers.

Flowers

Gayly nodding
Dancing by sunlight
Spelling color like Love
Blossoms!

These children were having no problems either of "discipline" or in learning. I have been to some schools where such a party would be a chaos: Most of the frosting in those tubes would have been squirted by the children at each other; much of the water in the overhead projector would have been splashed on the floor. Why the difference? Why indeed? I see it primarily as a project in which a group of teachers kept in touch with the children's world, and were able to communicate with them by using the communication techniques of their generation as well as descriptive language. The teachers disguised many difficult learnings through interesting activities, making the learning experiences relevant.

The Matter of Relevancy

We live in a world of change. Many of the cherished customs and ideas of the past are being trampled to death at the onslaught of change. Many of the concepts of the past are still relevant to modern life, but teachers have not presented them in a relevant or meaningful manner, so that students have failed to see their importance and have not learned them. One of the major problems of teachers from nursery school through college is how to present material in a manner so relevant to students that they understand its worth from the moment of presentation. One answer to the problem is to use creative methods of teaching: methods which motivate children, which use the techniques and hardware of their generation and get them so involved that their values are developed, their skills and knowledge expanded, and their behavior changed. The Psychodelic Light Party is an example of one such creative teaching experience.

Every planned unit and lesson should contain an answer to the question, "How relevant is this to the child of the space age?" or "How can I make this relevant to children living today?"

Relevancy cannot generally be detected by testing cognitive learnings. It deals with the affective domain as well as the cognitive. It can best be measured by observing the behavior of the students during the learning process; by careful observation on the part of the teacher on how well each student enters into the study, the enthusiasm and attitude of the students during the study, the ideas generated by the students, the materials they bring to the school, their willingness to spend time outside of school—these are measures of relevancy.

Even cognitive learnings are not always measured by a test as well as by the manner in which the learnings from any lesson are applied to life situations after the lesson is over.

Children should be able to give their teachers tests to indicate how well lessons have been taught. Lacking this sophisticated ability, they do, nonetheless, evaluate their teachers. These verbal evaluations are often clues to the effectiveness and relevancy of lessons.

The Acquisition of Language

Life is an adventure of action and interaction. A child enters this world with a physical and mental potential for language. His language ability will be determined to a high degree by his intellectual capacity and his physical well-being. He comes into a culture where a structure of symbols is already in use. How does he acquire this structure so that he too can become civilized?

According to Smith, Goodman, and Meredith,[1] two human qualities explain the development of language.

> The first quality is the capacity of man's mind to imagine and use symbols; the second quality is man's need to communicate. So universal is his need for communication that man invented language not once but perhaps many times, wherever, in fact, man congregated.
>
> The ability of children to think symbolically and to produce sound symbols makes it *possible* for children to learn language. The need for children to communicate makes it *necessary* for children to learn language.

Language is an abstraction from behavior; it is life being lived or life recorded, a system of meanings and a system of signs. It is because man has language that he is a high-level animal.

Smith, Goodman, and Meredith[2] also say this:

> Until the child assumes language he cannot separate himself from the all consuming moment. Like the other animals he is in the world without knowing he is in the world. Language makes it possible for him to objectify and conceptualize his world and himself and to share the responsibility for his destiny.

1. Brooks Smith, Kenneth Goodman, and Robert Meredith, *Language and Thinking in the Elementary School* (New York: Holt, Rinehart and Winston, 1970), p. 11.
2. Ibid., p. 4.

If language is so important to life, it is necessary for the teachers of language to keep in touch with the truths being disclosed about language by the linguists and the research specialists. For language, we have found, develops through natural stages in every human being. Just as one cannot grow a rose without first growing a stem, one cannot learn to read (without special devices or help) until he has developed visual acuity. It is natural for girls to be more advanced in language skills than boys, for instance. The environment into which a child is placed plays a dramatic part in his language development, of course, but equating normal children in normal situations has given us many clues about the natural life patterns of language development. A knowledge of these clues can be very helpful to the teacher in planning what is relevant to any child at any given time and will keep her from erecting barriers to his language growth by expecting too much from him before he is able to give it.

What are some of the latest generalizations that can be made about language development?

Generalizations About Language Development

Smith et al.[3] make certain generalizations from current studies which seem to bear significance to the child's language development as it relates to his learning processes.

1. The closer the language of the child comes to the speech norms of the adult community, the more effective his communication becomes.
2. There is a continuous tendency, therefore, for the child's language to move toward adult norms.
3. The more opportunity the child has to communicate, the more skill he will develop in use of language and the more acceptable will be his language by adult standards. He needs to be spoken to, listened to, responded to.
4. Anticipation of his needs by a parent or teacher before he communicates them will tend to retard a child's language development.
5. In literate societies, communicative need will play the same prime motivational role in the child's learning to read and write as it does in his learning to speak and listen with understanding.
6. Before change can be achieved in an individual's idiolect, the individual must feel strongly that the change will help him to communicate more effectively.

Other generalizations can be made from recent research studies.[4]

3. Ibid., p. 12.
4. Susan M. Ervin and Wick R. Miller, "Language Development," *Child Psychology*, National Society for the Study of Education Yearbook 62, Part 1 (1963), p. 20.

1. Language learning is not a natural part of maturation. Children who have been isolated from humans while maturing have not developed a language.

2. Every child achieves near-mastery of at least one language by the time he is five or six years old. Studies reported in 1963 indicate that the speech of most children of that age is a close approximation of adult speech in their immediate environment.

3. One of the most important learnings to have become accepted over the past few years is that language is not best learned in isolated fragments or "words." It is best learned in total situations. From the very beginning of life, a baby finds himself bombarded by sounds and words around him. From this smorgasbord of sounds, he eventually selects those that are best in meeting his needs. He sorts out particular aspects of a total situation and forms firm associations with these aspects before he is able to reproduce the sounds associated with them, or to speak.

This process may be the method most suitable for language development in the school situation, i.e., not to teach language in isolated words but in situations such as the psychodelic light party mentioned at the beginning of this chapter, and to focus on *particular aspects* of a situation only when a child needs help in forming certain specific concepts or in speaking certain words. Each of the adventures in communication recounted in this book is a total situation. The vocabulary development that results (both oral and written, and in that sequence) is relevant because (a) the words are used in meaningful context; (b) the child reacts emotionally as well as intellectually to the use of the words in the total situation; (c) he is able to incorporate the words into his own learning pattern in his own way; and (d) he is able to see other uses for the words because they are used in many ways, thus broadening his perceptions and forming concepts.

While it is true that children tend to use individual words when they first begin to communicate orally, this is due to the fact that young children do not have the physical coordination or mental development to utter a whole thought, although they use words (and actions) which convey a whole thought. Pointing to the water spigot, a child says: "Dink," which means "I need a drink." Pointing to his father and saying "Da-da" generally means "That is daddy" or "Help me, Daddy." Brown and Bellugi[5] report that children in their studies tended to repeat the most heavily stressed word in an utterance.

4. Because of the recent interest in the work of Piaget, some of his views on language development in children are pertinent to an understanding of language as part of the greater adventure called life.

5. Roger Brown and Ursula Bellugi, "Three Processes in the Child's Acquisition of Syntax," in J. Emig, J. Fleming, and H. Popp, *Language and Learning* (New York: Harcourt, 1966), pp. 3–12.

Piaget[6] has this to say about language:

> Words are probably not a short-cut to a better understanding . . . The level of understanding seems to modify the language that is used rather than vice versa . . . Mainly, language serves to translate what is already understood: or else language may even present a danger if it is used to introduce an idea which is not yet accessible.

Piaget felt that language was an outside agent that served the purpose of helping the child express his own symbols in a manner meaningful to society, and that his use of speech and language did not affect the development of personal symbolic structures. That is, each develops independently of the other. He indicates that children show that they understand many ideas through action which they cannot express in words. Piaget points out that when children are presented with an idea to be learned in adult language, structures are being forced on their thinking, and asks whether it is proper to teach the structure or to present the child with situations where he is active and creates the structure himself. He states that when we teach too fast, we keep the child from inventing and discovering himself. Piaget defines teaching as the creation of situations where structures can be discovered, not the transmission of structures which may be assimilated at the verbal level only. The material in this book has been presented with Piaget's concepts in mind: Teaching and learning situations have been created where structures can be discovered.

The Interrelatedness of Language

One of the most recent studies of children's language by Loban[7] shows certain interrelationships among the language arts. Loban drew the following conclusions:

1. Reading, writing, listening, and speaking were all positively related. Children who were low in general oral language ability tended to be low in reading and writing achievement. Children high in language ability tended to do well in gaining literacy skills.

It is the major premise of this book that the language experience concept is the most practical and logical for the teaching of the language

6. Jean Piaget in Eleanor Duckworth, "Piaget Rediscovered," *ESS Newsletter*, June 1964, Elementary Science Study, Educational Services, Incorporated, Watertown, Massachusetts, p. 15.
7. Walter Loban, *The Language of Elementary School Children* (Champaign, Illinois: National Council of Teachers of English, 1963), p. 89.

arts. Studies in language development in the past twenty years have repeatedly called attention to the fact that an effective language program in the elementary school must begin with a carefully planned, goal-directed program in oral expression (see Chapter 6). It would seem that Loban is re-enforcing the concept that a good reading or writing program is based on a sound program of speaking.

2. A positive correlation was found between health and language proficiency.

The vitality necessary to speak fluently can be generated only by a healthy body. Physical fitness and continual checks on the eyes, hand-eye coordination, and sleeping and eating habits of a child may be vital to his language development.

3. Reading and writing were related to sociometric position.

One wonders, as he reads Loban's conclusions, whether or not the commercial materials used in teaching children in atypical socioeconomic situations had a great effect on their language development. These studies seem to re-enforce the concept that the teacher must sometimes create the materials to be used with a child from any atypical environment, or with the child who deviates from the classroom norms.

4. Oral language ability and vocabulary correlated highly with success on group I.Q. tests.

Here Loban re-enforces a concept revealed by research studies of the past. There still seems to be a high correlation between intelligence and language usage.

5. Chronological age, effective use of language, and sociometric status correlated positively with complexity of grammatical structure in the speech of the children.

The use of language, especially at the spoken level, is one of the most successful ways of developing language usage. It is safe to assume, however, that in most schools, the emphasis is not on oral use of language: Most of the time allocated to the language arts program is utilized in completing written exercises. The reader of this volume should keep in mind that the author stresses a well-planned program in oral expression as a base for the successful development of all language skills, including reading.

Loban[8] points out an important fact: The major categories of language difficulties in elementary school children come from (a) the kind of teaching which presents language that is limited and inflexible and that does not serve the expanding needs of the child, particularly in school tasks, and (b) language that is considered nonstandard or socially unacceptable for educated members of the society to use. This should

8. Ibid., p. 89.

say something to all teachers. If langugage that is different, new, or unique is not used in school, children are being inhibited in their ability to develop and they are not assessing school learnings as relevant.

Life Patterns of Language Development

What are the life patterns of language development?

Research offers many studies of children's natural development, from pre-school years to adulthood. In the pre-school years, the home plays a vital part in launching the child successfully or unsuccessfully on his life pattern in language development.

MacGinitie[9] states:

> The home is obviously the prepotent source of environmental influence on language development. The extent and nature of language stimulation in the home reflects the play of many factors—the interest, affection, and ability of the mother, the presence of the father and other adults, the presence of siblings and the nature of conversation and verbal planning in the family. The strength of such influence is made abundantly clear when one considers Hess and Shipman's (1955) striking verbal examples of mother-child verbal interaction as being multiplied by days and years of more of the same. Obvious problems for school achievement come, of course, when the home teaches a different dialect or even a different language from that used in school. In such cases the language or dialect may be supported by peer-group or community values.

Although reports of research studies offer certain guidelines which may help the teacher in understanding the child, it must be remembered that the life pattern of language development for each child is a highly individual achievement, and that little is gained by comparing one child's language development with that of another except as a diagnostic procedure to locate areas in which further instruction may be of benefit to the child.

LeFevre[10] points out that a child incorporates all the forms of grammar about which he needs to know in his speech by the time he comes to school. Lewis[11] and others remind us that children the world over move through a succession and procession of definite sound patterns.

Studies of school beginners indicate the these children have a speak-

9. Walter MacGinitie, "Language Development," in *Encyclopedia of Educational Research*, Robert L. Ebel, ed. (New York: Macmillan, 1969), p. 696.
10. Carl A. LeFevre, *Linguistics and the Teaching of Reading* (New York: McGraw-Hill, Inc., 1964).
11. M. M. Lewis, *How Children Learn To Speak* (New York: Basic Books, 1957).

ing vocabulary of at least 8,000 words, and that they may know and understand over 20,000 words. Long ago, researchers[12] stated that the child at the age of six is likely to know 17,000 words plus 7,000 derivatives, and that he can reasonably expect to add approximately 5,000 words each year thereafter. With television and modern mass media prevalent in each home children today probably know many more words than this at the age of school entrance.

By the age of six, the child's spoken language has reached 90 percent of its mature level, when judged on the basis of sentence structure according to McCarthy.[13] The "only" child performs better than the singleton, and the singleton better than twins.

Hearing acuity affects growth in all language abilities. The age of six marks the beginning of complicated speech, manual performance, and behavior restrictions required of the child in adjusting to the school situation. Stuttering often begins at this time. Boys develop more slowly than girls in language, and there are more stutterers and more speech defects among boys than among girls.

Handedness is generally well established by the age of four.

Yedinack's research indicates that there is a strong relationship between readily disability and articulation defects at the second grade level.[14]

Loban[15] found that all the children in his study of eleven classes used all basic patterns of English sentence structure, even in the kindergarten. He found that the differences between groups of children who were rated high and low in language ability were not in the patterns they used. Children who read "poor" tended to use more partial utterances. Those who were rated as "better" users of language used more complete and more complex utterances. More subordinate clauses were used by the "high" group. Loban arrived at certain obvious conclusions about the general direction of language growth: As children become older, (a) they tend to use more language, (b) they tend to use more communication units (similar to sentences) when they speak, (c) the communication units tend to get longer, (d) the units tend to be more complex grammatically, and (e) language becomes more coordinated and more articu-

12. Robert H. Seashore, "The Importance of Vocabulary in Learning Language Skills," *Elementary English*, 25 (March, 1948), pp. 137–152.
13. Dorothea McCarthy, "Language Development in Children," in Leonard Carmichael, *Manual of Child Psychology*. 2nd ed. (New York: John Wiley & Sons, 1954), pp. 492–630.
14. Jeanette G. Yedinack, "Study of the Linguistic Functioning of Children With Articulation and Reading Disabilities," *Pedagogical Seminary and Journal of Genetic Psychology*, 74 (March, 1949), pp. 23–59.
15. Walter Loban, *The Language of Elementary School Children* (Champaign, Illinois: National Council of Teachers of English, 1963), pp. 81–89.

late. Less obvious is the fact that their language tends to express more tentativeness, more supposition, more hypothesis, more conditionality.

Loban also stresses the fact that children literally grope for words in the middle of an utterance. Those whose language is rated high tend to do less groping, but all children grope through "mazes" of words to some degree throughout elementary school.

Loban found that boys are at the extremes—they do very poorly in language when they are low in language ability, but excel when they are high in language ability.

In addition, he states that children who are rated as most proficient in language are also those who manifest the most sensitivity to the conventions of language.

Of importance to the teacher of language arts are additional findings reported in Loban's summary.

1. Both the low and high groups of subjects use the same number of words from among the 12,000 most commonly used words of the English language; after that, the low group shows a higher incidence of words selected from the next 20,000 of the most commonly used words (from 13,000 to 33,000). Thereafter, the high group gains ascendancy in the use of the least commonly used words of the English language.

2. For subject nominals, the low group depends almost exclusively on nouns and pronouns. The high group can use noun clauses, infinitives, and verbals.

3. Boys in the low group are clearly more limited in their repertoire of syntax than are girls in the low group. On the other hand, the boys in the high group tend to excel over the girls in the high group.

4. Problems with the use of verbs prove to be the most frequent type of deviation from conventional usage in the elementary school. Lack of agreement between subject and predicate, particularly in the third person singular, is a major difficulty. Consistency of verb tense is another problem.

5. Adverb and noun clauses are used by the total group much more frequently than are adjective clauses.

6. In this study, reading, writing, listening, and speaking show a positive relation.

7. The subjects in the lowest and highest quartiles in writing are also lower and higher, respectively, in reading achievement. Those who write well in grade three are also those who are above average in speaking and reading. Those who rate in the highest group in oral proficiency are also those who are completely above the median in reading for the random and low groups (also selected by a criterion of oral proficiency).

Smith, Goodman, and Meredith[16] have summarized recent research

16. Brooks Smith et al., *Language and Thinking in the Elementary School* (New York: Holt, Rinehart and Winston, 1970), pp. 17–26.

in an effective manner in their book, *Language and Thinking in the Elementary School.* They say:

> Throughout the process of language acquisition there are four continuing cycles: increasing experience, increasing conceptualization, increasing communicative need, and increasing effectiveness in communication. The last can be considered synonymous with increased control over language.
>
> Child language development can be viewed as a series of stages through which the child passes. These stages overlap; the child enters into higher stages well before he has completed earlier stages.

The authors then proceed to identify these stages and their characteristics. First comes the *Random Stage.* This is a prelinguistic phase in which the infant babbles and experiments with sounds. He produces sound as part of his reaction to discomfort and acquires a generalized ability to use sound purposefully as an attention-getting signal. He learns that sound can provoke responses from people at a distance who cannot respond to his body movements and other visual signals. He plays for long periods at noise-making, and his babbling is composed of consonant-vowel links such as "da-da-da." The peak of babbling is between eight and ten months of age. He mimics lip movements he sees; thus, the physical coordination necessary for speech begins before speech, although language development does not wait for physical maturation and coordination.

The second is designated by the authors as the *Unitary Stage.* The child begins to produce sounds purposely to express a need or desire. Often sounds are produced on cue but have no communicative value, as when a parent urges a child to say "bye-bye" and he does—he merely parrots the adult. Later, someone putting on a coat may provoke the sound "bye-bye" and the transfer has then been made to the communicative function. This phase is called the unitary stage because the child develops units of language—the utterance may be in one word, but the thought is a unit. Early sentences are not lists of words put together, but are utterances learned as wholes by the child, independent units of language. This retention of word order makes the child's communication effective. The phonemes of the child do not at this stage coincide with the phonemes of adult speech.

Next comes the *Stage of Expansion and Delimiting.* Here language is still a collection of utterances, but the utterances move in two directions at the same time. They are expanded from a one- or two-syllable utterance to fuller approximations of adult speech. This is not a process of combining words to make sentences, but is an expansion of the nucleus so that minor features are included—a filling-out of utterances rather than a building-up. They correspond closely to adult utterances, but they are still independent wholes.

At the same time, the child is delineating the use of his utterances. They come to be more and more precise in expressing more and more particular needs or wishes or feelings. The situations in which each utterance is used become increasingly narrow.

The *Stage of Structural Awareness* is characterized by the child's ability to generalize, to find pattern and order in the situations he experiences. He notices the common elements of similar utterances. He generalizes a pattern in which a series of things or people are inserted in the object slot, such as "I want milk, I want apple, I want Mommy," etc. In generalizing, the child must reflect on the utterances he uses, generalize a pattern, induce a rule, generate an utterance consistent with the rule, and evaluate the rule and modify it. Just as he had to learn the limits of each utterance, so must he now learn the limits of each rule. He becomes aware of words and phrases as well as of the complex interrelationships of these words and phrases.

A significant feature of this phase is that the child's language, which has been very grammatical up to this point because it has been highly imitative, may now appear to be highly ungrammatical because it is experimental. He is putting forms together in his own way to try to communicate and in so doing over-generalizes ("I taked it" instead of "I took it") or makes improper combinations according to adult standards.

The authors point out a very salient fact: Children who are prevented or discouraged from making errors in this stage may be reluctant to try out generalizations and may remain in the less effective stage of learned wholes.

It is at this stage that words or phrases begin to take on meaning instead of the utterance having one whole meaning. The child's large vocabulary of learned whole utterances serves as a check on his generalizations about language structure and word or phrase meaning, and he develops a feeling for language, a kind of intuition that is formed of many not wholly analyzed and understood language experiences.

The *Automatic Stage* is next. At this stage the child has internalized the grammar of his language. He can now generate utterances which he has—and has not—heard before that are fully grammatical. He does this with little conscious reasoning. The average child has reached the automatic stage of language by the time he begins kindergarten.

The *Creative State* is the last classification of the authors, and in this stage the child literally invents his own language. Up to now he has conformed to the language of the community, because this language has been his model and he had to know it in order to be able to communicate. His language has become a vast collection of clichés, trite expressions linked in trite ways. Children pass into a stage of creative manipulation of language which may be due to their increasing ability to conceptualize and think in metaphors and abstractions. New needs arise outside the realm of the "model" adult needs, so children invent new language to meet these needs, such as the teen-ager's creation of new language. Part of the latter can be attributed to the teen-ager's drive to be an entity—to be independent and to be identified with his peers rather than with his family. Much of this created language finds its way permanently into the language of the society.

Great storytellers and literary giants have retained this ability to create language. The authors have this to say about creative language:

Creative thoughts require creative language to express them. Emphasis on conformity in language in school or at home stifles not only expression but also thought. Fortunately, the tendency of children to be creative with language is almost universal. Parents and teachers can encourage this tendency. If they do, there will eventually be more adults with the courage to use language creatively.

Studies by Loban[17] and Strickland[18] follow the language development of a large group of schoolage children. Their studies relate language development to school achievement.

Summary

Smith, Goodman, and Meredith[19] make this statement:

Children have played key roles in the history of American English and will continue to make their influence felt as the language is molded today for the future. They are protectors of the language that was, conveyors of the language that is, and innovators of the language that will be.

The adventure of life can be lived to its fullest through the development of communication skills. These skills are not successfully acquired piecemeal in isolation from one another, but in full, rich, relevant life situations in which they are both acquired and used. Much of the teacher's ability to plan such experiences will rest on her knowledge and understanding of the normal life patterns of language development as revealed by research.

Her ability to teach communication skills effectively is dependent on her skill in fashioning these normal life patterns into relevant adventures in communication.

17. Loban, ibid.
18. Ruth Strickland, "The Language of Elementary School Children," *Bulletin of School of Education* (Indiana University) 38, no. 4.
19. Smith et al., ibid., p. 40.

To the Reader

1. If you are a teacher, observe the behavior of your students carefully for a week or more, and see whether you can identify those teaching acts which are relevant to them. Try some of the following assignments on them:
   (a) Give them a choice of any one of the following topics, and note which topics are chosen most frequently:

   Set I
   1. Write a story about the life of a slave in ancient Greece.
   2. Write a story about a trip to the moon in a spaceship.
   3. Write a story about your encounter one lonely night with a ghost.
   4. Write a story about your encounter with a strange creature called a Yippiedoodle.
   5. Write a poem about spring.
   6. Write a poem about your feelings when you lost your allowance.

   Set II
   1. Draw a picture to illustrate the coming of spring.
   2. Draw a picture of a Wiggley Woo.
   3. Draw a portrait of Abraham Lincoln.
   4. Draw a picture of the favorite members of your family.

   Set III
   1. Make a list of the inventions you can think of that will make your life easier.
   2. List all the uses you can think of for buttons.
   3. Make a list of your favorite books.
   4. Write about the most unusual friend you have.

   Can you develop some criteria for relevance from the choice of these assignments? For instance, do the children choose those which are personal to them? Do they choose those that demand recall or tease their imaginations? Do they choose those for which they have some familiar background? Those that are of their day and their time? Those with which they can empathize? Those that are important? Why do you suppose the Psychodelic Light Party became so relevant to the children in the incident in this chapter?
2. Encourage your children to write about color—or try it yourself. Why is color so relevant to life? Can you express this? Better yet, can you help the children realize how relevant color is to them?
3. In which of the stages of language development mentioned by Smith,

Goodman, and Meredith would you classify the poems written by the children in this chapter?

4. Loban's research indicates that children are often stilted in their language development by the manner in which they are taught. Think of all the ways this has been so in your own schooling or in your own classroom.

   How can the knowledge of normal developmental patterns of language be of aid to the teacher in planning her language arts program?

5. Questions for discussion:
   a. How do you suppose the teacher was able to get such exciting ideas from her students for the psychodelic light party described on pp. 2–6? (See Brainstorming.)
   b. What are the elements or principles behind creative teaching which make it different from ordinary teaching?
   c. Should a teacher teach "forms" of poetry before she has the children write poems?
   d. How can a sterile skill like letter-writing be taught creatively?
   e. How should teaching in a ghetto school affect the teacher's method of teaching language arts?

Selected Bibliography

Burns, Paul, Betty Broman, and Alberta Lowe. *The Language Arts in Childhood Education*, 2nd ed. Chicago, Illinois: Rand McNally and Company, 1971.

DeBoer, John J. "Some Sociological Factors in Language Development," in James C. MacCampbell, ed., *Readings in the Language Arts in the Elementary School*. Boston: D. C. Heath and Company, 1964, 77–89.

Dennison, George. *The Lives of Children*. New York: Random House, Inc., 1970.

Donoghue, Mildred R. *The Child and the English Language Arts*. Dubuque, Iowa: William C. Brown Company Publishers, 1971.

Emig, Janet A., James T. Fleming, and Helen M. Popp. *Language and Learning*. New York: Harcourt, Brace and World, Inc., 1964.

Hyman, Ronald T. *Ways of Teaching*. Philadelphia, Pa.: J. B. Lippincott Company, 1970.

Lenneberg, Eric H. *The Biological Foundations of Language*. New York: John Wiley and Sons, 1967.

Loban, Walter. *The Language of Elementary School Children*. Champaign, Illinois: National Council of Teachers of English, 1963.

LODGE, WILLIAM J. "Developmental Characteristics of Childhood Related to the Language Arts Curriculum" in James C. MacCampbell, ed., *Readings in the Language Arts in the Elementary School*. Boston: D. C. Heath and Company, 1964, 52–65.

MACCAMPBELL, JAMES C. "Child Growth and Development" in James C. MacCampbell, ed., *Readings in the Language Arts in the Elementary School*. Boston: D. C. Heath and Company, 1964, 42–47.

______. *Readings in the Language Arts in the Elementary School*. Boston: D. C. Heath and Company, 1964.

PIAGET, JEAN. *The Language and Thought of the Child*. New York: Humanities Press, 1959.

ROGERS, CARL R. *Freedom to Learn*. Columbus, Ohio: Charles E. Merrill Publishing Company, 1969.

SIGEL, IRVING, AND FRANK H. HOOPER (eds.). *Logical Thinking in Children*. New York: Holt, Rinehart and Winston, Inc., 1968.

SMITH, BROOKS, KENNETH GOODMAN, AND ROBERT MEREDITH. *Language and Thinking in the Elementary School*. New York: Holt, Rinehart and Winston, 1970.

TORRANCE, E. PAUL, AND ROBERT D. STROM. *Mental Health and Achievement: Increasing Potential and Reducing School Dropout*. New York: John Wiley and Sons, 1965.

WASHBURNE, CARLETON W. "Adjusting the Program to the Child" in James C. MacCampbell (ed.), *Readings in the Language Arts in the Elementary School*. Boston: D. C. Heath and Company, 1964, 375–385.

WELLS, CHARLOTTE. "The Child's Equipment for Language Growth," in James C. MacCampbell (ed.), *Readings in the Language Arts in the Elementary School*. Boston: D. C. Heath and Company, 1964, 66–75.

2
2

The Adventure of Communication

Bim Bam Boo and the Magic Talking Book

"Today," said Miss Ellis, "let's make a magic talking book!"

"Magic? How magic?"

"How can a book talk?"

"Is the talking part of the magic?"

"Oh, let's!"

I glanced down at the sheet of paper in my hand on which Miss Ellis had jotted her objectives. They read as follows:

As a result of this experience, the children will:

1. Have the opportunity to share their oral vocabulary, which will be used to develop a creative writing and a reading lesson.
2. Become aware of rhyming words and the rhythm and rhyme needed to create poetry.
3. Create a rhyming poem using their spoken vocabulary.
4. Create a choral poem using their own vocabulary.
5. Express themselves by use of new media: magic crayons and magic chalk.
6. Read familiar words in context.
7. Have an experience of organizing materials in a sequence.
8. Create a magic talking book (experiences in reading, oral expression, art, music appreciation, listening, and creative writing).

What a delightful way to begin—all the children were motivated at once! I looked up to Miss Ellis.

"We will have to wait and see!" she said. "First, I'd like to do some warming-up things to see how good you are. Let's make our book a poem—a fun poem. Is that all right with everybody?"

A unanimous "Yes" resounded to her question.

"Well," continued Miss Ellis, "to have a poem, we generally, not always, but generally have two things—rhythm and rhyme. Does anyone know what *rhyming* is?" She lettered the words on the chalkboard.

Charlie did. "It is putting two words together that sound alike at the end," he explained.

"Like what?" Miss Ellis probed.

"Ball and tall."

"Good," she said, "Let's try some more. What rhymes with beat?"

"Seat!"

"Man?"

"Pan!"

"Good—now just let's look a minute at these cards. See if you can tell me words that rhyme with the word I have printed on the top."

Miss Ellis then held up a card with the word BOO printed on it. "What rhymes with Boo?"

"Shoe."

"Glue."

"Blue."

"Moo."

"Zoo."

Miss Ellis printed the words. Other cards were filled out in the same manner, and set along the chalkboard.

"Now let's talk about this other word," said Miss Ellis—"this word rhythm. Does anyone know what it means?"

Marie thought it was a dance.

"It is a dance—Marie is right—but it is even more. When we move in movements over and over, or do the same thing over and over, we say we have rhythm. Joe, could you dance for us?"

Joe loved to dance and was on his feet at once.

"Do you see how nicely Joe moves his body and does some steps over and over? That is rhythm. Mary, could you walk for us, please?"

Mary walked.

"Does Mary have rhythm when she walks?" asked Miss Ellis.

The children agreed that she did.

After other demonstrations in which the children dramatized, Miss Ellis said, "In rhyming poetry and in poetry that *doesn't* rhyme, we have rhythm. Lots of words have rhythm—our names have rhythm. What is your name?" she pointed to a boy.

"John Mann," he said.

"John, clap the rhythm in your name."

John clapped: clap—pause—clap.

"Good," said Miss Ellis. "Let's all clap John's name."

Soon she pointed to Beverly. "What is your name?" she asked.

"Beverly Henderson," she responded.

"Beverly, can you clap the rhythm in your name?" asked Miss Ellis.

And Beverly clapped: clap-clap-clap-pause-clap-clap-clap.

"Good," said Miss Ellis, "and it is a different rhythm from John's name, isn't it? By putting these rhythms together, we can make another rhythm—like a song. Let's have half the group clap John Mann and the other half do Beverly Henderson and see what kind of new rhythm we have."

Other names were tried singly and in combinations. Finally Miss Ellis stopped the experimentation.

"Let's get back to our magic talking poem book," she said. "In it we will need to use both rhythm and rhyme, and I know now that you will do it well."

"I have here a word which I would like you to figure out," said Miss Ellis, holding up a strip of paper. "Raise your hand if you can tell me what it is—Jerry?"

"Bim Bam Boo."

"Right," said Miss Ellis, "Bim, Bam, Boo. Have any of you ever seen a Bim Bam Boo?"

The children all laughed, exclaimed, and showed amazement and laughter in their answers.

"Well," said Miss Ellis, "I have never seen a Bim Bam Boo either. A Bim Bam Boo can *look* anyway you want him to; he can *do* anything you want him to; he can *say* anything you want him to; and can *be* anything you want him to. Would it be fun to write our poem book about a Bim Bam Boo?"

"Yes."

"Let's."

"O.K.—then let's look at this card. Who can read it?"

On a series of long, heavy strips of paper Miss Ellis had printed words. The one on the top of the pile which she held up said,

"Have you ever heard of a Bim Bam Boo?"

Cherry read it.

"Good," said Miss Ellis, "Now look at this card." It read,

"He looks like a ______ ______ ______ ______ ______ ______ ______."

"Now what we can do to make a rhyming poem," said Miss Ellis, "is to get the same rhythm in the second line as in the first. Let's clap the first line while we read it together. Now let's clap the scond line the way it must be. You can see how many sounds we must make to give it the same rhythm."

After the children had experimented with this, Miss Ellis said, "Now what must we also do to make the second line rhyme with the first?"

"Put a word on the end that sounds like Boo," said Casey.

"Right," said Miss Ellis, "and here we have a whole card full of words that rhyme with Boo. Who can choose one and put it in at the end of a sentence that will have a rhythm like line 1?"

There were deep frowns and grinding wheels. Finally Bonnie said, "How about: He looks like a thing that left the zoo!"

The children were delighted with Bonnie's rhyme. They clapped the rhythm to be sure it fit.

Miss Ellis continued showing two cards at a time so the children could rhyme the second card with the first. They checked each of the companion lines for rhythm and rhyme. Miss Ellis had made enough lead lines so every child in the class would later have a line to work with. This is what resulted:

The Bim Bam Boo

Have you ever heard of a Bim Bam Boo?
He looks *like a thing that left the zoo.*
He lives in the swamp on the edge of the crop,
And he walks *like a frog about to hop.*
He eats peanuts, popcorn and cake
And gets *every day a belly ache.*
He talks through his nose like an old tin horn
And he looks *like he wished he wasn't born.*
He smells like cabbage and perfume, too.
He sneezes *like he had a case of flu.*
He runs like a cow with big, flat feet.
He cries *like no one you'll ever meet.*
He sleeps like a baby in his crib,
He drinks so *sloppy he needs a bib.*
He plays like a kitten with a ball of string.
He jumps *like a lion through a circus ring.*
He goes into town to have some fun.
He buys *cracker jacks and a water gun.*
He's funny, even funnier than you or me
And we find him *hiding behind every tree.*
He waddles like a duck on a rainy day,
He works *like a horse on the first of May.*

He weighs most a ton and is sloppy fat.
He holds his money in his old felt hat.
We'll try to get him back in the zoo,
Our big, old, funny, old Bim Bam Boo.

Thus was the text provided for the book. Objectives 1, 2, and 3 met! Motivation ran high!

"With such description about the Bim Bam Boo," said Miss Ellis, "I am anxious to see how you think he looks. And now comes the magic part of our talking book! This is what we are going to do!"

Miss Ellis then introduced the magic crayons and the black light. The children had experienced this medium before.

"I am going to allow you to choose a line from our poem story. Then take a sheet of this paper and go over to the table where I have hung the magic light, and draw a picture that will go with your line. If you use the magic crayons that are there, the colors will disappear when you take the picture away from the magic light. Number your paper in the corner the same as the line I give you—because this is where the magic comes in. I shan't be able to tell what picture goes with what line if you don't number them. Without the light I will see only a white sheet of paper."

The children enjoyed using the glowing colors under the magic light. Miss Ellis had two of the lights hung over a large table so there was plenty of working area for many children.

As soon as a child finished his picture, Miss Ellis gave him a large piece of colored construction paper on which he mounted his picture and the line of poetry that went with it. Three children who finished early made a cover for the book with large letters "The Bim Bam Boo." (See Figures 2 and 2–1.)

As the pages of the book were finished, one child was assigned to put them in the proper order. Then Miss Ellis helped put them together with two large paper fasteners.

Soon all the pages were in the book. What excitement prevailed in the classroom as the children placed one of the magic lights in front of the book and turned the pages so that they could see each other's work! Such weird, fascinating, and individual interpretations of the infamous Bim Bam Boo! When it was over, the children applauded—delighted and proud of their own creative product.

"It is beautiful—and such fun!" said Miss Ellis. "But I have something else in mind. Does anyone remember what I said we were going to make at the beginning of our project? Think hard!"

Hands were quick to go up.

"You said we were going to write a magic talking book," said Marcia.

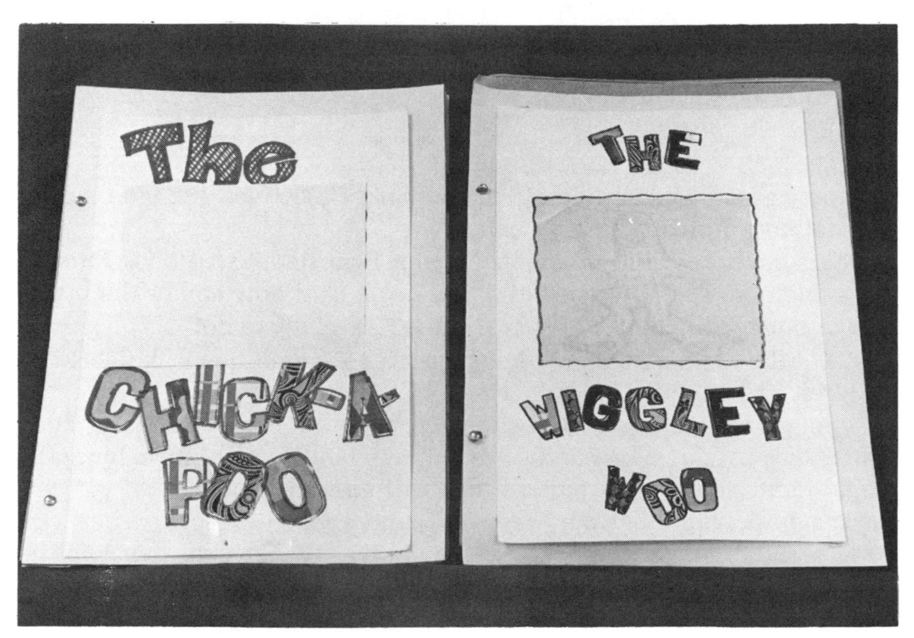

Figure 2 *Inspired by the adventure of the Bim Bam Boo, the author tried a similar idea in a first grade using the title, "The Wiggley Woo" and in a sixth grade, "The Chick-a-Poo." Both turned out to be creative adventures.*

Figure 2–1 *One page of a Bim Bam Boo book. The picture glows in the dark behind a black light.*

"Yes," agreed Miss Ellis, "and we did make a poem book, and we did make a magic book, but we did not make a talking book. Shall we make it a talking book?"

"Yes."

"Let's."

Hands clapping!

"All right. Now, how many of you can read the line of the poem on your page? Let's go through the book again and have each person read *his* line of the poem. If you need help, one of us will help you. Let's go." She then turned the pages again, and each child practiced reading his line while other children prompted. This gave Miss Ellis an excellent

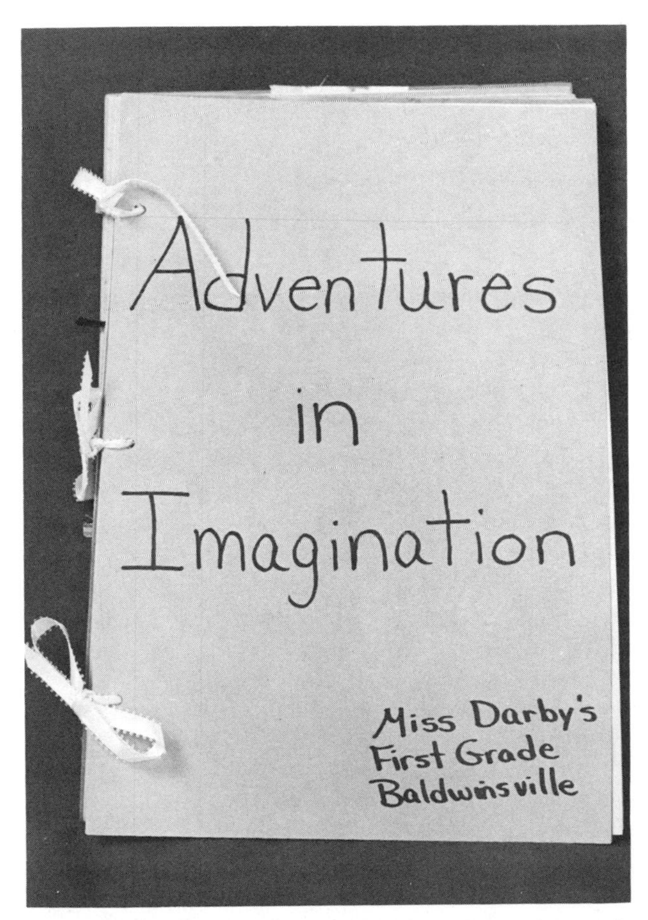

Figure 3 *Miss Darby had no black light so she used an adaptation of the Bim Bam Boo in her first grade with equally successful results.*

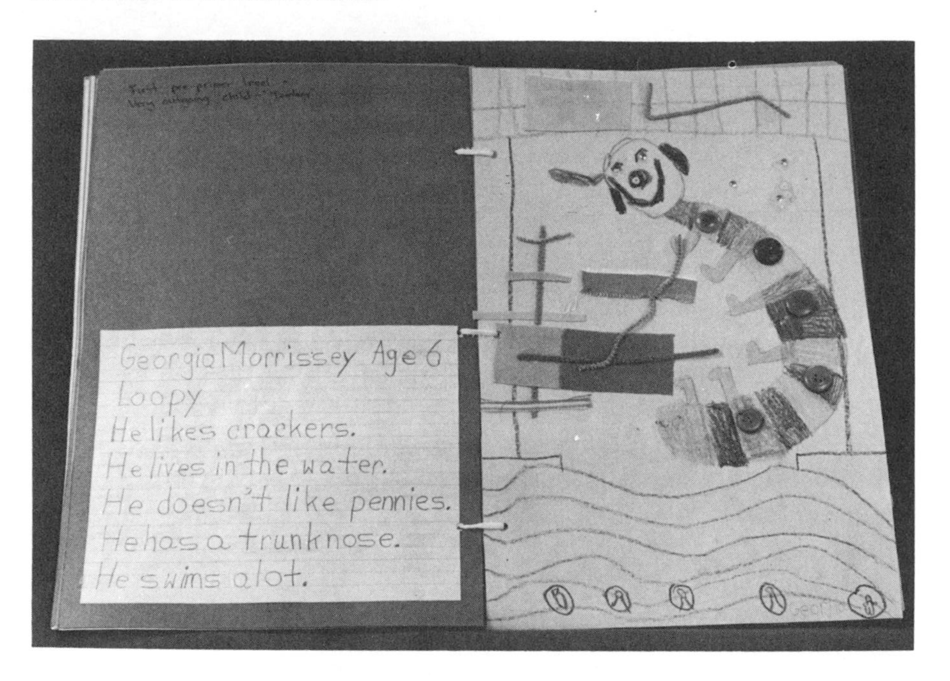

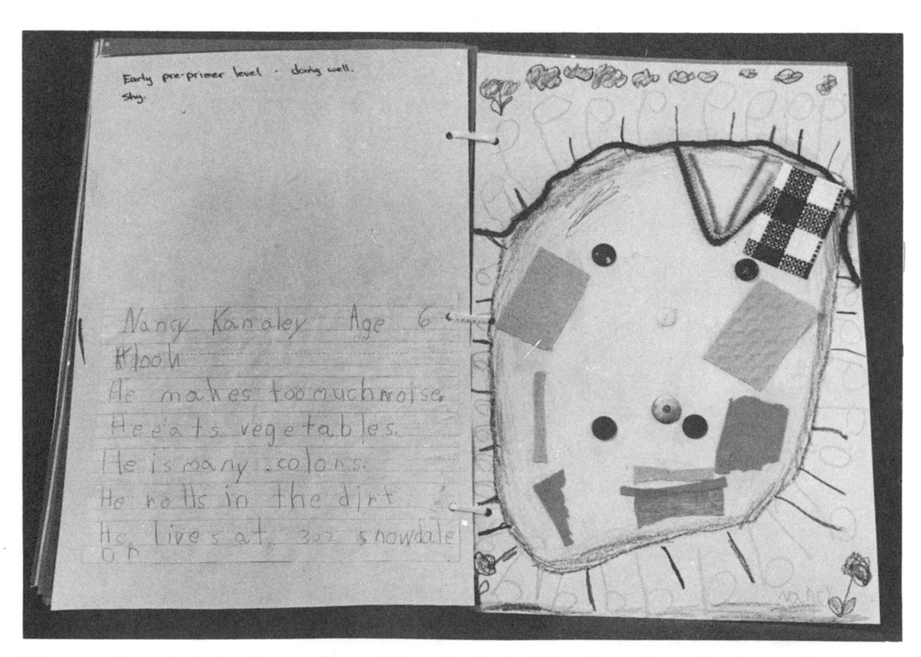

Figures 4 and 4–1 *Pages from Miss Darby's Bim Bam Boo Book used as a Big Reading Book.*

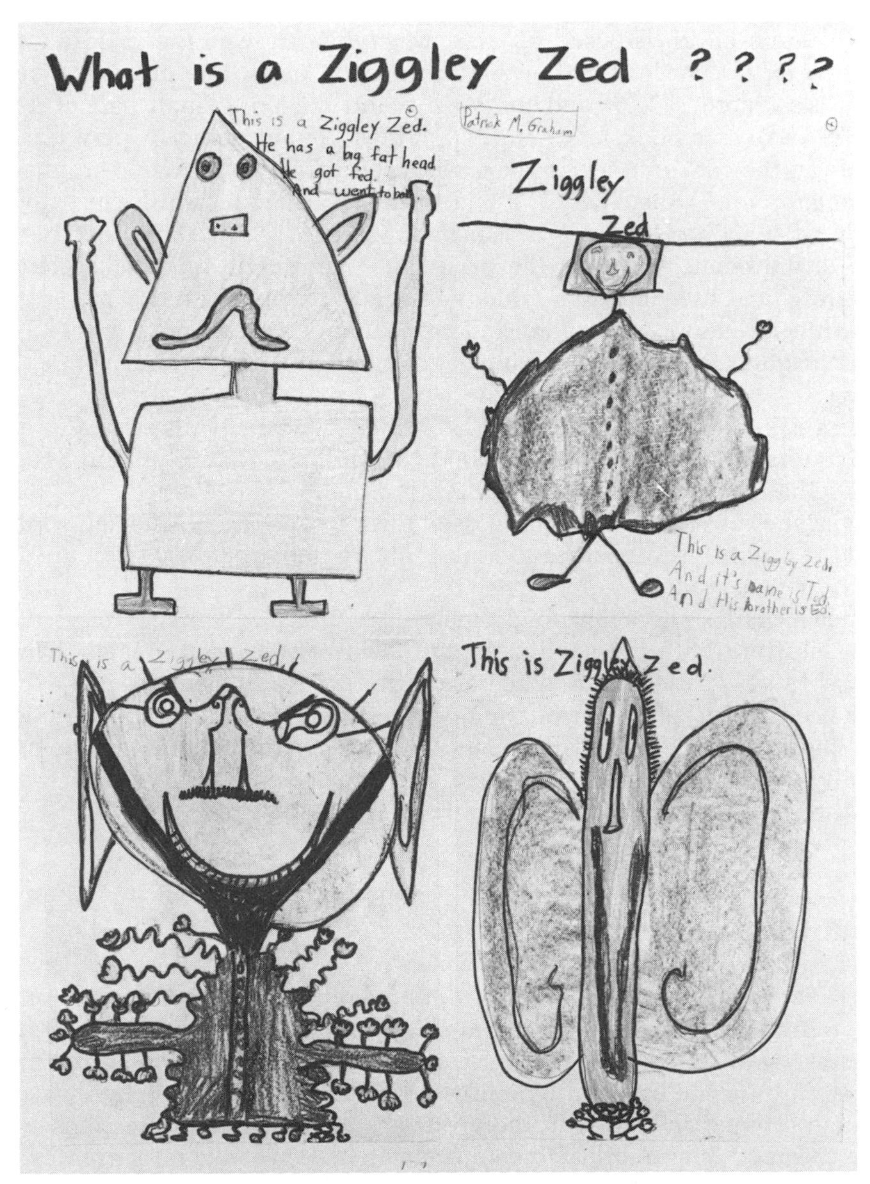

Figure 5 *Miss Smith's second grade created Ziggley Zeds and wrote stories about them: an excellent example of an open-ended teaching situation.*

opportunity to point out similar endings, like consonant sounds, and consonant blends.

After each child had read his line, Miss Ellis showed the children a cassette tape recorder that she had brought to class. She also showed them the record, "Peter and the Wolf," and played a small part of it.

"To make our book talk," she explained, "I am going to play this record in the background, and you will read your line of the poem into the microphone—then pass it along to the next person until everyone has read his line. When it is finished, we can set the tape recorder behind the book. As I turn the pages, the magic light will make your picture glow and your own voice will read the words on the page all the while the music is playing. And we will have a magic talking book."

Such squeals of delight—such exclamations of anticipation. Wonderful day!

Miss Ellis motioned for quiet. She started the record player. After a few strains of the music, she said into the "mike," "The Bim Bam Boo, an original poem story by Miss Ellis' third grade."

Then she turned the page and passed the microphone to Michael, who read the first page and passed the microphone to Marcia, and so on until the story was read.

Such a rich, creative morning! When the entire book was shown again, and this time with the sound, the enthusiasm was even greater than before! Miss Ellis had planned carefully indeed—all objectives met. No tests needed—no phony evaluation devices could ever test the learning and show the true behavior changes of these children. In this room creativity is a part of learning! In fact, almost all learning is based on the creative drive of children.

What Is Communication?

In the above story of the Bim Bam Boo, many kinds of communication were employed. I witnessed communication through speech, through pictures, through music, through color, through inflection, through gesture, by individual expression, by mass media, by poetry, by prose, through groups, and through individuals. Effective communication!

So common is our ability to communicate that we take it for granted. To understand what happens in the communication process, we need to take a fresh look at such processes.

How does communication take place? Smith[1] gives a simple account

1. James A. Smith, *Creative Teaching of the Language Arts in the Elementary School* (Boston: Allyn and Bacon, Inc., 1968), pp. 19–41.

of some of the concepts necessary to understand communication. He begins by describing the various levels of communication.

Levels of Communication

Communication is possible basically on three levels: the *experience* level, the *verbal* level, and the *conceptual* level. Figures 6 to 6–5 illustrates three types of communication.

In Figure 6 we see Mrs. Jones and Mrs. Fry making a cake. Verbal communication in this instance is possible with a minimum number of words spoken, since these two women are experiencing the total process together. New words take on meaning because they are introduced in context. But words are not the only means of communication in this picture. The two women communicate in many ways: speech, actions, demonstrations, gestures, facial expression, and movement. Once the cake is baked and eaten, both women can refer to this experience and relive it with a minimum number of spoken words. Mrs. Jones may meet Mrs. Fry at the shopping center and say, "Remember that cake you showed me how to make? Well, I tried it out on my family and they just loved it!" Mrs. Fry answers, "I just knew they would!"

A bystander would know from this conversation that Mrs. Fry had shown Mrs. Jones how to make a cake which she had tried out on her family. But that is about all. Mrs. Jones and Mrs. Fry, however, have communicated more to each other than simply the words spoken; they know the kind of cake Mrs. Jones made, the circumstances under which the making of the cake was first learned, the ingredients of the cake, and the number of people in the family who enjoyed the cake.

In Figure 6–1, we see Mrs. Fry talking to Mrs. Ellis. Mrs. Fry is trying to explain to her neighbor how to make the new cake. Because the communication is taking place on the verbal level without the background of the *common* experience, Mrs. Fry must use more words, and she must use more descriptive words to put across her ideas to Mrs. Ellis. What she really must do in order to be able to communicate here is to try to find word symbols from her own experience that match or nearly match those word symbols which identify similar experiences in Mrs. Ellis's background. She knows that Mrs. Ellis has experienced "½," she has experienced "cup," she has experienced "ripe," and she has experienced "strawberries." She is not so sure that Mrs. Ellis has experienced "avocado" so she embellishes the meaning for her by telling her what an avocado is, using words which are common labels to the past experiences of both women. These two women are able to communicate on this verbal level to the degree to which words (in the form of statements and

Figures 6 through 6–5 *Levels of communication.*

questions, gestures, facial expression, and voice inflection) make Mrs. Fry's experience meaningful to Mrs. Ellis.

In Figure 6-2, we see communication taking place on a conceptual level. Here the cooking class teacher is assuming that these mothers have already tried out (experienced) the avocado-strawberry cake recipe, and is talking on a level that requires a knowledge of a total experience and the ability to transfer or modify this experience to a new one. The teacher is dealing with concepts, and in order to understand her, each member of the class must have experienced the acts on which the concepts are based. The class member who has not had these experiences is very confused, because she has only a partial participation in the communication process that is under way. In every one of the three kinds of communication described here, common experience is necessary for full communication to take place.

Figures 6-3 to 6-5 show how the three kinds of communication function in a classroom. In Figure 6-4, the children of Miss Temple's first grade are visiting a farm. They see a tractor being operated and learn its name while watching it. They see the silo and the thresher and label these objects with a verbal symbol, or a word. These new words are very meaningful to them all because they are all experiencing them together.

In Figure 6-4, we see the children back in the classroom. Now they are making a reading chart of their experience. Miss Temple is letting them see their new oral vocabulary in printed symbol form. Communication is easy because the symbolic experience rises out of a common experience. All the children know and understand the *meaning* of the words.

Figure 6-5 shows these same children a few years later in the fourth grade. Since their original trip to the farm, they have had many other contacts with the same printed symbols. They have added new experiences to their old ones and have generalized these experiences into concepts. Therefore, when Miss Lavone says, "Modern farming equipment has helped the farmer produce more crops than our early ancestors from the same land," these children need no detailed explanation, because they have developed common concepts and communication takes place.

Learning at the verbal and conceptual level is actually a rearranging of old verbal experiences into new meanings, rather than living the experience oneself. When children have had a wealth of common experiences and have developed a reservoir of oral or verbal symbols to represent these experiences, the symbols *may* be rearranged into new understandings or new meanings in the child's mind so that new concepts are developed.

When teaching begins at the concept level without the base of the ex-

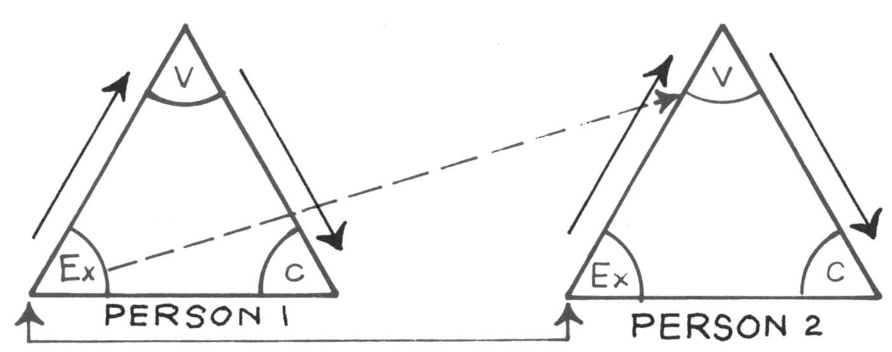

Figure 7 *Three levels of communication.*

perience level, communication breaks down. It is when we cross over from one level of communication to another that we fail to communicate. Figure 7 shows how this is likely to happen.

In Figure 7 each triangle represents a person. The solid line illustrates Mrs. Jones and Mrs. Fry communicating on the experience level. Their understandings are clear and concise. The dotted line shows a teacher who is talking on a concept level to a student; the verbalization is present, but there is meaning only if the student has the experience to interpret or translate the teacher's words.

Methods of Communication

In the above discussion, we have dealt largely with oral and written communication. Sometimes other forms of communication replace the verbal phase or the conceptual phase. Gesture is one such form. Such substitution is possible because a culture has developed common experiences which can be represented by a symbol of some sort. Examples of this might be: a cross, a Bible, a green light, a red flag, or a dove; all convey meaning since they appear in various places in everyday living.

Look at the problems listed below on a continuum. Try to do them.

1. Communicate some idea or thought by a pose; do not use movement or voice.
2. Communicate something by adding movement to your pose.
3. Communicate something through the use of movement and voice.
4. Tell about a trip you took recently. Allow the class to interrupt to ask questions.
5. Write about your trip.
6. Write about your trip in one paragraph.
7. Write about your trip in one sentence.

8. Write about your trip in one word.
9. Write about your trip in one letter of the alphabet.

In trying to communicate through the above techniques, which proved the easiest of all? Probably No. 4 enabled you to communicate more freely than any of the others. As you moved away from No. 4 both up and down the continuum, communication became more difficult. Let us see what might happen on each level of communication mentioned above.

No. 1: Communication here could take place by having someone assume a prayerful attitude by bowing his head and folding his hands. Persons entering a room and encountering someone in such a pose would probably drop their voices and even tiptoe to a seat. Because the pose has changed the behavior of a listener or observer, it has communicated something. Other poses might be assumed such as a salute, arms crossed on chest, the boxer's pose, or the pose of a runner ready to sprint. Each would communicate *something* to the observer. That *something* might be different to each observer, because the pose could be interpreted only in light of experience.

Figure 8 *Motions communicate.*

No. 2: Ideas can be communicated more easily by movement than by a pose. Many movements that have common meaning have been developed in every society: the thumb of a hitchhiker moving across his body as it follows the passing car; the circle motion of the finger winding around the ear as one child tries to show another that his teacher is a little "touched in the head"; the motion of the two index fingers making the pattern of a square as one teen-ager tries to describe the new boy in school to another; or the thumbs-down motion that indicates the rejection of a candidate by the club.

No. 3: Adding voice to movement makes communication easier for the speaker, but not always for the listener.

No. 4: This probably proved to be the most satisfactory kind of communication to both listener and speaker. Free to use his hands, voice, and facial expression, the speaker can put his ideas across. The listener can interrupt to ask questions and can put the speaker in a situation in which he must use words within the understanding level of the listener.

No. 5: Freedom to write as you choose makes communication easier than through simple gestures, but here are lost the tone quality of the voice, the facial expression, the right to question and to clarify statements. Here is a teen-ager's story about a trip:

My Trip

Last week I flew to Florida. When I left New York City the temperature was around zero. When I arrived in Florida the temperature was 78 degrees. Such a delightful change!

The flight down was perfect! We flew non-stop so it took only three hours. It was one of the most beautiful flights I have ever taken. The sky was a clear, azure blue all the way. At times cloud banks cut off our view of the earth, but most of the way the panorama of the countryside stretched out clearly below us in the bright, sparkling sun. It was a fascinating experience to watch the clean, white ground give way to bleak, barren terrain, which in turn became green and lush. We stepped into the plane in a cold, winter world and stepped out of it three hours later into a warm, summer climate. It was sheer magic!

My stay in Florida was just wonderful. I had such a good time! Our plane was met at the airport by a limousine which whisked us off to a swank hotel. As soon as we arrived we were invited to a reception on the terrace.

No. 6: To write about this trip in one paragraph becomes difficult, because much of the writer's excitement and feeling of the trip are lost. Of necessity, the writing becomes almost a summarized factual account of the experience.

My Trip

I flew to Florida for my vacation. The flight was delightful; the weather was perfect and the people were very friendly and gracious. From the moment I arrived at my hotel until the time I left to come home, I was busy with a variety of exciting activities. Needless to say, I had a wonderful time.

No. 7: Writing about this trip in one sentence handicaps the writer hopelessly. The result probably reads something like this:

My Trip

I went on a trip to Florida and had a wonderful time.

No. 8: What can one do here except to write "Florida"?

No. 9: This assignment becomes an impossibility.

We have taken a look at various types of verbal and conceptual communication skills, or substitutions for them. At some time in our own experience each type plays an important part. However, we feel most comfortable and communicate most readily when we operate in area No. 4, where we can communicate in a face to face manner employing all our resources.

The type of communication used depends on the situation. Communication without voice is difficult but possible. This is exemplified by the tourist in the foreign country where gestures and actions must be used to communicate because of the language barrier. The tourist does the best he can in a limited way. So does the hitchhiker who has to get across a message as quickly as he can. Short sentences generally are best suited to communicating one idea, not a whole series of ideas. Letters of the alphabet communicate almost nothing because they are less than ideas—they are fragments of ideas.

The Language Arts: Tools to Communication

The language arts are the tools of communication. They are not subjects in themselves for they have no body of content. We do not read reading or write writing or spell spelling. We read because we want to obtain a message or an idea from a printed page; we write because we wish to convey a message or an idea by symbols; we spell correctly because we wish to make our communication clear by utilizing those arbitrary written symbols agreed upon by our society. The fundamental objective of the language arts program is to develop relevant, correct, clear, imaginative, and effective communication. The full realization of this objective is possible only when the tools of language are used as *tools* and children practice the use of them continually.

Misconceptions About Language

There are many misconceptions about language which interfere with its use as a creative tool for the development of effective communication.

Smith[2] defines them as follows:

Misconception 1. Language and the Rules of Language Are "Set." Actually, there is little about language that is rigid. Because its purpose is to communicate effectively and efficiently, language is continually being changed. Verb forms that were frowned upon twenty years ago have now found their way into common usage.

There are really few pure forms of language and sentence structure used in common everyday speech. The drive for efficient communication within people resolves itself in a continual evolution in language usage: a virtual "trimming it down to size."

Which Sounds Natural?

I'll take the omnibus to the city.	*or*	I'll take the bus downtown.
Our high fidelity phonograph set has given us much pleasure.	*or*	We've had a great deal of enjoyment from our hi-fi set.

In many cases, the economical version communicates better than the more correct and proper version. By this criterion, the trimmed-down form is as acceptable as, or more acceptable than, the more proper forms as a medium for communication.

Great literature is written so that it communicates unusual moods, plots, ideas. On one page in a Nobel Prize book, there are twelve instances where grammar rules are violated so that the author can create a mood. This makes for powerful reading. Yet few teachers accept this type of writing in themes or stories. Regardless of the child's intent, these papers are generally marked with red pencil and returned to be corrected. Correct writing, in many instances, is dull and ineffective.

2. Ibid., pp. 42–57.

Misconception 2. Language and Rules of Language Are Determined by Experts. Language is determined by *common usage*. The words that are used in any given society are the ones which arise from the experiences of the people. After a short period of usage, these words appear in dictionaries.

Vocabularies within a language evolve, sometimes slowly and sometimes dramatically. A group of college juniors in teacher education compared two newspapers printed six months apart to show how dramatically language can change in a short period of time. One paper was printed in September 1957, previous to the launching of the Russian Sputnik. The other was printed in February 1958, six months after this historic event. The average newspaper is printed on the vocabulary level of the sixteen-year-old. Yet in the feature article of this newspaper, over seventy-five new words and phrases had come into common usage in six months time—almost a whole new language had been invented in order to communicate new ideas.

Experts serve the purpose of setting common rules by which language may be used for proper communication, but not always for most effective communication. They make their contribution to language in those instances when proper communication is needed, such as in business letter writing, formal textbook construction, reporting, and the like. However, the people of a society use the language to say what they have to say, according to the social setting in which they find themselves. In such instances, correct language forms may be abandoned for a more efficient or picturesque communication.

Misconception 3. Language Is Static. We have seen how language is continually changing. It is not static; it is dynamic, vibrant, and alive with change. Change replaces old phrases and words with new ones, gives us new spellings and more realistic language forms, new punctuation forms to coincide with our use of machines in communicating, and even alters the meanings of words.

New words are being born every minute while many words are falling into disuse:

Words Recently Born	*Words That Are Dying*
atomic	coal scuttle
mastic	blacksmith
supersonic	trolley car
drag-strip	hook and eye
fallout	buggy
megalopolis	knickers
space station	bloomers
countdown	carpetbag
antibiotics	bundling

Words Recently Born (cont.)

lunik
phonovision
astronaut
ballistic
minitrack
bibliotherapy
Telstar
aquanaut
cosmonaut

Words Almost Dead
(Rarely Used)
hobble skirt
buttonhook
surrey
waterglass
horseless carriage
gaslight
carfare
mumblety-peg
tenpins

Words Whose Meaning Is Changing

Decay: once meant decomposition of organic matter—now also means the deterioration of metal in outer space.

Fallout: once a command—now the radiation effect of nuclear blasts.

Pot: once a kettle—now a drug.

The symbols of language are constantly undergoing change. Children and adults are continually experimenting with language. When children cannot express an experience with a certain word, they put together other words to express the idea. Timmy, aged four, who does not have the word "boost" in his vocabulary says, "Will you please give me a *reach-up*?" when he wants to climb a tree. Stephen, aged five, describes the difference between a layer cake and a loaf cake by saying, "This is an *up* cake." Such experiments with language are called *verbalisms.*

We hear words in one context, reproduce them in another context, and absorb them into our own speech patterns if they are accepted by all listeners over a period of time.

Slang communicates too. Another common way in which language undergoes change is through slang. This use is often frowned upon in school, yet our language is peppered with slang which was once rejected. Such expressions as *O.K., savvy? classy, slick,* and *scram* communicate as no other words do. Slang has a unique feature—it seems to express a multitude of ideas and feelings with a minimum of words.

Slang fulfills many functions. To the teen-ager it is a way of asserting his independence and individuality by breaking away from adult restrictions and standards. It becomes a language all his own through which he can communicate with other teen-agers, but not with the adults who dominate his life. Yet, in most English courses, the use of slang as a means of communication is denied to children. This denial is an example of how teachers limit creative development by driving the use of words into the subconscious, rather than allowing it to remain accessible in the preconscious.

Even slang changes from generation to generation. Currently, one is "square" or "hip" by the words he uses in his speech.

Current Vocabularies

Square	*Hip*
nervous	up-tight
to leave	split or "flake-off"
cop (fuzz)	pig
excite	turn on
how things are	where it's at and like it is
exciting	like wow!
problem	hang-up
boring	dullsville
girl	chick
forsake	kopp out
with it	in gear
money	bread

When we refuse to allow children to use slang in school, we do not realize that what we are doing is refusing them the right to use their newly formed language (slang) while we are often using it ourselves (as we once knew it).

The creative teacher realizes the need for change in language. She accepts the creative forms of language being invented through common usage or by the children she teaches. She encourages the coinage of new words, recognizing the fact that creating a new word is as exciting as creating a painting.

Donald, aged 10, could not find the word he wanted to describe the sunny, golden day he was writing about in his poem, so he called it brightful. Shelley said there was no word to tell about the evening sky she was describing in her poem, so she invented pinksky. Ronnie, a teen-ager, named his jalopy "Shasta" because, said Ronnie, "Shasta have oil, shasta have gas, shasta have water everytime I drive her."

If we are to teach children to speak and write creatively, we must place all known resources at their disposal and not force language forms into the subconscious mind. The new patterns of speaking and writing are dynamic and changing; through them language becomes a creative tool.

Misconception 4. There Is a Single Language in a Culture. There may be many languages within one culture. Even though the same words are spoken, they may have different meanings among different sets of people. Lumberjacks, teachers, doctors, railroad workers, and laboratory scientists all have unique languages of their own. They also use words commonly employed by other sets of people, but often with completely different meanings.

There are languages within a language. Sometimes this is called "jargon." Educators have a jargon, as do most people involved in a vocation or profession. Spoken out of context, jargon is meaningless to some people. It actually represents communication at the conceptual level. (See Figure 9.)

Anyone who is hip will recognize the invitation by the cat to bring a girl friend to his house for dinner.

Figure 9 *Jargon communicates.*

In Figure 9, cooks in a short-order diner will recognize the order for two poached eggs on toast.

The statistician will recognize the language that tells about the falling of the data into the pattern of the normal curve.

Television crews and stagehands will respond by clearing the stage.

The marine interprets Figure 9 as meaning that the gossip about going to the swamps for practicing battle techniques is probably false.

These languages within the language require an interpreter almost as much as a foreign language does. Nonetheless, they give the language a beauty and a picturesqueness which make it exciting and colorful. Children who hear these subcultural languages are afforded opportunities to see how words can be used creatively to express different ideas. If their writing is to ring true, they must understand that certain words and sentences can convey many meanings.

Language often gives status. Knowledge of proper speech forms and correct grammar gives us a wider choice of usage. We can apply the forms of speech that we know to the social situation in which we find ourselves. Speech is, above all, a social process. One can be accepted or rejected in his social setting because of his speech. Many educated young men, in their drive to be accepted, abandoned their learned speech patterns while in military service and assumed the unique speech of the platoon in order to be able to communicate and hold status within that group.

Figure 10 *We change our speech patterns to gain social status.*

Just as there are many languages within the language, so there are many levels of language.

Levels of Usage

Illiterate	*Homely*	*Informal*	*Formal*	*Literary*
We've done et.	We just had chow.	We've just finished eating.	Dinner has been served.	Ah, how hath the groaning board been lightened of its burden.
He's maddern a hornet.	He's all riled up.	Boy, is he teed off.	He is extremely distraught.	The turmoil within him all but erupted in a volcanic outburst.
We're gonna shake a leg.	C'mon let's get with it.	How about a dance?	May I have the pleasure of this dance?	Let us bow and curtsey to the melodic strains of Strauss.

Effective communication may take place at one level as well as when levels are crossed. Often a child coming from a farm home or a bilingual home is confused by the phrasing of his teacher, because the words are used in different patterns or context from those he is accustomed to hearing. These children often experience spelling difficulties simply because they hear words as their parents say them and then spell them by sound. A farm boy in the sixth grade wrote "refrigeador," "stoopid," and "breffast" in a story. A visit to his home revealed this to be exactly the way his parents pronounced these words. Many years of listening had fixed these patterns so well in his mind that they predominated over his teacher's pronunciations. This boy needed to hear and see these words. He had a good phonetic sense, but he did not have the word sound or picture imprinted on his mind. This situation is a delicate one, because under no circumstances should the teacher cause a breakdown in communication between the parents and the boy, nor should the teacher do anything to cause friction or loss of respect in the boy-parent relationship. Yet the boy must see and hear the correct ways of saying and writing words.

Few people operate on any one level of language. Actually, most of us use all levels at one time or another, depending on the social situation in which we find ourselves. We fluctuate from the literary to the illiterate level frequently in the course of one conversation.

To help children cope with language and to better develop communication skills, it is important that they come to recognize levels of language, not as criteria for determining the social status of the speaker, but as a literary style or a means of communicating a specific idea within a certain context. Children are exposed to these levels of language all the time, and they need help in understanding, interpreting, and using them.

Every person has many vocabularies. Our grammar and reading books often refer to the child's vocabulary. This becomes a confusing concept because all people have many vocabularies rather than one vocabulary. As children acquire words, they categorize them within the memory operation of the brain. Some words they use continually, whereas others are stored away for special usage. Because language is a social skill, we select from our reservoir of stored-up words those which best suit each situation in which we find ourselves. Some words appear in all vocabularies, but many are unique to only one and are used only at one time. A child's comprehension vocabulary may differ from his speaking vocabulary; that is, he can hear and understand words he never uses.

Although there are many different vocabularies, we can sort out three basic ones for the language arts: the speaking, the reading, and the writ-

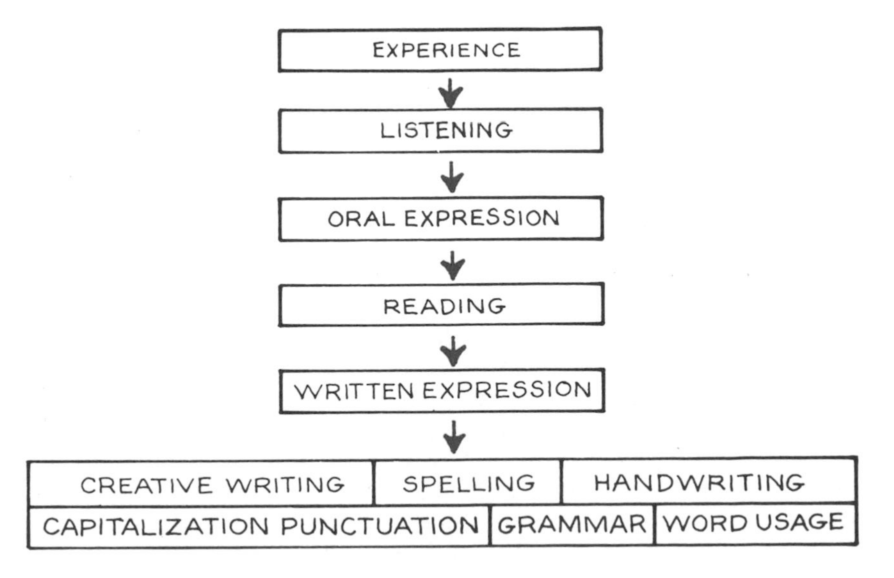

Figure 11 *Normal sequence of language development.*

ing vocabularies. In a child, the largest of these is the speaking vocabulary. Second largest is the reading vocabulary. Smallest is the writing vocabulary. In adults, the largest is the reading vocabulary, next is the speaking vocabulary, and smallest is the writing vocabulary.

It is important to note that the smallest vocabulary of both adults and children is the writing vocabulary. This is probably true because children never, and adults rarely, write words they do not say. All this bears significance when we realize that we must place a great deal of stress on the oral vocabulary of children in order to build the necessary vocabulary for effective reading and creative writing. (See page 47.)

How Language Develops

Language develops through a logical sequence. First in the sequence comes *listening*. Children learn the names of things by hearing them identified. Listening and experience go hand in hand. A child can understand the abstract verbal symbols we call words only when they represent a direct or a vicarious experience which he has had.

After the child has experienced and listened, he can *speak*. *Oral communication* is nothing more than the substitution of oral sounds for a vivid direct or vicarious experience. When the oral symbols or sounds become a fluent part of the child's vocabulary, he is ready to recognize them in print. This is *reading*. After his reading ability has developed sufficiently to afford him a true visual impression of these words, he is ready to imitate or reproduce these words in *writing*.

Spelling, *handwriting*, *word usage*, *capitalization*, *punctuation*, and *grammar usage* are refinements to the writing act. They make communication clearer but not necessarily richer. Actually, they are social courtesies learned in order that all people may communicate through writing. They are the examples of some of the necessary conformities of a society.

Figure 11 helps to explain the sequence of language development. This sequence is longitudinal as well as lateral. It is longitudinal in that it is the way language develops over a span of years. The baby listens for a period of time, varying from a few months to two years, to the people around him using verbal symbols in meaningful context. He listens and experiences. He hears his mother say "table" in a host of ways during this period of time. She says: "Helen, help Mother set the table"; "See the pretty flowers Daddy bought, in on the coffee table"; "Answer the telephone on the table in the hall"; and so on, until one day, when he is physically able and psychologically ready, he thumps his hand on the object in mind and says, "tabbul." He re-enforces his learning when Mother gleefully shouts, "Did you hear what he said? Say it again, Honey—tell sister. What is this?" Then he tells Daddy and all his relatives and so fixes the word in his mind. Here is an example of the word appearing in the child's vocabulary at the concept level, for he has generalized his experiences with many tables.

This sequence of development is also lateral in that the same process is used over a short period to introduce new words to children. For instance, a teacher calls a reading group to the front of the room. They are to construct a reading chart from an experience they had at the farm the previous day. They learn some new words such as silo, tractor, thresher, milking machine, milk-cooler, furrow, and acre by labeling their experiences. The teacher re-enforces their learning by showing pictures of these words, and the children recall the oral symbols. The teacher then introduces the printed symbol by use of the experience chart, and the children learn to read the chart. Some children, if they are advanced enough, may even copy the words in a story of their own later at their seats. In this situation, the child has widened his vocabulary and has developed language skills in one period, where he progressed from experiencing to listening to oral expression to reading and on to writing. This process is often called the language experience approach.

Intelligence enters into the picture here. It has been pointed out that intelligence is closely related to vocabulary development. Therefore, as the child progresses down through the above chart, his intelligence becomes more and more important in terms of his ability to use language. Slow-learning children do not read as well as normal or bright children, and we can never expect them to be able to punctuate, capitalize, and spell as effectively.

For effective teaching, the sequential development of language must always be followed; whenever it is violated, problems result. A primary teacher, about to give a reading lesson, often introduces a list of words on the board. If these words are not within the range of the children's experiences, they do not communicate effectively. The children can resort only to memory or name-calling of the printed symbol. Unless the word takes on meaning during the subsequent lesson, it does not become a part of the child's usable vocabulary. It is only a meaningless arrangement of letters looking like many other meaningless arrangements, and he will forget it due to lack of use.

Notice how clearly Miss Ellis introduced the story of the Bim Bam Boo at the opening of this chapter. She drew on the children's experiences to develop new words and to pull out familiar rhyming words—and in this exercise, listening and speaking were well utilized. Next, the words were put in rhyming sentence form, and the correct spelling, punctuation, and usage were automatically represented in the way Miss

Ellis placed the material before the children. Perhaps at some later date Miss Ellis might have the children *write* the poem, thus completing the normal language experience cycle.

Teachers once introduced spelling words for the week's lesson from a textbook. Many of the words were foreign to the child and unrelated to his experiences. When this was so, the teacher's first job was to see to it that the child experienced the word, then used it orally, next saw it in print, and then learned to spell it, so he could use it to help him communicate in his written work. (See Chapter 11.)

Unless these steps are followed, the motivation for learning the word becomes something other than communication. It may be fear of failure or desire to please the teacher. The child will memorize the word under this latter motivation, pass a test on Friday, and often not know the word on a succeeding test two weeks later. The word has never been a part of his total experience, and his memory of it has deteriorated. In a good language arts program then, much emphasis must be placed at the top level of this chart: *experience*. In the primary grades this experience must be, to a large extent, direct, so that the verbal symbol that represents it may be accurate and meaningful.

This sequence is vitally important in developing the creative aspects of the language arts. *It is only when children receive the opportunity to talk frequently and freely that they develop an extensive oral vocabulary. It is only when teachers make conscientious efforts to use normal experiences to build new vocabulary that children develop a rich written vocabulary. It is only when teachers contrive experiences to keep children using these vocabularies in new and creative ways that creative writing can take place. It is important to remember that children rarely write words they do not speak.*

Summary

Effective and creative teaching of the language arts must be founded on known truths regarding the nature of communication. These truths can be summarized as follows:

(1) There are three levels of communication: experience, verbal, and conceptual; (2) communication is possible through many techniques; (3) all communication is rooted in common experience; (4) verbal and conceptual communication are effective when meaningful symbols are assigned to common or like experiences; (5) there are many ways to communicate, but the most effective way is talking in face-to-face con-

tact; (6) the selection, arrangement, and fluency of words determine the degree of feeling and the accuracy of the information communicated.

All language arts teaching should begin with basic experiences. New vocabulary must develop from these basic (direct or vicarious) experiences, and eventually concepts should be built by adding depth and meaning to this newly acquired vocabulary. The story of the Bim Bam Boo demonstrates how this may be creatively done.

Ideas are the important factor in communication; the mechanics of communication are secondary. A creative teacher is concerned about the ideas she uses to communicate effectively to her students. She sets conditions for effective communication in her classroom by providing common experiences from which she can build a rich, imaginative language arts program. The creative teacher uses language with skill, aware of the sequential development of words and concepts. Language is her main tool for teaching, and her teaching skill is totally dependent on her ability to use language skills. The language arts are the tools of communication, and because communication is a complicated process, learning to use the tools is also a complicated process. There are many misconceptions about language which interfere with its creative use in developing effective communication.

Language develops in a logical sequence, and when this sequence is violated, the teacher may cause communication disability among the children. The importance of experience as the basis for language development cannot be overstressed.

To the Reader

1. Compare the account of the Bim Bam Boo with the language sequence chart on page 45 and note how well Miss Ellis followed the steps of the language experience concept.
2. Miss Smith, a second grade teacher, inspired her children to draw a Wiggley Woo and create the bulletin board on page 29. The children then wrote and read stories about their creations to each other. Is adaptation of this nature a form of creativity? Could Miss Smith develop the language sequence concept by the use of this activity? Refer to Chapter 3 and decide why this was a sound educational activity.
3. An excellent film which will give you new insights into the language structure is *Alphabet Conspiracy*, produced by the Bell Telephone Company. It may be borrowed from the company.

4. Make a collection of hippie words and note how many have become accepted in a few years by "the establishment." The words "hippie" and "square" are themselves two good examples.
5. Current magazines often publish a page of picturesque speech. Collect some of these sayings and analyze them. Why do they appeal to the reader so strongly? Would you say picturesque speech is creative?
6. It is a known fact that many of our current grammar rules to which we adhere so religiously were made up by the monks and scribes of the Middle Ages and by semi-literate Dutch printers in their attempts to standardize communication and eighteenth-century English grammarians who tried to make English obey Latin rules. It is ironic that the purists of language adhere so strongly to rules made up by this group. Research some of the origins of language and decide what mutations of language may have come from these origins.
7. Remembering the language sequence charted on page 45, think through the value of introducing new words for a reading lesson by printing them on the chalkboard. What would be a better way to do it?
8. On which of the objectives for teaching the language arts does your school place the most emphasis? Think of some way you could put more emphasis on them all.
9. Ask yourself, How do my children react to the lessons I teach in the language arts? Do they enjoy them? If not, is it likely they will use language skills freely? See what you can do to improve children's attitudes toward language skills.
10. You may properly conclude, after reading this chapter, that we set conditions for the creative teaching of language by understanding the function of language in our society and by teaching language skills to children. Children cannot communicate without these language skills. Once a skill is learned, each child is better equipped to create with it. Think of this and then discuss these questions:
    a. Where do you draw the line on the use of slang in school?
    b. Can the teaching of speaking and listening be creative?
    c. The use of proper forms in grammar and word usage is largely social courtesy. Are social courtesies necessary conformities? Why?
    d. In what ways would you handle the problem of the child who comes from a home where speech is almost always at the illiterate level?
11. The hippie uses a language of his own. Collect some hippie words and phrases. Discuss the purposes behind the hippie's choice of

vocabulary. Is this true nonconformity? Do you feel that any great writing, either poetry or prose, may emerge from the hippie movement? Why or why not?

12. From your reading in this chapter, list ten basic principles on which a teacher must build her language arts program.

Selected Bibliography

ANDERSON, PAUL S. *Language Skills in Elementary Education.* New York: The Macmillan Company, 1964.

ANDERSON, VERNA D., PAUL S. ANDERSON, FRANCIS BALLANTINE, AND VIRGINIA M. HOWES. *Readings in Language Arts,* 2nd ed. New York: The Macmillan Company, 1968.

BURNS, PAUL C., AND LEO M. SCHELL. *Elementary Language Arts Readings.* Chicago, Illinois: Rand McNally and Company, 1969.

CORCORAN, GERTRUDE B. *Language Arts in the Elementary School: A Modern Linguistic Approach.* New York: The Ronald Press, 1970.

CRARY, RYLAND W. *Humanizing the School: Curriculum Development and Theory.* New York: Alfred A. Knopf, 1969.

DALLMANN, MARTHA. *Teaching the Language Arts in the Elementary School,* 2nd ed. Dubuque, Iowa: William C. Brown Company Publishers, 1971.

DAWSON, MILDRED A., AND GEORGIANA C. NEWMAN. *Language Teaching in Kindergarten and the Early Primary Grades.* New York: Harcourt, Brace and World, Inc., 1966.

GREENE, HARRY A., AND WALTER T. PETTY. *Developing Language Skills in the Elementary Schools,* 4th ed. Boston: Allyn and Bacon, Inc., 1971.

HUGHES, JOHN P. *Linguistics and Language Teaching.* New York: Random House, 1968.

JOYCE, WILLIAM, ROBERT OANA, AND ROBERT HOUSTON. *Elementary Education in the Seventies.* Part IV, "Language Arts." New York: Holt, Rinehart and Winston, 1970.

LAMB, POSE. *Guiding Children's Language Learning,* 2nd ed. Dubuque, Iowa: William C. Brown Company Publishers, 1971.

LANGDON, GRADE, AND IRVING W. STOUT. *Teaching in the Primary Grades.* New York: The Macmillan Company, 1964.

LETTON, MILDRED C. "How Do Children Communicate?" in James C.

MacCampbell (ed.), *Readings in the Language Arts in the Elementary School*. Boston: D. C. Heath and Company, 1964, 48–51.

PETTY, WALTER. *Issues and Problems in the Elementary Language Arts: A Book of Readings*. Boston: Allyn and Bacon, 1968.

POOLEY, ROBERT C. *Teaching English Usage*. New York: Appleton-Century-Crofts, 1946.

REED, KATHERINE. *The Nursery School*, 5th ed. Philadelphia: W. B. Saunders Company, 1971.

SHUSTER, ALBERT, AND MILTON PLOGHOFT. *The Emerging Elementary Curriculum*, 2nd ed. Columbis, Ohio: Charles E. Merrill Publishing Company, 1970.

SMITH, JAMES A. *Creative Teaching of the Language Arts in the Elementary School*. Boston: Allyn and Bacon, Inc., 1968.

TORRANCE, E. PAUL, AND R. E. MYERS. *Creative Learning and Teaching*. New York: Dodd, Mead and Company, 1971.

TRAUGER, WILMER, *Language Arts in Elementary Schools*, 2nd ed. New York: McGraw-Hill, 1963.

VYGOTSKY, L. S. *Thought and Language*. Cambridge, Massachusetts: M.I.T. Press, 1962.

3

The Adventure of Creative Communication

THE HAUNTED ROOM

If you were a child and two weeks before Halloween you saw a sign like this one over the door of a small room which, up to this time, had been used as a conference room, wouldn't you be curious—and excited—and motivated?

This is exactly what happened to one group of children in a school I was visiting. Two of my student teachers were challenged by their co-operating teacher to plan some group work for an ungraded primary class which would result in some creative writing and some creative art work built around a Halloween theme. Of course, the master teacher had other objectives in mind, such as:

1. Building a speaking, reading, and writing vocabulary appropriate for the season.
2. Helping the children to see the importance of tone and inflection in reading aloud and in communicating ideas to one another.
3. Providing an incentive for the writing of stories, poems, and essays about Halloween.
4. Developing spelling tests for the next two weeks' work.
5. Developing individuality in each child.

The two young teachers conceived a series of lessons which resulted in one of the finest Halloween projects I have ever witnessed—truly an adventure in communication.

Miss Weissman and Miss Rauscher together wrote the following poem. Children enjoy knowing that their teachers write creatively, and this concept added to the motivation and interest of the experience.

Halloween

Tonight is the night
When dead leaves fly
Like witches on swithes
Across the sky,
When elf and sprite
Flit through the night
On moony sheen.

Tonight is the night
When leaves make a sound
Like gnome in his home
Under the ground,
When spooks and trolls
Creep out of holes
Mossy and green.

Tonight is the night
When pumpkins stare
Through sheaves and leaves
Everywhere,
Where ghoul and ghost
And goblin host
Dance round their queen.
It's Halloween!

To introduce the first lesson, Miss Rauscher and Miss Weissman read the Halloween poem in a flat, monotonous voice with no expression whatsoever. They then asked the children if they enjoyed the poem and if they could picture what had taken place in the poem. Most of the children responded (probably out of courtesy) that it was good, but that they didn't really know what it was all about.

The teachers then read the poem again, but this time they created an atmosphere: The lights in the room were turned off, children were instructed to put their heads on their desks, and the two student teachers read the lines with a great deal of expression.

The children felt that this was an improvement.

Miss Rauscher then introduced a bulletin board on which pictures had been placed, but the pictures were invisible because they were painted with invisible glow paint. "Scary" music was played, all lights were extinguished, and the black light was turned on to the bulletin board where the pictures burst into color and glowed in the dark. Again the poem was read, with the black light moving to focus on one picture after another, each appropriate to a particular line of a poem. The children were enthralled with the experience. They said they thought it was a different poem from the one read at the beginning of the lesson.

The teachers then asked the children what they had done to make the poem more interesting and easier to understand, and using fluorescent chalk, they wrote the suggestions of the children on black paper with the black light. This is the unedited list the children compiled.

Ways Poem Was Made Better:

1. Use props
2. Use color
3. Use sounds
4. Use magic light
5. Use scary stories
6. Use your voice
7. Set a mood
8. Use lightning (lights were flashed on and off at this point)

The teachers next asked the children if they would like to use these materials and ideas in communicating a Halloween poem or story. Of course, the children were immediately excited about it. The teachers then asked the children for some "scary" words which might be used in the story, and listed them on the chalkboard. Later they were put on a ditto master so every child could have his own list. Following is the list the children compiled:

goblins
witches
ghosts
scarecrow
footsteps
creaking door
bats
wind
trolls
sounds
skeleton heads
dead
cemetery

Frankenstein
dead leaves
rattling
pumpkin heads
black cats
owl
scary voices
trees
vampires
mummies
lightning
thunder
stormy

howling cats	cobwebs
shining	spiders
wolfman	monsters
eyeballs	ghoul
cloudy	sneaky
dark sky	black
stillness	silence

How far removed are many of these words from the lists printed in spelling books!

The following day the class was divided into two groups—one group used the magic chalk for making pictures and the other group began writing a story together. The next day the jobs were switched. There were enough sentences in the story so that each child could read one. The story was printed on a ditto master so each child could have his own copy.

Every child was then assigned a sentence and practiced reading it in the most effective way he knew how.

When the children were comfortable with their lines, they were all taken into the "haunted" room and together they read the whole story. They decided to collect "sound effects" to be used in the background. Then the story was put on a tape with the weird noises of shrieking ghosts and creaking doors added for effect.

All the pictures were then hung in the little conference room. Classes were invited in groups of ten to visit the haunted room. They sat on the floor, the door was closed, the tape was turned on with weird noises coming at the beginning, and then the magic light was turned on and the room burst into color with pictures of all the witches, goblins, and pumpkins glowing in the dark. The effect was delightful and the children were enthralled with the story. As a result of this experience, children from the other classrooms wrote about their experience in the haunted room and were motivated to write original Halloween poems and stories.

Creative Production

"Come to our room to see and hear our magic talking book about the Bim Bam Boo," said one child, pulling on my hand.

"No, come to ours and see our haunted room," another pleaded.

And there is more to come! Adventures with Hildegarde Magillicutty at the State Fair; Fun With Sally Flack and the Rabbit; a puzzle called Over, over, over, I, over, over, E, dot; and the Saga of the Kola-Kola Bird!

Right away my curiosity was aroused—is yours? If so, the first steps in the creative process have been achieved: motivation and involvement.

All these adventures about which we have read and will read are creative approaches to learning. Creativity is sweeping the world. Why?

For years and years very little was known about creativity. Long ago people believed that creativity was a divine gift doled out to a few select people, and they were thankful enough for this gift so that they cherished it and fulfilled it to the best of their ability. God was seen as the great creator, and these select few were chosen to continue his work of creating on earth.

Later, creativity was seen as a kind of neuroticism. Some creative people were even thought to be insane.

Still later, creativity was seen as a special kind of giftedness, again bestowed on a chosen few: Creative people were seen as geniuses.

It was not until modern times that the concept of creativity as a naturalistic phenomenon, a developmental trait inherent in all people, was accepted. The belief that all people possessed creative ability immediately established creativity as a behavior and therefore subject to change and growth through education. This whole new concept reawakened an interest in the area of creativity.

Among the naturalistic theories on which creativity is based is the Synectics Theory. Creativity is seen here as a problem-solving ability. The Synectic Process is based on: (a) making the strange familiar and (b) making the familiar strange. Research began in Cambridge, Massachusetts, in 1944 geared to uncover the psychological mechanisms basic to creative activity.

In 1955 J. P. Guilford[1] published an article in which he presented some hypothesis for research. This marked the beginning of an era when creativity was subjected to scrutiny and debate.

Interest in the area of creativity and creative teaching was accelerated with the launching of Sputnik, after which a realization swept the country that creativity had become a precious commodity. Research in this area has accumulated at breakneck speed since 1957. This research has had a great impact on all walks of life throughout the entire world. Its greatest effect is on the art of teaching. When this new knowledge is combined with new knowledge contributed by the linguists and the research communication centers at large universities, it results in some substantial guides for the creative teaching of the language arts.

Since 1955 much has been written and much study has been made about creativity. This work has come from all fields of endeavor: in-

1. J. P. Guilford, "The Nature of Creative Thinking," *The Meaning of Creativity*, Research Bulletin (Kutztown, Pennsylvania: Eastern Arts Association, 1954).

dustry, psychology, sociology, anthropology, the performing arts, the creative arts, and education. Some of the findings of that research and some of the current beliefs are summarized below.

A Definition

Although many authors in the field of creative studies would require a long definition of creativity written in behavioral terms, a simpler definition will suffice for the purposes of this book.

Creativity is defined here as the ability of an individual to sink taps into his past experiences and to come up with something new. This product need not necessarily be new to the world, but new to the individual.

The definition is illustrated beautifully in the story of the Bim Bam Boo at the beginning of Chapter 2 and the story of the Haunted Room at the beginning of this chapter. As you read on, you will better understand that which constitutes creative teaching.

Many of the processes required to develop something new can be considered as forms of creativity, such as the ability to see new relationships, the ability to be original, the ability to synthesize and define new problems. All these aspects of creativity are well demonstrated in the opening adventures in most of the chapters of this book.

The Nature of Creativity

The first basic truth about creativity is that all people are born creative.[2] It is true that there are varying degrees of creativity, but creativity must be viewed as a developmental process, greatly controlled by environment.

Some biologists consider the drive to create as part of man's drive to recreate—a part of the sex act. Creativity, like the ability to walk or talk, does not appear in the human being at birth. It develops *with* a child, and its stages of development can be recognized.

Applying this truth to the teaching of language arts means that we recognize the existence of creativity in all children; that we can provide an environment which will develop it or cut it off; and that we learn to recognize the stages or processes of creativity. It means that, because creativity is innate, it develops from the inner wells of every human

2. Edmund Sinnott, "The Creativeness of Life," in *Creativity and Its Cultivation*, Harold H. Anderson, ed. (New York: Harper and Row, 1959), Chapter 2.

being and cannot be imposed from without. It also means that we cannot really teach it except by re-enforcing it with praise when it does occur. In addition, it means that children must be afforded many opportunities to experiment, to make mistakes, to explore, and to discover without guilt feelings. In short, it means that the elementary school room is the place where experimentation with language is important to developing communication skills.

In Chapter 1, the creative aspects of language development are cited by Smith, Goodman, and Meredith.[3] They point out that great storytellers and literary giants have retained this ability to create language. It is an awesome thought that teachers, in their efforts to create literary giants, have taught in such a way as to destroy them.

Since the creative stage is a natural life pattern for children, how great is the contribution of the teacher who can make use of it and foster it in his students!

A second basic truth is that creativity is related to intelligence to some degree. In the studies by Getzels and Jackson,[4] it was found that intelligence alone did not insure creativity. High-level acts of creativity are performed by highly intelligent people, but all people are capable of creative acts.

Torrance[5] found that I.Q. tests do not identify creative people. If the I.Q. test is used as a criterion for selecting creative children, we lose 70 percent of the most creative. The I.Q. tests, like most tests constructed up to this time, do not measure those qualities of creative people such as flexibility, originality, depth of thinking, or intuition.

Guilford[6] explains the ineffectiveness of the I.Q. test in selecting creative people in his studies of the structure of the intellect. He defines two kinds of thinking, convergent and divergent. Guilford maintains that originality comes about through divergent thinking processes. This type of thinking was demonstrated in Miss Ellis' lesson. Guilford points out that, if education has the development of the intellect of students as its general objective, each intellectual factor provides a particular goal and every goal ability calls for certain kinds of practice in order to improve it.

In applying this basic principle to the language arts, we must first

3. E. Brooks Smith, Kenneth S. Goodman, and Robert Meredith, *Language and Thinking in the Elementary School* (New York: Holt, Rinehart and Winston, Inc., 1970), pp. 25–26.
4. Jacob W. Getzels and Philip W. Jackson, *Creativity and Intelligence* (New York: John Wiley and Sons, Inc., 1962).
5. E. Paul Torrance, "Current Research on the Nature of Creative Talent," *Journal of Counseling Psychology*, VI, no. 4 (1959), pp. 309–16.
6. J. P. Guilford, "The Structure of Intellect," *Psychological Bulletin*, LIII (1956), pp. 267–95.

note that language, like creativity, is related to intelligence. The intelligence test, however, is highly correlated with language art *skills*. The vocabulary test of the Binet I.Q. correlates most highly with the total test. Skill in using correct grammar and in using language correctly is thus a function highly related to intelligence. However, the *effective use of language skills as I have described it is related to intelligence only to varying degrees, and can be a function of all children*. We know that slow-learning children cannot achieve high degrees of efficiency in spelling, because vocabulary development is so highly correlated with intelligence; but we do know that they can use what vocabulary they have in many diverse and new ways—they can create with it!

If we are to develop the power of *effective* communication in *all* children, more emphasis must be placed upon teaching the language arts through divergent thinking processes—processes by which children use their knowledge to develop new and interesting patterns of speaking, writing, and expressing themselves (such as Miss Rauscher and Miss Weissman used in the lesson described above).

A third principle of which we must be aware is that creativity is both a process and a product. I have already mentioned that studies of the creative process show it to be developmental in many areas. Lowenfeld,[7] for instance, long ago observed the creative stages through which children progress in their paintings. As a result of his observation, we no longer impose stencils and patterns on children, realizing that this technique is not the way to develop creative painting. We now recognize and accept the scribblings and splashings of paint as the first healthy signs of creative art expression and encourage children in their non-schematic (manipulative-exploratory) stage.

Mary Lee Marksberry[8] has characterized the total creative process as a series of stages, each leading into the other until a final whole is realized. These stages seem to apply to both small and great acts of creativeness.

One of the most challenging questions of all research is why some people retain their creative powers whereas others do not. Many popular theories (not yet proven as truths) have been advanced to explain this phenomenon. Among the most commonly accepted is one by Lawrence Kubie.[9] Kubie's theory is centered around the idea that, as we ma-

7. Viktor Lowenfeld, *Creative and Mental Growth* (New York: Macmillan, 1947).
8. Mary Lee Marksberry, *Foundation of Creativity* (New York: Harper and Row, 1963).
9. Lawrence S. Kubie, *Neurotic Distortion of the Creative Process* (Lawrence: University of Kansas Press, 1958).

ture, cultural pressures and the drive for acceptance push many of our experiences into our preconscious mind. The role of the preconscious, he says, is to warp creativity. He feels that the creative person is an individual who, in some manner (which today is still accidental), has retained his capacity to use his preconsicous functions more freely than others who may be potentially equally gifted. Kubie argues that both the preconscious and the conscious processes act in such a way as to block the creative process. He feels that the essential quality of the creative person lies in his ability to allow preconscious material readily to achieve conscious expression.

In Harold Rugg's book on imagination,[10] he develops the concept that all life is lived as a continuum ranging from the unconscious to the conscious. Rugg feels that cultural forces drive many of our experiences into the unconscious. The rigid attitudes of society keep us from dipping into these unconscious experiences. The creative act is blocked at both rigid ends of the continuum. He proposes that, between the conscious and the unconscious, there is a threshold over which creative people pass and this leads them into a transliminal chamber. In this transliminal chamber, the creative mind is able to draw freely from both the conscious and the unconscious. People who are able to put themselves into this transliminal chamber are creative people.

Rugg's theory differs from Kubie's in one basic way. Kubie ascribes creative ability *only* to the preconscious, whereas Rugg holds that there is some creative, imaginative capacity in all sections of the continuum.

In applying these theories to the teaching of the language arts, we can draw the following conclusions: (1) To help children be creative in the communication processes, we must learn to recognize developmental stages of the creative process and not expect assignments to be accomplished full-blown at first attempts. Just as the child needs to manipulate and explore with paints, so must he manipulate and explore words, their meanings and uses, before he can apply them to creative patterns. (2) Children must be presented with stimuli, both natural and contrived, to prepare them for the creative act. Teachers must permit time for the period of incubation and recognize the coming of insight. Methodology must allow time for a period of evaluating, testing, and verification of creative acts. (3) Excessive pressure and excessive conformity must be eliminated so that children operate from their transliminal chamber and have access to all their life experiences in problem solving and creating. Excessive rigidity and excessive conformity are true enemies of creative development.

10. Harold Rugg, *Imagination: An Inquiry Into the Sources and Conditions that Stimulate Creativity* (New York: Harper and Row, 1963).

Another basic principle, which we must consider in planning for effective communication, is that creativity means individuality. The act of creating has been described as the ability to tap one's past experiences and arrange them into new patterns—not necessarily new to the world, but new to the individual. No person has ever become great by producing something exactly like that of any other person. Inasmuch as every human being experiences and perceives differently, he creates his own reservoir of unique experiences, and in drawing from these unique experiences, he produces a unique product.

This concept of individuality parallels the basic goal of the individual's role in a democratic society. In democratic political ideology, *individuals* count. Their contributions are important and they have certain freedoms. But for individuals to count, they must first *be* individuals. The aim of the school in the democratic society is to develop each individual to his fullest potential.

In applying this principle to teaching for effective communication, we can see the importance of discouraging the use of patterns in our teaching and the need for eliminating conformity in the products of verbal expression. Children cannot legitimately be given *one* topic about

Figure 12 *The assignment: From this pile of junk and one clothespin, make a Nutty-Bug which will be a character for your story.*

which to write or *one* set of words to spell. There must be *many* topics from which to choose, and these must be based on the experimental background of the children themselves.

Teachers should stress the value of individuality, praise differences, encourage uniqueness, and discourage commonness. Each child, because of his own pattern of intellect, experience, and maturation, may well be developing his own word lists, his own form of poetic expression, or his own technique of speaking, rather than conforming to preconceived patterns of the teacher or the textbook and being evaluated on his ability to do so.

Creativity is a set of traits, qualities, characteristics, and values. Research has shown us that children who have developed their creativity differ in personality characteristics from those who have not. They are more eager for new experience, more sensitive to problems, better able to analyze and abstract, more open to all life experiences, and more flexible. They have a fluency of ideas, are more original, have keener intuition and a good sense of humor.

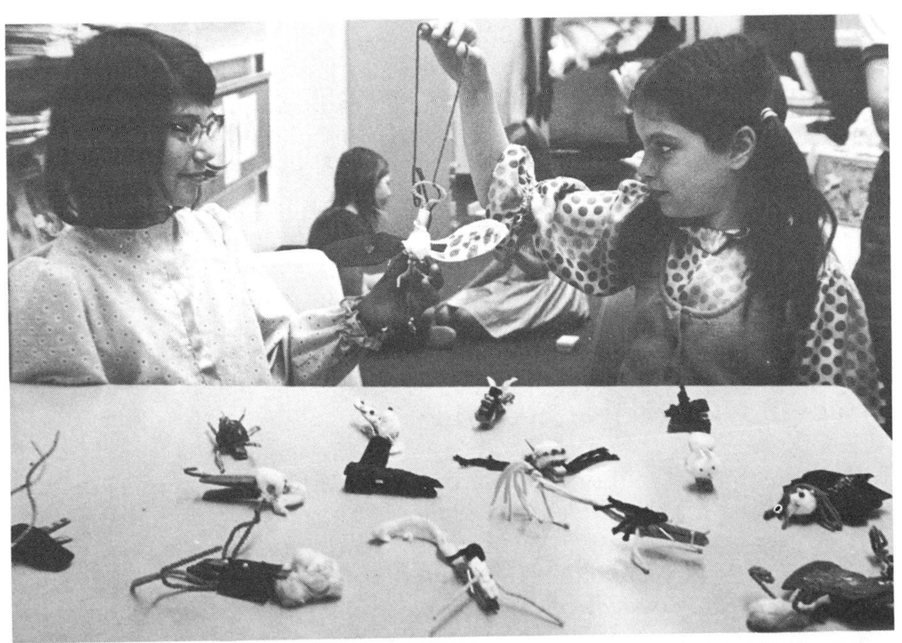

Figure 13 *The Nutty-Bugs are fearful and wonderful to behold! The stories about them are marvelous to hear! The creative process is shown in a creative product.*

We also know that the creative child is, on the whole, not well accepted by his teacher and is often treated along punitive lines. He does not identify with his teachers' immediate goals as the high-I.Q. child does. She tends to ridicule him, to scold him for his silly ideas, and to be annoyed by having him in her classroom.

Knowing about these characteristics can help us to take a new look at the children in our classrooms and to recognize their giftedness by means other than an intelligence score. This means that we can use other criteria for encouraging children in their class work. It means that we respect the child who tries to express himself orally and through written expression in unusual and different ways. We can encourage creativity as we equate giftedness to many criteria.

One last principle is that creativity is a way of learning quite different from the ways commonly taught in our schools. This has been implied previously. A body of research tells us that many people learn more quickly creatively, and that the results are better than from the purely convergent or cognitive methods of learning. And this is the greatest implication of all in reaching for effective and correct communication; to teach for creativity, teachers *must* try new methods—*they* must be creative too.

Creative teaching means for the teacher what it means for the children—a chance for the teacher herself to try out her own ideas in the classroom—to explore some of her own fads—to bring to teaching *her* personality and to make her classroom activities unique and cherished by her children. She operates on truths, of course, for truths form the foundation for scientific teaching, but the truths supply her with the security she needs to venture forth to try ideas of her own. The creative teacher becomes self-actualized in her own classroom—she realizes her potential as a teacher!

Principles of Creative Teaching

In 1967–68 Smith[11] published a book called *Setting Conditions for Creative Teaching in the Elementary School*. This book was the first in a series of books on creative teaching. In this book, Smith culled the research in creativity up to that time and devised a set of principles which identified the advantages of creative teaching over other types of teaching. Some of these principles are common to any good teaching, but

11. James A. Smith, *Setting Conditions for Creative Teaching in the Elementary School* (Boston: Allyn and Bacon, 1966).

others are unique. In the years following the publication of the creative teaching series, many teachers have applied these principles to their own teaching with outstanding success. Not all the principles apply to every creative teaching situation, but many of them do. As the reader studies these principles, note how many form the structural background of the adventures of the Bim Bam Boo and the Haunted Room.

1. *In creative teaching, something new and different results.* The first criterion for creative teaching is that the product or the process must be new. In the creative teaching of the language arts, children invent new poems, stories, patterns of poetry, word combinations, and even words. Miss Ellis was skilled in bringing this about.

2. *In creative teaching, divergent thinking processes are stressed.* Divergent thinking processes are not concerned with an absolute or correct answer. In divergent thinking, knowledges, facts, concepts, understandings, and skills learned through convergent thinking processes are put to new uses, and new answers result rather than one absolute or correct answer. Divergent thinking processes develop such qualities as flexibility of thinking, originality, fluency of ideas, spontaneity, and uniqueness, and are the basis of creative thinking. Creativity is a kind of giftedness. However, current I.Q. tests do not measure divergent thinking processes and consequently do not identify creatively gifted children; they identify only intellectually gifted ones.

The training of the divergent thinking processes in the elementary schools has been grossly neglected, because little has been known of the nature of creativity and how it develops. Research in the area of creativity has added substantial understanding of our thought processes. Neglect of training of this area of the intellect is no longer justifiable.

In teaching the language arts, the teacher has many opportunities to develop the convergent and divergent functions of the intellect. Learning the uses of a comma is an example of the memorization of absolute facts which are constantly applied in practical writing as a social courtesy. This is convergent thinking. Miss Ellis' lesson provided many instances for the use of convergent thinking, but she developed divergent thinking processes as well. All the words she drew from the children were put into new patterns, new ideas, and new modes of expression. No one answer was absolute or complete, but almost all were acceptable.

To develop divergency of thinking in children is to develop creativity. Every aspect of the language arts curriculum may be utilized to do this, even handwriting and spelling, as you will see in Chapters 10 and 11.

3. *In creative teaching, motivational tensions are a prerequisite to the creative process. The process serves as a tension-relieving agent.* From the opening statement in Miss Ellis' lesson to the very last state-

ment, children were constantly challenged to think. Miss Ellis was not content to allow them to slip into apathy at any time. Whenever ideas began to slough off, she built new tensions in the children by her own suggestions. All the children experienced tensions, relief, success, and satisfaction as they gave their ideas, which were accepted and used. In her planning, the teacher put strong emphasis on the motivational, tension-building forces she would use to get the children to think continually and to develop their divergent operational processes.

However, not every minute of every day in Miss Ellis' classroom was keyed to the tension illustrated by this lesson. Periods of relaxation, when energies of the children are not high-pitched, are also important for creative production.

4. *In creative teaching, open-ended situations are utilized.* After Miss Ellis introduced her topic, she posed questions which were worded so that they stimulated more questions. Open-endedness in teaching means that children are presented with situations in which they can put their knowledges, understandings, facts, and skills to work. Observe how Miss Rauscher provided open-ended situations when she asked for *unique* words to use in the poem.

5. *In creative teaching, there comes a time when the teacher withdraws and children face the unknown themselves.* Finally Miss Ellis told the children they were on their own to draw, and asked for ideas—as many *different* ideas as possible. She made certain that she had built highly motivating tensions in the children, and then she let them release these tensions in individual ways through drawing their own ideas.

6. *In creative teaching, the outcomes are unpredictable.* When Miss Ellis withdrew as a guide and leader to the children, she changed her role. Up to this moment she had been the organizer, the instigator, the leader, the *divergent* thinker, and the children were the responders, the helpers, the *convergent* thinkers. From this moment on the children became the organizers, the instigators, the leaders, and the main source of *divergent* thinking processes. Miss Ellis became the responder, the helper. She did not know what products would result from her motivations; she could only encourage the children and hope they would create. Her faith in them was obviously justified.

7. *In creative teaching, conditions are set which make possible preconscious thinking.* Miss Ellis encouraged the children to draw again and again from memory and from things they had heard or seen or felt. She accepted and used all their ideas. None were considered silly.

8. *Creative teaching means that students are encouraged to generate and develop their own ideas.* The poem and pictures which resulted from Miss Ellis' lesson show that Miss Ellis is a master at this.

9. *In creative teaching, differences, uniqueness, individuality, origi-*

nality are stressed and rewarded. Notice how Miss Ellis asked for *different* ideas. Her methods of inquiry and presentation, judged by the unique products she obtained, were successful.

10. *In creative teaching, the process is as important as the product.* The process of creative production has been defined by Marksberry as follows: (a) a period of preparation when the creator becomes involved with and identifies with the problem at hand; (b) a period of incubation when the creator lives with and is even tormented by the problem; (c) a period of insight when all parts of the problem seem to become clear; (d) a period of illumination or inspiration when the ideas or answers seem to come (this may also be classified as a moment of discovery), and (e) a period of verification, elaboration, perfection, and evaluation when the product is tested for its worth and tension is relieved.

Because Miss Ellis' lesson was one of minor problem-solving situations, all the steps of the creative process as defined by Marksberry are not as dramatically exposed as by some other illustrations which will come later. The period of incubation was short. It is a fact of creativity that it can be found in varying degrees. Lower degrees of creative problem solving do not require as long a period of time to reach a solution as do higher degrees of problem solving; however, each of Marksberry's suggested stages is present to some degree in the account of Miss Ellis' lesson.

11. *In creative teaching, certain conditions must be set to permit creativity to appear.* Creativity cannot be taught. We can only set conditions for it to happen, and then by re-enforcing its appearance through reward, encourage it to appear often. Among the necessary conditions are certain *physical conditions.* Miss Ellis provided a comfortable classroom, a comfortable and suitable seating arrangement, and all the necessary materials for her lesson.

Certain psychological conditions are also necessary. Miss Ellis provided these through establishing good rapport with the students and by developing an "air of expectancy" for creativeness in her classroom. She also developed a permissive atmosphere and a feeling of acceptance. Psychological security was provided through putting ideas on the chalkboard, building a vocabulary to which all could contribute and from which all could draw, and accepting and praising all contributions. Her lesson was, therefore, success oriented, and all the children became involved. Divergent thinking processes developed as the teacher encouraged the children to use more and different ideas.

Intellectual conditions abound in the challenge of creative thinking, in teasing the imagination, in keeping all the children thinking, in drawing on former words and experiences for material, and in putting this material into new patterns.

Sound social and emotional conditions were present in the rapport among the children, the acceptance of the teacher, and the freedom allowed to explore ideas.

12. *Creative teaching is success oriented rather than failure oriented.* In Miss Ellis' lesson, many children may have had a failure experience, but all were eventually resolved so they experienced success. There is a difference between failure experiences and failure. Failure experiences help children understand the true conditions of life and help build character, whereas repeated failure can only result in psychological damage.

13. *In creative teaching, provision is made to learn many knowledges and skills, but provision is also made to apply these knowledges and skills in new problem-solving situations.* Miss Ellis' lesson was a follow-up on other lessons in vocabulary building, word usage, punctuation usage, speech improvement, and composition. Every creative lesson cannot develop *all* the principles of teaching any more than any one lesson can teach all the uses of the comma. But Miss Ellis developed most of them. The problems she posed were not of great magnitude, but they were important in that they gave the children the practice needed to deal with larger problems encountered later on.

14. *In creative teaching, self-initiated learning is encouraged.* Miss Ellis' questions helped children to draw on their own experiences, to perceive in new ways, to recognize new relationships, and to produce new ideas.

15. *In creative teaching, skills of constructive criticism and evaluation are developed.* After the children finished the magic book, suggestions were given for a different word here or there. In some instances a whole new idea emerged. Miss Ellis then helped each child prepare his creation for the book by checking his punctuation and handwriting. Constructive criticism encourages creativity, but evaluation is better deferred in the creative act, as we shall see later.

16. *In creative teaching, ideas and objects are manipulated and explored.* Miss Ellis' lesson was a good example of this principle.

17. *Creative teaching employs democratic processes.* The exchanging of roles between pupils and teacher and the general tone of the classroom are good examples of the application of democratic principles.

18. *In creative teaching, methods are used which are unique to the development of creativity.*

Among these special methods are those suggested by Sidney Parnes[12] in his courses on Creative Problem Solving at the University of Buffalo:

12. Sydney J. Parnes, *Instructor's Manual for Semester Courses in Creative Problem Solving*, rev. ed. (Buffalo: Creative Education Foundation, 1963), pp. 32–36.

a. *Deferred judgement*—Notice that no evaluation of ideas was offered until after all ideas were out, and all picturesque speech papers were read.
b. *Creative ideation*—To stretch creative thinking, we suggest the following with creative products: new uses, adaptiveness, modification, magnification, minification, substitution, rearrangement, reversing, and combining. Dr. Parnes suggests attribute listing, forced relationships, and structure analysis.
c. *Brainstorming*—Brainstorming is a special technique by which creative ideas can be put quickly before a group in a limited length of time. Brainstorming is most effective in a group of ten to fifteen, although it can be used effectively with larger groups under certain circumstances. In brainstorming a problem has to be limited in scope: Too broad a problem generally leads to no specific solutions.

In brainstorming the following procedures are observed: The moderator poses the problem very specifically and generally sets a time limit for the session. A recorder is appointed to list the ideas as they are spoken. All ideas, no matter how foolish they may sound, are recorded. No judgement is passed on any idea until the end of the session. The

Figure 14 *Brainstorming! Mr. Smith dumped the waste basket in the middle of the table, and the children constructed stories around the contents: What happened in this room during the day?*

moderator may encourage the flow of ideas (creative ideation) by stopping the session and asking the recorder how many ideas have been thus far recorded. He may say, "In the first ten minutes we have come up with fifty ideas. Let's see if we can double it in the next ten minutes!"

In order to keep similar ideas together on the recorder's list, the hitchhiking technique is used. If one person gives an idea which sets off a related idea in another person's mind, the latter snaps his fingers and the moderator calls on him next so his "hitchhiking" idea will come after the idea that prompted it.

After the session is closed, a committee meets and leisurely evaluates the ideas that resulted from the brainstorming session. Some are immediately discarded as impractical: too expensive, too impossible, too involved, or too timely. The reduced list is often brought back to the main group for further discussion.

Brainstorming Put to Use: The Five Chinese Brothers

Can brainstorming be put to use as a technique for solving problems creatively with children? Indeed it can.

Following is an adventure in brainstorming in Mr. Adams' sixth grade class. It is an example of the skillful manipulation of unrelated experiences into a new product, new thought, or new experience—thus, a creative situation.

The children had decided to make a puppet show for their part of an assembly program for book week. Because the sixth grade was the highest grade in this particular school and all the children viewing the puppet show would be younger, Mr. Adams asked the children in his slower reading group to serve as a committee to choose the story to be dramatized—one that they had enjoyed very much and one that held universal appeal. They chose "The Five Chinese Brothers" by Kurt Weis.

Now, translating "The Five Chinese Brothers" into a puppet show presents many problems that are different from those of presenting it as a dramatization or in some other art form. Mr. Adams identified these problems as follows, and felt that they were excellent opportunities for brainstorming practice.

1. How will we show the first Chinese brother swallowing the sea in scene 1?
2. How can we show each Chinese brother going home to say goodbye to his mother?
3. How will we show the second Chinese brother's iron neck?

4. How will we show the third Chinese brother's legs "stretching and stretching" to reach the bottom of the sea?

5. How will we show the fourth Chinese brother being burned in the fire?

6. How will we show the fifth Chinese brother being smothered? How will we push him in the oven?

The ideas that the children came up with were delightful. Each was listed carefully on the chalkboard until no more ideas were forthcoming. Then Mr. Adams met with the committee that was responsible for each scene. Each committee was made acquainted with the technical problems and staging problems of a puppet show, and each idea was weighed for its practicability, general effect, possibility in terms of materials, expense and time and skills that might be needed to put the idea into effect. Sometimes one idea led to another—a new one. Then each committee reported to the entire class.

The creative ideas resulting from the first of the above problems were as follows:

1. To show the first Chinese brother swallowing the sea, the backdrop of the scene of the puppet stage was painted from the middle to the top to represent a Chinese fishing village tucked at the base of a mountain range. From the middle down, the backdrop was painted to resemble the bottom of the sea. It was a muddy color spotted with dead fish, old bottles, the hulk of an old boat, shells, and other debris.

In the proscenium arch, the children hung a piece of heavy cardboard with strings on the sides (invisible to the audience) so that the cardboard could be slowly lowered. The cardboard was cut along the top like the choppy little waves of the sea, and the rest of the cardboard was painted to look like waves with tiny white caps.

To give the illusion of the Chinese brother swallowing the sea, the first Chinese brother appeared with the little boy of the story on a wharf painted on the backdrop. He leaned over and made a great "slurping" noise. The cardboard was gently lowered with each slurp, giving the impression that the sea was lowering as the bottom with its dead fish, shells, and wrecked ship came into view. The little boy jumped down into the sea and ran around back and forth. When it was time for the first Chinese brother to release the sea and the little boy would not come back as he promised, it was simple for the first Chinese brother to make a huge noise as though he were spitting up the sea, the cardboard was then raised until the little boy was covered, giving the illusion that he had drowned. The realism of the scene held children and adults spellbound!

2. Mr. Adams pointed out to the children that the puppet stage was not very wide and that it would not seem real for the Chinese brothers

to walk across the stage solely to give the impression that each was going from the city out to his mother's home in the country.

Brainstorming with the concept of reversals, the children decided they could give the illusion of the brothers walking home if they would paint all their scenery on one big long mural and put it on rollers on each side of the rear of the stage, so the scene could be rolled like a scroll movie. At one end of the mural would be the fishing village, leading to the public square of the village, then on through the village with the thinning out of houses, on to the country and eventually the mother's house would come into view. By making the Chinese brother walk in place and having the scenery slowly go by behind him, the illusion was created that he walked from the village to the country.

3. The iron neck of the second Chinese brother was shown simply by using a small potted meat tin can which had the ends cut out and painting it to look as though it had bolts on it—somewhat like a Frankenstein effect. The can was dulled to resemble iron and every time the executioner hit the second Chinese brother with his axe, a child backstage slapped together two iron wrenches to give the sound effect of iron on iron.

4. To make the third Chinese brother stretch and stretch his legs, long legs were cut from cloth like pajama legs with heavy little lead feet attached to the bottoms. The tops were sewed up under a long kimono-type costume. Up the back of the puppet a long stick was fastened under the kimono-like blouse. When it came time for his legs to stretch and stretch, the feet were held to the stage, just below the level of the cardboard sea used in the first scene, and the child operating the puppet pushed the stick up and out of the puppet stage toward the audience. As he did so, the carefully folded cloth legs slowly unfolded and came down below the kimono, giving the effect of long, growing legs.

5. The children simulated a fire by daubing red, yellow, orange, and some blue color with flo-pens on an old large square white handkerchief and cutting it in from the edges with scissors. This they fastened to the wire cage of an electric fan. When the fan was held flat just below the eye level of the audience, the pieces of silk flew up and licked the fourth Chinese brother like fire. To add to the illusion, one child stood backstage and flashed a red floodlight around the stage to give the illusion of flickering flames.

6. An oven was made from a flat sheet of tin with big high doors which could be opened above and behind the proscenium arch. It was put on a shallow box, the back of which was covered with cotton balls. When the fifth Chinese brother was to be smothered, the great oven doors were opened, some of the "whipped cream" cotton balls spilled out and he dove in to have the doors close behind him.

When he emerged the next morning he had fluffs of cotton stuck to him.

The results of the brainstorming sessions which Mr. Adams held with his sixth grade gave this production a uniqueness and specialness that raised it far above the commonplace. These sessions provide an excellent example of divergent thinking processes.

Creative Teaching and Creative Learning

After observing hundreds of creative teachers at work, I make the following conclusions:

1. Creative teaching is a method of teaching, and it is a very effective method.
2. Creative teaching takes no more time than any other type. In fact, in terms of its results, it actually takes less time.
3. Creative teaching is not an additional task to be added to a teacher's heavy schedule: It takes place all day in all areas of the curriculum.
4. Creative teaching is cyclic: It produces creative results which provide aesthetic satisfactions, and it relieves tensions in teachers so that they are more willing to try new ideas, which in turn make children more creative, which in turn, etc.

Do children respond to creative teaching and to the kind of teaching which places them in open-ended situations so that they may be creative in finding solutions to problems? What better data than to seek the evaluation of such experiences from the children themselves!

Not long ago I corresponded with one class in Virginia. The teacher, Mrs. A., and I had conspired to carry out some letter writing with the hope that this activity would set the conditions for the children to write creatively and to create in other ways. Material flowed into my office. Mrs. A., I found, was a very creative teacher. Much of the illustrative material in this volume came from members of her class.

In one letter which I wrote to the class, I asked the children if they liked to do creative things, and why.

Following are a couple of the answers I received. None of the letters from the children was negative—the entire class was enthusiastic and excited about its creative work. Some of the letters themselves, I felt, were quite creative, especially Gail's.

April 15, 1971

Dear Dr. Smith,

After a pleasant vacation, and being a vacation it was welcome, we are back in school—wow! Actually, I guess I'm glad to be back—at least as far as English class is concerned. For English is one of my favorite subjects, at least the part where we get to write things.

You asked if some of us would send you some poetry or other writing—I'll be glad to, however when you receive a deluge of letters, it will be your own fault. But I'll start with one poem for today if you like it I'll send more, some of them are a lot more serious than this one.

The Crab

The crab was a he,
Who was looking for a she.
But his thoughts of love,
Were changed by him above.

For the Lord made the crab
  walk to the side
Although Heaven only knows
  the poor crab tried.

He could walk to the left,
  could walk to the right,
But he couldn't walk forward as
  he tried that fateful night.

He went to serenade Crabailia Brouse
He hoped to make her his spouse.
Crabailia was a lovely young miss.
He hoped someday to give her a kiss.

He got to the house,
Then caught sight of Miss Brouse.
He thought, "Now I will court her,"
But the Lord gave an order.

He said, "Walk to the side!,
You shan't take her for a bride!!"
So he walked sideways around the house
Till another crab wed Crabailia Brouse.

And so to this day
Crabs walk to the side,
Although Heaven knows
They've tried and tried.

I hope you liked it. I know you're very busy, but if you get a chance please drop a line and tell me if you like it. It doesn't have to be to me personally just mention it in a letter to the class.

Sincerely,
Gail Levinson

Figure 15 *Dana's Zouch.*

April 16, 1971

Dear Dr. Smith,

I really enjoyed the letter you wrote to the class. You asked us to write to you about what we have done that is creative and our ideas about creativity. For the first term we did puppetry. You might think that puppetry is creative only from the standpoint of art. But the way we did it, the project covered creativity in the field of not only art, but music, social studies, and English. How could we cover so much ground in this creative project? First, we created our own puppets. We decided who we wanted to depict. We made our own costumes. Each puppet showed the individuality and the different personalities of the people in our class. Then we wrote our own scripts. I wrote a parady on Greensleeves for my puppet skit. This was just one of the creative projects we have experienced this year.

Sincerely,
Dana Teitelman

P.S. (I drew the Zouch)

Creative Communication

Creativity has always been a precious commodity. Creative people have given us our advances in civilization, our great medical and scientific discoveries, our great literature and art.

Creativity has also been important in daily living. At one time creativity was a necessity for survival. The pioneer man and woman were forced to create from the materials provided by nature. With the advent of the industrial revolution, and subsequently mass production, much of the need for creativity in daily living was lost, and the task of creating was relegated to a few people.

Now we are again faced with a great need for creative people. Our survival may depend on our ability to develop it as a quality in the children of our schools today. In years past, a person could learn early in life a few things that would last him the rest of his life. This is no longer true. Our world is no longer so static. Knowledge increases daily, and with the increase of knowledge comes an increase in the number of world problems to be solved. Creative thinkers are needed to solve them.

One of the greatest needs of mankind is to develop creative means of communication. This implies a communication which is effective as well as correct, and the ability to choose the proper time to use both features or either.

Creative communication requires a fluency of ideas, original and ear-tickling thoughts, and the ability to relate words in unusual patterns and to select the right word for the right place. On the following pages, the concept of creative teaching is developed further, and examples are given to show how some teachers have brought about the creative teaching of language through placing children in provocative vocabulary-building, thought-centered, problem-solving situations.

Summary

We live in the age of the computer. It is currently fashionable and novel to "computerize" and mechanize everything, teaching included. Mechanization and computerization are justified in industry where the products are *things*, but the products in teaching are *people*, young people, and to mechanize any of the human processes is to deny people their right to realize full development, to become self-actualized—the very right to *BE*! In the democratic form of government, individuals count, and the *individual differences* in people are our greatest natural resources. To realize the development of individuals, teaching must remain, in itself, a creative act, concerned with the creative and intellectual development of *every* child who comes to school.

Creative teaching relates to the process of communication in many ways: (1) The objectives of teaching of the language arts must be concerned as much with the effective use of language as with the correct use of language; (2) creativity can be developed through the teaching of the communication skills; (3) to accomplish this objective, special *methods* of teaching must be employed; (4) outcomes will be different but more effective.

To the Reader

1. Following are some problems worthy of discussion with your colleagues:
   a. It would seem that creative lessons such as the Haunted Room and the Bim Bam Boo take a great deal of preparation time. Is it worth it in terms of results obtained?
   b. Can a teacher be creative in her teaching if she is not artistic?
   c. Can a teacher help children to be creative when she feels she is not creative herself?
   d. Can a teacher carry on a program to develop creativity when she is short of supplies?

e. If creativity is sinking taps into our past experiences and coming up with something new to the individual, is learning to knit creative, and can a person's first knitted sweater be compared to a Picasso painting?
f. What happens when a child must choose between fulfilling his own creative drives and gaining recognition and status from his teacher?
g. What happens to a child whose creativity has been greatly enhanced one year by his associations with a creative teacher when he finds himself the following year with a very uncreative teacher?
h. Can handicapped students be taught creatively and will they benefit from it?
i. Why is creativity not developed in our society? Does the social unrest of America have anything to do with the emergence of creativity in the past ten years?
j. Were the recent campus strikes a creative movement?
k. Is creative teaching a matter of convergent versus divergent teaching, or is it a fusion of both? What should be taught convergently?

2. In the appendix of this book is a check sheet of the characteristics of creative children most commonly identified by research. Duplicate some copies of it. Identify the five children in your room who you think are the most creative, and place their names at the top of the check sheet on the left of the paper. Place the names of the children who you think are the least creative on the right side of the sheet. Now observe their behavior for a week and then check the characteristics on the sheet in the boxes provided. Were you looking for the same behaviors as those identified on the check sheet? How near correct were you in your choices of the five most creative according to the characteristics listed? You can verify your choices by administering a form of the Torrance Tests of Creative Thinking and checking the scores against your choices and observations. Does knowing the accepted behavior of creative children make you more tolerant of them?
3. Keep a log for one week of something new or different that you did each day.
4. Discuss the advantages of the way Miss Rauscher and Miss Weissman built vocabulary in the lesson of the Haunted Room over the method commonly used in which the teacher drills on new words. What is the role of the teacher in lessons where vocabulary is developed as it is in the lessons on the Haunted Room?

5. Make a list of the principles of creative teaching as stated in this chapter and check your own teaching against them. How many of the principles have you developed in your own teaching?
6. Here are some ideas to stretch children's imaginations. Brainstorm them with children and note which children have the greatest number of ideas, which are more fluent, etc.
   a. How many uses can you think of for a paper bag?
   b. What two things in our classroom can we put together to make something new?
   c. How could we show a chicken being born in a puppet show?
   d. What are all the ways you can think of to show color in motion?
7. Under Title III of the National Secondary and Elementary Education Act, funds are available from the United States government to study or implement creativity in the nation's schools. In Des Moines, Iowa, Project IMPACT has been under way for three years. Each year a publication is printed telling of the progress and accomplishments of this study. What are these people finding out about creativity? You will enjoy these reports (see bibliography).
8. One of the most creative books your author has ever seen is "The Dynamics of Change" by Don Fabun. (See bibliography at the end of this chapter.) Read it, study the illustrations. Do you agree with him that books could be a great deal more creative than most of them are?
9. Perhaps the greatest center in the world for the study of creativity is *The Creative Education Foundation at the University of Buffalo*, Buffalo, New York. This foundation publishes a magazine, *The Journal of Creative Behavior*, to which teachers may subscribe. Innovations and research in creativity are reported regularly, and the author suggests that teachers contact the foundation for information.
10. If you want to see a dynamic idea put across in a creative way, read Lowell A. Siff's book *Love*, (New York: George Braziller, a Venture Book).
11. A great boon to the creative movement has been the establishment of the *Touchstone Foundation* in New York City, which exists for the express purpose of developing the creative talents of children. Mr. Richard Lewis, the director of the foundation, has published many books of children's work and has made some interesting tapes and recordings. (See bibliography.) Visit the Foundation when you visit New York, or send for their bulletin. (The Touchstone Center for Children, Inc., 430 East 56th Street, New York, N.Y. 10028.)
12. There are some excellent films which you may wish to ask your

A-V Department to rent for viewing by you and your colleagues. Among them:

Ape to Agape (Indiana University)
Christopher Film (Creative Education Foundation)
Creative Attitude (General Motors Corp.)
The Creative Cycle (Michigan State University)
Creativity (United States Management Association, Inc.)
Creativity: The Professional Approach (Michigan State University)
Garry Moore Film on Brainstorming (Creative Education Foundation)
The Golden Key (Creative Education Foundation)
Releasing the Energy of Ideas (Creative Education Foundation)
Why Man Creates (Pyramid Films)

Selected Bibliography

ANDERSON, H. E. (ed.). *Creativity and Its Cultivation*. New York: Harper and Row, 1959.

ANDERSON, HAROLD H. (ed.). *Creativity in Childhood and Adolescence*. California: Science and Behavior Books, Inc., 1962.

BAKER, SAMM. *Your Key to Creative Thinking*. New York: Bantam Books, 1968.

BARRON, FRANK. *Creativity and Psychological Health: Origins of Personal Vitality and Creative Freedom*. Princeton, New Jersey: Van Nostrand, 1963.

BERMAN, LOUISE M. *Creativity in Education*. Madison, Wisconsin: University of Wisconsin, School of Education, 1964.

CLARK, C. H. *Brainstorming*. New York: Doubleday and Company, 1958.

COBER, MARY E. "Creativeness in the Language Arts," in James C. MacCampbell (ed.), *Readings in the Language Arts in the Elementary School*. Boston: D. C. Heath and Company, 1964, 114–117.

EISNER, ELLIOT. *Think With Me About Creativity: Ten Essays on Creativity*. Dansville, New York: F. A. Owen Publishing Co., 1964.

FABUN, DON. *You and Creativity*. Beverly Hills, California: Glencoe Press, 1968.

GARDNER, J. W. *Self-Renewal*. New York: Harper and Row, 1964.

GETZELS, JACOB W., AND PHILLIP W. JACKSON. *Creativity and Intelligence*. New York: John Wiley and Sons, Inc., 1962.

GOWAN, JOHN CURTIS, GEORGE D. DEMOS, AND E. PAUL TORRANCE (eds.). *Creativity: Its Educational Implications*. New York: John Wiley, 1967.

GRUBER, HOWARD, GLENN TERRELL, AND MICHAEL WERTHEIMER (eds.).

Contemporary Approaches to Creative Thinking. New York: Atherton Press, Inc., 1962.

GUILFORD, J. P. "Factors That Aid and Hinder Creativity," *Teachers College Record*, LXIII (February, 1962), 386–392.

______. *Intelligence, Creativity and Their Educational Implications*. San Diego, California: R. R. Knapp, 1968.

HALPRIN, LAWRENCE. *Creative Processes in the Human Environment*. New York: George Braziller, 1969.

HYMAN, H. *Some Experiments in Creativity*. New York: Random House, 1961.

KAGAN, JEROME. *Creativity and Learning*. Boston: Houghton, Mifflin, 1967.

KARAGULLA, SHAFICA. *Breakthrough to Creativity*. Los Angeles: DeVorss and Company, Inc., 1967.

KNELLER, GEORGE. *The Art and Science of Creativity*. New York: Holt, Rinehart and Winston, Inc., 1965.

KORNBLUTH, FRANCES S. *Creativity and the Teacher*. Chicago, Illinois: American Federation of Teachers, 1966.

LOWENFELD, VIKTOR, AND LAMBERT W. BRITTAIN. *Creative and Mental Growth*, 5th ed. New York: The Macmillan Company, 1970.

MARKSBERRY, MARY LEE. *Foundation of Creativity*. New York: Harper and Row, 1963.

MARS, DAVID. *Organizational Climate for Creativity*. Buffalo, New York: The Creative Education Foundation, 1969.

MASSIALAS, B. G., AND J. ZEVIN. *Creative Encounters in the Classroom: Teaching and Learning Through Discovery*. New York: John Wiley and Sons, Inc., 1967.

MCKELLER, P. *Imagination and Thinking*. New York: Basic Books, 1957.

MICHAEL, WILLIAM (ed.). *Teaching for Creative Endeavor: Bold New Venture*. Bloomington: Indiana University Press, 1968.

MIEL, ALICE. *Creativity in Teaching: Invitations and Instances*. Belmont, California: Wadsworth Publishing Company, 1961.

MOUSTAKAS, CARL E. (ed.). *The Self: Explorations in Personal Growth*. New York: Harper and Row, 1964.

MURPHY, GARDNER. *Human Potentialities*. New York: Basic Books, Inc., 1958.

OSBORN, ALEX F. *Applied Imagination*. New York: Charles Scribners, 1963.

PARNES, SIDNEY, AND H. F. HARDING (eds.). *A Source Book for Creative Teaching*. New York: Charles Scribners, 1962.

PATRICK, CATHERINE. *What is Creative Thinking?* New York: Philosophical Library, 1955.

PLATTS, MARY E., SR. ROSE MARGUERITE, AND ESTHER SHUMAKER. *Spice: Suggested Activities to Motivate the Teaching of the Language Arts.* Benton Harbor, Michigan: Educational Service, Inc., 1960.

RATHS, LOUIS EDWARD. *Teaching for Thinking: Theory and Application.* Columbus, Ohio: Charles E. Merrill Books, 1967.

REED, E. G. *Developing Creative Talent.* New York: Vantage Press, 1962.

RUGG, HAROLD. *Imagination: An Inquiry into the Sources and Conditions that Stimulate Creativity.* New York: Harper and Row, 1963.

SHUMSKY, ABRAHAM. *Creative Teaching.* New York: Appleton-Century-Crofts, 1965.

SMITH, JAMES A. *Creative Teaching of the Language Arts in the Elementary School.* Boston: Allyn and Bacon, Inc., 1967.

———. *Setting Conditions for Creative Teaching in the Elementary School.* Boston: Allyn and Bacon, 1966.

TAYLOR, CALVIN W. *Creativity: Progress and Potential.* New York: McGraw-Hill, 1964.

TAYLOR, CALVIN, AND FRANK BARRON. *Scientific Creativity: Its Recognition and Development.* New York: John Wiley and Sons, Inc., 1959.

TAYLOR, CALVIN W. *Widening Horizons in Creativity.* New York: John Wiley and Sons, Inc., 1964.

TORRANCE, E. PAUL. *Creativity: What Research Says to the Teacher.* Washington, D.C.: National Education Association, 1963.

———. *Guiding Creative Talent.* Englewood Cliffs, New Jersey: Prentice-Hall, Inc., 1962.

———. *Encouraging Creativity in the Classroom.* Dubuque, Iowa: William C. Brown Company Publishers, 1970.

———. *Rewarding Creative Behavior.* Englewood Cliffs, New Jersey: Prentice-Hall, Inc. 1965.

———, AND R. E. MEYERS. *Creative Learning and Teaching.* New York: Dodd, Mead and Company, 1970.

WALLACH, MICHAEL A., AND NATHAN KOGAN. *Modes of Thinking in Young Children: A Study of the Creativity-Intelligence Distinction.* New York: Holt, Rinehart and Winston, 1965.

WERTHEIMER, M. *Productive Thinking.* New York: Harper and Row, 1959.

WILT, MARION. *Creativity in the Elementary School.* New York: Appleton-Century-Crofts, 1959.

ZIRBES, LAURA. *Spurs to Creative Teaching.* New York: G. P. Putnam's Sons, 1959.

4

Changing Experiences into Adventures Through the Language Arts

The Day of the ZERCH: A Remarkable Experience

One day Mr. Denning posted this sign on his bulletin board:

The children, of course, were on fire with curiosity.

"What is a zerch?"

"What does it mean—the day of the ZERCH?"

Mr. Denning explained, "I don't know what a ZERCH is any more than you do. It may be a poem, a story, a thing, something to eat—anything! But on Monday everyone is to bring to class a ZERCH—and we will spend the whole day doing things with our ZERCHES."

Secrets and plans flew about the room for the remainder of the week. On Monday exhibit tables were set up around the room and each child brought his ZERCH for display. There were strange and wonderful three-dimensional sculptures, wild drawings and paintings, zerch food, zerch poems, and from one child even a contraption which he called a "ZERCH" light.

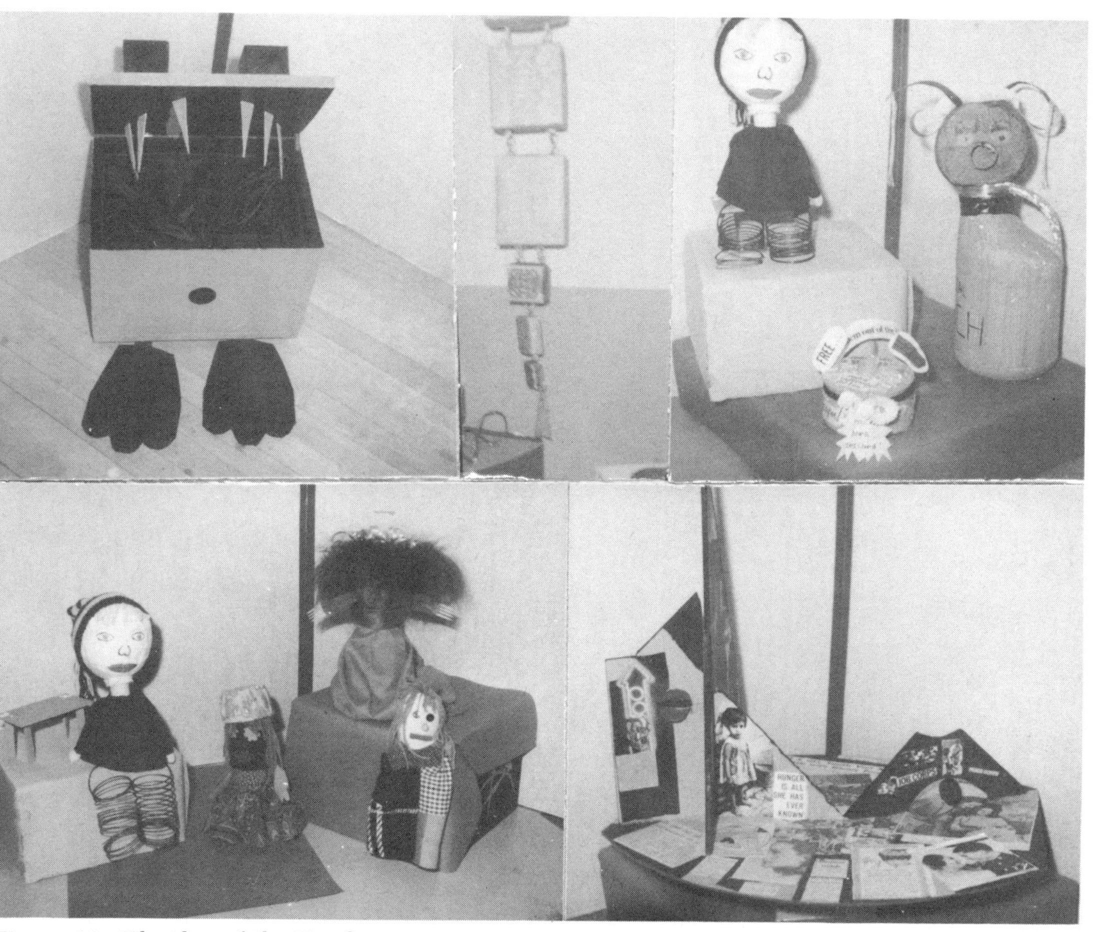

Figure 16 *The day of the Zerch.*

Figure 17 *What could you write about these Nutty-Bugs?*

Each child told about his ZERCH, and the remainder of the day was spent in making up plays using the zerches, writing stories about them, creating poems, and even working in some mathematics.

The Day of the ZERCH provided an excellent open-ended experience in which children could allow their ideas to run rampant, but it also gave Mr. Denning an opportunity to develop many language skills in a new and relevant manner. Not only were poems, stories, and plays created, but also many new lists of words were made for the children to study. Every aspect of language was incorporated in his plan: Good listening skills were developed, oral expression was encouraged, stories were written and read, rhyming words were used, word usage was explored, and grammar knowledge was put to work in meaningful ways. Making a zerch was an excellent exercise in divergent thinking.

Primary ZOUCHES

Miss Sterling, a primary teacher in Mr. Denning's school, was interested in his ZERCH day and decided to use an adaptation of the idea with her six and seven year olds.

She salvaged a pile of old manila folders from the office one day and cut the front of each folder in four strips, like this.

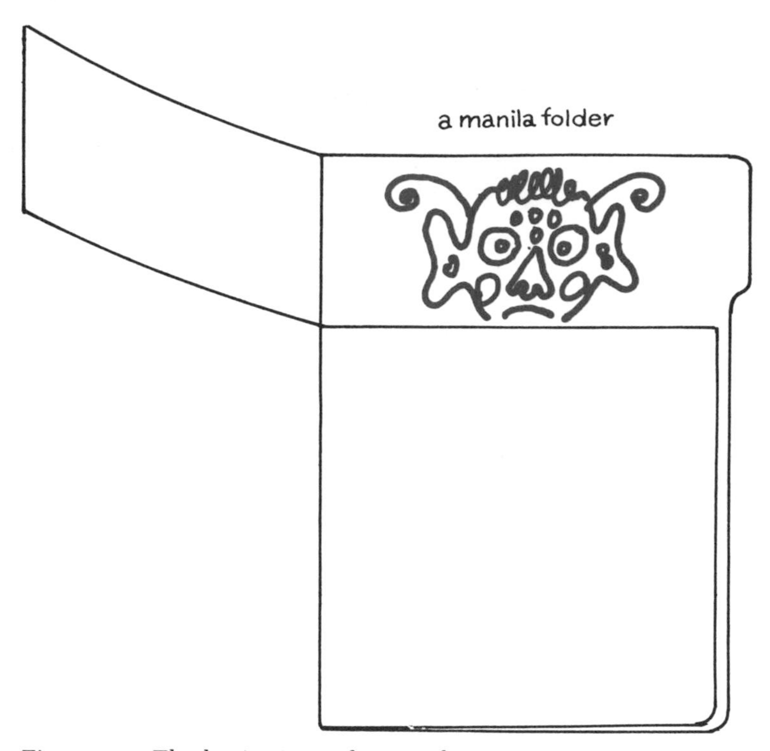

Figure 18 *The beginnings of a Zouch.*

Then she distributed the folders to the children and said, "Today we are going to make funny people called ZOUCHES. You have to promise not to peek and to listen carefully to what I tell you to do. Will everyone open the top flap of the folder on your desk and draw any kind of head and neck you want to—make it funny or serious, happy or sad. Anyway you want, only be sure to draw only as far as the neck. Put two marks at the top of the second strip to show where your drawing ends."

Then Miss Sterling had the children close the top flap, stick it shut with a small piece of masking tape, and pass the folder along to the child on his left. This child then began with the dots left by the first child and drew a part of a person from the neck to the waist, marking on the next section where his drawing ended. Again the flap was closed, sealed with masking tape, and passed along to the third child. This child drew a person from the waist to the knees. The next child drew from the knees to the feet.

The folder was passed along once more and the fifth child opened the flaps, bent them back, and displayed his ZOUCH. The drawings were hilarious and lots of fun. Each child showed the one he opened. Then

Figure 19 *The Zouch.*

Miss Sterling discussed rhyming words, and the children created a story or a poem which they wrote on the flaps. Here is onc of the products resulting from this delightful experience:

The ZOUCH

What is it?
Is it a beast or a man?
Can you figure it out?
I don't think I can!

—Sarah

A fourth grade teacher in Mr. Denning's school took the idea of the Zerch and adapted it to some problem solving in her own classroom.

Her children did not seem to have a comfortable understanding of phonetic sounds. So Mrs. Cross asked the children to make up lists of nonsense words. From these each chose one he liked and made a cut

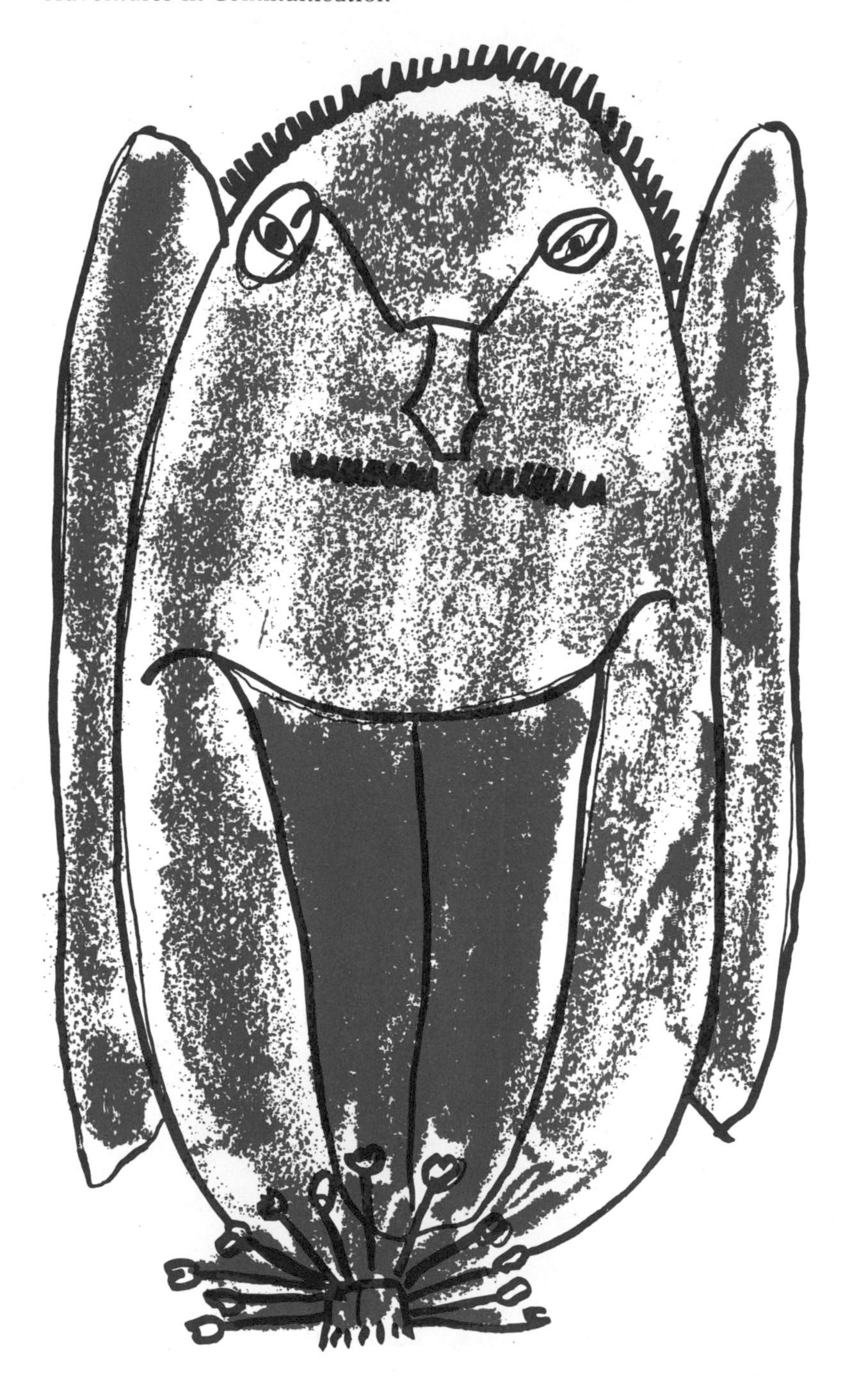

Figure 20 *The Oochy-Binky-Inka Blob: Daniel's fictitious character.*

paper poster of what he thought his word represented. Weird and fearful creatures adorned the walls of the room. The names assigned to these were as fearful as the creatures themselves, for there was a boosnozzle, a chicklerumper, a cartogenerian, a monsmonster, a phliphlopho, and a creatorouse, not to mention a horde of others.

Mrs. Cross suggested that the children write stories about their fictitious characters, and that they also try to invent new words from sounds which they might spell phonetically and use in their stories. The results were hilarious and very creative.

What Is an Experience?

Webster says that an *experience* is "the actual living through an event or events; actual enjoyment or suffering; hence the effect upon the judgement or feelings produced by personal and direct impressions; as, to know by *experience*." Another definition given by Webster is, "The sum total of the conscious events which compose an individual's *life*."

What Is an Adventure?

Webster defines an *adventure* as "a bold undertaking, in which hazards are to be met and the issue hangs upon unforeseen events; a daring feat; a remarkable experience; to venture or hazard oneself as *adventuring* upon paths unknown; to take the risk."

A sign faces you: "The Day of the Zerch." What do you predict? An experience or an adventure? Which is the more highly motivating: "Today we will write poems," or "The Day of the Zerch"? A workbook experience, or a folder cut into four parts? A chance to "do your thing," or following the teacher's instructions to the letter? A chance to take risks, or being guided perpetually?

According to Webster's definition, almost anything is an experience. Going to school is an experience; so is going to the circus. Eating dinner is an experience, but so is eating a *Japanese* dinner. Doing a workbook exercise is an experience, but so is seeing a magic flannel board story. Eating a cookie from the bakery is an experience, but so is baking and icing a cake all by yourself! Riding in a snowmobile is an experience, but so is building a soap box car for the derby! All are experiences, but certainly all are not the same calibre of experience! Some are more than experiences: They are adventures! Experiences can be enjoyable, like eating dinner; or miserable, like doing the workbook exercise. Experiences may be lived through, but not necessarily require involvement. Experiences may produce impressions which the individual may want to remember—or forget!

But an adventure is different. Adventures are enjoyable or exciting or unenjoyable—but, according to our definition, they must also be *remarkable*—a *remarkable* experience. Adventures may be miserable, but they are *remarkably* miserable! Adventures cannot just be lived through; they require personal involvement and risk, and consequently keen personal reaction. One must be willing to take risks—to venture onto paths of the unknown. When one has a remarkable experience, one really learns in an involved dramatic manner!

Dewey said, "We learn by doing!" He believed experience to be the basis of all learning. This author would like to substitute the word "adventure" for "experience." We learn by adventuring—by having *remarkable* experiences which deal with both the cognitive and the affective domain.

In the last chapter we discussed creativity and the characteristics of creative teaching. Notice the similarities between our description of an adventure and of creative teaching: (a) a bold undertaking, something new or different; (b) teachers (and children) must be willing to take risks; there comes a time when the teacher withdraws and leaves the children to face the unknown, something unusual, or original results; (c) children assume the responsibility for their own learning to a great degree, and (d) open-ended situations must be used.

Providing adventures instead of experiences for children makes all the difference. That is why I chose the title "Adventures in Communication" for this book; because it tells about *remarkable* experiences which teachers provide in the classroom for children to learn dramatically. If I were to write a single sentence for a definition of creative teachers, I would say, "The creative teacher is one who provides *remarkable experiences* (adventures) for her students!"

Objectives for Teaching the Language Arts

In this age of television, moving pictures, tape recorders, visual advertising, sound systems, and high fidelity, the child is bombarded with visual and audio stimuli from the time he arises until he goes to sleep. He learns from all this experience with sight and sound, he reacts to it and learns to accept it.

Unfortunately, least effective and least exciting of all his day may be the period between nine and three when he sits at his desk in a school room. Teachers have been reluctant to realize that today's child is accustomed to learning through the dramatic, and that his work in school must be dramatic also. Schools must compete with the teaching media outside the school. This is not to say that they will simply use the television, radio, tape recorder, etc., etc., as teaching aids; some teaching which I have witnessed where these media have been used has been every bit as boring and dull as the boring drill lessons for which they substitute.

What we forget is this: We have at our disposal the one thing which the mass media do not have—the child! He is an active, participating, thinking, risk-taking, problem-solving machine all his own—and no one child-machine is exactly like any other. This gives us an immediate advantage! In forming objectives for the language arts program in the elementary school for teaching and learning in the space age, it is essential that we make allowance for the changes in the times, for the needs and interests of modern children, and for their individual differences.

Basic objectives for the teaching of the language arts in the American public school have, in the past, centered largely around the teaching of the *correct* use of language. To this must now be added the teaching of the effective use of language—language which is clear, dynamic, forceful, imaginative, creative. To the goals of the teacher to teach this correct *and* effective language must be added the goal of developing creativity by teaching language creatively. In spite of the fact that modern man has now contrived more means of communication than at any other time in history, communication remains one of his greatest problems. Devices designed to facilitate communication make it easier but not necessarily more effective.

Basic objectives to be kept in mind in building correct, relevant, and effective communication skills are these:

Objective I: Each child needs to experience language (remarkably) *in dynamic and relevant ways all day, every day, so he can communicate comfortably in every way open to him, and without unnecessary pressures.*

The meeting of this objective implies that the skills learned in language arts and listed below in Objective II should be obtained in such a manner that their use is normal and natural to the child. Language cannot be learned effectively under excessive, negative pressures. When tensions build up, speech is the first part of the human system to break down. The communication skills must be taught in a relaxed atmosphere with positive pressures and wholesome motivation present. Language is part of the personality of the child and it grows with his personality. His attitude toward the use of these communication skills is as important as his ability to use them. Learning to read must be accompanied by success experiences, or the child will not learn to read for any purpose of his own; he will read to please his teacher. To be a reader, he must love to read; to write well, he must enjoy writing; to speak effectively, his speech must be satisfying and rewarding to him. A child's abilities in the language arts can be measured by tests for specific purposes, but in the long run these are meaningless measures of achievement. The factor which determines whether or not a school has a good reading program is not the grade levels on which the children read, but their attitude about books and the way they use them. Do they go home nightly with books tucked under their arms? Is the school library constantly filled with children? Do the children write profusely, leaving their creations on the teacher's desk as they leave the room each day? Can each child say what he wants to say in a class discussion without fear or embarrassment? If the answer to these questions is yes, the school has provided a facility and love of language that fulfills the purpose of a good language arts program.

Objective II: Each child must acquire necessary communication skills so that he may express himself effectively in all media.

This objective implies that there is a body of skills to be learned in order to use language effectively. Adventures in learning these skills are described in other chapters of this book.

Each child shall learn:

a. To listen effectively and for a variety of purposes (see Chapter 5).
b. To speak effectively in many kinds of social situations (see Chapter 6).
c. To spell acceptably as a social courtesy (see Chapter 11).
d. To write legibly and with ease (see Chapter 10).
e. To learn correct word usage as a social courtesy (see Chapter 12).
f. To use capitalization and punctuation as a social courtesy (see Chapter 12).
g. To use grammar correctly as a social courtesy (see Chapter 12).
h. To use reference material effectively (see Chapter 12).
i. To use word forms correctly (see Chapter 12).

Once these skills are acquired, adventures should be planned in which they may be applied; these should be not like the experiences children will have when they leave school. Such experiences should include adventures in storytelling, dramatics, creative writing, radio broadcasting, television broadcasting, tape making, film making, dictating and transcribing and editing written materials.

Objective III: Each child needs to come to appreciate the beauty of language itself, the effective use of words, and creative ways they may help him express his own original thoughts.

This is a study of language for language's sake. It is loving the rhythm of certain words; it is delighting in the way words are put together; it is using words and phrases to paint pictures. It includes the creative: the job of sorting, deciding, and choosing the right word for the right spot. It means that children evaluate words according to what they can do to make language forceful and effective. It means that children write their own literature and recognize beauty in the writings of others. It is the building of appreciation for authors, poets, and composers. It is the knowledge of that which lifts language from the commonplace to the beautiful. It is here that the objective for developing effective language fits.

Objective IV: Each child needs to find such satisfaction in his communication experiences that he will develop a healthy attitude toward communicating in all media and will develop his communication skills even without the assistance of the teacher.

In summarizing the objectives for the teaching of the language arts, we can see that effective communication does not necessarily take place when language is only correct (in the sense that all the grammar, punctuation, and sentence structure are perfectly written). Such perfection can, at times, impede communication. Effective communication means more than this; it means the ability to speak and write clearly, imaginatively, sensitively, beautifully, and effectively whenever the occasion demands.

To meet these objectives, relevant adventures must be encountered daily by the children in our schools.

The Problem of Writing Behavioral Objectives

The four major long-range objectives above designate the purpose of the language arts program. Each long-range objective now must be redesigned in the form of behavioral objectives which will state each cognitive learning of the language program in such a way that a predicted behavior change will occur, thus proving that the objective has been met.

"But," the observing student may ask, "if the outcomes in creative teaching (as stated above) are often unpredictable, *can* we predict behavior to the point where objectives for creative teaching in the language arts can be stated in behavioral terms?"

The question is well taken, and the answer is, "Yes—and no."

Most educational ideas and movements tend to create a bandwagon effect: Everyone hears about them and everyone hops on.

One such current movement is the writing of behavioral objectives for all cognitive teaching experiences, or in our own case, for all teaching adventures. The degree to which many teacher training institutions have latched onto this concept and promoted it has resulted in a fetish or faddism.

The writing of objectives in behavioral terms is a noble and sensible one. It springs from the concept that education is the process that changes human behavior. In order to teach effectively, therefore, the teacher must search for changes in the behavior of each student. To be a good teacher, then, she must be aware of the behavior that needs changing and the type of behavior that she hopes will result after her lesson or lessons—the changed behavior. If the resultant behavior is to be achieved, a system for measuring it must be included in the statement of the objective.

Mager,[1] a pioneer in this movement, lists the following criteria for a behavioral objective:

1. It names a specific overt behavior.
2. It tells exactly what the behavior consists of.
3. It may need to exclude related but unwanted behaviors.
4. It describes the conditions under which the behavior must occur.
5. It specifies the criteria of acceptable performance.

The term behavior refers to any visible activity displayed by a learner (student). Mager defines this as *overt action.* Terminal behavior refers to the behavior you would like your learner to be able to demonstrate at the time your influence over him ends.

The concept of behavioral objectives has not been fully accepted as logical or reasonable, especially in terms of creative teaching. Let us look at some of the criticisms of writing behavioral objectives in this context.

1. To write behavioral objectives according to Mager, the statement must specify what the learner must be able to DO or PERFORM when he is demonstrating his mastery of the objective. The behavior we observe may be verbal or non-verbal, but the teacher can only infer the state of condition of his intellect through observation of his performance.

This concept appears to be in conflict with the concept of creative teaching. This statement implies that the teacher must be able to predict the response that any given stimuli will evoke in a learner in order to be acceptable. While this may be possible in some cognitive learning, it is difficult at times to imagine that it can be accomplished even there. Take

1. Robert F. Mager, *Preparing Objectives for Programmed Instruction* (Palo Alto, California: Fearon Publishers, 1962).

the first year teacher, for instance. She has not yet taken her children through enough experiences so that she can predict the terminal behavior of the children, however much she knows about children at the age level of her students.

In creative teaching, direct, positive outcomes are unpredictable. If a certain amount of predictability is necessary to determine acceptable terminal behavior, then it is impossible to write objectives for the development of some types of creativity in behavioral terms.

2. Most of the texts define behavior as overt action, assuming that overt action can be interpreted by the teacher as a sign that the objective has been met. Overt action may be that a child is able to name the parts of an airplane. In her plan one teacher wrote: "As a result of this lesson each child will be able to name at least 90 percent of the parts of an airplane from a diagram." So the objective is met—the lesson is a success. Overt action may also be a child underlining a page of nouns in a workbook. This is the terminal part of an objective on recognizing nouns. But, in the true sense, has the child's "behavior," as we speak of it in terms of psychology, really changed? The teacher cannot tell at this point—she can only wait and observe whether this bit of knowledge changes the child's actions within the next days. Often the checking or testing of a bit of knowledge or a skill does not insure a change in behavior.

I have a friend who loves to sail. I go to his house to dinner. He talks continually about sailing. He takes me to the cellar and shows me the hulk of his boat which he is refinishing. My friend is enthusiastic; I enjoy listening to him and I learn a lot about sailboats.

But I am not particularly interested in sailboats. I leave his house, go home, go to bed, get up the next morning, and go about my business. I do not run down to buy a boat, I do not buy any books about boats, I do not rush to the seashore to see them sail. My overt behavior has not changed. Now, the chances are, had my friend said to me after telling me about his boat, "Let's see how many of the parts of the boat you can identify," or "Let's see how many of these questions you can answer," I could have told him most of the correct answers. But my *overt actions did not change.*

Writing the objective in behavioral terms (a) does not insure that the teacher will make teaching and learning any more relevant or creative; (b) will not insure the accomplishment of many objectives at the point when the teacher feels it is terminal; (c) will not insure a correct interpretation of the child's behavior at the terminal point; and (d) makes no allowance or measure for creative production, though it does not interfere completely with creative teaching.

3. A teacher's interpretation of children's overt action can be a risky business with the creative child. All our research to date draws attention

to the fact that teachers do not understand creative children and tend to misinterpret their behavior down the line. It seems that predetermined terminal behavior patterns allow for no originality or uniqueness of response in children—and the creative child who is already discriminated against becomes the victim of another "system."

4. It must be remembered that one of the goals of creative teaching is to develop divergent thinking. One of the characteristics of divergent thinking is that it does not have closure—or terminal behavior. Since behavioral objectives imply a terminal behavior, creative teaching cannot be stated in behavioral objectives.

5. In creative teaching, the outcomes are such that almost *any* response is acceptable, at least at the time it is offered. Judgement on ideas, poems, stories, and other creative products is deferred until the child feels himself finished; *then* the ideas are acted upon, the poem evaluated, etc. This cannot generally happen during a lesson—an incubation period must be allowed.

6. McAshan[2] says that the primary reasons for the current emphasis upon writing behavioral objectives are to: (a) aid in curriculum planning, (b) promote increased pupil achievement, (c) improve the techniques and skills of program evaluation.

In theory this concept seems valid. In practice it is difficult to achieve.

Perhaps one of the reasons why behavioral objectives are difficult to formulate in creative teaching is that behavioral objectives are designed primarily for cognitive learning experiences, and there are many experts in the field today who believe creativity belongs as much in the affective domain as it does in the cognitive.

In the taxonomies designed for grading thought processes and related questions,[3] creativity has been placed in the category of synthesis. No one studying creativity today will accept this categorization. Creativity is more than synthesis: As Carl Rogers[4] has said, "Creativity is problem solving plus." Synthesis is a high level of *convergent* thinking, whereas creative thought is *divergent*. To think and produce creatively, one must synthesize knowledge relating to a specific subject and then project or hypothesize something new that can be done with this synthesized knowledge. Our definition of creativity says it is taking our past experiences and putting them into something new or different. This is going on beyond synthesis. And because each individual has different

2. H. H. McAshen, *Writing Behavioral Objectives: A New Approach* (New York: Harper and Row, 1970).
3. B. S. Bloom et al., *Taxonomy of Educational Objectives: Handbook No. 1: The Cognitive Domain* (New York: Longmans, Green; David McKay, 1956).
4. Carl R. Rogers, "Toward a Theory of Creativity," in *Creativity and Its Cultivation*, Harold H. Anderson (ed.). (New York: Harper and Row, 1959), p. 72.

experiences and different knowledge, how can we say what he will create? We cannot. If we could, it would not be creative.

Perhaps one of the difficulties of stating all objectives for creative teaching in behavioral terms comes from a confusion as to whether creativity is a logical thought process or not. Research[5] has shown that, although there seem to be certain steps in creative processes, there are many kinds of creative thought patterns and many kinds of creativity. Perhaps creative thinking belongs to the affective domain: To be creative means to become involved, to respond emotionally, to give of the heart as well as the head. Affective learnings are not easy to describe in behavioral terms. I interpret the sparkle in the children's eyes as described on page 25 as meaning they are excited, happy, and pleased: but that is my interpretation. As a seasoned teacher, I can accept my own interpretation, but I will be much more cautious and reluctant to accept interpretation of this nature from a first year teacher.

7. In using behavioral objectives to guide learning and teaching, it must be remembered that the objective only sets the purpose of the lesson and the manner by which the learning is to be evaluated. The procedure of the lesson, that is, the teacher's methods can be as creative and unique as desired. In this sense, behavioral objectives may be used just as they are used in any other lesson. A statement such as the following does not indicate the method the teacher will use: As a result of this lesson, each child will be able to identify the use of commas, as evidenced by his ability to punctuate a selected work sheet. One teacher may open a book to page 69 and proceed to verbalize about commas with the children. Another may use the technique described in Chapter 12. Interestingly enough, Teacher 1 may give the selected work sheet and come off with results as high as those of Teacher 2. The *method* can be creative or not creative; the results the same.

However, this is exactly what disturbs this author. Both teachers are teaching for the same cognitive learnings, but Teacher 2 has other objectives in mind: She is also teaching for the development of *divergent* thinking processes as well as a *convergent* bit of knowledge. Divergency in thinking is developed over a long period of time and cannot be identified in one lesson, or stated in one objective. It is impossible for me to see how this objective, the more important one, can be stated in behavioral terms. Teacher 2 has led the children in her classroom toward the cognitive and affective learnings she has in mind, whereas Teacher 1 is going to fool herself that she has attained her goal. Actually, she may not have fulfilled her objective at all; she may have taught a piece of knowledge which may or may not *change the behavior* of the children.

5. Mary Lee Marksberry, *Foundation of Creativity* (New York: Harper and Row, 1963).

In either case, the true test of the effectiveness of the teacher's teaching and the students' learning *comes in the days following the lesson* when each teacher must observe any changes of the behavior of theme writing in the children!

8. When cognitive learnings are involved in a creative lesson, they may still be identified and written up in the original lesson plan, as in the story of Denny the Dinosaur in Chapter 12. One of the teacher's objectives read: "As a result of this lesson all the children will recognize describing words as adjectives by the manner in which they create and use adjectives in a nonsense story and in an original poem."

While such an objective is legitimate, it relegates creativity to the background and makes the cognitive learnings the most important part of the lesson.

This author questions the validity of this action, for he feels that the creative part of the lesson is more important and that the knowledges, though important, are incidental. Diagnosis by the teacher of the children's work after each lesson, and then remedial work with individuals, call for a *set* of objectives rather than a few, or, if needed, different objectives for each member of the class. Then the teacher teaches by groups, or to individuals, those skills or knowledges which each child has not yet mastered (see Chap. 12). This cancels the need for the latter part of the usual behavioral statement such as "The student is to be able to complete a twenty-five multiple-choice examination on parts of speech. <u>The lower limit of acceptable performance will be twenty items answered correctly within a period of twenty minutes</u>."

The underlined part states acceptable performance. Actually, no less-than-perfect performance is acceptable in mastering language arts skills. To deny a child the right of additional instruction in such a situation because he met the minimal requirements stated in an objective is to handicap him for life. Behavioral objectives, if not carefully controlled, may create sloppy and incomplete teaching.

In teaching language skills and knowledges, systems such as those above must be used in which individuals receive individual help and guidance—the goal being perfect performance, provided, of course, that the child is not somehow handicapped.

9. Too often we speak in terms of what a student—any student on any level—does instead of HOW or WHY he does it. In creative learning the HOW can be as important as the result, because creativity is a process and/or a product. Consequently, if behavioral objectives are to set means for measuring creative development, they must be more concerned with a process than with a terminal behavior at the close of a period of time.

To state objectives in any form is not to achieve them. The methodology is still the important thing. Evaluation simply tells whether the method worked and what the teacher must reteach.

Curriculum development involves a precarious combination of artistry, dedication, and experience, and a difficult mix of scholars, teachers, school administrators, and children. A more realistic emphasis in any program should be on the *method* best suited for each child to do what he is able, not as a statement of a final product expected from a total group, within which there are some children who cannot ever reach the goal and many who have already mastered the goal before the lesson begins.

Evaluating in terms of behavioral objectives means evaluating outwardly that which *appears* to be so in a given specific situation at one specific time. The long-range view is neglected: those changes in behavior which take place over a longer period of time—in essence, the REAL objectives behind each teaching act. The applications of learnings in this instance are largely the outcomes of a stimulus-response situation and are not concerned with the true changes in behavior that come after the lesson is over, as are the later applications of learnings in direct use in everyday living.

There is a certain amount of dishonesty in writing behavioral objectives if the constituency of the group is not known. This is true, of course, of the writing of any kind of objective. To be absolutely honest, a teacher must evaluate her own skill in teaching by evaluating the skills or knowledges the children already possess at the BEGINNING of the lesson. It is always possible that the terminal behavior is often the beginning behavior and that the child does not need the instruction. Discovering this at the beginning of the lesson at least does not permit the teacher to kid herself into believing she has taught something that she has not.

Some objectives for teaching in the affective domain can be written in behavioral terms. Part of the teacher's job is to identify such objectives. But, she should also be able to identify those objectives which cannot be measured in any immediate terminal behavior and these should be written in some other manner which is meaningful to her and which she may come to measure over a longer period of time. Many objectives for creative development will fall into this category.

The author does not intend to discredit the usefulness of writing behavioral objectives. Used in the proper context they clarify the teacher's goals, help her to select experiences to achieve the goals and suggest ways she can measure her degree of achievement. He does, however, emphasize the fact that behavioral objectives are not a panacea to the ills of teaching and to use them indiscreetly, especially in an area such as creative development where behavior is not always interpreted accurately or measured reliably may prove to interfere with the creative process.

Therefore, we must modify our concepts of behavioral objectives when we write for creative teaching. We can write only to a predictable point, and we cannot always describe the product as a behavioral change.

The following example may be classified as a behavioral objective, yet it recognizes creative teaching. *Objective:* As a result of this lesson, children will be able to brainstorm, as evidenced by the lists they invent of possible solutions to a given problem.

Teachers may be stifled or restricted because they cannot fit their creative teaching into the form of behavioral objectives. They should not be—this is not uncommon. Anything new or creative does not generally fit into an old mold.

"Objectives" a teacher must have—clear and distinct. But there are many ways of being creative, many ways of measuring creativity, and many ways to develop it. And no teacher should feel she must force her writing of objectives to fit a preconceived form. After all, objectives of any sort are only a guide to learning. There is still much to be said about capitalizing on teachable moments and changing objectives in mid-lesson; it is all permissible (and can be very creative) if the teacher keeps her new goals clearly in mind.

Our emphasis here is that children learn from adventures. Much of what they learn must be taken on faith: the willingness to take risks, the willingness to face the unknown, the courage to try, the willingness to experiment. Teachers should not be shackled by systems that prevent them from developing the same qualities in their own teaching.

Summary

Children learn best through adventures. Adventures are *remarkable* experiences. Creative teachers turn ordinary experiences into adventures so that children may not only learn effectively but will develop their own divergent thinking and creative thinking processes as well.

There are four general objectives for teaching the language arts. General objectives are goals that are attained over a long period of time. General objectives must be broken down into specific objectives.

Objectives for developing creativity cannot always be composed in behavioral terms. Outcomes from creative objectives are divergent, not convergent; ongoing, not terminal; process concerned as well as product concerned; primarily for real behavior change and not for knowledge and skill acquisition; for full potential development rather than a compromise adjustment; affective concerned as well as cognitive concerned; method concerned as well as objective concerned; child directed, not group directed.

It is possible that the attempt to compose objectives for creative teaching in any set pattern may be so thwarting to the teacher that it becomes a stumbling block to creative teaching.

Creative teaching also means creative planning.

To the Reader

1. Some questions for discussion:
   a. Psychologists are currently defending the students' rights to "feel good" as well as to "know good." They argue that we should, in school as in life, allow the emotional self to be as apparent as the logical and rational self. In the creation of Zerches, described in this chapter, how did the teacher help the children to "feel good" about their experiences?
2. Dr. Nyquist,[6] Commissioner of Education of New York State, said in a recent speech, "Perhaps there is some justice in the complaint of young people that we in education have become so concerned with refining mental capacities and honing rational processes for purposes set by the system—purposes of helping people make a living—that we have forgotten how to help people make a life. In Education lingo, maybe there is more than a little truth to the complaint that we have struggled for the mental forms and have lost the humanistic substance."

   Consider Dr. Nyquist's quote in light of the discussion of writing behavioral objectives in this chapter. Does the focus on writing behavioral objectives tend to dehumanize the curriculum? What part can creativity play in counteracting the concepts given in Dr. Nyquist's quote?
3. What are the differences between "behavioral objectives," "instructional objectives," and "performance objectives"?
4. Can behavioral objectives be developed in the "affective" domain?
5. How can instruction be individualized if behavioral objectives are not individualized?
6. Can behavioral objectives be used in teaching for the humanities?
7. Are there other ways of writing objectives which are effective but which do not exclude creative responses? What about writing ob-

6. Ewald Nyquist, *The Age of Humanity* (Albany, New York: University of the State of New York, Division of Humanities and Arts, 1970), p. 14.

jectives in terms of outcomes? What strengths and weaknesses are inherent in other plans?

8. Although the literature is replete with pros and cons about writing behavioral objectives, there is a startling lack of evidence as to whether school systems have attempted to train their teachers to write them; whether, in practice, the writing of behavioral objectives is practical; and whether its practice produces better teachers and better learners. One report from a school system which has done this is very interesting (Des Moines, Iowa, *Project Impact* [see Rowson, Joseph] in bibliography). Read this report and note again what these teachers concluded.
9. Advocates of writing objectives in behavioral terms state that the demand for *accountability* in teaching enhances the case for writing objectives in this manner. The author travels about the country a great deal, speaking and working with parents. It is true that parents and state boards are demanding accountability from teachers, but not entirely the cognitive-learning kinds. Questions often asked by parents are:

   "How can I get John to do his homework when he hates math so much?"

   "I always loved to read. Why doesn't my child love to read?"

   "What happens up here in kindergarten that makes my child hate kindergarten so?"

   "I have a creative kid and no one at school cares."

   How can accountability of this sort be measured? By test questions? By check sheets? Or, by observation—and long-range objectives? Does writing behavioral objectives provide for these problems?
10. From the bibliography at the end of this chapter, choose material about behavioral objectives which gives viewpoints for and against using them.

Selected Bibliography

ANDERSON, PAUL S. *Language Skills in Elementary Education.* New York: Macmillan Company, 1964.

ASSOCIATION FOR SUPERVISION AND CURRICULUM DEVELOPMENT. *To Nurture Humaneness: Committment for the 70's.* Washington, D.C.: Yearbook, 1970.

ATKINS, J. M. "Behavioral Objectives in Curriculum Design: A Cautionary Note." *The Science Teacher* (May 1968), 27–30.

Bernier, Norman. *The Affective Domain in Teaching.* Chicago, Illinois: Association for Student Teaching Speech—First Florence B. Stratemeyer Lecture, February 17, 1966.

Bloom, B. S., et al. *Taxonomy of Educational Objectives: Handbook No. 1: The Cognitive Domain.* New York: Longmans, Green, David McKay, 1956.

Burns, Paul C., and Alberta L. Lowe. *The Language Arts in Childhood Education.* Chicago: Rand McNally and Company, 1966.

Burns, Paul C. "Linguistics: A Brief Guide for Principals," *The National Elementary Principal,* 45 (September 1965), 37–42.

Clegg, A. "What Is a Humanizing Curriculum?" *National Elementary Principal,* 49 (February 1970), 8–12.

Cox, Benjamin G. "Behavior as Objective in Education," *Social Education,* 35, no. 5 (May 1971), 435–449.

Darland, D. D. "Accountable for What?" *Journal of Teacher Education,* 21 (Winter 1970), 467–68.

Dawson, Mildred, and Georgiana C. Newman. *Language Teaching in Kindergarten and Early Primary Grades.* New York: Harcourt, Brace and Company, 1966.

Eisner, G. W. "Educational Objectives: Help or Hindrance?" *School Review,* 75, no. 3 (1967 a).

Goldstein, Miriam B. *The Teaching of Language in Our Schools.* New York: The Macmillan Company, 1966.

Greene, Harry A., and Walter T. Petty. *Developing Language Skills in the Elementary Schools,* 4th ed. Boston: Allyn and Bacon, 1971.

Hayes, J. J., and J. D. DiSanto. "Implementation of Behavioral Objectives in Curriculum Development," *Education,* 96 (Summer 1969), 44–48.

Hersch, Richard, and Stuart Cohen. "A Case Against Behavioral Objectives," *Elementary School Journal,* 71 (May 1971).

Jackson, P., and E. Betford, "Educational Objectives and the Joys of Teaching," *School Review,* 75 (Autumn, 1967) 250–266.

Krathwohl, D. R. "Stating Objectives Appropriately for Program, for Curriculum and for Instructional Materials Development," *The Journal of Teacher Education,* vol. 16, no. 1 (1965).

Krathwohl, D. R., et al. *Taxonomy of Educational Objectives: Handbook II: The Affective Domain.* New York: David McKay, 1964.

MacDonald, James B., and Bernice J. Wolfson, "A Case Against Behavioral Objectives," *Elementary School Journal,* 71 (December 1970).

MacGinitie, Walter. "Language Development," *Encyclopedia of*

Educational Research, rev. ed., Robert L. Ebel (ed.). New York: Macmillan Company, 1969.

McAshen, H. H. *Writing Behavioral Objectives: A New Approach.* New York: Harper and Row, 1970.

McCampbell, James C. (ed.) *Readings in the Language Arts in the Elementary School.* Boston: D. C. Heath and Company, 1964.

Mager, R. F. *Preparing Objectives for Programmed Instruction.* Palo Alto, California: Fearon Publishers, 1962.

Nyguist, Ewald. *The Age of Humanity.* Albany, New York: University of the State of New York, Division of Humanities and Arts, 1970.

Petty, Walter T. *Issues and Problems in the Elementary Language Arts.* Boston: Allyn and Bacon, 1968.

Popham, W. James, and Eva L. Baker. *Establishing Instructional Goals.* Englewood Cliffs, New Jersey: Prentice-Hall, Inc., 1970.

______. *Planning an Instructional Sequence.* Englewood Cliffs, New Jersey: Prentice-Hall, Inc., 1970.

______. *Systematic Instruction.* Englewood Cliffs, New Jersey: Prentice-Hall, Inc., 1970.

Rowson, Joseph P. (ed.). *Impact '70.* Des Moines, Iowa: Polk County Board of Education, 1971.

Shane, Harold G., M. Redden, and M. C. Gillespie. *Beginning Language Arts Instruction with Children.* Columbus, Ohio: Charles Merrill Company, 1961.

Shane, Harold G., and June G. Mulry. *Improving Language Arts Instruction Through Research.* Washington, D.C.: Association for Supervision and Curriculum Development, 1964.

Trauger, Wilmer. *Language Arts in Elementary Schools.* New York: McGraw-Hill Company, 1963.

Yarger, Sam J. "Behavioral Objectives: Where and Where Not," *Phi Delta Kappa Record*, vol. 7, no. 4 (April 1971), 99–102.

5₅5

Adventures in Listening

Hildegarde Magillicutty Goes to the Fair

The following story was written for children from ages seven through twelve by a fifth grade teacher and his pupils. It was written as a "sound" story. The purpose of the story is two-fold: (1) to provide for the creative teaching of listening, and (2) to develop some meaningful phonetic training.

A "sound" story is one to which background sounds may be added softly by the listeners to heighten the mood and the effect of the story as it is being read, much as a choral poem is developed.

Careful listening is required so that everyone comes into the story on cue. Sound stories are most effective when they are spoken into a tape recorder and replayed so that the entire group may hear the final effect.

In developing a sound story, it is suggested that the story be first read in its entirety for pleasure. On the second reading, the listeners are alerted to identify all the sounds that could be made as background, and they are listed.

In the case of "Hildegarde Magillicutty Goes to the Fair," the sounds are very obvious and provide some good phonetic reading in a meaningful way.

Certain groups of children are designated to make the sounds in the proper place while one child (or a small group) reads the story. Generally, there is a build-up of noises until a din is reached and then the noises stop while the reader goes on alone.

"Sound" stories are fun for children and adults and may be varied greatly with the addition of musical instruments, rhythm band instruments, or other noises in the environment such as water pouring, feet stomping, or hands clapping.

* * *

Hildegarde Magillicutty lived by herself in a little, old, red farmhouse in the northern part of Onondaga County. It was a quiet, peaceful place and all Hildegarde Magillicutty ever heard when she awoke early each morning was the crowing of the rooster, the singing of the birds, and the sighing of the wind. Hildegarde liked it that way. If there was one thing she could not stand, it was noise!

One day, when she was shopping at the store down at Martins Corners, she saw a big, colorful poster in the window full of pictures of busy people and beautiful animals doing wonderful and fearful things. Across the top it read, "Come to the great State Fair—Sept. 9–15. Seven Glorious Days and Nights!"

Now Hildegarde Magillicutty had always wanted to go to the great State Fair down in the big city of Syracuse. Driving home in her little jalopy she thought about it. All that evening and all the next day she thought about it. On the second day, after she was awakened by the rooster crowing, she lay in bed and she made up her mind!

"I'm not gettin' any younger," Hildegarde said to herself, "I'm going to see that fair!"

So, early in the morning of September 9th she packed herself a lunch which she put in a shopping bag, and taking her umbrella, she got into her little jalopy and drove down to the railroad station and bought a ticket from Clem Peters for the only coach car on the 6:45 headed for Syracuse.

It was a glorious morning. The sun shone brightly. In the distance Hildegarde could hear the roosters crowing and the birds chirping. The speed of the little train made the wind sigh through the coach car. And, the clickety-clack, clickety-clack of the wheels on the tracks was a happy sound.

It seemed to Hildegarde that the train was just nicely under way when it began to slow down. Finally it stopped altogether.

Hildegarde leaned out the window to see what was the matter. She knew at once. They had stopped at a siding and there was a whole railroad car full of pigs waiting to be hooked on to the train. Such a noise they made! Hildegarde tried to call to the men standing by the siding but she couldn't make them hear her at all. So, she hurried down to the end of the coach clutching her shopping bag and her umbrella and stuck her head out the door.

"Where you goin' with all those pigs?" she shouted above the noise.

"Silas Jones is takin' them down to show them off at the big Fair in Syracuse," the station master called back.

Soon the car of pigs was hooked on and the little train was on its way. Only it was very different now. Hildegarde could not hear the crowing of the rooster or the singing of the birds. The pigs made so much noise with their oinking and grunting she could scarcely hear the clickety-clack music of the train. They were altogether too noisy, and she did not like it.

Hildegarde was hardly accustomed to the pig noises when the train slowed down once more. Again, she stuck her head out of the window. "What now?" she shouted to the station master, who was standing by the siding.

"Hi, Miz Magillicutty," he called back. "Goin' to the Fair? We'll only be a minute! Howie MacGregor's got a load of cows to hook on to the train. He's going to take them down and exhibit them at the great State Fair in Syracuse!"

And sure enough, there on the siding was a freight car full of Howie MacGregor's prize cows and bulls, all frightened and bellowing "Mooooo" and "Harumph."

In no time at all the car was hooked on to the little train and once again it hurried along the tracks to Syracuse. But Hildegarde was not too happy. She didn't like noise—and right now she had plenty of it! There was not only the clickety-clack of the train and the grunting of Silas Jones's pigs, but there also was the mooing of Howie MacGregor's cows and the "Harumph" of his bulls. The noise hurt Hildegarde Magillicutty's ears.

She wasn't settled comfortably before the train stopped at another siding to pick up a car full of Charlie Aspenwall's prize sheep. This time, when the little train started, Hildegarde could hardly stand the confusion. All she could hear was the clickety-clack of the train, the grunting of the pigs, the mooing of the cows, the snorting of the bulls, and the bleating of the sheep.

And, to make matters worse, the little train, which wasn't so little any more, backed into a siding and picked up a carload of Clayton Burn's chickens and geese and a car full of Byron Webb's horses—all going to the Fair.

This time when the train was under way, Hildegarde thought her head would burst, the noise was so great: She could hear the clickety-clack of the train, the grunting of the pigs, the mooing of the cows, the snorting of the bulls, the bleating of the sheep, the clucking of the chickens, the quacking of the ducks, and the whinnying of the horses!

She was never more glad in her life than she was when the train stopped and the conductor came into the coach shouting, "Syracuse—all out for Syracuse! Cars to the right take you right to the Fair!"

Soon Hildegarde stood before the gates of the Great State Fair. It was even more wonderful than she had dreamed. Flags were flying, cars were crawling past in long lines, state troopers were directing traffic, band music was pouring out of the fair grounds, and everywhere there were long lines of people waiting to buy tickets. She had never seen so many people in her life!

After she became accustomed to the busy scene, Hildegarde stood in line and bought her ticket. Inside the gates there was even more confusion.

The first building that Hildegarde came to was the Dairy Building, so she went in. Inside there were many interesting exhibits about milk and cheese and dairy products. Hildegarde went through one door and stepped into a huge room full of cows. She wondered if Howie MacGregor's cows were there so she started to look. It was hard to tell.

"Mooo," said all the cows as she walked past.

She couldn't find Howie's name on the signs so she kept on looking. Soon she discovered she had passed the cows and was now surrounded by chickens.

"Cluck, cluck, cluck, cluck, cluck!" they all scolded. Each one sounded as though it was laying an egg.

"Moo, moo, moo," said the cows in the background.

She hurried past rows of roosters in cages.

"Cock-a-doodle-doo—cock-a-doodle-doo," they all screamed.

"Cluck, cluck, cluck," scolded the hens.

"Moo, moo, moo," whispered the cows in the distance.

Soon Hildegarde came to a crate of ducks, all of which began to quack when they saw her.

"Quack, quack, quack, quack, quack," bickered the ducks.

"Cock-a-doodle-doo," screamed the roosters.

"Cluck, cluck, cluck," scolded the hens.

"Moo, moo, moo," whispered the cows in the distance.

By this time the din was terrible!

"I've got to get out of here!" said Hildegarde Magillicutty as she headed out the open door at the end of the building.

It was peaceful and quiet outside the Dairy Building compared to the inside. Hildegarde just stood and tried to relax for a while. Then she went on her way.

The next building she came to was marked "Farm Machinery." She had always lived on a farm so she decided to see what was new in farm machinery.

Hildegarde walked into the building. Once inside the door Hildegarde started to walk down the long aisles of exhibits.

First she came to a man demonstrating a milking machine.

"Farump, farump," sang the plungers as they moved softly up and down. "Farump, farump."

Hildegarde moved on. In the next booth there was a man demonstrating an electric drill.

"Rat-a-tat, rat-a-tat-tat," pounded the drill, and in the background,

"Farump, farump," whispered the milking machine.

In the next booth, a man was showing how a chain saw worked by cutting up logs. The saw made a frightening noise.

"ZZZinggg," screeched the saw.

"Rat-a-tat-tat, rat-a-tat-tat," pounded the drill.

"Farump, farump," whispered the milking machine faintly.

Hildegarde's ears were beginning to hurt so she moved on to a big open area. In it was a small airplane. Everyone should have one, the man said, to dust his crops.

He turned the propeller to show how easy it was to start the engine.

"A-chug, a-chug, Frrrruuuummmmpp," bellowed the plane, almost drowning out the "ZZZinggg" of the saw, the "Rat-a-tat-tat, rat-a-tat-tat," of the drill, and the "Farumpp, farump" whispering of the milking machine.

Hildegarde thought her ears would burst. She ran out a nearby door into the open sunshine. It was peaceful and quiet outside the Farm Machinery building compared to the inside. Hildegarde just stood and tried to be quiet for a while.

She sat and ate her lunch at one of the tables while she watched all the people stroll by.

After a while she saw something in the distance that fascinated her. It was the Midway, full of rides and hucksters selling exciting and colorful wares.

A man selling frozen custard was at the entrance to the midway.

"Frozen custard," he shouted, "Right here! Buy your frozen custard right here!"

The creamy, white stuff in the cones looked good so Hildegarde bought one. It *was* good. Easting her custard she strolled on until she came to a delightful sound. It was a merry-go-round.

"Tump-pa-pa-pa," sang the calliope on the merry-go-round.

"Frozen custard, step right up. Buy your frozen custard here," shouted the huskster in the background.

Hildegarde watched the children on the merry-go-round for a while and walked on.

"Popcorn, popcorn. Fresh buttered popcorn," shouted a man behind a little, red wagon.

"Fump-pa-pa, fump-pa-pa. Fump-pa-pa," sang the calliope.

"Frozen custard, fresh frozen custard," said the man faintly in the distance.

A screaming noise broke the silence!

"Put-put-put—Wheeeeee!"

Hildegarde was standing in front of a daredevil motorcycle sideshow. The men were racing the motors of the motorcycles to warm them up for the contest.

"Put-put-put—wheeeeee, put-put-put—wheeeee," the motors blasted as the men pushed the pedals.

"Popcorn, popcorn, fresh buttered popcorn," said the man behind the little, red wagon.

"Fump-pa-pa, fump-pa-pa, fump-pa-pa," hummed the calliope.

"Frozen custard, fresh frozen custard," whispered the man in the distance.

Hildegarde's ears were beginning to hurt again. She ran away from the noise of the motorcycles. But on every side voices were shouting over megaphones and loud speakers.

"Step right this way, Lady, three chances for a nickel!"

"Toss a ring, Lady—and win a prize!"

"Buy your tickets to the greatest side show on earth. Only fifty cents!"

"Step right over here, Ma'am, right over here. The show begins in ten minutes!"

"Put-put-put—wheeeee, put-put-put—wheeeee," blasted the motorcycles.

"Popcorn, popcorn, fresh buttered popcorn!"

"Fump-pa-pa, fump-pa-pa, fump-pa-pa."

"Frozen custard, fresh frozen custard!"

Suddenly there was a "Boom" that beat all the noises Hildegarde had ever heard.

"Boom! Boom! Acrack, crack, crack, boom! boom!" Daytime fire bombs! The sky was full of bomblike firecrackers going off.

Hildegarde thought her head would burst. She ran down the Midway away from the noise, back through the Industrial Building where everyone was still demonstrating everything.

She scooted out the front of the Dairy Building to the main gate. In a minute she was out the gate and into the little car that took her to the train. Clutching her shopping bag and her umbrella she got on the train and sat with a thump in her seat.

"Goin' home kinda early, ain't ya, Miz Magillicutty?" asked the conductor.

"Yup," said Hildegarde sitting up very straight, "I'm goin' home early. Just about had all I can take of the great State Fair."

So Hildegarde Magillicutty went back to her little, red farmhouse in northern Onondaga County, where everything is peaceful and quiet, away from the noises of the Fair. The only sounds she hears all day long are the crowing of the rooster, the chirping of the birds, and the sighing of the wind. She likes it that way.

* * *

Mr. Arnold made a tape of the "sound" story and it was broadcast over the communication system one morning to the entire school. Everyone enjoyed it. And Mr. Arnold's children learned a great deal about listening.

Listening as a Skill

Listening is the newest skill to be taught in the language arts program. Not long ago the teaching of listening was not felt to be important. Children were to be seen and not heard, and it was expected that they would listen. Indeed, there were few distractions to keep them from listening. Much of the time in the classroom was spent listening to the drone of the teacher's voice. Much of the time outside the classroom was spent listening to relatively few people and to familiar sounds day after day.

But times have changed. Today's child snaps on his radio or TV set as soon as he awakens, and many sounds fill his room. In a neighboring room his sister has tuned in another station. In the kitchen Mother has tuned in on the weather report in order to know how to dress the children for school. From the bathroom comes the sound of Dad's electric razor and the water running in his shower. Little sister has tuned in on "Captain Kangaroo" in the living room.

Soon he climbs onto the school bus where he sees and hears many children all chattering and telling about their home experiences. The bus unloads him at a large central school where he meets many people in small and large groups in the classroom, the gymnasium, the cafeteria, the library, and the auditorium. In the afternoon, he again rides the school bus, then drives to the shopping center with Mother, where he meets and hears more strange people in an hour than his great-grandfather heard in a year! Today's children are bombarded with sounds from the moment they arise until they retire.

The constant flow of words around them engulfs them to the degree that they quickly learn to shut off all those words and sounds that they do not wish to hear. This is perhaps necessary if they are to remain sane.

Because children are subjected to endless numbers of sounds, they do not always know *what* to listen to or *how* to listen. Even in the listening-for-listening's-sake situation, there are distractions present which make training in the listening skills necessary. For this reason, continued emphasis is being placed on the teaching of listening as a necessary language skill to be developed in the classroom.

Although speaking is the most common form of communication, it is ineffective without a listener. Listening constitutes half of the communication process.

Listening Must Be Taught

In a study conducted by Wilt,[1] it was estimated that children listened 77.6 minutes of the school day, according to the teacher. In her follow-up observations, however, Wilt estimated that children were actually supposed to listen more than half the time they were in school. The highest percentage of time children were supposed to listen was when they were listening to the teacher. The listening activity with the second highest percentage of "supposed-to-listen" time was when questions asked by the teacher were to be answered by one child. In the same study, the author concluded that the highest percentage of supposed listening time came in the first, third, and sixth grades. The lowest percentage occurred in the second grade, the second lowest in the fourth grade. Children are expected to spend more time listening than in any other activity, yet the writer concluded that teachers considered listening less important than reading and speaking. The writer felt she gained substantial evidence to conclude that teachers do not teach LISTENING.

Other studies in recent years have brought about a renewed focus on the teaching of listening. For instance, certain studies show that adults listen at the rate of 400 to 500 words per minute, whereas the average speaking rate is 100 words per minute.

Individual differences in listening ability have been found in children even as they enter school. These include differences in auditory acuity, discrimination, and comprehension. As in other areas of learning, these differences persist and the range becomes even wider as the child advances through the school system.

Listening is a mental process calling for reaction. In this sense it is like reading. Both processes call for thought and reaction.

1. Marion E. Wilt, "Study of Teacher Awareness of Listening as a Factor in Elementary Education," *Journal of Educational Research*, XLIII (April 1950), pp. 626–636.

Studies conducted by the Central New York Study Council showed the following to be true:[2] (1) Children in the elementary grades get information through listening; (2) children through the sixth grade level get directions better from listening than from reading; (3) listening results do not necessarily parallel reading achievement (slow learners are not necessarily poor listeners); (4) although sixth graders are both better readers and better listeners than fourth graders, there seems to be greater improvement in listening than in reading at the sixth grade level; (5) there is a limit to the number of things a child can listen to and recall (children seem to remember first directions better than the last); (6) there appears to be no significant difference in the listening abilities of the sexes from kindergarten through sixth grade.

Some conclusions which the researchers made were: (1) More direct teaching of listening could improve the quality of listening; (2) teachers should be conscious of teaching listening as a language arts skill; (3) listening is a good technique for teaching slow learners; (4) teachers should be aware of the limitations of the group and should give directions accordingly.

In another study, Pratt[3] found that even a short training period of five weeks can be instrumental in raising the general level of listening ability, thus reinforcing the idea that listening can be taught as a skill.

Setting Conditions for Teaching Listening

Not only can listening be taught, it can be taught creatively and with excitement. So often the teaching of good listening habits is interpreted as meaning a demand for attention or a demand for order. The author has seen countless numbers of teachers wasting precious minutes standing before classes of children, waiting until everyone was ready, or waiting because "John isn't quiet." He has also seen teachers who receive immediate response for each listening experience the children are to have, and the children come to the experience eager and excited.

The teaching of listening involves the setting of proper conditions so that listening can take place. These conditions may be *natural* ones. Natural experiences are those in which the conditions present themselves and the teacher makes almost no preparation because the motiva-

2. Central New York Study Council. *Some Helps For Building Guides for Skill Development in the Language Arts: Listening*. Report No. 7 (Syracuse, New York: Syracuse University, 1957).
3. L. E. Pratt, "The Experimental Evaluation of a Program For the Improvement of Listening in the Elementary School." (Unpublished Ph.D. Dissertation, State University of Iowa, 1953.)

tion is so high that the children all listen immediately. Conditions, on the other hand, may be contrived ones where the teacher plans, constructs, or utilizes materials, situations, or gimmicks to motivate children for the purpose of teaching listening skills.

One excellent example of such a contrived situation involved the construction by first graders of actual "listening ears" to be worn only when listening was required. This contrived experience is a creative way to help children to approach the beginning steps of attentive listening—simply paying attention! On the pages that follow are many suc-

Figure 21 *For creative listening: Miss Jones made an elf from plywood. He stood by the door at the front of the classroom. Every day his bag held a surprise for the Show-and-Tell period.*

cessful ways by which teachers have set conditions for effective listening. Some of these are skills, others are gimmicks. It is hoped that the reader, by reading these ideas and adding ideas of her own, will begin to see the possibilities of developing creative listening situations. The ideas have been categorized so that the teacher may better understand the specific situations in which they were used.

In the teaching of listening, there are certain important general conditions which should be considered before each teaching situation. They include the following:

1. Be sure the physical conditions are properly set up. Remove all the distractions that you possibly can—both noise and movement. Make sure that chairs face the right direction so that eye strain and uncomfortable sitting positions are erased. Place materials in a prominent place and remove materials that are not to be used. Make sure that each child is comfortable and that he can see well.
2. Speak in an animated and interesting manner, as though you yourself could hardly wait to tell the children what you have to say.
3. Make sure that your speaking speed does not exceed the children's listening speed.
4. Help the children make up rules for good listening.
5. Help the children to understand what they have heard, in much the same way as you would check comprehension in a good reading lesson. Ask such questions as, "What did Bill tell us about?" (selecting main idea); "What was the first thing that happened to Bill?" (sequence of ideas); etc.
6. Praise the children often for good listening. When you give directions and they are carried out well, motivation for listening is enhanced when the teacher says, "Good, I am proud that you did such a good job! It shows that we all listened well!"
7. Be a good listener yourself. Teachers so often only half-listen to a child as their eyes roam around the room taking in all the other children at work. Develop the habit of looking directly at a child when he talks and responding specifically to him.
8. Avoid needless repetition, especially in giving directions. It is better to say, "Do all of you understand that?" than "Listen once more and I'll say it all over again." The child who thinks he has it correct (and most of them will), will not listen the second time. This discourages good listening.
9. Avoid needless demands of pupil attention. Instead, try using interesting gimmicks and devices to gain immediate attention (see page 121).
10. Allow the children to talk. Remember that most teachers talk too much!

11. Adams[4] and Murphy[5] both emphasized four aspects to listening. These authors state that listening must be (a) purposeful, (b) accurate, (c) critical, and (d) responsive or appreciative.

12. Help children eliminate bad listening habits. Make a list of the poor listening habits you notice in the children. Bring these habits to the attention of the children. Let the children help to take care of them, perhaps by listing ideas for their correction.

13. Do not place too much emphasis on regurgitative material. A basic goal in education today is creativity. To foster creative listening, seek to develop an attitude of mental alertness in the children. Attitude or "set" toward listening is important. Much of the time that children are required to listen is for the purpose of reproducing what they hear. More emphasis should be placed on encouraging them to *think about* what they hear. Avoid overuse of these reproductive sets, and plan conditions for creative thinking sets.

14. In the teaching of listening, teachers should be sure that the children realize that there are varying degrees of attention required for different kinds of listening. Children can be helped to listen properly if they are told at the onset of each lesson just how important the listening for that particular lesson is, how they can best listen to get from the lesson what they should, and the guides or directions for the particular kind of listening needed for the lesson.

15. Above all, be sure that the child has something worthwhile to listen to, a valid reason for listening.

16. Present listening as a social courtesy, but explain that this is not the only or main reason for good listening.

Part of the task of the teacher is to set the mental and physical conditions necessary for listening in each new lesson throughout the school day.

Setting Conditions for the Creative Teaching of Listening

The generalizations stated above apply to the teaching of *all* listening experiences. However, there are certain basic differences between the general teaching of listening and the *creative* teaching of listening. The latter must include the above-stated principles, but most go a step beyond to include the following principles as well.

4. H. M. Adams, "Learning To Be Discriminating Listeners," *English*, XXXVI (January 1947).
5. G. Murphy, "We Also Learn by Listening," *Elementary English*, XXXVI (March 1944), pp. 127–128.

1. In the creative teaching of listening, a unique or original idea is used by teacher or children which obtains the required response, so that creative teaching may follow.

2. The creative teaching of listening not only develops the skill of and need for listening among children, but it also results in an unusual response from the children, or in a unique product as a result of the listening.

3. The creative teaching of listening accents highly motivational tensions; the listening experience is planned in such a manner that tensions are built immediately in children which make them want to listen. Little or no time is spent in waiting until John is ready or until all are quiet.

4. In creative listening experiences, the motivational experiences are planned so that divergent thinking processes begin to take place at once. Emphasis is not placed on the attainment of any *one* answer.

5. Consequently, the creative teaching of listening involves *all* children almost immediately—as shown in the opening situation in this chapter.

6. The creative teaching of listening utilizes many open-ended techniques.

7. The creative teaching of listening may require that some unique conditions be set.

8. Creative listening experiences are the motivational forces which build proper tensions so that creative teaching may follow. As such, they encompass or lead into the basic principles for creative teaching listed in Chapter 3.

The Sound Box: The following description of a lesson on the teaching of listening will illustrate the use of the above principles.

The teacher's objectives were stated in the following manner.

As a result of this lesson:

1. Each student will improve his listening skills as evidenced by oral, written and picture responses to a series of creative listening stimuli.

2. Each student will demonstrate by an original story, poem, or painting that appreciative listening can result in a creative product.

3. Each student will identify the fact that there are different kinds of listening as evidenced by a discussion and a resulting chart dictated by the class on ways of listening.

The teacher motivated the children by putting before the group a gaily decorated box on which she had printed the words Sound Box.

"What is that?" the children immediately asked, "What is it for?"

"It is a sound box," answered the teacher, "and everything in it is something to listen to. I have it here today to see how well you can listen and if you know what makes a good listener. Let's get ready to listen. All eyes up here, desks clear, lips closed. Good. Now what is in the box? Max, put in your hand and draw out the first thing you feel!"

Max pulled out a yellow card on which was printed "The magic word is *story*."

"This," said the teacher, "is a word everyone will listen for this afternoon. Every time I use this word today, the first one who raises his hand gets a point! Now, I will take something out of the box."

The teacher then took from the box a small tray covered with a cloth.

"Well," said the teacher, "we are going to see how attentive you can be. I am going to take the cloth off this tray and you will see many things on the tray which make a noise. I will walk among you with the tray and you will have to look hard and try to remember all the things you see."

She took the cloth off the tray to disclose an eggbeater, a Halloween noise-maker, a clamp, a small bottle of water, a piece of paper, a music box, two sticks, a pair of scissors, a baby's rattle, and a rubber band. After all the children had looked at the tray, she asked them to number a paper from one to ten, and then she put a folded cardboard upright on her desk behind which she made the noise of the object; she whirled the eggbeater, snapped the rubber band, tore the paper, sloshed the water, etc. After all ten noises had been made, she removed the cardboard and made the sounds in the same order so that the children could check their papers.

"Here is a book in the sound box," she said next. "Now I am going to read you the story to see how well you listen for fun—only you will have to listen and watch at the same time because you are going to help me read this story." She then read *Gerald McBoing Boing*, and every time a noise was mentioned, the teacher stopped reading, placed a card on the chalkboard, and the children filled in the noise. After the story was over and they had discussed it, the teacher said, "Well, let's see what else we have in the box. I have a game to play which will show how well you can listen. Each one of you may draw one of these cards from the pack. Look at it, but do not allow anyone else to see it." The teacher had a pack of cards with pictures pasted on one side. All the pictures were of noise-making objects. Each child then came to the front of the room and made the sound of the object pictured on his card while the rest of the class guessed what the picture was.

"There are two more things in the sound box," said the teacher, and she took out a recording and some drawing paper. "Oh, it is a record. I am going to play it, and while I do, you draw or write about something that the music means to you."

In about ten minutes the children shared their creative products. Some had written poems, some had drawn pictures, and some had written stories.

To summarize the afternoon's activities, the teacher said, "Well, the sound box is empty. How well do you think we listened today?" The children agreed they had listened well.

"Well, I agree—you did listen well and we did have a good time. Did we have to listen the *same*, that is, did we listen as *hard* or in the same manner to all the things we did? How would you say we listened to the different experiences we had?"

A lively discussion followed from which came the following chart:

Kinds of Listening

We listen hard—	*We listen easy—*	*We listen for fun—*
to hear small sounds.	to stories.	to games.
	to records.	to draw or write.
to put sounds and objects together.	for enjoyment.	to two things at one time.
to find one sound among many.		
to fit words in correct places.		
for special ideas.		
to directions.		

In this lesson the teacher applied the principles of creative listening, and although the children had not, at the third grade level, used the different labels of appreciative, attentive, analytical, and marginal levels, their summary chart shows a consciousness of these four levels of listening.

The illustrations of creative teaching which constitute the remainder of this chapter were selected because they meet the criteria outlined above. Many fine examples of the teaching of listening have been omitted due to lack of space. The author has concentrated on those instances in which *either* the teacher *or* the pupils applied the above criteria to obtain a creative product.

The Nature of Listening

There are basically four types of listening:

1. Attentive listening.
2. Appreciative listening.

3. Analytical listening.
4. Marginal listening.

Skills must be developed for each of these types of listening.

Berry[6] suggests six ways we can improve the listening of children: (1) by sensing relationships of listening to other phases of communication; (2) by understanding the psychological process of listening; (3) by providing general conditions conducive to listening; (4) by utilizing opportunities for children to listen; (5) by understanding the developmental levels of listening, and (6) by keeping alert to new inventions and equipment that will aid the program.

Attentive Listening

This is the type of listening in which most distractions are eliminated and the attention of the listener is focused on one person or one form of communication, such as a radio broadcast, a play, a television show, a recording, a lecture, or a telephone conversation. Attentive listening is used in many "natural" ways in the classroom:

1. Gaining attention of children to take roll, prepare for a lesson, etc.
2. In giving directions for assignments.
3. For daily planning and organizing of the class into groups.
4. For audience-type situation reading.
5. In making announcements and reports.
6. For dramatic presentations and puppet shows.
7. For lectures or presentations by the teachers.
8. For announcements and programs over the school's sound system.
9. For giving directions on the playground and in the gymnasium.
10. For taking examinations.
11. For taking notes.
12. In searching for answers to questions in reading assignments.
13. For listening to tape recorders.
14. For teaching rote poems and songs.
15. For teaching music and for playing instruments.
16. For ordinary conversation.
17. The Show-and-Tell period.

Attentive listening may or may not involve two-way conversation. In some cases it is a one-way communication process.

6. A. Berry, "Listening Activities in the Elementary School," *Elementary English Review*, XXIII, (February 1946), pp. 69–79.

Contrived Ways to Get Attention: Formal teaching cannot take place until there is order in the room and children are listening attentively. In any large group, however, children have much to say to each other and they shut out sounds that do not pertain to their immediate interests. Teachers can use several devices to bring children back to order so that it is accomplished quickly and pleasantly.

Create one or more signals at the very beginning of the school year which tell the children they should stop what they are doing to listen at once. These signals may involve lights, music, holding hands up high, or other devices.

Develop a variety of phrases that help the children to direct their attention to you immediately. Use different ones so the children do not "tune you out." Here are a few that teachers have found successful:

- "May I have your attention, please?"
- "Here is something you will all want to hear."
- "Let's zip our mouths and open our eyes." (Do this with movement.)
- "I am ready to talk. Are you ready to listen?"

The primary teacher can take roll (or dismiss children) by saying, "Will all the children wearing blue stand up," or "All the children who have red on may get their wraps."

The above are commonplace attention getters. Some more creative ones follow. These tend to get attention immediately if not overdone, and they follow the principles of creative teaching mentioned previously.

The teacher may make such statements as these:

- "Let's all listen and tell if we can hear the grass grow."
- "Let's listen to the snow fall (the clock tick, the rain fall, the wind blow, etc.)."
- "I'd like to see the color of everyone's eyes."
- "I'd like to see how wide everyone can smile."

Games are always enjoyed by children. Here is an attention-getting listening game. The teacher touches a child and says, "Shh," by putting her finger to her mouth. That child, in turn, touches another and does the same thing. Every child who has been touched may touch others so everyone is quiet as quickly as possible. The object of the game is to catch on quickly and be quiet, and *not* to be the last one talking. The last one talking pays a penalty; he has to do some little job such as putting the books away.

Make an irrelevant statement and begin a discussion with the children around you—or write the statement on the board. Soon all will come to see what is going on. Some statements to use:

"I wonder how long it takes to go by rocket to Mercury."
"I wonder what Christopher Columbus really looked like."
"I wonder who invented cheese."
"I wonder what it would be like with no sunshine."

Lower your voice almost to a whisper and say something humorous or tell a funny story. When the children around you laugh, the rest will come to see what they are laughing about.

Use words of praise as much as you can. Children always respond to praise. "My, what a bright happy group of faces I am looking at today" generally creates bright happy faces.

Instead of speaking all the time, turn and write or print simple directions on the board.

Sing commands or directions for a change. This is especially effective in the lower grades.

Also effective in the lower grades is singing the child's name for taking roll. The child sings back his name to the same tune or to a tune that completes the tune. For example, the teacher sings to the tune of "Frère Jacques":

"Are you here,
Are you here,
Mary Brown?"

And Mary sings:

"Yes, I am."

Different tunes can be sung to each child. Tape this. Sometimes results are delightfully creative.

Creative Teaching of Attentive Listening

Attention getters serve the purpose of getting children ready for any lesson, but they should not be confused with actual lessons planned to develop attentive listening skills. Suggestions for the creative teaching of attentive listening follow.

1. *Read stories* that draw attention to the value of listening to sounds, words, letters, or sentences. Examples: "Stories in *The Listening Book* by Dan Safier; *Ounce, Dice, Trice* by Alastair Reid; *The Listening Walk* by Paul Showers; *Word Bending with Aunt Sarah* by Al Westcott.

2. *Use of puppets.* In the primary grades, the children may have a friend who comes to talk to them once a day. In one room it was Jo-Jo, the puppet. The teacher had made a laundry bag from some colorful material. The laundry bag had a slit in the back through which she put

her hand. Inside the bag lived Jo-Jo. Every once in a while Jo-Jo came out. He was shy so he only whispered to the teacher, and she had to relate to the boys and girls what he said.

Jo-Jo always had a surprise in his bag. Some days it was a letter or an invitation from another class. Some days he had a new book or a new game or a new story. One day he had a packet of seeds to plant. On another day he had a note from the principal telling of the Halloween party plans. All the teacher had to do was to stand by Jo-Jo's bag and there was immediate silence.

3. Choose ten "sound" makers. Fold a piece of cardboard to make a screen on a table concealing the ten items. Suggest to the children that they number a paper from one to ten. Call a number and make the sound. Let the children write down what they think it is. Younger children may raise their hands when they know instead of writing it down.

After this game has been played a few times, the teacher may ask the children to work by two's and think up sounds they can use on the rest of the class. When a group is ready, a few minutes may be used each day to develop listening skills.

4. Another variation of this game is to have the children categorize sounds under such topics as "Sounds Heard on the Playground" (the thud of a ball being thrown into a mitt, the sound of a medicine ball bouncing, the smacking of a ball and bat, the thud of the football on the ground, etc.). Other categories might be "gym noises," "cafeteria noises," "hall noises," "classroom noises," "party noises," etc.

5. Teachers may carry this idea further by taking home a tape recorder over the weekend and making a recording of kitchen noises, living-room noises, outdoor noises, etc. Many variations can be taped and used in many ways with the children.

6. Children, too, can tape noises and bring them to school.

7. Children can make up stories, but instead of telling them with words, they can tell them with sounds. Adding pantomime is fun, too!

8. Begin the period by playing records or playing a variety of musical sketches on the piano. Have children listen for music that is alike or different. Use some of these ideas for comparisons.

a. Alike in rhythms.
b. Alike in tone.
c. Fast—slow.
d. High notes—low notes.
e. Folk music—classical.

9. Read stories to the children in which the plot is constructed around a breakdown in communication due to faulty listening. Discussions of these stories help bring out the need for careful listening. Examples are:

a. "The Hot Weather Mix-Up" (*Jack and Jill*, July, 1957).
b. "The Story of Slow Joe" (Safier, *The Listening Book*).
c. "The Tar Baby" by Joel Chandler Harris.

10. *Group discussion* provides rich opportunities to develop listening skills. A variation of the group discussion is the panel discussion. Some good samples of good group discussion are described in *The Teaching of Speaking and Listening in the Elementary School* by W. Pronovost.[7]

11. A good "audience-type" situation can be provided for listening by inviting a consultant to speak to the children and preparing them for specific things to listen to. Some people to ask might include: a parent who has an unusual occupation or hobby, the librarian, the school physician, a forest ranger, a town person who has just returned from a trip, the school nurse, the principal, the custodian, a state trooper, a fireman, a policeman, a visitor from a foreign country, etc.

12. Children spend large blocks of time listening to television. This listening can be put to good use by assigning children homework such as the following:

a. Watch "Saturday Morning Movietime" to see if they tell the story as it is written in this book I am about to read to you.
b. Listen and watch the President's Press Conference and jot down the points he makes which tell how he feels about the education bills now in Congress.
c. The television awards will be given tonight. Here is a sheet which tells in what categories the awards will be made. See how many of the blanks on this sheet you can fill in.
d. It is difficult to produce mob scenes on TV due to the small screen area. See how "Treasure Island" is produced tonight to give the illusion of a mob during the mutiny.

A television guide can be of invaluable use to teachers in planning structured listening experiences for their children. Programs such as "Sesame Street" provide many excellent opportunities for primary listening experiences. A guide to the Sesame Street programs may be purchased at a nominal fee.

13. To sharpen children's sensitivity to listening, it is sometimes fun to make a list such as the following:

What Interfered with Our Listening Today?

a. The lawnmower outside.
b. People interrupted.

7. Wilbert Pronovost, *The Teaching of Speaking and Listening in the Elementary School* (New York: Longmans, Green, 1959), pp. 74–110.

c. An airplane flew over.
d. The fire bell rang for fire drill.
e. We were worried about getting our work done on time.

14. Listening signs placed around the room can help to develop listening habits. Examples:

a. What did you hear today?
b. The magic word today is *time*. How many times will your teacher say it during planning period?
c. Listen: What is the new sound in our room?

15. Certain machines help promote the teaching of listening. Through the use of the tape recorder, the teacher may dictate special assignments on tapes and one group may listen in, even though many other activities are going on in the classroom.

16. Children can reproduce sound effects from the stories in their basic readers while other children guess the stories.

17. *Obvious endings:* The teacher makes up poems or stories with obvious words missing and accepts any logical rhyming words such as:

> Once there was a little mouse
> He lived in a little ______
> Every day he said, "Oh please,
> May I have a piece of ______?"
> "Cheese," his mother then would cry.
> "You will get some bye and ______.
> Right now with me you'd better scat
> For down the street comes Tommy ______."

Encourage the children to create some for each other.

18. Have the children clap for various reasons when they are being read to. For instance:

a. Clap at every word that rhymes with *hat*. (Use Dr. Suess' books, "The Cat in the Hat" and "The Cat in the Hat Comes Back.")
b. Clap for every word that is a noun.
c. Clap for every word that describes something.
d. Clap for every word that begins with a certain sound.

19. Have children play at television broadcasting. A good audience-type listening situation may be created by cutting a hole in a large box, painting the box like a television set, and having one child appear in the opening as Uncle Don or the Space Boy to tell stories or reread the textbook story to his audience.

20. Several games to teach listening are listed on pages 169–172 of

Beginning Language Arts Instruction with Children by Shane, Reddin, and Gillespie.[8]

21. *Creating sound:* In the early grades children enjoy the opportunity to translate real sounds into word sounds. Allow the children to listen to sounds and then substitute a word sound to take its place. For example:

a. For pounding clay a child said, "Bim, bam."
b. For pounding with a hammer a child said, "Bang, bang."
c. For a ringing bell, a child said, "Bong, bong."
d. For a pound-a-peg board, one child said, "Boom, boom, boom."
e. Squeezing clay, one child said, "Squashy, squashy."

22. *Some Good Games to Develop Attentive Listening:*

a. *Whisper:* Teacher (or a child) whispers ten sentences, words, or sayings; each is in a softer voice and children try to see how many they can hear.
b. *Gossip 1:* One child starts a sentence down his aisle or around his table by whispering a sentence *once* to the child next to him, who, in turn, passes it on until the sentence reaches the last child. This child tells what he thinks he heard. The first child tells what he said, and children can compare to see how well they whisper and listen. Variations in the upper grades may be that children use sayings, proverbs, book titles, etc.
c. *Fruit Basket Turn Over:* Give each child the name of a fruit. One child becomes "It." He calls the names of two or more fruits. The fruits called exchange seats. "It" tries to get into one of the vacated seats. The person remaining without a seat is "It." Every once in a while "It" shouts "Fruit Basket" at which time everyone exchanges seats.

   Variations of this game may be played on many occasions, such as the beginning of the year when everyone is learning the names of classmates. They may call names directly, and call "Register" instead of "Fruit Basket." On Halloween, each child may be assigned a Halloween name (witch, cat, ghost, spook, pumpkin, broomstick, etc.) and exchange seats. "Witch's Ride" may be the signal for all to exchange seats.
d. *Keep Talking:* This is an excellent game for older children. It originates from a popular television show of a few seasons past. Some children are each given a phrase. At the signal from the teacher, Child 1 begins a story. He tries to include his phrase in his story without

8. Harold Shane, Mary E. Reddin, and Margaret G. Gillespie, *Beginning Language Arts Instruction With Children* (Columbus, Ohio: Charles E. Merrill, 1961), pp. 169–172.

giving it away to the rest of the group. The teacher taps a bell every thirty seconds and the next child must keep talking, picking up where the first child left off, and trying to include *his* phrase in the story, and so on until all the group has had a chance, whereupon they start at the beginning again. If, at any one time, one child guesses another child's phrase, the child who loses his phrase loses his chance.

e. Sometimes the holidays lend themselves very well to the teaching of special listening skills. Not only are there directions to follow in making decorations and gifts, but also stories and poems and special music to hear, assemblies, films, filmstrips, and tape recordings to listen to, and games to play.

Many good holiday games can be designed to teach listening skills. One good technique used by Miss Watts to develop attentive listening was for the distribution of gifts at Christmas time. Each child brought a wrapped quarter gift. Miss Watts read *The Night Before Christmas* and every child held a gift, but passed it on every time the word "and" was read. At the end of the reading of the poem, the child opened the gift he held in his hand.

f. *Airplanes Fly:* Games similar to "Simon Says" and "Airplanes Fly" call for attentive listening. Children stand by their seats. The leader, standing before the room, says "Airplanes fly" and the children raise their arms and flap them. When the name of something that does not fly is called, such as "Chairs fly," the arms are not flapped. After two misses, the children drop out by sitting.

g. *Barnyard Frolic:* Assemble two sets of word cards with the name of one animal commonly found on a farm on each, e.g., dog, duck, goat, cat, and chick. Print the word "barnyard" on one of the cards. The leader keeps a complete set of cards for himself and then distributes one card to each player. When the leader holds up a card with the word "dog" on it, the child who holds the matching card must "Bow-wow" like a dog and so on. When the leader holds up the card with "barnyard" on it, each child responds with the sound made by the animal on his card.

23. *Mouthing—Lip Reading:* Teacher (or a child) mouths a sentence, using exaggerated lip movements, but makes no sounds. Children try to guess the sentence.

24. Encourage the children to tell or read aloud their own stories to the rest of the class. Children always enjoy listening to each other's stories.

25. Some worthwhile oral reading activities (by pupils) requiring group listening include:

a. Rereading to answer a question.
b. Rereading to prove a point.
c. Rereading of descriptive passages.
d. Rereading of humorous passages.
e. Preparation for dramatization.
f. News reading (children's news publications, regular newspapers, magazines).
g. Stories, poems, magazine articles.
h. Informational sources—encyclopedias, etc.
i. Personal creative products—poems, stories, rhymes, riddles.
j. Prepared oral reports.

26. Young children enjoy the rollicking sounds of Mother Goose rhymes. They can be encouraged to say these rhymes and add rhyming sounds to their own, such as "Hickory, dickory, stockory, mockory" and "Muffet, tuffet, puffet, stuffet," etc. If the teacher records these invented sound words as she hears the children saying them, they can later be read to the class who will add more sounds.

27. Give the class three titles and ask them which one best fits the story or poem to be read to them.

28. Begin a rhyme and let the children make up a new ending. (See the Bim Bam Boo, pp. 21–30.)

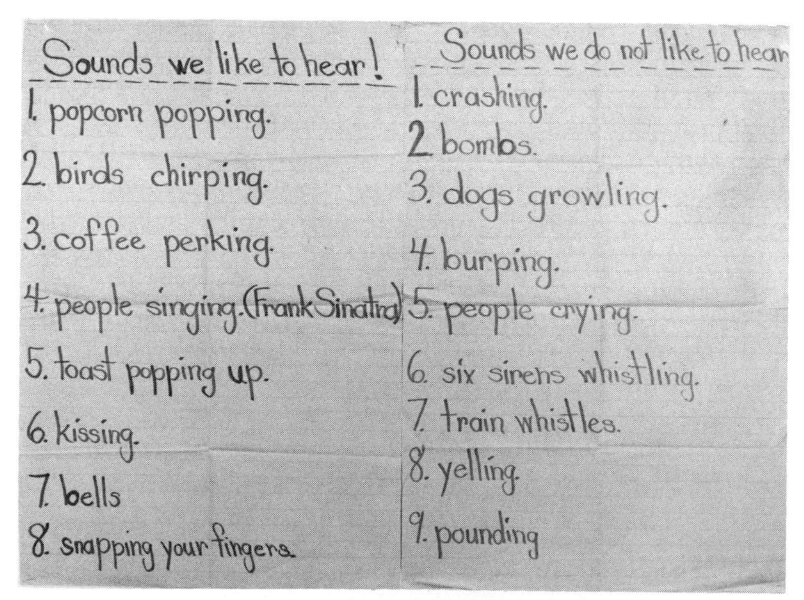

Figure 22 *Sound charts made in a first grade to develop listening skills: an excellent way to introduce vocabulary in a meaningful way.*

Appreciative Listening

Appreciative listening is the type used when one listens for enjoyment. Appreciative listening is not as concentrated as attentive listening. It is more relaxed, and the listener is in a less tense state. Appreciative listening was demonstrated above when the children listed to "Gerald McBoing Boing." They react to this type of listening in pleasant or emotional ways. Suggestions for the use of appreciative listening in the classroom follow:

1. Listening to musical or art recordings.
2. Listening to radio and television programs for enjoyment.
3. Listening to a play or puppet show, and other types of dramatizations.
4. Listening to a concert.
5. Listening to stories or poetry being read.
6. Choral speaking.

Creative Contrived Situations That Develop Appreciative Listening

1. *Reading stories and poems:* Some stories lend themselves to *listening* exercises. Noises are repeated which children can reproduce. Every time the teacher comes to a certain word, the children are told to make the sound that goes with it. For example, the word *dog* evokes a "grr," the word *telephone* evokes a "ding-a-ling." Some very good stories for this and other kinds of listening activity are: "Gerald McBoing Boing," Anonymous; Walter de la Mare's poem "Someone"; "I know An Old Lady Who Swallowed a Fly" by Burl Ives; "On a Steamer" by Dorothy Baruch; "Growl Bear" by Margot Austin; "Wait Till the Moon Is Full" by Margaret Wise Brown; "Ten Little Fingers: A Book of Finger Plays" by Priscilla Pointer; "Time of Wonder" by Robert McCloskey.

2. Play some beautiful records and have the children paint, draw, or fingerpaint while the music is playing. Suggestions: "Nutcracker Suite" by Tchaikowsky; "Slavonic Dances" by Dvorak; "Peer Gynt Suite" by Grieg; "William Tell Overture" by Rossini; "Sleeping Beauty" by Tchaikovsky; "A Summer Place"; "Tara's Theme"; "Rhapsody in Blue" by Gershwin; and "Blue Star." A variation is to play the music, listen carefully, and then have the children draw, paint, or write what it means to them.

3. *Choral speaking.* Choral speaking provides endless opportunities for careful listening so that children may work out patterns of their

own. Much of choral speaking should be with the children's own creative work and with familiar selections. (See chapter on Oral Expression.)

4. Use a round-robin listening drill: one child says a word, the second child repeats it and adds another, a third child repeats both and adds a word and so on until a story results.

5. Listen to recordings and dramatize the ideas suggested by the music—or the stories.

6. Often a poem such as "The Sugar Plum Tree" by Eugene Field can be read. Then the teacher asks the children to draw a picture showing everything they can remember about the poem.

Poems that are adaptable to this sort of activity are: "Wynken, Blynken and Nod" by Eugene Field; "My Shadow" by Robert Louis Stevenson; "Song for a Little House" by Christopher Morley; and others.

7. Finger plays are excellent devices to foster good listening habits, especially when the children write their own.

8. *Game:* The Tiger Hunt: Almost every teacher knows the story of the tiger hunt where children use their hands to dramatize the story as the teacher tells it. Try other stories that include the children's experiences, working out the accompanying sounds. Samples: The Haunted House, The Playground Accident, The Wild Ride for the Doctor, A Day in a Lumber Camp.

9. *Television Commercials:* Ask the children to listen to and reproduce as closely as possible their favorite television commercials or the opening phrases of their favorite television shows, and then to change them to suit themselves.

10. Listen in order to learn to do folk dances or ballroom dances to popular music.

11. Listen to interpret the music with simple rhythm instruments.

12. Courtesies in listening should be taught—but courtesy is practiced also through listening. Have the children dramatize social courtesies such as introducing a man to a woman, introducing a child to an adult, conducting a club meeting, answering the telephone properly, asking a girl to dance, etc.

13. A Picture Book of Sounds may be made with several ideas being used in it. One page might be devoted to sounds at home, with pictures for the lower grades or words for the upper grades. Children might also use this in connection with reading, by finding pictures or using words beginning with various sounds, blends, etc.

14. One of the most creative results from training in listening skills can result when children become so sensitive to the sounds in their environment that they write poems and stories about them. A sixth grader wrote the following poem about sounds:

Sounds

Tolling bells, honking cars,
Zooming rockets going to Mars,
People talking, leaves a rustling,
Silverware clattering, ladies bustling.
The tick-tick-ticking of a clock,
The different sounds the bluejays mock,
Children's chatter, grownups talk,
Sparrows singing while you take a walk.
Symphonies playing the classic ballet,
Jazz and other sounds so gay,
Sounds are happy, sounds are grey,
All sounds help to make a day.

—Renée Chapel

Analytical Listening

Analytical listening is attentive listening plus, because the listener is expected to respond in one way or another. This means that one thinks carefully about what he hears. Instances in which analytical listening are used naturally in the classroom are as follows:

1. Listening to solve arithmetic problems.
2. Reading-discussion assignments where children are:
   a. Reading and discussing to find specific points.
   b. Reading and discussing to outline.
   c. Reading and discussing to select main ideas.
   d. Reading and discussing to determine the true meaning of a word as it is used in a new context.
3. Discussing social problems, i.e., seeking a solution to a playground fight or solving problems through a school senate.
4. Any discussion involving a decision, such as, "What day shall we go on our trip?" or "Which textbook is correct?" when the texts do not agree on certain facts.
5. Analyzing a selection of poetry, literature, or music.
6. Analyzing a speech, television program, tape recording, or radio presentation.
7. Discussions on what should fill restricted space in a school newspaper, etc.
8. Listening in an oral reading situation to:
   a. Find a sequence of events.

b. Find supporting details.
c. Find emotional persuasion.
d. Draw comparisons.
e. Make judgements.
f. Find relationships.
g. Make inferences.
h. Follow directions and instructions.

Creative Contrived Experiences Which Promote Good Analytical Listening

1. *Analysis records.* Both children and teachers can do this. How aware are we of the sounds in the world around us? Each can keep a diary over a given period of time wherein each lists all the sounds he can remember having experienced during the day, from the ringing of the alarm clock early in the morning to the playing of the "Star Spangled Banner" on television late at night.

2. Science experiments and demonstrations provide excellent situations for developing analytical listening.

3. Children may number a half-sheet of paper as for spelling words. Teacher asks, "Where do you hear the "t" sound?" The teacher then pronounces words such as report, tinkle, tank, part, etc. When the child hears the sound he is listening for, he marks it on the left side of the paper if it is found in the first part of the word, on the right side of the paper if it is found in the last part of the word. He then adds all the words he can think of to fill in both sides of his page.

4. Using a flannel board, build listening skills for details, for main ideas, etc. For instance, the teacher places a cutout of a girl in a blue dress holding a doll, and a girl holding a doll in a blue dress. The teacher says, "The girl in the blue dress is holding the doll," or "The girl is holding the doll in the blue dress." She asks which picture goes with the sentence just read. Children take over by compiling imaginative combinations of words.

5. Quiz games provoke good listening.

6. Use motion picture films with creative listening assignments. For example:

a. How does the musical score help to tell the story?
b. Look and listen for these three important facts. (List them.)
c. How does the opening line of the film set the theme for the rest of the film?
d. Toward the end of the film there is a line which tells the main theme

of the whole film. Can you find it? It comes during the prison scene. What other ways might this theme be developed?

7. *Scramble.* Oral sentences are scrambled and children arrange them in correct order. They make up scrambled sentences for each other.

8. Read a short paragraph containing several words that have the same or similar meanings. Children are to pick out the words that mean the same. Older children may write them down.

Example: Soon the *little* man came to a *small* dining room. He peered through the *tiny* door and saw a lovely, *petite* room all set up with *miniature* furniture. There were even *minute* dishes on the dining room table.

Encourage children to write paragraphs of this nature for each other.

9. Ask children to listen on the way to school to special sounds, which they reproduce (when possible) in the classroom where lists are constructed. Categorize them on charts into such headings as building noises, play noises, beautiful noises, funny sounds, etc.

10. Have the children close their eyes and see how many sounds they may hear in a two-minute period. Make a list.

11. A good way to begin a unit with sounds is to say something like this: "Everyone put his head on his desk and close his eyes. I am going to open the window for two minutes. Listen to hear all the sounds that were not here when Columbus discovered America." The class tries to see how long a list it can get. *Variations:* "Since the Wright brothers flew their first airplane," "Since the covered wagons went West," etc.

12. Read poems to the children which require responses. Examples:

a. "The Children's Calendar" (*The Listening Book*, pp. 87–98).
b. "The Humming Song" (*The Listening Book*, pp. 99–102).
c. "Soon, Soon, Soon" (*The Listening Book*, p. 155).

13. Have a toy telephone in the room. Encourage a child to talk into the telephone as though she were calling her mother, her father, or a friend. The children try to guess what the person on the other end of the line is saying by listening to the one-sided conversation.

Middle grade students are especially clever at this. One sixth grade boy used only the word, "Yes," but he said it in fifteen different ways. The children had to listen carefully to that conversation. The next day one of the girls carried on a similar conversation using the word "Oh" with twelve expressions.

14. Have the children tell stories or read into a tape recorder and listen to their own presentation in the play-back.

15. Use the records, *Sounds Around Us* by Scott-Foresman and Company for Developing Listening Skills, and *Listening Activities* by RCA Victor Record Library for Elementary Schools (Volumes I–II).

Records suitable for this use in the primary grades are: *Come to the Fair*, Young Peoples Records; *Muffin in the City*, YPR; *A Walk in the Forest*, YPR; *Let's Play* (Children's Musical Action Stories by Kay Ortman. Set I—Farm Lands, Set II—Adventures in the Forest), Kay Ortman's Productions; *Sounds We Hear* (Illa Polendorf), Grosset & Dunlap; and others.

For the intermediate grades: *The Shearing Piano* (George Shearing), Capitol; *Peter and the Wolf*, Columbia Long Playing; *Hansel and Gretel* (Basil Rathbone), Columbia; *Caught in the Act*, (Victor Borge), Columbia; *Rusty in Orchestraville*, Capitol; *Big News Series*, Columbia; *Alice in Wonderland* (Jane Powell), Columbia.

Marginal Listening

Marginal listening is that kind of listening in which there are two or more distractions present. Children listen to the radio while doing their homework, apparently with no ill effects. An example of marginal listening was when the children wrote and drew in the lesson above while the record was playing. Instances where marginal listening might be used naturally in the classroom are as follows:

1. Teacher provides music for the children as a background for creative writing.
2. Teacher plays music for rhythms.
3. Children paint to music.
4. Teacher counts while children learn a folk dance or popular dance.
5. Children are planning together and writing plans on a chart or the blackboard.

Creative Contrived Experiences to Develop Effective Marginal Listening

1. Use a series of pictures that describe an event or a process such as frosting a cake, making a valentine, carving a jack-o'-lantern, etc. Tell about the picture, but omit one of the steps and have the children find the step omitted.

In the upper grades, the same procedure can be followed using words without the pictures.

2. Riddles are fun. Children can create their own.

3. A visit to a museum or an exhibit requires careful listening in the planning as well as in taking the trip, and also in the follow-up discussion.

4. Take the children on a field trip around the school to listen to all the sounds around them.

5. Run a short cartoon film, then shut off the sound and have the children tell the story or reproduce the speaking parts while the film is rerun.

6. "Musical Chairs" is a good marginal listening game.

7. Dramatize action poems that require careful listening. Examples: "The Horsemen" by Walter de la Mare; "A Stick for a Horse" by Sybil Fountain; "Mrs. Hen" by M. A. Campbell; "The Elf and the Dormouse" by Oliver Herford; and others.

For intermediate grades: "Casey at the Bat" by Ernest Lawrence Thayer; "Stopping by Woods on a Snowy Evening" by Robert Frost; "The Duel" by Eugene Field; "The Pied Piper of Hamelin" by Robert Browning; and others.

8. Listen to records which can be dramatized or interpreted that require special listening skills such as *Peter and the Wolf*, Serge Prokofiev; *I Went for a Walk in the Forest*, Young Peoples Records; and *Children's Corner Suite*, Debussy.

Listening Disabilities

Normal children love to listen—witness the hours spent in front of the television set, or listening to a good story-teller. When normal children do not listen, something is wrong; either the teaching lacks motivation, the child is ill or fatigued, or he is abnormal in some respects.

There are some children who are not normal in the real sense. These children may have physical, intellectual, or psychological problems. A teacher needs to ascertain whether or not children have listening problems other than normal ones at the outset of the school year.

Most common of all reasons for poor listening is *physical discomfort*. This chapter points out the need for proper conditions for listening, and physical conditions top the list. A room may be too warm, too humid, or too chilly. It may be too noisy. The speaker may not be projecting or may not speak in a pleasant voice. The acoustics of the room may be poor. Before good listening can take place, these factors must be adjusted.

Physical discomfort may also come from within the child. He may be unable to hear sounds or unable to distinguish between sounds of different frequencies. He may be unable to recognize similarities and differences in sounds of words and word elements. He may have poor eye-ear or ear-hand coordination. He may have specific disabilities such as partial deafness, partial blocking of the eustachian tube, a middle ear infection, enlarged tonsils or adenoid difficulty, excessive nervousness, poor auditory memory, or inability to adjust home sounds (such as foreign accent, sectional speech, mispronunciations, etc.) to school speech.

All children should be given tone audiometer tests to detect such abnormalities as soon as possible. The school nurse should be consulted and an attempt made to help with the child's diet or to refer him for special help with any problem he may have. He may need to be placed nearer the teacher than other children, or he may need a hearing aid. Some of the special exercises in this chapter will help him in learning to coordinate his school and home speech.

Mental discomfort is well up on the list near physical discomfort. A rasping voice, an angry voice, or a nagging voice can make a child create a block to learning. Unfamiliarity with a subject can turn him off. Lack of listening readiness can shut him off too. With some children, other factors enter into a lack of listening readiness: poor hearing, poor general health, lack of purpose, lack of desire to learn, poor muscular coordination, low mentality, poor language mastery, lack of adequate and pertinent listening vocabulary, lack of good speaking and comprehension vocabularies, and a short attention span.

Such children have little to gain by participating in long listening sessions. The teacher will need to increase the child's background experience, give him simple and short oral directions, allow him to work with concrete materials, use materials such as the ones presented in this chapter to help him become interested and involved, give him practice in listening to answer specific questions, and help him to interpret what he hears, reads, and experiences.

Some children show a lack of interest in the classroom activities. While this may be due to the fact that the activities may be uninteresting and do not motivate the child, the teacher will need to be aware of other possible causes. Lack of interest may be the result of meager experiences in listening—or even none at all. A child who has had unhappy out-of-school experiences is generally not eager to listen to the experiences of other children. He may not see a purpose in listening—or the listening material may be below the child's interest level and present no challenge to him. On the other hand, the material may be too mature for him.

In such instances, the teacher must try to motivate the child and give him a purpose for listening. The material used must be related to the child's personal experiences and concerns. He should be encouraged to talk (and listen) about experiences of interest to him and should be drawn into listening activities. Many of the creative listening activities in this chapter will appeal to a child like this.

Some children do not listen well because they have little or no purpose—they have not been taught to listen for pleasure as against listening for information or appreciation.

Personality traits can interfere with a child's effectiveness in listening, especially the middle school and older child. Characteristics such as prejudice, egocentricity, narrow-mindedness, antagonism, resentment, boredom, nervousness, and an improper attitude toward school, teacher, subjects, or speaker all have their effect on the child's ability to listen. It takes a teacher with a will of iron to cultivate fairness and objectivity in such a child. Often it can be done with a series of creative, interest-provoking activities.

Emotional maladjustment may have a multitude of causes; almost all the symptoms mentioned above can develop into emotional maladjustment if allowed to persist for too long a period: auditory impairment, conductive deafness, self-consciousness, speech defects, nervous tensions and frustrations, speech disabilities, oversensitiveness, inferiority feelings—all may cause or be the result of specific listening patterns. The causes of emotional maladjustment are not easy to identify. They may be multiple or simple: the child's inability to master his work, lack of parental interest in the child's school life, excessive tension in the school or home, too much confusion in the child's life, poor social background, too much competition, excessive mobility during his school life—who knows.

Some of these children can be motivated and rehabilitated in the classroom when proper situations and conditions are set so that they learn in a relaxed, congenial environment, and when their needs are met effectively. Some will need referral to the school psychologist.

Whatever the defect, it must be remedied to the best of the teacher's ability in order for the child to learn at all; for listening is the base of all learning, and the time spent on teaching effective creative and meaningful listening habits is always worthwhile. When the teacher takes time to teach creatively, she can resolve many of the problems listed above.

Summary

There are basically four kinds of listening: attentive listening, appreciative listening, analytical listening, and marginal listening. Each type can be developed creatively and with creative results in the elementary school classroom. The creative teaching of listening requires different skills and produces different outcomes from regular listening experiences.

In a democratic society where we must learn to respect each other's viewpoints and contributions, children must be taught the skills and courtesies of listening so that effective communication can take place. We have seen how these skills may be developed in interesting, meaningful, and creative ways when the proper conditions are established. These conditions are affected by the following factors:

1. The child's maturity level.
2. The child's general ability.
3. The child's interest in the topic at hand.
4. The child's previous experience with the material being presented.
5. The type of material being presented.
6. The listening "climate" created by the teacher.
7. The children's rapport with the teacher or the speaker.
8. The quality of the teaching.
9. The attitude and ability of the teacher (or speaker) to relate to the child.
10. The demands made on the child during the listening period.
11. The child's listening readiness.
12. The child's established listening habits.
13. The child's ability to adjust to any abnormal or unpredicted situation.
14. The physical-emotional tone of the room.
15. The child's acquired listening skills.
16. The adjustment of speed of reception with the speed of delivery.
17. The creative set to listen.
18. The child's general health and the social-emotional climate of his home.

To the Reader

1. At the close of any given day, see if you can recall instances when you used *each* type of listening.
2. A great deal of research has been done concerning the effect of mass media on communication. Have some of your classmates or colleagues (whichever the case may be) work with you on preparing a report on this topic.
3. If you are a teacher, keep a record on any given day of the time you use waiting for your students to listen. Examine your record to see

where you might cut down on this time by using more creative approaches to the listening situation. If you are a college student, observe how one of your professors motivates you to listen. Also note at your campus club meetings how much time the president wastes getting the members to listen.

4. Notice particularly the times your students (or friends or classmates) tune you out. Keep a record over a week's time to see if any pattern evolves: For instance, do they listen less at the beginning of the day; are they better listeners during any special period or activity; do they listen best when it is a marginal or analytical situation; do they listen to each other (or to other people) better than to you? Whatever the answer, seek to discover the causes. To what degree do physical conditions enhance the listening situation? Emotional conditions? Social? Intellectual? Can you improve your listening power by changing your approach?
5. For one day keep an informal record of the amount of time you spend listening: Be sure to include conversations, television, concerts, plays, lectures, etc. Average a week's listening time.
6. Some questions for discussion:
   a. Does marginal listening as practiced by teen-agers doing their homework interfere with their grades in school or the effectiveness of their homework? Research has been conducted on this topic.
   b. What part does perception play in analytical listening? What is perception?
   c. Under what type of listening would you classify humor as used in witticisms and funny stories?
   d. Considering the chart on page 45, would it be safe to say that slow-learning children learn best by experiencing and listening?
   e. In what category would you place the type of listening when a Marine sergeant gives orders to his men in a drill team? When a football player receives orders from his coach? When a student receives help from his advisor? When a girl is being loved by her fiance? When a mother listens to her year-old baby?
   f. How would an accepted international language improve communication? Is it the new language we need, or new listening skills in existing languages?
7. One of the most creative innovations in listening and in the development of creativity is the publication of a series of recordings by Bert F. Cunningham and E. Paul Torrance (Ginn and Company) on a variety of subjects. One called *Messages for Millions* is the Alexander Graham Bell story. It tells of a great creative moment in history, and then, on the flip side in a presentation called *Commander of*

Communication, helps the children to understand how one creative idea makes possible the development of another creative idea.

One other record, *Sights and Sounds*, is especially motivational toward producing creative thinking. At this printing there are about a dozen of these records available. Each is accompanied by a teacher's manual. They are linked in with Social Studies, Language Arts, Creative Arts, and Science.

8. Send for the Sesame Street Magazine. Even if you cannot watch this popular children's program, you will find the magazine loaded with helpful suggestions for creative listening and creative doing. (*Sesame Street Magazine*, The Children's Television Workshop, 1865 Broadway, New York, N.Y. 10023.)

Selected Bibliography

ANDERSON, RHEA, LUCILLE MINSHALL, AND IRIS TRACY COMFORT. "How to Teach Better Listening," *National Education Association Elementary Instructional Service Leaflet*. Washington, D.C.: National Education Association, 1962.

BORTEN, HELEN. *Do You Hear What I Hear?* New York: Abelard-Schuman, 1960.

BROWN, CHARLES T. "Teaching Listening Comprehension," *Journal of Communication*, 3 (November 1953), 127–130.

CANFIELD, ROBERT. "How Useful Are Lessons For Listening?" *The Elementary School Journal* (December 1961), 147–151.

COMMISSION ON THE ENGLISH CURRICULUM OF THE NATIONAL COUNCIL OF TEACHERS OF ENGLISH. *The English Language Arts*, Chapter XIV. New York: Appleton Company, 1952.

———. *Language For Today's Children*, Chapter IV. New York: Appleton Company, 1954.

DENBY, R. U. "NCTE/ERIC Report on Research in Listening and Listening Skills," *Elementary English*, 46, no. 5 (April 1969), 511–517.

DEVINE, THOMAS G. "Reading and Listening: New Research Findings," *Elementary English*, 38 (March 1961), 170–174.

ERNEST, CAROLE H. "Listening Comprehension as a Function of Type of Material and Rate of Presentation," *Speech Monographs*, 35, no. 2 (June 1968).

GREEN, HARRY A., AND WALTER P. PETTY. *Developing Language Skills in the Elementary Schools*, 4th ed. Boston: Allyn and Bacon, 1971, 152–184.

HALL, EDWARD. "Listening Behavior: Some Cultural Differences," *Phi Delta Kappan*, 50, no. 7 (March 1969).

KELLER, PAUL W. "Major Findings in Listening in the Past Ten Years," *Journal of Communication*, 10 (March 1960), 29–38.

LUNDSTEEN, SARA W. "Language Arts in the Elementary School," in *Teaching for Creative Endeavor*, W. B. Michael (ed.). Bloomington, Indiana: Indiana University Press, 1968.

MACCAMPBELL, JAMES C. (ed.). *Reading in the Language Arts in the Elementary School*. Boston: D. C. Heath Co., 1964, 132–140 and 141–147.

MONAGHAN, R. R., AND J. G. MARTIN. "Symbolic Interaction: Analysis of Listening," *Journal of Communication*, 18 (June 1968), 127–130.

PETTY, WALTER T. "Listening: Directions for Research," *Elementary English*, 39 (October 1962), 574–577.

PRONOVOST, WILBERT. *The Teaching of Speaking and Listening in the Elementary School*. New York: Longmans, Green, 1959, 338.

REDDIN, ESTOY. "Characteristics of Good Listeners and Poor Listeners," *The Journal of the Reading Specialist*, 7 (March 1968), 109–113.

ROSS, RAMON. "A Look at Listeners," *Elementary School Journal*, 46 (April 1964), 369–372.

RUSSELL, DAVID, AND ELIZABETH RUSSELL. *Listening Aids Through the Grades*. New York: Teachers College, Columbia University, 1959.

SAFIER, DAN. *The Listening Book*. Caldwell, Ohio: Caxton, 1954.

SHANE, HAROLD G., MARY E. REDDIN, AND MARGARET C. GILLESPIE. *Beginning Language Arts Instruction With Children*, Chapters VIII and XII. Columbus, Ohio: Charles E. Merrill, 1961.

SMITH, JAMES A. *Creative Teaching of the Language Arts in the Elementary School*, Chapter IV. Boston: Allyn and Bacon, 1969.

TAYLOR, SANFORD. *What Research Says To The Teacher: Teaching Listening*. Washington, D.C.: National Education Association, 1964.

TIEDT, SIDNEY W., AND IRIS M. TIEDT. *The Elementary Teachers Complete Ideas Handbook*, Chapter IV. Englewood Cliffs, New Jersey: Prentice-Hall, 1965.

WAGNER, GUY et al. *Listening Games*. Darien, Conn.: Teachers Publishing Corp., 1962.

WILT, MARION. "Children's Experiences in Listening," Chapter VII in *Children and the Language Arts* by Virgil Herrick and Leland Jacobs. Englewood Cliffs, New Jersey: Prentice-Hall, Inc., 1959.

———. "A Study of Teacher Awareness of Listening as a Factor in Elementary Education," *Journal of Educational Research*, 43 (April 1950), 626–636.

6 6 6

Adventures in Oral Expression

Sally Flack and the Rabbit

Miss Jennings made a large flannel board which had a hinge in the middle so it could bend. Today she stood it on its side; it was to serve as a simple puppet screen or stage.

She purchased a colorful, cheap book of animals in the five-and-ten-cent store, and cut out the animals and stapled each to the end of a dowel. One of the animals was a rabbit.

At the end of another dowel, Miss Jennings had fastened a little doll with a cute, impertinent face, similar to the Eloise doll so popular a few years ago.

She started her lesson with the following comments.

"We have had so much fun reading stories together and telling stories to each other and listening to some people make up stories of their own that I thought you might enjoy trying something today that we have never done before."

A chorus of "yes" came from the group.

"I thought we might have fun trying to tell a story together—and if it works well, perhaps Miss Jennings can put the words in a book so we can learn to read it later.

"Because we haven't tried this before, I thought I might start by introducing you to my friend. Every story should be about some*one* or some*thing* and I thought we might make up our story about my friend. Here she is—and her name is Sally Flack."

Miss Jennings brought out the doll on the stick. The children smiled

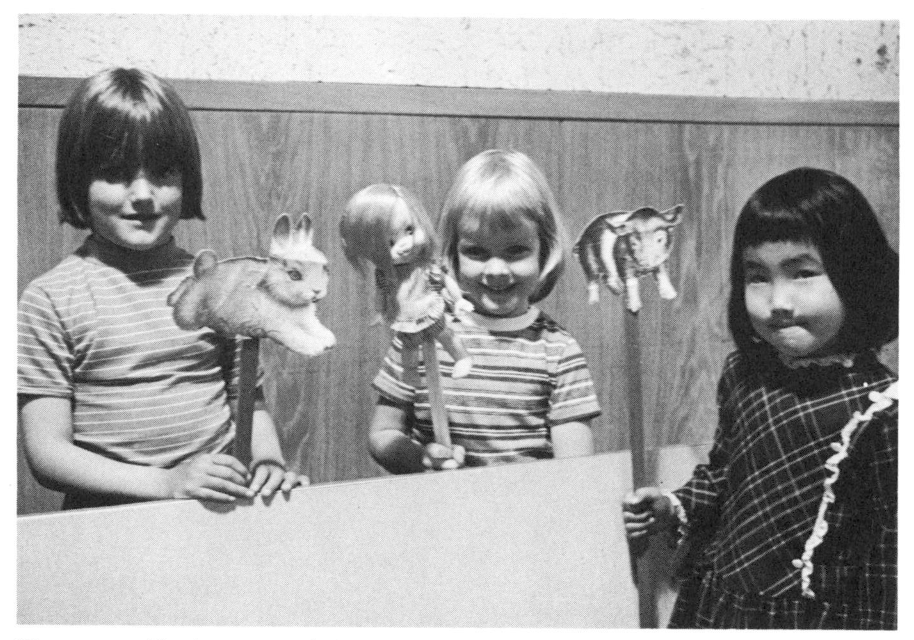

Figure 23 *Kindergarten children create the story of Sally Flack and the Rabbit with stick puppets.*

and commented, "She's cute." "Could I hold her, Miss Jennings?" asked one little girl.

"Yes," said Miss Jennings, "You be Sally Flack's voice," and she gave Marcia the doll on the stick.

"Now I have another character for our story," said Miss Jennings and she pulled the rabbit from her box. "And I must tell you something about him. He does not have a name and he is very sad. He is sad because he was left over from Easter—no one wants him—here it is November. Let's see on our calendar how many months it is since Easter."

They soon figured that it was five months. "And all that time," continued Miss Jennings, "our rabbit has wanted someone to take him home so he will have a nice place to live—but no one has. Something must be the matter. What do you suppose it is?"

"He's bashful," said Eric.

"I know! He's got B.O.," said Jeannie.

"He's mean," added Pete.

"He's dumb!" commented Eddie.

"I bet he hates kids," was Allen's contribution.

"Those are all good ideas," said Miss Jennings, "and I am sure we will want to use one in our story. I'll tell you what we'll do—let's see what else I have in this box and then we'll let Marcia and someone else play out the story so we can see why our rabbit doesn't have a home."

At this point about five more children slid along the floor and joined those at Miss Jennings' feet.

She then held up for display each cardboard animal on its stick, and distributed them to each child with such comments as: "Martha, you be the voice for the lamb," and "Shelly, you be the voice for the horse."

"Could I be the pig?"

"I want to be the baby calf."

The enthusiasm of the group was destroying the situation. Miss Jennings paused and put her fingers to her lips.

"In making a story," she said, "it is very important to listen so you will know what has happened before it is your turn to speak. All right—now all listen to Miss Jennings. Good! First, does everyone have an animal? Let's see if you can make some of the animal sounds. Good! All right—now you will be that animal's voice. As we go along, we will try to get each animal in the story. Peter, I see you have the rabbit. Let's let you and Marcia squat behind the flannel board, put your stick puppets above the board like this, and act out the beginning of the story. Do you want to talk together first?"

"I don't know what to say," Peter said shyly.

"Well, we'll help you," said Miss Jennings.

"What could happen in the first scene of our story?"

"Peter could ask Sally to take him home," volunteered Eddie.

"Sally could say she was looking for a nice rabbit to take home," said Ellie.

"All right, let's see how it goes," said Miss Jennings.

Peter and Marcia took their places behind the flannel board and pushed the cardboard figures above the rim of the board. The rabbit was on the left side. Sally moved in toward the rabbit.

"Oh, dear," said Sally, "I wish I had a pet. And most of all I would like a rabbit."

There was a pause and suddenly Peter's head appeared above the flannel board.

"Hey, Miss Jennings," he said, his eyes wide with discovery, "rabbits don't make any noise!"

Miss Jennings jumped in and seized the golden opportunity offered by such a teachable moment.

"Peter is right—and I think he has discovered the reason why the rabbit has no home—he can't talk."

"Yeah!" said Peter, his eyes still wide, and his mind fairly clicking.

"Yes," echoed the class, all very pleased with themselves.

Peter's head disappeared below the flannel board. Immediately the cardboard rabbit hopped away from Sally Flack. A highly strained "put-on" falsetto voice came from behind the flannel board.

"Boy—look at that cute little girl. I'd like to go home and live with her—but I can't ask her to take me because I can't talk."

"Oh, what a cute little rabbit," said Sally Flack. "I would like to take him home with me. Mr. Rabbit, would you like to come home and live at my house?"

The rabbit puppet moved, but it did not answer.

"Well," said Sally impatiently, "would you?"

Still no answer.

"What a dumb rabbit," Sally said in a disgusted voice. "I don't think I want such a dumb rabbit," and she disappeared behind the flannel board.

"Oh dear, dear," said the rabbit, "she doesn't know I can't talk so I can't answer her. What will I do? What will I do?"

Suddenly the stick puppet leaped up and down. "I know what I'll do—I'll learn to talk," said the rabbit and he disappeared from view.

"Wasn't that good?" asked Miss Jennings. By now all the children were seated on the floor before the flannel board. "I think Peter has made it possible for all the rest of us to get into the story. Let's have the rabbit go in search of someone to teach him to talk. He could ask each of the animals to help. Is that a good idea?"

"Yes," they answered enthusiastically—and all wanted to be next. Miss Jennings said, "To save time and to not break up the story, Miss Jennings or Peter will choose who will go next. So, let's let Mr. Rabbit meet Mr. Lamb."

Martha went and squatted behind the flannel board. A dialogue followed between Mr. Rabbit and Mr. Lamb.

Peter's head appeared again above the flannel board. "Now I'd like Sally to talk to," he said.

Marcia returned to her place behind the flannel board. There was a whispered conversation. Soon the puppets of Sally and Mr. Rabbit appeared on top of the flannel board. The rabbit hopped toward Sally. Another dialogue followed in which Miss Horse also participated.

And so the story continued. Each animal had its turn. Each scene was similar and yet different. Some children elaborated on the conversation extensively; others talked in clipped, short sentences. Occasionally Miss Jennings offered a suggestion or gave a few words of help, but as the story progressed, it gathered momentum and she became more and more a part of the background.

Each animal taught Mr. Rabbit to talk his own language, and each time Mr. Rabbit went to Sally Flack to talk as animals do to humans, Sally laughed at him and went off and left him.

After each child had participated, there was a short discussion on how the story should end. The final scene went like this:

Sally: Oh, there's another rabbit. Maybe this is the one I want to take home.

(Rabbit comes slowly over to Sally and moves as if licking her feet.)

Sally: Oh, isn't he sweet? Mr. Rabbit, would you like to go home with me?

(Rabbit puppet becomes active—moves up and down as though rubbing and licking Sally.)

Sally: Oh, he loves me—he loves me! And he doesn't make a lot of silly noises like all those other animals. My mother won't care if I have him, because he is nice and quiet. Mr. Rabbit, I am going to take you home with me!

* * *

Miss Jennings said enthusiastically, "What a wonderful story!"

The children clapped. "Yes." "Boy, that was great!" "Hey, Miss Jennings, that's real cool!" Other comments came from the group.

"Well," exclaimed Miss Jennings with her eyes sparkling and her voice full of enthusiasm, "we set out to see if we could make up a story together and I guess we did it, didn't we?"

The children clapped in their enthusiasm.

"And now," she continued, "now I have a surprise for you. All the time you were making up the story I had the tape recorder running and we have the whole story on tape."

"Let's hear it—let's hear it!"

Miss Jennings tactfully pointed out that they had been working on the story a long time and that they had best wait until the afternoon to hear the tape. Now it was snack time.

Later in the day the children did listen to the story and decided what parts should be altered or cut out. Miss Jennings later wrote the story from the tape onto chart paper, and it became the base of many reading lessons for the children who were learning to read. It was kept and later used again and again for enjoyment and for reading, as other groups advanced to the reading chart stage. Of course, pictures were drawn of each "page" of the chart book and a cover was put on it. It was the stimulus for many original stories which followed in the succeeding months. Some of these were made into talking books (see page 21).

I have only envy for Miss Jennings' ability to develop the creativity of the children in her classes, and to use creativity as the base of all that constitutes the language curriculum of her classroom.

Miss Jennings is guided by a curriculum bulletin planned by her school, which includes objectives for these specific activities for children at each age level, skills they should master as they progress, and many suggestions for meeting these objectives and developing these skills. It *does not* contain dogmatic directions as to how the objectives or skills shall be accomplished; that is left to the creativity of the teacher. The bulletin is loaded with available resources and information that helps the teacher to understand the rationale behind the program. But it places the actual act of teaching with the teacher, where it rightfully belongs.

During the discussion with Miss Jennings after school, she showed me her notebook of plans. She was enthusiastic over the things she was doing and would do with the children. She pointed out that she had a "mixed" group and that such a group provided her with a challenge. She stated the many values in having a mixture, indicating that they were learning not only language from each other, but values and abilities as well.

I believe that the rationale behind Miss Jennings' creative approach is the sound one for today's changing world. I cannot imagine children in classrooms with teachers like this being bored or having time to get into trouble.

First of all, everything she did was *relevant:* that experience came from the minds and hearts of those youngsters. While there is a place for book-learning in every classroom, it can be effective only when it is made relevant to the children by the teacher. And *adventurous* learning experience is still the most relevant kind of learning.

Secondly, *all children were involved*, all were stimulated, and all were creatively contributing in varying degrees.

Thirdly, Miss Jennings was developing language the way professionals know language develops naturally, as described in Chapter 1 in this book. The children were *experiencing* and *adventuring* together—and *listening*. Occasionally Miss Jennings introduced new words, but *in context*, so their meanings were obvious. The words were repeated *orally* many times in the telling of the story. Again the children *listened* and used the words, and when Miss Jennings felt that their meanings were clear, they were introduced on charts to *read*. From the ability to read new words came the ability to *write* them so other stories could be written later in the year. This exercise also gave Miss Jennings a base for *spelling*, and the opportunity to note *grammar* and *word usage* defects so she could help individuals in later study periods.

Miss Jennings is able to do this because she keeps clearly in mind those objectives which her school faculty have drawn up for the primary block: All children are not expected to accomplish all objectives or master all skills at one time; the school is ungraded, yet heterogeneously grouped. This is the children's first year—and each child has a cumulative record folder in which Miss Jennings periodically makes entries so that any substitute or a new teacher may quickly be informed of the place to begin instruction with any individual.

Miss Jennings does not plan her day in jerky, piecemeal lessons. She tries to plan each day into an easy flow, varying large-group work with small-group work and work with individuals. She attempts each day to alter physical activity with sitting-down mental labor. Above all, one of her values is that *each* individual is important, so she tries to teach for individuals as much as possible and give individual help whenever needed. She understands that for each child to function fully, his self-concept must be strong. And the best way to develop a strong self-concept is to make sure that each child's unique and special talent or idea is used: his creativeness.

A look at the objectives for this particular unit in Miss Jennings' plan book shows why she does not have to divide her day into small, isolated (and often uninteresting) classes. She accomplishes a great deal in one larger period by watching closely the children's physical needs, and by integrating her work into *meaningful, relevant* learning situations.

Creative Teaching of Oral Expression

Teaching of creative oral expression is the resultant behavior of a teacher's own set of values.

If the teacher values creative production, she will seek for new and exciting ways to bring about self-expression in the children; if she values her time, she will not spend hours of it correcting work books of dubious value, but will, instead, spend the same amount of time preparing materials to help individuals to come up with creative ideas; if she really values the individual ideas of her children, they take precedence over the textbooks as the materials on which her curriculum is built.

Too often teachers and educators know what is good teaching and good learning behavior, but do lip service to the principles of sound, creative teaching while their behavior in actual practice is something quite different. Knowing that a good reading and grammar program can best be based on a carefully developed program in oral expression, a teacher does not then proceed to spend a major portion of her day telling children to be quiet. Neither does she allow the children to all talk at once or at any time. A sound, creative program in oral expression is carefully planned with definite objectives in mind, is structured in its execution, and is evaluated in a manner appropriate to the objectives.

Miss Jennings is a teacher who does more than lip service to her knowledge of sound educational principles. Miss Jennings is teaching in a first year class in a middle-class suburb on the rim of a large industrial city where she has a group of children well mixed in races, in ethnic backgrounds, and in socioeconomic settings. Part of her job is to encourage freedom in speaking among the children.

At the beginning of the year many of them were too shy to speak to each other. One little boy did not speak directly to Miss Jennings until the fifth week of school!

Learning cannot take place without a flow of communication, much of which is oral in the first years of school. Part of Miss Jennings' technique was to provide so many exciting adventures in creative oral expression that the children forgot themselves and consequently talked about the things they were doing.

There is one effective way to evaluate a good program in oral expression—while it is in progress, watch and listen; watch the faces and actions of the children; listen to what they have to say. I watched and I listened.

I must admit I was as excited as the children were during the creation of Sally Flack and the Rabbit. Their faces glowed in anticipation, their hands waved in eagerness, their eyes sparkled in enthusiasm. Once during the lesson I walked quietly to the front of the room to observe their faces. They did not even notice me! And I shall never forget those faces! I can best describe them as being almost in direct contrast to the faces of children watching television: How often I have seen that slack-lipped, dull, impassive look, staring at the "boob-tube" with an occasional wan smile, back humped, legs crossed, hands limp in the opening made by the crossed legs.

But these children were not like that! You could see the wheels go round. No passivity here—faces aglow—expressions quickly flitting from a smile of pleasure to a frown of thought—hands waving enthusiastically, bodies up and down, tense one minute and relaxed the next; each engrossed in the act of creative production and learning.

The greatest tribute that could be paid to any teacher happened to Miss Jennings that day. When she began the adventure, the children were sitting in their seats, arranged around four large tables in the room. By the time she was ten minutes into the lesson, every child had quietly left his seat and had seated himself at Miss Jennings' feet. No disorder, just plain interest and excitement. She just smiled as each came forward and let it be. Children need to help set their own conditions for comfortable learning. Lessons such as the one described above provide the opportunity for them to do so.

This chapter describes many such oral adventures in communication. The adventures were observed in various classrooms of creative teachers, or were experienced by the author himself in working with children. They are not recounted here with the intent that teachers should repeat them in their own classroom, for that would be a violation of the concept of creativity itself. Creativity is not defined as copying what someone else has done. But one form of creativity is *adaptation*, and adapting an idea to one's own classroom is a permissible concept on the basis that one idea adapted may spark another and then another, so that soon the teacher and the children are able to create on a higher level of productivity by coming up with ideas of their own: the teacher with ideas so creative that the children learn quickly and well; the children with ideas that help them to learn, but which develop their own creativity as well.

The categories below indicate the opportunities present in every classroom where speech may be developed; the illustrations are presented to serve the purpose of stimulating the teacher's imagination as to how the categories may be utilized to achieve the objectives of a sound program in oral expression.

I am aware that some illustrations are far less creative than others. Their inclusion is deliberate. They may help teachers who feel they are not creative to see that some of the things they do can lead to creative teaching. A challenging program in oral expression leaves a situation open-ended, so children must think through to the conclusion of the situation. This has been the basic principle behind the selection of the materials included in the remainder of this chapter.

I have not graded the material presented because it is adaptable to all grades. In many instances I have given an illustration of the adaptation of the same stimuli to both primary and intermediate grade levels. Creativity, like learning, is based in the child's past experiences. It is necessary, then, not to begin with a grade but with a child. Because of an impoverished background in some areas, the creative work may well begin on a very simple level with many children.

Classroom Situations

Ordinary classroom situations which may be used effectively to build a controlled, sound creative program in oral expression listed on the following page:

Discussions
Writing the morning news
The Show-and-Tell period
Composing original stories such as the one above
Flannel board stories
Book reports
Presenting Social Studies reports
Panel discussions
Finger plays
Choral speaking
Chalk talks
Reciting poetry
Creating original poems
Dramatizations
Reading to each other: audience-type situation
Conversations
Telephone dialogue
Simulated radio and television shows
Shadow plays
Scroll movies
Puppet shows
Programs over a loud-speaker system
Assembly programs
Planning periods

Children's Speech

Smith[1] proposes that one way to produce creative oral expression is to listen to children's dialogue and note the many creative things they say. Smith, Goodman, and Meredith[2] say that one stage of the child's language development is the creative, and capitalizing on this natural stage may do a great deal to encourage creative oral expression, and consequently effective communication.

Smith,[3] in his book *Creative Teaching of the Language Arts*, gives some illustrations of the creative expressions of children.

1. James A. Smith, *Creative Teaching of the Language Arts in the Elementary School* (Boston: Allyn and Bacon, 1968), p. 97.
2. Brooks E. Smith, Kenneth S. Goodman, and Robert Meredith, *Language and Thinking in the Elementary School* (New York: Holt, Rinehart and Winston, Inc., 1970).
3. James A. Smith, *Creative Teaching of the Language Arts in the Elementary School* (Boston: Allyn and Bacon, 1968), p. 98.

Lloyd, age 7, says on a foggy day, "If the church steeple didn't hold the fog up like a tent pole, it would all fall down and smother us."

Marcia, age 8, says, "Love is kinda like heart trouble."

Mark, age 9, returning from a cub scout overnight hike says, "The moon is a flashlight in the sky."

Kevin, age 5, says on a blustery day, "Gosh, the wind is grouchy today."

Marion, age 12, says, "Loneliness is being all by yourself even when there are people around."

Smith points out that children experiment with speech just as they experiment with art materials. They manipulate words and try them out to see if they understand their true meanings. These trials are called verbalisms. Adults use verbalisms also, as they manipulate and experiment with speech.

Verbalisms may be considered a part of the experimental stages of speech development. It is hoped that children will progress from this

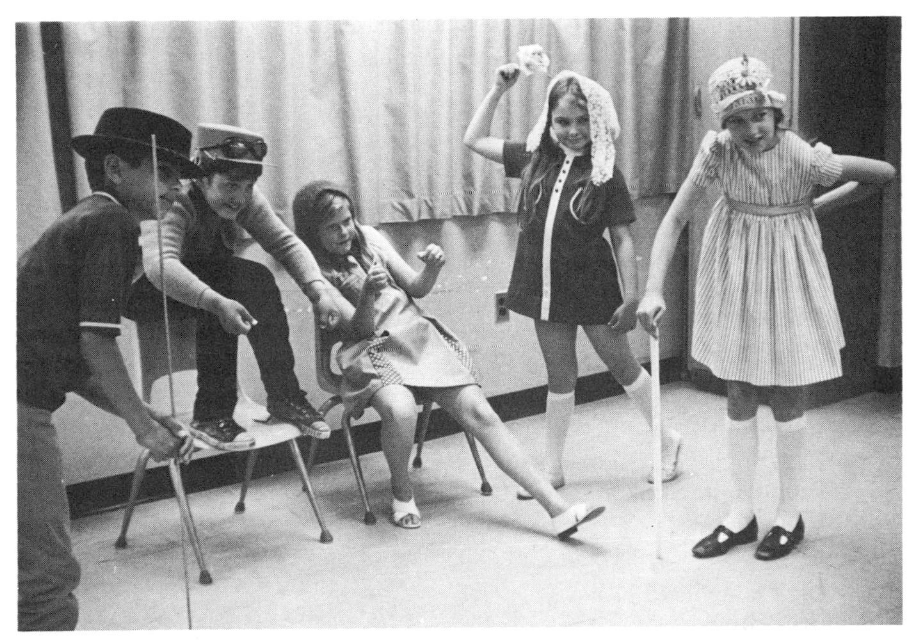

Figure 24 *The children were asked to choose a hat from a box of hats, put it on, and pantomime the character suggested by the hat.*

They were then given ten minutes to plan a play in which all the characters might meet in a logical manner. In the scene above, a motorcycle kook stops his cycle, a woman driver brakes her car at a street crossing while an old lady crosses the street to be interviewed by a TV announcer.

stage on to the aesthetic stage, where they find enjoyment in arranging words just for the beauty of the words themselves and for the word pictures they can paint with them.

From an early age, youngsters go around the house chanting words which fall pleasantly off the tongue. Teen-agers pick up new words and make their discovery obvious by using the word six or seven times during the course of one conversation.

Playing with Words

Often, when new words are introduced into oral conversation by a child or the teacher, the word can be "played with" to help develop its meaning and its use. This is true for all sorts of words.

On a rainy day, for instance, Miss Eckhart, second grade teacher, played with the word "rain," and the children listed all the words they knew that contained the word "rain."

Further discussion included oral descriptions of each word, or how it would be used in effective writing. A class poem resulted:

DRIP, DRIP, DRIP,
Splashy, Splashy,
BLURP, BLURP, BLURP.

On a rainy day I see . . .
Rain clouds,
Worms,
Lots of snails,
Mud puddles,
Raindrops,
Mud,
Wet trees,
Hail,
People in raincoats,
Umbrellas,
Wet sidewalks.

On a rainy day I hear . . .
Drip, drop,
Birds chirping,
Rain splashing,
Lightning striking,
Clouds bumping together,
Raindrops on the roof,
Thunder booming,
My dog pouting to get out.

On a rainy day I feel . . .
Cool, damp,
Wet,
Good when I'm walking,
Warm,
Cold, soaking,
Comfortable.

It's fun in the rain!

—Twelve 2nd Graders
Lemon Ave. School
La Mesa Spring Valley School District

Mr. Parnes asked the children to give as many meanings as possible to new words. The children in his fifth grade gave some imaginative descriptions and definitions to some words:

Question: What is *ordinary?*
Answers:
Ordinary is anything that turns you off.
Ordinary is anything that needs something else.
Bread is *ordinary.*
A ride on a school bus is *ordinary.*
Ordinary is a girl in blue jeans.
Question: What is *experience?*
Answers:
Experience is doing something instead of reading it.
Experience is using all your senses instead of just one.
Life is *experience.*
Experience is like eating from a smorgasbord.

Following sessions such as this with a creative writing session often improves the quality of the creative writing. In this case, Mr. Parnes encouraged the children to use an experience of their own and write about it—but to make it an emotional experience. Dana wrote the following:

Experience

I hesitated and I gingerly approached the ski lift. What would it be like? What would happen? In the midst of my thought I had missed the car. A feeling of safety came over me as I gave a big sigh of relief. But look! The next car! Here it comes! It's either now or never so. . . . Up I went. The course looked so frightening. How I hated the snow and mountains. To me they were just lurking there, waiting for some unsuspecting victim to be trapped there, luring innocent victims to their deaths. There's the top! "Stop! Let me off!" I tried to scream, yet nothing came out. The tears rolled down my eyes. "Save me! Save me from this horrible fate!"

I was on the top. I was on the bewitching, desolate, frightening top. But I had to do it. There I went! Could it be true? It was actually fun! A thrilling sensation filled my body as I slid down the icy, snowbound slopes. I was a bird! I could almost fly! How stupid I felt. How could I have imagined those terrors and fears I had in my mind. Why this was the most fantastic, fascinating, wonderful sport I had ever experienced.

—Dana Teitelman
Norfolk, W. Virginia

Cinquain poetry such as that mentioned in Chapter 9 is an excellent way for children to put into writing descriptions of experiences for which they are using new words.

Mr. Ames felt the children should be impressed by the fact that *one* word could change the entire meaning of a whole passage. He wrote a list of numbered phrases on the chalkboard. He asked the children to number a sheet of paper like the list on the chalkboard. After each number the children wrote the word *they* thought was appropriate to finish the phrase, supplying a word Mr. Ames had omitted. The children read and compared their words, indicating the variety of images which had filled their minds at the suggestion of the phrases.

Two of Mr. Ames's phrases were:

1. the ______ light in the young girl's eyes.
2. the ______ sound of the bell.

The variety of words supplied for number 1 is indicated by the list below, which is a composite from twenty-five children:

happy	cold
sad	bitter
heartbreaking	friendly
joyous	glad
mischievous	delighted
devilish	sparkly
hard	excited
defiant	sleepy
angry	snappy
dreamy	dangerous
hazy	alert
soft	

Almost a different word for every child!

Mr. Ames was quick to point out that, although the children had selected a wide range of excellent words, authors could not often be so liberal in their selection of words: they had to make certain that they chose the *proper* word for the proper place. Authors were clever in making words work for them, but they must paint pictures with words, and their skill was challenged when they wanted every reader to see the exact same scene; they must build excellent descriptions.

"Let's see how words work for us," said Mr. Ames. He placed a card on the chalk tray which said: *The Right Word Counts.* Next to it he placed another card which said: *Words Take Us Far Away.*

"Now," said Mr. Ames, "think hard—when have words ever taken you far away?"

Mary finally volunteered. "Well," she said, "the other night I was in my room reading and my mother called me for dinner three times before I heard her."

"Why was that, Mary?"

"Well, Mr. Ames, I was reading Heidi and I wasn't in my room; I was in Switzerland on the side of the mountain with Heidi and Peter the goatherd, and Grandpa and the blind grandmother. I didn't hear my mother; the words had taken me far away."

"What an excellent idea," said Mr. Ames. "Now look at this card and see if you can give me an example of it."

He placed a card on the chalk tray which said: *Words Make Us Happy.*

Several hands went up on that one. Mr. Ames called on Bruce.

"Well," said Bruce, "I like to read the funny papers and lots of times they make me laugh!"

"Good example," said Mr. Ames. "Darryl?"

"I like to read jokes and they make me laugh," said Darryl.

"Very good ideas," said Mr. Ames approvingly. "Now take a look at this next card." On the chalkboard he placed a card which read: *Words Work for Us.*

"I know we have just shown how we can use words to do things to us and for us, but can you think of a way that words actually did some work for you, some physical effort, that is, and you didn't have to do it?" asked Mr. Ames.

"Yes," said Dick, "when I was sick last week, I had a fever and I rang a little bell by my table and my mother came right away. I asked her for a drink and she got it for me; the words did the work for me. I didn't have to get out of bed and do it."

"Very good," Mr. Ames nodded. "Let's try another." This time the card read: *Words Make Us Sad.*

There were many volunteers for this one: reading sad stories that made you cry, or sad poems, or hearing sad songs. One child remarked that a cross word or a scolding from her father made her sad.

"I am sure we can see how important it is to choose the *right* word and get it in the *right* place," said Mr. Ames, "and I am certain we will think a great deal about words when we are choosing them to express our ideas aloud or on paper."

Oral Definitions

Another aspect of playing with words is the creating of definitions. Definitions should come at the close of an experience. A very common but effective example of developing creative and effective speech is the use of Peanuts cartoon characters in recent years in tickling the imagination of children with incomplete phrases such as: Happiness is ______ ______ ______ and Misery is ______ ______ ______.

Some responses collected by the author from various ages follow:

Happiness is bringing home a dog and being able to keep it. (An eight year old)
Happiness is a new baby. (A four year old)
Happiness is bread with peanut butter on both sides. (A six year old)

These definitions could not be written, obviously, until each junior author had first of all experienced his own kind of happiness.

Teaching which begins with a definition, then, can be a rote memory process with little or no real meaning or value to a child.

Smith[4] gives an example of a definition that was developed as the result of an experience:

In a combined fourth, fifth, and sixth grade in a rural school, a teacher had provided his children with many rich vocabulary-building experiences. One day Pat, a girl in the sixth grade, asked what adjectives were. The teacher asked where she had heard the word, and Pat replied, "I have a sister in junior high school who is studying adjectives and she spends all her time at home underlining words." Soon the whole class was interested in the word "adjective." What were they? The problem of helping these children draw from their experiences the meaning to go with the verbal symbol confronted the teacher. The fourth graders did not have the background the sixth graders had, so the task was not an easy one.

However, he worked out a plan. He gave each of the children a sheet of drawing paper and some crayons. Then he wrote on the board, "The house stood on the hill under a tree," and asked the children to interpret this sentence through a drawing. When the drawings were finished, they

4. Ibid, pp. 103–104.

were placed before the class and discussed. As might be expected, there was a great deal of variety in the interpretations. There were steep hills and squatty ones, tall houses and rambling ones, high trees and low ones. The teacher then led a discussion on how an author would paint a picture with words instead of brushes—especially if he wanted his readers to get a definite picture in mind because of its importance to his story. The suggestions from the children for adding more words soon resulted in rewriting the sentence this way: "The low, rambling, ramshackle house stood on the gently sloping hill under a tall elm tree."

This time, when the children drew their pictures, there was more of a similarity among them. Next the teacher led the group to verbal expression by having them put their heads on their tables while he read the sentence: "The brook ran through the meadow past the mill."

The children described what they had "seen," and again it was decided there were not enough words to paint a clear visual picture. So again the teacher asked that they close their eyes and attempt to see this picture: "The winding, bubbling brook ran through the daisy-dotted meadow to the old deserted grist mill."

Pat, at this point, raised her head and said excitedly: "Hold it, Mr. Jones! I've got 'technicolor'!"

And adjectives, to that group of children, became technicolor words. This is a definition that far surpassed any in the books and was never forgotten by that group, for to them it was rich in meaning and experience.

Vocabulary Building

Vocabulary building should "pepper" the school day. Teachers should seize every possible opportunity to awaken children to the joy of hearing, repeating, and understanding new words, and should provide opportunity for children to discover and invent new words themselves.

Vocabulary building is essential if the teacher is to help equip the child for creative expression. Too often the concept of vocabulary building is linked solely to the reading program, and little is done to help children learn new words outside the reading or spelling class. This is unfortunate, since the speaking vocabulary of children is many times greater than the reading vocabulary; learning new words for everyday speaking must come first.

Developing a feeling for words is not difficult if the teacher bases her teaching at the early childhood level on the resources the child already has. The wonderful sense of rhythm inherent in children expresses itself through words as well as through bodily movement. From the time the child can speak, he repeats sounds and nursery rhymes, not because they bear a particular meaning, but because of the natural rhythm of the words or the line. Repeated consonant sounds or well-mouthed vowel sounds fascinate the child. Thus, he sings and hums nonsense rhymes from an early age, and entering the gang stage in his intermediate grade experience, he works out gang-calls that are full of rich sound expression:

Hip-Ka-Ninny
Ka-Ninny-Ka-sock
Ka-boob-a-ley-ock
Ka-Yoo-Hoo.

This may be meaningless to an adult but music to a child.

A feeling for words may be developed through a variety of forms. One way to develop expressive oral speech is to dwell on the describing words in the language which add tone, humor, and color to ordinary speech. This can be demonstrated to children in many ways.

The teacher can describe these words (largely adjectives and adverbs) as words that paint pictures. A discussion of the importance of the describing words can lead to a comparison between them and the strokes of color an artist puts on a canvas to paint his "paint picture" as we sometimes paint "word pictures."

Demonstrations of the effectiveness of word pictures may be developed in various ways.

Mr. Elkins asked all the children to sit quietly and, without using their mouths and only by using their fingers, to show him how the describing words changed an idea. On a pocket chart in front of the room, he put a card on which was printed the word *water*. "Now I am going to put other words in front of the one," he said. "Show me with your fingers how they change the idea each time." In front of the word *water* he placed a card bearing the word *running*.

Immediately fingers began to wriggle up and down, to move along, to dance gently. "Look," said Mr. Elkins, "our fingers are moving in a somewhat similar way, yet they are all different too. Now watch while I add another word." This time he put the word *dancing* before the word *water*. At once fingers made fountains or danced in a variety of patterns across the desk, each different from the other. "Very good," Mr. Elkins went on. "Now, let's try this," and he added the word *quiet*. Other words added were *angry, tumbling, cool, deep*. In each instance he evoked many interpretations from the children.

Almost any noun can be used in this manner if the teacher is sensitive to the many forms of describing words which create visual images in the youngsters' minds. The word *cat*, for instance, brings to mind one's own cat. Add words such as *pussy*, *tiger*, *black*, *soft*, and *pretty*, and the vision changes. Add other sets of words such as *frightened*, *angry*, *nasty*, and *foolish*, and a whole new set of images appears. Words like *minister's*, *teacher's*, *educated*, and *captain's* placed before the word bring forth another whole set of pictures.

Rhymes and songs are good media for helping children build a sensitivity to rhyming words.

The teacher says, "Afraid, afraid, who's afraid?" and any child who can think of a rhyming word says it, as when Mary said in response to the above, "The maid!" The answers can be sensible or nonsensical, whichever the class agrees they should be. Almost any sentence can be made into a rhyming one.

This idea can be further developed by the teacher, who might have a question box on her desk which she uses to phrase rhyming questions. The teacher asks, "Why is a rabbit's nose so twitchy?" and the children will invariably reply, "Maybe it's because it's itchy!"

Pictures may be used very effectively for building an enriched oral vocabulary. Smith[5] offers many suggestions about their use. He says:

> At no time in the history of the world have beautiful pictures been accessible to teachers as they are today. Almost every scene imaginable has been depicted by pictures—cartoons, photographs, paintings, drawings and reproductions. All of these are free for the asking from calendar companies, educational supply houses, poster agencies, travel agencies, current magazines and newspapers.
>
> Teachers have always used pictures in their teaching, but not always have they attempted to exhaust the possibilities pictures have for developing oral vocabulary. The most common use of pictures is to tell a story or to decorate a bulletin board. While these are two excellent ways to excite discussion, they are only a beginning.

He proceeds to list ways of setting up thought-provoking conditions for the creative use of words through the use of pictures.

Pictures that appeal to the senses help evoke a group of expressive words.

In a second grade where Figure 25 was shown, these words came from the group:

yummy	thick
warm	wet
good	hot
comfortable	

The teacher suggested a few more such as:

tasty	rich
delicious	creamy

5. Ibid, p. 121.

Figure 25 *How does it taste?*

From the second picture came this list of words:

cool	refreshing
soft	delightful
wet	wonderful
grand	

Figure 26 *How does it feel?*

When a picture of a child watching an airplane was put on the bulletin board and the sounds were discussed, children in a third grade made these analogies. They said, "It sounds . . .

. . . like bees
. . . like flies buzzing
. . . like airplanes far away
. . . like Daddy's razor
. . . like mosquitos
. . . like burrs in my head
. . . like millions of telephones far away"

When children draw analogies such as this, poetic expression is beginning to emerge. Poetry results as a combination of mind and heart, and these children have begun to put the feeling into their work which gives it a poetic quality.

Sometimes two or more questions can be asked about a "situation" picture to help children see that new words are required to describe different points of view.

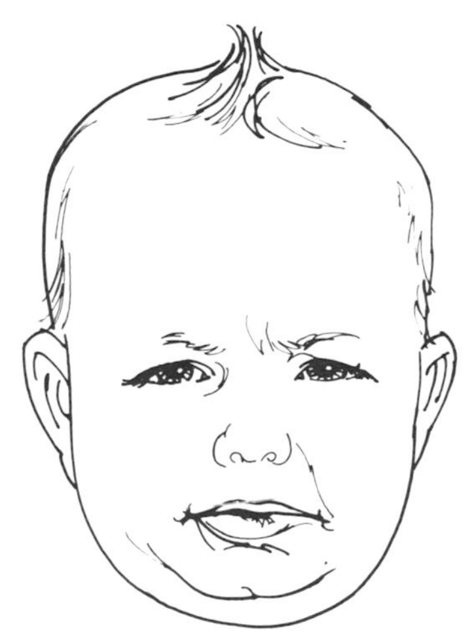

Figure 27 *How does baby feel? What does baby see?*

Figure 27 also helped to develop empathy in the children when the teacher asked them to make a face like the baby, and then said, "What would you be looking at to make a face like the baby?" The question brought out these suggestions:

a dog
a bear
a lion
someone hurt
a car wreck
his rattle on the floor
his milk spilled over

Figure 28 *What happened? Tell a story.*

Pictures have always been good starters for telling a story. The picture with the unusual twist is a strong motivater for the unusual story. Instead of the phrase "Tell me about this picture," children are often stimulated to explore feelings more deeply and to search for expressive words when asked the question, "What happened?" or "How could this have been avoided?" or "Who was responsible for this?"

Figure 28 brought forth some creative suggestions from fourth graders who were asked, "What happened?" which were completely different from those of another group of fourth graders who were asked to tell the story of the picture.

The group that told the story labeled the items in the picture. Little imagination was displayed as to what happened before or after the picture was taken. The other group had many unusual ideas, however, going into long build-ups to the situation depicted in the picture and offering solutions or logical endings to their stories.

Some pictures show a situation which has become unmanageable (Figure 29).

Figure 29 *What happened before this picture was taken?*

A whole flood of ideas will come forth if a teacher asks: "What happened *before* picture was taken?"

There are pictures which are especially good to use in asking the question, "What happened *after* the picture was taken?" Norman Rockwell magazine covers often show children and adults in various predicaments which supply excellent material for discussions built around this question.

Magazines and advertising material are filled with pictures of beautiful desserts, salads, and other enticing foods. Some of these pictures, mounted attractively on a bulletin board, can bring out some imaginative prose or poetry when the label, "How does it feel to be your favorite dessert?" is attached.

Find pictures of people using one-way communication systems, such as a person telephoning, a man or woman talking on TV or using a public address system. Put captions such as these over the pictures:

"What is she saying to you? Answer her."

"What is he saying? Tell us."

Encourage children to take turns being the person in the picture and adding the sound to it. The label, "Make a sound picture out of me" is a good one to use on the bulletin board with many pictures.

Find unusual pictures, pictures that are misty, or that show a scene taken through a window down which the rain is pouring. Ask the question, "What words describe this picture?" Unusual words are needed to describe unusual pictures. Find pictures that tend, in themselves, to depict some quality such as strength, or beauty, or joy. Use it to develop a specific vocabulary about specific parts of the picture.

Figure 30 *Using parts of pictures to develop new vocabulary.*

These questions were asked of Figure 30:

"Notice the man's arm in the picture. How could we describe it to others who could not see the picture?"

(Some of the words offered by a fifth grade class were: *strong, tense, taut, tight, muscular,* and *manly.*)

"Look at the line. How could we describe it?" (Words which were used included: *strong, tight, taut, strained, stretched, heavy.*)

Now let's look at the fish and tell about it. (Words such as these were offered: *powerful, slick, slippery, wet, shiny, fluid, beautiful, graceful, strong, resistant.*)

Often magazines publish pictures of beautiful designs. The caption at the top of the page asks, "What is it?" Close scrutiny proves the lovely circles to be onion rings, the beautiful flowing rivers turn out to be the cross-section of a cabbage, the gorgeous sunbursts are crystals of sugar, all enlarged by the magic of the microscope. These pictures are excellent for classroom discussion, especially when their use results in making children closer observers of the beauty in the common things around them.

A variation of this use of pictures is to cut out an attractive picture for a bulletin board. Over it hang a piece of oaktag with a small hole in it revealing only a part of the picture. The caption, "What is it?" creates the motivation for a discussion. Often a plate of spaghetti may look like a chocolate-chip cookie when only a part of it is exposed through a round hole. After children have tried to imagine what is under the oaktag, it is lifted for all to see.

This can be a springboard for other discussions on how things often are not what they seem. Frequently this can lead into the telling of mystery stories.

There are many pictures which can be partly covered, and by so doing, the whole idea of the picture is changed. Watch for pictures like this. Mount them on a bulletin board with a piece of tag board over part of the picture. If it covers the bottom part, put this caption over the picture: "What do you think the bottom of this picture is about?" On the tag board write, "Talk about it, then lift me up and see."

Children's imaginations can run rampant in a situation such as this, and the words will flow. The surprise of finding out what is really under the oaktag is fun too.

Pictures of inanimate objects are excellent to stimulate imagination. A caption such as, "If They Came Alive, What Would They Say?" can lead to a discussion or a dramatization, in which different children assume the roles of the objects in the picture. Projection of feeling into inanimate and animate objects helps to develop a good "feeling" vocabulary.

Figure 31 *How does the horse feel?*

Instead of asking children to tell about Figure 31, the teacher asked, "How does the horse feel—what does he think?" This brought out a flow of interesting "feeling" words: *angry*, *frustrated*, *violent*, *unhappy*, *enraged*, *wild*, *vicious*, *furious*, *destructive*, etc.

The use of pictures to develop vocabulary is unlimited. In the introductory chapter to this section, the point was made that oral vocabulary develops meaningfully when it grows out of the children's experiences. These experiences may be direct or vicarious. Pictures provide vicarious experiences for children. From these experiences comes a sharing of the vocabularies of all the group. Then new words, words developed this way, have meaning to the child and equip him with the tools he later needs to do creative writing. Children rarely, if ever, write words they do not say. The core of a good creative writing program and a good reading program lies in building a good oral vocabulary. Children ought to enjoy building their oral vocabularies—learning new skills should always be satisfying and fun.

Children enjoy playing and experimenting with words. Instead of shoving words down their throats, it is fun to stop and discuss words and their value. The fact that children enjoy playing with words and may think a great deal about them may be noted in Debbie's story on facing page:

A World Without Words

What would we do if we didn't have words? Wouldn't it be terrible? Everything we know revolves around books. If we didn't have words, there would be no books and we wouldn't know about anything. And we wouldn't have all of the modern conveniences that we have today.

We also would not be able to have peace talks to help stop wars. If we could not have the peace talks, the wars could get so bad the world would be one big war.

There would be no poems or stories, either, for knowledge or enjoyment. We wouldn't have the *Bible*, *Torah*, or "The Ten Commandments." Also, all of the poets and authors would be out of a job.

Of course, we couldn't do all of these projects and papers and things in school and we couldn't get in trouble for talking either. Words have their good points and bad points, I guess.

—Debbie Kenner
Norfolk, Virginia

The Vocabulary Chart

Experiencing, hearing, speaking, and reading: If the sequence of language development is to be maintained, children should *see* the new words they bring into their speech. One way to present the visual image of new words is a vocabulary chart which is hung in a conspicuous place in the classroom.

Many teachers have a flo-pen hanging on a string beside this chart so it is available at all times for children and teacher to enter new words on the chart at any time of the day. Such a chart serves a fourfold purpose: It provides a place to record new words; it creates a good reference chart for children who wish to use new words in their work and spell them correctly; it keeps the visual image of a new word before the class; and it provides the source of spelling lists for the following week. An accumulation of such charts over a period of time will show a wealth of new words which do not appear in the books, but which arise from the children's experiences.

The flow of words that comes from children should never be checked —controlled and utilized perhaps, but never checked. The children bring new words to school to share just as they bring in new toys to share. Teachers can make use of these natural experiences.

And if at times the river of verbal symbols tends to dry up, then the teacher should have up her sleeve many clever and contrived situations to give children the opportunity to develop a rich oral vocabulary and to have fun using words. Every single second spent in the development of good oral vocabulary is time well spent, because a good oral vocabulary is necessary before reading, handwriting, or creative writing can be taught.

Many highly creative children "tune out" what is going on in a classroom simply because the sounds around them are not worth listening to. A purposeful oral expression program keeps the sounds around children in the classroom more interesting than those going on in the corridor or out the window, and keeps the children challenged, because they must think and pass judgement to be certain that the right word goes in the right place.

Specialized Vocabulary Charts

Word charts that are less general in nature than the vocabulary chart described above can serve the same purposes as a vocabulary chart, but can also help children to classify and categorize.

For instance, Miss Smith asked each child to draw a specific picture on one side of a large sheet of manila paper. These pictures included: an elephant, a clown, an exercising dumbbell, a baby chicken, a house, etc. Miss Smith took one of these sheets of paper at the beginning of each day and told the children they were going to brainstorm words which could be placed appropriately on the chart. For elephant words the children wrote *plod, clomp, heavy, weight, lumber, huge, tremendous, large, massive, immense, two-ton, gigantic, Dumbo,* etc. On the sheet of paper with the clown, Miss Smith printed FUNNY WORDS and the children put these funny words on the paper: *laugh, titter, guffaw, giggle, joy, happy, silly, foolish, delightful, capricious, joke, clown,* etc. By the exercising weight she printed HEAVY WORDS and the list included *elephant, ton, fat, obese, lead, solid, cumbersome, dinosaur, iron,* and *weight.* The baby chick inspired a collection of SOFT WORDS such as *light, airy, fluffy, furry, dainty, milk, weak, gentle, kind, peaceful, snow, milkweed, tender, pleasant, blurry.* WORDS FOR HOUSES included not only descriptive words but unusual names which children had seen on houses as well: *rambling, haunted, stately, deserted, ranch, colonial, Cape Cod, apartment, modern,* and names such as Linger Awhile, Dew-Drop Inn, The Pillars, Don Rovin, Dad's Dreams, Lane's End, and Mortgaged Manor.

These charts were bound into big books and left on a shelf in the reading center where children could easily refer to them when they desired to write a story about any topic in the book.

The Show-and-Tell Period

I once met a teacher who somewhat forlornly said to me, "My 'Show-and-Tell' period has turned out to be more of a 'Bring-and-Brag' than anything else!"

I am inclined to agree with her that this is one of the many ills that have grown out of the misuse or misunderstanding of the Show-and-Tell period.

In theory it should be the most valuable time of the day, a time when the teacher can listen carefully and make note of the words the children are hearing from each other. It is a time when she can present new words which she plans to introduce later on in the reading program, so that the words are spoken in context and with meaning before they appear in printed form. It is the most important part of the language development sequence stated on page 45 and the place where most reading programs break down.

However, teachers who have forgotten this purpose often view the Show and Tell merely as a sharing period—children bring things from home and show them, then sit down, and on to the next child, with the word and language development of the lesson almost accidental.

The Show-and-Tell period, although often misunderstood and misused, can be a highly effective method of developing vocabulary at the spoken level. Children do not write (and rarely read) things about which they do not talk, so the introduction of new words as suggested in the sequence (see page 45) at the spoken level is of the utmost importance. Following is a sample of a series of Show-and-Tell periods of a creative nature, developed by a first grade teacher, which resulted in some excellent language experience.

Mrs. Lomax, the kindergarten teacher in one particular school, was retiring. She was greatly loved by all her students, especially those in the first grade who had been under her guidance the preceding year. Miss Fry, the first grade teacher, was sensitive to the needs her class seemed to have to express their love and gratitude to Mrs. Lomax.

On the Monday preceding Teacher Recognition Week, she suggested that the children talk about Mrs. Lomax's retirement, and also told them about Teacher Recognition Day. The words "retirement" and "recognition" were discussed and printed on a vocabulary chart.

One child suggested that each one bring a present for Mrs. Lomax. Miss Fry, knowing that all children could not afford a present, made the following suggestion.

"That's a good idea, Marion. I wonder if Mrs. Lomax might like as a present something which you yourself have made. She would be happy if you each had a part of the present so she could remember each one of you. I have an idea! This morning, why don't each one of you paint the thing you would like most to give to Mrs. Lomax, and then each morning this week we will have five people show what they have painted at Show-and-Tell time, and maybe we can come up with an idea as to what we can do with the paintings. Do any of you remember what Mrs. Lomax likes?"

"She likes flowers," said Pat.

"She always liked rabbits 'cause we always had rabbits and they got them again this year," volunteered Mike.

"She likes kids," said Perry.

"I gave her some pink soap at Christmas and she told me it was her favorite present," said Phillip.

"I think it is important to make something Mrs. Lomax likes—or something you think she will like," said Miss Fry.

On each of the succeeding mornings, five children who were ready showed their paintings and a discussion was held. The dialogue from one of the discussions follows:

Pat had drawn a paper full of bright, beautiful flowers.

"I made flowers, 'cause Mrs. Lomax loves flowers," she said as she displayed her painting.

"It is a beautiful painting, Pat," said Miss Fry. "Boys and girls, does it remind you of anything else we have seen?"

"A garden," said Jimmy.

"A tablecloth my mother has," said Hazel.

"Wallpaper on our living room," said Mary Ann.

"Anyone else?" asked Miss Fry.

"No? Then can you tell me how Pat's painting looks to you? Can you give me some words to describe it?"

"It is colorful," said Joan.

"Pretty," said Brian.

"Happy," said Peter.

"I think it is gay," said Pat.

"We have four good words: *colorful*, *pretty*, *happy*, and *gay*," said Miss Fry. "Let's see how they look." And she added them to the chart in the front of the room.

"Now tell me how Pat's painting makes you feel," she suggested. "Are there any words up here that suggest a feeling?"

"Yes, *happy* and *gay*," Brian quickly volunteered.

"Good," said Miss Fry, "let's think of some more!"

"It makes me feel funny," said Bill.

"All right. *Funny*. Anything else?"

"It makes me feel giggly and bubbly," said Marcie.

"*Giggly* and *bubbly*, two wonderful words to describe how we feel," exclaimed Miss Fry. "I'd like to add two more. Pat's painting makes me feel *lighthearted* and *joyful.*" She printed the words on the chart. "Let's look at those two words and see if we can figure out what they mean. What would it mean to have a light heart?"

In the discussion of the four other paintings, vocabulary was developed in a similar way. Often Miss Fry pointed out the fact that some words sounded alike, or rhymed, such as the words "bright" and "light" used to describe Brian's picture, a gift of a pile of gold he wanted to give to Mrs. Lomax. On Friday all the paintings were placed before the class and the words unique to each were placed under them. Miss Fry suggested that each child then write something to Mrs. Lomax about his picture gift, that it could be a letter, a story, or a poem; that it could be written by those capable of writing their own, but that those who could not write dictate it to her and she would print it; that they try to use the new words to make each idea beautiful in words as well as in paint.

Here are a few of the children's written (or dictated) materials:

Colorful flowers
Pretty flowers
Happy and gay flowers
Make you feel
Giggly and bubbly
Lighthearted and gay

Like Mrs. Lomax.

—Pat

Dear Mrs. Lomax,

If I could get you anything in the world

I'd get you a ton of gold so bright

You'd never have to have a light.

Love,
Brian

If I could choose anything in the world to give you

I'd give you a rabbit to keep you company when you retire.

—Jan

On Monday of Teacher Recognition Week, Miss Fry had each painting hung around the room with the message to Mrs. Lomax below it. The children discussed a possible way to give all the material to Mrs. Lomax. One advanced child, reading in a Big Book, suggested they be put in a Big Book. Miss Fry then suggested another idea.

"I have another idea," she said. "Have you ever seen a talking book?"

"No," they said, "what is a talking book?"

"How would you like to get a talking book for a present?"

"Yes," they responded enthusiastically.

So the project culminated in a talking book. Each child mounted his picture and his message on a large sheet of Chip Board, and each was bound into a large book. A flyleaf was left for a dedication and another page for a table of contents. True, Miss Fry printed the title of each poem or letter, but each child printed his own name after the title. For number work the pages were numbered, and each child placed the proper number of *his* page after his name on the Table of Contents page. A cover was painted for the book. After much discussion, a title was agreed on and painted on the front: "To Mrs. Lomax with Love."

The talking part of the book came when each child "read" his message on a tape through the tape recorder. (See the Bim Bam Boo, pp. 21f.) Miss Fry brought in many records and placed them near the record player in one corner of the room. Before and after school each child was encouraged to select a record which he wanted played in the background when he read his part of the Talking Book. The class together listened to music and chose music to play at the beginning and ending of the tape. Miss Fry helped the children who could not read to memorize their selections.

On Teacher Recognition Day, Mrs. Lomax was invited to the room while a student teacher took her class. The children escorted her to a chair. The Talking Book was on an easel before her. One child stood on each side of the easel. Another operated the tape recorder behind the easel.

Music from *Tales of the Vienna Woods* flooded the room. Then a child's voice said, "To Mrs. Lomax with Love—a talking book, made for her by her friends in the first grade." The children turned the pages of the book until the first poem appeared—the music then stopped for a moment to be replaced by *The Dance of the Sugar Plum Fairies* and Patty's voice in the foreground reading, "Colorful flowers, pretty flowers, happy and gay."

Needless to say, the Talking Book was a success, not only for the gratification and joy the children felt in presenting it to Mrs. Lomax, but also in the excellent experience they had in developing vocabulary creatively for two weeks. Miss Fry had introduced many new words at the speech level, and the children had the opportunity then to read them and use them in their own creative writing.

Show and Tell in this illustration is a creative situation. Miss Fry used a unique school occurrence to help children explore their past experiences and find new combinations and relationships for placing these experiences into a new experience. She set conditions for this to happen.

How can a teacher liven her Show and Tell and gain full value from it? Below is a composite of many good and often creative examples from several different schools.

Miss Kay Ward sent me a charming booklet of creative writing which came from her class about a variety of topics. Here are some of the excerpts (illustrated) from the booklet, showing that one way to conduct exciting, relevant, and meaningful Show-and-Tell periods is through *using a variety of topics*, a different one each day, and setting aside certain days for sharing things from home. One or two topics well developed is perhaps as good as, if not better than, several which are lightly passed over. Observe the unusual (yet important) topics Miss Ward develops from her Show-and-Tell period into creative writing and for her homemade reading books.

Figure 32 *Pages from Miss Ward's Holiday Book.*

NIGHTMARES

Nightmares come when you are asleep.
Dark shadows creep along the wall
I call, "Mommy! Mommy! I'm SCARED!"
She comes - and there's nothing there
At all.

Figure 33 *Page from a first grade magazine, "Nightmares and Cats."*

Ca[illegible]e loving - sometimes.
They are fluffy, furry,
soft and purry.
They are happy when you feed them.
Sometimes they are gone,
when you need them.

Figure 34 *Page from a first grade magazine, "Nightmares and Cats."*

Figure 35 *Happy snowman. Page from a first grade magazine.*

Figure 36 *Wind and ice. Page from a first grade magazine.*

Nightmares

Nightmares come when you are asleep
Dark shadows creep along the wall
I call, "Mommy! Mommy! I'm SCARED!"
She comes—and there's nothing there
At all.

Cats

Cats are loving—sometimes.
They are fluffy, furry,
  soft and purry.
They are happy when you feed them.
Sometimes they are gone,
  when you need them.

The Happy Snowman

  Mr. Snowman, fat and jolly
With your funny clothes and face,
  When the sun shines down on you
We'll find a puddle in your place.

Wind and Ice

Wind and ice are not very nice.
Wind blows your hat and makes you cold.
Ice makes cars and people slip and slide
Some people like them—
  but most of us don't.

Grandmas

Some grandmas make things for you. They hug you when you get a bump, or when you are sad. They take you shopping and out to eat. We love them.

Grandpas

Some grandpas do nice things for you. When you are sick, they bring candy and read stories. They love you—and always know what's wrong.

The children were very proud of the booklets made periodically from these discussion periods and read often during the weeks after their creation.

Figure 37 *Grandmas and grandpas.*

I visited their classroom one day and told them the story of "The Sugar Plum Tree" with the magic light. Then they created a story with me. They had so much fun, they did not want me to leave. The day after my visit they wrote me this letter, and Gina copied it from the chalkboard (Figure 38).

When Mrs. Ward asked if they had something they might share with me to show their appreciation, immediately they suggested that they send me one of their books. This was a gift of love—something highly relevant to them because it *was* "them" expressed through a creative product. It was highly relevant to me too.

Imagination in the Show-and-Tell Period

A graduate student in my class on Creative Teaching wrote the following poem.

The Show-and-Tell Fairy

I saw a fairy yesterday,
Her face was sweet and fair.
Her hands and feet were full of grace,
She had lovely yellow hair.

She had the prettiest silver wings,
With hint of blue so rare,
And rose and yellow intermixed.
She was like a rainbow there.

I was picking flowers in my yard,
To make a spring bouquet.
For teacher always loves them so,
I pick some every day.

The fairy peeked at me above,
The tulips gay and bright.
Twas just a second that before,
I saw a bird alight.

I think the yellow bird had come
To bring her down to see
The pretty fragrant flowers,
And to say, "Hello!" to me.

At Show and Tell I told my class
About the lovely sight.
But sad to tell, my teacher
Said I didn't tell it right.

I'd just imagined it, she said,
Things aren't what they seem.
Just for an instant there, I thought,
It must have been a dream.

But sure I am I saw her with
Her lovely silver wings.
Peeking around the tulip cup
I heard the bluebells ring.

And when again I see her,
I know she'll give to me,
Her tiny lacy hankie,
For everyone to see.

Then I am sure that all will know,
That I did really see,
That lovely rainbow fairy,
Peeking out at me.

I'm sure my teacher knows a lot,
About a lot of things,
Like, "seas and ships and ceiling wax,
And cabbages and kings."

But grown up folk sometimes forget,
That you and I can see
The fairy folk and many things
That they refuse to see.

—Lillian Moyes

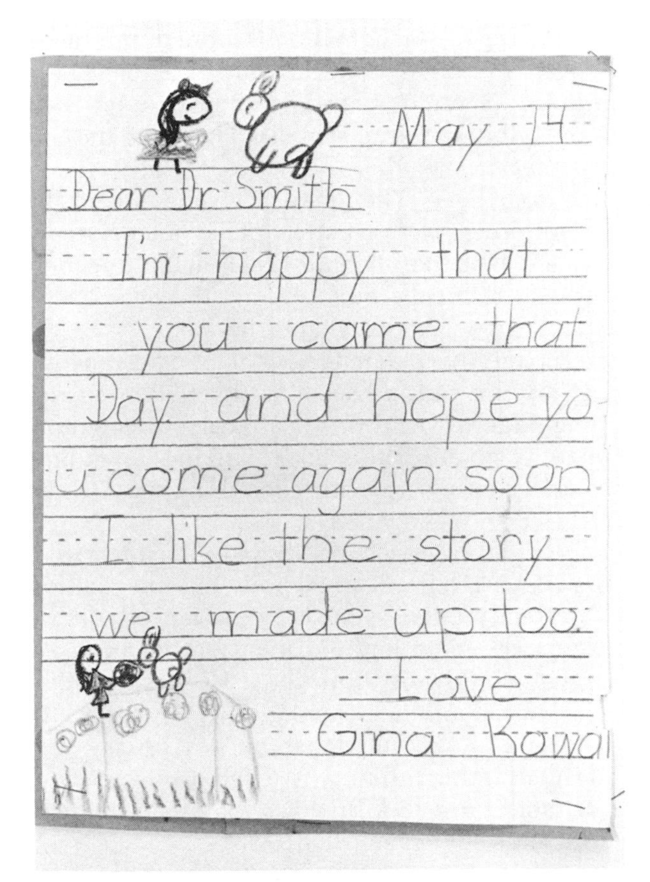

May 14

Dear Dr Smith

I'm happy that you came that Day and hope you come again soon I like the story we made up too.

Love
Gina Kowa

Figure 38 *A letter from Gina.*

How well my student captured the essence of a serious problem in her creative way! For some of the researchers tell us that children do have vivid and exciting imaginations, and that one of the blocks to creative production is when adults refuse to let them express themselves imaginatively. Teachers tell me, "Well, you can't have him telling fantasies all the time. He's got to learn to differentiate the truth from make-believe."

He has also got to keep that wonderful imagination in order to survive in this problem-torn world! And if he is to be a contributing member of society and not merely an "existing" member, he must keep his ability to create.

Teachers are overly concerned about the problem of children deviating from the truth. The students of child development tell us clearly that a vivid imagination is a normal part of growth and development, and that at certain times in a child's life this imagination is more pronounced than at others. Take the seven and eight year olds, for instance. These children are now adventurous: They go away from home under their own steam for certain errands, they ride the school bus or take the bus by themselves to the local theater. Yet their activities are still highly controlled by the adults in their lives. They may go to the end of the street but not across it, or not down the next street. They may ride the school bus, but not *any* bus. What they cannot do in actuality, their minds do for them—take them off on the bus or along the next street. Their imaginations satisfy their urge to know what is there.

Imagination alone is not creativity, but it is a vital part of creative production. Imagination is simply putting what is in one's mind together into new and exciting patterns. And this is almost a direct quote from the definition of creativity given in this book: sinking down taps into our past experiences and coming up with something new to the individual.

When a child tells a story about a green two-headed monster with a body like a horse and legs like a giraffe, it is obvious his imagination is working. He has never, directly or vicariously, experienced such a monster, *but* he *must* have experienced (either directly or vicariously) *each* of its components, or he could not think thus. He has, in other words, experienced green and head and horse and giraffe. His creativity is working when he puts these into new relationships, and he can do it because he is flexible and fluent in his thinking. We call it imagination. Whatever we call it, we cannot afford to kill it. We may feel, in some cases, that it needs to be directed—but never killed!

How does a teacher give direction to imagination and help the child to separate real from make-believe? With most children this is unnecessary—the child himself makes the necessary change—he "outgrows" it. Teachers can "play along" with his make-believe for a while, but sometimes the other children themselves may ridicule a certain child. To avoid social or psychological problems, teachers can, in a situation such as this, say, "That was a good *make-believe* story that John told us, wasn't it, class?" Some days she may say that *only* make-believe stories can be told that day—on other days only true stories can be told for Show and Tell.

Guidance may be needed in developing the imagination, but guidance means providing a positive and acceptable outlet for it as against cutting it off completely.

Following is a sample of a make-believe story told at Show and Tell after such an assignment was made. This one comes from an eleven year old.

The One Winged Angel

Once upon a time there was a angel with only one wing. No one liked her. Or should I say no angel liked her. She only had the one wing so when they flew away she was far behind and no one cared.

But one day one of the angels dropped a star, which the little angel was under. She caught it for knowing each child born has a star of its own, this might have been someones star. But it wasn't it was god in that star, testing the angels the angels were so happy they forgot she only had one wing.

And God gave her one more wing.

The angel who had dropped the little star was very sorry but much relieved when she saw the angel catch it and they became the best of friends.

—Norma O'Looney
Utica, New York

Choral Speaking

In most instances where choral speaking has been used in recent years, it has contributed little to the child's vocabulary development or his creative development. The common practice has been for the teacher to select a passage that will make a good choral poem; teach it to the children, who memorize it or learn to read it well; assign parts to the children to speak; and then "drill" them until the sounds fit the teacher's conception of a good choral poem.

The objectives of: (a) introducing vocabulary at the spoken level; (b) making new words meaningful; (c) developing creativity; and (d) developing good speech in children are often negated when teachers rely on books that provide choral-speaking selections with parts to be assigned to individuals, rows, and groups, and when tense and strict drill is used to master the selection. This does not set proper conditions for learning or for creativity.

When used properly, choral speaking *can* be a very creative and effective way to set conditions for good vocabulary development. It becomes creative when children identify so closely with a passage that they want to learn it or say it. The children can then decide how the

Figure 39 *Cover and illustration from Norma's original story "The One-Winged Angel."*

passage shall be spoken, and work out an effective pattern of recitation with the help of the teacher. Even more creative is the group which writes its own passages and poems to be set to choral-speaking rhythms. Many of the writings of children can be used in this manner.

The poem developed on page 188 is a good example of how choral speaking can come from a classroom situation, using the children's work as the content.

Choral speaking is especially effective when *all* children become involved. *All* children need to say words in order to acquire them so they may be used later in their creative writing, reading, and spelling. The shy child, who rarely volunteers in a class discussion, can enter into a choral-speaking exercise with all the poise and security of the confident child. All children learn new words, because the words are spoken in meaningful context. Choral speaking must be conducted in a relaxed, happy atmosphere where the product becomes secondary to the process. The learning comes in the doing and not in the end result. Often the children will be so pleased with a passage they have created that they will want to perform for someone else. In this case, time should be spent in "polishing it up." Most choral speaking should be carried on for the joy of using words in rhythmical patterns, much the way singing is.

Some suggestions for beginning creative and effective choral speaking follow:

1. Develop a sense of rhythm in the children through various techniques. One which I have found very successful appears on page 23.
2. Smith[6] proposes an excellent use of familiar material for children to develop skill in developing creative patterns of choral speaking. Here is how one teacher used "Hickory Dickory Dock" to develop a good sense of choral work.

Miss Nellis asked if anyone had ever seen a grandfather's clock. Teddy had, so she asked Teddy to show how the pendulum worked. Teddy clenched his fist and swung it through the air at arm's length like a pendulum. The children talked about the grandfather's clock, and the teacher showed a picture of one for those who had never seen one. Then Miss Nellis developed her theme as follows:

She asked the children to say the nursery rhyme in time to Teddy's swinging fist.

"What does the grandfather's clock say?" Miss Nellis then asked.

"Tick-tock, tick-tock," Teddy volunteered.

"Well, let's put the tick-tock into our poem," said Miss Nellis. "How will it be if this half of the class says, 'tick-tock' while Teddy swings

6. Ibid, p. 131.

the pendulum, and this half will say the poem. Watch me for the signal and we'll have the tick-tock begin first."

After this was done, Miss Nellis asked if the children had ever heard of any other kind of clock.

"My wrist watch," said Martha.

"Listen to it and tell me what it says," said Miss Nellis.

"It says 'tick-tick-tick-tick'," said Martha.

"Let's put Martha's watch into our poem," said Miss Nellis. "This time these two groups will be the wrist watch, these two will be the 'tick-tock,' and these two will be the poem. Watch Teddy and we will let the 'tick-tick-tick-tick' go first, then the 'tick-tock,' and then the poem."

It went according to this pattern.

Group 1	*Group 2*	*Group 3*
1 2	1 2	1 2
tick-tick-tick-tick	tick-tock	Hickory Dickory Dock
tick-tick-tick-tick	tick-tock	The mouse ran up the clock
tick-tick-tick-tick	tick-tock	The clock struck one
tick-tick-tick-tick	tick-tock	Down he run
tick-tick-tick-tick	tick-tock	Hickory Dickory Dock.

The children were delighted with the result. Miss Nellis asked for other ways they could do it. Sally suggested they all shout, "Tick-tock" at the end. The children were pleased at this, and Miss Nellis taped the results so the children could hear for themselves how nicely it went together.

When this same technique was tried later in a sixth grade, a group of boys added the sound of Big Ben as they imagined it. They were studying Great Britain, and Big Ben had been a fascinating part of their work. They sang "Bong-Bong" in a deep bass. Other children added the clicking of their tongues to the chants of the group. One boy wanted to try to end the chant with "Cuck-oo" for the cuckoo clock. All these creative ways of saying this rhyme stimulated the imagination of the children.

Mr. Howard used a technique in his classroom which the children enjoyed very much. Each Friday morning the children chose membership in a specific group and appointed a chairman. As part of their library trip on that morning, the chairman was to find a poem which each group could work into a choral presentation. On Friday afternoon the groups met and worked out their choral patterns. After half an hour, each group presented its work to the others. Often the whole class decided to tape some of the presentations. After a while the class had a whole tape of interesting poems to listen to.

3. Another way to provoke creative thinking with choral speaking is to give the children a poem which lends itself to many adaptations and allow them to explore various ways of presenting it. Here, again, is an opportunity for several groups to be working at one time and then to share ideas after each has worked out its pattern for presentation.

4. Poems can be chosen which *must* be walked or dramatized to be effective, such as "The Merry-Go-Round" by Dorothy Baruch. Part of the class chants the poem while a group in front of the room becomes horses, working out various ways of going up and down like a merry-go-round.

5. Nursery rhymes are always good for establishing the idea of using words to rhythms. With little children they can be dramatized, such as "Jack Be Nimble" with the children jumping and hopping to accent the lines, or "Hickory Dickory Dock" as was used above by children in the intermediate grades.

I asked an intermediate grade group of girls recently if they could think of a nursery rhyme with many sounds which might be used in a choral poem. They suggested "Ding Dong Bell." We listed possible sounds as follows:

Bells tolling
The cat crying

They worked out a delightful choral poem in dialogue which went like this:

Group 1	*Group 2*	*Group 3*
(Ding-Dong)	(Ding-Ding-Ding-Ding)	Ding Dong Bell
		Group 4
(Ding-Dong)	(Ding-Ding-Ding-Ding)	Pussy's in the well.
		Group 3
(Ding-Dong)	(Ding-Ding-Ding-Ding)	Who pulled her out?
		Group 4
(Ding-Dong)	(Ding-Ding-Ding-Ding)	Little Johnnie Stout.
		Groups 3 & 4
(Ding-Dong)	(Ding-Ding-Ding-Ding)	Now wasn't he a naughty boy To do poor pussy harm?

All Groups: Me-o-oo-ww (voices falling off like a siren)
SPLASH!

6. I always find it easier to go from these beginning steps to using material that was created by the children, rather than to try commer-

cially prepared materials. After all, they have an emotional tie to it—and it gives the material importance to use it.

Here is an illustration of a lesson which worked out well from an idea given to me by a child.

"Let's make up our own Christmas carol," he said. So we did. We decided that the background noises could be real bells, and the children brought in bells from home. A few were salvaged from the school music room. Together the children worked out a harmonious melody with the bells. The big cow bell tolled the whole-note time, a sleigh bell was rung for the half-note time, wrist bells played quarter-note time, and a tiny porcelain bell played eighth-note time. The bells were varied during the speaking of the following poem which the children wrote.

The Bells Tell of Christmas

The bells, the bells!
Ring out the sounds of Christmas.

Sleighbells ring
Clocks chime
Horns honk
It's Christmas time!

Church bells toll
Carolers sing!
Shoppers shout!
Cash registers ring!

The bells, the bells!
Ring out the tastes of Christmas.

Plum pudding covered with juicy sauce,
Popcorn balls crisp and sweet,
Candy canes all peppermint and bright,
Turkey with dressing and spices.

Applesauce and ribbon candy,
Mincemeat pies and pumpkin, too,
Snowflakes fall on my chilly tongue,
Hot chocolate and cold eggnog.

There were additional verses telling of the smells and sights of Christmas.

The "carol" was done with a tape recorder so that the entire class could enjoy the delightful effect. Later it was played over the school's sound system on Christmas Party day.

7. *Choral Speaking With Music:* When children find pieces of literature that they like, use them dramatically. Decide how you will say them, and use a background of music to add to the effect. Taping such

productions allows the children the joy of hearing the entire production. For instance, try "Stopping by Woods on a Snowy Evening" with the children singing or a record softly playing, "Jingle Bells." Try the Twenty-Third Psalm with the music of the "Battle Hymn of the Republic" playing in the background. Do "The Highwayman" with a Rock-and-Roll beat; "The Bells" with a chime record; "Paul Revere's Ride" with "America, the Beautiful" and "Columbia, the Gem of the Ocean."

Helping children to blend music and words leads to helping them get feeling into their words, which, in turn, leads to creative experimentation.

Miss Jarvey, a third grade teacher, played three or four pieces of music on a record player. She then asked the class to select the one composition they considered to be the most beautiful. In this instance the children chose "Blue Star." Miss Jarvey asked each child to think what was the most beautiful thing in the world to him. When each child said he had an idea, Miss Jarvey had the children sit in a circle. In the center of the circle she placed a tape recorder and a record player. She then played "Blue Star" and recorded the opening theme on the tape recorder. Then she handed the microphone to the first child, who said, "The most beautiful thing in the world is my mother." While the child was speaking, Miss Jarvey turned down the volume of the record player. As soon as he finished, she increased the volume, and passed the microphone on to the next child. When he spoke, she again decreased the volume, and so on around the circle until each child had recorded his idea.

In the playback she got, first of all, beautiful music, which softened when a childish voice said, "The most beautiful thing in the world is my mother," then swelled forth, and softened again as another childish voice said, "The most beautiful thing in the world are the stars twinkling in the sky at night," and so on. This created a very effective tone poem.

Variations of the idea may be employed on all grade levels, using different themes such as:

The saddest thing in the world
The loudest thing in the world
The softest thing in the world
The ugliest thing in the world

On some holidays special recordings can be taped. On Halloween, for instance, the children may create a tape on "The spookiest thing in the world" spoken with "Danse Macabre" or "A Night on Bald Mountain." Fourth of July can bring about the question, "What is the noblest (or most patriotic, or finest) thing in the world?" recorded against military music.

Experiences such as this often tend to grow into experiences which are even more creative. Miss Roehm's class talked about signs of autumn and how we know it is here. She then played a record of "Autumn" by Mantovani. One of the children wrote a poem about autumn to go with the record.

8. *Using the Children's Own Poems:* Encourage the children to find music to be played in the background while the class reads a poem.

Appropriately enough, Dana, who was inspired by the record, "La Mer," wrote a poem about the sea, and then played the record while the class did the poem in choral speaking.

A second grade teacher wrote me how she did some creative writing with her second grade which she used as tone poems for choral speaking. She says:

Since first graders have quite a limited reading and writing vocabulary in December, I decided to have the children tell me what to write and I would write it for them in their words.

We discussed the following topics and they thought about what each one meant to them.

I taped four large pieces of chart paper on the chalk board and labeled them:

1. I can feel Christmas!
2. I can smell Christmas!
3. I can hear Christmas!
4. I can taste Christmas!

The following is the result I had after some discussion. Each idea is the way the children expressed themselves and is written in their words.

1. I can feel Christmas!
    I can feel presents.
    I can feel the spirit of Christmas:*
      Giving gifts and receiving gifts.
    I feel happy.
    I wish everybody to have a Happy Christmas!
2. I can smell Christmas!
    I smell candy canes.
    I smell Christmas bulbs.
    I smell Christmas trees.
    I smell fruit cakes.
    I smell turkey.
3. I can hear Christmas!
    I hear bells.

* The child had said: "I feel the spirit of Christmas." I asked him to tell us what he meant by the spirit of Christmas and he said: "Giving gifts and receiving them."

I hear people talking in whispers.
I hear footsteps coming down the stairs.
I can hear Santa.

4. I can taste Christmas!
   I taste candy.
   I taste Christmas cake.
   I taste candy canes.
   I taste fruit.
5. Christmas is a happy time
   We wish everyone a Merry Christmas and a
   Happy New Year!

If I had had more time, I would have had each child illustrate his idea. We would have assembled this material into a book that they could reread, and then make it into a delightful choral poem.

Children express their thoughts in words quite simply and adequately if allowed to do so. After this enriching experience, I see more and more why we should provide the opportunity for them to start expressing themselves verbally, as well as orally and artistically.

9. *Structuring Original Oral Stories and Poems.* Sometimes teachers can structure a poem or story so that it falls into a pattern which readily lends itself to choral speaking.

One example comes from an ungraded classroom of mixed intermediate ages. Noting the children's interest in pollution, Mr. Clayton developed some creative material after the children had studied the problem rather thoroughly.

He wrote the following four lines on the chalkboard:

Dust, dirt and rust
  Sewage, junk and grime
Foul air, water and earth
  Will kill us before our time.

Then he wrote these lines, leaving a large space between each.

What does it mean?
P
O
L
L
U
T
I
O
N

Mr. Clayton then challenged the children to make up two-line rhymes to express their feelings on this topic.

> Put out the fires
>   Clean up the smoke!
> Out with detergents
>   Or streams will choke!
> Leave clean the forests
>   Make the streams clear
> Litter no highways
>   Put all your gear
> Under the ground
>   Leave sidewalks hosed!
> Take all your garbage
>   To be decomposed.
> Incinerators must have
>   Smoke filters instead
> Old cars reclaim
>   For iron and lead.
>
> Never, no, never
>   Think you are free
> For POLLUTION is caused
>   By you and by me!

When the poem was made into a choral poem, various groups of children spoke the lines while one group chanted "Pollution, pollution" softly in the background. The result was very effective.

10. Reports for social studies may be written in such a way that they read as a cross between prose and poetry, and can develop a definite rhyme. With a little practice, children can write such reports, which may be put on ditto paper, distributed to the class, and then chanted onto a cassette tape. A very creative teacher friend of mine, over a period of a few years, had her whole social studies curriculum on cassette tapes in a multitude of types of choral poems. Here is a section from one of her tapes:

> Across the river by the water there
> Stood Paul Revere—waiting, waiting
> For a light to appear in the old North Church,
> Waiting, waiting.
> One if by land and two if by sea.
> And the night passed by—
> Waiting, waiting!
> Suddenly a light in the old North Church
> A light, a light—by land they come!
> Alert the farmers—tell the world

The British are coming!
Prepare, prepare!
Be off—spread the word"
No more waiting, waiting!

Chalk Talks

Chalk talks help develop in children: (a) good speaking vocabulary, (b) good speaking voice, (c) a concept of a logical sequence of ideas, and (d) a creative imagination. Most children enjoy a chalk talk which has a climax. However, a climax is not absolutely necessary. Children enjoy hearing other children tell stories as they draw pictures. The addition of colored chalk adds variety to the presentation.

One form of chalk talk which stimulates oral creative expression is that which uses abstract color blocks as an agitator to creative thinking. The teacher uses colored chalk directly on the chalkboard, or tapes large sheets of manila paper to the board and then proceeds to apply large blocks of color. The children are instructed to volunteer when the emerging design reminds them of something.

This is the way it went in Miss Sheckell's third grade. She took the colored chalk in her hand and started to make large circles.

"Boys and girls," she said, "I am going to put some pretty colors on this paper. When they remind you of something, you raise your hand and tell me." She applied yellow and red until Anne said, "It makes me think of a clown."

"All right," said Miss Sheckells. "A clown it shall be. And while I am making a clown out of my colors, let's think of a poem or story that tells about him. I'll make him sad; maybe we could begin like this: Here we have a sad, sad clown."

She drew the mouth with the corners turned down and then put in a little perky nose with black chalk. "What can we say for our next line?" she asked, and Bobby said, "His nose turns up, his mouth turns down!"

"Good," said Miss Sheckells as she continued drawing on a clown hat and fancy buttons down his front. "Now what else can we say about him?" and she drew large feet on him.

"His feet are big," said Dale.

"That's fine, and we can put another idea with that line," said Miss Sheckells.

"Well, his hands are wide," said Marcia.

"Very good," said Miss Sheckells and she read the poem again. "Perhaps we can add one more line that rhymes with 'wide'—any ideas? Why is he sad?"

Judy volunteered the answer, "His nose pulls off. I know. I tried."

As in other situations, the greatest value from this kind of chalk talk comes when the teacher asks if someone would like to put on blobs of color while the class makes up a poem to go with it.

Wayne, in the third grade, used purple to make this design:

Figure 40 *Wayne's design.*

Some child said, "A light bulb," so while Wayne proceeded to make a light bulb from his color, the children made up this rhyme.

There once was a purple light
It was a lovely sight
For it shone a funny bright
To make a purple night.

There are other types of chalk talks. Some are excellent motivation and inspiration for children who will later write one for the class and demonstrate it. Following is an old folk tale handed down from generation to generation, one my mother used to tell me when I was a little boy.

The Old Man's Adventure

There once was an old man who lived in a funny old house. It looked like Figure 41.

Figure 41 *A chalk talk.*

One day his children, who were grown up, went away to seek their fortunes, so the old man decided to make two houses out of his house. He built walls down through the middle, cut the front door in half, put on another chimney, and rented it to a young couple. Like Figure 42.

Figure 42

Because he had almost no room left for his furniture, he built a little shed in the back yard, away from the house, like Figure 43.

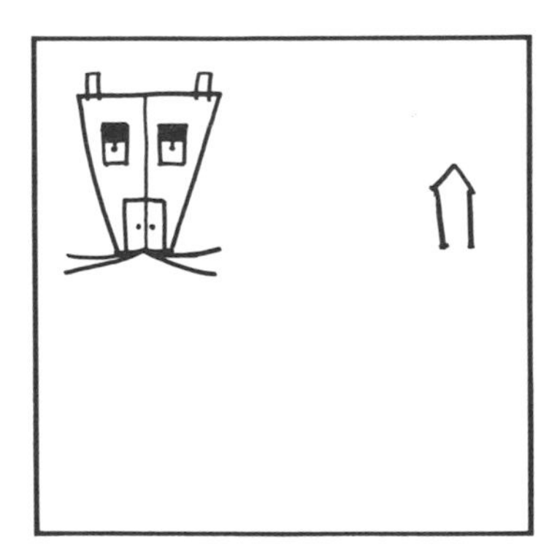

Figure 43

Then, because he was lonesome, he bought a few chickens to take care of and he kept them out in the shed.

One night the old man heard a strange noise out in the shed. He grabbed his gun and ran from the house into the yard. Now it happened to be a very black night and he could not find his way so he roamed about the yard, like Figure 44.

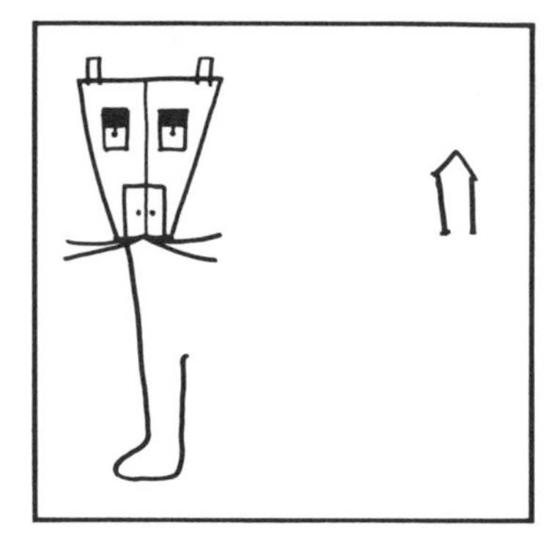

Figure 44

Finally, he realized the noises were gone so he went back into the house and went to sleep. The next morning he went out into the shed, and, sure enough! Something had run off with one of his chickens.

The little old man was very angry so the next night he put his gun right by the side of his bed and waited. Before long, he heard it again—something was making noises in his shed.

The old man grabbed his gun and dashed out of the house. It was a dark, dark night again and he soon lost his way. He ran around the yard just as he had done the night before. He fell down twice, like this (teacher retraces pattern from door to where she left off), and continued on to fall down again, like Figures 45 and 46.

Figure 45

Figure 46

And again, like Figure 47.

Figure 47

Finally, he did find the shed. Inside the shed he lighted a lantern—something was gone. Something had carried off another of his chickens.

This made the old man very angry. "I will fix whatever-it-is," he said. "I will fix him good." So, the next morning he awoke early. He went out to his shed and he fastened an electric light on the top of it, like Figure 48.

Figure 48

He put the button right next to his bed—very near his gun. When night came, he lay down and went to sleep.

Soon he was awakened by the noise in the shed. But this time he was prepared! He grabbed his gun, snapped on the light, bolted out the door, and headed straight for the light on the shed, like Figure 49.

Figure 49

And this is what he found stealing his chickens – this wildcat!

After hearing this story, George, a sixth grade boy, created his own chalk talk.

George's Story

One Easter time my brother and I asked my mother if we could have a real, live Easter rabbit.

"No," said my mother, "Every year your Dad and I have bought you something new for Easter. This year I am going to get something new. I am going to get a new Easter hat. There will be no money left for a rabbit!"

My brother and I pleaded and pleaded with my mother but she said, "No." She wanted her new Easter hat.

So one day just before Easter, my mother took the car and drove into town to get her new Easter hat. She saw one with big flowers and feathers and she liked it very much so she bought it. The clerk put it in a big hatbox like Figure 50.

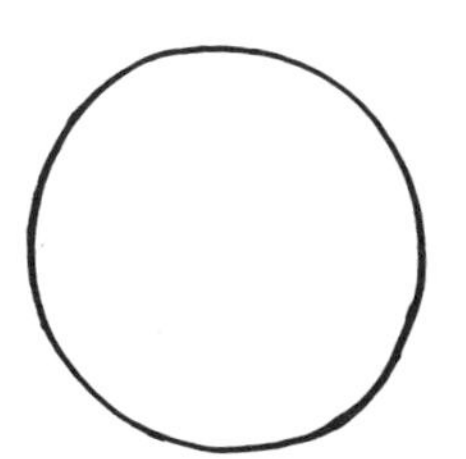

Figure 50 *George's chalk talk.*

. . . and Mother started back home.

Now the road was bumpy and the clerk hadn't fastened the hat box very well so it kept bouncing around on the seat of the car. Finally Mother hit a bump and the hat bounced right off on the floor. Mother reached for it with one hand and pulled it back on the seat, but the top had come off and the two feathers popped out, like Figure 51.

Figure 51

Before long Mother hit another bump and the box jumped off the seat. The cover fell off the hatbox again. Mother pulled it back on the seat, but this time one of the big flowers popped out of the box like Figure 52.

Figure 52

In a little while the same thing happened once more, and this time a little flower would NOT go back into the box like Figure 53.

Figure 53

By this time, Mother was home. As she pulled into the driveway, we ran to meet her. "Did you get your hat?" we called to her.

"Come and see," she said.

We looked in the car. She took off the cover of the hatbox and this was in it (Figure 54)

Figure 54

—our bunny. She hadn't bought the hat at all. Mothers are like that! (Figure 55.)

Figure 55

Figure 56 *Here are two pictures. Put them with the two pictures in Figure 57 and create a story about the characters. Half the class should make the story follow the sequence presented here.*

Figure 57 *The other half of the class may mix the pictures in any sequence they prefer.*

Sound Stories

Chapter 5 is introduced with a sound story. There are other types of sound stories which can be used for good listening devices and for developing a good oral vocabulary. Many commercial stories lend themselves to becoming good sound stories, such as "Gerald McBoing Boing," "The Tiger Hunt," and "The Sound Book" (Margaret Wise Brown).

Often the teacher can set up a beginning situation to create a sound story, and the children can take it from there. Putting such stories on tape contributes to their enjoyment, because children hear the total effect better in the playback than they do while making up the story.

A sound story must be one that can have sounds added to it in much the same way a "round-robin" story has words added to it. Think of noisy situations to get your clue: a visit to a factory, the circus, the carnival, a state or county fair, a living room with TV set, radio, hi-fi set, and people talking, or a busy store. Start a plot by having a main character enter this situation, and add to the plot by adding sounds as the plot develops. Then the children in the room add the noises until the whole story reaches a climax.

Reading charts in the lower grades can also provide some interesting material for creative oral work.

If the teacher keeps an eye on the charts that children construct, she will often find one that lends itself well to choral speaking. Or she will find many charts which lend themselves to making a "sound" story.

Miss Kennedy's first grade had visited a farm. From this experience she had built her first reading experience chart. This was how it went:

The Farm
We went to the farm
We saw cows
We saw ducks
We saw pigs
We saw horses
We had fun.

Figure 58 *Miss Kennedy's reading chart.*

On the day after the children had written the chart, Miss Kennedy said, "Boys and girls, after we read about our trip to the farm today, I would like to make a new story from it." Some of the children read the story, and then Miss Kennedy showed the children a card bearing the word "heard."

"This is a new word," she said. "It says heard. If we can learn this one new word, we can write a whole new story." The children then found the word in various places around the room where Miss Kennedy had concealed it. Miss Kennedy had also put the sentences of the story on strips of tag board so the children could reconstruct the story in the pocket chart.

After the story was reconstructed in the pocket chart, Miss Kennedy said, "Now, let's see if we can change our story by changing one word." She then put the word "heard" over the word "saw" on each line of the chart where it appeared. The children then read the story. Miss Kennedy then said, "Now let's make our sound story. What did we hear the cows say?" The children answered "Moo-moo." Miss Kennedy completed the story this way (Figure 59):

The Farm

We went to the farm.

We heard cows
They said,"Moo-Moo."

We heard ducks
They said,"Quack-Quack."

We heard pigs
They said,"Oink-Oink."

We heard horses
They said,"Neigh-Neigh."

We had fun.

Figure 59 *The sound story.*

Lap Stories

"Lap stories" are fun for all age levels. Instead of telling a story some day, the teacher sits down in the middle of a group where all can see and holds a simple piece of wall board on her lap. With a few props, she tells or retells a story by acting it out on her lap board. The one way a lap story differs from any other storytelling is that the teacher gets the children involved in telling it. Here is a description of how Miss Issacs, a first grade teacher, used a lap story.

Miss Issacs was retelling the story of the "Three Billy Goats Gruff." She used the following props:

some blue construction paper
some green construction paper
some brown construction paper
a small jewelry box which had contained a bracelet
four balls of soft clay

This is how the story developed:

"Today I thought it would be fun to let you help me tell one of our favorite stories a new way. We haven't heard 'The Billy Goats Gruff' in a long time, so I thought we might enjoy that one again. Billy, Marjery, and Peter, you take the ball of clay and each make me a billy goat. Peter has the small ball of clay, so his will be the little billy goat. Marjery has the middle-sized ball of clay, so hers will be the middle-sized billy goat. And Billy's will be the big billy goat. Henry, you take this ball of clay and make me a funny old troll.

"Now, while these people are making our characters for us, will the rest of you look at my lap and we'll make the scene. What will we need in our scene?"

"The river," said Mickey.

"All right," said Miss Issacs. "You tear this piece of blue paper so it will go across this board to make a river. Now, what else will we need?"

"A green field," said Joe.

"Well, then, you tear this piece of green paper to make a nice green field on this side of the river. Now what kind of a field is on the other side of the river?"

"One where the grass is nearly gone," said Susan.

"Susan, you put this brownish-colored paper on the other side of the river to show the worn-out field. Now, there is something else we need."

"The bridge!"

"Yes, and I wondered if this little box might not make a good bridge."

The children agreed it would as the teacher put the box in place.

"So, our scene is ready," said Miss Issacs. "How are we coming with the goats and the troll? Oh, those are fine; I guess now we are ready for our story. Let's put the troll under the bridge, Henry. Peter, Marjery, and Bill, you put the three billy goats in the old worn-out field, and I guess we're ready. Once there were three billy goats . . ."

And Miss Issacs began the story, allowing the children to tell as much as possible while she manipulated the figures on her lap.

Miss Issacs' ultimate goal was, of course, to encourage the children to tell lap stories of their own and prepare the props for them.

Lap stories can vary from the simple to the complex. Nursery school and kindergarten teachers can begin with the simplest forms—a candle in a candle holder and a doll or cardboard image of Jack, for "Jack Be Nimble." Almost all the nursery rhymes lend themselves to lap stories; then there are "The Gingerbread Boy," "The Three Pigs," "The Three Bears," "The Three Little Kittens," and "Henny Penny."

In the third and fourth grades, children enjoy doing "Hansel and Gretel," "Snow White and the Seven Dwarfs," "Peter and the Wolf," "Jack and the Beanstalk," and "Rapunzel."

Older children can do more elaborate lap stories, working in committees with each child doing a different scene. Some stories which lend themselves well to lap stories on this level are:

Robinson Crusoe
"The King's Stilts"
"Homer Price"
Paul Bunyan stories
Scenes from *Robin Hood*
Scenes from *Treasure Island*
Scenes from *Little Women*
"The Golden Goose"
"The Wind in the Willows"
"The Tar Baby"
"The Pied Piper of Hamelin"

Lap stories provide an excellent device for making book reports.

Figure 60 *Flannel boards can be used very creatively. This one was especially effective in motivating several classes to enjoy "The Sugar Plum Tree" because it glowed in the dark when a blue light was turned on it.*

Flannel Boards

Telling stories by use of a flannel board is an excellent way for children to share words they know and to add new ones to their vocabularies. Commercial cutouts can be used for flannel board stories. Pictures from any old worn-out books provide a wealth of material if they are cut out and a small piece of flannel is pasted on the back so they will stick to the board. A new dimension in creativeness is developed, however, when children design and paint their own figures and symbols for use on the flannel board.

Flannel boards serve many purposes besides the telling of stories. Because children must *tell* about the materials they are putting on the flannel board, vocabulary may be developed in all subject areas.

Here are a few creative ways in which teachers have used the flannel board to develop oral vocabulary:

Literature: Miss Carmen asked her fourth grade children to give a third dimension to their flannel board stories by making the figures and objects from construction paper and designing them so they moved or opened. In presenting the "gingerbread boy," the children found that by bending one leg of the figures, they could give them the appearance of running. They made the barn door open; the oven door opened so the little gingerbread man could be shut in; the mowers' pitchforks were separate from the mowers so they could throw them down; and a big gingerbread boy folded his arms and legs, and finally his head disappeared.

As part of a Christmas program, Mr. Fuller's fifth grade presented "The Small One" by Charles Taswell in the following manner: The children read the story and listed the eight major scenes on the chalkboard. They then signed up for the scene on which they preferred to work. Working in committees, they first made large flannel boards of the same size by taping outing flannel over cardboard cut from towel cartons. Then each group made characters, scenes, and props to tell about its part of the story. The night of the program, the curtain opened to reveal the eight blank flannel boards resting on easels across the stage. Christmas music was playing softly in the background. A spotlight picked up a narrator standing on the side of the stage. The narrator began to tell the story and the spotlight moved to the first flannel board. Two children came forward from the back of the stage and proceeded to build their scene as the narrator told the story. Then the spotlight shifted to the second scene and down the line until, at the end of the story, the footlights were brought up, revealing a mural across the stage of the entire story. The children, grouped behind the pictures, sang a Christmas carol to end their portion of the program.

Original Flannel Board Stories: After the teacher has utilized the flannel board effectively with the children, creativity is evidenced in using it as a motivator for their own creative work. The ultimate goal is to have children create their own stories and use their own ideas to present them.

Miss Hawkins went through some magazines and tore out pictures of a variety of things children like, ranging from food to toys. She asked the children to cut them out in their spare time and to paste pieces of flannel on them. Then Miss Hawkins found a figure of a boy to use as the central figure of her story and backed it with flannel too.

One day she said, "We have been using our flannel board to tell many stories and to make pictures of the stories we have read. Today let us see if we can make a flannel board story of our own. Will each of you select a picture from this box of pictures you have all helped to cut out and we will try to make a story out of it? Are we ready?"

"Once upon a time there was a little boy named Tommy, and here he is," Miss Hawkins said. She put the cutout of Tommy on the flannel board.

"One day Tommy brought a note to school to his teacher. It said, 'Dear Miss Hawkins. May Tommy be excused from taking the bus tonight? Instead, I shall meet him at the Sears Roebuck parking lot at 5:00. Today is Tommy's birthday and he has some money to spend. I would appreciate it very much if you would allow Tommy to do this. Cordially, Mrs. Smith.'"

"Well, Tommy was very proud that day. When all the children lined up to get the bus, Tommy strolled off down the street toward the stores to spend the twenty-five cents his father had given him. The first store he came to was the dairy store. Tommy pressed his face against the window. What do you think he saw? Does anyone have a picture of anything Tommy saw when he looked in the dairy window?"

"I do," said Kevin.

"So do I," said Mary Ann.

"Me, too," said Douglas.

"Well, good," went on Miss Hawkins. "Put them on the flannel board so we can see what they are."

Kevin put a bottle of milk on the flannel board; Mary Ann put a package of cheese on the flannel board. Douglas had a luscious-looking dish of ice cream.

"Well," Miss Hawkins went on, "Tommy was awfully hungry, because almost every afternoon right after school his mother gave him milk and cookies or a sandwich. But even though these things looked good to him, he didn't spend his quarter on any of them. Can anyone guess why?"

The children thought a minute and then Alvin volunteered, "Because it would spoil his birthday supper."

"That's a good reason," said Miss Hawkins. "So," she went on, "Tommy went on to the next store and it was the florist shop. Does anyone have any pictures of anything Tommy saw in the window of the florist shop?"

Jimmy offered a rose and Thelma had a vase.

"These were very pretty," said Miss Hawkins, "and Tommy thought how nice it would be to take one of them home to his mother, but he decided against it. Can you guess why?"

"Well," said Dora, "it was summer and his mother had lots of flowers in her yard. She had lots of vases too."

"Good reasons," said Miss Hawkins, "so Tommy went on. Next he came to the Ben Franklin Five-and-Ten-Cent Store. Does anyone have any pictures of things he saw in the window there?" . . . and so on from store to store until all the children had placed their objects on the flannel board. Each time Miss Hawkins called for objects as Tommy went from store window to store window, she talked less as the children caught the idea of the story and talked more. After the last child had placed his object on the flannel board, Miss Hawkins said, "Poor Tommy. It is almost five o'clock and he hasn't spent his twenty-five cents yet. Let's see if we can remember the whole story so far."

Pointing to the first object, Miss Hawkins said, "The first store Tommy came to was ______"

"The dairy," said the children.

"And in the window he saw ______"

"Milk and cheese and ice cream," said the children.

"But he didn't buy them because ______"

"It would spoil his supper," finished the children.

"So he went on to ______"

"The florist."

"Where he saw ______"

"A rose and a vase."

"Which he didn't buy because ______"

"His mother already had some."

"So ______"

"He went on to the Ben Franklin Five-and-Ten and he saw a toy doll, a little truck, a game, a book, and some crayons which he thought he might buy for his little brother and sister, but he didn't, because the money was for *him* for *his* birthday. So he went on to Tony's fruit market and he looked at the oranges, the apples, and the plums, but he didn't buy any, because he wanted something different for his birthday. Then he went on to Ellie's Pastry Shop. In the window he saw cakes and candy. He didn't buy any, because he was going to have a birthday cake at home. The next store he came to was the drug store, and he saw pills and medicine, but he didn't buy them because he wasn't sick. In the window were comic books, a pen, a notebook, a game, and a baseball, all marked 25 cents and on sale, but he didn't buy them, because he already had most of them as presents for his birthday."

"Poor Tommy," Miss Hawkins again took up the story, "here it was almost five o'clock and he hadn't spent his birthday money. Well, right at this time he was at Sears Roebuck where he was to meet his mother. He noticed by the clock that he had only a few minutes left. He noticed, too, that Sears Roebuck was all decorated with bright-colored flags waving in the breeze. Big signs all over said, 'Carnival Days at Sears—Big Sales!' Just as Tommy was about to look away, he heard a strange and beautiful noise."

At this point Miss Hawkins started a music box which she had concealed in a bag behind her chair.

"What do you think it was? Well, Tommy was all excited. He followed the music. Around the corner of the store he went and into the parking lot. Then he stood still and stared. There before him on the parking lot were a Merry-Go-Round, a Ferris Wheel, and a Tumble Bug. And, what was even more wonderful, there was a big sign which said, 'Carnival Days at Sears—Rides for the Kiddies—3 Rides for 25 cents.' Now, how do you think Tommy spent his quarter?"

Taping these stories as they are told provides children with a good listening situation.

Sequence stories can be built on any common everyday incident. Children can create stories and share words when stimulated by the simplest idea.

Dramatizations

Dramatics provide one of the most natural ways for children to use their voices in dialogue. Much improvisation can be encouraged in speaking aloud in the various forms of dramatization such as role playing, sociodrama, role reversal, and free dramatics. Children naturally imitate and absorb the words of their elders and peers in free play and dramatic play situations.

New words may be introduced through situations set up by the teacher. Some of the obvious means of utilizing oral vocabulary are:

1. Dramatization of favorite stories and poems
2. Spontaneous imitation of a recent event, or role playing a situation of interest

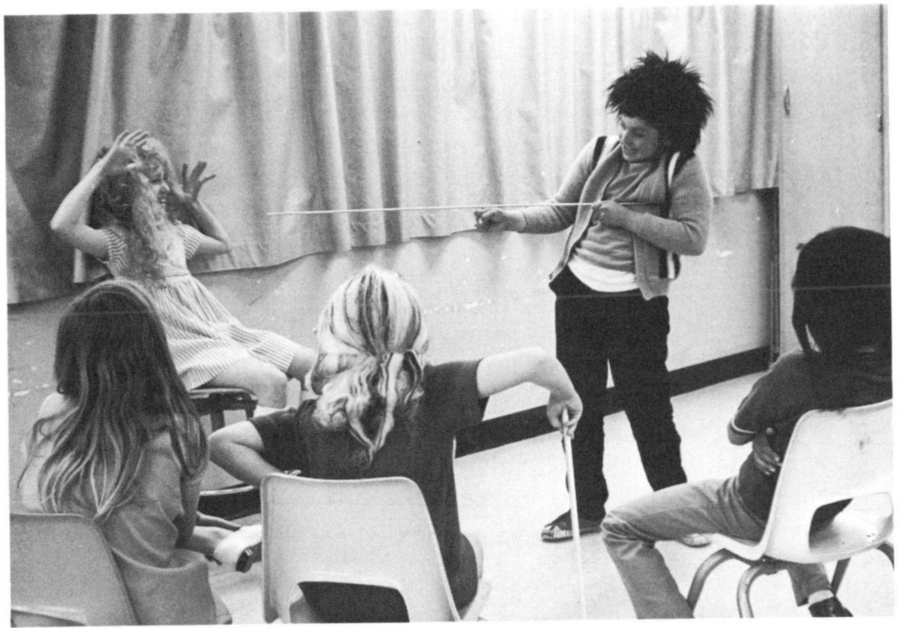

Figure 61 *Each child chose a wig from a box of wigs and then dramatized the character he became when he wore the wig.*

A challenging assignment was then presented to the children: Prepare a skit showing how all these characters meet in a logical situation. In this scene a motley audience consisting of an old man, and old lady, and their daughter are watching an actress and a hippie emote in a play.

3. Dramatizing problem stories
4. Writing and producing scripts
5. Acting out telephone conversations, social courtesies, scenes, etc.

When the main purpose of a dramatization is to develop meaningful oral vocabulary and clear speaking quality, a polished, finished product is of little consequence unless the dramatization is to be used as a production for the public. Then the situation becomes a public relations problem, and a new dimension is added. A certain amount of "polishing" is needed.

Following are a few ways I have used forms of dramatization with children to help develop oral expression.

Role Playing and Role Reversal: A careful observer of children at play will notice that, after playing through a situation once, they replay it with a shifting of roles. Thus, a child who was mother in a dramatic play often becomes the father, or the baby, or the postman.

Through their play, children learn what it is like to be and speak like a postman, a milkman, a dog—or what it is like to be dead. They are not content to merely see and hear the various roles of life being enacted around them, they must *feel* what it is like to be a mother, a father, a postman, a dog, or dead! Through mimicking words and actions as they see them, they come to feel like the dog who cannot talk. They feel how it is black and quiet when one is dead. They feel how tired the milkman may become, jogging from place to place in a monotonous routine. They also *feel* how mother becomes angry at children who do not do as they are asked. They *feel* how it is to be nasty, to be sympathetic, to be loving, to be hated. And through these imitations and these feelings, they learn a great deal about human nature and the reasons behind action, and how to express their feelings in spoken symbols.

It is this ability of children to *feel* that makes it possible for them to understand. Through empathy, they come to recognize the other fellow's viewpoint. This is a creative approach to the understanding of problems which breaks down emotional barriers and develops emotional understanding. Helping them to verbalize their feelings is important.

Figure 62 *Harold and Jim have donned masks to role-play the meeting of two parents who try to solve a school integration problem.*

Role playing is a conscientious attempt on the part of the teacher to use these natural tendencies of empathy for constructing natural group relations. In the first grade, two children have a quarrel over the possession of a ball. Instead of moralizing the conflict, the teacher may ask each child to become the other one, and then to give reasons why he should claim ownership. Thus, each child is pressed into feeling and acting like his opponent and is therefore more understanding. In a succeeding verbalization of their feelings, the children, more understanding at this point, are often able to arrive at their own solutions and work out a way to handle the situation. The teacher has encouraged understanding and left the solution up to the creativeness or inventiveness of the individuals concerned. She is leading them to an independent solution of their problems and to emotional maturity.

A child in the fourth grade feels he has been treated unfairly at home and comes to school with a chip on his shoulder. He is ugly and cross. Finally, when confronted with the need to account for his actions, he spews forth his ill feelings concerning his father, who was overdemanding of him before school time. By being encouraged to play the role of the father while another child plays *his* role, he may be able to more readily understand his father's actions—to identify the true reasons behind them. He learns through empathy plus analytical discussion that what appears to be annoyance on the father's part may actually be motivated by concern and love. Any social eruption taking place within the classroom which is a group problem can be dramatized in order to give the class a firsthand experience with the situation. Once the group sees the problem presented by the dramatization, a discussion on the facts of the situation (which are clearly known) can take place.

Mr. Anderson, a fourth grade teacher, found two boys from his classroom running in the hall, chasing another boy for a hat. Running in the hall was against school rules. Mr. Anderson brought the boys into the classroom to talk over the problem. Each seemed to feel that the other was to blame for the situation. Mr. Anderson asked them if they felt they could remember enough of what had happened to dramatize it before the class. The boys were willing to do this.

After they had dramatized the situation that brought on the hat snatching, Mr. Anderson stopped the dramatization at the point at which he had stopped the running in the hall, and asked, "Now how do you boys feel? Now that you have acted out the situation, do you see it any differently?" Each boy still felt the other was to blame, so Mr. Anderson turned to the class to ask for opinions.

Mr. Anderson did not express his opinions to the class. He did not moralize, nor did he make the children feel guilty. He simply approached the situation as a social problem for which his fourth grade class had a responsibility. And the children took the responsibility. At the end of the discussion, they had thought of five ways the boys could solve the problem.

The Structured Dramatization: The structured dramatization differs from role playing in that it has been written beforehand. Children memorize the lines or simply read the lines and "walk out" the play.

These dramatizations are situations dealing with social problems. They are useful in building values, appreciations, and understandings. Children's plays that pose a social problem can often be used. Many upper grade children can be encouraged to write their own.

Generally, a teacher uses a structured drama in the classroom when she is having problems in social behavior that are founded on a lack of a sense of values or appreciations. She finds (or writes) a play built around a theme that shows a lack of a sense of the same values or appreciations. In a reading class or social studies class, children read the parts, and a discussion follows. Again, it is not the purpose of the teacher to moralize, but to provide an open-ended experience. The children discuss among themselves ways in which such a situation might be handled, and thereby determine their values or help develop values. Dialogue in this situation is purposeful, and words of emotion can often be learned in meaningful context.

Free Dramatization: Actual historical scenes or events in other countries can be dramatized to help children feel the event more fully. Often the entire class can take part in such dramatizations with no audience to watch, because the emphasis is on participation and involvement to develop creativity and empathy. One group dramatized a Mexican Christmas, a pinata party, and a Mexican fiesta. Every child role-played his part in keeping with the situation. Another group dramatized a medieval fair. Other events that lend themselves to total-group dramatization are: a medieval tournament, a visit to a Spanish market place, the election of a president, a day in Plymouth, a trip to New York, an evening around a campfire, the meeting of an Indian council, a visit to a carnival, a day at Fort Niagara, etc.

Games: Some games encourage dramatizations, such as *Who Am I?* One child sits before the group and tells about himself. Once in a while he stops to act out certain parts of his life. The rest of the class guesses who he is. In Mr. Jones's class, one boy acted as Ben Franklin and told about his boyhood. He dramatized his experimentation with the kite to discover electricity and his invention of the Franklin stove. This particular dramatization was so well done that Mr. Jones used it as a means of introducing "Ben and Me" to the class.

Another technique for developing individual dramatic interpretation is the *You Are There* game. Children dramatize an historical event and the rest of the class tell what it is. The Boston Tea Party, the assassination of Lincoln, the launching of a space ship, and innumerable other events lend themselves well to this sort of treatment.

Historical events can be dramatized in social studies to make history more realistic and to develop creativity. Many scenes lend themselves well to such dramatic interpretation: the landing of the Pilgrims, the signing of the Declaration of Independence, a meeting of the United Nations Security Council, the inauguration of the president, the daily life of a cowboy, a day in a colonial school, and many others.

A popular radio program of a few years back called "Minute Dramas" lends itself well to creative oral development. An opening scene is described, and the children make up and dramatize an ending with no preparation; they do it as they go along. Example: "You are at the airport waiting for a plane, and suddenly a strange man rushes up to you, clasps your hand, calls you by name, and says, 'I haven't seen you for years. It's just luck that I should see you now! I am in deep trouble and I need your help!'"

Various forms of dramatization lend themselves well to creative book reports.

Contrived dramatizations introduce many new words into the child's oral speech. Place five unrelated objects in a bag, such as a thumbtack, a water pistol, a hair curler, a stick of gum, and a measuring cup. The class is divided into groups of five. Each group takes a bag and must construct a story using all the five objects, which they then dramatize for the rest of the class. Children enjoy making up the bags for each other.

Most children enjoy playing fractured dramas. Instead of dramatizing stories exactly as they are written, children are encouraged to change the endings and "ham" them. Thus, in *Casey at the Bat*, Casey does *not* strike out. Comic relief is encouraged, and children have a way to expend the wisecracks which they so enjoy at this age, in a legitimate and acceptable manner. A modern parody on *Red Riding Hood* by one sixth grade had Red Riding Hood playing the part of a communist spy, and the wolf was a symbol for Russia. The entire production was hilarious and creative.

One sixth grade group performed a "fractured" interpretation of Romeo and Juliet. The entire balcony scene was played with Romeo using television commercials in wooing Juliet, such as "Thine eyes glow like coals, my love. Does thou use Maybelline? And thy lips—

truly a product of Helena Rubenstein with the smile of Gleem so easy to come by."

Children are jolted into breaking away from traditional patterns of thinking in developing new ideas or inventing new endings. The imaginative aspects of their thinking are brought into play. Creative ideation through the use of modification, minification, elaboration, substitution, and other techniques mentioned in Chapter 3 is brought into play.

It is important to realize that taking such liberties with established pieces of literature should not destroy the literature itself. It can add meaning and beauty to it if the children are able to catch the feeling of the author's writing, or show his skill by the use of contrasts.

The ability to form analogies is a part of creative thinking. The constant use of symbolism in the incident where Red Riding Hood was a Russian spy was a rich experience in creative thinking for the children. Empathy was developed, analogies were created, subtleties were imagined, and symbolism took on real meaning. Each of these skills is a strong force in developing creative thinking.

Tin can telephones are easy to make and fun to use, especially if one child can go out of the room with his "telephone" and talk to another within the room.

In developing oral vocabulary, the teacher will do well to remember, "All the world's a stage!"

Puppets

There are many kinds of puppets and many ways in which they can be used to develop good speaking habits and good vocabulary. Figure 63 shows some ideas for using them in the classroom.

Fist puppets can be made quickly. With the children crouched behind a table, they can hold the fist puppets in view and have them carry on conversations or create jingles to recite to the class.

Paper bag puppets can be made quickly and used for rhythms, for dramatizing stories, or for solving problem stories. (See Figure 64.)

Stick puppets also serve to help children create ways to express themselves. (See page 144.)

A Kleenex box or small shoe box makes a small theater for two children to present shows to each other or to small groups (Figure 65). The tips of fingers can have faces put on them with colored chalk, colored pencil, paint, or make-up to represent puppets.

Finger puppets can also be made with the fingers used as the legs, thus providing many opportunities for desk-top dramatizations (Figure 66).

Figure 63 *Using puppets to develop oral expression.*

Figure 64 *Paper bag puppets.*

Figure 65 *A small box makes a mini-theater.*

Figure 66 *A finger puppet.*

Papier-mâché puppets provide excellent opportunities for all sorts of dramatizations. Children may be given boxes of junk or bags of materials which may be useful in making puppets, and encouraged to make the puppet using a variety of these materials (Figure 67).

Teaching children to make puppets will help them in perfecting skills. The creative puppet will be the one the child invents to make a character to help him solve a life problem with which he is closely identified.

A puppet play may be used as a projective technique to present a current classroom problem to a group. Puppets are sometimes more appropriate for telling stories than for an actual dramatization. They are a superb device for tapping a child's creativity. Not only do they provide an opportunity for purposeful vocabulary development, but they also afford one of the best opportunities possible for developing voice control, the power of projection, and clear speech.

Figure 67 *Papier mâché puppets.*

Finger Plays

In the primary grades particularly, finger plays provide an excellent opportunity for children to use words orally. Certain work with finger plays can be very creative, especially when the teachers and children write their own.

A sample finger play is included here to illustrate how teachers and children may communicate together when they repeat the poems and perform the action of finger plays.

Five little snowmen happy and gay	All fingers up.
The first one said, "What a beautiful day!"	Thumb rigid while others slouch.
The second one said, "We'll never have tears."	First finger rigid while others slouch.
The third one said, "We'll stay here for years."	Third finger up.
The fourth one said "What will happen in May?"	Fourth finger up.
The fifth one said, "We will all melt away!"	Fifth finger up. Then all curl slowly into a fist.

Other popular finger plays are:

Miss Polly

Miss Polly had a dolly who was sick, sick, sick.
(arms rock dolly)
So she telephoned the doctor to come quick, quick, quick.
(hand to ear and mouth)
The doctor came with his bag and his hat
(hand on head—other hand swings at side)
And he rapped at the door with a tap, tap, tap.
(rap in the air)
He looked at the dolly and he shook his head
(shake head)
And he said, "Miss Polly, put her straight to bed!"
(shake index finger)
And he wrote on his paper for some pills, pills, pills.
(write on hand)
"I'll be back in the morning with my bill, bill, bill."
(hand on head—swing other at side)

Christmas Is Coming

Here is Santa's workshop (hands form pyramid)
Here is Santa Claus (thumb)
Here are Santa's little elves (fingers)
Putting toys upon the shelves.
Back and forth they scamper
Busy as can be (run back and forth)
Now they help to chop and trim
Santa's Christmas tree (chop and trim)
On Christmas Eve when I'm asleep (rest head on hands)
Down the chimney he will creep (fingers run down left arm)
And if I'm good as I should be (palms together)
Perhaps he'll leave some toys for me.

Stretch

I stretch and stretch my arms out wide (stretch)
As if to make them longer (stretch more)
I stretch and stretch and stretch (stretch even more)
For that will make me stronger.

I stretch and stretch my arms up high (arms above head)
As high as they will go (raise arms higher)
I stretch and stretch and stretch
For that will make me grow. (stretch even more)

Action Poem

Stretch up high
Stretch down low
Raise your arms
And away we go!

Make a circle in the air
Sweep your arm around
Now the other—do the same
And jump up off the ground.

We like to bend
We like to stretch
We make our muscles strong
Bend, stretch, bend, stretch
All the day long.

First I bend my knees
Then I stand up tall
Down, up, down, up
Like a rubber ball,
First I'm short
Then I'm tall.

The most effective and creative finger plays are those created by the teacher and/or the children, such as the following one composed after a class trip to the circus.

We went to the circus (hands with fingers touching like a tent)
We saw a clown (hands to face—one on each side of mouth
pulling mouth into a wide smile)
He juggled eggs (hands in juggling motion)
And jumped around (forefinger and one next to it make jumping
motions on desk top)
We saw big elephants (hands become waving, floppy ears)
And horses too (two fingers prance across desk top)
A cage full of monkeys (arms bent at elbows—out from body—
hands hang loose like a monkey's)
And a kangaroo, new (hands hop across desk top)
We ate cotton candy (lick fingers)
And apples on a stick (pantomime)
And had peanuts and popcorn (pantomime)
And ice cream to lick. (pantomime)

Shadow Plays

Shadow plays provide another excellent way to introduce words into the child's oral vocabulary. Here are some ways shadow plays may be used.

Hang a sheet before the room. Place a bright light behind it. Children can make simple scenery by using cardboard to create shadows, or simply by cutting newspaper and pinning it to the sheet to make shadows. Turn out the light to change the scenery. Be sure the children perform close to the sheet so that they will make clear-cut shadows.

Take a large carton such as a paper towel carton, and cut a hole in it to represent a stage. Tape a piece of sheeting or unbleached muslin over the hole. Put a bright light behind the carton (Figure 68). Using the towel carton stage, encourage children to cut out cardboard figures and tape them to long wires. Wire coat hangers, when pulled straight, are excellent for this purpose. These figures can then be pressed against the muslin to create shadows without the operator's shadow showing. The operator must sit or stand behind the light that creates the shadow.

Figures can also be cut from cardboards with a tab on the bottom so that they may be operated from beneath the carton simply by putting a slit in the back of the carton and pushing the figures up onto the screen, then moving them about by manipulating the tab.

A simple way to make scenery for this type of shadow box is to paint the scene with thick tempora paint or black flo-pen onto a heavy-grade Saran wrap. The scene can then be pressed firmly against the muslin and it will stick. When the light is turned on, the paint or flo-pen ink casts a shadow, making a fixed scene against which the movable figures can act. This technique provides an easy way to change the scenery quickly.

Figure 68 *Shadow plays.*

Ideas!

Following is a list of suggestions that set certain conditions under which children can develop some very creative ideas and words. Try them out some day when things seem to be dull!

1. Place single, unusual, or beautiful objects in separate bags. Allow the children to select a bag, take out the object, and describe it. How does it look? How does it feel? How does it make you feel?
2. Place five objects in a bag. Pass the bags out to groups. Each group will dramatize a play using all five objects.
3. Make fingerpaintings or drawings about words such as fear, love, anger, hate, condense, etc.
4. Make rhymes by bouncing a ball. Someone bounces the ball to the rhythm of the rhyme, and anyone can say the rhyming word, such as
   a. Yellow, yellow
What is yellow?
(one child said a fellow!)
   b. Big, big
What is big?
("a pig!")
5. Collect baby pictures from magazine advertisements and other accessible resources, and write captions under them about your classmates.
6. Make charts of words that have many meanings. Print the word at the top of the chart, and brainstorm in small pictures to put on the chart a word such as hot: *hot* dog, *hot* day, *hot* rod, *hot* water, *hot* items (stolen jewelry), *hot* seat, etc.; or fair: *fair* girl, state *fair*, a *fair* game, etc.
7. Make up a new game and explain the directions.
8. Take three unrelated words such as *astronaut*, *pineapple*, and *paperclip*, and make a story from them.
9. Have the children make a tape recording about themselves; it could serve as a nice Christmas gift for Mother or Father.
10. Collect animal pictures and write captions under them about your classmates.
11. Ask children to work in groups of two or three and present their favorite comic strip to the class some morning by cutting out the figures and dramatizing one particular incident.
12. Have children act out "jokes" this way.
13. Ask children to take turns in telling "tall tales," "whoppers," etc.
14. Children can create their own jokes and comic strips.
15. Little children can dictate stories to the teacher, who can type them with a primary typewriter or put them on chart paper. When

the teacher reads the story to the children, the stories can be illustrated as reading charts or bound to make "Big Books."

16. Place something soft, or something rough, or something sticky in a bag. Pass it around and encourage the children to put a hand in the bag and feel of it. Then have them tell about how it felt.
17. Have the children make a string painting (this is a painting made by dipping string in paint and laying it on, or folding it in paper). Have them tell what they see in the abstraction.

Summary

In the years ahead, it is likely that our children will often be called on to speak before large groups of people, either directly or by means of radio or television. During one presidential election, the candidates talked to over 60,000,000 people at one time. The ability to speak effectively before groups and audiences is a needed skill in the space age. This is a skill that needs to be developed in the elementary school. Oral communication is the most effective, the most common, and the first means of communication among men, and it is the basis for a sound program in reading, handwriting, spelling, word usage, and creative writing. To learn to speak effectively means to speak creatively, inasmuch as words are put into new patterns for expressing ideas.

Children can and will learn to speak effectively if the situations in which they learn oral vocabulary are relevant to them. A rich, full repertoire of spoken words is necessary for the development of other language skills, for children never write what they do not say, and they cannot read with comprehension words that are not used in context in their everyday speech.

To the Reader

1. Some questions for discussion:
   a. When does dramatization in the classroom cease to be a learning experience, and when does it become a public relations experience?
   b. Discuss this statement: It is possible for a teacher who does not understand the concepts of creativity to appear to be teaching creatively when actually the opposite is true?
   c. Should the program in oral expression be the same in a city ghetto

area as in a wealthy suburban area? An inner-city school? A deprived rural school? Why or why not?

d. Would you say that a creative program in oral expression cannot be a planned, structured one? Does encouraging fluent oral expression mean that chaos must result?

e. Puppetry has often been referred to as a projective technique. Would this enhance or detract from its value as a means to develop vocabulary? I once had a sixth grade boy who stuttered. He volunteered for the Announcer's role (a clown) in a puppet show the class produced. To my surprise, he did not stutter when he announced each "act" as a puppet. Why?

2. Check the principles of creative teaching as they are listed on page 64 against Miss Jennings' lesson on Sally Flack, and decide to what degree you feel Miss Jennings was a creative teacher.

   Also check out Mr. Ames's lessons on page 156 and Miss Fry's, page 171.

3. Try to write some haiku and cinquain poetry of your own—read it to your class (or to a group of children) and note their reactions.

4. Check your own Show-and-Tell period, and note whether it is still "teaching" new vocabulary, or whether it has fallen into a traditional rut and accomplishes little or nothing. How can you use some of the ideas in this chapter to revitalize it?

   If you are a student, see if you can arrange to visit a neighborhood primary school and observe the Show and Tell as objectively as possible for the reasons mentioned above. How would you change it?

5. What are the basic objectives, would you say, of Miss Jennings' planned experience of "Sally Flack and the Rabbit"? (pages 143–149.)

6. If you are a teacher, try to keep a running account for one day of the amount of time you allow your children to speak. Note the number of times they are asked to put something in writing instead of speaking. If you are a student, observe the same situation in your college classrooms. How does it compare with your dorms or living quarters? In which instance does communication flow most easily?

Selected Bibliography

BAMMAN, HENRY J., MILDRED A. DAWSON, AND ROBERT J. WHITEHEAD. *Oral Interpretation of Children's Literature*. Dubuque, Iowa: William C. Brown Company, 1964.

BATCHELDER, MARJORIE H., AND VIRGINIA COMER. *Puppets and Plays: A Creative Approach*. New York: Harper and Row, 1956.

BYRNE, MARGARET. *The Child Speaks.* New York: Harper and Row, 1965.

BURGER, ISABEL B. *Creative Play Acting: Learning Through Drama.* New York: The Ronald Press, 1966.

CALDER, CLARENCE R., JR., AND ELEANOR M. ANTAN. *Techniques and Activities to Stimulate Verbal Learning.* New York: The Macmillan Company, 1970.

CARLSON, BERNICE W. *Act It Out.* New York: Abingdon Press, 1965.

CHAMBERS, DEWEY W. *Literature For Children: Storytelling and Creative Drama.* Dubuque, Iowa: William C. Brown Company, 1970.

CROSSCUT, RICHARD. *Children and Dramatics.* New York: Charles Scribners' Sons, 1966.

CULLUM, ALBERT. *Shake Hands with Shakespeare.* New York: Citation Press, 1967.

GRAYSON, MARION. *Let's Do Fingerplays.* Washington, D.C.: David McKay, 1962.

GREENE, HARRY, AND WALTER T. PETTY. *Developing Language Skills in the Elementary Schools,* 4th ed. Boston: Allyn and Bacon, 1971, 185–233.

GROFF, PATRIK. *What's New in Language Arts: Oral Language.* Washington, D.C.: American Association of Elementary-Kindergarten-Nursery Educators, N.E.A. Center, 1970.

KOSKEY, THOMAS. *Baited Bulletin Boards: A Handbook for Teachers.* San Francisco, California: Fearon Publishers, 1954.

LEWIS, M. M. *How Children Learn to Speak.* New York: Basic Books, 1957.

MCCASLIN, NELLIE. *Creative Dramatics in the Classroom.* New York: David McKay Company, Inc., 1968.

PETTY, WALTER T. (ed.). *Research in Oral Language.* Champaign, Illinois: National Council of Teachers of English, 1967.

MURRAY, RUTH LOVELL. *Dance in Elementary Education.* New York: Harper and Row, 1963.

PIERSON, HOWARD, "Pupils, Teachers and Creative Dramatics," in James C. MacCampbell (ed.). *Readings in the Language Arts in the Elementary School.* Boston: D. C. Heath and Company, 1964, 151–160.

PRONOVOST, WILBERT. *The Teaching of Speaking and Listening in the Elementary School.* New York: Longmans Green, 1959.

RASMUSSEN, CARIE. *Speech Methods in the Elementary School.* New York: Ronald Press, 1962.

SHANE, HAROLD G., MARY E. REDDIN, AND MARGARET G. GILLESPIE. *Be-*

ginning Language Arts Instruction with Children, Chapter XI. Columbus, Ohio: Charles E. Merrill, 1961.

SHAFTEL, FANNIE R., AND GEORGE SHAFTEL. *Role-Playing for Social Values*. Englewood Cliffs, New Jersey: Prentice-Hall, Inc., 1967.

SIKS, GERALDINE B. *Children's Literature for Dramatization*. New York: Harper and Row, 1964.

______. *Creative Dramatics: An Art for Children*. New York: Harper and Row, 1958.

SMITH, BROOKS E., KENNETH S. GOODMAN, AND ROBERT MEREDITH. *Language and Thinking in the Elementary School*, Chapter IV: "Language in Communication." Boston: Allyn and Bacon, 1971, 189–246.

SMITH, JAMES A. *Creative Teaching of the Language Arts in the Elementary School*, Chapter V. Boston: Allyn and Bacon, 1969, 97–156.

WILLIAMS, HELEN V. *Puppets Go to School*. Philadelphia: Winston Company, 1955.

7

Adventures in Reading

Will the Bluebirds Please Come Forward?

Bobby was a typical ten year old. He read in the Bluebird group. I asked him to read for me from a social studies text to check out his comprehension abilities. He read normally aloud—stumbling over a few new words but reading on with ease and confidence.

Then I asked him to return to the opening sentence of the selection. It read as follows:

"Northern Mexico is a hot, arid region."

"Bobby," I said, "I'd like to talk to you about that one sentence. Now what does the word *northern* mean to you?"

Bobby lives in a little town called Mexico in New York State. It is located on Lake Ontario. To the east is Oswego; to the west is Rome and south is Syracuse. The lake is north and across the lake is Canada. People in Oswego and Mexico get their bearings from the lake. One never drives very far north or he falls in the lake. Children, when lost, locate the lake so they can find their way home, so it was not unusual that Bobby said, "There," and pointed across the lake—"Canada," he added.

"I see," I said, "and what does this word mean to you?" I pointed to the word Mexico.

"That's where I live," he responded promptly.

"So it is. Have you ever heard of another place by that name?"

"Yes," he said. "There's a country somewhere by that name. I heard about it and once in awhile I see pictures of it on television."

"Tell me some of the things you know about that Mexico," I encouraged.

"Well, it's hot there. People wear big hats to keep the sun off, I guess. They wear blankets some of the time and I should think they would be very hot. They have cute little donkeys to haul their stuff around. One thing that's funny is that they take naps every afternoon. They have big celebrations, too, and almost everybody goes to a plaza to shop."

"You know a lot about that country named Mexico," I said. "Which Mexico do you think the book is talking about—that Mexico or yours?"

"That one," he said.

"Bobby, what does the word *hot* mean to you?"

He thought for a minute. "Lots of things," he finally said.

"Like what?"

"Well, last week it was 96 degrees, and that is hot."

"O.K.," I said, "hot weather—what else?"

"Well, hot dogs," he said. "I like them."

"Anything else?"

"My brother is making a *hot* rod. My mother puts *hot* sauce on my spaghetti. She cooks good *hot* cross buns."

"Wow! You do know a lot of ways to use the word *hot*. Which way do you think it is used here?"

"Weather hot," he answered promptly.

"Now," I said, "let's look at the next word. What is 'arid'?"

He hesitated a moment and then said brightly, "It's a deodorant they advertise on television."

I laughed but said, "And region?"

"Well," he said, "before my dad was sick we used to drive down to Syracuse to the *regional* market. It's a place where all the farmers bring food and things they make to sell to the grocers. We had lots of fun and I guess that's what a region is: a place where people come together to sell stuff."

Now I ask you what can this intelligent, sharp ten year old get from the sentence: *Northern Mexico is a hot, arid region?* Something like this, maybe: Across the lake in Canada is a country with a name, Mexico, like my town, and there is a hot deodorant which they advertise on television where men and women come to sell stuff.

Words, unless backed by (1) experience and (2) spoken symbols incorporated into oral usage can be no more than verbal garbage and can restrict the communication process rather than help it.

If teachers, especially in the beginning reading stages, are not clever enough to develop reading materials from the child's own spoken vocabulary until such time when he will encounter a minimum of new words at the written level in his reading, then they must be certain that the words introduced each day as a prologue to the reading lessons in current manuals are introduced meaningfully (not in memorized form but in meaning form) at the oral or spoken level as an outgrowth of classroom or out-of-class experiences.

It is the violation of this basic understanding of the reading process which results in so many reading failures and comprehension in reading problems.

It is not difficult to understand why young children, before they can really learn to read, must have a wide range of experiences to which they have attached a multitude of oral symbols. We can see, too, why the primary program in reading must be loaded with experiences to which children and teachers apply symbolic expression. Thus the children are constantly building up new words in their speaking vocabulary so that they will be able to read them.

Reading is the ability to recognize, say, and understand the printed symbols on a page. Reading is a skill or tool which helps an author communicate with the reader. Children read because they want to know what is on the page. The reading itself is not sacred. It is what the reading *tells* the child that is important. Reading is an important means of communication but it is not the only one, nor is it the best. To insure the development of a good primary reading program children must have: (1) a large background of experiences, (2) the ability to listen well, and (3) a good oral vocabulary which labels their experiences meaningfully. They must also have the required intelligence and no serious physical, social, or emotional problems.

The Nature of Reading

Reading falls into the natural sequence of language development after good listening and oral expression skills have been developed (see page 46). When a child is speaking many words and using them as an integral part of his personality, he is ready to read them. In teaching reading to young children, this is often the first place where we go wrong: we pull words from thin air and try to put them into the child. Often we make matters worse by putting these strange words into printed context outside the realm of the child's experience and expecting him to read—and he cannot.

Children can read any word they speak. One of the greatest hoaxes in all of educational pedagogy is that which says that reading vocabulary must be developed in a predetermined logical sequence. It just isn't so. Linguists tell us that when a child comes to school he has all the language equipment he needs in order to learn reading and all the other skills of language. The trouble is that we don't use his equipment. We contrive artificial systems of language development and methods of teaching reading, and we impose them on children. It is almost as though the child has to learn two languages in order to be able to read—one for communication and one to "get through" his reading books.

More research has been done in the area of reading than in any other area of the elementary school curriculum. This is justifiable because reading is an important skill needed for learning. But it is not the most important method of communication. It is important only to the degree that it *communicates!*

Much confusion exists about this research. This is the second place where we go wrong; we have built up a vast storehouse of knowledge about reading, but *all* the needed knowledge is not yet known. And, because there are great gaps in that knowledge, we have turned to the next best source—the opinions of the experts in the reading field. What is more, where the knowledge is lacking, we have filled in with the opinions so that we often confuse the two. The result is that many experts have advocated their "systems" of teaching reading, basing them on known truths but filling in the gaps with their own ideas. Schools have often adopted these systems so wholeheartedly that teachers are not permitted to skip one page of a basal reading book or omit one single exercise in the reading manual that accompanies the text. Many teachers have simply become middlemen, transmitting the ideas of the authors of a basal series to the children and not daring to use their own ideas to teach reading as a communication skill. This takes all the sense out of language skill development and reduces the role of the teacher to that of a puppet. Certainly no creativity can break through such rigid conformity.

Teachers are *teaching* experts. Their training has made them this. Reading experts can help with a multitude of ideas but they cannot possibly know the problems of any *one* teacher with any *one* group of children. Basal readers and teacher's manuals work *only* if they are adapted to the group of children using them, and they can be invaluable when used this way but are almost worthless when they are not.

Most of the reading books on the market today are written by the experts, and these experts are all concerned with making a living. Consequently, they plug their reading systems. One reading expert recently told me he was almost frightened by the dogmatic way in which his reading series was being used by school people. He has a good basic series, and in the introduction of the teacher's manual he states clearly that the series must be adapted to the children and makes many logical suggestions for this adaptation. Apparently some teachers do not read introductions to teacher's manuals; they plunge into Lesson I without first learning the primary objectives of the series and its basic philosophy.

We teach *children* reading. Any system of reading that does not consider the *particular* group of children and *each child in that group* first is pseudoscientific in its approach. Only a teacher can know the children she teaches—and know them she *must* before any significant gains can be accomplished.

The author feels strongly that reading becomes vital only when the teacher becomes the source of the plan of the teaching and when she is able to utilize the experts' books, materials, gimmicks, devices, and ideas to help her develop her *own* plan for her *own* particular group of children. Teaching is a creative role, not a mimetic one, and the teaching of reading must be a creative process.

Linguistic research of the past ten years has provided us with implications and some contradictions as to how reading should be taught.

Linguistics and Reading

Educators often refer to the "linguistic method" of teaching reading which focuses on the systematic relationships of phonemes to graphemes (sounds to letters).

Wardhaugh[1] says that linguistics can contribute to the study of reading; but it does not offer a method for teaching reading but a body of knowledge about language that reading researchers and teachers can draw on in their work.

Wardhaugh, a linguist, states that when a person reads a text, he is attempting to discover the meaning of what he is reading by "using the visual clues of spelling, his knowledge of probabilities of occurrence, his contextual-pragmatic knowledge, and his syntactic and semantic competence to give a meaningful interpretation to the text."[2] He points out that reading is an active process, in which the reader must "make an active contribution by drawing upon and using concurrently various abilities that he has acquired." These abilities should be taught to children and according to the linguist, are essential for a child to know.

Wardhaugh lists these abilities as follows: the ability to associate certain sounds and certain letters; the ability to react to significant rather than nonsignificant visual clues; the ability to use both short- and long-term memories effectively during the processing involved in read-

1. Ronald Wardhaugh, *Reading: A Linguistic Perspective* (New York: Harcourt, Brace and World, Inc., 1969), p. vii.
2. Ibid., p. 133.

ing (this includes semantic and syntactic processing in addition to processing the visual signals).[3] This processing requires a competent knowledge of the language. Wardhaugh feels that the subject matter of reading should touch on something within his experience or be relevant to that experience in some way so the reading task will be a meaningful one.

Wardhaugh states that considerable emphasis must be placed on teaching the association of orthography to phonology at the beginning stages of reading. Although Wardhaugh warns against the linguist prescribing any particular method for teaching reading inasmuch as reading is not linguistics, nonetheless he makes several suggestions inferred from knowledge of linguistic research. He feels it is apparent that children learn to read by being helped with the task of reading and not by learning rules about it, especially rules that are too sophisticated, too complicated or too inconsistent to be applied. They must learn that grammatical signals of written language are basically those of spoken language, and to use contextual clues in the deciphering of written texts. He feels that teaching children long lists of unordered phonic generalizations has little real benefit. A child does learn a rule by repeated experience of its use in context but it is unnecessary for him to be able to verbalize them. The notion of "mistake" and "error" in reading could be discarded in favor of arriving at an understanding of the unconscious rules a child is applying or not applying to his reading tasks.

Children require perceptual skills not required for spoken language.

Linguists criticize current reading methods. The "look-and-say" method recognizes that meaning is important and that English words are often irregularly spelled; the "sentence" method treats the sentence as a unit of thought and emphasizes the child's experience as a key to his success in learning to read. These methods are considered inadequate because they feel that repetition does not guarantee learning, that words are not language in any significant sense, and that sentences can assume such a diversity that to rely on sentences produced at random by children for the content of a reading program is to have in reality no program at all.[4]

They advocate a return to a basic concern with reading as it relates to language, so that a more rigorous examination can be made of such relationships as sounds to letters, words to meanings, sentences to sense, and so on.

The one great linguistic innovation which has been quite successful is the Initial Teaching Alphabet. The Initial Teaching Alphabet is con-

3. Ibid., p. 133.
4. Ibid., p. 12.

cerned with the regularizing of English phoneme-grapheme correspondences through the use of a modified alphabet for beginning reading texts.

Linguistics offers important insights into many problems that confront the reading teacher and the reading researcher. To that extent it offers each a perspective from which he can profitably view the various tasks he faces in teaching reading, in experimenting with different methods and techniques, and in devising remedial programs.

Linguists do not agree among themselves how the new knowledge gleaned in linguistics shall be applied in a reading program.

A pioneer in linguistics, Bloomfield[5] felt that children should be trained in visual discrimination and then be taught to associate visually discriminated objects such as letter and word shapes to already known sounds and meanings. Bloomfield, along with other linguists, felt that comprehension of materials read was irrelevant in the beginning stages of learning to read. Phoneme-grapheme correspondences were important so that the child came to understand the basic structure of words. Learning the letters of the alphabet was a must. Naming the letters of a word from left to right guaranteed both visual discrimination and correct word attack; but naming the letters had nothing to do with "sounding out" words. Bloomfield insisted that words, although spelled by letters, be pronounced by wholes.

Because the major task in initial reading was concerned with the interpretation of words and not with guessing at their meanings, Bloomfield rejected pictures in readers. Other linguists believe in this concept.

Because Bloomfield saw the basic task of the child was that of understanding the spelling system of English and not the meanings of English words and sentences, nonsense syllables and nonsense words could be used in achieving this mastery. In the beginning reading stages, the job of the teacher was to teach children to break the code of a new word and not to teach the children a new message.

Recent linguists have altered some of the concepts found in earlier writings. Most linguists acknowledge the need for learning some sight words so that stories can be made interesting.

Sofietti[6] who re-enforced much of Bloomfield's writing went so far as to advocate an early introduction of the skills of written communication in an ordered approach.

Fries[7] later contended that there are regular spelling patterns in

5. Leonard Bloomfield and Clarence Barnhart, *Let's Read* (Detroit: Wayne State University Press, 1961).
6. James B. Sofietti, "Why Children Fail to Read: A Linguistic Analysis." *Harvard Educational Review*, vol. 25 (1955), pp. 63–84.
7. Charles C. Fries, *Linguistics and Reading* (New York: Holt, Rinehart and Winston, 1963).

English, and it is the reading teacher's task to teach these patterns from the beginning by presenting them in carefully arranged sequences and giving beginning readers practice in recognizing them. Fries saw reading as a new visual task for children, one requiring a high sense of visual discrimination. He favored the exclusive use of upper case letters in teaching children to read. He believed that children would find written words composed out of twenty-six uniform letters easier to perceive than the corresponding words composed out of twice that number of letters.

Fries advocated contrastive word patterns because he considered the principle of contrast basic to linguistic structure *and* to visual discrimination. He did not feel children needed to spell out words. He emphasized focus on whole words. He emphasized oral reading because he felt that the written message was but a representation of the oral message but his goal was silent reading. Fries felt content and meaning were important and he acknowledged the need for some sight vocabulary to tie stories together sensibly. He did not, however, emphasize comprehension. He felt meaning was gained through an awareness of structure. He felt reading was a high-speed recognition of meanings already familiar to the reader. In Fries concept of teaching reading, there is no concern over the teaching of reading in later stages because all the problems would be overcome by good initial teaching.

Wardhaugh,[8] in summarizing a discussion on linguistic approaches to reading observes that it would not be unfair to say that what has become known as the linguistic method of teaching reading relies heavily on the work of Bloomfield and Fries. It entails little more than the presentation of regular phoneme-grapheme, or sound-spelling relationships in beginning reading texts," . . . a kind of new phonics with a good, undoubtedly much needed, dose of linguistic common sense added."

Exceptions to this methodology would be exemplified by LeFevre[9] who is one of the few recent linguists who attempts to apply the knowledge in linguistics to the method of reading.

LeFevre is concerned with a broader view of linguistic knowledge than Bloomfield or Fries. He feels that it is not enough to consider only phoneme-grapheme relationships and the ordering of difficulties in spelling. He is concerned with structures and patterns, particularly sentence patterns. His entire method emphasizes the whole sentence approach; he feels that words acquire meaning only through their contexts and that teaching children words in a list (as advocated by Bloom-

8. Ibid., p. 25.

9. Carl A. LeFebre, *Linguistics and the Teaching of Reading* (New York: McGraw Hill, Inc., 1964).

field and Fries) is no more than word calling and can hardly be considered reading. Sentence patterns contrast with each other, he feels, not word patterns. Patterns of the written language reflect the patterns of the spoken language over which children already have control at school age. Children must be taught to recreate the sounds of the spoken patterns from the marks on the printed page. In order to do this they must be taught phoneme-grapheme correspondences and they must also be taught how to relate groups of written words to groups of spoken words, and punctuation symbols to intonation patterns. Much emphasis is placed on reproducing the original spoken sentence in correct intonation, pitch, voice emphasis, accent of voice, etc. so the sentence will "sound right" to the child.

Modern linguists see reading as processing information.[10] Wardhaugh[11] feels it is fair to say that children must be taught the following in the initial stages of learning to read: (1) the left-to-right sequence in reading; (2) identification of the discriminating attributes of letters; (3) association of written symbols with spoken words on a basis which takes into account the fact that children already know all the sounds, most of the grammar, and a considerable part of lexicon of the language; (4) acquisition of a familiarity with the main patterns of inflection and derivation as represented in English spelling; and (5) making intelligent guesses as to what any particular group of letters represent. When checking out these suggestions with techniques already used in other reading programs, none appears new.

The teaching of reading may well be on the brink of a revolution in method. The linguists have contributed valuable information about the structure of the English language. Whether or not this knowledge can be effectively transposed into teaching methodology with large groups of children with varied problems and abilities remains to be seen. If it can, and some usage indicates that it can, a new era in the teaching of reading may lie before us. Much of the material proposed by the linguist, however, is no more motivating or exciting than some other current material in other methods of teaching reading. Linguists admit that such factors as motivation, psychological "set," physical well-being, intelligence, and environment affect the reading act. Many of the individual reading problems of the past have resulted because of inattention to such matters: there is still no evidence that they cannot negate the method proposed by the linguist. When all has been said and done, there is still very little evidence that knowledge of the structure of language and methodology built around this structure can be any more successful than the methods

10. Ibid., p. 52.
11. Ibid., p. 117.

used in the public schools in the past which have already taught millions of people to read. Some educators feel that the one problem in reading lies with those who do not appear able to learn to read by any modern method and ask whether the knowledge proposed by the linguist can be made into a method simple or meaningful enough to reduce the number of nonreaders or problem readers among these children. As yet, there is no proof of this. The other problem about which educators fret is that many children learn to read but appear to dislike reading so much that they rarely read outside the pressure of the school. Again, a fundamental question arises: can knowledge of the structure of words in specific and language in general motivate a child to read? This too, remains to be seen.

What Is Reading?

Reading is the ability to decipher and understand the printed symbols of the child's spoken vocabulary. Printed words, as well as spoken ones, are meaningful to the young child only insofar as his field of experience overlaps that of the author of the printed text. The old cliché, "You can take from a book only what you bring to it," is, in essence, true. The reader learns from a book only if he is able to understand the printed symbols and rearrange them into vicarious experiences in his mind. His ability to think, to reason, and to conceptualize makes it possible for him to receive new ideas from a printed page without actually experiencing the new idea, *but he must have experienced each symbol that helps make up the new idea!*

Teaching reading as a subject rather than a means for communication can be deadly for children. No one reads *reading*. He reads *something*—letters, books, poems, stories, newspapers—and he reads with a purpose. Each reading experience with children should have meaningful content, a purpose obvious to the child, and pleasant associations.

Not all children are ready to read at the same time. The wide socioeconomic and experiential backgrounds of children, combined with their physical development and intellectual ability, will determine the points at which children are able to begin the formal reading process effectively. Children often reach this stage at the first-grade level; therefore the formal reading program should generally begin in the first grade, when the average child has a mental age of about six-and-one-half years. The first-grade teacher is responsible for the continued development of the child as a whole. To deprive him of a rich variety of experiences so that he may spend time reading from books is the quickest way to insure reading difficulty among children, both in ability and attitude. School personnel have been guilty of spending long hours having children read laboriously from good books which the children soon come to hate. The biology of the child is violated in long, tedious, uncomfortable sitting periods, in tiresome repetition, and in meaningless or dull stories.

When a first-grade teacher sees the teaching of reading as her major objective and consumes a major part of the child's day with reading, she is capitalizing on the excellent experiences the home and the kindergarten have provided for the child. For, after all, these give meaning to his reading stories, which, at the first-grade level, are based on his first-hand home and school experiences. She may flatter herself on the excellent reading ability of her children and be smug in her knowledge that she can teach any child to read! What she fails to realize is this: unless she continues to provide suitable additional experiences in social studies, community contacts, literature, music, and so forth, she is depriving succeeding teachers of their privilege of doing a good job in teaching reading. This explains why, too often, children start out as good readers but experience reading difficulty by the time they reach third grade. They lose meaning in their reading because planned background experience stops when formal reading begins.

To children of the Space Age, who have radio, television, automobiles, fine recordings, and lovely books, most of the beginning reading stories in reading texts must seem insipid and cannot be expected to hold their attention long. Their real first interest in reading lies in their joy at discovering they *can* read. To exploit this joy, and to use it for needless repetition, means to soon destroy the only motivation the child has. The subject matter of a primer does not hold the child; we cannot, as a rule, expect him to be interested in these first "stories" for long. In the average classroom, the child not only hears these stories read and reread by every member of his group; he has heard them read dozens of times by preceding and succeeding groups working at various ability levels.

How Does a Child Learn to Read?

To understand how a child learns to read means first to understand how he learns anything, especially how he learns to apply symbols to the world around him. It is a well-known fact that children the world over are born with the same physical equipment for producing sound. M. M. Lewis[12] has shown that all children make the same initial sounds in

12. M. M. Lewis, *How Children Learn to Speak* (New York: Basic Books, Inc., 1959).

crying, babbling, and gurgling. But children in different cultures *hear* different sounds; at a very early age the child begins to listen and to imitate those sounds which he hears or is able to reproduce and which meet his personal needs. The first sounds he is able to make require little tongue or lip agility and no teeth; they are made largely by blowing air through the lips with variance in the force of the air and differences in the shape of the lips. Thus "mama," "papa," and "nana" (for grandmother) are often among the first sounds American babies imitate.

Soon the child repeats other sounds, and then, with the development of the tongue, lips, and teeth, and with repeated experience, the child realizes that all objects in his life can be identified with a verbal label. He soon learns that all actions also can be labeled, and before long he is forming his sounds into accepted words and repeating them over and over—testing his ability to label those things with which he is familiar.

The child must memorize a word for every object in his environment and for every action he performs, and he must also learn the words that tie actions and objects together to make sensible sentences. This means he must recognize actions (such as walk, dance, run, jump, and crawl) and label them. It also means he must learn the shape of every object in his environment and remember it so he can label it. He must remember what a chair looks like, what a stove looks like, what a spoon looks like. Recognizing the shape, he can say the symbol that identifies it.

Children speak several verbal symbols on the conceptual level from the first time they are uttered. The word "table" is not only a label for a specific table; it is a concept because it is a generalization from several experiences with many different kinds of tables. The child has learned that tables are objects with a flat top and four legs, which look somewhat alike, although there can be variances in size and shape.

Other conceptual words such as "hot" take on new meanings from new uses as witnessed by Bobby's interpretation at the beginning of this chapter.

Most children learn to recognize the symbols for objects in the same way they memorize the object—by its shape. At the beginning of the learning experience the word "table" is easily read because of its shape. Children do not need to know the phonetic sounds of the letters or the names of the letters themselves. To introduce these skills may slow the beginning reading power of some children, because then they have many things to learn and apply, and they do not need some of these things yet. Just as they learned to identify the table by making its sound, they will learn to read "table" most quickly by recognizing its shape. Most children pick up a wealth of words by recognizing their shapes ("sight" vocabulary).

Acquiring a sight vocabulary has its complexities. So many words are so nearly alike in shape that they become confusing, especially if they are also rather abstract in meaning. Study the words below:

1. on no
2. saw was
3. then there
4. grandmother
5. hippopotamus
6. submarine

It is easy to see how a child can become very confused by the first three sets of words in this group. They are much alike in shape. A beginning reader often has difficulty developing a left-to-right concept because he has learned to recognize objects whether he sees them frontwards or backwards; he does not always look at a word from left to right and often calls *on, no* and *no, on*. Simple words, therefore, often create more reading difficulty in a child than the more complex words 4, 5, and 6, above. Each of these words has an unusual shape, as well as emotional or physical associations. Grandmother is very dear to most children, and the smaller word "mother" may be familiar to them. Therefore the word "grandmother" has many pleasant associations and is easily remembered. All the circles (o's) in hippopotamus may help the child remember it is about the big, fat animal the teacher showed them in a film. The shape of the word "submarine" even looks like a submarine, which may enable some child to remember the word after very few exposures to it.

A child learns to read his first words mainly by recognizing their shapes. After he is using many words fluently in his speech (sound images) and has many words in his sight vocabulary (visual images), skills are developed from these sight *and* sound images which help him to read all other words as well as to read independently. These skills include phonics application, word analysis, and structural analysis.

Stages of Reading Development

There are basically four recognizable stages in the normal development of reading:

1. The readiness stage.
2. The beginning reading stage.
3. The stage of rapid growth.
4. The stage of reading power.

The first three stages generally constitute the normal growth pattern of the primary-grade child. The stage of reading power is developed, as a rule, in the intermediate grades. The first three stages, when broadened, indicate the instructional tasks of the primary teacher.

The primary teacher is faced with six major instructional tasks:

1. Providing a good reading readiness program.
2. Developing a beginning program in reading—developing a basic sight vocabulary.
3. Developing good reading habits (eye movement, etc.).
4. Developing reading skills—work with words, phonetic analysis, structural analysis, speed, and comprehension.
5. Developing independent reading.
6. Developing creativity.

Each of the stages and tasks of the primary teacher will be considered on the following pages.

The Readiness Stage

In order for children to be able to read, certain conditions must be present.

First, the child must have a wide *experiential background*. Reading is the visual presentation of an oral vocabulary derived from experience. As stated above, to be able to understand the visual symbols, the child must have a direct or vicarious experience to back them up.

Second, the child must be *developmentally* ready to read. This means he must be physically, socially, and emotionally mature enough to read. Physical readiness means that his eyes must be developed enough so that they can focus properly on print about 12 inches from his face. It means that he must be able to hold a book and sit fairly quiet, and his attention span must be long enough so that he can concentrate for ten or fifteen minutes on a single thing. Physical readiness means that he has enough eye-hand coordination to react to printed symbols and handle reading materials automatically. His fine finger muscles must have matured to the point where he is not clumsy in his use of reading materials. And he must have developed certain physical skills, such as auditory and visual discrimination ability.

Social and emotional maturity means the child must be psychologically ready—he must have the correct attitude toward reading. He must feel emotionally secure and socially at ease; he must feel that he has status as an accepted member of a congenial group. Emotional disorders can provide blocks in the reading process. The child must feel accepted by his teacher and be comfortably at ease with reading materials. He must also feel challenged and motivated by the reading experience.

Third, the child must be *intellectually* ready to read. He must be able to conceptualize, to recognize symbols, and to understand the meaning of reading. Although very intelligent children may be ready at an earlier age than normal children, and the refinement of communication processes such as television in the home may have upgraded the figures given, early studies showed that most children were physically, psychologically, emotionally, socially, and intellectually ready to read at the mental age of 6.5.[13] Since intelligence and reading ability are highly correlated, there will be vast differences in the reading abilities of children within any given grade.

Setting Conditions for Reading Through Skill Readiness

In addition to experiential, psychological, and intellectual readiness, there are certain skills which must be developed in each child before he is able to read.

Children must have a desire to read. The teacher sets conditions for all reading by making clear to the children the *need* for reading and the joy which comes from being able to read. Some ways teachers have done this follow:

1. Read to the children every day for enjoyment. Let them experience the fun in books.
2. Use books frequently to look up material for them. When children see the teacher use books to identify objects or to find out about them, they will want to learn how to use them too.
3. Keep many picture and simple story books around the room where they will be easily available to the children.
4. Keep bulletin board exhibits, displays and other exhibits, book jackets, and peg-board exhibits of good books in your classroom all the time.
5. Use books and stories as the basis for puppet shows, dramatizations, shadow plays, roll movies, and various other activities, as described in Chapter 6.
6. Make simple books of children's experiences. They can contain paintings, magazine pictures, and simple stories or sentences.

13. M. V. Morphett and C. Washburne, "When Should Children Begin to Read?" *Elementary School Journal*, XXXI (1931), pp. 496–503.

7. Letter notes and messages to the class on the board. List on the board questions children ask. Even though the children cannot read them, the teacher can read these questions to the children and they will come to recognize the value of reading and writing as a method of keeping records.

8. Utilize the immediate school environment fully. Take children on simple trips to observe the fall foliage, to hear the sounds on the playground, to observe the play equipment and possible science resources in the school yard. Use these trips as an experiential background for making simple picture books when the class returns to the schoolroom.

The first step in the creative process is creating such strong motivational drives in children that they are almost driven by a passion to learn. When reading is regarded as problem solving, and teachers consider the building of a strong desire to read as a motivational-involvement process, they are accomplishing the first step in all good learning, especially creative learning. The desire to read can fire a child to explore the reading process and the structure of language so that creative teaching can follow.

Children must develop the ability to listen. See pages 105–141 for ideas of creative ways to help children to learn to listen.

Children must develop a large oral vocabulary. Refer to Chapter 6 for creative ways to develop a large oral vocabulary.

Children must have developed the left-to-right concept. Children do not easily acquire this skill. In observing objects for the first six years of their lives, they study them from every angle and learn to recognize and name an object such as a chair from the front, the side, the back, from underneath, or over the top. Then they are presented with reading material and must always remember to look at it one way: from left to right. Many ways of helping children develop this concept can be employed. Some children will have no difficulty with this skill, while others will need a great deal of practice.

Children must develop audio acuity. In order to be able to read, each child must develop a sensitivity to sounds. An infant recognizes gross sounds such as the clanging of a bell, the honking of a horn, or the barking of a dog. As his sense of listening develops, he is soon able to hum, showing he can differentiate pitch. His hearing skill must be developed until he becomes sensitive to sounds in words that are very much alike—*men* and *man*, *catch* and *ketch*, *we're* and *were*. Finally he must develop a good ear for phonetic training, a sensitivity to sounds themselves such as *m*, *n*, *pl*, *ch*, *ā*, *à*, and so forth. Many suggestions for developing listening skills may be found in Chapter 5.

Children must develop a keen sense of visual discrimination. Research shows that creative children have a particularly keen sense of visual discrimination. Thus, in developing visual discrimination for reading purposes, teachers are also helping a child to develop his creative powers.

Children are called upon to note minute differences in word shapes and then in letter shapes in order to read. First a child recognizes shapes of objects about him: a drum, a ball, a swing, an automobile. Then he notices differences within objects of the same or similar shapes: dull or shiny, sad face or happy face, brother or sister. He also develops the concept of related shapes at a very early age: large and small, big and tiny, long and short. To read he must be taught to select the one shape that is different from the others, and eventually to see differences in word shapes, such as *mother* and *grandmother*, and *on* and *no*. In the end he must discriminate between little shapes that are very much alike, such as an *o* and an *a* or a *b* and a *d*.

In a sense all kindergarten activities are natural readiness experiences in visual perception. The work and play which children do with blocks gives them the necessary experience they need to work later with shapes and objects. From their work with paints, clay, cut paper, finger paint, doll furniture, dolls, miniature furniture, toys, and other materials, they gain the experience and concepts essential to the beginning reading program. In this sense the kindergarten program becomes a most important part of a child's formal schooling.

Children must develop a comprehension ability. Research on the creative personality has shown that creative children are more sensitive to problems than noncreative children are. They like to redefine and rearrange, to bring order and understanding out of disorder and disorganization. They like to produce; they have strong intuition and identification ability. Since all these skills are also part of the total concept of comprehension skills in reading, a teacher is also developing those aspects of creativity in children. The mastery of comprehension skill is closely linked to the child's intellectual development and his ability to listen, to conceptualize, and to organize well. Many general activities can be used to check the children's comprehension ability in kindergarten and first grade: interpreting the main idea of a story; retelling a story with some specific questions by the teacher to check depth of comprehension; encouraging children to react to a story; interpreting a picture story in sequence; finding missing details in pictures and stories;

following directions; anticipating endings in stories and poems; finger plays; following sequence in games such as "Looby Loo"; and general discussions with children about material read to them.

Most of these activities are of the type that develop convergent thinking processes. Some that develop comprehension skills *and* creativity are making roll movies; developing stories or story endings after a fragment of the story has been read; dramatizing stories or poems; pantomiming stories or making puppet plays or shadow plays from them; interpreting the ideas in a story by reading a sequence of pictures; and using the stories as a basis for making pictures, murals, dioramas, and other art work.

It has already been pointed out that much of the material used in commercial workbooks tends to jeopardize the child's creative development by giving him too many patterns to trace or imitate. Excess use of this sort of activity should be avoided. Instead of using exercises that say, "Draw like this," comprehension can be readily checked in more creative ways, where the directions say, "Fold your paper into 4, number each box 1, 2, 3, 4. In Box 1 draw something that lives in a tree, in Box 2 draw the part of the story that was funny," etc. This gives the child the opportunity to apply his own creative powers and, at the same time, tells the teacher what she needs to know.

With all the devices, gimmicks, and methods which can be used as an aid in developing comprehension, none is as effective as that of making certain that children fully understand each word when it is first introduced. Comprehension failure can generally be traced to the child's attempting to decode phonetically a cluster of unfamiliar sounds which are not a part of his field of experience and which, when decoded in sound, have no frame of reference in thought.

Children must develop skill in concept formation. The ability to understand concepts comes largely from experience with the use of words and their application to new situations. Suggestions for concept development have been given on page 33.

Many words are concept words; they have more than one meaning and their meaning can only be known from the way they are used in the sentence. Remember Bobby in the illustration at the beginning of this chapter and all the meanings he gave to the word *hot*?

Research on creative personalities indicates that creative children are better able to conceptualize than noncreative children. Helping children to form concepts contributes to their reading skill and their creative development.

Suggestions are given in a previous chapter (Chapter 6) and a later chapter (Chapter 9) on playing with words and abetting concept formation.

Children must develop a knowledge of the alphabet. As soon as children begin to hear sounds of letters, the letter should be introduced as a symbol to represent the sound. Letters will be learned individually before they are learned in alphabetical sequence. The latter can be taught as soon as most of the children recognize and associate sounds with their letter symbols. Little use is made of the alphabetical sequence as such much before the upper primary or early intermediate grades, but the letters should be recognized early in the reading program.

The Beginning Program in Reading

The beginning reading program is concerned with:

1. Developing a sight vocabulary.
2. Developing good eye movement across the page.
3. Developing a comfortable rate of speed in each child.
4. Making sure the child understands what he reads.
5. Introducing him to books within his range of ability.
6. Beginning to develop a phonetic sense in seeing likenesses and differences in words, both in sound and shape.
7. Beginning to help each child read some materials independently.

How does a teacher know when a child is ready for a formal reading program? Basically, when he begins to read! A child brings material to the teacher to read. He may pick out phrases or words with his fingers and read them. He seems to have a high motivation toward figuring out the printed symbols. He sees differences in words and shapes. He has a good sense of audio discrimination. He talks freely and expresses himself well. He is physically mature. And at this psychological time, he should be taught to read. Grade level has nothing to do with it.

There are ways a teacher may determine whether or not a child is ready for formal reading. Careful observation is the first. As the children work and play at kindergarten and first-grade activities, the observing teacher notes that George cannot put simple puzzles together; he has no concept of the relatedness of shapes. At clean-up time Ellen persistently tries to put a long block back on a short shelf. Alice tries to shove a large doll carriage through a smaller doorway. Marcia cannot tell one note from another. Jerry cannot sit with the group for a discussion.

None of these children is ready to read. George, Ellen, and Alice need more direct experience in developing visual acuity; Marcia needs more direct experience in audio discrimination; Jerry is too immature to concentrate. The teacher will provide more direct experiences for these children to prepare them to read.

Many check lists are available to help teachers determine the child's readiness. Check lists serve the purpose of directing the teacher's observation to specific acts in the child's daily routine which indicate whether or not he has mastered certain readiness skills.

Reading readiness tests may also be given to help a teacher determine whether her interpretation of the child's behavior is logical. Has he mastered the fundamentals prerequisite for success in formal reading?

Many readiness workbooks are geared to checking this readiness, but a wise and observant teacher can tell many of these things without printed devices, which do not appeal to all children. Workbooks used as a check for readiness are justifiable, but, when used as instructional material at this stage, they often create more problems than they solve. Overuse of the workbook may mean that children are not getting the meaningful experience background necessary to understand the material to which they will later be exposed. Workbooks can deal only with various sorts of printed symbols; they do not replace direct experience in any way.

The teaching of reading must be individualized. While much reading can be taught by group work, time should be allotted each day for personal instruction for those children who need it. Often the whole class may read together. But no teacher can teach a child to read without knowing a great deal about him, his likes, dislikes, home life, neighborhood experiences, and the level of experiences he has from day to day.

The best teaching of reading requires both group and individual work in the classroom. Each child is ready to read at a different time, and because each child is unique he may need a different approach or different techniques when he reaches the formal reading stage. The large classes confronting elementary teachers in our classrooms today prohibit to some extent this kind of teaching, though more of it could be done. The use of groups has been developed, and children are organized into areas of "like" problems which facilitate the teaching of reading, or any other subject, for that matter (see page 262).

Probably the first sign of a child's readiness to read is his ability to read pictures, which are often his first symbolic experiences. In our culture the use of picture symbolism has reached such proportions that we cannot conceive of a child who does not understand its use to some degree when coming to school. Yet not so many years ago in a little rural school, a teacher showed a young child of Polish descent the picture of a cow and the child said: "What is that?" "Why, it's a cow," the surprised teacher said. And the child smiled wisely and answered, "Naw, this no cow! The cow—she's big, she's fat, she's round and soft . . ." and in his broken English he proceeded to describe the cow with the aid of his waving hands.

This child, of limited experience, could not identify the very first step in symbolism: the picture of the actual object. It is difficult for us to imagine children today with so little background and experience that they have never before seen a picture! Yet somewhere (incidentally, perhaps) but certainly at an early age, every child comes to recognize a picture of an object as his first understanding of the meaning of symbolic representation. It is another step, and sometimes a difficult one, for him to recognize the printed words as symbols representing the pictures. In our modern books pictures provide a bridge for the gap in the understanding of written symbols. Many adults still find that pictures are easier to read than printed words, and many modern magazines capitalize on this knowledge and tell their stories in pictures to a wide reading audience.

The concept of symbolism develops within a child as he matures. At first it is difficult for him to associate the noisy, screaming, racy, bright red object that tears down the street with the dull, inactive symbol *fire engine*. As he learns that everything can be represented symbolically, and as he remembers best the names of unusual objects, he remembers best the unusual words. The shape and contour of a word helps the child to retain its visual image.

Developing a Sight Vocabulary

Developing a sight vocabulary in children means exposing them to phrases and words used in many different contexts so that they remember their shapes and recognize them "at sight." The creative teacher will find many ways to do this.

The experience chart. The most common way to build a sight vocabulary is the experience chart. It is a sound, logical method because it follows what we know to be sound in the development of language. The teacher takes the children on a trip (common experience) to a farm. Here they talk about what they see (listening and then oral labeling). "What is the man riding, Miss Allen?" "It is a tractor, Bill," "What is that tall thing?" "That's a silo." "What is it for?" "They store ensilage in it," and so on. The teacher and children return to the classroom and record their experiences on a series of simple charts.

We went to the farm.
We saw a barn.
We saw a silo.
Ensilage was in the silo.
We saw the cows.
They ate the ensilage.
We like the farm.

First they learn to read the chart in whole sentences or phrases. The teacher helps them to recognize and remember the words by making a duplicate chart and cutting it into strips. Children match the sentence on the strips with the original chart by reconstructing the story on a pocket chart. The children may then have fun mixing the sentences and creating a new story with them.

Obviously, work with the first reading charts is largely memorization. Children have memorized whole stories long before they come to school. Every parent has had the experience of reading "The Three Bears" to his three or four year old only to find that, in attempting to omit a line or two, he was prompted by the child who knew every word by heart.

The purpose of beginning reading charts must be kept clearly in mind: to memorize words and phrases to build a sight vocabulary and a base for the understanding of phonics and word structure. Memorization of the entire chart is necessary before memorization of the individual words is very logical.

Charts need not all be *experience* charts—though they should obviously use words that children are using orally and which are based on their own experiences. As soon as a few words are known, they can be used in many ways on different kinds of charts. Thus children may have the opportunity to read them over and over in new situations.

Individualized reading. Teaching children to read individually does not imply that each child is always on his own reading program. Common experiences give children common understandings and these can be employed for group work. Individual teaching does imply that certain individual needs, problems, and interests must be met, for each child may need extra help or attention at some time.

Labeling. Objects in the room may be labeled with cards and tags to make simple sentences. Signs such as "This Is the Reading Table" and "Our Library" help children to visualize many words over a period of time.

Dramatizations. Dramatizations can be used to develop reading skills. After the teacher reads a story, labels can begin to play a part in dramatizing it. The imaginary scenery can be labeled "This is a tree" or "Here is a house." Characters can be labeled "I am Dick" or "I am the mouse." Actions and sounds can sometimes be read from cards instead of being enacted.

Vocabulary charts. Occasionally a word or phrase that takes on great importance to the children comes up in the classroom, and the teacher may print it on a vocabulary chart for future reference. Words that arise in an experience such as the Show-and-Tell period reported on page 171 is one such example. Words around holiday time may be printed out of context on a vocabulary chart and still have a great deal of meaning to the children. Vocabulary charts are excellent ways to keep the picture and the spelling of current words before the children and are of special value after children begin to write and can use the phrases and words in their stories and poems.

To encourage the development of a vocabulary for special days such as holidays, clever, highly-motivating gimmicks can be used. One teacher constructed a bulletin board which was a huge kettle painted on white paper under which was a fire. Over the kettle, printed with a flo-pen, was the jingle

Our Halloween Witches Stew
What can you add Boo!

Each child was encouraged to come to the bulletin board and add any word to the witch's stew that could be used in writing stories for Halloween. These are some of the words written in the kettle:

worms	turtles
milk	tails
pumpkins	frogs
corn	cats
crayons	bats
cement	grease
mud	weeds
banana skins	gas
rotten tomatoes	peanuts

The Use of the Basic Text

A creative teacher will make a careful study of the reading books she intends to use with her class so that she becomes very familiar with their content. The introduction of the preprimer can be a highly motivating experience if the teacher is so aware of the vocabulary the child will encounter there that she has helped him to learn many of the words in his experience charts beforehand. The introduction of any reading book should be an exciting experience for every child.

Once a child begins to read in books, his chart experiences should not cease. Chart-making may shift from story charts to those concerned with gleaning information, planning charts, vocabulary charts, evaluation charts, and such, but charts still play an important role in having the reading experiences of the young child grow out of his spoken experiences.

There are two points of view regarding the use of a basic text in developing a sound reading program. Some teachers avoid the use of the basic text until very late in the reading program because they feel it does not have meaning for many children. Basic texts present the lives of neither the subcultures nor of mixed racial groups. Nor do they represent children of low socioeconomic levels. Consequently, to some children these basic texts are as much outside the realm of their experiences as are the ancient fairy tales. Second, the teachers feel that the basic texts tend to give the impression that unless they are followed page by page the children will not develop good reading ability. Third, they believe the beginning stories in most basic texts are insipid and stupid, and consequently very disappointing to children after they have been making their own exciting charts. These teachers often use a basic text as a supplement to a well-developed reading program for the purpose of teaching skills, evaluating pupil growth, and securing material for a variety of purposes very quickly.

On the other hand, other teachers feel the basic text has been prepared by experts, and the step-by-step guidance offered in the teacher's manual is the most scientific way of teaching reading known to man.

Actually, a combination of the two points of view probably produces the best program in reading instruction. In teaching reading, as in all other teaching, the variable that makes the difference is the teacher. The creative teacher will use all materials and will make them work for her.

Often the child is introduced to books through the use of the "big book" used at the front of the room. This is a natural transition for him, because the big book resembles the charts his teacher has made. After the big book has been read by the class, each child will be happy to discover that he can read the small copy of the same material in his own hands.

Time should be taken at this point to help children understand the difference between the basic texts and the books they have been looking at and trying to read. If children understand clearly that a basic text is designed to help them learn to read, they will realize that it performs a different function for them than books of children's literature which they want to read.

Some children develop such a rich sight vocabulary that they literally breeze through preprimers and primers. Contrary to popular belief, every page of a reader does not have to be covered. The one best guide for the development of a reading vocabulary is to listen to the words the children are *speaking* with meaning. If these words are the same as those used in the basic text, the children are ready for it. But the basic text should not constitute the total reading program of any classroom.

Easy books for beginners. Lately, the reading program of many classrooms has been enriched by the introduction of "easy beginning books" written especially for beginning readers. These books often do what the beginning readers do not. They tell a sensible, exciting story in a simple, direct way that rewards the children by making the reading of the story worthwhile.

Along with the easy beginning books has come much criticism as to their literary value. Literary value or not, they are far superior to the beginning stories in most basic text series. A visit to any classroom where these "easy books" are being used will show how eagerly they are accepted by children. Words are repeated over and over in such a way as to help the child develop a broad sight vocabulary. Various root words, beginning word sounds, word endings, prefixes, and suffixes are so simply introduced and so repeated that children often begin to use phonetic and word analysis skills to figure out the new words for themselves, thereby enabling the teacher to launch into a sound word-attack program at the time the child is most ready for it.

Many bright children have taught themselves to read with the "easy books," and many other children have delighted in their ability to read these books after one or two readings by the teacher.

Criticism or not, the "easy books" have made their way into the reading programs of most children, at least out of school, where parents have seen these books as one means to satisfy the hunger of the highly motivated beginning reader. The books can be put to profitable use within the school program if they are carefully integrated into the total reading program.

Developing Good Reading Habits

Good reading habits are developed at the onset of the reading experience. Children develop good eye movement across a page because they are taught to see and read for ideas rather than words.

Physical conditions must be appropriate to develop good reading habits. The presence of books, bulletin boards, daily stories, and all the other motivational devices previously mentioned is necessary. One part of the room should be set aside for quiet reading time. Distractions should be removed. Simple rules for reading time should be established. Above all, reading should be enjoyable.

Reading is a tool or a skill to be used in many ways and for many purposes. Therefore, reading goes on all day—not just during a reading period. The children plan their day together and teacher prints their plans on the board. The children read these plans as soon as they are able, along with their individual notes and surprises. The teacher writes the news on the board when they "share and tell" and thus provides another chart. Billy and the others read their surprise charts to the group after the surprise is known; the class writes a chart of Billy's experience. Teacher reads stories to the children. Long-term plans for a puppet show are printed on a chart. A list of "Things We Want to Know" constitutes another chart of questions the class will ask on their train trip. And at some specified time during the day, teacher meets with groups or individuals for individual reading experiences or help in techniques.

Such a program shows the need for reading to the children and places reading in its proper place meaningfully. Children do not read just for the sake of reading; they do it to communicate, to hear what others have to say. Reading can be established as a habit for communicating when the skills taught during the reading period are put to use all during the school day.

Reading is also geared to the individual ability of each child. Children are not given special graded reading material at one period and thrown into a standard social studies text the next period. Spelling lists are geared to the children's capabilities. In all language experiences children are grouped according to common problems and not by the arrangement of materials in a book.

Developing Reading Skills

As soon as a basic sight vocabulary has been learned and the reading habit has been established, and children are reading charts or books, the first-grade teacher must begin to build skills that will lead the child into independent reading ability. All these skills center around developing techniques in word recognition. These techniques may be listed as follows:

1. The use of picture clues to identify words.
2. The use of verbal context clues.
3. The use of word-form clues.

4. The use of phonetic analysis.
5. The use of structural analysis.

One instructional job of the teacher in developing independent reading skills is with the use of independent seat work. She must also be concerned with expanding the children's reading range through the introduction of new topics and supplementary reading materials.

Using Picture Clues to Identify Words

Picture clues provide necessary vicarious experiences (see page 248) and often bridge the gap between a real experience and the printed symbols of that experience.

When children have had extensive work with pictures such as those suggested in Chapter 6, they develop the ability to study pictures closely and to be sensitive to many of their component parts. Ability to read a picture well will ultimately help a child to read the printed symbols that appear under it. In his desire to make his reading have sense, his eyes wander back to the picture to find the pictorial image of the word.

Using Verbal Context Clues

Context clues also help children understand the meaning of words—or help them to put meaning to them. Children can often decipher a strange word encountered for the first time simply because using it makes sense in a sentence.

While pictures may help children in reading many beginning stories, there are some instances when they do not. Here the child resorts to searching for clues in the context of the story itself. In the reading readiness program, he developed many verbal context skills in the work with audio discrimination, visual discrimination, listening, and oral expression.

Using Word-Form Clues

Word-form clues are those which deal with the outward appearance of the word. Recognizing likenesses and differences in words, recognizing beginning sounds and endings, and noting the lengths of words are the first kinds of word-form clues which a child uses to figure out the pronunciation of a word. The phonics program expands this ability and a program in structural analysis tends to complete it.

In developing a sight vocabulary, children build a base for skills in using word-form clues. Continued work in oral vocabulary building as described on page 152 to 224 is necessary so that the spoken words of the child may be meaningfully recognized in print.

Using Phonics Analysis

The comprehensive use of phonics is reliant on the memory of known words or word fragments like "p" and "an" and their application in familiar patterns ("sight" words) before they can be used in unfamiliar words. To ignore the building of a sight vocabulary of many words in a program using the phonics approach is to leave to chance the most important stage in the child's reading development.

Phonics serve the purpose of unlocking the sounds of familiar words —words already in the speaking vocabulary of the child, words he has *heard* before but he does not remember *seeing* in print before. They do not really serve to teach new words in reading.

All phonics instruction must be based on letters or groups of letters or words already known by the child; he cannot understand the reason for the sound of *p* until he knows the letter *p*, or the sound of *gr* until he has experienced *gr;* nor can he sound *in-to* until he has experienced compound words.

Although teaching phonics is not teaching reading, nonetheless, phonics play an important part in learning to read. In the reading readiness program, phonics sounds are often used to refine audio discrimination. Children learn the consonant sounds such as "m" and the vowel sounds such as "a," The speech consonants and consonant blends such as "ch" and "br," and so on, less as a technique for teaching them to read than as a technique to help them hear and see minute differences in sounds and shapes. When these exercises are taught as games, or in meaningful ways, they are fun. It has been pointed out that children create sounds and use them in their speech and early writing. Teachers can capitalize on the "ch-ch-ch" for "train" and have the children reproduce this sound to accomplish the same ends as the more formal lessons in the manual. There is the "sh" sound when rocking baby to sleep; the "da-da-da-dat" sounds of playing at shooting machine guns, the "whrr-whrr" for the airplanes, the "z-z-z-z" sound of an automobile, and a multitude of others.

Learning sounds in the readiness stage of reading does not insure the child the ability to decipher phonetically, however, for that is not the purpose of sound consciousness at this stage. Many children do carry over this knowledge later into their reading but they should not necessarily be expected to. Most children learn to read initially by recognizing the *shapes* of words as they learn about people, animals, and things by *their* shapes. To a little child, all men may be classified as "Daddy" because they have a similar shape. Dogs soon become "bow-wow" regardless of size, because the shapes are similar; coffee tables, end tables, dining-room tables, and bridge tables are all "tables" at first due to their similarity of shape. It is later that the details of shapes within the shapes begin to make for discrimination. The child notices the unusual parts of objects and sees differences. Thus the tail of the dog, which is always moving, and the head, which is always barking, eating, or licking, come to his attention; differences are noted, and a more definite classification results. "Dog" becomes "cocker," "dalmation," "collie"; "Daddy" becomes "man," or "grandpa," or "Mr. Jones." "Table" becomes "coffee table" or "dining-room table."

So the child learns to identify words by shape and then the peculiarities within the words draw his attention. He sees wiggly "g's" and tall "T's," and when he notes differences within shapes he is also ready to notice they stand for the differences within the sounds he is making. This is the time when phonics should be taught as a reading aid and a step toward independent reading. Now the child needs techniques for attacking new words so he may eventually read independently. Again, the element of discovery can provide an excellent motivating force if the teacher teaches phonetics skillfully enough so the child discovers new words through sounds. Many teachers prefer to begin phonics apart from the reading groups themselves, through word games. This is perhaps wise in that it does not interfere with the child's eye span or slow up his reading when he is in the initial stages of establishing the reading habit. After a series of sound games have been played and the basic consonant and vowel sounds and consonant blends have been established, the teacher naturally makes the transfer to the reading situation by having the children sound some of the words they do not know in their reading books. This can be discovery, it can be fun, and children can spend time sounding out new words they meet daily.

It must be remembered, however, that phonics is but one way to recognize words which the child does not recognize, as yet, in print and is no more important than a number of contextual clues.

Because the creative personality enjoys seeing the order and logic behind life, an understanding of the structure of words can contribute to this aspect of the child's creative development.

Using Structural Analysis

Almost as soon as he begins to read, the pupil will find likenesses in words. In studying phonics he will notice a familiar base sound with a new consonant beginning, such as "night" and "sight." Often he will recognize small words in larger ones, as "mother" in "grandmother." When this begins to take place, children are capable of understanding the structure of words; now they may be taught the variations and deviations of words, which will help them in developing independent reading. A study of structure of words involves an ability to:

1. *Recognize base words in derived words.* A child reads: Helen was playing the record. He recognizes the word "play" and is able to apply his knowledge of prefixes and suffixes to "sound out" the word. Once he says the word to himself, he recognizes it as one he already uses orally and he has brought meaning to the sentence.
2. *Recognize compound words.* Knowing the words "rain" and "fall," he quickly recognizes a word, "rainfall."
3. *Find a little word in a longer word.* Discovering the word "let" in "letter" helps the child figure out the total word.
4. *Divide words into syllables.* Knowing that each syllable contains a vowel helps the child to properly pronounce the word "at-ten-tion."
5. *Recognize contractions* (see Chapter 12).

The teaching of structural analysis begins in the development of visual discrimination. Some suggestions which help to develop structural analysis skills are:

Seeing how many words can be built from *one* root word and noticing how the new words are all related to the root word in meaning. Examples: Root word "law." Words built by adding suffices, prefixes, and compounds: "lawyer," "lawless," "lawsuit," "lawful," "unlawful." Root word "rain." Built words: "raincoat," "rainy," "raindrop," "raincheck," "raining," "rains."

Making collections of compound words whose meanings are obvious and some that are not. Mrs. Marr's third grade produced the following two contrasting charts:

Words That Tell Us Their Own Meanings	*Words That Do Not Tell Us Their Meanings*
evergreen	tidbit
shoelace	shamrock
scarecrow	slipshod
teabag	sandwich
boxcar	fanfare
sidewalk	ketchup
tiptoe	horse-radish
sandman	iceberg
airplane	handsome
seashore	nightmare
tattletale	

Making collections of words that go together but are not compounded. Mrs. Farr's list looked like this:

Words We Say Together But Do Not Put Together
tie tack
mince pie
eye ball
candy cane
window sill
window pane
lake shore
state fair
hope chest
ice cream
ferris wheel
fish pole
golf ball

Increasing skill in identifying endings on nouns without change in base forms.

(1) Endings "s," "'s" and "s'" without adding an extra syllable (*boats, uncle's, girls'*).

(2) Endings "s" and "es" adding an extra syllable (*pieces, watches*).

Increasing skill in forming compound words.

(1) Making "solid" compounds (*today, another*).

(2) Building hyphenated compounds (*make-believe, far-off*).

Increasing skill in forming contractions by substituting an apostrophe for one or more letters (*I'm, can't*).

Increasing skill in identifying "s," "es," "est," "ed," "er," "ly," as forms of familiar words by:

(1) Naming the root word.

(2) Using the root word to make new words.

(3) Looking through a story or book to find words that were made by adding an ending to a known word.

Studying word endings by:

(1) Observing word endings "s," "es," "est," "er," "d," "ed," "ly," "ing."

(2) Identifying root word in attacking new words (*open, opening*).

(3) Making new words from a root word. *Example: want, wants, wanted, wanting.*

(4) Choosing correct word ending to complete sentences. *Example:* Jane (*play, plays*) with her doll.

Some games and gimmicks are suitable in developing structure awareness in children:
(1) *Word Pyramid.* Start at the top of the pyramid with the word *A.* The players take turns adding another letter to form a new and longer word and to build the pyramid. If the first player adds "t," the pyramid may develop as follows: *a, at, eat, meat, steam, steamer, teamster.* The pyramid may be built on the chalkboard.

Developing Independent Reading

The development of good reading habits and basic reading skills should place the child well along the road toward independent reading. Most children enter the stage of rapid growth in reading as soon as they begin to read independently. The main jobs of the teacher at this point are to continue to develop those skills which will give the child independent reading power and to supply a wealth of material geared to the reading ability level of each pupil. In addition to the reading act, there are certain mechanics of reading which greatly aid the child in the use of books and increase his power to work with books by himself.

Mechanics to Be Developed by the Primary Teacher for Independent Use of Books

1. Teach the alphabet names (very soon after the reading act is established).
2. Teach the order of the letters of the alphabet.
3. Teach the mechanical features of a book.
4. Teach care and handling of books.
5. Use alphabetical skills in other books such as:
   a. Dictionary (picture and others).
   b. Telephone book.
   c. Address books (make some).
   d. Reference materials in children's encyclopedias.
6. Develop an interest in authors and publishers.
7. Develop library skills by:
   a. Learning card catalogue in library a-b-c order.
   b. Learning that encyclopedias are in a-b-c order.
   c. Looking for pictures on given topic.
   d. Locating materials on library shelf.

The Intermediate Grade Program

The intermediate grade program in reading is often misunderstood or neglected because it is interpreted as a continuation of the primary program. The instructional tasks of the intermediate grade teacher may be the same as the primary teacher's, but they also go far and above those tasks developed in the primary grades.

Reading power is developed in the intermediate grades. When analyzed into its many parts, reading power is seen to come from the acquisition of many desirable and necessary skills. Developing these skills is the job of the intermediate grade teacher, who must concentrate on:

1. The continued development and expansion of primary reading skills.
2. Continued independent reading.
3. Expanding the vocabulary and range of materials.
4. Developing more refined techniques of effective comprehension.
5. Developing the techniques of critical thinking.
6. Developing techniques for effective reading rates.
7. Developing the skill of reading carefully for directions and details.
8. Developing skill in oral or audience-type situations.
9. Developing more skilled approaches to word study and word attack skills, such as:
   a. Building word meanings.
   b. Mature techniques of word recognition.
   c. Advanced word-analysis skills.
   d. Skill in using the dictionary.
10. Teaching the efficient use of reference techniques:
    a. Ability to locate information.
    b. Note-taking.
    c. Outlining.
    d. Summarizing.
    e. Use of library resources.
11. Teaching how to apply reading skills in these ways:
    a. Dictionary skills.
    b. Book skills.
    c. Skills in locating information.
    d. Selecting main ideas.
    e. Skimming.
    f. Reading for beauty—interpretative and appreciative.
    g. Reading for detail.

   h. Reading dialects.
   i. Reading charts, maps, and graphs.
12. Developing organizational skills.

As children begin to utilize their word-attack skills and sight vocabulary by reading books on their own they generally enter a stage of rapid growth in reading. At this point, their interests and problems become so diversified that grouping by ability is likely to retard rather than help many children in the development of independent reading.

Grouping

Something needs to be said about grouping and its direct relation to reading in the intermediate grades. One common conception of grouping is that the class is divided into three or four groups—the fast readers, the average readers, and the slow readers. This type of grouping implies that we are concerned with reading rate: the best (fastest and with greatest comprehension, generally above grade level); the average (about where they should be in terms of rate, comprehension, and grade level); and the poorest (slow readers, below grade level). Reading is concerned with much more than speed or rate. Comprehension or meaning (the acquisition of the thought the author is attempting to communicate) is much more important. Speed and comprehension are related, but both must be "taught." There are other important skills involved in the reading process which children will need help in developing. Vocabulary building is one. The ability to select the main ideas from different selections, to skim and to read differently for different material, to attack and discover meanings for new words, to summarize, to outline, to read for information, to read poetry—these and a host of other skills must be acquired by children if they are to be effective readers.

Teachers can discover who needs help in these areas and *group the children according to similar problems.* This is possible at any level once the reading act has been efficiently established. The creative teacher can work up a series of lessons to help children gain skill in selecting the main ideas from stories or paragraphs regardless of their reading ability level. She may, for instance, run off on a ditto machine a story aimed at the poorest reader; her purpose is to teach a skill, not to worry over the reading matter itself. Everyone reads the story, and through discussion they select the main ideas and may even outline the story on the board. The teacher then gives the child a book to read on his own reading level, and he practices with a story from the book. There are advantages in this heterogeneous grouping in that children who read well can help those who do not. Good social relationships are developed in this process and the "sights" are raised for the slow child while the quick child gains status in the group. The slower child also stands a stronger chance of responding to and discovering answers so that he, too, gains status in the group.

Ability grouping is necessary to some extent. The problem the teacher confronts here is raising the ability in reading, if possible. But this is not the only reason for grouping. It is important that teachers remember that the best way to help children become better readers is to teach them the skills that will help them read independently. Fast readers as well as slow ones often have difficulty selecting main ideas, attacking new words, or understanding what they have read. When children are grouped to work on problems, the groups constantly change, and the stigma attached to a slow reading group dissolves. Real ability grouping implies flexibility. The grouping described above is really "content" grouping although it is often misnamed "ability" grouping.

Another logical way to keep children reading independently at the peak point of their ability level is through the personalized reading program. In this type of reading program the major portion of the child's time is spent reading as an individual, not as a member of a reading group. Inasmuch as this is the way most people read in life, it seems to be a rewarding and practical way to teach children to read.

Success in obtaining independence in reading is based largely on the conditions set in each classroom for making reading an integrated, useful skill to be used throughout the school day. When children are successful in applying skills, they hunger to master more skills to attain more success. Success at each step of reading development is necessary to produce the psychological atmosphere where achievement can develop.

Continued Development and Expansion of Primary Skills

Continued work in developing visual perception, oral vocabulary, sight vocabulary, phonetic and word analysis, word attack skills, and the use of various context clues continue throughout the child's reading instruction program.

Continued Independent Reading

Power in reading at the intermediate grade level comes from many experiences including:

1. The *mastery of word-attack skills* described on page 254–260.
2. The *careful building of a meaningful vocabulary* as each child is exposed to many topics in his science, social studies, arithmetic, and other studies.

It must be remembered that word-attack skills only aid a child in pronouncing a word; they give no clue to its meaning. Consequently, new words should be introduced for the first time at the meaningful experience level, which can be either a direct or a vicarious experience.

The Continued Development of a Sight Vocabulary

Many words can be learned all through life simply by remembering the shape of the word. The continuous building of a sight vocabulary provides the teacher with a backlog of known words on which she can build phonic generalizations and exceptions, and on which she can develop reading skills.

Mrs. Ames used a homemade tachistoscope for quick recognition of many words. She cut a piece of oaktag about 5 × 8 inches and folded it back one-half inch along each of the long sides. This served as a tray to hold her printed materials. She cut an opening in the center of the oaktag strip wide enough to allow for the usual size printed material and fastened another piece of oaktag over this opening with a piece of masking tape to make a hinged shutter. Printed words on slips of paper cards were slipped into the folds on the back of the oaktag and the shutter was flipped for a second to see if the children could recognize new words at a glance. Children used this device in drilling each other.

Books and Materials on All Levels of Reading and About Many Topics

An essential requisite of all reading abilities and problems is an accessible abundance of material for many levels of reading. The materials for the upper elementary reading program should include copies of many textbooks, many commerical trade books, SRA materials, reading machines, some workbooks for individual practice, and programmed reading materials for some children. A school library is a *must* for a good intermediate-grade reading program. Three or four sample books from many sets of social studies, science, and arithmetic books are a wiser choice in stocking room libraries than are twenty-five books from one series which are all alike. At least one newspaper and several magazines should be available to children.

Individual Records of Reading Growth and Power

Careful records must be kept of each child's reading power. At this age this is possible because children can keep their own records. The SRA materials offer help in this direction. Teachers and children can devise check sheets and record sheets which keep a record of each child's problems, the books he has read, his reading power, and the areas where he needs help.

Strong incentives for reading are necessary in order to help each child read independently.

Expanding the Vocabulary and Range of Materials

In the intermediate grades, the child is often introduced to a world of new words through the social studies program of the school and through the expanding, varied number of activities in which he finds himself. Up to this time, most children have been reading material in their social studies books which is familiar to them. They have studied their own community, contrasting communities, and then the history of communities. In each instance, the children have added unique words to their base oral and reading vocabularies, but the bulk of the words were learned in studying their own communities. These vocabularies were developed with meaning, since most of them were derived from the child's common, local, everyday experiences. These base vocabularies made it possible for him to transfer meanings into a study of other communities because all communities are alike to a degree.

In the area of science, especially in topics related to the space age, children have acquired a unique vocabulary by the time they reach the fourth grade. Through television, newspapers, movies, and other forms of mass media, children at this age have often integrated a larger vocabulary in some of these areas than their teachers. In selecting and constructing reading and instructional materials, teachers need to recognize this fact, threatening though it may be to some of them.

Also, by the time the child reaches the fourth grade he has learned many things from reading. He is now capable of living many experiences in his mind; that is, word symbols suggest experiences about other people which he can visualize and which he no longer has to experience directly or vicariously in order to understand. His own vast background has given meaning to word symbols to the degree that he can now use them in new thought patterns and imagine the experience being described on the printed page. This ability makes it possible for children of this age to learn a great deal more from books than the early primary child who can only read with understanding about those experiences which are much like his own.

One precaution should be taken in order to avoid reading disability at this time, however: *new* words should still be introduced at the experience level. Social studies books, at best, are a collection of important concepts, and any one page may contain several concepts outside the realm of the child's comprehension. One of the first jobs of the teacher is to be sure that the vocabulary of new words to be introduced for any social studies unit is done at the experience level. For instance, a group of children who are going to study Mexico will need to develop a vocabulary unique to that country in order to be able to use these words with meaning as the unit develops. Such a list might contain such words as "adobe," "sombrero," "serape," "fiesta," "siesta," "tortilla," "frijole," "burro." All these words can be meaningfully introduced through a good film that shows each and where the teacher stops the film to discuss with the children those parts which give meaning to the words. A word is assigned to an object or an experience in meaning and context so that it has equal meaning when read later in the context of the social studies book.

In addition to the ever-expanding social studies vocabulary of the middle grades, there are several other experiences for which the children need to build new vocabulary—current events, regional experiences, introduction to new heroes, sports and political events, and the ever-widening world of the child as he travels with his family. Reading power can be developed most logically if the child is helped to develop the meaningful oral vocabulary first, then see the words he is speaking put into print as suggested by the language sequence chart on page 46.

Developing More Refined Techniques of Effective Comprehension

Reading without comprehension is not reading. Throughout the primary grades reading comprehension is checked with each day's reading lesson in a variety of ways. Comprehension will be no problem if the child's reading is based on material within his own experience. When he begins to read widely and independently, however, he meets many words he has not experienced, or his experience is limited, and the word does not make sense as applied in a new situation, so comprehension often breaks down. More frequent checks on comprehension are needed, and skills in helping children obtain the meaning of new words and old words used in new situations need to be taught.

Developing the Skill of Critical Thinking

Critical thinking is problem solving which is directed toward some goal. It is more objective than creative thinking. It is taking a group of facts, synthesizing them and then making decisions and passing judgments consistent with those decisions.

Critical thinking can be stimulated by situations in which children find themselves forced to pass judgments or make decisions. Sometimes the motivation for critical thinking comes from the questions teachers ask or those listed in a textbook.

Many questions asked by teachers and textbooks serve the sole purpose of checking comprehension. The answers can be found simply by rereading parts of the text. This is not to be confused with critical thinking. When social studies are taught by the reading of a textbook through a question and a read-to-find-the-answer period, little can be claimed for it in terms of meeting social objectives. The program is little more than a series of lessons in reading comprehension using a social studies text.

An example of such a comprehension question, taken from a current textbook under the title of critical thinking follows:

"Why did the pioneers often take their stoves with them in their wagons when they went West, although space was so precious?"

The answer can be found on page 163.

The following questions were taken from the plans of two teachers who were concerned that their children should learn to think critically. The difference between this type of question and the one listed above is obvious.

1. What effect has the St. Lawrence Seaway had upon our country?
2. What were the desirabilities and undesirabilities of plantation life?
3. Why were a desert state (Nevada) and a swamp state (Florida) the two fastest growing states in the 1960's?
4. What were some of the differences and similarities of settlers in Virginia in 1607 and in California in 1849?
5. Where would you want to live if you moved to Alaska? Why?
6. Do you suppose Russia is sorry that she sold Alaska to us?

Developing Techniques for Effective Reading Rate

In a culture where much reading material is available and where the average citizen must read a great deal to remain literate in national and world affairs, speed in reading becomes an essential skill. But speed in reading is a skill only if the reader comprehends what he reads. Part of the problem in developing speed in reading is helping the child *think* about what he reads. The *type of thinking* must help determine the speed. Is he, for instance, reading to think *critically, evaluatively, imaginatively, appreciatively, analytically?* The purpose of reading determines the proper speed for reading. Part of the problem in developing speed for reading, then, is to help the reader recognize material which should be read with speed and that which must be read slowly. Parts of the daily newspaper may be skimmed without losing the essential point of the article, while other parts must be read with great care in order not to confuse essential points of any given issue. Much of the work of the teacher in developing reading rate is to help children determine the intensity of speed to be used with any given article. Children may make lists of material which should be read carefully and that which should be skimmed.

Developing the Skill of Reading for Directions and Details

Some reading must be slow to the point of being laborious in order to be effective. Reading for directions and for details may fall into this category. In teaching children to read carefully without destroying the speed essential to other kinds of reading, probably the first step again is to help them recognize material that will require slow reading.

In Mrs. Mead's fourth grade, the children made an analysis of their reading over a period of two weeks and listed all the material they had read slowly and carefully.

Developing Skill in Oral or Audience-Type Situations

Oral reading is used much less than silent reading in actual life experiences. Consequently, it is not emphasized as heavily in the reading program as it once was. Excessive oral reading reduces rate in speed and comprehension. The use of oral reading in the classroom should be restricted to those purposes for which children use oral reading in life.

Developing More Skilled Approaches to Word Study

Among the word-attack skills developed in most intermediate grades (if they have not already been developed in the primary grades) are the following. Each child:

1. Gains auditory perception of digraphs and diphthongs, as "oa," "ea," "oo," "ow," "ou," "oi," "oy."

2. Recognizes phonograms useful in attacking new words ("aw," "ou," "ight," "ick," "ack," "ock," "ing," "old," "ill," "all," "est," "ake," "orn," "ong.")

3. Recognizes "x," "k," and "s" sound alike (books, fox).

4. Recognizes "s" sometimes has sound of "z" (visit, busy).

5. Recognizes words with both voiced and unvoiced "th" (*they, their, thin, thought, through*).

6. Knows that "wh" has sound of "w" in *wh*en, *wh*ere.

7. Knows "wh" has sound of "h" in *who*, *whole*.

8. Learns the principle of contractions (apostrophe used in place of one or more letters) (see Chapter 12).

9. Learns meaning and uses of common suffixes and prefixes, as "ful," "less," "re," "un."

10. Receives continued development in using the context to develop meaning in passages read.

11. Learns that words can have more than one meaning, as "run *fast*," or a "*fast* color."

12. Learns that meanings of words may shift from line to line or page to page.

a. Make cards showing this:

> It was a *fair* day.
> The Joneses were going to the *fair*.

13. Learns that some words have no meaning until seen in context, such as the word "cleave."

Example: The butcher will *cleave* the beef into several parts. The barnacles will *cleave* to the side of the ship.

14. Learns that there are exceptions to all rules.

Example: The prefix "in" often negates a word, as in "destructible" and "indestructible"; "valid" and "invalid."

Exception: "valuable" and "invaluable." Meaning not negated—both mean "valuable."

Teaching the Effective Use of Reference Techniques

To become independently adequate in applying reading skills to the subject-matter areas, the intermediate-grade child will need to master many reference techniques. Specific skills he will need are:

1. The ability to locate information easily (see Chapter 12).

2. The ability to take notes (see page 495).
3. The ability to outline (see page 480).
4. The ability to summarize (see Chapter 12).

Teaching the Application of Reading Skills

No reading skills should be taught without direct application of the skill to the reading. For a highly developed teaching program, a few skills must be extracted from a reading program. Then the learned skill should be applied through continual usage in reading material. These skills are often taught as another part of the language arts program and then applied to reading.

A list of skills needed in the intermediate grades (if not developed before) in order to promote independent reading and reading power would include:

1. Dictionary skills (see page 506).
2. Book skills (see Chapter 12).
3. Skills in locating information (see Chapter 12).
4. Skills in selecting main ideas (see Chapter 12).
5. Application of skills in reading for beauty and appreciation (see Chapter 9).

Reading Levels

Throughout the reading program the teacher must realize that all children operate on three basic reading levels: the independent, the instructional, and the frustration reading level.

At the independent reading level, the child can read with enjoyment and without help from his classmates and teacher. It will generally be below the level of instruction. At this level many easy books are read, and most children enjoy rereading stories they have previously enjoyed. The independent reading level is recognized by the fact that the child can read almost 100 percent of the material selected.

The instructional reading level is that level of reading where the child reads fairly well but needs help in certain reading skills or in the mastery of new vocabulary. It is at this level that actual teaching occurs. The criterion for the instructional level is that the child is reading 95 percent word recognition and 75 percent comprehension of the selected material.

The frustration reading level is that at which the child cannot read well enough to receive enjoyment or understanding from his reading.

The criterion is that he reads little of the selected material with comprehension—anything less than the criterion at the instructional reading level.

Evaluating the Reading Program

A teacher can best evaluate her reading program by noting how the children read, their attitudes toward reading, and their selection of reading materials. Many good reading tests are available, although their frequent misuse has spoiled their effectiveness. Standardized tests help teachers find the ability levels of their students and, in many cases, will help the teacher identify the specific problems of each child. When utilized in this manner the tests can be of extreme value, but when teachers spend their time trying to get children up to "grade level" they are defeating the purpose of such tests. They must remember that the tests are based on norms and norms are averages and, by that very token, half the class must fall above the midpoint and half below. If this is not true, the chances are that the teacher has either a brilliant or a retarded group.

The best readers are those who have a wide background of experience and basic reading skills from which to draw, and who enjoy reading immensely. The most effective way of evaluating a reading program is through the use of individual check sheets that show each child's abilities and needs in reading and indicate clearly his frustration level, his independent level, and his instructional level. Such charts used over a period of time will clearly show the child's progress and will remove threatening grade-level classifications and useless grade indicators. Children can help teachers keep these charts in diagnosing their own difficulties, in planning their own instruction, and in evaluating their own growth. Many excellent charts and scales are available commercially, but children and teachers can do some creative thinking in making their own. The activity of constructing such a chart helps the children understand the teacher's objective for the entire reading program and creates a high motivational interest in their own reading progress—the first step in the creative process.

Remedial Reading

Little has been said about remedial reading in this chapter because the author believes that remedial reading implies what it says—a remedy—that something has gone wrong. He has seen too many limp, unhappy, meaningless remedial reading classes to have much faith in them. Some corrective reading may be necessary in any program. Children have illnesses, or defects, or need extra help, or misconceive, or misinterpret. A good reading program diagnoses children's ability *continually*—every day, in fact—and these flaws are *corrected* before whole blocks of remedial reading teaching are needed. In the creative teaching of reading, children at times read as an entire class (see page 172), at times in small groups (see page 262), at times individually to the teacher (see page 253), at times to each other (see page 87), at times to themselves (see page 183)—but rarely in a strange room to a strange person with strange material. Creative teaching should eliminate the need for remediation in reading because creative teaching does not see the deficiencies of a child as something for which he is to blame. Creative teachers accept what a child *has* and draw it out to help him to grow, and they do it in such a way that his own creative powers and his passion to learn lead him forward into new discoveries, into continuous growth, and toward self-realization.

Summary

Reading is a complex process consisting of the mastery of many specific skills. Much is known about the teaching of reading, but much research is still needed before specific methodology can be proven.

Meanwhile, evidence would indicate that current reading programs are no more successful than the methods of yesteryear for which they were substituted. Reading problems increase in spite of all the hardware and personnel the public school has acquired to prevent reading problems.

This author proposes that much of the problem may be in the dull, conforming way in which reading is taught. He feels that more creative, child-centered reading approaches need to be installed in our schools. Creativity *can* be developed in the teacher and the student through the teaching of reading. Some of the systems for teaching reading currently used in our schools provide little chance for creative development, while some appear to provide countless opportunities for it. Some plans of classroom organization deny the full development of teacher and student to their creative potentials; others seem to promote it. Almost no independent reading materials currently used in our schools consistently provide for creative development. A careful scrutiny of teaching plans, organizational plans, and teaching materials must be made if the teaching of reading in any school is to promote creative teaching among its teachers and creative thinking among its pupils.

The imposition of pseudoscientific methods of reading on children destroys creativity in teachers, which conversely cuts off the creative teaching of reading. Uncreative teachers become rigid conformists in their slavish addiction to manuals and textbooks, and somewhere in the shuffle *individual* children from whom we expect *differences* are lost. Such teachers quickly lose sight of the importance of individuality and the need for a variety of ways to teach reading. Reading is a skill that develops as a result of a mixture of instruction and the many components making up the personality of the child. Basic to all reading instruction is the awareness on the part of the child that, through reading, he may find the answers to many of his problems and curiosities and experience adventures far removed from his own life. To each child, reading is a personal thing—it serves to round out the knowledge, experience, and concepts his own living cannot afford him. It is a skill he must acquire in order to live effectively in his society.

The teaching of reading must, above all, be exciting, practical, and individual. No child should be hindered in his reading by being forced to wait for a poorer reader. Nor should any child be pushed into material that does not communicate to him. No child should waste time learning skills he already knows, nor should he be handicapped in his reading ability through lack of adequate materials that are on his level and interesting to him.

The basic purpose of teaching reading is to refine the skills to communicate. The development of these skills gives the child the ability to do new things with his life. Reading, for many children, can unlock the doors to creativity. Most of the skills needed for the good reader are the skills necessary to develop creative people.

To the Reader

1. Problems for Discussion:
   a. On page 235 the value of pictures in aiding a child to read is mentioned. Early linguists proposed reading texts without any pictures appearing. They feel pictures interfere with the child's ability to concentrate on sounds and visual images of letters. What do you think?
   b. Some authors feel that the ideal reading situation is when a teacher and a child sit face to face and work individually on reading. This author does not feel that way. He feels that children learn too much from each other to be reading isolated from each other much of the time. He also feels there are times where group

experiences are *more* valuable in helping children to learn to read than individual sessions with the teacher. He feels that the main problem in most reading systems is that we tend to go for individual *or* small group *or* large group reading, when actually a blend of all three is more ideal toward accomplishing the goals of any reading program. What do you think?

c. Read Clymer's study (see bibliography) and discuss this problem: which rules for phonics which often appear in our reading manuals should *not* be taught as generalizations in your opinion?

2. Discuss these statements:
   a. An integrated language arts program is more meaningful than isolated periods of reading, spelling and grammar.
   b. It is important that every child read to the teacher every day.
   c. All children who do not read up to grade level should be referred to the remedial reading teacher.
3. Think of five ways you might increase your own reading rate and reading comprehension. If your college or school has a reading clinic, check to see what methods are used to increase reading speed and comprehension in adults. Are any of these methods applicable to children?
4. How can you turn a heterogeneous grouping of children in a classroom into an asset in the teaching of reading?
5. What changes in an average reading program must be made if you are to be successful in teaching reading in a ghetto school? In a class of slow learners? In a class of children with IQ's of 125 and above?
6. Examine the teacher's manual of any reading series. How many lessons can you find which might be classified as creative?
7. Take *any* lesson in phonics and brainstorm all the ways you might teach it creatively.
8. Look at the words below and sound them out. Check your pronunciation with the dictionary. Often when children sound out words they encounter the same problem you will encounter. Knowing this, can you be more patient with children's experimentation with words? Of what value is phonic analysis in this instance? Might it not be more practical to drill on the memorization of the word?

   tapetum
   iatrophysical
   erythrocyte

9. More Questions for Discussion:
   a. Which plans of grouping currently in vogue in the schools best meet the needs of individual children and set conditions for the most creative experience in reading?

b. Which of these plans of organization seem to work *against* creative teaching: the non-graded school, departmentalization, un-graded classes, ability grouping by grades, the Joplin Plan, self-contained classroom grouping, the Lakeland Plan?

c. Why do so few reading manuals indicate the objectives for each lesson? The next time you meet with a reading group ask yourself, "Do these children really know why they came to this group? Do *they* know what I am trying to teach? Did I actually teach them anything?"

10. Design some independent reading activities that will develop creativity in children. Evaluate some that you are already using as to their effectiveness in teaching language or in developing creativity.
11. In one of his first books on the teaching of reading, Paul McKee presents an interesting gimmick which helps the reader empathize with children and their feelings much the same way that he does in the story, "Will the Bluebirds Please Come Forward." See pages 23–38 of Paul McKee, *The Teaching of Reading in the Elementary School* (New York: Houghton-Mifflin Company, 1948).
12. Did you ever think of all the ways you could teach children to write the alphabet other than just copying it? Start with the Alphabet Funnies on page 492 and brainstorm all the ways you can think of to make children aware of the shapes of the letters of the alphabet.

Selected Bibliography

ANDERSON, VERNA DIECKMAN. *Reading and Young Children.* New York: The Macmillan Company, 1968.

BLOOMFIELD, LEONARD, AND CLARENCE L. BARNHART. *Let's Read.* Detroit, Michigan: Wayne State University Press, 1961.

BOND, GUY, AND EVA BOND WAGNER. *Teaching the Child to Read*, 4th ed. New York: The Macmillan Company, 1966.

BUSH, CLIFFORD L., AND MILDRED H. HUEBNER. *Strategies For Reading in the Elementary School.* New York: The Macmillan Company, 1970.

CARTER, HOMER L. J., AND DOROTHY MCGINNIS. *Diagnosis and Treatment of the Disabled Reader.* New York: The Macmillan Company, 1970.

CHOMSKY, NAOM. *Syntactic Structures.* The Hague, Mouton and Company, 1957.

CLYMER, THEODORE. "The Utility of Phonic Generalizations in the Primary Grades." *Reading Teacher*, vol. 16 (1963), pp. 252–58.

CUTTS, WARREN G. *Research in Reading for the Middle Grades.* Washington, D.C.: Superintendent of Documents, Government Printing Office, 1963.

DAWSON, MILDRED A., AND HENRY A. BAMMAN. *Fundamentals of Basic Reading Instruction.* New York: David McKay Company, 1963.

DEBOER, JOHN, MARTHA DALLMAN, AND WALTER J. MOORE. *The Teaching of Reading,* 3rd ed. New York: Holt, Rinehart and Winston, 1970.

DECHANT, EMERALD. *Improving the Teaching of Reading,* 2nd ed. Englewood Cliffs, New Jersey: Prentice-Hall, Inc., 1970.

———. *Detection and Correction of Reading Difficulties.* New York: Appleton-Century-Crofts, 1971.

DURKIN, DOLORES. *Phonics and the Teaching of Reading,* rev. ed. New York: Bureau of Publications, Teachers College, Columbia University, 1969.

EDWARDS, JOHN L., AND NICHOLAS J. SILVAROLI. *Reading Improvement Program.* Dubuque, Iowa: William C. Brown Company Publishers, 1969.

FITZGERALD, JAMES A., AND PATRICIA G. FITZGERALD. *Fundamentals of Reading Instruction.* New York: The Macmillan Company, 1967.

———. *Teaching Reading and the Language Arts.* New York: The Macmillan Company, 1967.

FRIES, CHARLES C. *Linguistics and Reading.* New York: Holt, Rinehart and Winston, Inc. 1963.

GRAY, WILLIAM. "Reading as Experiencing, Thinking and Learning," in James C. MacCampbell, ed., *Readings in the Language Arts in the Elementary School.* Boston: D. C. Heath and Company, 1964, 411–425.

GREENE, HARRY A., AND WALTER T. PETTY. *Developing Language Skills in the Elementary School,* Chapter XIV. Boston: Allyn and Bacon, 1971, 464–501.

GUNDERSON, DORIS V. *Research in Reading at the Primary Level.* Washington, D.C.: Superintendent of Documents, Government Printing Office, 1963.

HARRIS, THEODORE. "Reading" in Robert Ebel, ed., *Encyclopedia of Educational Research,* 4th ed. New York: The Macmillan Company, 1969, 1069–1104.

HEILMAN, ARTHUR W. *Principles and Practices of Teaching Reading,* 2nd ed. Columbus, Ohio: Charles E. Merrill Books, 1967.

HENDERSON, RICHARD L., AND DONALD R. GREEN. *Reading for Meaning in the Elementary School.* Englewood Cliffs, New Jersey, Prentice-Hall, Inc., 1969.

HERR, SELMA E. *Learning Activities for Reading,* 2nd ed. Dubuque, Iowa: William C. Brown Company Publishers, 1971.

HINMAN, DOROTHY, AND RUTH HINMAN. *Reading for Boys and Girls.* Illinois: Illinois State Library, 1970.

JONES, DAISY MARVEL. *Teaching Children to Read.* New York: Harper and Row, 1971.

MACCAMPBELL, JAMES C., ed. *Readings in the Language Arts in the Elementary School*, Part VII, "Reading Instruction." Boston: D. C. Heath and Company, 1964, 283–331.

MCKEE, PAUL, AND WILLIAM K. DURR. *Reading: A Program of Instruction for the Elementary Grades.* Boston: Houghton Mifflin Company, 1966.

MORRISON, IDA E. *Teaching Reading in the Elementary School.* New York: The Ronald Press, 1968.

ROBINSON, H. ALAN, AND SIDNEY J. RAUCH. *Guiding the Reading Program.* Palo Alto, California: Science Research Associates, 1965.

SCHUBERT, DELWYN G., AND THEODORE TOGERSON. *Improving Reading Through Individualized Correction*, 2nd ed. Dubuque, Iowa: William C. Brown Company Publishers, 1968.

SILVAROLI, NICHOLAS J. *Classroom Reading Inventory*, rev. ed. Dubuque, Iowa: William C. Brown Company Publishers, 1969.

SMITH, FRANK. *Understanding Reading: A Psycholinguistic Analysis of Reading and Learning to Read.* New York: Holt, Rinehart and Winston Company, 1971.

SMITH, HENRY, AND EMERALD DECHANT. *Psychology in Teaching Reading.* Englewood Cliffs, New Jersey: Prentice-Hall, Inc., 1961.

SMITH, JAMES A. *Creative Teaching of Reading in the Elementary School.* Boston: Allyn and Bacon, Inc., 1968.

SMITH, NILA BANTON. *American Reading Instruction.* Newark, Delaware: International Reading Association, 1965.

______. *Reading Instruction for Today's Children.* Englewood Cliffs, New Jersey: Prentice-Hall, Inc., 1963.

SPACHE, GEORGE D., AND EVELYN B. SPACHE. *Reading in the Elementary School.* Boston: Allyn and Bacon, 1969.

STAHL, STANLEY S., JR. *Teaching of Reading in the Intermediate Grades.* Dubuque, Iowa: William C. Brown Company Publishers, 1965.

STAUFFER, RUSSELL G. *Directing Reading Maturity as a Cognitive Process.* New York: Harper and Row, Publishers, 1969.

______. *The Language-Experience Approach to the Teaching of Reading.* New York: Harper and Row, Publishers, 1971.

______. *Teaching Reading as a Thinking Process.* New York: Harper and Row, Publishers, 1971.

STERN, CATHERINE, AND TONI S. GOULD. *Children Discover Reading: An Introduction to Structural Reading.* New York: Random House, 1965.

VEATCH, JEANNETTE. *Reading in the Elementary School.* New York: The Ronald Press, 1966.

VYGOTSKY, L. S. *Thought and Language.* Cambridge, Mass.: MIT-Wiley, 1962.

WARDHAUGH, RONALD. *Reading: A Linguistic Perspective.* New York: Harcourt, Brace and World, 1969.

ZINTZ, MILES V. *Corrective Reading.* Dubuque, Iowa: William C. Brown Company Publishers, 1966.

———. *The Reading Process: The Teacher and the Learner.* Dubuque, Iowa: William C. Brown Company Publishers, 1971.

8

Adventures in Children's Literature

The Saga of the Kola-Kola Bird

Mrs. Palmer's middle school group thoroughly enjoyed Rudyard Kipling's story "The Elephant's Child." Mrs. Palmer seized the opportunity to teach many language skills by developing this much-loved story as a class project. Some of the experiences Mrs. Palmer hoped to provide for her children were as follows:

Art

She hoped to give her class experiences with these media (which they had never had):

Making papier-mâché puppets
Making a mural
Cardboard construction (the stage)
Wire sculpting
Tie-dyeing for curtains

Creativity

She planned to provide experiences in:

Poetry writing
Brainstorming
Art (above)
Voice inflection
Dramatics

Listening

Skills she hoped to develop were:

Ability to select main ideas
Ability to place events in a proper and logical sequence
Ability to develop courteous listening habits
An appreciation of good children's literature
Ability to interpret ideas in dramatics form

Oral Expression

Mrs. Palmer hoped her children would develop:

The ability to read with expression
The ability to make a "tape" which they had not as yet experienced
The ability to use sounds to help develop the humor and tone of a classic piece of literature

Reading

Mrs. Palmer knew that she could:

Introduce new words in a meaningful context
Develop interpretation of new words through painting and dramatization
Introduce new words at the experience and oral level, and then at the reading level in scripts
Develop good audience reading abilities

Refinements of Handwriting: Word Usage, Grammar, etc.

Mrs. Palmer felt that she could teach such skills as script, writing, punctuation usage, grammar, and the spelling of new words.

The project provided her with an opportunity to fulfill her objectives and much more. The children's interest ran so high that other jungle stories were sought from the school library and read. Book reports with pictures followed. Posters were made to advertise the puppet show when it was decided to present it as an assembly program, and Mrs. Palmer brought in the art teacher to teach print skills in making the programs for the show.

In keeping with the language sequence charts, Mrs. Palmer first made certain that the children had encountered words such as "precession" and "equinox" in their daily conversation so they would not interfere with the flow of the story. Then she read the story to the children.

She next provided copies of the story for the children, using dittoed sheets on which she had numbered the paragraphs. Each child chose a paragraph to read. Mrs. Palmer was careful to give guidance to the poorer readers to be certain each chose a paragraph within his reading ability. Children were afforded the opportunity to practice reading their particular paragraph, securing help if necessary from Mrs. Palmer or from a neighbor. When everyone felt he was ready, Mrs. Palmer discussed with the children the possibility of having a musical background all during the puppet play. Records were listened to, and finally "The Elephant Walk" on Henry Mancini's record was chosen as being particularly appropriate.

The children sat in numerical order in a circle, and while "Elephant Walk" was played on a record player in the middle of the circle, each child read his passage into a battery-operated cassette tape recorder which was passed along with one child holding the recorder while the next child read his lines. Martha suggested that the tape be opened with the following announcement, played against a musical background: "Mrs. Palmer's middle school class presents 'The Elephant's Child' by Rudyard Kipling"; and someone had to conclude the show by saying "The end" at the close of the last scene.

After the sound track was made, the puppet show action was planned. Many specific problems arose, which were put on the chalkboard before the room. They included these:

1. From what available materials can we make our puppet stage?
2. From what materials can we make our curtains, and how can we color them?
3. How shall we make our puppets?
4. How do we make papier-mâché?
5. How can we show the elephant's child walking through the forest?
6. How can we make the elephant's child's nose grow longer and longer?
7. How can we have the crocodile open his jaws?

For problems 2 and 4, Mrs. Palmer introduced tie-dyeing and making papier-mâché. Once the skills were acquired, the children began making curtains and some puppets.

Problems 1, 3, 5, 6, and 7 were used as a technique to introduce brainstorming (see page 69). Brainstorming provided some excellent creative thinking and oral expression experiences with the following results:

1. The puppet stage was made from a television carton, painted, decorated, and supplied with curtains.
2. Although the elephant's child and other elephants were made of papier-mâché, it was not an appropriate medium for all puppets. The Kola-Kola bird was eventually made from wire and feathers loosely put together so that she flapped and flipped around. The Hairy Uncle, the Baboon, was made from wire and fur; the Bi-Colored Python Rock Snake was made from a long coiled wire covered with soft cloth so he could stretch and slither. He was operated by a series of wires from above. The Crocodile was made from a stocking, with the toe and heel made into enormous jaws lined with cardboard teeth so he could snap beautifully.
3. The illusion of the elephant's child walking through the forest was obtained by making a long jungle mural in art class, then rolling it on dowels and using it along the rear of the puppet stage so the scenery could move while the elephant's child walked in place, thus giving the illusion of a walk through the jungle.
4. A hole was left in the front of the elephant's child's face where the nose was to go. A long spring was covered with soft gray felt and pushed into the hollow head to give the illusion of a "mere-smere nose." As the nose grew, the child whose fingers were inside the hollow elephant head pushed on a stiff wire fastened to the tip of the nose, thus extending the felt-covered spring farther and farther into the stage, giving the illusion that the nose was growing longer and longer.

These are but a few of the ideas that Mrs. Palmer used to make the project a successful creative experience in language and the creative arts. (Figure 69.)

The puppet show was so successful that other teachers and children who heard about it asked if they might see it. Invitations were sent to other classes, and the show was repeated.

An additional thrill was provided for the children when they were able to see and hear the puppet show themselves. One of the fathers, a professor from a neighboring college, brought in a simple super 8 mm camera and set up a cassette tape recorder, photographed the presentation, and made a running account of the sound track. This simple

Figure 69 *Puppets can be simple or elaborate. This is a creative presentation of "The Country Mouse and the City Mouse."*

operation gave the school a permanent record of a most enjoyable experience.

Children write their own literature if they are encouraged to do so. And once they have done so, they develop an enormous capacity for the good literature of others. Sharing their literature sets conditions for the development of quality. Witness how it is done!

The "Literary Group"

One fourth grade teacher, Mr. Bell, formed a literary group to encourage his children to write creatively. Any class member could become a member of the literary group by submitting some creative writing each week. But this was not all. The group discussed various forms and types of literature, shared good writing of various authors, and were taught about writing by their teacher. In this way, quality in writing was developed in the children. Many of the excellent poems and stories in this book were sent to the author by members of Mr. Bell's literary group. The last packet of material was accompanied by the following letter:

May 27, 1970

Dear Sir,

Enclosed are some stories and poems that we have been working on for quite some time. Mr. Bell thought that you would enjoy seeing them so we collected them to share with you.

Our literary group has been working very hard on these stories and poems. We are now trying our skill on plays.

Thank you so much for your time and interest.

Sincerely yours,
Mr. Bell's Literary Group

One of the stories in the packet was written about a dog by Jeanette and appears below. I am sure the reader will see that writing quality in fourth grade can be developed when proper psychological and intellectual conditions are set.

Bullet

Bullet raced ahead of Joany and Susan who were riding their horses, Apache and Black Magic. Joany was 9 and Susan was 11.

They were all very happy this spring morning, and the smell in the air seemed to tell them something exciting was going to happen. Bullet had seen a rabbit and was off after him. The rabbit bounded off through the tall weeds, and although Bullet could not always see him the smell was strong. The rabbit sensed that he had to do something fast or he would be caught. He turned and dashed into the thick woods. Bullet was confused, but only for a moment. Then he was after the rabbit again. Soon the rabbit came to a hole by a tree and scrambled down it. Bullet sniffed and scratched at the hole, but the rabbit was safe inside, so he turned slowly around and started back to Joany and Susan.

Meanwhile Joany and Susan were trying to find Bullet.

"There he goes," cried Susan pointing to a brown and white tail that was racing along through the weeds.

"Oh, I see him too," replied Joany.

They galloped after the bobbing tail. Soon they met Bullet again.

"Let's go up in the mountains today," suggested Joany.

"O.K., I'll race you," answered Susan.

"Come on, Bullet."

They galloped through the rest of the field and started up the hillside. It was rough going for the horses, so the race wasn't as exciting as it started out to be. The horses picked their way slowly around boulders and fallen logs.

"I won," Susan declared, as she reached the top, just a few steps ahead of Joany.

"Oh no you didn't," replied Joany, "Bullet did."

And sure enough there was Bullet sitting on a log looking proud and happy.

"All right, Bullet, lead on," commanded Susan.

Bullet jumped off the log and ran slowly over the mossy ground just ahead of the girls and their horses.

"We'd better be careful of the cougars," warned Susan.

"Oh yes," answered Joany. "I hope nothing happens."

As they continued along they came to a big oak tree in the middle of a small forest at the top of the mountain.

"Oh, let's climb that tree," begged Joany.

"All right."

They got off their horses and tied the reins to some tree branches. Then they ran to the oak and started climbing it.

"Let's play tree tag," said Susan.

"All right," agreed Joany. "I'm it."

They ran along the strong supporting branches. Joany tagged Susan and swung up to a higher branch.

"Now you can't get me," she declared.

"Oh yes I can," answered Susan as she too climbed higher. Joany got on another branch and then jumped to one below it. Susan jumped too and tagged Joany on the head.

"I told you I'd get you," she exclaimed.

"But I'm going to get you too, so watch out."

The girls ran around on the branches and soon Susan came to a wide gap where a branch had cracked off. Joany came up behind her so fast that Susan fell to the ground below.

"Are you all right?" asked Joany worriedly.

"Yes," answered Susan. "The ground is soft."

"I didn't mean to push you," said Joany climbing down. "But I couldn't help it. I fell forward when I stepped on the branch you were on."

"That's all right, but we'd better go home now. It's getting towards evening and it's chilly."

"Yes. I can't wait 'till we get into the middle of spring; it will be even lighter at night."

The girls mounted their horses and rode slowly off. Bullet, who was dozing quietly in the grass, jumped up and ran after the girls. He startled a pheasant, which took off in a flurry of wings. A chipmunk, just going into his nest in a tree, scolded them. Even at dusk spring was a very nice time of year.

"That was a blast," said Joany happily.

"Yes," answered Susan. "I'm coming back tomorrow."

"Me too."

"Maybe we can go further."

"We might even be able to pack a lunch and bring it with us."

"Oh, I hope so."

Suddenly from above them they heard a low growl.

The horses bolted in fright. Above them the girls could see the huge form of a cougar. He jumped from boulder to boulder. Susan's horse was farther away than Joany's, so the cougar leaped at Joany's horse. The terrified horse reared and threw Joany into a ditch. The cougar landed beside the horse. So the horse took off as fast as he could down the mountain side. Susan got off her horse and let him go, but she didn't know how to help her sister.

Just then Bullet came dashing out of the bushes. The cougar wheeled around to face him. Bullet moved in, and then attacked. The cougar cuffed him on the neck and climbed higher. But Bullet was not going to give up. He leaped up after the cougar and lunged at him. He nipped the cougar slightly on the shoulder, and dodged the cougar's paw. Then he lunged again and bit into the cougar's front leg. Since the cougar could go no higher, he leaped to a ledge below Bullet and turned to face him. Bullet crouched and then leaped upon the cougar. This sent them both rolling down the hillside. The cougar saw his chance for freedom and pulling free dashed up the hillside. Bullet did not bother to chase him further.

Susan climbed down from the tree she had hidden in while Bullet and the cougar fought. She ran to the ditch and jumped in beside her sister.

"Are you all right?" she asked.

"Yes, but my leg is stuck under a log."

"I'll pull on it but you'll have to be still."

"I will."

Susan took hold of the end of the log and pulled. It moved slightly but then it would not move at all. So she took a long tree branch and put the end under the log. Then she pushed on the other end of the branch. The log rolled slowly off Joany's leg.

"Does it hurt?"

"No. It was just sitting on my leg, but I couldn't move it."

Susan helped her get up and then they climbed out of the ditch. Susan ran over to Bullet, who was resting in the grass.

"Oh, Bullet, you're bleeding," she exclaimed.

Joany came up and hugged Bullet.

"It's awfully dark now," said Susan. "We'll have to stay here all night and go home in the morning."

The girls stayed close to Bullet all night. They tried to stay awake but they could not.

In the morning Susan woke up to find Joany still asleep. Apache and Black Magic had come back and were grazing a few feet away.

"Where are we?" asked Joany sleepily.

"Oh, you're awake now. We're in the mountains, remember?" answered Susan.

"Oh, yes."

Joany started to get up but fell back.

"Oh, my leg hurts," she groaned.

"Let me see it."

Susan pressed gently on Joany's leg.

"I'd better go for help."
"Who will stay with me?"
"Bullet."
"All right, but how are you going to go?"
"The horses came back."
"O.K."
Susan mounted and waved good-bye. Then she was off. She had to go slowly down the mountain. Soon she reached the field and galloped off. After a while she came to her farm. Her father and several other men were getting horses ready.
"Dad," she called.
Her father galloped to meet her.
"Are you all right? Where's Joany?" he asked.
"She's up in the mountains. She's hurt. Bullet saved us from a cougar and he's with her now."
"All right, lead us to them," he said. "Come on men."
They were off across the field. Then they climbed slowly up the mountain. Soon they came to where Joany was. Her father examined her leg and then put her on his horse.
"We'll have to call the doctor as soon as we get home. And we'll fix up Bullet too."
He picked up Bullet and laid him across one of the men's saddle. Then he climbed up behind Joany and they rode home.

The End

The Place of Literature

Literature is what learning to read is all about! Reading skills are learned so that children may be able to read the literature written for them. No school can honestly boast a good reading program, then, unless that school has an excellent, well-stocked library.

Children's literature makes definite contributions toward creative development in boys and girls, and offers many opportunities for creative teaching. Literature is the creative product of the minds of creative people. As a painting serves to fire the imagination, so does a fine story, a well-composed poem, or a good book. Children who write their own literature are always eager to see what others write. True literature stimulates the imagination and contributes to the children's concept of the use of imagination in creating. The creative teaching of literature can contribute to creative development in many ways:

1. It can stimulate children to write for themselves.
2. It can provide a means of therapy for troubled children.

3. It can help children build skills in expression, in defining, and in elaboration.
4. It can help build a colorful vocabulary that will assist each child to express himself better.
5. It can serve as the basis for constructive daydreaming and complete identification with a problem (so necessary for creative problem solving).
6. It can make children more discreet in passing judgement and making choices, especially in the use of words.
7. It can be the perpetual source of creative stimulation for every child.
8. It can develop a sensitivity to places, sights, sounds, words, life problems, and people.
9. It helps children build a set of standards and values regarding creative writing.

Literature should not be "taught"; it should only be *read* and *enjoyed.* The teacher's job in sharing a story or a poem with children is a simple one: She is an intermediary between the author and his audience, and her major duty is to try to put across the author's ideas as though she were a substitute for him.

Through literature the child develops his tastes in reading for pleasure. If he experiences satisfaction in the stories the teacher reads, he will seek out this satisfaction in other stories. Satisfaction, happiness, contentment, fun, joy, positive release, pleasure: All these feelings should accompany the literature period in the classroom.

Literature fulfills a need in the modern school which does not confine it to the language arts alone. It touches on every aspect of living and therefore should become an integral part of the entire school program. At least once every day, and in some instances many more times than this, a teacher should read a poem or story to the children regardless of age range or grade placement. The wealth of available material gives her resources for every occasion.

Although literature is often classified among the fine arts, in the elementary school it can be combined with any area of the school curriculum. Social studies books can, at best, be only a summary of facts about a country or a period in history. They cannot consume space to give to children the feeling for the way of life in any given country or any period of time. Without the "feeling" element, facts cannot help children understand life in a time or place different from their own. Reading about Switzerland in a social studies book is one thing, and reading *Heidi* is another. Facts about the Revolutionary War cannot impart to children the terror, the suspense, the fear, the bravery, the courage, the compassion, or the hatred which war arouses in the hearts of men, whereas reading *The Matchlock Gun* or *Drums Along the Mohawk* can. Social studies books reach the minds of children, but literature reaches their hearts.

Good literature recaptures the *mood* rather than the *facts* of life. The life of a bygone period of time is reconstructed, a strange place comes alive, or a feeling or mood saturates the reader to the extent that the author is able to communicate in an imaginative manner. It is not the *story* of Tom Sawyer and Huckleberry Finn that makes it a delightful book—it is the author's unique ability to make every boy today feel a kinship with Tom, because he understands Tom through the genius of the author's communicative power. Tom makes fires glow in the hearts of fathers, bringing back the carefree adventurous feeling of their own boyhoods; he evokes nostalgic memories through the magic grouping of words. So literature can transplant us to another world or another period of time; it can create an emotional situation, a mood or tone, a feeling. We experience sadness, love, joy, disgust, hatred, sympathy. This we do through empathy, our ability to project ourselves into the situation and live within the consciousness of the characters created by the author.

The therapeutic value of literature must be recognized. Creative writing provides emotional release, and, in reading the writings of others, many children are able to project themselves so that they receive help with their own problems. They come to understand human nature by learning that their problems are not unique.

The field of literature, then, belongs in the area of the creative arts for the aesthetic values it has; it belongs to the field of language arts, for it is the most perfected use of symbolic communicative tools; it belongs to the area of the social sciences for the knowledge and understanding it develops. More intimately than any other subject matter area, literature, as children write and read it, goes hand in hand with the goals of the modern school. It *is* communication through creative experiences.

Criteria for Choosing Literature for Children

Literature is concerned more with the telling of the story than with the plot. It is the raising of the commonplace to the beautiful by caring enough to choose exactly the right word for the right place. Six criteria for the selection of literature to read to children are:

1. The story must be relevant to the children and to the situation.
2. The story should have a fresh well-paced plot or relate a relevant, exciting incident.

3. It must have unique individuality.
4. It should contain plausible, direct conversation.
5. It must have well-delineated characters.
6. The story must have authentic outcomes.

Leland Jacobs[1] feels that good children's literature must be free from obvious sentimentality while being rich in honest sentiment; it must be free from direct moralizing but rooted in genuine spiritual and moral values; it must be free from cuteness and triteness but vigorously unhackneyed and distinctive; it must be free from talking down or misunderstanding of children's abilities. He feels good literature has "memory" value—there is a residue of meaning after time lapses.

Periodically, surveys are developed to assist the teacher in the selection of appropriate literature at various age levels. These surveys show that children tend to have specific interests at different ages, but that with the changing interests, there remain some persistent overall ones. Children tend to maintain an interest in machines, nature, everyday experiences, holidays, love, fun stories and poems, and make-believe.[2]

Young children prefer literature that has one main plot. They want to be able to anticipate the outcome of the story. They like literature that sets a mood, and they like "direct" conversation. They enjoy colorful "tongue-tickling" words and prefer simple, natural climaxes in their stories. They like stories developed around one main character, and generally they prefer one acceptable boy or girl hero, although sometimes an animal hero may act as an acceptable substitute. And they like literature with illustrations that also tell the story.[3]

As children grow older, they develop a keener interest in animals, especially specific animals such as horses or cats. Older children like folk literature and stories of American folk heroes. They like modern magic, stories about contemporary experiences, historical fiction, regional fiction, and intergroup fiction. They enjoy reading about child life in other countries, and like biographies and books about science. They also enjoy stories built around such themes as sports, games, religion, arts, crafts, heroes, humor, mystery, travel, nature; or stories about children with their own characteristics and problems.[4]

In choosing books for children's reading, or in guiding children in the selection of their own reading, teachers will keep in mind the following

1. Leland Jacobs, "Children's Experiences in Literature," in *Children and the Language Arts*, Virgil Herrick and Leland B. Jacobs (eds.), (Englewood Cliffs, New Jersey: Prentice-Hall, Inc., 1955), p. 194.
2. Ibid., pp. 196–198.
3. Ibid., p. 198.
4. Ibid., p. 198.

sources: contemporary literature, great stories and classics, realistic tales, fanciful tales, stories of fiction, stories of information, current material in periodicals, popular materials and distinctively literary reading matter, anthologies, and inexpensive books on children's literature.

Creative Teaching of Literature

A good story or a good poem will stand by itself; it needs no embellishment. Because this statement is obviously true, librarians and teachers sometimes frown on any activity that detracts from the story or poem being read to the children.

While the basic criterion for using any piece of literature *is* that it communicate effectively and beautifully, much can be done to develop children's taste in literature. Today's children are exposed to much cheap, yet often impressive, writing. They become confused when no attempt is made to help them distinguish between good and poor literature. Children are not born with a set of standards and values. These they develop as a result of the understandings they glean from their experiences. Setting conditions for the creative teaching of literature means that the teacher provides experiences that help each child to become more selective in his reading, more critical of the type of material he reads, and more sensitive to good writing. It is likely that Mrs. Palmer's children will always look upon "The Elephant's Child" with fondness and affection.

Inasmuch as empathy is necessary in order to experience literature, and the ability to project oneself into any situation is dependent on one's own related experiences and feelings, it is not enough that children hear good literature in the classroom—they must *experience* it. This means that though sometimes the reading of a poem or story will suffice in itself, in most instances conditions must be set so that the children can experience or live the material being read. It is this additional attention paid to the "good" stories and poems that makes children realize they are special. By living and feeling the story with the characters, and by learning to express their own feelings in carefully chosen words, they come to see the skill of the author—and to appreciate the quality of the work. Through classroom experiences with literature, they build their own values and standards, and learn to evaluate the writing of others.

In setting conditions for developing a love and appreciation for literature, there are a few hints a teacher might follow:

1. *Remember that it is not only the plot that makes the story a good one; it is the way it is told.* Encourage the children to use the author's

words as much as possible. Be sure that the Elephant's Child does not look only for the crocodile, but also for "the great grey greasy Limpopo River all set around by fever trees."

2. *Children can interpret the author's words only in light of their own experiences.* Do not try to force your interpretation of a story on them. Let them dramatize or retell it in their own way. Although their interpretation may not be the same as yours, the retelling does give you an opportunity to correct gross misconceptions.

3. *Enjoyment of the piece of work, not perfection of performance, should be the goal.* Should some child's or some group's contribution be exceptionally well received, the class may work on it to "polish it up" for other classes or for parents. This should happen only occasionally, for polished performances take too long to prepare. Children should receive enjoyment from experiences with literature every day.

4. *Continually draw attention to phrases or words in the writing that make it unique or give special delight.* All over America children love to chant:

> He meant what he said
> And he said what he meant
> And an elephant's faithful
> One hundred percent.

and

> Listen, my children, and you shall hear
> Of the midnight ride of Paul Revere—

and

> "The time has come," the Walrus said—

and

> Speak for yourself, John

and

> Fourscore and seven years ago

Phrases lifted from literature are as much a part of life as learning itself. To know them is part of the children's rightful heritage.

The teaching of reading and the enjoyment of literature go hand in hand. In skill-building reading periods, children learn the tools needed to unlock the joys concealed in the world of books. Children come to school with a reservoir of literature of some kind in their background. Much of this can be used to teach reading. Miss George, for instance, printed the favorite phrases of her children on a chart before the room, and these children learned to read them as they learned to read an experience chart.

The first reading chart composed by the class may well be their first experience at composing literature. A sensitive teacher will make certain that these first charts *are* well composed, simple as they may be. A good program in the enjoyment of literature and poetry may grow out of the first compositions of the children. As soon as children write their own stories, the stories may be placed on charts and read and enjoyed by other children. Every topic suggests a work of literature or a poem that will help children understand the power of effective communication. An understanding and appreciation of good literature develop most readily when children write their own and then discover that others enjoy the power of expression through words.

General Classroom Conditions Necessary to Build an Appreciation of Literature

A teacher must work at keeping good literature before her class. Some activities employed by successful teachers are listed below:

1. Have a library corner with good books easily available.
2. Keep a bulletin board of good books before the class. Discarded book jackets, posters, and pictures of favorite authors will help make these bulletin boards attractive.
3. Read a poem or story to the class at least once a day.
4. Encourage children to share the good books they have read by providing time during "sharing" periods.
5. Provide time every day for children to choose favorite books and to read silently.
6. Encourage the children to tell and write stories, poems, and books.
7. Take the class to good motion pictures of great pieces of literature or show these films in the classroom.
8. Use film strips, such as those of the Weston Woods, to create an interest in new books.
9. Use creative book reports for children to share each other's literature experiences.
10. Draw or paint pictures of favorite poems, books, or characters.
11. Encourage children to share their home libraries with the class. Ask them to bring three or four books from home and tell the others about them while they show the pictures.
12. Encourage frequent trips to the town library or the school library.

13. Reserve time occasionally for the school librarian to come into the room and show new books from the library or tell a story.

14. Encourage children to take advantage of local children's theater groups or traveling companies who do a notable adaptation of some piece of children's literature.

15. Watch the paper for good commercial television shows that portray some great children's literature.

16. Play some of the better commercial recordings of dramatizations of children's stories, such as *Hansel and Gretel*, *The Littlest Angel*, *The Christmas Carol*, *Peter and the Wolf*.

17. Organize a Book Club or a Literary Group that meets once a week in your classroom.

18. Children can make their own book jackets for their favorite books.

19. Make up good book lists for parents and have them dittoed to be sent home. This may be done around Thanksgiving time as a guide for parents in purchasing children's books for Christmas gifts.

20. Watch for radio programs that dramatize children's literature.

21. In art class, have the children make posters of books they like. When made in three dimensions, these posters add interest to book exhibits, library displays, and bulletin board exhibits.

22. Devote a few assemblies each year to programs about books. If each grade would take responsibility for putting on one assembly program during the year to which other classes were invited, the children would be constantly exposed to books on all reading levels and all topics.

23. Celebrate Book Week with assemblies, exhibits, visits from authors, library trips, story hours, displays, and special programs. Be sure all children have a part in preparing for Book Week. (Many ideas for Book Week programs may be found on the following pages.)

24. Hold at least one or two Book Fairs a year where the materials made by the children may be exhibited. However, a fair should expose children to hundreds of new and exciting books. It will be necessary to arrange for traveling commercial exhibits and book companies to exhibit. The books should be covered with strong plastic covers so that they may be handled and skimmed by children.

25. Correlate literature with all your classroom work. In social studies, read great books to help children understand the life of any given country. *Heidi* correlates well with a study of Switzerland, *The Secret Garden* with England. Kipling's stories relate well to India, and *The White Stag* is perfect reading when studying the countries of central Europe. Many books provide excellent material for dealing with social problems.

26. In grammar classes, styles of writing may be studied by reading from various authors. Much literature has been set to music, such as "The Lord's Prayer," "The Owl and the Pussycat," "Little Boy Blue,"

"A Nautical Ballad," "Cradle Hymn," "The Nutcracker." Less notable ones that are, nonetheless, part of the children's rightful heritage, are "The Night Before Christmas," nursery rhymes, and folk ballads of the West, the mountains, and the plains. Music and literature can be closely correlated by singing some of the great poems set to music, or by hearing them sung by great artists on high-fidelity recordings. Every aspect of the school curriculum may be correlated with some great children's story or poem.

27. Art work is a close companion to literature. Correlations in art have already been suggested in: bulletin board displays; creative book reports; drawing and painting pictures of stories, books and poems; making posters and book week exhibits and displays. Other ways art may be correlated are:

a. Use cut-out illustrations for children's favorite selections.
b. Use crayon sketches.
c. Use block print designs for posters and for covers for Book Week programs.
d. Have the children fingerpaint pictures of the literature they read.
e. Spatter paint designs can be used as variety in illustration.
f. Make silhouette designs of favorite scenes from their readings.
g. Colored chalk lends variety to illustrations, especially in covering large surfaces such as murals or backdrops for scenes.
h. Favorite characters can be depicted with soap carvings.
i. Sand-table scenes of favorite stories may be constructed.
j. Wood models may also be constructed.
k. Dolls may be dressed to represent storybook characters (real and paper dolls).
l. Prints (potato prints, cork prints, and linoleum prints) may be used to make book covers, program covers, and invitations to Book Week programs.

Methods and Techniques for Building an Appreciation and Standards in Literature

Dramatization

Most obvious of all the ways to live literature is through dramatization, which helps the children get the feel of the characters and sense the mood of the story. Many stories and poems lend themselves well to dramatization. The dramatizing of a poem or story can be creative in itself if children are encouraged to interpret characters, improvise props, and develop moods.

If we apply the principles of the creative situation to dramatization, however, we must go beyond a simple dramatization of a story in order to build up those qualities which make for creative and critical thinking. Mr. Brooks, a sixth grade teacher, read *The Adventures of Tom Sawyer* to his children. They then chose to dramatize the fence-painting scene. Many children volunteered to play the parts. Mr. Brooks chose a cast and gave them a few minutes to get simple props and to establish a crude setting. Then the group dramatized the scene. When they had finished, Mr. Brooks and the rest of the sixth grade told what they had liked about the scene and also made suggestions as to how it could be improved.

Then another cast depicted the scene. In the discussion that followed, Mr. Brooks pointed out that the differences in the interpretation were good, since different characters could be portrayed in different ways without spoiling the plot of the story. The children also noted that the character of Aunt Polly lent itself least to a varied interpretation.

Through evaluation of this sort, children come to understand characterization very well. They also use words that describe the characters they are portraying, thus developing a good oral vocabulary for later use in their own writing.

Dramatization does not always have to be a story. Little children dramatize freely—they will mimic ducks, chickens, and pigs as easily as they mimic people. Intermediate grade teachers might well make use of this technique to build up the idea of character. Here are some kinds of dramatizations, other than stories, that teachers may use.

1. Pretend you are an animal. Act like the animal you choose, and let the class guess what you are.
2. The next time you go to a shopping center, watch one person closely. Then dramatize this person for us and we will see if we can tell what he was doing.
3. Show anger, pain, hunger, fear, joy.
4. Working in groups, dramatize a scene you saw during the past week at home or in school. Use no voice, just pantomime.
5. Dramatize a holiday using no sound, only action.
6. Dramatize a day and have the class guess what the weather is like on that particular day.
7. Dramatize such words as "airy," "beauty," "hopeful," "tremble," "painful," "exciting."
8. Dramatize your spelling words.
9. Dramatize one line of poetry.
10. Pretend you are in a circus. Show us what you do.

Figure 70 *A fourth grade dramatization includes a scene of "Johnny Appleseed."*

Poetry also lends itself well to dramatization. Mr. Palmer's sixth grade dramatized "Casey at the Bat"; Miss Hobart's third grade did "The Elf and the Dormouse." In both instances the children came to understand the drama and humor in the poems.

Some books lend themselves to other kinds of dramatizations such as pageants, shadow plays, or puppet plays. (Figures 70, 71, and 72.)

Telling and Reading Stories

Both telling and reading stories have a place in presenting good literature to children. Certain stories, poems, and plays are written in such a way that to tell them would be to spoil them. This is especially true of books where the script rhymes, or where especially beautiful words are used to set a specific tone for the story. Dr. Suess's rhyming books need to be read (unless the teacher can memorize the script). Robert McCluskey's *Time of Wonder* is a book that needs to be read because of the way this particular author uses the soft sounds of "s" and "c" to give the impression of the softness of fog and rain, and the way he uses other sounds to develop an audio atmosphere for his story.

Other books should be read because of the close relationship between the story and the pictures. Many primary books are written in such a way that the pictures help tell the story. McCluskey's *Blueberries for Sal* and

Figure 71 *A scene from a sixth grade production of* The Wizard of Oz.

Make Way for Ducklings are good examples of such books. When books of this nature are read, it is essential that the teacher set proper physical conditions so that all children can easily see the pictures.

When the teacher *tells* a story, something different happens. When read, the book is the focus of attention for both teacher and children; however, when a story is told, the focus of attention is the teacher's face. Her voice inflections, her expression, her degree of animation, and her own enthusiasm play the major part in putting the story across. The art of storytelling has almost become a lost one. It is due for a revival. Children gain something unique and special from this kind of experience with literature.

In telling stories, the teacher need not memorize; this often makes for a stilted and wooden performance. She needs to know the story well, with the logical sequence of events carefully organized in her mind. Even more important than this, she must memorize the words, lines, or phrases that give the story its personality and charm—and repeat them in exactly the right places.

Because folk tales have always been passed along from mouth to mouth, they lend themselves especially well to telling. Such stories as "The King of the Golden River," "The Man Who Kept House," "The Gingerbread Boy," "East of the Sun and West of the Moon," and "The Princess of the Glass Hill" are especially suitable for telling. Legends and fairy tales fall into the same category.

Proper physical conditions are essential in storytelling. All distractions should be removed. Children should probably sit facing the quietest wall in the classroom. The teacher should stand if children are

Figure 72 *Miss Liberty dramatically welcomes settlers to the shores of America in a fourth grade original play, "The Melting Pot."*

seated—at any rate she must be easily seen. Her own voice must be sure and clear. Her face must show the animation and expression necessary to project the story as well as the mode or feeling of the words. She must see herself as the author, telling the story directly to the audience for which it was written.

Storytelling becomes highly personal in that it is person to person, with no barriers or distractions. It is communication in its most elementary and most beautiful form. The great literature of the past was all passed along this way before man could read and write. All children should experience the joy of hearing their teachers tell stories, since this is the way young children will communicate at home before *they* can read and write. Storytelling is an art that children should be encouraged to keep through their lives to pass along to their own children.

Making Films

Film making is less expensive today than it was, and children can have many worthwhile experiences making a real movie and showing it to other children. Actually, making a moving picture is not much different from making a play—only much more permanent! An 8 mm camera can be used with black and white or colored film. Taking movies is so simple with modern built-in view-finders that children can be quickly taught how to do it.

Mrs. Briggs's fourth grade enjoyed reading "Hansel and Gretel" so much that they decided they would make a moving-picture film of it. Mrs. Briggs borrowed a camera for the shooting of the film. The children had raised some money for classroom activities, and they used it to purchase the film.

First they rewrote the story into a script. Then, since they had no indoor lighting equipment, they obtained some large sheets of cardboard from a box manufacturer, and on this they painted a cottage scene to set up outdoors. For the woods scene, they used the woods behind the school. They also painted, on heavy cardboard, a gingerbread house to set up in the woods.

Costumes were simple and were made for the most part from crepe paper. Props were gathered from around the school or brought from home.

A book on moving-picture making was obtained from the library. The children learned a movie-making vocabulary and talked in terms of "going out on location" or "building the set."

The case of main characters was chosen through a discussion in which criteria were established for each part; then children tried out for the parts. Voting was done in terms of the established criteria and checked against performance.

Although only a few children were chosen for the main parts, they all took part in some way. Some made titles, some painted scenes, some cared for costumes. There were scene designers, directors, camera men, editors, and a make-up crew. All the children took part in one dance, "Brother Come and Dance with Me," which they called their "production number."

The scenes were shot in true Hollywood style, not in sequence but whenever they were ready, provided, of course, that the weather was suitable.

After the film was developed, returned, edited, and shown, the children decided to put the songs, music, and script on a tape to go with the moving picture.

The entire project cost $12.00 and keeping track of the expenses provided some excellent arithmetic experiences.

The children showed the film at a P.T.A. meeting, where Mrs. Briggs explained the learning values that came from the work. They called this showing their "World Premiere" and advertised it as such.

These children lived this story with every fiber of their beings. Such an experience made them appreciate good stories and gave them the opportunity for many social and academic experiences.

Book Reports

There are many ways of giving book reports so that they are creative and challenging to children. Too often, books are read for the primary purpose of making a report on Book Report Day, which makes the literature secondary. Book reports assigned in this manner often make a child hate a book. If he has liked the book, he will *want* to tell others about it! The inventive teacher will find many ways to encourage the child to *tell* about his book.

* * *

Miss Wagner organized her class into a Book Club that met from one to two o'clock every Friday. Each Friday morning the members of the class were divided into five groups. Then the children took their weekly trip to the library where, in addition to other books, each child chose one book he wanted to read for fun and brought it back to the classroom.

During Book Club time the groups met around five tables, and for the first five minutes everyone looked at the books each child had chosen for fun reading. Then each group selected one book and a child to read it to them. The five groups sat at different places in the room where a story was read to them. After half an hour they discussed whether they wanted to report on their book to the rest of the class. If they did, they decided on interesting ways in which they might present the book, and selected one. During the following week they had time to prepare their report.

The last fifteen minutes of each Book Club meeting were spent in the presentation of one group's report. Thelma's group read "The Five Chinese Brothers," and with Miss Wagner's help they gave the following presentation."

The six girls on the committee made flowers for their hair from colored facial tissues. They made their eyes look oriental with an eyebrow pencil. Then each made a picture of one of the Chinese brothers, accenting his unique feature—such as the legs that stretched or the neck that could not be cut off. These pictures were made on wrapping paper so they rolled up easily. Each girl brought an oriental Halloween costume from home, or a kimono or house coat.

At the beginning of the presentation, the children played the record, "The March of the Siamese Children." Then Thelma tiptoed into the room and stood before the group. The five other girls minced in behind her, holding their rolled-up pictures, and stood in a row behind Thelma. Thelma bowed deeply to Miss Wagner. "Honorable Teacher," she said. Then she bowed to the class, "And Honorable Classmates," she added, "I would tell you a story about five Chinese brothers. Now each brother had something very strange about him. One had a neck that could not be cut off." At this line, Becky tiptoed to the front of the improvised stage and let her picture unroll. Each character was introduced in this way.

After this, Thelma invited the class to read the book to find out what happened to them, and the six Chinese sisters minced out of the room while Miss Wagner turned off the record player.

Bill and Sid gave their book report by using a flannel board. It worked out very well for *Robinson Crusoe*, because new characters and objects could be added to develop the scene as they went along.

A group of five boys gave scenes from *Treasure Island* by using a sheet with a light behind it to make a shadow graph. Scenery was made by simply tearing or cutting shapes from wrapping paper and pinning them to the sheet so that the shadow made a setting. Another group chose different scenes from their story and pasted them in sequence on shelf paper from which they made a roll movie.

Projects such as these not only arouse children's creative thinking, they also serve the additional objective of making literature live.

Bulletin Boards

Bulletin boards can be exciting condition setters for experiences with good literature. Throughout this book, frequent mention has been made of the bulletin board as an instructional device. Bulletin boards may be arranged for a variety of objectives; in the realm of children's literature, some of them are:

1. Motivation to interest children in new books or poems.
2. To have the children share their writing and reading with their classmates.
3. To summarize an experience in literature.
4. To impart information.
5. To provide individual instruction or individual work for the children.
6. To share beautiful passages, phrases, or words.
7. To encourage creative writing on the part of the children.

8. To advertise or announce new books and events about books.
9. To display first editions, unusual books, or illustrations in books.

Let us see how one teacher used the bulletin board to fulfill these objectives.

* * *

Miss Nelson used her bulletin board a great deal as a summary of experiences with literature. After her fourth grade had read Kipling's "How the Camel Got His Hump," the children built a scene of the story from cut construction paper.

On another occasion Miss Nelson used Carl Sandburg's "Fog" as motivation for some creative writing on a foggy day. She printed the poem on a cardboard and centered it on a bulletin board. After the children had discussed it, and then discussed the fog, they made up phrases and poems describing the fog, which were posted around the poem. One child suggested the title "Foggy Ideas," which was printed and placed over the bulletin board.

Miss Nelson brought in an armful of old magazines one day. After she read them the poem, "America the Beautiful," the children went through the magazines and found pictures to illustrate the poem. These were then mounted on the bulletin board around a printed copy of the poem. On another occasion, the children drew their own pictures.

Miss Nelson used the bulletin board a great deal to integrate social studies with literature. Bulletin boards built around such topics as "Stories about Mexico," "Children in Other Lands," "Children in Trouble," "Books about Living Together" helped Miss Nelson direct the children's attention to the literature dealing with the topic being studied.

When the fourth grade was studying Indians, Miss Nelson introduced the unit by reading "The Song of Hiawatha" while she played soft drum music on the record player. From this reading came a dramatization followed by questions about Indian life. This led to a bulletin board built around the questions, and pictures of Indians depicting the answers.

Bulletin boards can be very creative and helpful in setting conditions for the enjoyment of literature. To be creative, they must be ingenious, fresh, and interesting so as to provide an outlet for creative expression much as a painting or a clay modeling does. Here are a few suggestions that should be considered in making bulletin boards that place no restrictions on the creator.

1. The overall effect of the completed bulletin board should be as well

designed and as pleasing to the eye as a painting. Too much material can make bulletin boards confusing and cluttered.

2. Any lettering should be as much a part of the total design as the other material on the bulletin board. It should not be tacked on as an afterthought.
3. Bulletin boards are more attractive if material is grouped according to related ideas rather than simply spread out in any manner. Rest spaces for the eye help the purpose of the bulletin board to become more apparent.
4. Every bulletin board should be centered around an idea or purpose, and that idea or purpose should be outstanding enough to be both immediately recognizable and conveyed across the room. The main idea should attract the children so that they are drawn to the bulletin board to read or see the subtopics. Importance can be obtained for the outstanding idea by having it larger in size, brighter in color, or more prominently placed than any other idea on the bulletin board.

Displays and Exhibits

Displays and exhibits can help children develop a love of books. Many schools have Book Fairs during Book Week when all the grades display the creations they have made which relate to good children's books. Often, assembly programs are given to stimulate an interest in stories and poems. Exhibits of commercial books, original sketches for various books, and bulletin boards of the authors and their lives can add a great deal of interest to such an exhibit. To make the exhibit even more meaningful and "live," films may be scheduled at various times. Many schools invite an author to be present to tell stories or to sketch for the children.

Commercial publishing houses will supply catalogues for such exhibits. Children should have the opportunity to handle books and to help select those that are to be purchased for the school library. Good children's magazines and periodicals should constitute a portion of the book exhibits.

Often the neighborhood library advertises a children's book exhibit. School personnel should take advantage of these exhibits by taking children on excursions to see them.

The value of displays and exhibits is enhanced when children have a part in setting them up. This involves careful planning, however. Haphazard exhibits are often so confusing that they become ineffective. Material should be grouped topically, by authors or by reading level. When tables are used, they should be elevated at the back in some way

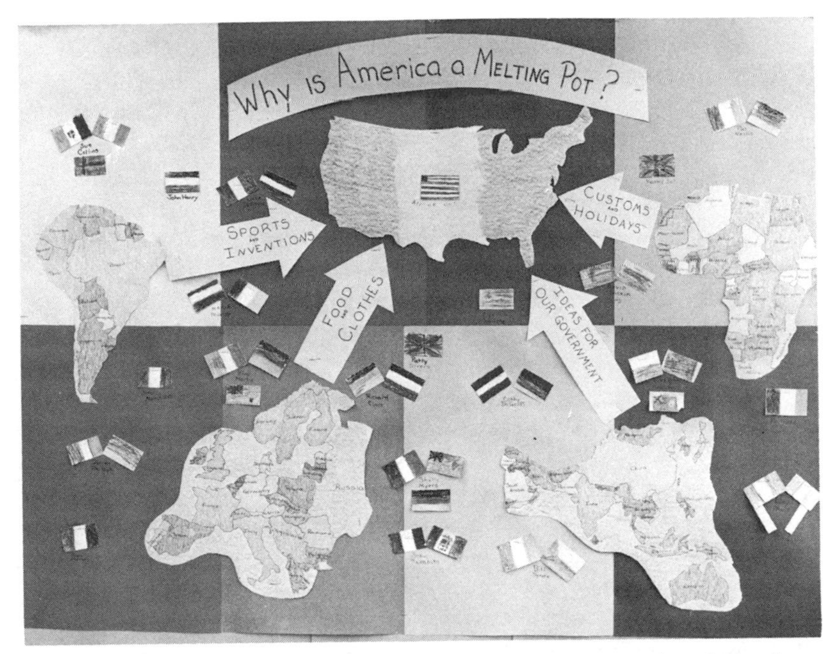

Figure 73 *Bulletin boards can be very creative. Here a fourth grade committee has put across an important idea in an economical, creative manner.*

so that all books are readily exposed to view. Books that are to be handled should be on tables low enough for the children to see them easily. Often a theme for the exhibit (such as "A Book Is Like a Ship" or "Adventures Through Books") makes it possible to organize the exhibit more logically and interestingly.

Although a large exhibit once a year is a worthy activity for any school, smaller exhibits and displays should be used constantly. The school library should always have displays of new books, and bulletin boards which excite an interest in reading. A showcase near the main entrance of the school building can provide notice of the new books in the library as well as develop an interest in a special gem recently acquired. Such a showcase or bulletin board can also keep children informed of the worthwhile television shows built around children's literature. It can draw attention to fine films in town based on great writing. The showcase can be used to announce unusual events such as the Book Fair, special noon-hour film showings, and current neighborhood library displays. Such announcements and displays create even more interest among children when they have had a part in creating them. (Figure 74.)

Figure 74 *Creative people adapt old things to new uses. Trial blow paintings, string paintings, and polymer and tissue paper paintings were not discarded by the teacher: They were cut by the children into shapes to create a spring wall mural—an inspiration for creative writing.*

Contacts with Authors

Nothing is more thrilling for a child than to become acquainted with an author through his writings and then to correspond with that author or, what is even more exciting, to see him. Teachers can develop in children a great love for literature, and for reading, by writing to live poets and authors, or by influencing a local organization to bring one to visit the children during Book Week or at any appropriate time. Writers of children's books love children—and are most gracious with them. Acquaintance with these fine people is a constructive and inspiring experience for children.

Box Theaters

Box theaters provide another form of dramatization which can be adapted to many different uses in presenting children's literature. Box theaters are actually dioramas with some sort of movement added. Sometimes the movement comes simply from slits in the bottom of the box through which stick figures make their appearance on the stage. Larger box theaters can be used with hand puppets.

One group of children who were studying magnets used a box with a thin cardboard bottom and made their characters move about the stage through the use of magnets. This was done by making cardboard figures and inserting a paper clip in the base that held each figure upright. The powerful magnet, when touched to the cardboard floor, attracted the paper clip. By moving the magnet about on the underside of the floor, the children made the figures in the box theater move about also. To stop them in a particular place, the magnet was simply pulled away from the cardboard floor. One group of children used this technique very effectively in dramatizing *Hans Brinker and the Silver Skates*, where the magnet was especially effective in making the skaters glide.

Box theaters can be adapted to finger puppets or simple marionettes, or to using commercial figures. They are especially effective if the teacher wants to depict a scene or a story without too much preparation. In presenting the poem, "Wynken, Blynken and Nod," Miss Carey used a box theater and made the wooden shoe sail about the sky simply by making a cardboard shoe and fastening it on a thin dowel with a tack. The dowel was left protruding from the back of the box; a slit was cut there so that Miss Carey could grasp the dowel and, by moving it in the slit, could give the illusion of a wooden shoe sailing the skies. She also used this simple idea to present "The Duel." The gingham dog and the calico cat could really fight when she moved the dowels protruding from the back of the box theater. With this simple device, trains and cars can move, ships can rock, Jack can climb the beanstalk, and Humpty Dumpty can fall.

Box theaters are effective for giving book reports, for use at school exhibits, and for sharing books read at home.

Shadow Projects

Shadow dramatizations are excellent for depicting favorite stories when the scenes are complicated or foreign to the natural environment of the children. A realistic dramatization of a story can be obtained by fastening cardboard figures on wire coathangers (which have been straightened) with masking tape, and then moving the figures about on a screen of unbleached muslin pasted over an opening cut in a large box. A light between the child and the figure being manipulated casts a clear-cut shadow on the screen. Scenery of detailed design can be made on heavy plastic wrap with a black flo-pen and then simply pushed against the unbleached muslin. To change scenes, the children turn out the light, pull off one piece of plastic wrap, apply another, turn on the light, and continue with the story. Shadow dramatizations are especially effective when one child reads the words from the story and others shadow-play it. Stopping at intervals to allow the players to speak parts adds interesting variety to the scenes.

A simple yet equally effective way of casting a "life-size" shadow so that characters may move about the "set" is to place an overhead projector *behind* a sheet. Tiny objects laid on the overhead and focused cast the shadow on the sheet for a necessary scene. The light is simply turned off to change the scene. Beautiful, weird, and unusual effects may be obtained by using plain color transparencies on the overhead. If the projector is far enough back from the sheet, the shadows are life size and the children may act near the sheet, casting their shadows against the sheet in a very lifelike manner. Actually, then, a child climbing on a beach that has three palm trees may be a real, average-sized child, yet the palm trees need only be cut from cardboard about two inches tall. On the screen they are in proper perspective. (Figure 75.)

Shadow boxes. A large shallow box can be made into a shadow box that will serve as a focal point for arousing interest in good literature in the classroom. The front of the box can be cut out, leaving a frame. It is then painted and hung on the wall. Because of its depth, three-dimensional objects may be displayed in a variety of ways to obtain many interesting effects. A feeling of greater depth may be obtained by paint-

Figure 75 *A shadow play: The child is life-size, but the tree and the hut are only about one inch high, cut from cardboard and projected from the rear of an overhead projector.*

ing heavy cardboards to represent various aspects of a scene and placing them one behind the other. Sometimes lights (the Christmas tree variety) can be added to gain more realistic effects.

* * *

Miss Arnold's fourth grade made an interesting shadow box of "The Night Before Christmas." They poked holes in the back of the shadow box to allow light to come through to represent stars. The back of the box was then painted a deep blue. Near the bottom, about one-half inch from the back of the box, they set cardboard mountains covered with snow. In front of this they set a cardboard row of fir trees covered with snow. Along the very front of the box, they made flat cardboard houses, with windows cut out and covered with tissue paper. Using a string of Christmas tree lights, they set some blue lights in front of the trees and mountains, and some colored lights behind the windows of the cardboard houses. To top off their scene, they cut out a cardboard Santa and reindeer and suspended them on threads between the top of the box and the houses, giving the illusion of a Santa flying before a star-studded sky.

Shadow boxes can provoke a great deal of interest in poems and stories, and they can provide rich creative activity when the children themselves make them. Often they can serve as a place to put an exciting or colorful object—e.g., a lovely arrangement of driftwood and flowers, a place to suspend two or three lighted Japanese lanterns, a coveted shrine to exhibit an artistic madonna, or a center where objects to be seen and not touched are displayed.

Shadow plays. Shadow plays are the same as shadow pictures except that the children themselves act out the parts, casting their shadows on a sheet behind which there is a bright light. Scenes for shadow plays can be made by cutting simple shapes from wrapping paper or newspaper and pinning them to the sheet. Almost any story or poem lends itself to shadow play. Shadow plays may be done in pantomime or with voices and movement.

Peg-Board Displays

Peg board is invaluable in the modern classroom. With the variety of hooks, metal pockets, and bars manufactured for the peg board, the teacher is able to display three-dimensional objects very effectively as part of her bulletin board display. The books themselves can be placed in the pockets; through the use of the adjustable wires, they can be displayed open to selected passages. Pegs help to hold pictures in place.

Bars make it possible to construct simple shelves on which clay modeling or other three-dimensional objects may be displayed. Peg board is very adaptable to many uses and purposes, especially in the promotion of children's literature.

Dioramas

Dioramas serve the purpose of providing children with a three-dimensional picture of the images created in their minds by the stories and poems they read. Similar to a shadow box in construction, the diorama provides an opportunity for the creative use of materials in group or individual projects. They can be made from cardboard cartons, or can be constructed as a real art form with heavy cardboard and wood.

Dioramas are especially effective at book fairs and exhibits. A series of them can show scenes from several stories or poems, or several scenes from the same story. Sometimes dioramas can be made in various forms to add uniqueness to an exhibit. (Figure 76.)

Each child in Mr. Rogers' sixth grade made a small diorama. The children worked in groups and built three or four scenes for each of several stories. They then framed their dioramas by cutting poster board in the

Figure 76 *Patty's diorama of Sir James Barrie's* Peter Pan.

shape of an open book. A hole the same size as the diorama was cut in the open book so that the resulting effect was a three-dimensional picture on one page of the open book. On the page facing the diorama was the name of the book, the author, and the passage that best described the diorama.

Later in the year, Mr. Rogers' group tried to depict various moods with the creative use of materials in dioramas. One group of children made the locked-up room in *Great Expectations.* They created the illusion of the old, dusty wedding table by spraying a table set with miniature dishes with Christmas snow. Across the front of the box they used string to suggest cobwebs. Old strips from plastic bags cut with ragged edges hung from the ceiling like cobwebs and dust.

Another group depicted *McGillicutty's Pool* by painting the inside of their box to resemble water and suspending the fish and undersea animals on strings from the top of the diorama to give the illusion of swimming. Across the front they pasted pale blue cellophane to complete the impression of an underwater scene.

Lap Stories

For a discussion of this technique, see page 204.

Commercial materials are often well adapted to the lap story technique. Miss Ames found the characters of Red Riding Hood printed on a post toasties box. She punched them out and used them for a lap story. The paper dolls were designed in such a way that Miss Ames could insert two fingers in the holes near the base of the figures and thus, by moving her fingers, make them walk. "Dr. Suess" figures, purchased at the department store, also served as the core for a good lap story. Paper dolls can well be used for this purpose.

Sometimes children's toys lend themselves to use in a lap story. Michael received a miniature steam shovel for Christmas; he and Miss Ames used it to tell the story of "Mike Mulligan and His Steam Shovel." Building blocks often provide good props for lap stories. Arthur brought a cardboard castle to school, and it was used to tell several lap and "table-top" stories of "King Arthur and His Knights." Edith made puppets that fit over her hand so that they walked when she moved her fingers, and her puppets danced, talked, and walked when she told "Hansel and Gretel" as a lap story.

Often little objects cannot be used for audience-type situations because they are not visible in an auditorium or classroom seating arrangement. Some of these objects (delightful dolls, intricate carvings, and clever gimmicks) can be easily and advantageously put to use in the informal closeness of a lap or table-top story.

Felt-O-Grams and Flannel Boards

Felt-o-grams and flannel boards are especially effective for stories that are developed by adding a character or two as the story progresses (such as "The Gingerbread Boy"), or for those stories where there are not many scene changes but there is a building up of one or two scenes (such as "The Duchess Bakes a Cake").

Stories with several scenes can be effectively depicted by tacking several layers of flannel along the top of a board and drawing a simple scene on the flannel with crayon. The pieces of flannel can then be flipped as the scenes unfold and the characters and scenes added in their logical sequence.

Many creative effects can be developed with the flannel board if children are cautioned to keep alert to find all materials that might adhere to the flannel. Colored pipe cleaners can be bent quickly into many shapes, and they will readily stick to felt or flannel. Blotters will also stick to felt and flannel, and many figures and objects can easily be cut from them. Decorative materials, such as glitter or Christmas snow, also adhere to flannel and can create interesting illusions.

In telling the story of "The Night Before Christmas," Mr. Torsey sprinkled Christmas snow over the last scene as he said, "Happy Christmas to all and to all a good night!" Mrs. Cohen used silver glitter on her flannel board to create the illusion "Sailed on a river of crystal light, into a sea of dew" from "Wynken, Blynken and Nod."

Lightweight tiny objects can be backed by flannel and are effective in telling stories.

Another unique way of telling stories is from the use of glow paper on the flannel board, using a magic light. This is especially dramatic with stories of magic and make-believe because of the unreal, brilliant colors created by the glo-light.

Mr. Smith cut a sugar-plum tree full of goodies from glo-paper—a lollipop sea, a "shut-eye" row of houses, some trees and bushes, a chocolate cat, and a gingerbread dog. He told the story of "The Sugar-Plum Tree" to the delight of the children. This led to the telling of many stories with the glo-light, especially at Halloween. Finally children wrote their own stories to tell with the magic light.

Peep Boxes

Peep boxes are constructed much like shadow boxes. They allow the children to put into visual form the images created in their minds by words from their favorite stories. They are especially useful for individual projects. The element of mystery added by "peeking" at the scenes is high motivation for children. Peep boxes can be used effectively in school book exhibits, at book fairs, and for book reports.

Mobiles

Mobiles are especially fascinating when units on literature are being taught. Miss French's second grade was reading Dr. Suess. The children and the teacher read all the Dr. Suess books they could find. They also read and collected material about Dr. Suess as an author.

Their five favorite Dr. Suess stories were listed on charts. Each child signed his name under the story he liked best of the five. Then the children met by groups and planned what they would like to put on a Dr. Suess-mobile. Each group worked out its mobile, which was suspended from the ceiling, in its own way. One group used a tree branch, which they painted white. From it, suspended by threads, were Horton, Mazie, the two hunters, an egg, a circus tent, and a ship. Another group crossed sticks and balanced many grotesque and unique animals to represent *If I Ran the Zoo*.

In the center of the room hung a mobile with a picture of Dr. Suess surrounded by tiny books on which were printed the names of every book he had written.

Mobiles lend themselves to an excellent representation of poetry and well-written prose. The movement of the floating mobile symbolizes the flow of characters and words through the child's mind. An imaginative teacher can find many ways to match the free, fluent action of a mobile with the free-flowing words of a good poem or story.

Finger Plays

Many works of literature lend themselves to adaptation of finger plays. This is especially true of nursery rhymes and counting poems. Children can make up rhymes for finger plays, or they can use their fingers to create table puppets to act out stories or selections (see page 219).

Games

Certain games, such as charades, lend themselves to developing an interest in literature. Children can act out the titles of books while the rest of the class tries to guess what they are. Games such as "Who Am I" or "What Am I" also contribute to descriptive word usage.

Often the games that children play regularly in gym periods can be adapted to a game dramatization. Bombardment is an excellent game to play along with the reading of *The Adventures of Robin Hood* or "The Charge of the Light Brigade."

One game many children like is "telephone conversation" where they tell about a book over a toy telephone and the class must guess the book.

Of course, in the primary grades imitative rhythms can be readily applied to the stories the children read. They hop like Peter Rabbit, strut like Paul Bunyan, chug like the little engine, and generally pantomime the characters they love.

A physical education teacher will have many suggestions as to how games may be adapted to literature in such a way that children "live" it.

Reading with Moods

Since literature often creates a mood, teachers should be conscious of the mood or "tone" of stories and should set conditions for the full enjoyment of these stories.

Some, such as ghost or mystery stories, are effectively told with the lights out in the classroom and the shades drawn. One candle burning on a table in the center or at the front of the room often lends additional mystery to the situation.

Some stories are told more effectively against a background of soft music. This is especially true of poetry, which lends itself to mood very well. Interesting combinations of voice and music can be developed, both when the teacher reads to the children and when they read to each other.

Sound effects sometimes enhance the feeling of a poem or story. A music box makes an excellent background for reading Dorothy Baruch's "The Merry-Go-Round." The teacher can work with a child who will add sound effects as she reads a mystery story—a creaking door, a loud bang, the sound of footsteps, a dripping faucet. Some commercial recordings are excellent for providing "sound" introductions to stories or sound effects during the story.

The children's positions also can be used to develop a mood for a story. Some stories are best felt when children put their heads down on their desks and close their eyes; others lend themselves to reading or telling while children are stretched out on the floor ready for a mid-morning nap. Some stories are best told when the children are grouped at the feet of the teacher, others when they are seated at their desks.

The weather may help decide the mood of a story. Foggy days help set the mood for certain poems, just as rainy days, snowy days, and sunny days do for others.

In all instances, the teacher should take advantage of every possible opportunity to set the appropriate physical conditions for presenting literature to children. Often the initial association that a child has with a story or poem determines at once whether he enjoys it and whether it will bear repeating. Every attempt should be made to recreate the author's mood when he wrote the selection. If a similar mood is experienced by the child, the message is communicated. Children come to understand the importance of using the right word in the right place. They get to the heart of the selection so that it becomes an emotional, as well as an intellectual, experience for them.

Creating Ballads

Another way that music and literature can be correlated is to help the children put their favorite stories into ballads. They can pretend they are singing the story just as the old minstrels did long ago. In free or rhyming verse, the story can be retold. Atmosphere can often be added if someone in the room strums a guitar or the teacher plays a recording of guitar or string music. Often one child begins the story and points to another to continue. Children who cannot make rhymes are not pressured to do so; they just tell their portions of the story in their own ways. The musical background will help to determine the tempo and rhythm with which they tell it.

For an account of one approach to writing ballads, see Chapter 13.

Dance Interpretations

Many poems and stories lend themselves well to dance interpretation.

After the children in the second grade had read "The Elf and the Dormouse," Miss Bradford asked them if they would like to dance the story. A large umbrella was used as the toadstool; it was set up in the middle of the room. Some of the children then made up "elf" steps. Others made up "mouse" steps. The children selected two interpretations they liked best, and then Miss Bradford composed music to go with their steps. After one group had danced the story, another group gave its interpretation.

In Miss Harmon's fourth grade the children made up a dance for "The Night Before Christmas." There were many step patterns to be planned—the prancing reindeer steps, the heavy, plodding "Ho-ho-ho" steps of Santa Claus, the airy steps of the sugar plums "dancing through their heads," the fast steps of the "dry leaves before the wild hurricane fly." Miss Harmon used a Fred Waring recording as a background for this dance. At another time her children dramatized "The Elves and the Shoemaker," and she composed music for the dance.

A group of fifth grade girls and boys created a dance for their Book Week assembly program from "Snow White and the Seven Dwarfs."

Whenever possible, children should have the opportunity to see literature translated into dance interpretations; for example, a corps de ballet dancing the *Nutcracker Suite*, *The Red Shoes*, *Peter and the Wolf*, *Hansel and Gretel*, *Cinderella*, *Robin Hood*, and other famous stories.

Scroll Movies

Scroll movies can be an excellent way to introduce stories and poems, to develop the sequence of a story, or to utilize the author's language to translate words into visual imagery.

Miss Fry's class made a roll movie of trees as a result of reading "A Tree Is Nice." Almost all stories lend themselves to roll movies, which provide a fine opportunity for children to express themselves creatively in a group project.

Radio and Television Shows

Almost all children these days have the opportunity of putting on a live television or radio performance. But too often the "showy" aspects of a school program are exploited in such presentations. Children's literature could be used for these programs much more than it is. This would not only help educate parent viewers as to good literature for children, but would motivate child viewers to watch better television shows. Simple or elaborate props can be used. It is important for the teacher to remember that it is the beauty of the words that makes good literature, so the author's words should be used as much as possible. Many of the suggestions in this chapter are well suited to television programming: choral speaking, puppet shows, shadow plays, dramatizations, reading with music, dance interpretations, pantomimes, book reports, displays and exhibits, dioramas, interviews with authors, flannel boards, pictorial maps, and impersonations.

It is well to remember that, although most of this material should grow out of regular classroom work, the class is justified in striving for a polished performance when it is to be presented before the public.

Choral Speaking

Both poems and many prose selections lend themselves well to choral reading or choral speaking exercises. In Chapter 6 some illustrations of the effective use of choral speaking were given. Choral speaking can enrich the enjoyment of literature by giving the teacher a method of using the words of the author in beautiful and varied ways. It can often be used *with* many of the activities for promoting children's literature which have already been mentioned in this chapter. Choral speaking provides an excellent background for shadow plays, puppet shows, and pantomime. Probably no other device is as effective in enriching a child's oral vocabulary.

Murals

Literature can be expressed very well in mural painting. Tempera paint, cut-out construction paper, and colored chalk lend themselves well to the creation of brightly colored murals for the classroom, the school corridors, or the school library.

Murals can grow out of the telling of one story or poem, or they may be a composite of many of the works of literature which the children have read.

* * *

Mural making may be the motivation for art work also. Mr. Harrison taped a long piece of mural paper over the chalkboard along the side of his classroom one day. Then he said to the children, "In the center of this paper I am going to draw a crossroads with this colored chalk. This is where four roads meet. It is Banbury Cross. Remember how all the people came to Banbury Cross to see the fine lady ride on the fine horse? Now each of you will take a section of the paper, and we will chalk in all the people, the animals, the houses, the trees—everything, with everyone running to Banbury Cross. Let's see how many different ideas we can get and how well you can connect your work with your neighbor's." The result was delightful.

Murals may be developed like this to convey impressions, or they can be carefully planned in order to express more lasting ideas. Variations of mural making may be obtained when children make them three-dimensional. Pieces of discarded cloth can be pasted on for clothing; green burlap can represent grass; yarn can be glued on for wires; corrugated cardboard, flannel, and novelty papers can represent house fronts; cereal can represent bricks or pavement blocks, and so on.

Murals can be used for scenery in puppet shows. Large murals painted on big sheets of cardboard cut from mattress boxes or obtained from box companies make excellent backgrounds for the enactment of plays at assembly programs, especially when the cardboards are taped together with wide masking tape and can be folded accordion-wise as the play progresses.

Pictorial Maps

Picture maps serve many purposes in helping to develop a love for literature.

Mr. Jones's sixth grade made a large outline map of the United States. In each state they located the authors about whom they studied as a class during the year.

The children in Mr. Barrett's third grade made a small book of every book they read by folding a piece of construction paper and printing the title and author on the front page and their own names on the inside page. These were then pasted on a large outline map over the state about which the story was written.

More elaborate maps made by some children had flaps that opened. On each flap was a clue about a great piece of literature, such as "A story was written here about a famous rabbit." On lifting the flap, one read, "'The Tar Baby' by Joel Chandler Harris." Another clue read, "Spare your country's flag!" and under the flap was printed "'Barbara Fritchie' by John Greenleaf Whittier."

Pictorial maps tend to help develop concepts of time and place in children as they relate to authors and their creations.

Poetry Is Fun

A special word must be said about the teaching of poetry. So few children above the primary grades seem to know and love poetry that it seems essential to give poetry some extra attention and explore ways of reviving an interest in it.

Poetry is part of a child. It exists in the rhythm of his walking, his speech, his dancing, his movements, his singing. By setting the proper conditions for learning, teachers can bring out the poetry to be expressed in written form. Once a child writes his own poetry, he needs little motivation for enjoying the poetry of others. However, teachers should constantly present poetry in new and exciting ways so that the children may gain deeper appreciations and skills in using it as a creative outlet. Much of the tension in children can be positively released if they can put their feelings down on paper in a creative form. A revival of interest in poetry is a must in a world full of the tensions of the space age.

All the ideas suggested in the preceding pages are applicable to setting conditions for the creative teaching of poetry. Because poetry is a unique form of written expression, however, some additional suggestions are entered here.

1. Use choral speaking for the teaching of many poems.
2. Write a poem on the chalkboard and divide the class into groups. Encourage each group to think of a different way to present the poem through choral speaking.
3. Print a rhyming poem on a large sheet of paper. Cut the poem into rhyming strips and pass out the strips. Allow the children who have the strips to go to the front of the room and reassemble the poem by rhyming it. Then allow them to do the poem in choral speaking.
4. Create special moods by reading such poems as these to the children:

"The Song of Hiawatha" (with drum beats).
"The Bells" (Edgar Allan Poe) (with bells).
"Gerald McBoing Boing" (with "boings" and other sounds suggested by the story).

5. Read action poems and then have the children create sounds or actions to go with them:

"Jack-Be-Nimble," while some children jump over the candlestick.
"The Midnight Ride of Paul Revere," while children make the clip-clop noise of the horse in rhythm to the reading.
"The Highwayman" with accompanying hoof beats or music.

Summary

No reading program is complete without a planned parallel program for the enjoyment of literature. All the language arts become meshed in a final product when children write their own literature and read the effective writing of others. All the teaching of listening, speech, oral expression, reading, and handwriting skill is directed to this end. None of the teaching of any of these skills of communication is of any substantial value unless it all results in the application of the skills in effective writing for oneself and enjoyment of the writings of others.

Literature is the record of man's living which contains his feelings as well as his way of life. Children can capture the spirit of literature because they have inherited the same feelings as other men, even though they live in a different age. Literature is a common bond of communication of feelings across the continents, across the countries, and across the years. The beauty of living in all times is captured in it. It is the rightful heritage of all children everywhere. Teachers can help children relive and refeel the history of the world by helping them read and experience their great literary heritage.

Doing "special" things with good pieces of literature helps children build an appreciation of them and develops a taste for writing with quality. Somewhere in Mrs. Palmer's room may be a future author of a saga of the kola-kola bird! He needs encouragement!

To the Reader

1. Can children's books be as exciting to adults as they are to children? This author thinks so. One such book is *A Wrinkle in Time* by L'Engle.[5] Read it and see if you agree.
2. By what criteria would you grade children's creative writing? Grade the story of Bullet by Jeanette on page 284. Ask three or four of your colleagues also to grade it (use the A, B, C, D, E basis). How much agreement did you get on the grade? Ask a few other colleagues to grade it, using your criteria. Is there more or less agreement on the grade? Does the matter of "taste" enter into the evaluation of literature? How would you grade "The Elephant's Child," "The Five Chinese Brothers," "Horton Hatches the Egg," "A Wrinkle in Time"? Does literature need to be graded? Should the creative literature of children ever be graded?
3. Questions for discussion:
   a. What is a children's classic? What criterion can be used to determine a classic? What are some of the classics of the past? Do you think any classics are being written now? May "A Wrinkle In Time" become a classic?
   b. To what degree should a teacher impose her standards for good literature on children?
   c. Do you think that the filming of a children's classic can destroy the joy of reading the classic? Why or why not?

5. Madeleine L'Engle, *A Wrinkle In Time* (New York: Farrar, Straus and Giroux, Inc., 1962).

d. Examine the TV Guide and note the number of great pieces of children's literature that are being made into good TV movies or productions. Among recent ones are the perennial *Wizard of Oz* and others such as *Hans Brinker and the Silver Skates*, *Cinderella*, *The Pied Piper of Hamelin*, and *Heidi*. View some of these (with children if possible) and react to them: Do they enhance or destroy your enjoyment of the books?

4. Design a plan for teaching the history of the United States through the use of children's literature.
5. Collect specific stories from children's literature which lend themselves to:
   a. an understanding of life in France.
   b. the building of values.
   c. understanding of the terror of wars.
   d. an understanding of prejudice.
   e. the development of appreciations.
   f. the importance of mastery.
   g. the development of empathy.
   h. the seriousness of murder.
6. Make a collection of picturesque speech from passages in children's literature that will be appropriate to use on cards or charts for children to read and learn in any given classroom.
7. There is a great deal of trash in the form of children's literature on the market today. Have each member of the class bring a book of recent publication to class. Using the criteria for selecting children's literature as defined in this chapter, evaluate the books brought in.
8. There are many children's magazines on the current market. Some are excellent; others are junk. Collect copies of various kinds of children's magazines and assess them for their literary value.
9. In planning your next unit, use the *Periodical Guide to Children's Literature* to see how many ways literature can be used in correlation with social studies, science, arithmetic, and the creative arts.
10. Obtain a copy of the report of the National Library Association's Annual Conference and look for these facts:
    a. How many children's books were published in the past year?
    b. How many children's books were published in 1940?
    c. Note those books which were the most popular with children. How many of them do you remember as being translated into a TV show?
    d. From these observations, can you tell whether children are reading more or less than they did twenty years ago, and can you draw some conclusions about the effect of television on children's reading?

e. Check other evidence to determine whether or not films encourage or discourage the reading of the book.

11. Make a list of the ten favorite stories you remember from your childhood. Check them out with today's children—are any of them still popular? Why or why not do you suppose this is true?

Selected Bibliography

ANDERSON, PAUL. *Flannelboard Stories for Primary Grades.* Minneapolis: Dennison, 1962.

ADAMS, BESS PORTER. *About Books and Children.* New York: Henry Holt and Company, 1953.

ARBUTHNOT, MAY HILL (compiler). *The Arbuthnot Anthology of Children's Literature.* Chicago: Scott, Foresman and Company, 1953.

———. "Developing Life Values Through Reading," *Elementary English*, 43: 10–16, January 1966.

———, AND DOROTHY M. BRODERICK. *Time For Stones.* Chicago: Scott, Foresman and Company, 1968.

———, AND SHELDON L. ROOT, JR. *Time For Poetry*, 3rd ed. Chicago: Scott, Foresman, 1968.

ARNSTEIN, FLORA J. *Poetry in the Elementary Classroom.* New York: Appleton-Century-Crofts, 1962.

BAMMAN, HENRY A., ROBERT J. WHITEHEAD, AND MILDRED A. DAWSON. *Oral Interpretation of Children's Literature.* Dubuque, Iowa: William C. Brown Company Publishers, 1964.

BREWTON, JOHN E., AND SARA W. BREWTON. *Index to Children's Poetry.* New York: H. W. Wilson Company, 1942. First Supplement, 1954, Second Supplement, 1969.

CARLSON, RUTH KEARNEY. *Literature For Children: Enrichment Ideas.* Dubuque, Iowa: William C. Brown Company Publishers, 1970.

CHAMBERS, DEWEY W. *Children's Literature in the Curriculum.* Chicago: Rand McNally and Company, 1971.

———. *Story Telling and Creative Drama.* Dubuque, Iowa: William C. Brown Company Publishers, 1970.

CIANCIOLO, PATRICIA. *Literature For Children: Illustrations in Children's Books.* Dubuque, Iowa: William C. Brown Company Publishers, 1970.

CLARK, MARGARET. *Keeping Up With Children and Books*, 1963–1965. Chicago: Scott, Foresman and Company, 1966.

COLWELL, EILSEN. *A Storyteller's Choice.* New York: Walck Publishing Company, 1964.

CULLINAN, BERNICE E. *Literature for Children: Its Discipline and Content.* Dubuque, Iowa: William C. Brown Company Publishers, 1971.

CULLUM, ALBERT. *Greek Tears and Roman Laughter: Ten Tragedies and Five Comedies for Schools.* New York: Citation Press, 1970.

———. *Push Back the Desks.* New York: Citation Press, 1968.

DOYLE, BRIAN (ed.). *The Who's Who of Children's Literature.* New York: Schoeken Books, 1968.

EAKIN, MARY K. *Good Books For Children, 1948–1961.* Chicago: University of Chicago Press, 1962.

GEORGIOU, CONSTANCE. *Children and Their Literature.* Englewood Cliffs, New Jersey: Prentice-Hall, 1969.

GILLESPIE, MARGARET. *Literature for Children: History and Trends.* Dubuque, Iowa: William C. Brown Company Publishers, 1970.

GUILFOILE, ELIZABETH. *Books for Beginning Readers.* Champaign, Illinois: National Council, Teachers of English, 1962.

HAVILAND, VIRGINIA. *Children's Literature: A Guide to Reference Sources.* Washington, D.C.: United States Government Printing Office, 1966.

HUBER, MIRIAM BLANTON. *Story and Verse For Children.* New York: The Macmillan Company, 1965.

HUCK, CHARLOTTE S., AND DORIS A. YOUNG. *Children's Literature in the Elementary School.* New York: Holt, Rinehart and Winston, 1968.

JACOBS, LELAND B. (ed.). *Using Literature with Young Children.* New York: Teachers College Press, Columbia University, 1965.

LADLEY, WINIFRED C. *Sources of Good Books and Magazines for Children.* Newark, Delaware: International Reading Association, 1970.

LAMB, POSE (ed.). *Literature for Children Series.* Dubuque, Iowa: William C. Brown Company Publishers, 1970.

LARRICK, NANCY. *A Teacher's Guide to Children's Books.* Columbus: Charles E. Merrill Books, Inc., 1963.

LUCK, JAMES T. *Creative Music for the Classroom Teacher.* New York: Random House, 1971.

MACCAMPBELL, JAMES C. (ed.). *Readings in the Language Arts in the Elementary School.* Part VIII. Boston: D. C. Heath and Company, 1964, 210–215, 332–358, 359–365.

MONTEBELLO, MARY. *Children's Literature in the Curriculum.* Dubuque, Iowa: William C. Brown Company Publishers, 1970.

REASONER, CHARLES F. *Releasing Children to Literature*. New York: Dell Publishing Company, Inc., 1968.

SMITH, DORA V. *Fifty Years of Children's Books*. Champaign, Illinois: National Council, Teachers of English, 1963.

TOOZE, RUTH. *Storytelling*. Englewood Cliffs, New Jersey: Prentice-Hall, Inc., 1959.

WAGNER, JOSEPH A. *Children's Literature Through Storytelling*. Dubuque, Iowa: William C. Brown Company Publishers, 1970.

WHITEHEAD, ROBERT. *Children's Literature: Strategies of Teaching*. Englewood Cliffs, New Jersey: Prentice-Hall, Inc., 1968.

WITUCKE, VIRGINIA. *Literature for Children:* Poetry in the Elementary *School*. Dubuque, Iowa: William C. Brown Company Publishers, 1970.

9

Adventures in Creative Writing

Spring

The slush and sleet of the Spring thaw,
And the gushing waters that I saw,
Told me something
Something I couldn't quite put my finger on.

The sun was peeking from behind the clouds,
And birds were coming in seasonal crowds.

There had to be something that was going on
I could feel it in the air,
Flowers were popping up everywhere,
Animals were sprouting out,
And fisherman were catching trout.

I know what it is,
I've heard it before
It's Spring!
At last it's come knocking at my door!

So writes Elizabeth, a fourth grader.

Setting Proper Conditions for Creative Writing

Children rarely write what they do not say. Prerequisite to a creative writing program is a rich, broad program in oral expression and a sensible, meaningful program in reading. Such a program in reading is one that utilizes the oral vocabulary of children to make classroom charts, labels, and stories *so the children may see their own words in manuscript or written form.* When the visual images of these words are stamped on the child's mind, he is ready to reproduce them in his own handwriting. He then has the tool he needs to write the beautiful things he has to say.

When an individual writes creatively, he is communicating on paper in his very best way. As a communication technique, the ideas he writes are predominantly important. Misspellings and imperfections in grammar are secondary considerations. Too much emphasis on spelling and grammar at this point checks the flow of ideas or frustrates the writer so that he abandons writing as a communication form. Because of this, spelling and grammar should not be taught during the process of creative writing, but should be taken care of in the editing that follows. Editing is necessary for the child to share his writing with others; it must be put in the common acceptable forms of grammar so that others may read it.

Teachers set conditions for creative writing in several basic ways:

1. They provide for many experiences with smell, touch, sight, and sound in the classroom, or capitalize on the children's sensory experiences outside of school.
2. They help the children put these experiences into spoken words in beautiful, descriptive ways.
3. They provide the children with the visual image of the words so they learn to read them.
4. They help the children reproduce these words in handwritten form.
5. They provide the permissive, experimental atmosphere necessary to all creative endeavors.
6. They then stand off and let the child write.

Purposes for Creative Writing

Creative writing serves many purposes for the individual.

First, it is a means of *self-expression*. By this we mean that it gives the child the opportunity to express his own intimate thoughts and feelings about the experiences he has from day to day in the way that is most effective and rewarding for him.

Secondly, it is a means of *communication*, and if it is truly creative, it is communication in a unique, different, or unusual manner. It is a way for children and adults to communicate beautifully and effectively—as Nancy does so well in "Nature's Blessing."

Nature's Blessing

The grasses are covered with morning dew.
And the day is crisp and bright,
Nature calls its melodious song
And the birds take rest from flight.

The small bird chirps a lovely note
And it spreads its graceful wings,
Then it falls to the ground with a pitiful bound!
But the innocent bird still sings.

Now life has changed for the helpless bird.
For now he's big and strong,
The hunters will shoot him for use as a meal
And his life won't last for long.

Always running in fear of death,
As long as the bird will live,
God made him as he is,
The hunter's fugitive.

Life is a blessing for all to cherish.
Its beauty is oh, so rare,
But it is even prettier
If in other lives we may share.

—Nancy Kaplan

Thirdly, it provides a *psychological catharsis* for the writer. Some communication comes off best after a lapse of time—an incubation period for arranging one's thoughts in an expressive way—as against an oral "off-the-cuff" comment. Children may need such time to adequately rid themselves of negative feelings, or to work out the meaning of happenings they do not understand. Often this takes the form of a projected vicarious experience.

The following essay is an excellent example of the way a teen-age girl struggled with her feelings about suicide and received a kind of mental catharsis in projecting herself into a dramatic situation.

A Suicide Note to the World

I am alone now. The room is still and quiet. Darkness engulfs me. I wish to leave; to go forever is my fondest desire. It would not take long and I am not afraid. Nor am I a coward. I am not running away; I am giving up!

Nor am I old; I am young, but perhaps this is more of a reason, for now it is up to me. The old have lived their era. Now it is my turn. I talk, I call, I cry but no one listens. I feel like an outsider looking in a window. I knock on the pane but no one looks up! They're all too busy! Their cruel, self-centered, miserable lives are all they care about. "Let the other fellow die. I don't know him." "Black-skins aren't allowed in here." "Go away, leave me alone!" So let them miss the real meaning, I no longer care!

The noise is too loud, the people too great in number, the truth too hidden, the pace too fast. Call me what you will but it is I who feel sorry for you. I can see—you are blind. I can hear—you are deaf. I understand—you never try. I love—you only hate. I believe—you have no God.

Therefore do not call me a coward. I am tired but soon I shall have peace.

—Susan

Creative writing also provides a *balance to life experiences*, in which the writer may use his own and other's writings to indicate that problems happen, but that there are ways to find solutions.

In addition, creative writing makes provision for children who possess literary talent to secure encouragement, help, and improvement in quality in their writing. Certainly the children who wrote the passages above fall into this category.

Creative writing can and should become the basis of the total program in written expression.

Most of all, creative writing arouses a sensitiveness to good literature.

Kinds of Writing

There are basically two kinds of writing: the practical and the creative. Burrows, Ferebee, Jackson, and Saunders[1] distinguish between them as follows:

. . . We recognize that there are two fundamental kinds of writing. One is practical, the other personal. There is a gratifying sense of power that comes to any individual when he can fulfill the practical writing demands of his own life, whether it be the first brief direction that goes from school or the lengthy treatise that terminates an original study. And even more telling in its expansive effect is the personal writing that wells up out of the depths of the spirit.

Practical writing deals with those formal matters of communication which must be taken care of in order to function socially in a culture: the writing of invitations, formal business letters, notes of appreciation, thanks, and the like. This is not to say that these types of communications cannot be creative. Indeed they can, but the form and formality of

1. A. T. Burrows, J. D. Ferebee, D. C. Jackson, and D. O. Saunders, *They All Want To Write*, rev. ed. (Englewood Cliffs, New Jersey: Prentice-Hall, 1952), p. 2.

the message are more likely to communicate the basic message, because this is an accepted cultural form.

It is when we add a heart and mind to writing that it becomes creative. When children begin to coin words, when they manipulate and explore them, when they begin to draw analogies and create metaphor and simile, when they see relationships in their environment and draw comparisons in word experiences, when they paint word pictures and become unique and novel in expressing themselves, we have creative writing.

Getting Started

Teachers sometimes experience difficulty in beginning creative writing . . . If the creative abilities of children have been stifled over long periods of time, it is not enough to provide motivation and time and then expect unusual or high-quality results.

With some groups of children who have not developed the ability to express themselves creatively in their writing, some structure and much encouragement are needed. Sometimes the teaching of certain skills such as punctuation, capitalization, or letter formation is necessary to give the child assurance and security so that he can feel free and competent to express his thoughts on paper. This is not to say that children *must* be able to spell, punctuate, and write well in order to write creatively. The mechanics of writing should ordinarily be taken care of in the editing of the child's work. However, *some* children who have been extremely unsuccessful in mastering handwriting skills may be so completely insecure in writing creatively that *one* approach is to provide them with greater security in learning the necessary skills. Often these skills can be taught in such a creative manner that some creative writing can result from the teaching process itself, thus providing the child with confidence in his beginning attempts.

Sometimes children experience difficulty in creative writing due to an impoverished written vocabulary. A great deal of emphasis is placed on vocabulary building in this book. This author almost always precedes his creative writing sessions with children with a "Fun With Words" warm-up (see page 154). Children enjoy learning new words. As soon as they speak new words, it is a good idea to have them see them in printed form. A pooling of known words in any group always means that each child is learning new words known by his neighbor. Of course, as a member of the group, the teacher makes her contribution too.

Often this means that the teacher must precede the creative writing period with a great deal of shared talk; not just any "talk," but talk directed toward a purpose. It may be that the teacher wants to build a descriptive vocabulary for winter; in that case, some situation must be planned which will evoke winter words and descriptive phrases that can be put on the chalkboard before the children. The teacher must assume that children can learn to read any word that they are using orally in a meaningful way. Thus, the purpose of the oral expression period is to get words meaningfully into the oral vocabulary so that children say them, then read them, and finally write them.

Beginning creative writing experiences means that children must have many adventures with oral expression. Following is a simple situation in which a second grade teacher tried to tap the oral vocabulary of her students soon after school started. She also wanted to check on their ability to use descriptive words and at the same time introduce them to rhyming words and some creative writing.

Who Am I?

Interested in knowing each child and how he felt about himself, Miss Lemmick distributed a dittoed sheet to each child on which she had printed the following.

Who Am I?

My hair is ____________.
I have a ____________ nose.
My eyes are ____________.
I smell like a rose.
My ears are ____________.
And ____________ is my name.
I look like a ____________.
And that's a shame!

Miss Lemmick said she wanted to know more about them so they were going to talk about words that would tell about themselves. They could then fill in their own poem to describe themselves. They could make it funny or serious.

In discussing the first line, after the whole poem was read, most of the children told Miss Lemmick their hair color. So, after she had listed the colors on the chalkboard, she reminded them that there were other ways to describe hair besides color; thus, words such as *blonde, brunette, long, short, clipped, straight, curly, soft, fluffy, pretty,* and *different* appeared on the list.

The children were encouraged to fill in the remaining blank spaces in the poem, and Miss Lemmick drew their attention to the fact that there were four lines on the bottom where they could add their own idea if they liked. About half the class did. John wrote:

Who Am I?

My hair is blonde
  I have a flat nose
My eyes are merry
  I smell like a rose
My ears are small
  And Corky is my name
I look like an ostrich
  And that's a shame!
I like to run
  And I would enjoy
Being a deer
  Instead of a boy!

A Magic Talking Calendar

Some children do not need as much structure as Miss Lemmick's group. In another second grade where a study of the calendar was a social studies requirement, Miss Cooper was able to get her children writing couplets. The experience was so pleasant that the children went on writing poems of their own; Miss Cooper encouraged this by introducing new situations which required creative thinking. It was not too long before she received some high-quality material.

The problem of introducing the calendar again for December bothered Miss Cooper. The children had struggled through learning number concepts and reviewing the days of the week in composing a September calendar. By November they were less enthusiastic, and Miss Cooper wanted to rekindle their interest because she felt that there was much the children could yet learn from the use of the calendar.

It was her custom to begin each month with a discussion on what that month would bring, including of course holidays, birthdays, weather conditions, special events, etc. While deliberating over a new way to do this, she came up with the idea of the magic talking calendar.

Miss Cooper drew squares for the days of December on a large green cardboard with a flo-pen. On the top she printed the couplet:

December is here!
Winter is near!

She then cut lightweight white pieces of cardboard which, when folded down the middle, fit the boxes for the days that she had drawn on the green cardboard. On the cover of the first folded card, she made a pretty number "one" and decorated it with snowflakes.

The children immediately wanted to know why the calendar was there and asked if they were going to make a new calendar for December.

"Yes," said Miss Cooper, "but today we are going to do something different with our calendar. Let's make a magic talking calendar!"

That's all they needed. "How?"

"I have an idea how," said Miss Cooper. "Do you want to hear it?"

"Yes," hands clapping—everyone running to his place so all could hear about the talking calendar and get started.

"Well, first," said Miss Cooper, "You are going to help me decide what the calendar will say. So let's start. I want you to think of all the *sounds* you will hear during December which you will not always hear the rest of the year:

"Sleigh bells"
"Strong wind"
"Christmas carols"
"Church bells"

Miss Cooper printed these ideas on the chalkboard. When John said, "fire in the fireplace," Miss Cooper encouraged John to use a word to describe the fire, and he said, "crackling fire." Thus, she kept the pattern of the ideas.

As soon as the children began to run out of ideas, Miss Cooper printed the word "sights" on the chalkboard. "Let's look at this idea," she said, "What are some of the *sights* you see in December that you don't see much at other times of the year?"

Hands waving, eyes sparkling, ideas coming in a torrent:

"Christmas trees"
"Snowstorms"
"Christmas wreaths"
"Ice and sleet"
"Christmas stars"
"Salvation Army Santa Claus"
"Santa Claus"
"Reindeer"

"Decorations"
"Church windows"
"Children playing in the snow"

After the list was as long as Miss Cooper had room for, she asked for the *tastes* of December.

"Snowflakes on your mouth"
"Turkey"
"Plum pudding"
"Peanut brittle"
"Pumpkin pies"
"Mince pies"
"Popcorn"
"Candy canes"

Then a list was composed of the *smells* of December.

"Wood burning in fireplaces"
"Cookies baking"
"Bread baking"
"Evergreen trees"
"Scented candles burning"

"Now," said Miss Cooper, "we must do something to organize all these wonderful ideas. I am going to give each of you a card with a number on it just like the one I have up here already on the calendar. You may decorate yours later as I have decorated mine, but right now we are going to work on the talking part of the book, so look now at this paper."

Miss Cooper had printed the numbers from one through twenty-five along the left-hand side of some lined primary paper, leaving two blank lines after each number. "Now, because I have the number one on my card, I am going to make up a rhyme to go with one—and here it is:

I am December one,
Summer is done.

"How is that?"

The children approved.

"Using some of the ideas that we have on the chalkboard, or an idea of your own, see if you can make a rhyme to go with your number. Just raise your hand when you are ready, and I shall place it here on the chart. Use smells, tastes, sights, or sounds of December. We will help you if you haven't an idea.

Deep concentration. Then a few hands. Billy is first. He says:

"I am December three
Today we'll buy a Christmas tree!"

"Great," says Miss Cooper as she prints it after 3 on the chart. "Billy has the idea. Anyone else?"

Oh yes, Marcia is ready. She says:

"I am December four
A Christmas wreath is on the door."

Soon many hands are raised. Some need help—they have numbers hard to rhyme. So Miss Cooper shows them that the words may be changed around. The finished couplets, omitting the weekend days and making possible the contribution of each of the *twenty-one* children, look like this:

1. I am December One
   Summer is done
2. I am December Two
   Skies are cold and blue
3. I am December Three
   Today we'll buy a Christmas tree
4. I am December Four
   A Christmas wreath is on the door

(December 5 and 6—Saturday and Sunday)

7. I am December Seven
   Snowflakes fall from heaven
8. I am December Eight
   Icy sidewalks is what I hate
9. I am December Nine
   Snow piles on the trees of pine
10. I am December Ten
    Merry sleigh bells ring again
11. I am December Eleven
    Brightly shine the stars in heaven

(December 12 and 13—Saturday and Sunday)

14. I am December Fourteen
    I like the smell of evergreen
15. December Fifteen now is here
    With shiny sled and bright reindeer
16. December Sixteen—what am I?
    I smell of mince and pumpkin pie

17. December Seventeen—man, oh man
    Popcorn's popping in the pan!

Now school was out for the Christmas holidays, but the children made the calendar continue through Christmas day.

Miss Cooper and the children were happy with the words for the talking calendar. "This is what our calendar will say," said Miss Cooper, "but let's talk a while about *how* it will say it.

She made certain that each child could read his two lines—each received help and practice from the teacher or his neighbor. When the poem was read well, she called the numbers in order and the children lined up in the front of the room. Miss Cooper then played a recording of the bells at the Yale bell tower, and with the bells playing in the background, each child stepped to the microphone of a battery-operated cassette tape recorder and read his lines.

To complete the talking calendar, each child drew a picture with crayons on the inside of his card to illustrate the lines he had written. He also decorated the number on the front. Each child then placed his card in the proper space on the big calendar before the room.

Then the children sat still to hear the calendar talk.

Miss Cooper put the tape behind the illustrated calendar and played it. As each number was mentioned, she opened the card on the calendar so that the appropriate drawing was revealed.

"Oh, that was good!"
"It really talks!"
"I liked your picture, Marcia."
"Can't we do it again?"
"Kevin was funny!"
"This is the best calendar we ever made!"

And on and on! The talking calendar served as an opening-day activity to prepare the children for each day of December. Every morning the first thing they wanted to do was to hear the talking calendar. They decided, after they had heard it, that they would leave the card for the day open so they could enjoy the drawing for the day.

Miss Cooper's plan consumed the greater part of a morning, but in it she had (a) developed vocabulary; (b) introduced new words in print in a purposeful way; (c) provided a meaningful experience with numbers; (d) construed some excellent oral expression experiences; (e) provided some excellent listening experiences for that particular morning *and* for every subsequent school day in December; (f) worked with rhyming words; (g) developed the concept of a couplet; (h) provided some excellent reading material; (i) initiated some art work; (j) developed organization and classification skills; and (k) provided the children with an experience which, although structured, set conditions and provided security so they could explore and experiment with their own creative ideas.

Truly the children of Miss Cooper's class had an adventure in communication on that cold first day of December.

Other Ways

There are other ways of getting children started in their creative writing with enthusiasm and security.

One way is to write the beautiful things they say on a chart before the room and thereby give them importance.

Such sayings as "It is colder than the inside of our refrigerator" and "The puppy feels like warm silk" begin the flow of words needed to do writing from the heart.

Have children write about single words in much the same way they talked about them as suggested on page 152. The teacher writes on the chalkboard: "What is quiet?" or "What is love?" The children then write their descriptions of these words.

How Would You Say It?

From the time that children first learn to read, they come across phrases which appear again and again in their reading to the point where they become almost meaningless. Groups of words like "the starry sky," "pretty as a picture," "the silvery moon," "sweet as a rose," "the desert sands," "the whispering pines," and others are hackneyed and trite.

Teachers can alert children to novel and colorful ways of expression by drawing attention to these phrases in their books and asking children to collect them. The teacher can then put an envelope on the bulletin board with the phrase, "How would YOU say it?" printed on it. Below it she can place a pile of 5 × 8 inch cards. As children find these phrases, they come and write them on a card and place the card in the envelope. After several have been collected, the teacher may use them as a springboard for a discussion on different ways of saying them. These new ways can be written on the back of each card. Then the teacher can encourage children to write the new ways of saying the phrases whenever they like—thus providing a stimulating independent activity. The new phrases will later appear in their creative writing.

On the back of a card which said, "the starry sky," a fifth grade girl wrote, "There in the heavens, the GREAT JEWELER spread all his diamonds on black velvet."

Why and How?

Smith[2] tells of one technique he used to begin writing. He encouraged children to ask questions in class, when he could not answer them immediately, by writing them on a slip of paper and dropping them into a question box provided for this purpose. These questions not only provided the bases for many excellent oral experiences in discussion, but also became the base for many creative experiences.

Since many questions began with "why," these were singled out. Over a period of time it was noted that many questions ended in words that rhymed. By trying various combinations and with a little class "doctoring" with rhythm and rhyme, a series of "why" poems were created.

Here is a why poem written by his sixth grade with material from the question box.

Our Why Poem

Why must parents tell us "No!"
  Why do children always grow?
Why are winters bleak and cold?
  What is old?

Why is the earth so big and round?
  Why do plants grow from the ground?
Why do we get stung by bees?
  Explain a sneeze!

What is it that makes fire burn?
  Why does milk to butter churn?
What makes curlers on a fern?
  Why learn?

Similarly, "When" and "How" poems may be composed from questions which reflect the children's natural curiosity.

Creating a Mood for Creative Writing

Special moods may be set as part of the conditioning for creative writing. Generally, writing done while children are in the mood produces groups of words not commonly used under other circumstances.

2. James A. Smith, *Creative Teaching of Language Arts in the Elementary School* (Boston: Allyn and Bacon, 1967), p. 192.

There are many ways a teacher may create moods:

1. By supplying various sounds.
2. By playing music.
3. By reading poetry or stories.
4. By drawing the shades.
5. By using an affected voice.
6. By dramatizing a scene.
7. By using a film.

Some teachers take a great deal of time to develop the feeling concept, because good literature creates a feeling or mood in the reader. Children discuss how they felt when the firebell rang, or when they were late, or their reactions to their first airplane ride. Vocabulary to express these feelings is developed by the teacher and children working together.

In one classroom the children were asked to react to the playing of music from the *Nutcracker Suite*. Some immediately responded and danced and dipped to the recording. Some shy ones could not bring themselves to perform, so the teacher encouraged them to write about the dancers and how they felt about them. Frieda wrote about Helen and the music.

Helen's hand goes up and down
She's drawing ocean waves—
Green and swirling
She's drawing cool, tall mountains.
I would draw flowers with long tangled stems
Warm and bright
And drenched with sunlight.

In another classroom the teacher had the children construct a still-life picture from material around the classroom. Then, while the teacher played "Blue Star," she asked the children to write about spring as it was suggested by the picture. Sandra wrote:

Beautiful! Beautiful!
Beautiful Day!
A golden daffodil
Two ducks at play
And heavenly music
And rainbows near
It whispers softly
That Spring is here!

—Sandra
Grade 5

The light, provocative music of Tchaikovsky evoked this lovely little ballad from Janet.

The Elves Dance

Around about, around about
  In a fair ring-a,
Thus we dance, thus we dance
  And thus we sing-a,
Trip and go, to and fro
  Over this green-a,
All about, in an out,
  For our brave queen-a.

—Janet Wilmot
Grade 5

Using Music to Set Moods for Creative Writing

The teacher can select musical recordings and ask the children to write what comes to mind as the music is playing. Later, these can be read while the music is played softly, and the combination can be taped. During the playback, children will see how a mood can be created by blending together the words and the music.

Imagine if you can the beautiful music of "Le Mer" playing softly in the background and a child's voice reading the following poem.

The Sea

The sea,
All blue and gray.
With the whitecaps,
And the mist
When it crashes
Against the rocks.
Do you see it?
Isn't it lovely?
That great, big sea
Just waiting for you.

—Debbie Kenner

The following poems were inspired by a picture of two beautiful butterflies and were read against the joyous sounds of *Tales of the Vienna Woods.*

Butterflies

Butterflies fly,
Across the sky,
They wing their way,
At break of day.

Their colors are numerous,
Black, white, yellow, and red,
And many others
That I have not said.

Their homes are near,
But I wonder where,
Where do they fly,
When night comes by?

Many things
We do not know,
About butterflies,
And where they go.

—Liane Godsey

Haiku

The writing of haiku poetry is enjoyed by most children. It is a good example of the fact that creativity does not require an unlimited, unrestricted *setting* in which to flourish. Haiku is a highly structured type of oriental poetry with five syllables in the first line, seven in the second, and five again in the third. In spite of the limitations of this restricting pattern, children are often challenged to write beautiful thoughts. Sometimes, then, restrictions or pressures can be a stimulant for creative production as well as a stricture to it. This type of creativity is probably comparable to the high-level creativity which men in the space program produce while under extreme tension and competition.

Haiku writing appeals to children of all ages, as these samples indicate.

Crickets

The evening has come.
Some young crickets sing a song.
The night is still fresh.

The Sea

The sea is lovely.
Especially the high tide
With waves splashing high.

Oh, the gorgeous sea!
With the surfers in the waves
And swimmers by shore.

—Debbie Kenner
Norfolk, Va.

An extension of haiku is tanka which is an oriental verse of exactly thirty-one syllables arranged in five lines of five, seven, five, seven, and seven syllables.

Tanka

Flowers are budding,
The small birds enjoy the spring.
It is beautiful.
The young animals come out.
I can almost feel the dawn.

—David Audlin
Grade 6

Cinquains

Children who like haiku will enjoy proceeding to cinquain poetry. Cinquains serve to develop good describing words (adjectives), verbs, and synonyms, and to help establish good vocabulary usage. Children may want to develop their own cinquains, but cinquains are also fun to use at a party where each line is written on a piece of paper folded back and passed along to the next person. Used in this way, cinquains become nonsense poetry.

An easy way to develop cinquains is as follows: Give each child a dittoed sheet like the one in Figure 77.

CINQUAIN POETRY

____

________ ________

________ ________ ________

________ ________ ________ ________

________ ________

Figure 77 *A form for cinquain poetry.*

Then instruct them to write in the following pattern:

LINE 1: One word (title)
LINE 2: Two words (describe title)
LINE 3: Three words (an action)
LINE 4: Four words (a feeling)
LINE 5: One word (refer to title)

Here is a sample of a cinquain done by fourth grade children.

Kittens

Softly purring
Sleeping on the hearth
Cozy, and warm, contented
Felines.

Shapes

One way to stir the imagination of a child who has difficulty getting started is as follows:

Draw a strange shape on a ditto sheet and have the children make something of it. When they have finished, name it, then write about it: What it does, what it eats, how it walks, what it says, etc.

Joe drew a queer-looking creature which he called:

The No-Grammar Grunch

Can't eat
  Ain't got no mouth.
Can't see
  Ain't got no eyes.
Can't feel
  Ain't got no hands
Can't talk
  Or tell no lies.
Can't smell
  Ain't got no nose
Can't walk
  Ain't got no feet
Can't climb
  Ain't got no toes
Can't write
  His grammar's beat!

Myself

Ask the children to bring their baby pictures to school. First have a bulletin board of baby pictures with numbers under each, and encourage them to guess each other by numbering a sheet of paper the same as the pictures and entering the names next to the appropriate numbers.

Then encourage each child to think up clever captions for his picture. Each child can write a story about himself—as he was in the picture—who were his friends, what were his joys, his needs, his interests, his likes and dislikes?

The Baby

Soft cuddly baby
Eyes big and bright,
No hair, no teeth
Everything right
Can't talk, can't sing
Gorgeous to see.
Long long ago
Could you be me?

—Jenny
Grade 5

Beginning Sentences

Write beginnings of sentences (several) on the chalkboard, and have the children select one (or create one of their own) about which they might write.

Some ideas:

Snow is diamonds from heaven ______
Before I was born ______
If I were God, I ______
Happiness is ______
Maybe someday ______
I was never more excited (upset, hurt, unhappy) in my life than ______
If I were a dinosaur, I ______
I wish I was a camel named ______
When I was a member of Robin Hood's Band ______
The time I was cabin boy for Columbus ______
I walked into a Time machine and ______
The day I was teacher of my class I ______
The sun has repainted the earth ______

Jack Frost has been making lace again!
The sky is a sea of fog ______

Beth wrote the following poem after thinking about the snow line above:

Snow

Snow is diamonds from heaven—
  Snow is odd.
It stays in the clouds until
Jack Frost comes
Then it comes daintily down
It covers the sidewalks,
the houses and streets.
I like snow.
It brings santa claus
with presents for good boys and girls.
It's beautiful, fluffy and white.
The snow oh snow please come again soon.

—Beth

Last Sentences

Conversely, ask children to write stories which *end* with one of the following sentences:

—I was so glad to find it was only my brother Bob!
—Was I relieved to see my uncle Charlie!
—It was such a relief to find it was all a dream.
—I shouldn't have worried because suddenly he was gone as quickly as he came.
—You can bet I never did that again!
—So they lived happily forever after.
—And that's how the pig got his curly tail.

Known Topics

Use topics which you are sure children *want* to write about, such as PETS. Phyllis loves dachshunds.

Dachshunds

Dachshunds are dogs known for their long bodies and short legs. They have a cone-shaped head, a slim tapering muzzle, and long drooping ears. They have a long pointed tail and short smooth hair. Their glossy coat is usually black or tan, but it may be red, yellow, gray, spotted, or striped.

Dachshunds are strong, hardy, and alert dogs. They have a good sense of smell and make good pets. In Germany, where Dachshunds originated, they are considered national dogs.

Dachshunds are very cozy dogs. They love to curl up on your lap and put their necks over your arm. If there is no one around to curl up on, the fury lining of a coat, a pillow, some blankets, or anything soft will do.

Dachshunds love to run around on soft carpets and rugs, and rub their stomachs on them. They especially like you to rub their belly with one hand and let them bite on your other hand at the same time.

They love to run around outside and sit on soft grass in the sunshine.

When Dachshunds get mad they growl and start nipping on you, but they are truly great dogs!

—Phyllis White
Grade 7

One third grader who loves all animals—but especially dogs—writes as follows, displaying a delightful sense of humor!

Dogs

There are dogs of all kinds.
Even dogs striped with lines.
There are dogs with tiny spots.
Imagine dogs with polkadots!
If I like dogs and so do you,
There's one thing we ought to do.
Get a dog and that is that.
If you don't like dogs you could get a cat.
Cats are nice but dogs are better.
I especially like an Irish Setter.

—Beth Mattheus
Grade 3

Phrases

Sometimes these instructions may work: Write a story using these three phrases:

an old wilted rose;
a weatherbeaten mansion;
a snow-white horse.

or

flashing black eyes;
dying, wilted lettuce;
an old, familiar shoe.

Any combination of such phrases can produce interesting results.

Open-Ended Topics

One good idea is for the teacher to keep posted in the room an everchanging list of titles that are open-ended; that is, they leave the topic wide open. Some children who cannot "write about anything" and yet resent having to write just to complete an assignment will choose one of these topics and do some very creative things with it.

Such headings might include:

An Awful Experience
The Terrible Ending
You Don't Understand
Who Was It?
The Last Three Days
Two in The Zoo
The River
The *Twisted* Tree
The First Rain

Common Topics

Many natural and common topics often persuade children to write, such as: writing autobiographies; keeping diaries; writing about their own experiences; writing jokes; making up tall tales; writing pen-pal letters; making poems for birthday cards, valentines, or Mother's Day cards; writing announcements for reading over the school loud-speaker system; and writing plays or puppet show scripts.

The Writer's Corner

In your classroom, have a writer's corner set off from the room by a screen. To this corner all writers may go to be alone. Put a table, a chair, and plenty of paper and pencils in the corner. If a typewriter is available, it adds a new dimension. A signal on the outside of the screen indicates that the "corner" is being used—a red circle means STAY OUT.

Other Ideas Worth Trying

1. Little children can dictate stories to the teacher, who can type them with a primary typewriter or put them on chart paper. When the teacher reads the story back to the children, it can be illustrated as a reading chart or bound with others to make big books.

2. Keep a poetry file or a poetry drawer where poems and stories may be filed—both original and collected.

3. Keep an *idea sheet* in the front of the room, where anyone may put down an idea and anyone else may use it for some writing if the spirit moves him.

4. Keep a changing bulletin board of something beautifully written—by an author, a poet, one of the children, or yourself.

5. Have the children make a string painting. (This is a painting made by dipping string in paint and laying it on or folding it on paper.) Have them write what they see in the abstraction.

6. Sick cards: Children can make their own cards, write letters, or prepare surprises for a sick classmate who is absent. A chart is made of the number of days the student is apt to be absent. An envelope containing a number of the cards is mailed every day, so the sick child receives a packet of cards every day he is away from school. These cards and letters can be a strong motivation for some very creative writing.

7. Passing notes: The teacher can capitalize creatively on the children's natural desire to pass notes to each other. A mailbox can be constructed from an old carton—especially one which has separate sections (such as a paste carton). Children are then assigned a box, and are encouraged to write notes to each other and to the teacher and to mail them. The notes are distributed just before the children go home. This gives the teacher a chance to write special notes, assignments, or suggestions to children who need them most.

8. Organize a literary club where children may read together the things they write and evaluate each other.

9. Read some poetry or a beautiful piece of prose each day.

10. Use beautiful recordings frequently as background music in the room.

11. Use changes noted outside the classroom windows to discover descriptive words.

12. Breed an air of expectancy in your classroom. Children will write when they know it is expected of them.

13. Have each child write a description of another child. The description should include five clues. Then the composition is read to the rest of the children, who try to guess whom he is describing.

14. Have each child write about himself—physical appearance, likes, dislikes, hobbies, etc.—with his name written only on the *back* of the paper. The descriptions are then read and posted on the bulletin board. Only when other children have exhausted all possibilities may they peek to see who it is.

15. Write a word picture of the kind of music which comes from each musical instrument or from the orchestra as a whole.

16. Plan and make a class yearbook.

17. Encourage children to spin yarns and sea-shanty stories.

18. Use your units of work in social studies for new topics or ideas for creative writing.

Topics for Creative Writing

The joy of being creative is that you can write about anything or nothing, and in most any manner you like. You can write serious stories or nonsense poems. You can try limericks, riddles, or book reports. All that's really needed is that skill of writing, a good open-ended situation, and creative conditions under which you may work!

On the following pages I have listed many topics used by teachers everywhere to excite children to write. The results of their choices are evidenced in the sample writings accompanying the topics.

The secret of stimulating effective creative writing is simple: (a) encourage children to write about *their* experiences—and they are experiencing *something* every day of their lives, and (b) set proper conditions so that they can write freely.

Common Objects

Use intriguing subjects; Mark decided to write about trash cans!

Trash Cans

Although the trash can's job is poor he's always
 happy and gay,
No one ever thinks of him except when it's his day,
And just because he smells a lot we know he's not to blame,

It's the person who keeps dumping trash into him that really should be
shamed,
Of all the many trashcans, none of them are named,
It's just trash can and garbage can; to the trash man they're all the same,
Now, if I were a trash can, I'd be happy too,
Cause if I were a trashcan, I'd have lots and lots to do,
So, be sure to be nice to a trash can, what ever you do,
Cause do unto others as you would have them do to you.

—Mark Hubal
Grade 6

Animals

The Chipmunk

There the Chipmunk stands,
Looking for his prey, over the broad lands.
But there are so many animals bigger than he.
I'll bet he wishes he were me.

—Steve Griffin
Grade 6
Norfolk, Va.

Nature

It is interesting to note how two different age levels reacted to the Tree. First, let's look at Donald's poem (Grade 3).

The Children's Tree

I was a seed.
I turned into a tree.
I grow a little each week.
The people water me.
I like the people—all I see.
When I get big—10 or 15 years old.
I'll let the children climb on me.

Some day I would like to see,
One other just like me.

—Donald Stewart

Now JoAnne's poem: "Nature's Trees." JoAnne is in Grade 4.

Nature's Trees

Trees being planted,
Flowers start to sprout,
A nest in a tree,
A bright rainbow trout.

The winter comes and we find
Nature has given us a white blanket of snow.
She has shortened our day and sent
A howling wind which does nothing but blow.

The fall months arrive
And send leaves dancing in air
The animals begin to take stock of their food
The weather is cooler so we add sweaters with care.

The sun gives us heat from dawn until dusk
Swimming in brooks, rivers and streams.
Flowers are reaching their fullest bloom
Thank you, Mother Nature, for completing our dreams.

—JoAnne Marzadri

Holidays

Teachers everywhere need not be reminded that the unique mood of every holiday affords excellent opportunities for developing vocabulary words, especially those dealing with the senses, to be used in creative stories and poems.

However, children are exposed year after year at holiday times to the same stimuli. Teachers can be creative if they become more selective in the types of creative writing experiences they provide for their students. The Halloween story on page 53 is an excellent example of how an experience may be expanded after the children have lived through Halloween in school for a few years. The quality of the results achieved continues to improve from year to year.

One technique for motivating creative writing is to choose PART of a holiday and have the children write their feelings about it. Cathy, for instance, expresses her thoughts of Christmas morning as follows:

Christmas Morn

In the morning children rise,
Looking forward to the big surprise,
They run downstairs, straight to the tree,
And cry, "This is for you, and this for me!"
There're presents for everyone, mom and dad,
It's the nicest day you've had.

For the children there are toys,
Dolls for girls and drums for boys,
And, in the end you all pause,
And then you say, "Thanks, Santa Claus!"

—Cathy Miceli

With a little encouragement from the teacher, a first grade wrote this poem for Halloween. It is about a scarecrow they found on the bulletin board one morning whose name was Jack-O.

Jack-O

I am a little scarecrow.
I have a pumpkin head.
  I wear an old green jacket.
  I never had a bed.
I stand up on a stick,
I stand there night and day.
  I have a scarey face.
  To chase the crows away.
I live out in the field,
The corn is all I see.
  If you come by on Halloween,
  Please stop and visit me.

—Miss Smith's
First Grade Class

Current Topics of Interest

Children enjoy writing about their problems, and about the beauty and the mysteries of their world. When conditions are set to bring about free discussion, to introduce new words in meaningful context, and to tease imaginations, not only do learnings of subject matter take place and concepts develop, but creative outlet is highly accelerated.

After a discussion of man's proposed trip to the *Moon*, one child was inspired to write as follows:

Who Are You, Moon?

Who are you, Moon?
What do you look like?
Are you cold and gray?
Or are you full of life beneath the surface?

Are you green and pretty?
Do you have hills?

Do you have mountains and plains?
What is in those dark craters?
What is in those dark corners?
Why won't you show us your prettiness?
Are you afraid to show us?
Are you afraid of us?
If you are afraid, don't be.
We won't hurt you.
So moon, show your true self!

—Liane Godsy
Grade 6

Seasons

One teacher encouraged the children to use their feelings and thoughts from a class discussion about the seasons in poetic form, with the following results:

The Signs of Spring

The sign of spring is a great delight,
For anyone young or old.
It gives you a warm and happy feeling,
That anyone can behold!

The birds coming home, the grass turning green,
And no more snow coming down.
The flowers blooming everyday,
With fragrance fit for the crown.

All of these are signs of spring.
But there are many more.
For it shares with us so many things,
Because that is what spring is for!

—Phyllis White
Grade 6
Norfolk, Va.

Nature is an Artist

She paints the world beautiful.
She paints the sky majestic blue.
For the sea she blends greens, yellows, and blues.
She leaves the land every possible color that exists.

—Robert Gardner
Grade 6
Norfolk, Va.

Inner Thoughts

Some teachers encourage children to write about their *INNER THOUGHTS*. And how beautiful they sometimes are, as evidenced by Ann's "Reflections."

Reflections

The moody humor of the day has been swept aside
And before you, you see nothing.
Through this nothing you must walk quietly, slowly, with thoughts pounding through your head.
The lonely nothing has no green bushes, no flowers.
The furnishings are pictures of your thoughts; mirrors of your memories; clocks, ticking away your life.
For each minute you take a step,
Life is a long gray corridor; reflecting and ticking.

—Ann S. Hirstein

Catastrophe and Calamity

Catastrophe and calamity are not unique to adults. Writing about harassing experiences serves as a catharsis for children who have been emotionally moved by some situation. The words they must seek to express their feelings can greatly enrich their ability to express themselves, as seen from the words used by this fourth grader to describe the awful experience of being lost.

Lost

Howling winds came rolling by,
Tripping over the long endless railroad tracks
let in agony and I wanted to cry.
As tired as I was I tried to lie down, although
I felt I had to keep going 'till I was found.
The wolves in the woods and the snakes in the grass,
Gave me chills all over my body so fast,
That I ran and ran till my weary legs could hold
me no longer,
I stopped to rest 'till my heartbeat go stronger.
Then I started to walk through the wild dark
wilderness.
No longer was I to search for my long lost home.

—Liz Saunders
Grade 6
Norfolk, Va.

Historical Events

Dana was inspired to write a song about *AN HISTORICAL EVENT.*

There once was a girl
And her name was Betsy
And she'll ne're be forgotten
By you or by me.
And this young girl
With her talented hand
Made the United States flag
Which now flies so grand.

Chorus:
Betsy Ross made the U.S. flag
Out of needles and thread and bits of old rag.
Betsy Ross is remembered by me
And she'll ne're be forgotten in history.

She was a fine woman.
She was a fine lass.
Her flag is the present.
Her work is the past.
Her talent will live
Through her glorious flag
Which was made out of needles
And bits of old rag. Repeat chorus

—Dana Teitelman
Grade 6

Sports

Attendance at sports events or participating in a sports event is often a new and exciting adventure to children. Let them tell you about it.

Mark loves to sail:

Sailing

The sea was very quiet,
and it was as smooth as glass.
We had just set sail,
When I saw a big fat bass.

Suddenly a breeze was stirring up,
and the air was getting cool.
The catspaws were racing across the water,
and I felt like a fool.

The sea was getting windy,
and it was getting cold.
We were playing poker,
and I had to fold.

We were keeling at 45°,
and the waves were getting rough.
We were in the middle of a storm,
and our captain was very tough.

The captain started yelling,
and the boat started to rock.
We had just seen land,
when the captain saw our dock.

—Mark Burnett
Grade 6

Stories of Make-Believe

Children of all ages enjoy stories of make-believe and love to try a hand at writing them. Add to this joy a dose of knowledge of the folklore and customs of a country such as Finland, for instance, and you may get a class book with illustrations, such as the following book "The Fauni Trolls" created by a fifth grade class.

Quite a long time ago, in the forests of Finland, there lived many tiny troll-like creatures. They were from one to three inches high and a variety of shapes and colors. For instance, someone could have a bright purple body and long green hair. (See Figures 78, 79, 80, and 81.)

Living together in small groups, they managed quite well, Because they made small huts of moss, leaves, and bark, they were well protected from the bitter winter weather. For food they planted gardens of mushrooms and shiny red lingonberries. Icy water from streams was the only thing to drink, but it served the trolls well. So, for many hundreds of years, they lived peacefully and happily.

Now up in the barren tundra land of Northern Finland lived a terrifying old witch feared by all people. Her name was Noita-Akka, which simply means witch.

Noita-Akka loathed these troll-people with all of her crafty, wicked heart. What carefree, happy things they were, just lazing around while she, yes she, the great witch of the north toiled night and day! Such impudence! For years she planned and plotted, and finally came up with a spell which would turn them into harmless dolls.

Soon the trolls were to have a special two-day celebration which every

Figure 78 *Illustration from* The Fauni Trolls.

Figure 79 *Illustration from* The Fauni Trolls.

Figure 80 *Illustration from* The Fauni Trolls.

Figure 81 *Illustration from* The Fauni Trolls.

troll was obligated to attend. Having heard of this, Noita-Akka planned to come secretly to the celebration and hide until the Grand Assembly.

Then came the first day. Every Fauni troll was present. Anywhere you looked you could see trolls feasting, dancing, singing, and having a gay time.

When it was all over, the Grand Assembly began. Just as the eldest troll began to speak, a fearful, shrieking creature leaped out of the woods. Noita-Akka!

"Aha! Now I have you, the whole lot of you no-good, silly trolls!" she screamed. "Beware if anyone tries to flee!"

"What do you want from us?" cried the eldest troll. "What have we done?"

"You know I have despised you lazy things for many years! Now at last I can put an end to you! Quite harmless though, unfortunately," she replied.

Then she screeched, "Now!" and a bright blinding light flashed. All the trolls stood statue-like. They had all been turned into toys.

"From 12:00 midnight to 5:00 you shall be alive again, but if a human ever sees you in that form, none of you will ever move again!" she said.

Then Noita-Akka took out a huge sack and put all the trolls into it. They were very tiny to her. Quickly she made herself look like a peddler. For many months she walked from town to town, selling the bewitched trolls for gold.

After they were all sold she went back to the tundra where a poisonous snake slithered up to her and said, "I saw what you did, and because the trolls once helped me, I shall now help them." His fangs snapped on Noita-Akka's finger and she died instantly.

* * * *

Even today many children own these toy trolls who were called the Faunis. But at night, at the certain time, the trolls come alive and dance and play as they did at the festival before they were bewitched.

Fables

Children enjoy fables. After reading some, such as Kipling's "The Elephants' Child" or "How the Camel Got Its Hump," suggest that they write their own. Examples:

How the Zebra Got His Stripes
How the Dog Got His Bark
Why the Cat Has Claws
How the Woodpecker Got His Red Head
How the Ostrich Got Her Long Neck

Movies

Write about popular *MOVIES* the children enjoy. Here is Debbie's poem written as a postlude to the movie, "Oliver."

If Time Went Back

Foggy towers in the morning
All around us beaming,
Dirty rooftops show us that
The sweeps have not been sweeping.
But as the day gets warmer
And markets open wide,
And in comes the country farmer;
London shows her pride.
Ducks and geese are being sold,
And plucked on Scalding Deley,
Being sold are beakers of gold,
And tickets for a rally.
Such a wonderous sight,
Stone horses might
Start coming alive in Hyde Park.
And beaks are yelling,
Left; right! left; right!!!
And cornish fishers are selling blue shark,
And here and there; . . .
And there and here; . . .
You'll see wallets disappear.

—Debbie Pryor
Grade 6

Wishes

All children enjoy writing about their *WISHES*. Murray wrote the following:

The greatest wish I could have would be for eternal peace. Because the whole world could work together, not separated, but united. All of the great men thinking together, helping us journey further than we ever have been. Instead of "One nation under God," it would be "One world under God," indivisible, with liberty and justice for all. Nothing is impossible, not even peace!

—Murray Rosenb
Grade 6

Glorify the Commonplace

Creative writing is a medium through which the simplest of things can be glorified.

Mr. Bell had the children list things that were so common that they didn't notice them too much—things the children were apt to take for granted. Then each child chose a topic and wrote about it.

Some of the poems he received appear below.

Firefly

Firefly, firefly light your light
Make it bright to walk at night
Make it right so I'm not in plight
Firefly, firefly light your light.

Firefly, firefly with a light
Turn it dark or turn it bright
See anything even at night
Firefly, firefly light your light.

Firefly, firefly in your light
See everywhere even at night
Firefly, firefly never in plight
Firefly, firefly you've got your own light.

—Elizabeth
Grade 4

Figure 82 *Shapes—illustration for Elizabeth's poem.*

Shapes

There are many shapes in the world today,
They are all so different in every way.

There are round shapes,
And square shapes which have lines that meet,
There are squiggly shapes that can't be beat.

There are triangle shapes that point to the sky,
And rectangle shapes that meet eye to eye.

There are so many shapes in the world today
And they are all so different·in every way.

—Elizabeth Saunders
Grade 4

Personification

What would *things* say if they could talk? *Animals? Colors? Written words?*

In one delightful class I attended, the teacher was asking the children to list all the things they could think of that might want to talk that day. They listed these ideas:

Red
The Sun
Our Stuffed Elephant
The Eraser
The Light Bulb
The Bulletin Board
The Pencil Box
An Automobile

The teacher had them choose *any* topic (even one not on the list) and write as though that topic were talking. After sharing the papers, she pointed out the principle of personification. It is interesting to note here that the definition of personification which the children determined came out at the close of the experience, not as a prologue to it.

Neighbors

Mrs. Ayers and her class began a unit on developing understanding of people of the world with a discussion of neighbors—ways they were alike, ways they were different, and why neighbors were nice or not nice. Mrs. Ayers' objective was to show the children that the same problems existed with "world" neighbors as with "street" neighbors.

The discussion took a turn toward sentimentality when the children talked about the many nice neighbors they had and how lucky they were. The discussion ended with one sixth grader concluding that the "differences" in people helped to make them interesting.

Mrs. A. suggested that they might want to write a vignette, a poem, or an essay on the neighbors they liked. Almost all the children did. It seemed to me that Gail's poem reflected the tone of the entire discussion.

Testing the Neighbors

A kindly young man moved in
Among ourselves we shared a grin
We thought, "Ah, yes, a joke,"
And across our faces mischief broke.

He laughed at the skate on the stair,
Said he'd just leave it there.
We knocked on the study door and hid,
He opened it and smiled—that's all he did.

And once we discovered he was kind
No loss of temper we'd ever find
It was that very same hour
We left our welcome—a woodland flower.

But how about his spouse,
A quiet country mouse?
A pie left on the window ledge
Tempted us across the hedge.

She laughed and was filled with glee,
At least it seemed that way to me.
I'd often see her tending her lawn
Or nursing to health the sick baby fawn.

And now that they are old and gray
It is with great pride we can say,
"We love each smiling feature
Of the kindly wife and friendly preacher."

—Gail L.
Grade 6

Humor

Creative children have a wonderful sense of humor. Their humor at times may vary greatly from the humor of adults, but if we understand their humor, we enjoy it. In the classroom, common use of oral and written humor can do much more than build good rapport between teacher and students. It can develop creative imagination in expression and a certain amount of wit. Wit is a result of good thinking plus an opportune moment. Witty remarks and a good sense of humor provide a means of creative communication and promote a type of social relationship in the classroom that no other form of expression can accomplish.

I a Sox

I am a sock. I have been married for five years to Bobby Sox. We're the happiest couple in the clothes basket. I met my husband six years ago. We were both hanging on a line between a pair of underwear. It was love at first sight. And soon we were united in holy thread lock. I loved the way his threads were sewn together.

Last week we had our first fight. We really socked it to each other. One day one of my threads got loose and I became very ill. Bobby Sox ran to the sewing basket and pleaded help from the needle and thread spools. Soon I was back in shape. But Bobby Sox had been so worried we pledged by rubbing heels together never to fight again and to stay together reunited in that clothes basket in the sky.

—Rebecca Lantzy
Grade 6
East Detroit, Mich.

Ambitions

We must never forget that children have dreams and ambitions and enjoy writing about them. These ambitions and goals are subject to change yearly, even monthly, in the growing child: all the more reason to use them for his own personal creative writing.

Following is an essay written by a sixth grade girl whose dreams and ambitions were not quite so changeable: she *is* now a second grade teacher:

I would like to be a second grade teacher. I think this for about five reasons. First, I had a lovely, wonderful second grade teacher and I wish

I could be just like her (Mrs. Martin) even though it is not possible. The next reason is a little silly but I like to check papers. Also, I want to go to Syracuse University. I like seven-year-old children and I think I would like to teach them. The last reason is that I have been very lucky all through school to get such wonderful teachers, and friends and I want other kids to be as lucky as I.

—Dotty
Grade 6

Upside-Down and Backwards Stories

Tickle the imagination of the children by having them write about an "Upside-Down" or a "Backwards" day, year, month, event, or lifetime. The following sample shows how imagination can be employed by an eight year old.

A Backward Upside-Down Christmas

Once upon a time there was a upside-down Christmas tree. The people who owned it had a boy and a girl in the family. The boy's name was Jack Kcaj and the girl's name was Jill Kcaj.

Christmas time was coming and the upside-down Christmas tree was set upside-down. Then Christmas time came. The whole family went to bed early. Then Claus Santa came up the chimney and he put all the presents on the ceiling and put all the Christmas tree decorations in the lamp. The next morning when the children got down they walked across the ceiling and opened their presents and had a very merry upside-down backward Christmas.

—Joe
Grade 3

Daydreams and Night Dreams

Daydreams are imagined experiences which we project into the future or into the realm of fantasy, seeing ourselves as we would like to be, hoping and wishing for things we would like to own, going places we would like to go, imagining what it will be like "when" and "if." Daydreams provide a continual motivation for creative writing and can be a legitimate outlet for the creative expression of children who have secret wishes and desires. As for a technique for developing vocabulary, they are unsurpassed. Witness the following "daydream" composition which came from a sixth grader when the class decided to write about things they would like to own:

What I Would Like to Own

I would like to own a 3.9 liter Alfa-Lotus competition touring car. The car is aerodynamically shaped, it is magnesium alloy and fiberglass. It also has an aluminum engine block.

The companies that make the car are leading companies. Alfa, an Italian make combined with Romero are making some of the best cars in the world. Lotus also makes fine lightweight cars.

Those are the main reasons I would like to own a Alfa-Lotus.

—Jack
Grade 5

Other "Daydream" topics are:

A Place I would Like to Be
What I Want to Be When I Grow Up
If I Inherited a Million Dollars
If I Were Rich
If I Were Taller
If I Ran the Circus
A Trip to the Moon
Life As An Astronaut
If I Were My Father

"Night dream" stories are generally of another variety, often conducive to the development of an entirely different spoken and written vocabulary: more often words describing frightened feelings, confusion of mind, weird and unexplainable sensations (such as falling) come into play and may be explored.

On writing about "a nightmare," Mary penned the following:

Drowning

O, unbearable current,
Why do you pull at me?
Tossing me about like a toy,
Oh, help!

Brilliant blue sea,
Aren't you a friend to me?
Your violent surging waves,
Are pulling me in.

Oh, you deadly waves,
Why can't you leave me be?
To play on the shore,
With shovel and pail.

I once knew you as a quiet calm friend,
But now my life is at its end.
Oh, help!

Other topics for "Night Dream" stories are:

An Unreal Experience
After I Shut My Eyes
The Twilight Zone
My Other World
An Unconscious Life
Out of My Mind
Sleep Without Rest
My Other World

Pictures

There are so many beautiful and wonderful pictures available that teachers need never be without material to inspire children.

One teacher showed the children colored pictures from "In Wildness is the Preservation of the World" by Eliot Porter. The children were inspired. One of them wrote about the wintry, woody picture as follows:

On a Winter's Night

On a winter's night, not long ago,
The rain stopped its plight, and it began to snow,
And I discovered something I didn't already know,
That lightning may accompany snow;

It came in thrashes across the sky,
And sullen lashes to imply,
That this sky was conquered by its will,
As I speculated from the window sill;

We bundled in our winter's cloak,
As the hour of seven softly broke,
Each sleeping child joyfully awoke,
Each envied by an older folk;

Our shrills were heard, muffled by snow,
The wind's sweet chills, softly did blow,
And then through the sky, came our foe,
It fell once more, the conquered snow;

When we retired from the cold,
The lightning was weak, that was once so bold,
Its conquering strength, now frail and old,
It perished and died, in the winter's cold;

—Kathryn Ackley
Grade 6

Another single picture viewed was a lovely colored print of a bird's nest full of eggs couched in the crotch of a mossy tree.

Experience which cannot be observed in the classroom may be brought into the classroom through pictures.

One Day

I wandered through the woods one day
On a bright sunny morning in May.
When I stumbled upon the nest of a bird
I was careful and silent as not to be heard,
I was in hopes that the bird to whom these belonged
Would be somewhere near and just pass along.
So I waited and waited and waited some more
I waited and waited and got very sore.
I had to get up and stretch for a while.
I felt I could walk for many a mile.
As I walked away and looked down at the nest
There sat the bird with a bright blue vest.

—Renée Chapel
Grade 6
Norfolk, Va.

Actual News Reporting

Excellent motivation for writing may be obtained by encouraging children to write true-life experiences, or to take true-life experiences and fictionalize them.

Ideas to Try ★

Try these ideas some dull day when both students and teacher need a lift. The results may just save your day!

1. *Character Transplants:*
   Take the leading character from a reading-book story and transplant him or her into a new story; of course, the character's personality, physical characteristics, and attitudes must remain unchanged.

2. *Proverbs and Sayings:*
   Encourage children to write stories or poems about famous sayings or proverbs such as "A Stitch in Time Saves Nine" or "She turned me off." Afterwards, it is fun to fantasy about the origins of such sayings.
   Drawing pictures about famous sayings can be highly creative and amusing. This type of activity provides an excellent lead into the teaching of metaphor. Some writers believe that the ability to make metaphor is the greatest difference between creative and non-creative people.

3. *Historical Transplants:*
   Describe what would most amaze George Washington, Benjamin Franklin, Abraham Lincoln, or Christopher Columbus about America today. What would make them most unhappy?

4. *Unrelated Objects:*
   Have each pupil bring an object from home. Divide the class into small groups of five or six each. Then have the pupils pool their objects in the middle of their group. Write a story or a play utilizing each object contributed.

5. *Unusual Names:*
   What does a name like Bradford Bullwinkle make you think of? Agnes Mellacoppie? What kind of person do you think would have a name like Adamson Farmweather? Make up a story that includes people like these whose names you would invent.

6. *Inanimate Objects:*
   Pretend to be something that is not exactly alive and write about it—tooth, paper, eyebrow, teakettle, football, etc.

7. *Imagery:*
   Make pictures of "new" animals by combining existing animal names—such as an elephanteater, a doggoat, a zebronco—and write a poem or story about the animal.

8. *Pantomiming:*
   Encourage individual children or groups of children to pantomime an activity. After it is guessed, write the activity on the chalkboard in a sentence such as: John is opening his Christmas presents.
   Then embellish the sentence with colorful, descriptive words such as: John is nervous and excited as he eagerly opens his beautifully wrapped, breathtaking Christmas presents.

John then does his pantomime again, and the children can see how the embellished sentence better describes the picture John is attempting to portray.

9. *Hailstones and Halibut Bones:*
Read Mary O'Neill's *Hailstones and Halibut Bones* to the children as a good example of setting a mood for creative writing. Most teachers find that poems seem to come naturally with children as a result of listening to this charming book.

10. *The Senses:*
Literature, both prose and poetry, appeals to the reader when it touches his heart as well as his head. The "feeling" of a passage makes it memorable. Attempts to appeal to the senses of children help to develop "feeling" in their writing. Sometimes it is advantageous to dwell on one sense alone.

The Sense of Smell. Blindfold four or five children and let them hold your hand while you go to the office for something. Take them by a devious route and, when you return, let them: (a) tell where they have been, and (b) tell how the smells they experienced made them feel. They will have recognized the twang of the ditto ink as they went by the principal's office, the odors of cooking foods when passing the cafeteria, the smell of detergent as they passed the janitor's closet, your own perfume, and the smell of perspiration in the gym.

Place objects, such as horseradish, mustard, vinegar, ginger, vanilla, etc., on a tray. Blindfold the children and let them smell each item. They should not only identify it, but also tell how it feels to them.

Mary Lou said, after sniffing horseradish, "It felt as though I stuck my nose into a porcupine."

Peter, age 9, said about vinegar, "My jaws itched to be away from it."

Marcia, age 12, said about cloves, "They make me think of old things, like chandeliers, hoop skirts, and pretty music. I felt old and long ago."

Children will also have fun collecting smells they like and putting them in poems, either collectively or individually.

The Sense of Hearing. Such trips as those mentioned above may be followed by "Hearing" trips. Children can close their eyes and listen to sounds and try to guess where they have been. Also, open the window on a warm day and let the children listen to the noises in the street. Then they can make up a story or a poem about what they have heard.

The Sense of Sight. There are many ways children can sharpen their observations to put what they see into words and eventually into their writing; many have been mentioned in the previous paragraphs – puppet shows, bulletin boards, TV viewing, dramatization, and working with all media.

11. *Unforgettable Character:*

Try *"Someone I Admire"* or the *"Most Unforgettable Character I Ever Met."*

An Adult I Admire

One person that I admire is my brother. He is the kind of person that is fun to talk, play, and be with. He is married and his wife's name is Mickey. They are both nice to me and the rest of my family. He doesn't come over too often because he has to work, but when he does come over we all have fun. He teaches me many things like how to shoot a gun, how to wrestle and things like that.

To me, he is the best brother any boy could ask for.

—Greg Moore
Grade 6

12. *Limericks:*

Write LIMERICKS—and then, if possible, put them into a folk-song pattern.

Hannah & Kenny

Once a young lady named Hannah,
From the big state of Montana,
Lived in a farmhouse and had a pet hen,
And she fell in love with a nice boy named Ken.

Chorus:
Deedle de-de
Deedle de-do
Deedle de-di and
Deedle di-da

Kenny came over and gave her a kiss,
He was in love with this pretty young miss,
He said, "I love you" and he called her his hun,
And out came her pa, and he had a big gun!

Chorus

Soon they got married without pa's consent,
They were so happy and very content
Then one day Hannah, she did hear a shot,
And out came her pa, a new suit he had got.

Chorus

He said, "Oh my Hannah, I'm rich as can be,
I have plenty gold, and I'm sure you'll agree".

She said, "Oh no papa I hope you will see,
Farmlife was meant for both Kenny and Me".

Chorus

—Beth Cohen
Grade 7

13. *Emotional Situations for Creative Writing Projections:*
Encourage children to project themselves into emotional or physical "make-believe" situations such as: being smaller, bigger, happier, sadder, etc.

Land of the Giants

One day at the supper table I felt sick so went to lay on the couch and went to sleep. When I woke up I had a funny feeling. Then I realized what had happened: I had shrunk. All of a sudden I heard a loud shriek, and then I heard an earth quake. I closed my eyes and plugged my ears. When I opened my eyes, a huge body was going to sit on me. It was my mother. I yelled out "Help!" She stopped and looked around and found me. She took me to a laboratory and they gave me a potion and I was back to size that week. Our house was filled with people and reporters. That morning I was on the front page.

—Mark Wyham
Grade 4

My Small Adventure

One day when I walked in the school, I felt that I was shrinking. When I walked I shouted, "Watch out where you are walking!" Then I said to myself that I must have drink a potion. Then I walked out of the school. I was looking for a little ship to go sailing on. I found a little ship sitting there. I sailed to Lilliput. It was fun in Lilliput. Then I went around the world. Then I went back to Lilliput. I said, "To a man, Lilliput is the best place in the world."

—Debbie
Grade 4

14. *Unlikely Titles:*
Select at random a group of things which seem the least likely subjects for poems or essays. Some children will be challenged by making such a list as well as by the writing of a poem or essay suggested by it.

Miss Wilkins asked her children to make such a list on the chalkboard. Here is how it looked:

A Cannonball
An Eraser
A Tin Can
Chalk Dust
A Map Puzzle of the States
The Globe
A Pair of Rubbers
An Earache
A Dirty Floor
Six Nails

15. *Using Leading Questions:*

Use unusual, thought-provoking, open-ended questions to trigger the children's imagination to produce creative thoughts.

To the question "What Color is Happiness?" one teacher received the following responses:

Yellow because it reminds me of sunshine which makes me happy.
Red, white and blue because it reminds me of our flag.
White because it reminds me of winter.
Brown because it reminds me of autumn.
Red because of the color of your lips.
Red, purple and yellow because they're my favorite rainbow colors.
Red because when someone blushes, their face gets red.
Blue because when you see it in the sky, it won't rain that day.
Green because it's the color of money.

Other questions which may be used to provoke unusual groupings of words are:

"What color is a baby's cry?"
"How does a rainbow feel?"
"What does a cloud smell like?"
"If you could eat it, how would the sun taste?"
"What color is sadness?"
"How wide is the sky?"

16. *Slides and Sound:*

A set of slides can be made around an original story—the story can be taped and shown with the slides. A variation of this idea is to use commercial slides and allow children to write a story to go with them.

17. *What Happened:*

Use "What happened" beginnings for children to complete such as:

I opened the cellar door to call my dog and all I heard was a queer noise. I snapped on the light, calling, "Here Sport," but he did not answer, so I started down the stairs to investigate the queer noise. I stopped dead in my tracks: waddling across the cellar floor was a huge duck!

I had put my hand into that potato bin hundreds of times. I just pulled out potatoes of all sizes in the dark. But tonight, when I stuck my hand in the bin as usual, instead of a potato, my hand closed on something warm and furry!

18. *Unusual Questions:*

Put a series of questions on the chalkboard and have the children select one to write about.

Example: What does your shadow think of you?
What is it like being a milkweed pod?
How big is trouble?
What do rainbow colors remind you of?

Cindy wrote the following poem about her shadow:

My Shadow

My shadow goes where I go;
It plays with me all day,
It sleeps when I am sleeping.
It eats when I am eating.
My shadow does most anything.
When the sun is up—
Not down.

—Cindy
Age 8

19. *Surprise Stories:*

Write about these: You go to see your dog's new puppies, and there under her is a rabbit! You sit at the table to eat, and suddenly everything before you that is glass begins to melt!

20. *Beginning Letters:*

Use the names of holidays or important events as the beginning letters of each line of a poem.

Here's what Nancy wrote about Christmas:

C is for candy canes so tall,
H is for holly hung on the wall,
R is for reindeer that lead Santa's sleigh,
I is for ice and snow on the way,
S is for snowman so funny and cold,
T is for tinsel all silver and gold,
M is for merry, that's what we'll all be,

A is for angel at the top of the tree,
S is for stars so shiny and new,

That's the end of my poem,
MERRY CHRISTMAS TO YOU!

—Nancy
Grade 4

21. *Suggested Topics For Creative Writing:*

Although not completely open-ended, topics for creative writing are free enough to spark the imagination of some children:

Life Inside a Ping-Pong Ball
The Life of a Pencil
If I Were a Dirty Car
The Day I Forgot
A Rhyming Advertisement
A Television Commercial
If I Were a King (or Queen)
The Opposite of a Rock
If I Were Santa Claus
If I Were Blind
Life as a Baseball Bat
If I Were a Penny
Life as a TV Set
My Life as a Sandman
When I Was a Boogie Man
My Visit to Peanuts and Lucy
Footsteps
If I Never Had to Eat
What Color Is Hate?

22. *Radio and Television Shows:*

If children have the opportunity to present real live radio or TV shows, some excellent script writing can result.

23. *Animated Cartoons:*

Show an animated cartoon to the class, *but* cut off the sound track and have the children write their own dialogue.

24. *TV Commercials:*

Write your own TV commercial about a real or fictitious product. Timmy (age 11) wrote this about a cereal he invented:

They don't sizzle
They don't pop
They don't drizzle
They don't plop

Fruit as silk
White and tan
They just sop up
Milk in a pan!

25. *Roll Movies:*

Have everyone in the class draw a picture. Paste them all on a long sheet of paper and make a roll movie. Now write a story that includes each picture as it comes into view. Try to connect the story logically.

26. *What Happens:*

Write stories about what happens to . . .

An old automobile tire
Old razor blades
Cigarette butts
An improperly addressed letter
Golf balls
A cancelled stamp

27. *Directions:*

Practice writing directions for new games. (Figures 83, 84, 85, 86, and 87.)

Figure 83 *A sixth grade writes its own version of* The Wizard of Oz, *and produces it.*

Figure 84 *This set was left from a school play. The sixth grade teacher divided the class into four groups and said, "Here is a place. Something happened here. Each group is to decide what happened and then act out a scene for us!" This is an excellent example of using an open-ended situation in creative dramatics.*

Figure 85 *Idea! Who says that snowflakes must be white? These are blue and orange. They were an inspiration for several poems and stories.*

Figure 86 *A performance evaluation. A scene from a fourth grade production of* The Melting Pot.

Figure 87 *Each nation is represented by a colored streamer and at the finale of the play they are symbolically woven together in a creative adaptation of the Maypole dance.*

Evaluation of Creative Writing

Creative writing can be evaluated, but it is a question of great concern as to whether or not anything creative should ever be "graded" or "marked." A teacher goes beyond her role when she attempts to judge a child's creative ability. Consequently, the emphasis should be on improvement of quality of writing, but not at the expense of enthusiasm, which also produces quantity. If children are to be "graded" for their creative writing, the whole purpose of the writing is defeated, because this simply means that the child must write about those things which please the teacher and in a manner which pleases the teacher. Research shows that the content of the same themes can vary in grade from A to E when read and marked by different teachers. It is questionable whether or not elementary school teachers themselves are creative enough or know enough about creativity to evaluate the creativeness of children's writing.

What is needed in evaluating creative writing is discussion about content, help in vocabulary building, and help in developing the skills which make possible the recording of the writing the child wished to put on paper for others to read.

On the other hand, the teacher who strives only to have students increase their skill in writing correctly or in using the correct forms is wasting her time unless the children are interested in wanting to write, in having a purpose for writing, and in writing with honesty and responsibility.

The teacher who has poems, compositions, and stories placed on her desk each day has the material at hand that will help her diagnose the needs of her class and the core for designing her language program.

Mr. Smith used a very simple technique to identify the needs of his children. From his register he made a master ditto with all the children's names along the left-hand side of the paper. A series of title boxes after each child's name made it possible for him to read the children's poems and stories, and to put a check after each child's name to indicate the skill in which he needed help. On page 379 is a portion of Mr. Smith's diagnosis sheet for punctuation and capitalization skills.

A glance at the sheet which Mr. Smith marked after reading two sets of stories from the class shows some interesting things: (a) the entire class has mastered the use of the period and the question mark; (b) Joe Adams, Peter Barkan, and Molly Durkin do not, as yet, know how to properly use exclamation points; (c) seven children need help with commas; (d) seven need help with quotation marks; (e) Joe, Peter, and Molly also do not use capital letters in writing titles; (f) Joe also needs

TOPIC: *Punctuation—Capitalization*
DATE: ______________________

									Caps.		
Class		?	!	,	“”	;	:	-	T.	S.	N.
Adams, Joe			X	X	X				X	X	X
Arlott, Helen				X	X						
Barnes, Margaret					X						
Barkan, Peter			X	X	X				X	O	
Bason, Janice				X	X						
Crane, Helen											
Danes, Mary											
Dell, Shiela				X	X						
Durkin, Molly			X	X					X		
Eaton, Charles											
Ester, Alice											
Frank, Marge				X	X						

help in capitalizing letters. Mr. Smith can also note that Joe and Peter are very weak in capitalization and punctuation skills. How will Mr. Smith handle this situation?

On the Monday after he filled out this diagnosis sheet, he motivated the class for some creative writing; after the children were busy, he took Joe, Peter, and Molly aside into a little group and retaught a creative lesson on the use of exclamation marks. Margaret, who is very good at punctuation, met with the group at Mr. Smith's invitation, and when Mr. Smith reached that part of the lesson where he wanted the children to drill, he was able to go help the other children while Margaret took over and helped the children in the group.

The next day Mr. Smith called Joe, Helen, Peter, Janice, Shiela, Molly, and Margaret together and retaught a creative lesson on the use of the comma.

Each day of the week Mr. Smith taught the skills needed by grouping the children together who needed the help. The other children, who had mastered the skills, were applying them in creative writing forms. Children who needed help were getting it and individual differences were being met. Of course, Mr. Smith spent a great deal of time with Joe and

Peter because they needed constant help—and continued reinforcement of any success they had.

Teachers must not forget that they are in the classroom to teach—and not to test, except as a means of identifying progress. Teaching means diagnosing followed by remedial teaching or "new teaching," then checking. Of what purpose, then, is the "grading" of creative writing?

Anderson[3] gives some guides for teachers who are interested in developing the quality of children's writings. He suggests that we not be concerned as much about content as about the following:

1. What prompted the student to write the paper? What limitations did he have? What does the paper really say? What are its strengths and weaknesses?

2. Oral and written criticisms should encourage students and suggest further effort in writing. Any comment made by the teacher, even though it is critical, should indicate respect for what the student has written.

3. A student who truly understands that adherence to the conventions of language is a courtesy to the reader and an aid in conveying the meaning intended by the writer will be more inclined to write correctly than will a student who thinks of spelling, grammar, and so forth, as something aside from "thought."

4. If a teacher places undue emphasis on form, he or she is penalizing the bold, original, aggressive thinker whose ideas sometimes get ahead of his command of written language. Teacher and class should have a common understanding of the relative "weight" to be assigned to content and form.

5. Marginal symbols are useful in showing a student where his writing is weak. Teachers recognize, however, that certain kinds of weaknesses (particularly in structure of sentences) cannot be easily explained by any symbol, but must be discussed orally with the student or elaborated on in a written comment. (This is where Mr. Smith's technique mentioned above is sound. He is able to return the papers at once and hold a discussion, either individually or in small groups, as to the merits and deficiencies of the paper.)

6. Teachers in the upper grades need not make a correction for a student. Rather, they might indicate the point of error or weakness and let the student, with whatever help he needs, work out the correction himself. It is equally important to mark strong points in a student's paper.

7. Teachers will always want to be cautious in suggesting that students "vary sentence patterns," "subordinate" a particular idea, or the like. The relationship of ideas shown in complex sentences by the use

3. Paul S. Anderson, *Language Skills in the Elementary School* (New York: Macmillan Company, 1964), p. 411.

of modifying phrases is a highly individual matter. What the writer means to say will determine his sentence structure, as far as subordination is concerned. If the meaning in a given sentence or paragraph is not clear, the student—not the teacher—must decide how sentence structure should be changed to clarify the student's ideas. This can often be worked out best in an individual discussion.

8. The extremely poor speller frequently has some psychological or emotional disturbance. Ignoring his spelling until some diagnostic and corrective work can be done is sometimes the best course of action.

9. Older students should expect to revise and rewrite, or copy, their work. Because revision is important, they must be given time to think about it, time to do it, and help when they need it. However, if a student can correct a minor error or two without completely recopying a paper, he should certainly be allowed to do so. (See below: The Editorial Box.)

10. All teachers know that "it is poor teaching to demand what the teacher knows cannot be done." Criticism and suggestions for revision, therefore, must be in terms of an individual's capacities.

11. Highly general suggestions for revision are fruitless. To say to a student, "Make this more interesting (or entertaining, or effective)," will probably result in baffling rather than helping the student.

The Editorial Box

Teachers often complain that there is not time to read all the material that comes from children, and if a teacher is good at getting children to write, this can often be a justifiable objection to the conscientious evaluation of children's work. There are several ways that teachers can cut down on the time consumed in evaluation processes.

Workbooks: A Problem?

If workbooks are used judiciously, they can be of great help to a teacher and can save her many hours of preparation. However, when they are used simply as a "busy work" device to keep all children occupied, whether or not they need help in the specific skill on the workbook page, they are a violation of the education process and the child's psychology. One way to use the workbook effectively is described below in the narration of the Editorial Box. Teachers generally feel compelled to correct workbook exercises. This time might be more gainfully spent in reading children's creative writings; when properly handled and organized, the reading of children's material takes no more time than the "correction" of twenty-eight workbook sheets, is much more purposeful if some system such as Mr. Smith's plan is worked out, and is even enjoyable.

The Box

As the year progressed, Mr. Smith cut down considerably on the time needed for reading, evaluating, and rereading of children's work by instituting the following system:

Through his diagnostic charts, he was able to identify those children who were continually able to master grammar forms, punctuation forms, etc. In this case, he put Helen, Mary, Charles, and Alice on an Editorial Committee.

In a conspicuous place in the classroom, Mr. Smith placed a file drawer (an old apple box painted bright red). He gave each child a tabbed manila folder. On these folders, Mr. Smith asked the children to print their last names, followed by their first. On the day the folders were distributed, he also had each child make a cardboard flag, like that used on a rural mailbox. He taught a creative lesson on alphabetization so that the children understood the concept; at the close of the lesson, their folders all appeared in the box, arranged alphabetically.

These folders became a medium of exchange within the classroom. Mr. Smith also had his own folder in the box in its proper alphabetical order. Often, when Mr. Smith found a student who needed special drill in some skill, he would tear a sheet from a workbook, clip a note to it (such as, "Charlie, you are having some trouble with commas. Read this, work the sheet, and drop it in my folder, please. Mr. Smith"), and drop it in the student's folder. Work finished during the day was placed in Mr. Smith's folder. (It also proved to be a legitimate place for children to drop "mash" notes to the teacher. Many of these were unsigned.)

When a child wrote a poem, story, essay, or any creative venture, it was understood that he could write it on scrap paper or however he liked until he was ready to share it.

Then, as a social courtesy, it had to be in the best form the child could put it in before being submitted to the teacher.

Mr. Smith had said to the class at the beginning of the year, "Boys and girls, I like to write. Sometimes I write stories or articles, and sometimes I write books. When I am writing, I use scrap paper, I scratch on it, I write over, I scribble, and I cut chunks of my writing out. Sometimes my ideas come so fast I cannot write as fast as I can think, so my sentences are not complete or properly punctuated—and that is all right. But, when I finally get it the way I want it and it says what I want it to say, I write it in my best handwriting so a secretary can read it easily in order to type it, and I send it to the publisher. It is only courteous to them and helpful for me to do this. So, this year, even though you see notes on my desk which are scratched or poorly written, they are just for me and it doesn't matter. But when I write you notes, or when I write on the chalkboard for you, I shall write the very best I can. That is only proper and courteous. And when you write for yourself, you may scribble too, but when you write for me or for the rest of the boys and girls, we expect you, too, to write your very best.

So after a child had written his material on scrap paper well enough for an "editor" to read it, he would put it in his folder and put up the flag. Helen, Mary, Charles, or Alice, at any time of the day when they were not busy, would see the flag up, go to the folder, note the name of the child, and look to see if that child was occupied. If not, the "editor" took the folder to the child's desk. Together they went over the writing, making corrections and preparing it for the final draft. Then the author copied the creation in his best handwriting and as neatly as possible on a clean sheet of paper, and it was placed in Mr. Smith's folder. Both the author and the editor signed the copy given to the teacher. In this way, Mr. Smith had to read only the best work of the children all the time. Also, if mistakes in punctuation, capitalization, grammar usage, or spelling were made, Mr. Smith put a check after both the editor's and the author's name on his diagnostic sheet to indicate that there was one area in which they both needed help.

Summary

When proper conditions are set, children will express themselves in writing as soon as they have mastered sufficient writing skills to do so. The language of the child is beautiful, expressive, and, generally, very effective. It is unfortunate that our schools have emphasized the "proper" skills of writing over the *effective* skills of written expression, thus reversing the technique by which creative adult writers are made. It is equally unfortunate that the schools have substituted textbooks and workbooks for the child's own writing as a basis of a language skills program.

If individuals are ever to be the core of a democratic society, their effectiveness in written communication will depend on the individuality of their writing. Our schools have matured to the point where the writing of the children must become the basis of the language program rather than a garnish to it as it now is in so many educational systems.

To the Reader

1. Make a diagnostic chart such as Mr. Smith made on page 379, and follow his plan of teaching for one week by diagnosing the chil-

dren's language problems from their creative writing and teaching individually or by small groups. If you are a student teacher, you may be able to do it with part of a class. Examine what you accomplish with the children at the end of the week. How do you feel about it?

2. Some questions for discussion.
   a. The examples of children's writing presented in this chapter lack quality.
   b. Knowledge of parts of speech and word forms will make better writers of the children whose works appear in this chapter.
   c. Imagination and creativity are one and the same.
3. Instead of launching into a story the next time you plan to read to children, take out a "PLAY BOX." A play box is any box brightly covered and filled with objects from a well-known story such as *The Little Rabbit Who Wanted Red Wings* or *Tom Sawyer's* whitewashing scene. For the latter, this would include a paint pail, a paintbrush, a bandage for Huck's toe, a fishpole, an apple, a marble, a dead frog (preferably paper), and a bonnet (for Aunt Polly). Ask the children to play out a scene using all the items, *or*, if they are old enough, to write a play or scene using all the items. After you have enjoyed the children's creations, share with them how Mark Twain put these objects together in a story.
4. Several books and materials have been produced to stimulate divergent thinking in children and to encourage creative writing. Some of these appear in the bibliography at the end of this chapter and have an asterisk before them. Study them, but better yet, use them.
5. Send to Ginn and Company for E. P. Torrance's records, *Sounds and Images* and *Messages for the Millions—Alexander Graham Bell: Commander of Communication.* These provide excellent materials to stimulate divergent thinking and creative writing.
6. Try out an idea from this chapter yourself—one you have never done before. As well as you can, analyze the process you go through. Do you better appreciate the efforts of the children who wrote materials for this chapter once you have tried to create something yourself?
7. By using the writings of the children in this chapter, find instances that prove the following statements:
   a. Children are capable of a high degree of symbolism.
   b. Even primary children can conceptualize.
   c. The ability to use metaphor may well be a sign of high creative potential.
   d. Cuteness is a form of creativity.
   e. Children are capable of building suspense.

f. With little or no instruction, children seem to understand the concept of "plot."
g. Children seem to be born with a sense of rhythm and rhyme.
h. Young children write as they talk.
i. In order for children to write creatively, they must have a rich program in oral expression.

8. What sort of experiences do you feel the girl who wrote the suicide note on page 327 had in her own life? Was she projecting or unhappy? You have perhaps wondered. She was a well-adjusted girl who wrote poetry to express her feelings about all aspects of life. The writing indicates her interest in some suicide cases she had read about in the papers. She was projecting. Can you see dangers in trying to interpret children's writings on any basis other than creativity? On the other hand, do you see how they might be helpful to a psychologist?
9. From the children's writings in this chapter, which of the following emotions would you feel these children have experienced—and deeply? Find poems and stories that support your choice.

anger	hate
fear	love
frustration	remorse
happiness	disgust
goodwill	harassment
joy	loyalty
suspense	pride

10. Make a collection of the beautiful or unique things children say—just listen to them and encourage them; do not try to lead the conversation. Write down some of their sayings. How could you use them to persuade other children to try some creative writing? Today, for instance, I heard the children outside my window say in their play:

    "My Daddy's tire died."
    "We couldn't write because we lost his zippie."
    (I figured he meant zip code.)

11. Try some haiku or cinquain poetry. It is easy and fun. After you have a few, read them to children; notice how they react. Did you ever notice that sometimes certain children will not sit still or pay attention to some stories—even the classics, and yet they always seem to sit spellbound when the teacher or other children read stories that they create?
12. Creative writing does not have to be grandiose and flowery, but can

be quite brutal or grim—and about very common things. Try writing about some common topics such as those listed below:

A Spatula	The Back Fence
An Old Pair of Jeans	A Gallon of Gas
Water	Two Million Straight Pins
A Toothbrush	

Selected Bibliography

ANDERSON, PAUL S. *Language Skills in Elementary Education.* New York: Macmillan Company, 1964.

*APPLEGATE, MAUREE. *Helping Children Write.* Evanston, Illinois: Row, Peterson, 1954.

ARBUTHNOT, MAY HILL (compiler). *The Arbuthnot Anthology of Children's Literature.* Chicago: Scott, Foresman and Company, 1953.

*ARNSTEIN, FLORA J. *Children Write Poetry: A Creative Approach.* New York: Dover Publications, Inc., 1967.

———. *Poetry in the Elementary Classroom.* New York: Appleton-Century-Crofts, 1962.

BREWTON, JOHN E. AND SARA W. BREWTON. *Index to Children's Poetry.* New York: H. W. Wilson Company, 1942. First Supplement, 1954, Second Supplement, 1969.

BURROWS, ALVINA T., JUNE D. FEREBEE, DORIS C. JACKSON, AND DOROTHY O. SAUNDERS. *They All Want to Write.* New York: Prentice-Hall, 1952.

CARLSON, RUTH KEARNEY. *Literature for Children: Enrichment Ideas.* Dubuque, Iowa: William C. Brown Company Publishers, 1970.

CHAMBERS, DEWEY W. *Children's Literature in the Curriculum.* Chicago: Rand McNally and Company, 1971.

———. *Literature for Children: Storytelling and Creative Drama.* Dubuque, Iowa: William C. Brown Company Publishers, 1970.

COLWELL, EILSEN. *A Storyteller's Choice.* New York: Walck Publishing Company, 1964.

FARRIS, HERBERT J. "Creative Writing Must Be Motivated," in James C. MacCampbell (ed.), *Readings in the Language Arts in the Elementary School.* Boston: D. C. Heath and Company, 1964, 261–262.

GREEN, HARRY, AND WALTER T. PETTY. *Developing Language Skills in the Elementary Schools* 4th ed., Chapter 8. Boston: Allyn and Bacon, 1971.

*LEWIS, RICHARD. *Journeys: Prose by Children of the English-Speaking World*. New York: Simon and Schuster, 1969.

*______. *Miracles*. New York: Simon and Schuster, 1966. (Poems by Children of the English-Speaking World.)

McCASLIN, NELLIE. *Creative Dramatics in the Classroom*. New York: David McKay Company Inc., 1968.

MEARNS, HUGHES. *Creative Power: The Education of Youth in the Creative Arts*, rev. ed. New York: Dover Publications, 1954.

MURRAY, RUTH LOVELL. *Dance in Elementary Education*. New York: Harper and Row, 1963.

*MYERS, R. E., AND E. PAUL TORRANCE. *Can You Imagine?* Boston: Ginn and Company, 1965.

*______. *Plots, Puzzles and Ploys: Adventures in Self Expression*. Boston: Ginn and Company, 1966.

PEASE, DON. *Creative Writing in the Elementary School*. New York: Exposition Press, 1964.

*PETTY, WALTER T., AND MARY BOWEN. *Slithery Snakes and Other Aids to Children's Writing*. New York: Appleton-Century-Crofts, 1967.

REASONER, CHARLES F. *Releasing Children to Literature*. New York: Dell Publishing Company, 1968.

*Smith, Allen H. *Don't Get Personal With a Chicken*. New York: Perma-book, 1959.

*______. *Write Me a Poem Baby*. Boston: Little, Brown and Company, 1956.

SMITH, JAMES A. *Creative Teaching of the Language Arts in the Elementary School*. Boston: Allyn and Bacon, 1969, 97–156.

*SMITH, ROBERT P. *"Where Did You Go?" "Out." "What Did You Do?" "Nothing."* New York: Norton, 1957.

*TANNEN, ROBERT. *I Know A Place*, Books 1–2–3. Boston: City Schools Curriculum, 1969.

WALTER, NINA WILLIS. *Let Them Write Poetry*. New York: Holt, Rinehart and Winston, 1966.

WHITEHEAD, ROBERT. *Children's Literature: Strategies of Teaching*. Englewood Cliffs, New Jersey: Prentice-Hall, Inc. 1968.

10

Adventures in Handwriting

"Over, Over, Over, I, Over, Over, E, Dot!"

That's what Miss McCarthy used to chant while my class practiced writing the word "mine." Previous to this, we had practiced push-pulls and contact ovals. Those long, tedious, dull days of irrelevant drill seem humorous today, but I often wish I had the time that was spent then to use in more exciting ways now.

Miss Perkins, a first grade teacher teaching the alphabet, focused attention on the formation of the letters by having the children study the basic shape and then make an *Alphabet Funny*. An *Alphabet Funny* is a picture made with a letter serving as the basic structure to the picture. After each picture was completed, the children were encouraged to write a story, poem, or limerick about their Alphabet Funny. These were put on ditto masters, and everyone in the class eventually received an Alphabet Funny book to take home. Here are a few examples. (Figure 88.)

Figure 88 *Emerson.*

E is for Emerson.
Emerson lived in a crooked house.
His chair was full of hair.
His rug was full of bugs.
And Emerson didn't like his house.

Then a man came. He said,
"The trouble with your house is
You have hair in your chair,
You have bugs in your rug."
Emerson didn't like what the man said
And he never hated his house again.

—John Turner

Mrs. Paps used similar techniques in teaching cursive writing in the third grade. To draw attention to the shape and structure of the letters, Mrs. Paps had the children make the letters on cards as she taught them. The letters were made with a thick, black flo-pen. Then the children were encouraged to make something out of the letters. Some weird and fantastic creatures resulted. The shape of the letter was not destroyed in the process, nor was the visual image distorted, because the black of the flo-pen was so much darker than the crayons that the children used in the drawings. This helped the children to visualize the good sample of each letter and made the process of reproducing the letters on paper an easy one.

Mr. Armour tried to help his handicapped children in the primary grades to write their names. These children had cerebral palsy. Mr. Armour spread plasticine in a cookie sheet and lightly scratched the first letter of the child's name in the soft clay with a popsicle stick. Then he handed the stick to the child and let the child dig the letter into the clay.

Mrs. Markson was having trouble getting some of her slower children to see the formation of the letters in manuscript writing. She had the children make the letters in gooey, brightly colored finger paint. The transfer to smaller paper was then a simple matter.

These techniques for teaching handwriting are much more dramatic and more individual than those I experienced with Miss McCarthy. They have come about through a greater understanding of handwriting over the past years through research, and because of a renewed interest in handwriting in the past decade.

Handwriting Is Developmental

Handwriting is a developmental process. It develops in children as an art form. In the beginning, the child first shows his creative tendencies on paper through the scribble stage. While he experiments with scribbling, the child naturally learns the basic strokes required to make manuscript letters. Figure 89 is a composite of forms taken from children's paintings. It shows how a child's inherent abilities enable him to make, with no instruction, the seven strokes required in manuscript writing.

We can find the seven strokes in the picture we if we examine it carefully. (Figure 90.)

Figure 89 *A composite of strokes children make in their paintings.*

Figure 90 *The seven basic strokes of manuscript writing.*

When the teacher or the parent sees a child making these basic strokes in his paintings, she knows that the child is ready to write. The first word that most children write is their name, and this name usually appears as part of a painting. This is probably because the child sees his teacher writing his name in manuscript on each of his paintings in the nursery school and kindergarten, and eventually he begins to copy what he sees, using a very clumsy tool, the paintbrush. At this point in his development, he is not necessarily recognizing his name or the individual letters in his name; he is only reproducing a shape. His visual acuity is not too refined, and very often the *n*'s have the bar going backwards, *e*'s and *s*'s are painted backwards, and many other letters are not true to the real form. Nonetheless, this is an indication to the teacher that the child is interested and ready to print or write. In his development in art, the child goes through the manipulative and exploratory stage to the communicative stage. The communicative stage occurs when adults can begin to recognize objects and forms in the child's art work. It is at this time that the name begins to appear in the painting—or at least parts of it. A careful study of a sequence of any one child's paintings will show a gradual evolution from simple daubings as straight bold strokes into circular strokes and strokes that cross to form crude letters. From this scribbling and daubing, handwriting is born into the child's life experience as an art form.

From the very beginning, handwriting is a visual skill. A good readiness program provides time for a child to paint letters and to experiment and manipulate letters and letter forms. As with the teachers above, the child may get the feel of a letter by pulling its shape in clay or through finger painting. Often it is wise to start with large movements with a brush over large sheets of paper or with finger paint to enable the child to experiment and reproduce letters and words without the muscular strain imposed on him when he finally begins to use a primary pencil on lined primary paper. Some teachers even cut the letters out of sandpaper or foam rubber so that the child may have a sensory experience in feeling the letters before he is called upon to draw them. When the young child writes, he is really reproducing forms that he sees; a sharp sense of visual perception must be developed. In the sequence of language development, handwriting comes after reading, for a child must have many experiences *seeing* a word before he can reproduce it. Soon after children are able to recognize words on their experience charts or in their reading primers, they will want to draw them. A first grader gave a story to her teacher one day not long after she had been introduced to the reading primer. Linda had selected a picture from the box of pictures that her teacher kept handy for the development of oral expression and visual acuity. Linda announced, "I guess I'll write my story today instead of telling it." She then went to her seat, took out her primer, and laboriously selected the words she needed from the page. These she used, with the words she had already visualized, to write her first story. In terms of our definition of creativity, it was a piece of creative writing, for

Linda took parts of her past experiences and assembled them into a new one.

Highly motivating experiences in handwriting are essential if children are to use it fluently as a tool of communication. Each exciting and new experience in handwriting provided by the teacher at the beginning stages of instruction should be rewarding and satisfying to the child. His attitude toward handwriting will determine the extent to which he will write effectively during his total school experience.

Classroom Conditions for Teaching Handwriting

Smith[1] lists certain conditions that should be set for the teaching of handwriting from both the practical and the creative viewpoints. They are as follows:

1. Handwriting materials (paints, art paper, large pencils, regular pencils, ball-point pens, writing paper, fingerpaint, fingerpaint paper, scissors, paste, sandpaper) should be kept in a place where they are easily accessible to the child so that he may write in any form and at any time he likes.

2. The atmosphere of the room must be relaxed, congenial, and pleasant. Recent research shows that children do their best handwriting in a comfortable, encouraging atmosphere where some tension is present. Lack of tension tends to create a lackadaisical sort of writing, whereas too much tension creates a tense type of handwriting.

3. An air of expectancy and certain positive tensions stated above tend to produce better handwriting in children than no tensions at all.

4. The visual image of the letter or the word to be written must be present somewhere. In the beginning stages of the child's handwriting experience, these images should be handy in physical form for ready reference in the classroom: on the chalkboard, on charts, on cards above the blackboard, or in some simple handwriting book placed before the child. With the older children, the image of the shape of the word will be present in his mind and no actual image is necessary.

5. The visual form of the word or letter placed before a child should not be considered as a pattern that he will be expected to reproduce exactly. There are basically two objectives in the teaching of handwriting —legibility and fluency. Because handwriting is personal and maturational, no two children can possibly write alike. In the first place, each

1. James A. Smith, "Handwriting" in *Creative Teaching of the Language Arts in the Elementary School* (Boston: Allyn and Bacon, 1968), pp. 201–220.

starts with different equipment. Children differ in their physical growth. We cannot expect a short fourth grade boy to reach as high as a tall fourth grade boy, nor can we expect children to turn out precise, similar written work. Some children have long fingers; some have short fingers. Thickness of fingers, wrist development, and bone structure vary in the child's hand. With these differing characteristics to begin with, teachers cannot expect children to produce similar products.

6. To a great degree, the teaching of handwriting must remain personal with individualized instruction. Unpleasant writing experiences result for most children when they are forced into reproducing patterns which are too difficult for them. The frustrations that children undergo in an attempt to write in an unnatural and awkward way advocated by certain writing systems cause children to shy away from the handwriting experience. The use of writing scales is also a frustrating experience for many children who simply cannot reproduce the type of writing represented on the scale. On page 399 there are suggestions for a realistic use of handwriting scales.

7. Handwriting instruction must correspond to the child's individual growth. Manuscript writing is used at the beginning of instruction, because the child's fingers contain muscles that develop later than any others in his body. At the stage when the child first wants to write, he is capable of making large, definite strokes. Manuscript writing, based on these strokes as shown above, provides the quickest way for the child to get into the writing act. As the muscles in his fingers develop and his finger usage is refined, he can easily make other strokes of greater complexity and variety. Little by little he prepares for cursive writing.

Excessive attention has been given in the lower grades to the grade level at which cursive writing should be taught, rather than to the time the child is ready to write cursively. Cursive writing should be taught when the child is ready. Some educators feel the teaching of cursive writing is no longer necessary, that our culture demands so much manuscript writing that it would be well to devote our time to perfecting this technique. Manuscript writing can be done as quickly as cursive. However, as long as both types are used in modern living, it is only fair that children should know how to read and write both ways.

When a teacher detects a group of students who are copying the cursive writing patterns from the chalkboard or from a chart which she has prepared, she may feel sure that they are ready to put their scribblings into patterns. She can begin to give instructions to this group by permitting them to imitate large samples of cursive writing from the board, or from individual sheets she has prepared. The grade level at which this takes place is unimportant so long as the children are ready and are not forced into these complex acts before they are *comfortably* able to perform them.

8. Many *purposes* for writing must be apparent at all times. Hours of endless, meaningless drill can quickly dull the child's desire to write. At first he enjoys and welcomes the opportunity to reproduce the sample the teacher sets before him, but he soon tires of attempting to refine his work so that it looks exactly like the teacher's. This tiresome and wasteful drill can be avoided. More meaningful writing practices develop when children write letters, invitations, or announcements that are actually sent. At first these may be no more than a copy from the board of a master made by the teacher, which the teacher and pupils have composed together. Later, as the child gains spelling and writing skills, he may create his own letters and invitations. He may compose stories and poems to be read by others from a bulletin board. When the handwriting program is built from a program in creative writing such as that described in Chapter 9, children write perpetually to communicate ideas which cannot be expressed orally because the time or place is inappropriate. In an effective handwriting program, the teacher creates many *purposes* for which the children need to write. The teaching of writing is not necessarily a period set aside to practice meaningless scribblings, but a time in which children enjoy learning another technique which will pave the way to greater fluency in recording their thoughts and ideas.

9. Good attitudes should be developed about handwriting practice. Few adults are able to compose and write correctly and beautifully with the original draft of their writing. In like manner, when children are writing for aesthetic values, or for reports to the class, it is unrealistic to expect the original draft or even the first few writings to be in perfect style. All of us have several kinds of handwriting. We write notes differently from the way we write a business letter; we write a note to a friend more hastily than we write a letter to someone who is not well known to us. The purpose of writing determines its stage of refinement. When all the writings children do are judged by high adult standards, children become discouraged. We should recognize and accept that they write differently for different occasions. Some suggestions for handling the situation are given in Chapter 9 on creative writing.

10. The handwriting program must be adjusted to meet the changing times and the needs of children in everyday living. Children should write in school with the same tools they will use outside of school. From the beginning, children should have practice with the felt pen and the ball-point pen rather than with the obsolete steel-point pen. Common sense tells us that no child is ever going to use the steel point pen after

he leaves school, and this primitive tool should be eliminated for the use of the more modern one. Felt pens are easier to use, less messy, and more easily taken care of, and should facilitate the teaching of writing. Much of the change in style of accepted handwriting through the ages has been brought about by the invention of more efficient and more practical handwriting tools.

11. The teacher should continue to recognize and teach handwriting as an art form. Today's children are exposed to all kinds of writing. They see billboards, posters, television commercials, newspapers, magazines, books, advertising, road signs, and neon lights, and are exposed to mass exploitation of various writing forms at every turn. Because children see so many kinds of handwriting in these forms of communication, they must learn to read many kinds of handwriting and printed script. Some handwriting is obviously used as an art form, such as that which appears in an ad on the subway or in an advertisement in *Vogue* magazine. Children will recognize that certain kinds of handwriting are prettier than other kinds. This is the recognition of the art value of the writing. Exposure to many patterns of handwriting makes the job of the teacher less difficult on the one hand and more difficult on the other. Because handwriting is a visual skill, children *see* many forms of handwriting both in and out of school, and the image is impressed more readily on their minds. This should make the teaching of handwriting easier and quicker. But because these impressions are not standard, and because the children often see words and letters represented in *many* forms, the teacher's job is also difficult. She must help children see the purpose behind different forms of handwriting, and she must also help them select the forms that are most legible and easy for them to use in performing the handwriting act for themselves. The skills of (a) selecting a form to fit a purpose and (b) selecting efficient and legible handwriting for common usage were not a part of the instructional job of the teacher in the past when her own pattern of handwriting was the most constant (and sometimes the only) pattern to which children were exposed. A creative teacher will have children collect many patterns of handwriting in various art forms. These can well be used to build standards in legibility, efficiency of use, and beauty as related to purpose.

12. Much nonsense has been published about posture in handwriting. While it is necessary to check to see that children assume the most effective posture while writing, it is ridiculous to assume that all children write their best sitting the same way. The best handwriting is produced when the writer is most comfortable. Handwriting position is correct only when it produces good handwriting, and that will be when

the child is released from uncomfortable, unrealistic strain during the act of writing.

13. Finger movement is necessary in developing effective handwriting. The fetish for wrist movement so popular several years ago has subsided to a more realistic understanding that legible, fluent handwriting results when a combination of wrist and finger writing is used. An excessive use of either impedes the communication process; thus, guidance should be given at the beginning stages. Moving pictures of excellent writers show that they employ both the wrist and the fingers. The child's fingers are the most useful tools he has in developing written expression. To interfere with the use of these tools is to impede his writing development. Any method used to help a child write is justifiable if it makes handwriting easier, quicker, and more legible.

14. In the space age, children use the typewriter at a younger age than ever before. However, the typewriter will replace handwriting only to a certain degree. Note taking, personal writing, editing, and other forms of handwriting cannot be replaced by the typewriter. The typewriter has been a help in improving formal communication skills and makes its major contribution in that area. Children will benefit from instruction in typing, but the typewriter will not replace the need for legible handwriting.

The Creative Teaching of Handwriting

"I have something interesting to show you," said Miss Ames. "Look at these samples which I have in my hand."

Miss Ames held up a copy of the Constitution of the United States. "This is a very important document," she said, "I'm sure that some of you will recognize it." Many of the children did. "Why do you suppose that it is written as it is and not printed?" asked Miss Ames. It was not long before the children concluded that the Constitution was written before the printing press was available.

"I would like to show you a copy of a letter which I received from my grandmother when I was just a little girl," said Miss Ames. "Let's compare the writing on the Constitution with the writing in this letter." The children held a very interesting discussion about the differences in the writing in the Constitution and the letter from Grandmother. The main difference was the thickness of the letters.

"The letters are thicker in the writing of the Constitution because the men who wrote it used a quill pen and my grandmother wrote with a steel pen," said Miss Ames. "This is a letter I wrote when I was a little girl. My mother has saved it in a scrapbook." Again the children looked at the sample that Miss Ames had mounted on a piece of cardboard. The fourth sample which Miss Ames held up was a letter that she had written the previous week. It was written with a thick, black, highly legible ink. Miss Ames then encouraged the children to discuss why they felt the handwriting in each of these four letters, written over a period of more than one hundred years, had changed so much. Eventually she held up a picture of a quill pen, a steel-point pen, a ball-point pen, and a felt pen. Some of these were cut from pictures in magazines and others were from advertisements. In the ensuing discussion, the children concluded that the instrument employed determined to a great extent the image that resulted from its use.

This is one creative approach to handwriting. Miss Ames was attempting to show the children that our handwriting does not remain constant, and that everyone's handwriting is not the same as everyone else's. There is a tendency to feel that, because the act of handwriting means that we try to help children reproduce letter forms that are as close to the perfected letter form as possible, handwriting cannot be taught creatively nor can it develop creativity in children. This is, of course, conformity and imitation in their purest sense. Many people feel that we work in such a situation to eliminate the differences in children and work for a common product rather than a different one. In this sense, handwriting must then not be creative.

Handwriting is non-creative to the degree that conformity to several basic regulations is necessary. In imitating the letter forms supplied by the teacher, the child is indeed non-creative. Handwriting is imitating; it is copying; it is conforming. It is one of the skills used in daily living in which conformity and imitation are necessary. In any culture there are many times when conformity is necessary, and part of the job of the teacher is to help children determine those times when they must abandon individual drives and needs because it is best for the good of everyone concerned. However, though conformity is necessary, there is still room for individuality. Because people are all different, the *way* they conform is different. In the history of the development of handwriting in this country, there is ample evidence to support the fact that the practice of teaching any specific method of handwriting has been successful only to a limited degree. Few adults write according to the method by which they were taught. Though they spend endless hours in school practicing specific forms of letters, they abandon these letters as soon as they are outside the range of vision of their teacher. If the form being practiced does not come easily for the writer, he adopts a more efficient, but still legible, style of handwriting. His personality affects his handwriting and it becomes different from that of anyone else. Handwriting analysts can often do a skillful job in telling about a person's personality through his handwriting. In this sense, handwriting remains creative in spite of all our efforts to stereotype it.

In his book, *Creative Teaching of the Language Arts*, Smith tells how the teaching of handwriting can be creative:

1. Handwriting is a personal thing and no one pattern can be successfully reproduced by all children. Therefore, the goals of legibility and efficiency should be stressed above other goals.

2. Different kinds of handwriting are used for different purposes and in different situations. The child's *best* handwriting should be expected for those papers which are to be shared with others. Other kinds of handwriting are acceptable when he is writing for himself, or when he is composing first drafts of material to get his ideas on paper quickly.

3. Handwriting is a tool by which a child communicates. It is *what* he writes that is important and should be given priority over all other considerations. *How* to write correctly and acceptably comes after ideas are put down in their desired form. Final drafts of material should be used to develop the best handwriting.

4. There are certain basic principles for all good handwriting. Instruction in handwriting should stress these basic principles as much as it stresses the finished product.

5. Handwriting scales and patterns of adult handwriting can be very frustrating and discouraging to the child, because he is not physically equipped to match them. A realistic handwriting program is based on the improvement of handwriting rather than on the attainment of some unobtainable goal. If handwriting scales are to be used to evaluate children's handwriting, they must contain many acceptable forms of handwriting so that each child may find one enough like his to identify with and work toward. He should first have help in analyzing the differences between his own handwriting and the sample on the scale.

A more realistic approach to evaluation of handwriting is to help each child analyze his own specimens according to the basic set of principles mentioned on page 406, and then to use them to improve his own writing. Here the emphasis is creative; it is on improvement and change (a creative concept) rather than on imitation (a non-creative one).

6. Left-handed children need not be handicapped in handwriting performance. If the paper is slanted to the left instead of to the right, the left-handed child can form letters and write in exactly the same way as his right-handed classmates. However, overhand writing must be discouraged.

Attitude is important here. No ridicule or pressure should be placed on the "southpaw" because of the difference in his method of writing. It will help him to realize that many great men, such as Harry S. Truman, Leonardo da Vinci, King George VI, Babe Ruth, and Cary Grant were all left-handed. With a minor adjustment of paper and seating position, handwriting instruction need not be special for the left-handed child.

The teaching of handwriting can be creative when the teacher emphasizes *change, individuality*, and *improvement*, rather than imitation and conformity. It can be creative in the ways she sets up a variety of *purposes* which place children in conditions where continual handwriting skills are practiced. It can be creative when it is used as a *tool of communication* for the entire day and not as an isolated, meaningless drill period.

Opportunities for Adventures with Handwriting

Primary Grades

The following experiences provide meaningful opportunities for children to write their names:

1. Label their lockers.
2. Make nameplates for their books.
3. Label their own chairs and tables.
4. Label napkins for mid-morning lunch.
5. Label their paintings.
6. Make tags to identify their art objects.
7. Sign the dittoed letters sent home to parents.
8. Write their names on cards to be used in the primary grades.
9. Write their names on apples cut from construction paper (used each day to check attendance when each child sets his apple in a slit in the construction paper apple tree). This technique can be varied by using other objects when the group interest is high.
10. Sign their own milk money receipts and bills.

Other opportunities for handwriting in the primary grades are provided through encouraging the children to:

1. Write labels (see above).
2. Write stories.
3. Write poems.
4. Write simple plays.

5. Write letters—gradually filling in words to the completion of the entire letter (see page 475).
6. Write simple invitations.
7. Write letters of thanks.
8. Copy and write announcements.
9. Copy and write letters to parents about school events.
10. Print daily school cafeteria menus for the bulletin board.
11. Label exhibits and displays in the classroom.
12. Write simple stories about paintings.
13. Write self-portraits.
14. Write store signs and label prices of objects.
15. Keep weather reports.
16. Write the daily news on the chalkboard.
17. Make booklets.
18. Write autobiographies.
19. Plan the daily program for the class and write it on the chalkboard.
20. Write captions under pictures.
21. Write greeting cards.

Intermediate Grades

Every day experiences in the intermediate grades that provide purposes for handwriting are:

1. Writing labels.
2. Creative writing experiences.
3. Writing stories.
4. Writing poems.
5. Writing letters.
6. Writing plays.
7. Writing reports for social studies.
8. Writing book reports.
9. Writing invitations.
10. Writing letters of thanks.
11. Writing announcements.
12. Writing for the school newspaper.
13. Writing letters to classmates.
14. Keeping lists or records.
15. Keeping accounts of science experiments, etc.
16. Keeping bills, writing checks, etc.
17. Writing letters to government and other public institutions, to firms, etc., for information on making arrangements for trips and for materials.

18. Ordering supplies and booklets.
19. Taking minutes of club meetings or school meetings.
20. Keeping reports on the weather.
21. Keeping attendance reports.
22. Keeping reports on book sales, attendance, etc.
23. Writing autobiographies.
24. Making a class directory.
25. Making a book of stories, poems, important social science information, etc.
26. Planning the daily program in the classroom.
27. Making long-term plans.
28. Making book lists.
29. Keeping a vocabulary list of new words.
30. Writing up interviews held with people for information in social studies, science, etc.
31. Taking notes.
32. Making outlines.
33. Organizing materials.
34. Writing plans for assembly programs.
35. Writing captions for pictures and movies.
36. Writing for a school newspaper.
37. Writing stories or sentences dictated by the teacher.

Creative Adventures in Handwriting

Primary Grades

1. Use large sheets of paper and paintbrushes to introduce children to experimentation with word and letter forms. Children can develop basic movements for letter formation by painting them first.
2. Because handwriting can be pretty and some papers can look nicer than others, it is interesting to have the children, in the initial stages of learning to write their names, paint their names with a wet paintbrush on a folded paper. As soon as the child has finished painting his name, fold the paper and make a blotto. When these are opened, children can mount the resulting blottos on pieces of heavier paper and hang them around the room to show the pretty designs made by their names.
3. Allow children to begin handwriting practice on the chalkboard with fat chalk and plenty of space so that the child's attempt to reproduce letters is not inhibited.

4. The dotted-line technique can be used to guide children in the formation of more difficult letters and numbers. Many writing manuals and workbooks contain such exercises.
5. Spread plasticine in a shallow cookie sheet and scratch a letter on the surface of the plasticine with a sucker stick as mentioned above. The child who is having difficulty with any specific letter may get the feel of making it by pushing the sucker stick into the plasticine and digging the letter into the soft clay.
6. Sometimes children can get the feel of letters if they have a chance to manipulate them. Many toy blocks are cut out in the shapes of letters. Some teachers have cut the letters out of flat sheets of styrofoam so that the child could trace the letters with his fingers.
7. Sometimes letters can be cut out of felt and used on a flannel board to form children's names and words that they know. Again, in feeling the felt, the child gets a better sense of the formation of the letter.
8. Some teachers have played a game at lunch time or at recess time by having the children go into the new-fallen snow and make the shapes of letters in the snow.
9. Allow beginning writers to work with letters and words on large sheets of paper with colored felt pens to get the feel of the letters. Also, finger paint is a good medium to use in the beginning stages of writing.
10. Working with a wet paintbrush on a dusty chalkboard allows freedom in using large muscles when the child is making the transition from painting to manuscript writing.
11. There are many recipes available for plaster or play dough. The children can form this dough into the shape of a heart. Words like "love" can be made out of play dough and stuck onto the heart. When allowed to dry, these objects become extremely hard and can be painted. If a paperclip is stuck into the top of the heart before it dries, it forms a loop onto which the heart may be hung with a piece of bright-colored yarn, thus making a necklace. Peace symbols may also be made this way, and the children thus learn to make a variety of letters.
12. Often a child may cut his initials into a potato that has been sliced in half with a dull, saw-toothed, plastic knife. This may then be used as a block print by spreading paint over the potato and pressing it onto small sheets of paper. Thus, the child makes himself some personalized writing paper which he will enjoy later when he desires to write notes home or to his teacher.
13. The formal writing period may begin in this manner:
    (a) Transfer the writing readiness practice from the chalkboard to large, unlined paper, then to lined paper; (b) change writing tools from brush, crayon, or chalk to large pencils and then to smaller

ones; (c) write all letter forms in manuscript, both capital and small (upper and lower case); (d) write first and last names; (e) write the figures from one to ten; (f) write sentences, poems, stories, and letters on the chalkboard from messages dictated by the group.

14. Cover a wall or a portion of a wall with plain white paper to make a graffito wall. On this wall children are encouraged to paint or write their names or messages as soon as they are able to write. This will greatly encourage children who are practicing letters to apply them in a new situation.
15. Instead of having children write meaningless words out of context, correlate handwriting drill with Social Studies, Science, and other subject areas. This may first be done simply by labeling centers and later by making lists of pets or farm animals, etc.
16. Have each child make his own picture dictionary with illustrations.
17. Encourage children to label objects in the room.
18. Encourage children to label bulletin boards and exhibits.
19. Make records of group experiences to be bound into individual reading books, such as, "We Make Applesauce," "Our Trip to the Pet Store," etc.
20. Make titles for books and posters.
21. Use jingles to create interest in letter or figure formation, such as

   Big and round and tipped this way
   Is the very best way to make an a.

   Round the tree and round the tree
   This is how we make a 3.

   Tall and straight as it can be
   With a cross on top, that's T.

   Across the sky and down from heaven
   That is how we make a 7.

22. Write number rhymes to practice numbers, such as

   1, 2, buckle my shoe.
   3, 4, shut the door.

   or

   1, 2, 3 little Indians,
   4, 5, 6 little Indians,
   7, 8, 9 little Indians,
   10 little Indian boys.

23. Write the number of children in the room, in a row, at a table, etc.

24. Make up a dittoed address book for each child. Leave room for each child to write his name, address, and telephone number. Pass the books around and have each child write in all the other books until they are complete.
25. Make calendars on dittoed sheets for practice in number writing. Children can draw pictures to illustrate the calendar. (See page 331 for development of the calendar concept.)
26. Make number booklets. Have the children write a number at the top of the page and then draw pictures to illustrate each number.
27. When practicing letters, help the children to know where to begin the stroke by marking this place with an arrow or a colored dot.
28. In transferring from manuscript to cursive writing, use cards which point out the difference in the formation of the letters.
29. In transferring from manuscript to cursive, write sentences or stories on the chalkboard in manuscript and directly below each line write the same story in cursive, using a bright-colored chalk. Encourage the children to try cursive when they appear to be ready.
30. Study the early history of handwriting. Include in this the fact that Indians used drums and smoke signals to communicate, early cultures used picture signs and scrolls, the Monks of the Middle Ages made handmade books, and finally writing was greatly facilitated by the invention of the printing press.
31. Lines to help children write evenly on the chalkboard will last several hours and stand several erasings if they are drawn with chalk when the chalkboard is wet.

Intermediate Grades

Children in the intermediate grades will be eager and anxious to improve their handwriting if they are exposed to creative adventures in using it. Many of the suggestions given above for the primary grades may be adapted to the intermediate grade level, especially those that are concerned with the making of love and peace symbols, painting of words to make blotto designs, and the graffito wall which children at this age love to fill with all kinds of exciting slogans. This concept may even be developed to the point where a new graffito wall is established each week with a theme for the week, such as a Play on Words Week where the children might write "Eating is the weigh to go," Cartoon Week where they will draw funny cartoons with a saying, a Springtime Week where they may make wisecracks about each other's love affairs, etc. Other suggestions for developing some specific handwriting situations follow.

1. When a child is absent from school for a week or more, have the children make get-well cards with pictures and messages, as suggested on page 347.
2. Adopt a merchant marine ship for a year and correspond with the captain and crew. Let them help you plot their trading routes all over the world. You need to apply for the waiting list if you desire to do this. Write to: Merchant Marine, Battery Park, New York City.
3. Write to children in foreign lands as pen pals.
4. Collect various forms of "arty" writing from letters, magazines, and newspapers, and make a chart or bulletin board display from them.
5. Examine historical documents to see how styles of handwriting have changed.
6. Elaborating on the potato print idea given above, have children carve their names in block prints or do lettering in block prints to make designs for individualized correspondence paper.
7. Collect greeting card salutations from family scrapbooks and records, and note how writing forms and styles have changed.
8. Try writing with a quill pen. Notice the difference in the style of writing that results. Compare the styles of writing with a steel point, a fountain pen, and a ball-point pen.
9. Make up check lists such as in Figure 91 for the evaluation of handwriting.

Name: ____________	Very Good	Good	Fair	Poor
1. Do I keep my letters tall?				
2. Do I leave my oval letters open?				
3. Do I write all my letters with the same slant?				
4. Do I leave attractive margins on my paper?				
5. Do I end my words well?				
6. Do I space my letters well?				
7. Do I space my words well?				
etc.				

Figure 91 *A check list for self-evaluation—handwriting.*

Evaluation of Handwriting

The self-evaluation check list above is one way to help children continually check and evaluate their own handwriting.

The teacher evaluates continually in terms of legibility and fluency. When papers are not legible, something more than red check marks or a verbal reprimand is needed to help the student remedy his handwriting deficiencies.

Analysis of handwriting skills has shown certain basic principles to be consistent in all legible handwriting. Mr. Edwards used the following method to bring those basic principles into focus for his fifth grade group.

Early in the term, he asked each child to write this sentence in his best handwriting:

The boy and the man were excused from the class for the entire day.

He composed this sentence because it contained one type of each letter made by various stroke combinations. It also contained all letters except g, j, k, p, q, and v.

Each child wrote his sample on a piece of paper. No names were affixed to the papers. The papers were then collected, and Mr. Edwards explained to the children that he was going to use the papers to show each child how to improve his handwriting.

Mr. Edwards then selected one very legible sample and one which was not as legible and threw them on a screen before the class by using the opaque projector. The children were asked which of the two samples was easier to read. The more legible sample was identified. Then Mr. Edwards asked the children why.

As the children discovered various reasons, Mr. Edwards wrote them on the chalkboard. Then he used two other sets of the sample papers to further develop an analysis of basic handwriting principles.

From this class, these basic principles evolved.

Handwriting Is Easier to Read When:

1. All the letters slant the same way.
2. Tall letters are really tall, and even and low letters are really low and even.
3. The tops of rounded letters are round (as in m, n, and h) and not pointed.
4. Oval-shaped letters (such as e, a, and o) are left open, but closed at the top.
5. Words are spaced about two letter o's apart on a line.

6. Each letter has a space after it and does not run into another letter.
7. Looped letters are carefully closed (e, l, f).
8. "Trick" letters cause the most difficulty, for example, the letters t (improperly crossed), e (confused with i), a (left unclosed, could be o or u), and r (when not flattened on top, confused with i, u, e, etc.), and must be checked carefully.
9. Words rest on the line.
10. Arrangement on the page is carefully made. Margins help to make reading easier.
11. The papers are neat.

Once this set of basic principles was established, Mr. Edwards showed the class some of the other handwriting samples he had collected from the class. These samples were checked against the basic set of principles in terms of legibility. Many children freely identified the samples as their own and noted how they could improve their own handwriting. The rapport between teacher and pupil and between pupil and pupil in Mr. Edwards' classroom was such that children were not afraid to see their own handwriting used for analysis. In classrooms where such rapport does not exist, the teacher may collect handwriting samples from other classes to analyze, thereby removing the threat of criticism.

After the children had practice in analyzing handwriting together, they were asked to write another sentence at the top of a sheet of paper and did a self-analysis of their own handwriting. Using the set of principles on the chalkboard as a guide, each child copied under his own writing sample those principles on which he needed to concentrate. This became the basis of a series of individualized handwriting lessons during the following weeks.

In order to help each child evaluate his progress in handwriting, Mr. Edwards dictated or wrote on the chalkboard a short paragraph once a week. Each child wrote the paragraph in his best handwriting and gave it to Mr. Edwards. He examined each paper carefully and checked it by writing a series of numbers on the top of the paper. These numbers corresponded to the basic principles for legible handwriting that Mr. Edwards had printed on a chart which now hung before the room. Children checked the numbers with the principles.

Mr. Edwards discovered that some children continued to have difficulty with specific letters. In such cases he made out an individual worksheet or wrote the child a note referring him to a certain page in a workbook or handwriting manual. Children worked on these sheets during the day when other work was finished or whenever they had free time.

Mr. Edwards insured a carry-over from practice to use by utilizing the same code for basic principles when he read reports, stories, and other written materials submitted by the children. Each child kept a folder containing his weekly analysis sheet along with a sample of his best handwriting. These dated sheets helped to show his progress. Often Mr. Edwards used the folder of one child who showed excellent progress, and displayed his papers (written over a period of time) by placing them in the opaque projector. Thus, all the children were allowed to see how each other's handwriting had improved.

Occasionally Mr. Edwards used a handwriting scale with an individual child so he could compare his own handwriting to a form accepted by the experts. In such instances, however, Mr. Edwards pointed out the discreet use of basic principles which made the handwriting legible, rather than emphasizing the suggestion that the child should be writing exactly like the sample on the scale.

When creativity is seen as problem solving involving both critical and creative thinking, we can see how Mr. Edwards' approach to handwriting is much more creative than having children compare their writing to someone else's pattern.

Summary

The teaching of handwriting can be raised from the realm of boring, time-consuming drill if children discover the basic principles necessary to improve their handwriting skill, and if they see purposes for using this skill all through the day as a means of communication. Many of the myths associated with handwriting from the past, when the actual nature of handwriting was unknown, must be abolished and replaced by more meaningful practices in handwriting experiences. A legible, attractive hand is an essential social courtesy.

The teaching of handwriting calls for more conformity than do most of the language arts skills, but it can be creative in the following senses: (a) It develops judgment and evaluation; (b) new products result from this judgement; (c) it develops an understanding and application of basic principles; (d) it can serve as a tension-relieving agent; (e) the teaching can be open-ended to some degree; (f) it can be individual as well as efficient and legible; (g) certain conditions must be set for good handwriting to develop; (h) it can be success oriented; (i) knowledge and skills are learned and applied to new situations; (j) it *can* be developed as a problem-solving process; (k) self-learning can be encouraged; (l) ideas and materials can be manipulated and explored; (m) it may be used as a tool for written creative expression; and (n) the results, though somewhat conforming, will also be somewhat individual.

To the Reader

1. Problems for discussion:
   a. Because modern society often demands that people print for legibility, children in our schools should continue to develop skill in the use of manuscript writing throughout their formal schooling.
   b. Handwriting should be evaluated by letter grades on a report card.
   c. There is a high correlation between high intelligence and good handwriting.
   d. Fast readers are generally good penmen.
   e. Inability to write comfortably can greatly interfere with creative production.
2. How might you, as a teacher, teach handwriting on an individual basis in the intermediate grades?
3. Brainstorm ways you can teach handwriting with the help of an overhead projector.
4. Handwriting has become a neglected area of the school curriculum in the past five years. To what do you attribute this phenomenon?
5. Try out some Alphabet Funnies on your children or classmates and compare the results with those in this chapter.

Selected Bibliography

BURROWS, ALVINA I., JUNE D. FEREBEE, DORIS C. JACKSON, AND DOROTHY O. SAUNDERS. *They All Want To Write.* Englewood Cliffs, New Jersey: Prentice-Hall, 1952.

EDIGER, MARLOW. "Essentials in Teaching Handwriting," *Education*, 86 (1965), 37–65.

FELDT, LEONARD S. "The Reliability of Measuring Handwriting Ability," *Journal of Educational Psychology*, 53 (December 1962), 288–292.

GREEN, HARRY, AND WALTER T. PETTY. "Improving Children's Handwriting," in *Developing Language Skills in the Elementary Schools* 4th ed. Boston: Allyn and Bacon, 1971.

HANDWRITING FOUNDATION. *Handwriting and Related Factors, 1890–1960.* Washington, D.C.: Department of Education, 1961.

HANIGAN, LEVIN, AND GRACE HILDEBRAND. "Handwriting in the Primary Program" in James C. MacCampbell (ed.), *Readings in the Language Arts in the Elementary School.* Boston: D. C. Heath and Company, 1964, 170–178.

HERRICK, VIRGIL E. (ed.). *New Horizons for Research in Handwriting.* Madison: University of Wisconsin Press, 1960.

HORN, THOMAS D. (ed.). *Research on Handwriting and Spelling.* Champaign, Illinois: National Council of Teachers of English, 1966.

MYERS, EMMA. *The Whys and Hows of Handwriting.* Columbus, Ohio: The Zaner-Bloser Company, 1963.

OTTO, WAYNE, AND DAN W. ANDERSON. "Handwriting," in Robert L. Ebel (ed.), *Encyclopedia of Educational Research*, 4th ed. New York: The Macmillan Company, 1969.

ROBERTSON, WANDA. "Creating a Good Environment for Writing," in James C. MacCampbell (ed.), *Readings in the Language Arts in the Elementary School.* Boston: D. C. Heath and Company, 248–254.

SMITH, LAWRENCE. "Handwriting and Child Development," in James C. MacCampbell (ed.), *Readings in the Language Arts in the Elementary School.* Boston: D. C. Heath and Company, 1964, 167–169.

TEMPLIN, ELAINE. "Handwriting—the Neglected R" in James C. MacCampbell (ed.), *Readings in the Language Arts in the Elementary School.* Boston: D. C. Heath and Company, 1964, 179–182.

11

Adventures in Spelling

"Write It Ten Times, Hubert!"

I recently visited a classroom where the children were having their spelling papers returned from the previous week's test. Each incorrect word on each paper was marked with an angry red check, and a percentage grade was boldly emblazoned across the top of the paper.

I was sitting near Hubert, and the teacher slapped his paper on the top of his desk and said, "Someday, Hubert, maybe you'll study your words. Write each one that you missed ten times!"

Hubert looked sullen and hurt. I slid nearer to him. He looked at me with eyes reddened with unspilled tears.

I couldn't believe my ears. I thought that kind of teaching went out in the Middle Ages. I was in sympathy with Hubert—I remembered the teachers who had said those very words to me. They weren't teaching me—they were punishing me for their own poor teaching. The few times I ever had one hundred percent they beamed on me.

Hubert, it turned out, had studied quite hard for his test on Friday. It also turned out that, of the twelve words he had missed (from a total of twenty), he couldn't even read six. He showed me his spelling book when I asked where the words came from. It was ironic that the class was studying the northern states, and yet the spelling lesson contained words like *palm*, *coconut*, *cocoa*, *kimono*, *surf*, etc. I also observed that nothing was done about all the words those children missed except that the grades were entered into the teacher's class book and they were told, in a threatening voice, "You had better take them home and study them because someday I'll put them in with our test of regular words!" I had expected the teacher to announce that they would have one of those humiliating spelling bees to which I was subjected when I was a child!

A Spelling Lesson

Many of the problems in the teaching of spelling arise from an improper diagnosis of the child's deficiencies or from a misunderstanding of the way words are learned. Years ago the greatest emphasis in spelling was placed on the oral reproduction of words. The old spelling bee was very popular. More recent studies in spelling and the art of communication show us that such devices are really poor methods of teaching spelling. Almost never does an average or slow learner *learn* spelling by use of the spelling bee. The bright child who can visualize keenly and reproduce his visual perceptions on an oral level is the winner of most spelling bees.

Many of the older methods of teaching spelling have been shown to be ineffective in the long run. A look at some of these ideas will help us to see how difficult spelling can be when viewed from children's eyes.

* * *

A SPELLING LESSON

mandice	torsepen
pondak	apne
cryeno	joph
hotsen	kiopk

Apne upon a time a little old cryeno had a hotsen full of pondak trees.

The pondak trees grew joph and the torsepen of pondaken grew near the tops of the trees.

The pondaken grew so joph that the little old cryeno kiopk not get them down.

---

1. Write the two-syllable words.
2. What words have three syllables?
3. Find the word that is *plural* (means more than one). What letters show that it means more than one?
4. Write the plural of *mandice;* of *pondak;* of *hotsen.*

* * *

Let us imagine that the page reproduced above is a list of new words as presented by the spelling text commonly used twenty years ago. This lesson is presented in this fashion because we believed in these things:

1. All children should learn the same words inasmuch as they were to take part in a common adult culture.
2. Words would be selected from the vocabulary lists made of adult speech. By doing this, we were preparing children for adulthood.
3. Spelling was best taught through a knowledge of the phonetics system and a knowledge of word structure. Syllabication was very important to good spelling.
4. The greatest portion of spelling drill was oral.
5. Spelling rules must be learned in order for spelling to be taught effectively. Then the exceptions to the rules must be memorized.
6. Spelling was learned through the Stimulus-Response psychology, and the way to learn to spell was to drill, drill, drill. This drill was generally accomplished by having children spell words orally many times, or by having them write them ten times.
7. The more difficult the word, the more challenging it would be to the child. Difficult, remote words were the real test of a good speller.
8. All children should learn all words.

The child was told to open his book to the new spelling words. Inasmuch as the words were obtained from adult lists, the reader's reaction to the page above must be similar to the reaction the child felt when he opened his page to the "new words."

Our educational pedagogy at that time dictated the arrangement of this page because of many supposedly sound reasons.

First, the words to be studied were introduced at the top of the page. Each word was pronounced by the teacher; someone was asked to give its meaning and to use it in a sentence. The word was next divided into syllables, the accent mark was placed on it, and the proper markings for the vowel sounds were applied.

The story followed so the children would be able to see how their new words might be used in context.

Exercises were given at the bottom of the page to re-enforce the children's learning and to test their ability to apply previously learned words and rules.

The method of teaching from such a page was to follow the procedure suggested above, but to supplement the material in the textbook by having children write the words ten or more times.

If you follow the procedure prescribed here, you will look at the eight words at the top of the lesson. None is familiar (they were invented for this lesson).

You go through the words—there are no clues to the meanings. So you read the story below because you have been taught to read for context clues.

You conclude that apne probably means once; you cannot imagine what a cryeno is, or a hotsen. Perhaps it means a grove. Pondak is a kind of tree. What do joph, torsepen, and pondaken mean? Could joph mean tall—perhaps? And what about kiopk?

Putting it all together, you still do not know what the story is about, what the words mean, or how they are spelled. The teacher says it is essential now to pronounce the words and verbalize the meanings. Some of them may be important to you—however, none of them may be of importance. You may remember the word for a short time—long enough to use it in a sentence. The story *could* be read with some meaning as long as the meanings of the words are remembered.

The exercises are not difficult if the student remembers the rules:

1. The two-syllable words (a vowel in each syllable) would be: man-dice, pon-dak, cryen-o, hot-sen, ap-ne, ki-oph.
2. There is one three-syllable word: tor-se-pen which could also be a two-syllable word like horse-pen.
3. The plural word could be found—pondaken—the *en* suffix making the difference.
4. Therefore, the plurals required would be mandicen, pondaken, and hotsenen.

Now the words could be written ten times, but the child might write ten m's, then ten a's and so on—not really *seeing* the entire word at all.

We can properly ask: What has all this word manipulation to do with spelling?

From this lesson we can make some conclusions and observations, most of which blast to pieces the beliefs we held years ago. Let's re-examine those beliefs in the light of recent sociological developments and in reference to recent research.

The Truth about Spelling

Spelling is a polishing-up technique—one of the refinements that comes after the basic concepts of speech and recorded communication have been established. In a culture where sounds have been borrowed from many other cultures, and where words have a multitude of meanings, spelling is a difficult process at best. Let's take a look at those assumptions mentioned on page 415.

1. All children should learn the same words inasmuch as they are to take part in a common adult culture.

In the age of specialization in which we find ourselves, nothing could be further from the truth. Certainly adults living in the space age have many vocabularies, all categorized in the brain to be used at the proper time. Each adult has a common usage vocabulary for everyday living purposes. This vocabulary includes such words as gasoline, groceries, house, freeway, weather, storm, school, college, etc. But each also has a unique vocabulary or two: one which is common to the person because of where he lives and his socioeconomic status, and one because of what he does for a living. A college professor speaks commonly of statistics, homogeneity, normal curves, validity, reliability, curriculum, and grants because of his job, and of colonial architecture, antiques, ranch houses, suburbs, azaleas, flagstones, stocks, investments, and increments because of where he lives and his socioeconomic status.

Children, too, live in these specialized cultures within cultures in the space age. They do not speak from the same backgrounds. They do not read the same materials. Nor do they all need the same spelling instruction to satisfy their many needs. The basis for the effective and creative teaching of spelling, as with handwriting, lies in the teacher's ability to diagnose each child's spelling problems and to give him the individual instruction that will remedy these problems. The main problems in spelling generally evolve from the following causes: improper visual image of the word, inability of the child to syllabicate, inability of the child to use phonetic sounds, utilization of words which have no meaning to the child, difficulty with exceptions to common spelling words, and difficulty with parts of words such as reversals or non-phonetic words.

Children must be motivated to *want* to spell correctly. This is accomplished through the same devices which make him want to write legibly. Spelling is another refinement of the handwriting act. From the time that children begin to write their own words, stories, or poems, diagnosis for causes of misspelling can take place on an individual basis. Teachers can group children who have common problems or use techniques to help individuals who have unique problems.

Suggestions for Keeping Spelling Individualized

a. Some children are natural spellers. They see a word a few times, and it seems to be photographed in their minds to be reproduced easily. These children need not spend much time on spelling drill. They can benefit from a plan such as that described on page 427, known as the test-study-test method. If they know the words for the week, they are excused for other work, or they are given more complex words.

b. For children who need instruction in spelling, the study plan described on page 427 allows the teacher to spend most of her time with the children who need her most.

c. The teacher may use the stories, poems, and articles which children write to diagnose their spelling problems. If a series of charts with spelling rules are left in the room after children have constructed the rules, the teacher may number the chart and then edit the child's papers by placing a number over the misspelled word which tells the child where to look for help.

d. A 5 × 8 inch card for each pupil can be used to list the basic spelling principles with which he is having trouble. These cards can be used as a basis for grouping children with similar problems or for individualized instruction.

e. Spelling scales can be used to help teachers determine individual difficulties (Gates, Dolch, Horn, Betts).

f. Standardized tests will help diagnose children's spelling difficulties.

g. Some teaching machines help children to progress at their own rate in spelling ability.

h. Poor spellers can be assigned fewer words to learn during the week, with the understanding that as soon as the list is learned, they may have more words to learn.

i. Instill in children a purpose and desire to be good spellers by trying to:

   i. Impress upon students that spelling errors make a poor impression in letters and other written work, causing them trouble in such matters as applying for jobs.

   ii. Show students that the words they are learning in their spelling lessons are those which they can and do use now and will continue to use in the future.

   iii. Provide definite evidence of progress to convince students that they can improve their spelling ability—comparison of scores on first and final tests of the week, progress charts, etc.

   iv. Allow children to assume responsibility for learning to spell by setting up their own goals and taking the responsibility for reaching them.

   v. Give many opportunities for writing, so that students will feel a need for spelling.

   vi. Lead children to take pride in correct spelling in all written work and to proofread for spelling errors.

   vii. Emphasize mutual helpfulness rather than competition in the classroom. Games, contests, devices, and working for marks should be used to supplement the more basic appeals listed above, not substituted for them.

viii. The teacher must be interested in spelling herself! Enthusiasm and sympathetic understanding of the needs of individuals will go a long way toward obtaining desired results. A little praise for small improvements made by poor spellers may bring about greater improvements.

2. Words should be selected from the vocabulary lists made of adult speech. By so doing, we prepare a child for adulthood.

The source of word lists must be considered carefully. A reference to the language sequence chart shows us that spelling becomes essential to children only after they begin to write. Children write those words which they use in their oral vocabulary, and oral vocabulary is a verbalization of their own experiences. Words that are not drawn from their experience are meaningless to children and only tend to clutter up their organized vocabulary resources, or confuse the spelling of words they already use. The teaching of spelling is more realistic and brings better results when it is based on actual experience. The teacher who takes the children on a trip to the dairy, or who helps her class live through the experience of producing a play, has little difficulty in teaching the multitude of words that arise from such an experience. Children need these words for their charts, scripts, poems, and stories, and they learn them best by using them. If a vocabulary chart is kept in the room and new words are added daily, a long list soon results. From this list of fifty or sixty new words each week, the class can choose twenty which they must learn how to spell. This should be the spelling lesson for the week—composed of words which the children understand, know, and need.

Textbooks in recent years have greatly improved in the presentation of word lists. These lists are now derived from the vocabularies of children rather than from those of adults. They are compilations of the words most commonly used by children. As such, they serve as a check to the average teacher or as a resource for her in planning spelling lists for her own class. She can introduce many words at the oral level of communication, if she feels a need for the children to know words presented in the text.

One thing the textbook does not do is to teach words which children need at a special time, or to teach words which are newly coined and used constantly by children. In the first category fall such words as "robin" and "mumps." While adults probably use the word "robin" a great deal in the spring as they look for signs of spring, the child uses it often during the year because he is always interested in birds. An epidemic of mumps creates the need for the knowledge of the spelling of the word so that children may send letters to the afflicted persons and use the word in writing the daily news, poems, and stories in school.

Local and regional words that are of great importance to children cannot be put into textbooks. A child living in a farming region has many words in his oral vocabulary (such as *fertilizer, silo, crops, stanchion, thresher*) which his city cousin does not. His city cousin commonly uses other words such as *boss, strike, station wagon, picture window, suburb, ranch house,* etc. The teaching of these words in each case should come at different times—but in each case at a time when they are most needed by children for their written communication.

In the category of newly coined words fall such ones as *rocket, missile, astronaut, dragstrip, orlon, megaton,* and words which have been applied to common usage since any particular textbook was published or since the word list studies were composed.

One day recently, the author visited a nursery school. Two boys had constructed a one-windowed, six-sided frame house from blocks. Over the top they had placed a cardboard. A hole in the cardboard allowed a string to extend from the structure. One boy was sealed inside the structure; the other was walking with his arms and legs extended. His movements were done in slow motion. Our conversation ran as follows:

Author: Joel, what are you playing?
Joel: I am an astronaut taking a space walk.
Author: What is Jerry doing?
Joel: He is the astronaut inside who is managing the controls.
Author: I see. Why are you walking like that?
Joel: Because I am out in space and there is no gravity to hold me to the ground.
Author: And what is this? (pointing to the string)
Joel: It's my lifeline. I get oxygen from it to breathe.

And so on. Look at the words Joel is using meaningfully in context: *astronaut, space, managing, controls, gravity, lifeline,* and *oxygen.* And Joel is four. The author finds it difficult to conceive that no beginning reading book contains any of these words, and that Joel will not be presented with these words as spelling exercises until the fifth or sixth grade. The chances are that he will learn to read them by himself, without formal instruction and because he is bright, and that he will maintain their visual image on his mind and learn to spell them by himself too. Children are not only exposed to the sound of these words on television, radio, and daily conversation, but also *see* them on bus advertisements, on television, or in the newspaper. They are a vital part of a child's written communication and must be utilized in a realistic communication program.

Words foreign to the child's experience have no place in his communication system. They are an added attraction, remote from his regular experience, an imposed task to be mastered, and often a boring chore. Attitudes toward spelling, and an insight and desire to spell, are not fostered by sterile lessons of learning such words. Even the most skillful teacher has difficulty in teaching words so removed from meaningful content, and many of our teachers, lacking this skill, become slaves to the book which tells them so precisely what to do. In the most extreme cases, where we have midyear promotions, many teachers teach the lessons in sequence and have the children learning Christmas words at Easter.

Probably the best textbook for use is one which lists words children have in their daily experiences at each level of growth, but which makes ample provision for all other new and necessary words that children must learn.

We have come to realize that childhood has vocabularies unique to itself, and that all the basic principles needed to be a good adult speller are better taught using the vocabularies of childhood. Such a sound foundation insures spelling proficiency—we do not have to teach for the future.

3. Spelling is best taught through a knowledge of the phonetics system and a knowledge of word structure. Syllabication is very important to good spelling.

An understanding of phonetics and word structure should be meaningful and should arise from the child's experience. Good listening habits are necessary in teaching children to spell phonetically. The many suggestions offered in Chapter 5 to develop good listening habits and to develop audio perception have as much bearing on learning to spell as they do on learning to read. The phonics practices suggested in Chapter 7 also develop spelling abilities in children. A good phonics program builds the skills essential to good spelling.

Many of the words in the English language are non-phonetic, and these words must be memorized. Children should not be misguided into believing that phonic rules apply to all cases. Exceptions should be taught along with the rules so that a realistic concept is formed. (See 5 below.)

The matter of syllabication is another problem. Syllabication is far from standardized. Teachers and children should know this. They are victims of an arbitrary judgement made by the authors of whatever dictionary they are using.

Since much of our spelling is based on Latin, and the open syllable is natural to the Latin language, the syllabication in English words as they appear in most dictionaries results in a group of open syllables rather than closed syllables, which would give the language a natural unit. The new graphoneme concept recognizes the closed syllable and calls for a new, more reasonable and standard system of syllabication.[1,2,3]

Consequently, some spelling problems may well arise from our lack of a standardized syllabication system. A child changing schools (as a great percentage of our children now do) may change dictionaries or systems and become highly frustrated in the lack of continuity in his instruction.

Syllabication is no panacea to spelling difficulty. With regular words it may help, but then children rarely encounter difficulty with the regular words.

Children learn more from us than we think—it is only because they cannot always apply what they learn that we feel they have not learned. We need to know what they are *thinking* to know what they are learning.

A teacher friend of mine writes to me and I share an excerpt from her letter with you:

"They have odd ways (maybe) of figuring out spelling—a bit unorthodox! Barbara asked how to spell 'er.' I asked what she wanted to write. She said, 'I *know* how to spell moth and I want to make mother.' And Doug was crushed when he found out yesterday that 'ghat' is not the way most people spell fat. After all cou*gh* has the same sound! I told him I figure it's fine because one could tell what he means to say but most people use the dictionary spelling. He threw his pencil down and announced, 'I give up!' I can't blame him!"

4. The greatest spelling drill is oral.

Spelling is basically a visual skill. What makes a child a good speller? Primarily, it is when he has stamped on his memory a visual image of each word that he can reproduce on paper. All the mechanics of teaching spelling may help a child a great deal in his spelling ability. Phonics will help him guess at the spelling of new words. Rules for spelling (such as the *i* before *e* rule) help him in remembering unique features about troublesome words. But in the long run, in order for him to spell correctly, the word he writes must match the perception of that word which he has stamped on the marvelous mechanism of the brain.

When our image of a word is fuzzy or incomplete, we are not sure that it is spelled correctly. We sit down to write a letter to a friend. We write, "We gave our school play tonight. It was a big success." We are not sure

1. Virginia Jones and Evelyn Wiggins, *Utilizing the Graphoneme Concept in Teaching the Independent Decoding of Reading Vocabulary*. Mimeographed Material, 1968.
2. Virginia Jones, "Training Teachers of English for Alaska's Native Children," *Elementary English* (February 1971), pp. 198–202.
3. Virginia Jones, *The Graphoneme Concept*. Mimeographed Material, 1967.

of the spelling of the word success, so we turn to someone in the room and say, "How do you spell success?" The someone says, "s-u-c-c-e-s-s" and we promptly answer, "That's what I have but it doesn't *look* right." What we mean is that the word we have written does not conform to the shape and image in our memory, or our memorized image is fuzzy and we want to check it. Because spelling is a visual skill, more emphasis should be placed on the "look" of the word than was formerly put on the sound of it. Children learn to identify things by shapes: people, dogs, tables. The shape of the total word is the way the child first sees it. This visual image is the pattern impressed on his mind. Any distortion of this pattern is likely to cause misspelling.

When the child is asked to write a word ten times to learn to spell it, we may be asking him to learn it the hardest way for him. He is not hearing the word, and unless carefully supervised, he may be seeing each letter separately and missing the total word pattern. The value of this type of learning is dubious.

The way a word *looks* is as important in teaching spelling as the way it sounds. And we do not mean the way the letters look, letter by letter. Rather it is how the total word looks, each letter in its proper place in relation to the others. Good teaching accepts as its first responsibility the idea that the child should see and hear the word correctly. He closes his eyes and attempts to see the word; he checks his visual image with the board or a book; he again shuts his eyes to see it, and says it *softly;* then he checks by trying to write it and by comparing it to the model. When he is able to reproduce the word correctly, he goes on to study the next word.

When children do not have a clear visual image of a word, they resort to auditory perceptions, trying to apply the phonetic rules they have learned. In this case, misspellings are often the result of incorrect auditory reception. A child spells "I don't wanna go," because he hears "want to" that way. He spells "encyclopedia" as "ensighklopeedia" because he has never noticed the spelling of the word before, nor has he been called on to spell it, and he applies phonetic spellings he already knows.

The basic emphases in the teaching of spelling, then, should be on seeing the word and hearing it correctly. Most misspellings are due to a deficiency in these two areas.

5. Spelling rules are learned in order that spelling be taught effectively. Then the exceptions to the rules must be memorized.

Spelling rules, like all definitions, must grow out of experience and should not precede it. Exceptions to rules must be understood. Primary children write their first words simply by the reproduction of shapes. As they become phonetic and structure conscious, they gain techniques to attack new words in reading and to write new words (or spell them). Exceptions to phonetic and word structure rules may be noted when the child first comes upon them and notices that an application of the rule does not work. Children may begin to make charts of these exceptions until they have enough evidence to formulate a rule. If the exceptions and the generalizations grow out of the children's experience and are kept on charts or in a class-made book, the children will understand these exceptions, using the charts and books as a ready reference when solving spelling problems.

Miss Watson's third grade noticed that when two vowels appeared together in a word, only one was heard. Miss Watson suggested that the children collect such words from their reading books and from their experience. She printed these words on a chart over a period of a few days. She made two separate lists as the words were suggested. Her lists looked like this:

1	2
boat	pear
beat	tear
meat	bread
leak	book
mean	took
tear	about
oar	would
feel	our
peach	ready
cheer	chief
read	brief
your	break
seen	heard
each	does
please	goose
sheep	
tail	

After the list was large enough to show a rule *and* some exceptions, Miss Watson used it for a lesson. She asked the children to look at the double vowels in each word in list one. They pronounced the words together. Miss Watson reminded them that they had collected these words because only one vowel was heard in each; the other was silent. The children went through the list and found which vowel was silent. They noted that in each case it was the second vowel.

Miss Watson then drew their attention to the first vowel in each word by circling it with a red felt pen. She asked the children to read the sound of each vowel she had circled. Then they were asked which sound of the vowel was used in each case. They identified the long sound.

"Do you suppose we could make up a rule about double vowels when they appear in a word that will help us to know how to read and spell that word?" asked Miss Watson.

The definition suggested was as follows: When there are two vowels in a word, the first one often says its own name and the second is silent. Miss Watson printed this definition on the bottom of the chart. Then she introduced this list of new words, taken from the children's reading books.

coat	bean
peel	dear
reach	hear
steam	neat
poet	

The children applied the rule to each word to see if it would work.

Miss Watson then introduced list number two. She asked the children to read the words. The principle was then applied to each word; they could see that it did *not* work. Miss Watson asked if they could use their rule in all instances. The children agreed they could not. Billy suggested they print at the top of the list, "except these words." The children were then encouraged to watch for words which did not follow the rule and to print them on the chart.

The first rule was later applied when Miss Watson gave the children a series of drill exercises with words to spell, such as *rear, foam, goal, reel, gear, toad.* In each case the children had to memorize the silent vowel which made the first vowel *say its own name.* An understanding of spelling rules and their exceptions results when the rules grow out of the experiences of the children and are not imposed on them.

Words which do not follow the rules of ordinary spelling can only be memorized as non-phonetic words are memorized in reading. Research shows a high correlation between reading and spelling ability. A good reader sees many words over and over in many situations, and the images of these words become clearly imprinted on his mind. It is easier for him to reproduce these words on paper than it is for the child who has not seen the word as many times in print.

6. Spelling is learned through the Stimulus-Response psychology, and the way to learn to spell is to drill, drill, drill! This drill generally consists of saying spelling words orally several times or writing them ten times (shades of Hubert!).

Spelling is now regarded more through the Gestalt psychology approach: that correct spelling means being aware of the *structure* of the word and of its wholeness, as indicated in 4 above.

If Hubert wrote his words ten times with the teacher standing over him to say the word each time and to be certain that he wrote *and saw* the entire word each time he wrote it, this drill *could* be worthwhile.

Children seem to spell better when they *see* a word in ten different situations during a day than when they *write* it ten times.

A fifth grade teacher recently told me that her children made the solar system to scale from papier mâché and hung the planets from strings on the ceiling. The children were exposed visually to the names of the planets over a period of a week in the following ways:

1. They listed them on the chalkboard so each child could sign up for a committee to construct a planet.
2. They labeled a map of the solar system with the names of the planets.
3. They read about each planet in their science books.
4. They made cards with the names of the planets and put them in a pocket chart at the front of the room. They computed the distance of the planet from the sun on the back of each card.
5. The name of the planet was suspended from the bottom of each papier mâché planet.
6. They were given dittoed sheets on which the planets were listed, to classify them in relation to their distance from the sun.
7. The names of the planets were copied from the chalkboard into their science notebooks.
8. They read the names of the planets many times on a dittoed science test on their knowledge of the planets.

At the end of this exposure, which every child experienced (some used the names many more times in labeling drawings, in writing essays, etc.), my friend put all the cards out of sight and gave the children a spelling test on the names of the planets and other words used in visual form before the group, such as *papier mâché*, *planet*, *star*, *meteorite*, etc.

Of twenty such words on the test, only five children missed any. The highest number missed was five.

Effective and meaningful drill does not have to take place in a "formal" spelling period. It can be planned and integrated into lessons such as that reported by my friend. The time ordinarily spent on irrelevant drill was spent in more relevant ways.

Necessary to relevant spelling drill is a congenial, helpful atmosphere in the classroom. A permissive atmosphere must prevail in the classroom so that children will feel free to explore words and to question their structure. Vocabulary charts, word games, a typewriter, certain kinds of textbooks, word files, and other devices which give the children the chance to explore and enjoy learning to spell, help to make correct spelling important to them. Success experiences are essential to every child. These successes come in the practical application of the words to his daily work, in praise and congratulations from the teacher when he spells correctly and when he contributes new words which aid in the group communicative process.

7. The more difficult the word, the more challenging it will be to a child. Difficult, remote words are a real test for a good speller.

Difficult words do not test the good speller. Good spellers probably can spell difficult words, because they have an excellent memory, a high intelligence, and good study habits. A good system of study will help a child spell almost any word.

Conditions should be set to develop efficient study habits in spelling. Good study habits are basic, and the children and teachers should work out a *plan* for studying their spelling words. Different children learn in different ways, and the plan for study need not be the same for all children. Children can study independently by making up a plan that suits their needs. Independent study removes boredom on the part of the student and is often time saving for the teacher.

A plan for learning the weekly spelling list is important, and many good spelling texts tell of such plans. The teacher can work out one which works best for her group or for individuals in her group. A sample of one such plan employed by one teacher follows, not to serve as a pattern, but rather to provide an idea of how the actual mastery of the words may be obtained, while considering group and individual needs and interests.

In this particular grade, on Monday the teacher and the children went through the vocabulary chart from the previous week's work and underlined in red twenty words they felt they should learn. Knowing that some children had already learned many of them, the teacher gave a pretest so that each child could make a list of the words he would study for the week. Before this test, the words were discussed and their meanings associated with the occasion that prompted their appearance on the chart. Other meanings for the words were discussed, the words were used in other ways, small words within large ones were discussed, and word derivations were sometimes brought out; for example, *lawyer* contained the word *law*, etc.

The test was then given. After the test, each child checked his own paper by comparing it with the teacher's master copy on the board. He made out a new list of the words that he had misspelled. These were the words to study for the week. The teacher checked each list to be sure every child had the spelling of each word copied correctly on his paper. Notebooks were sometimes used to keep a running record of troublesome words.

On Tuesday, those who had all words correct were dismissed to do other things. The children who missed words brought their lists to the teacher and met in a group. The words were discussed, put on the board, and explained carefully.

The whole list was pronounced, with each child saying the pronunciation aloud. Then each child was told to look at his first misspelled word and to try to see the entire word. He then shut his eyes and tried to see the word. Then he checked with the writing on his paper. Then he looked at the word and spelled it to himself, and next closed his eyes and tried to *see* each letter and spell the word. He tried to write it on a piece of paper and checked it again with the original. If he wrote it correctly, he studied his next word. If not, he repeated the entire process for the word that he missed.

In this way, each child studied different words under teacher guidance, and good study skills were developed. When a child finished his list (as those who missed only a few did), he helped the next one to finish by hearing him spell his words aloud or by dictating them to the child so that he might try writing them all again.

On Wednesday, everyone joined in some games with words. Then the teacher dictated the entire list and the children took the test again. This helped to check up on any pupils who had merely guessed correctly on Monday. After the test, the words were checked by the children and new lists of words were made out for study. Only the few who had real spelling difficulty were left with misspelled words.

Thursday's period was left for those who had such lists. The other children worked at other jobs, and the teacher worked with those children who needed more help than any others. Again the words were studied as on Tuesday. Dictionary work and word analysis skills were developed. More games and drill work were employed to help those students. Generally, a careful check was made at the end of the lesson of each pupil by the teacher.

On Friday the test was given again. Any words missed at this time were placed on a 5×8 inch card or in the spelling notebook and studied at odd times by the children. Words missed weekly and added to the card gave the child an account of all the words he had missed during the year. On short weeks (when vacations occupied some of the school days), the teacher and children restudied their cards for their review spelling lessons.

The teacher may judge the effect of her teaching by the manner in which the children use the words they have learned in their written classwork. If the words appear and are spelled correctly, she is giving her children additional tools for communication and is fulfilling the objectives for teaching spelling. She is also giving them a tool which they can employ for creative communication purposes.

8. All children should learn all words in each week's lesson.

We have seen under 7 above how, through a pretest, the teacher can weed out the children who already know their spelling words and may then be directed to other worthwhile experiences.

Spelling is a maturational as well as a learning process. All children are not ready to spell as many words or the same kinds of words at the same time. Provision must be made to meet individual differences in the spelling program.

Some of the words used in school will not need to be memorized; their life use is too infrequent. They should be copied from the dictionary when needed. Children should not be forced to learn to spell words which they will seldom, if ever, use in life situations. Constant use of the dictionary should be encouraged for the proper spelling of unusual and rarely used words. If, with a basic vocabulary well learned, the habit of consulting the dictionary when in doubt is established, the child will be well equipped to meet his ordinary spelling needs if he has some idea of the spelling of the word.

Our chart of language development shows us that spelling is far down in the sequence of language development. It is a sophisticated skill in many ways. There is a correlation between spelling ability and intelligence. Slow-learning children may never master an adequate spelling vocabulary.

Objectives in Teaching Spelling

In light of the above discussion, some obvious objectives seem to arise for the teaching of spelling in the space-age school.

1. To help each child learn to spell correctly those words which he will need in order to express his own ideas in writing.
2. To develop in each child a basic set of principles and concepts that will help him to spell familiar words.
3. To create interesting drill exercises and techniques to help each child fix in his memory images of those spellings which are essential to social courtesy, but which are exceptions to the principles and concepts of ordinary spelling.
4. To instill in each child a desire to spell correctly and an attitude that good spelling is a social courtesy in the communication process.
5. To help each child form good study habits in spelling which help him to attack unknown words intelligently. This includes the intelligent use of reference materials.

Ideas for Relevant Drill in Spelling

Games

Spelling lends itself well to games, and games serve as motivators to learning. A few precautions must be exercised in using spelling games, however.

1. The purpose of the game should always be to teach the spelling words. Many games become so involved that the purpose is lost in the development of the game and it contributes little to the learning of the word. Games should be kept simple, with emphasis always on the correct spelling.

2. Visual impressions are important. In introducing spelling words, games should not be used which distort the image of the word. Games such as scramble, where words are listed on the board with the letters in incorrect sequence for the children to unscramble, are inappropriate because they often confuse the child more than they help him. *Games used at the onset of the spelling teaching experience should not distort words.* After the words are learned, games such as scramble may serve as testing devices, but only when the teacher is certain that children have a visual impression of the word firmly established in their minds. (See below.)

3. Games should include every member of the class or group, and at no time should any of the children be eliminated completely. The fallacy of the old type of spelling bee was that the children who were poor spellers were eliminated almost at once, leaving those to practice who needed it least. Poorer spellers need to participate *more* than good spellers—and their participation must be active. The visual form of the word must appear many times during the course of the game. Some provision must be made for all students to participate, even when the game calls for some to drop out. The dropouts then become checkers or help in the playing of the game.

Some commercial games and aids are excellent for teaching spelling. These include:

- spelling lotto
- anagrams
- spelling wheels
- the typewriter
- word cards
- word-building cards
- self-instructing teaching machines

Games: Primary Grades

Inasmuch as success in spelling is due largely to the child's ability to visualize a word, spelling words can be written or printed on cards with a flo-pen and placed on a flannel board where they can be moved about for a variety of reasons. As words are mastered, they can be easily removed, leaving before the children only those which are more difficult. Some children may have the card with the word on it on their own desks where they see it repeatedly over a period of time. Words on cards can be filed alphabetically after they are mastered, and may be used frequently on the flannel board for review, or used in the file as a check by any child who is not sure of the spelling.

1. Miss Ashforth helped her primary children to develop visual images of their spelling words by making, from a cardboard box, three small houses, which she placed at the front of the room. Each was labeled with a sign: "Sally's Playhouse," "Dick's Ranch House," and "The Gingerbread House." Large pieces of gray paper were cut to represent stones. Words from the spelling lesson were lettered on these stones and they were placed a few feet apart, leading to each house. The children were divided into three groups. One child started at the opposite end of the room and walked to the house by stepping lightly on each stone and naming and spelling the word as he did so. If he failed to recognize a word, another child picked him up. A record was kept of the child's progress inside the house in an envelope. Eventually all reached their goal; then new stones were substituted.

2. The teacher selects words in the spelling lesson which can be pictured. She prints eight words on the board and numbers them. The children fold a sheet of paper into eight folds and number the blocks made by the folds. Then they copy the word from the board in the top of the block and illustrate the word. It is important that the teacher check each paper to be sure that the child has copied the word correctly. Later these papers may be cut apart and the illustrated words used for study or for playing other spelling games.

3. Use clever devices to motivate children to good spelling. Mrs. Bickel made a large Christmas tree out of poster paper. Each week from Thanksgiving to Christmas the words for the week appeared in the colored balls on the Christmas tree. When the test was given on Friday, the children wrote their words on a dittoed sheet on which was drawn a Christmas tree with circles that were left plain. The children wrote the words in the circles. If the word was correct, each child was allowed to color a design in his circle, making a Christmas tree ball. This left the misspelled (but corrected) words exposed to be colored as quickly as

the child learned the word. Variations of this idea can be used throughout the year, for example:

a. Draw circles on the board to represent snowballs. If a child spells his word correctly, let him write it in one of the snowballs.
b. Cut out bells or stockings for children to write words on during Christmas week. Booklets can be made from the week's spelling papers.
c. Have him write his Easter words on eggs and all can be placed in a basket on the bulletin board.
d. September words can be written in leaves dittoed on a page. October words can be written in pumpkins lined up on a fence. For November use a row of turkeys or pilgrim hats. January can be snowflakes; February, hearts; March, shamrocks; April, umbrellas; May, flowers. Other ideas might be balls, pitchers' mitts, houses, or any form appropriate to a social studies unit.

4. Use a round-robin drill with the spelling words. One child says a word he remembers and spells it, the next one repeats that word and adds one of his own, a third child repeats both and adds another, etc. This goes on until one child misses, and then it begins again. The missed words are always written on the chalkboard.

5. Disappearing words: A child takes a word he would like the rest of the class to guess, such as "grown." He might say, "Change one letter and the word disappears. A new word takes its place." (*drown* for *grown*)

6. Each child chooses a partner and acts out any words in the spelling lesson. The children watching guess the word and write it down.

7. The Owl Game: Individuals or small groups working together with paper have fun figuring this out. In this Owl Game, the teacher gives definitions of words which all end with owl.

A noise from a canine in distress	(howl or yowl)
To rove about stealthily	(prowl)
A feathered friend	(fowl)
To make a fierce noise	(growl)
A monk's hood	(cowl)
To make a distorted face	(scowl)
The lower part of the face	(jowl)
A concave vessel, hemispheric	(bowl)
etc.	

Other ending sounds can be used. Children can work this game in reverse by dividing in groups, making up their own definitions, and trying them on each other.

Games: Intermediate Grades

1. Garbled Words: After the spelling words are known and the visual image of the word is so well fixed in the mind of the child that the teacher is certain he can spell it correctly, Garbled Words or Scrambled Words can be used to check the spelling or to tease the child's thinking and cause him to focus on the individual letters of the word.

Scrambled words is the old game, often played in the primary and intermediate grades, where words are purposely mixed and the child unscrambles them, i.e., usohe is house. In the primary grades, the beginning letter (and sometimes the end letter) is left in its proper place to make the game less difficult for little children, such as h-u-o-s-e.

Garbled words are something different and can generally be used most effectively with children in the upper grades. This is a game which exploits the concept that the same letters appear in many words but in different arrangements or sequence. Thus, the word *rat* can become *art* or *tar*.

The object of the game is to find the word in poems such as the following, which, when its letters are rearranged, will make a new word and will fit the other blanks. The epitome of the task is when children create their own rhymes (utilizing such words) for each other.

Try this:

A ______ old lady (vile)
On ______ bent, (evil)
Put on her ______ (veil)
And away she went;
"______, my son" (Levi)
She was heard to say,
"What shall we do to ______ today?" (live)

A sixth grader created this one:

Once upon a ______ (time)
A tiny ______ said: "Stop! (mite)
I will ______ a yell (emit)
For each ______ in this shop!" (item)

The creative aspect of this game comes when the teacher challenges the children to find words which can be used in this way, and to make up poems for the rest of the class.

Stephen, grade five, submitted the following:

Mother stopped scrubbing her ______ (pots)
Dirty from cooking the roast
And said, "______ playing with your ______ (stop, tops)
And take this letter to ______. (post)

Some starters for fun are:

stone (notes, tones, onset)
time (mite, emit, item)
tears (stare, rates)
rats (arts, star, tars)
mile (Emil, lime)
pat (tap, apt)
meat (team, mates)

2. Write a long word on the board. Then have the children try to make a list of as many different words as they can find in the long word.

Example:	extraordinary	
	extra	ordinary
	or	din

Later, after they have learned the long words, they try to make as many different words as they can from the letters in the long word.

3. Individual progress charts or individual graphs can be kept by each student to record his own growth in spelling. These graphs and charts provide for self-incentive and maintain comfortable learning conditions in the classroom.

4. Vocabulary Building: Slang often takes a back seat in "school" communication, yet it is most efficient, expressive, and used more out of school for dialogue among children than the so-called proper language taught in school.

Slang contains a great deal of metaphor and humor. Sensing the young child's eagerness to imitate his older brothers and sisters, Mrs. Wills asked the children in her middle school classes to make collections of slang words and expressions. When the lists were long enough so that each person in the class could have one, Mrs. Wills asked the children to select a word and write a picture definition of it.

Some of the results were a delight:

kopp-out: a kopp-out is when you spend a whole week trying to get up the courage to ask a girl to a movie, and when you finally get the nerve to call her up, you ask for your homework assignment instead.

turn-on: to turn on is to be starving and be placed in front of a smorgasbord.

flack: flack is the truth changed to gossip.

5. Encourage each child to select and paint a spelling word to be labeled and placed along the top of the chalkboard in the classroom. Children will find it easy to paint words like palm, engineer, and astro-

naut, but their creativity will be challenged by painting words like without, especially, and exactly. The colorful images of the word above the printed word will re-enforce the visual concept.

6. Applying Phonics: After children have learned phonics skills, encourage them to play detective, using phonics clues to unlock the mystery of a word. Pronounce words which they do not know how to spell but which have phonetic spelling, and have them figure them out on the chalkboard. A variation of this game is to use nonsense or non-existent words to see how many in the class can use sounds correctly (Examples: redenter, forsitill, marinking, etc.).

7. The Mixed-Up Story: The teacher (or a child) writes a story using as many of the spelling words as possible. The spelling words are printed on cards—the story is printed on oaktag or on the chalkboard. After the story is placed before the group, the cards are put on indiscriminately with a roll of masking tape. Children take turns in changing the story to its correct form by changing two cards around. Each child has a chance.

8. Word Meanings: On twenty-eight cards the size of playing cards, write different words in black. On twenty-seven cards, write the meanings of twenty-seven of these words in red. One word is left without a meaning card. Shuffle the cards and deal. Play according to the rules of "Old Maid," each drawing a card from the player to his right. When pairs are found, they are placed in the center of the table. Drawings continue until one child is left holding the word without a meaning card.

9. Definitions: Definitions should come at the end of an experience. Once definitions are pulled together, or knowledge is amassed, a creative way to test knowledge and definition is through the construction of a crossword puzzle. Figure 92 is one made by a fifth grade group; correct spelling is essential to fill the blanks properly.

Some definitions can be written in poetry form, putting spelling to use. For example:

What Is Spring?

Spring is the time when robins are seen,
Spring showers will come and make everything green.
Buying new kites that you'll fly in the breeze,
Hoping your kite won't get caught in the trees.
Your heavy old coat will be set aside.
Then get out your bike and you'll go for a ride.
For spring is the best time of the year.
Spring is the time when fun is near.

—Cynthia Cupelo
Grade 5

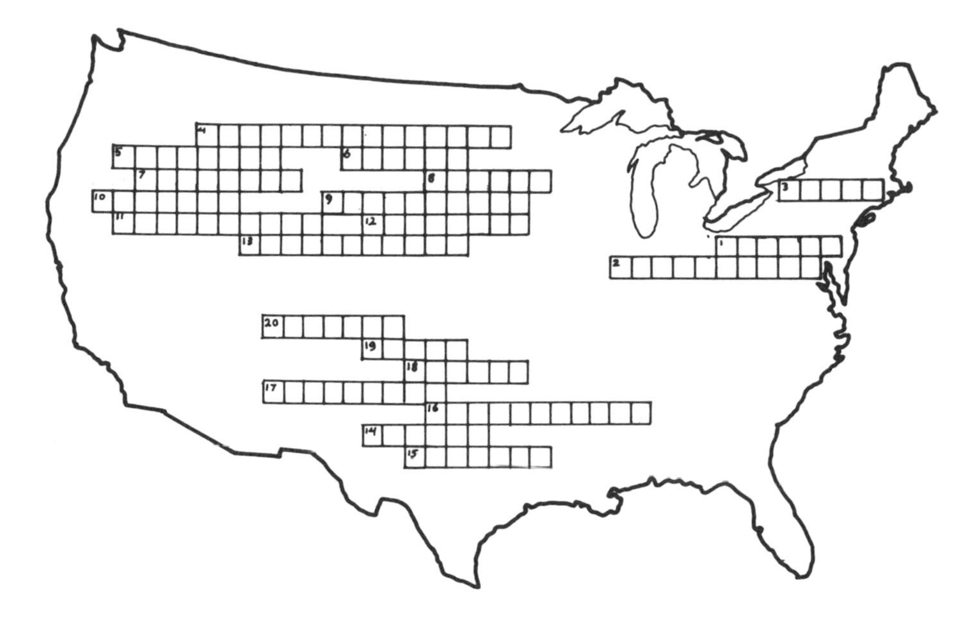

1. Delicately beautiful
2. Bold
3. Bright
4. A special skill or ability gained by study or training.
5. Having a pleasing appearance.
6. Power or capacity to be active.
7. As different as possible.
8. A space that is included within certain limits, as measured in cubic inches or feet.
9. Rules of conduct.
10. Fearlessly, courageously.
11. Having to do with or made by machinery.
12. Having a firm idea or purpose; determined.
13. Settlements of disputes, reached by each party giving up part of his demands.
14. An important city in Massachusetts-Puritans founded this city.
15. Any information, notice, news, or instruction sent from one person to another.
16. An important scource of energy which is found in nature.
17. A receptacle.
18. At a distance; yonder.
19. A warning of danger.
20. The condition of being able.

Figure 92 *A crossword puzzle.*

10. Stories from Spelling Words: Some children are challenged by trying to see how many of their spelling words they can use in a comprehensive story. "Winter Fishing" shows how one ten-year-old boy was able to incorporate eleven of fifteen words in a story. Jim certainly knew the meanings of these words!

Winter Fishing

One cold winter day Uncle Jim and Peter got into the new family *automobile* and went down to the *river* to fish. They *walked* out upon the *ice*.

"I brought two lines," Uncle Jim said to Peter. Mine goes here and *yours* goes there."

Peter stood by the *round* hole in the *ice*. The water looked black and cold.

"You should not get too close," said Uncle Jim. "I will show you where to *stand*. Watch out!"

But it was too *late*. Splash! Uncle Jim *fell* into the *water!* Peter helped him *climb* out. They ran back to the house.

"Did you catch any fish?" Aunt Mary called. "No," said Peter, "but I caught one big, wet Uncle."

Evaluation in Spelling

The real measure of a child's spelling progress is how well he carries over this learning into his writing. Guides for this kind of evaluation include the following questions:

1. Does the child spell commonly used words correctly in all his written work?
2. Does he keep a list of the words he misspells?
3. Can he study independently?
4. Can he apply simple generalizations?
5. Does he use the dictionary frequently?

When the child develops a positive attitude toward spelling; when he can write the most common words with ease and accuracy; when he feels secure in his ability to face new words and use a variety of approaches with them; when he takes pride in his written work and feels satisfaction in it as a means of personal expression of his feelings, thoughts, and ideas; then it is realistic to expect that he senses its value. He has developed a tool which helps him to be more creative in his writing.

Summary

Many misconceptions exist concerning the teaching of spelling. The concept that it is a dull "happening" which must be experienced as a necessary preparation for life is perhaps the greatest of these misconceptions. Spelling *can* be taught in a highly motivating, highly relevant manner, provided that teachers are willing to take a new look at its function in the space age and are ready to make it more relevant than writing the word ten times—Hubert!

To the Reader

1. Listen to any group of children at play. List the unusual words (or common words) they use. Check a spelling text for the child's age level and notice how many of the spoken words are or are not included.
2. Obtain a collection of material written by children of any age level. Make lists of the words most commonly misspelled in this material. Analyze the lists and note whether any unique patterns of misspellings run through them. Can you conclude anything? Sometimes, developing one or two misconceptions about spelling in a given classroom can increase spelling power by as much as 50 percent.
3. What do you remember about spelling in the grade school when you were younger? What parts do you remember as pleasant or unpleasant? Can you remember any special thing the teacher did that seems relevant to you now?
4. Some statements for discussion:
   a. Phonics training is more helpful in spelling than in reading.
   b. Spelling *can* be interesting, but it is the one time when children must be highly conforming in order to get by. You can't be a creative speller. Therefore, spelling cannot be taught creatively.
   c. There is a high correlation between good spelling and intelligence. Muscular coordination? Reading?
   d. The old-fashioned spelling bee was better as a socializing device than as a method of teaching spelling.
   e. What is needed in the space age is an international language with an international spelling system.
5. Make a file of interesting techniques, games, and gimmicks for teaching spelling.
6. Almost every year someone attempts to pass a bill through Congress which will put the English language on a phonetic spelling basis. Can you see advantages to this? Why do you suppose the bills never get as far as committee?
7. A bright child submits a story to you with these misspellings: refrigeador, Sattidy, stoopid, ole, cum, triger, breffast. Can you diagnose some of his problems? What remedies would you apply?

Selected Bibliography

BLAKE, HOWARD. "Studying Spelling Independently," in James C. MacCampbell (ed.), *Readings in the Language Arts in the Elementary School*. Boston: D. C. Heath and Company, 1964, 183–187.

FITZGERALD, JAMES A. "Spelling: Diagnosis and Remediation," in James C. MacCampbell (ed.), *Readings in the Language Arts in the Elementary School*. Boston: D. C. Heath and Company, 1964, 188–194.

GROFF, PATRICK. "Research on Spelling and Phonetics," *Education*. November, 1968, 132–135.

HAHN, WILLIAM P. "Phonetics: A Boon To Spelling," *Elementary School Journal* (April 1964), 383–384.

HODGES, RICHARD E. *What's New in Language Arts?: Spelling*. Washington, D.C.: American Association of Elementary-Kindergarten-Nursery Educators, NEA Center, 1970.

HORN, ERNEST. *What Research Says to the Teacher: Teaching Spelling*. Department of Classroom Teachers and American Educational Research Association. Washington, D.C.: National Education Association, 1967.

HORN, ERNEST (ed.). *Research on Handwriting and Spelling*. Champaign, Illinois: The National Conference on Research in English by the National Council of Teachers of English, 1966.

SHANE, HAROLD, MARY E. REDDEN, AND MARGARET C. GILLESPIE. *Beginning Language Arts Instruction with Children*, Chapter VI. Columbus, Ohio: Merrill, Inc., 1961.

YEE, ALBERT H. "The Generalization Controversy on Spelling Instruction," *Elementary English*, (February 1966), 154–161.

12

Adventures with Words, Structures, and Forms

The Ballad of Denny the Dinosaur

Miss Ricker was teaching a unit about dinosaurs. The children had learned many new words during the unit, along with the identity of all the different kinds of dinosaurs.

One way that Miss Ricker used to check the children's knowledge was to have some of her students draw the various kinds of dinosaurs on poster paper. She then cut them into puzzle pieces which, when put together, not only showed the shape of each dinosaur but also spelled out his name.

Miss Ricker saw the opportunity to do some excellent vocabulary development and to do it in a creative way. One day she asked the children, "Why do you think one of our gasoline companies uses the dinosaur as its emblem in advertising?"

It did not take the children long to suggest that the dinosaur exemplified power, strength, and superiority in size, which is what the company tried to say about its gasoline. They also suggested that it represented the age when the gasoline was formed.

Miss Ricker then asked the children to make a chart of all the words they could think of that mean big or strong, and to put the words strength, power, and superiority at the top of the list. The list soon grew to include:

King-Kong
enormous
fat
ton
elephant
blubbery
obese
gigantic
huge
colossal
great
superman, etc.

Miss Ricker then reminded the children that they had learned that dinosaurs lived millions of years ago, and that that was indeed very old.

A chart of OLD words then evolved, which included *ancient, antique,* and others.

Another chart of HEAVY words was made.

Miss Ricker suggested that they use these words in the stories they might write about dinosaurs. In fact, she had a game, she stated, that would afford them the opportunity to use the words at once. They were going to write a foolish story, she explained.

On a transparency Miss Ricker had printed a story, leaving a space for all the adjectives. On an overlaying transparency she had drawn a small box where each adjective would be used on the first transparency. She projected the transparency with the boxes upon the screen and said, "Now, from all these charts of new words, you take one that describes something, or else make up a describing word, and I will let each one of you tell me your word and I will put it in one of these boxes."

The children took turns in suggesting the words. Then Miss Ricker told them that they really had helped her write the words in a story she wrote about dinosaurs, and now they would see how their words fit into her story. With this, she put the first transparency over the second, and where she had left spaces, the children's words now completed the sentences, making the fun story below. (The underlined words are the ones the children supplied.)

A Foolish Dinosaur Story

Once upon a time there lived an enormous mouse named Doris. She lived in a cooky, antique mouse hole under a gigantic, sissy tree. She lived with her blubbery father, her weak mother and her fat-cat sister whose name was Martha.

One day Doris went for a walk with her ancient sister Martha. Her fierce mother said, "Martha, you be very careful and watch for old Benny, the fat Brontosaurus! If he ever steps on you he could squash you flat!"

"We will be careful," said Doris and Martha together. Everyone was afraid of two-ton Benny, the Brontosaurus!

Doris and Martha were not far from home when they heard a big-mouth noise. The antique earth shook! They were frightened. They ran to a weak tree and hid behind it. When they dared to peek out, they saw Benny, the jet-set Brontosaurus. They wanted to run home and hide they were so scared but Doris noticed something.

"Look," she said, "Skinny-Bones Benny is crying. He is crying because his tail is caught in that vine and he cannot turn around to bite it off! Come, we must help him!"

At first, crazy Martha did not want to go but after a while, Doris persuaded her and they went out and stood before enormous Benny.

"Don't cry, gigantic Benny, the strong Brontosaurus," said Doris, "We will help you!"

And Doris and Martha ran up to the elephant vine and gnawed and chewed until they ate right through it. Obese Benny, the Brontosaurus, was free.

"Thank you, thank you," said superman Benny, the Brontosaurus, "You are my friends. I shall never let anyone in the King-Kong forest ever, ever hurt you!"

So old Doris and heavyweight Martha became the heroes of the day and never had to worry when they went for a stomping walk in the forest.

* * *

The children were delighted with the nonsense story, and Miss Ricker pointed out that she was aware that they knew the meanings of the words by the fact that they laughed when some of the words came in improper places.

This activity led to the creation of many nonsense stories by individual children later on in the weeks that followed.

When Miss Ricker saw how highly motivated the children were over writing a story, she decided to use the dinosaur unit as the basis of teaching rhyming words and of writing original poetry.

On the top of a piece of construction paper, she printed words such as *dinosaur, ago, tree, breaks,* etc. She then talked to the children about rhyming words. Placing the children in pairs, she gave each pair a sheet of paper. They were to write all the words they could think of that rhymed with the key word in a five-minute time limit.

When time was called, all the papers were posted along the chalk tray, and each pair of children read the words they had put on their chart. In some instances, more words were added. In others, a few that were obvious misfits were crossed out.

Miss Ricker then placed on the bulletin board a strip of paper on which was printed this line.

In the forest lived Denny, the dinosaur.

"Now look at our chart of words rhyming with dinosaur," said Miss Ricker, "and see if anyone can pick a word that can be put at the end of this sentence, but with words filled in so it will make sense."

And on the bulletin board, below the first sentence, she added:

He ate ______ ______ ______ ______ ______ ______.

Finally Charlie volunteered, "He ate all the time and wanted more." The children were delighted, so Miss Ricker put up another line.

He lived on the earth many years ago.

And she said, "Now finish this with a word that rhymes with 'ago'."

Which was ______ ______ ______ ______ ______ ______.

Soon Debby raised her hand and said, "Which was long before the ice and snow!"

They were off. The following poem resulted. Italicized words indicate those supplied by the children.

The Ballad of Denny the Dinosaur

In the forest lived Denny, the Dinosaur
He ate *all the time and wanted more,*
He lived on the earth many years ago
Which was *long before the ice and snow*
He loved to lie in the cool, cool shade
He ate *little beasts and drank lemonade*
He walked very clumsy like a big old man
And he never *never never ran.*
One day he went to a mountain top
To get some *air and a new rag mop*
But he slipped and fell with every step
Until he *lost all his pep*
He lay in the mud and there he died
And *dust and dirt soon covered his hide*
Three billion years later he came to the top
Denny, the dinosaur *carrying a mop!*

The children wrote many poems after this kickoff. Many were illustrated and bound into individual books. Miss Ricker had indeed made word usage and vocabulary building a relevant activity for her pupils.

In the above experience we see the children discovering how language is structured. The children are identifying many types of sentences and are expanding the sentences into new structures by adding words, phrases and clauses. They are discovering, also, that certain morphemes sound alike and may be used in creating rhyme when used at the ending of a word.

Later, after many creative experiences of this nature with the use of words and sentences, Miss Ricker selected kernel sentences from the children's work on which to build lessons for the purpose of exploring English sentence patterns.

The teacher took the basic subject-predicate pattern of

Dinosaurs eat

and helped the children expand the structure in the following ways:

Giant dinosaurs eat. (expansion through addition of an adjective)
Greedy dinosaurs eat.
The enormous dinosaur eats greedily. (addition of a determiner—an adjective and an adverb)
All dinosaurs eat food. (addition of determiner and object)

Teaching punctuation, word usage, capitalization, and grammar should result from exercises in creativity such as this. Miss Ricker, in using grammar forms properly, sets models before the children which they can copy when they need them. A steady diagnosis of their individual papers tells Miss Ricker those language forms which need to be taught.

The Mechanics of Written Expression

Although capitalization, punctuation, correct word usage, and correct forms of written expression are often taught as part of a grammar or English program, a justifiable case could be presented to include them in a handwriting program.

Handwriting is a visual skill, important to the individual only when he wishes to communicate on paper. In developing this skill, his visual perceptions must be refined to a high degree.

Punctuation is also a visual skill; it does not appear in speech. It is used as an attempt to communicate some of the voice quality, voice inflection, and natural division of thoughts from oral speech into written speech. It exists only on paper. It is logical that it should be taught along with handwriting (or reading), which also exists only on paper.

Like punctuation, capitalization is a visual, written skill.

Many of the problems of correct word usage are problems that appear only when we write them and not when we speak them. When a child says, "I am going to the store," to communicate an idea, it is unnecessary for him to know that there are three spellings for the word "to" and that only one of them is correct. It is only when he begins to write his ideas on paper that this knowledge becomes necessary, or that he confronts the problem of deciding which spelling he must use.

Forms of written expression such as letter writing are also handwriting rather than oral skills; they involve visual perception. A child must learn to visualize his handwritten page before he writes a letter, because form is the thing that will "make" the letter.

Forms of written expression include:

1. Various types of sentence structure
2. Paragraphs
3. Outlines
4. Poetry
5. Forms of correspondence such as business letters, friendly letters, letters of thanks, invitations, announcements, greeting cards, and note cards
6. Alphabetization
7. Note-taking
8. Script writing
9. Punctuation

Like handwriting itself, the mechanics of handwriting require standards of conformity in order to be effective. Teachers may question whether or not the teaching of such skills, already made rigid by common use, can be creative. In the sense that teachers can set conditions which lead children to discover the purpose of writing mechanics, and that children can be helped to apply these standard accepted forms to make their own written communication more creative and more effective, these skills *can* be taught creatively. The creative person is neither compulsively conforming nor compulsively non-conforming, but is free to be one or the other, depending either upon his values or upon what is more effective or logical in any situation. Therefore, the creative child will learn the correct use of the forms of written expression and will adapt them to handwriting situations as a social courtesy to the reader. Like all children, he will learn the forms well if they are taught creatively.

General Conditions for Teaching Mechanics of Handwriting

Smith[1] lists the following conditions necessary for the teaching of the mechanics of writing.

1. Because the mechanics of writing and the use of correct word forms

1. James A. Smith, *Creative Teaching in the Language Arts in the Elementary School* (Boston: Allyn and Bacon, 1968), pp. 221–274.

and communication forms are *visual* skills, it is important that children "see" these forms. One of the major criticisms which can rightfully be leveled against commercial workbooks is that they often do not differentiate between written and oral skills and try to correct speech problems through written exercises. This is language teaching in reverse of its natural sequence. Correct oral forms are taught on the oral level. Inasmuch as children write in the same way they speak, the carry-over from speaking to writing will be taken care of. The reverse seldom occurs. Correct use of auxiliary verbs such as "I have finished" and "I had finished" and correct speech forms such as "I haven't any" and "it is I" are oral problems and should be handled in developing correct oral expression.

Correct use of certain words, such as *their* and *there*, and uses of punctuation and capitalization are visual or written language problems, and can therefore rightfully be taught and corrected on paper. The important principle to be observed in teaching the mechanics of writing is that, as much as possible, emphasis must be placed on *visual* perception of the form.

2. Dealing with punctuation, capitalization, correct word usage, and correct written forms is working in the abstract and conceptual forms of communication. For this reason, children need to have extensive concrete experiences with writing and speaking before they are taught the abstract structure and mechanics of language. Slow-learning children may never be able to deal effectively with these abstractions. Normal children will encounter difficulty if the abstractions are not built on several meaningful experiences which gradually lead the children into an understanding of the rules and concepts that build a language. In other words, definitions "grow out" of experiences; they do not precede experiences.

A definition is a concept. It is also a generalization. Generalizations are reached after a series of experiences show that all these experiences have common elements. In teaching the mechanics of handwriting, many experiences with each of the mechanics is necessary if children are to understand the generalization.

3. The atmosphere of the room must be such that children are not afraid to experiment with punctuation and various word and written forms. The system often called "spoonfeeding" is justifiable in teaching writing skills. Spoonfeeding is that technique, used by some teachers, which almost never allows the child to see incorrect writing forms. In the intitial stages of teaching any new skill, the teacher makes certain that all children see the form correctly, even if she must show them individually several times on their own papers or on the chalkboard. The children are allowed to use the form only when the teacher is certain

that it will be used correctly. Inasmuch as forms are visual skills, the purpose in spoonfeeding is to make a correct visual impression on the child's mind, much the same as the teacher does when she builds a sight vocabulary in reading. This technique is in contrast to the one where the teacher teaches a lesson on some handwriting mechanic and then the children are tested by completing a workbook exercise. The danger in the latter system is that, unless the child has learned the mechanic or form in one lesson, he may complete the workbook exercise incorrectly. This tells the teacher that he has not understood the lesson, but it may also distort the visual perception of the mechanic which he is learning. Unless corrected immediately, he may carry this incorrect visual impression in his mind.

4. The mechanics and forms of writing should be taught as art forms. Every child will want to make his paper "look nice" and "look pretty." This is the aesthetic value of written compositions. Comparisons between margins and mounts on the children's art work can be made to show that each accomplishes the same purposes: framing the material, providing a rest space for the eye, and creating a focal point in the center of the page. Written composition forms have many correlations with art forms. The beauty of a well-written and well-formed page can be as pleasing to the eye as a well-done painting.

The mechanics of writing and written forms do not, by nature, stem from the child's experience, but they are inherited from the distant past. Some of them do not make sense, because they were established at a time when the structure of the language was unsettled and not completely understood. Consequently, the rules of the language are not pure; there are exceptions to them all. These exceptions exist for no realistic purpose and even interfere rather than promote communication. They are taught to children by rote memory and regarded as accepted forms.

Handwriting mechanics and writing forms are highly sophisticated skills. The teacher must take the naive child at all levels of his development and contrive experiences that will lead him to an understanding of the purpose and use of language forms. Research has shown that creativity is enhanced when the basic principles underlying an act are understood.

5. Language is not taught in a language period. There should not be a period in the day for only language—language is the tool of communication used throughout the day. Teachers will take time on certain days to teach specific language skills which grow out of the needs of the class or of individual children. Often such periods will be devoted to a group needing special help, rather than to the entire class. When mechanics of writing or speaking and written language forms are used, the effectiveness of the lessons is evaluated by the manner in which this material is

put into common practice in relation to the entire curriculum throughout the school day.

6. The teaching of the mechanics of writing and of accepted written forms must be kept on an individual level due to the element of intelligence and experiential background which plays a large part in each child's readiness.

7. Purposes for the use of writing mechanics and written forms must be apparent at all times. With all the normal experiences which arise out of children's daily needs, there is rarely any justifiable reason to teach mechanics and written forms in isolation from other work. The teaching of handwriting mechanics and written forms may grow out of the child's needs to write letters, to create books, to send invitations, to write social studies reports, to write book reviews and articles for the school newspaper. Once a purpose is established, meaningful teaching and meaningful learning can take place.

8. The author has stated previously that there are certain social levels of language rather than the "right" or "wrong" usage. This means that teachers within the same cities but in different schools may be following different language or grammar programs for that which is acceptable language usage in one school may not be in another. Reference to the word "correct" in this chapter means what is correct for the school or culture. This is not to say that standard English is not promoted under these circumstances. It does mean that standard English forms are not recognized as the only means of communication, but rather as an alternate way.

Grammar

Modern linguists define grammar as the study of the structures of English speech, the language as it operates: the syntax. In expanding this definition some writers[2] note that grammar is a study of the way a language works encompassing morphology (meaningful forms), syntax (sentence structure) and phonology (sounds).

In studying the structure of English speech clarification has been made in order to isolate that which is classified as grammar and that which is classified as "word usage." Misconceptions about grammar have been identified and discussed. In some instances, linguists have found it simpler to identify that which *is not* grammar rather than that which is.

2. Metropolitan School Study Council, *Structural Linguistics: An Introduction for Teachers and Administrators* (New York: Teacher's College, 1961), p. 2.

Grammar is not usage. It is not that which we have labeled "good English" in the past. Concepts of correctness or incorrectness in language pertain to usage. Consequently, grammar is not "parts of speech." Nor is it the mechanics of composition (punctuation, capitalization, etc.).[3]

Modern grammar based on structural linguistics and generative grammar emphasizes learning about grammar by engaging in the work of the linguist; examining the language itself. The student can discover word classes, sentence patterns and methods of expanding them.

Linguists have invented many labels and many classifications for "grammar" for the English language. These include traditional grammar, historical grammar, structural and generative or transformational grammar.[4]

Types of Grammar

"Traditional" grammar, according to the linguists is an inaccurate representation of English sentence structure. This is the label given to the type of teaching and learning of the old school. The rules for "proper" and "improper" grammar were based on the rules of Latin.

Linguists have concluded that the teaching of traditional grammar or formal grammar as we used to call it has had a negligible (and even harmful) effect on the improvement of writing.

Historical grammar deals with the origins of English words, the development of the languages and changes in spelling and pronunciation.

Structural grammar is a descriptive grammar which separates the structure of language from its meaning, or a study of syntax from semantics. Studies of structural grammar led to new concepts such as phonemes (the sounds of English), morphemes (the meaningful units of language), and phrase structure. The scholars of structural grammar devised a new system of classifying the words in a language—on syntax rather than meaning.

The structuralists discovered that all nouns are distinctive from other words in that a noun can be made plural and possessive. This is a property unique to nouns.

Generative grammar or *transformational grammar* extends the concepts of structural grammar to include semantics of language. In the story of Denny, the Dinosaur an illustration is given of the process of structural grammar development. The teacher helped the children

3. Iris Tiedt and Sidney W. Tiedt, *Contemporary English in the Elementary School* (Englewood Cliffs, New Jersey: Prentice-Hall, Inc., 1967), p. 21.
4. Owen Thomas, "Grammatic Content," *English Journal* (May 1963) Reprinted in *Linguistics in the Classroom* (Champaign, Illinois: National Council of the Teachers of English), p. 6.

identify a core sentence: Dinosaurs eat. This is a simple declarative sentence with no elaboration. Then Miss Ricker expanded the children's concepts by supplying rules (through questions) which transformed the core sentence into such sentences as: Giant dinosaurs eat, The enormous dinosaurs eat greedily, etc. (see page 445). The teacher could then proceed to lead the children to identify *obligatory* and *optional* transformations. An obligatory transformation is agreement between a subject and a verb such as: Dinosaurs eat (not eats). An optional transformation is an elaboration of the core sentence such as: The enormous old dinosaur eats greedily all day long.

Generative grammar has developed very exact rules for transforming sentences and these rules are usually stated in a formula.

New concepts of grammar as designed by the linguists offer much promise for constructive changes in the teaching of written language. Because of the newness of the entire field of linguistics, many schools still function under the old concepts of formal grammar. Tiedt and Tiedt[5] express the problem as follows:

> It will be some time before these definitions are assimilated by the teaching profession and even longer until the public understands, for example, that there is a distinction between grammar and usage. When critics of education cry, therefore, for a return to the teaching of grammar so that our young people will gain skill in composition, we can be certain that these representatives of the public really want the classroom teacher to stress the teaching of "correct usage."

Because children come to school *speaking* fluently and using all forms of words and clusters of words, the raw material with which to teach grammar is in the minds and mouths of the children.

Tiedt and Tiedt state that a wise approach to the study of grammar is to impress the student with his own knowledge of grammar rather than to stress the esoteric, difficult nature of the study on which the class is embarking.[6]

Rather than teaching for "correct" or "incorrect" grammar, linguists recommend that we teach the concept of varied levels of usage. One level of varied usage is standard English, another might be a dialect, another is slang.

About the only logical purpose for examining the structure of English sentences and experimenting with methods of expansion is to foster the student's ability to generate (or create) sentences of his own which are meaningful to him and help him to say well that which he wants to say. Exploration of sentence structure should help students develop their own style of writing.

5. Tiedt and Tiedt, ibid, p. 22.
6. Tiedt and Tiedt, ibid, p. 28.

Word Classifications

Structural linguists suggest a new classification for words. Of the eight parts of speech or form classes identified by traditional grammar, structural linguists maintain seven as still useful and identify other function words which appear in English sentences. The first classes: noun, verb, adjective, determiner, intensifier, and adverb are open classes. Open classes are those to which an indefinite number of words can be added. The other classes are called *function* or *structure* words: prepositions, conjunctions, subordinators, auxiliary words, and pronouns.

These classifications are defined as follows:

Noun: A noun is a word that can be made plural or possessive and may follow the words *the, a,* or *an.*

Verb: A verb is a word that can be changed from past to present and usually (except for forms of *to be*) adds *s* when patterned after *it, she, he.* The morpheme *ing* may be added to a verb.

Adjective: An adjective patterns with the word *very,* and the adjective can follow a linking verb.

In the terms of the modern linguist, some words formerly treated as adjectives are identified as *determiners.* They signal that a noun follows. Included in this class are *the, a, an, every, each, this, that, these, those, my, one, two, three, four, most, more, either, neither, our, your, their, his, her, its, no, both, some, much, all, any, several, few.*

Intensifiers pattern with adjectives and adverbs and include such words as *very, somewhat, rather, quite.*

Prepositions signal that a noun follows, usually a prepositional phrase which serves an adjective or adverb function. Common prepositions include *about, above, across, in, into, up, off,* and the like.

Conjunctions are linking words which join equal words or groups of words (*and, but, for, either-or, neither-nor, not only-but also, yet*).

Subordinators are linking words that join subordinate subject-predicate word groups (classes) with independent subject-predicate word groups (classes). Included are *who, when, until, unless, that, since, if, what, which,* and others.

Auxiliaries signal that a verb follows. Some auxiliaries may also serve as independent verbs, and only two (*be, have*) pattern with the past form of verbs.

Pronouns do not pattern with determiners, but they substitute for nouns or proper nouns.

One of the most effective ways to introduce children to these parts of speech is to use a creative approach where students make discoveries for themselves.

Ideas for Teaching

1. To build a speaking vocabulary in referring to word classification, Mrs. Felshaw gave the children many experiences with nouns, verbs, intensifiers, pronouns, etc., from which the children arrived at definitions. The names for classes of speech were printed on long strips of tag board with the definitions after them. The names were cut apart from the definitions with an unusual cut of the scissors. Not only did the children have fun matching the definitions with the names, but any student who did not remember the definition could match the cut in the tag board much like putting a puzzle together.

2. *Word Classification Game:* Give pupils cards that have a noun, verb, adjective, etc., on them. All pupils who have cards that can make a plural or a possessive exchange seats. All pupils who have cards that express action and can be changed from past to present change places. All pupils who have cards that pattern with the word *very* may change places, etc. If one seat is removed, one child will be left standing each time and he may call for the next exchange.

3. *Prepositions:* A game: Place a box on a table. Put an object in, under, beside, below, above, or on the box. List the words which describe where the object is and label them as prepositions. Show that they signal that a noun follows and a prepositional phrase.

One day in Miss Stone's sixth grade, the children painted prepositions for art. Some beautiful abstractions resulted when children painted their ideas of: across, under, and around.

4. *Consequences:* Equipment: A long slip of paper and a pencil for each player. The leader holds the following list of descriptions:

1. An *adjective* to describe a man
2. A man's name (proper noun)
3. An *adjective* to describe a girl
4. A girl's name (proper noun)
5. Where they met (prepositional phrase)
6. What he wore (noun)
7. What she wore (noun)
8. What he said (quotation)
9. What she said (quotation)
10. What the world said (quotation)
11. The consequence (sentence)

Each player writes the first statement at the top of his slip, then folds the slip down and passes it to the right. The second statement is written beneath the first, folded down, and passed on. When the list is completed, each slip is passed once more, and the players all read the complete stories they hold.

5. *Adjectives and Adverbs:* Take small, short sentences lacking in descriptive words and have the children build them into longer, more exciting sentences.

Miss Aaron's fourth grade class changed a sentence as follows:

The birthday cake sat on the table.

to

The snowy, white, delectable, three-layer birthday cake sat proudly on the gaily decorated party table.

6. *Adjectives:*

a. Mr. Johns placed pictures from magazines on his bulletin board, below which he placed a clean sheet of paper. Children were encouraged to write words that described the pictures.

b. List nouns on the board such as *bird*, *house*, *rocket*, *astronaut*, and *space ship*. Have the class list, in front of each word, all the describing words they can think of.

c. Print phrases on strips of cardboard, leaving out the describing words. Have the children write words that might be used in the blank spaces. Show how one word properly placed may change the whole meaning of the phrase.

Mr. Ellis used this phrase in his class:

the ______ smell of smoke

For the blank space, the children listed such words as:

suffocating
pungent
horrid
terrifying
awful
frightening
tantalizing
clean
stuffy

The children discussed the fact that the use of each of these words suggested a whole new story to them.

d. For excellent examples of descriptive word building, refer to the account of "Adventures in Listening," Chapter 5, "Adventures in Oral Expression," Chapter 6, and "Adventures in Creative Writing," Chapter 8.

e. Writing cinquains and haiku are excellent devices for developing describing words. (See p. 341 and p. 340.)

7. *Nouns:* Singular and plural nouns are generally introduced in the intermediate grades. In most cases these are spoken skills, but the exceptions to the general rule are written skills. The exceptions require a memorization of the visual image. After discovering the general rule by

studying nouns which follow it, a chart of the exceptions should be made and kept in the classroom in a place where children may go to it for easy reference. Children will have fun finding exceptional plurals and adding them to the chart.

8. *Proper and Common Nouns:* One child thinks of a common noun that can be described specifically. This child calls out his noun and then asks another child to give an appropriate proper noun to go with this. If the child succeeds, he may then give the next common noun and call upon another, etc.; e.g., first child says "school," next, "Roberts Street"; "city," "Detroit"; etc.

9. *Verbs:* Have the child perform an action and the rest of the children guess or write the verb.

A game for verbs: The players are divided into two groups, one of which leaves the room. The remaining group selects some verb (such as *sing*), to be guessed by the other group. The group outside is then told a word that rhymes with the chosen word (such as *spring*), whereupon they decide on a word which they think might be the right one, enter the room, and act it out without speaking a single word. If the inside group sees that the correct word has been guessed, they clap. When the word has been correctly guessed, the sides change places.

One child does something to show action, as he might walk to the drinking fountain. Other children think what action word was represented. Stick figures are made to show the action carried out, and a sentence is used with and without modifiers (adverbs) to tell how, when, or where the action was displayed.

10. *Parts of Speech Review:* Mrs. Osborne read the book *I Love My Anteater With an A* to the children and they made several sentence commentaries on various animals. All nouns, verbs, and descriptive words were to begin with the same letter (any letter a child chose). Dictionary usage was encouraged and done with zest. Children enjoyed sharing each other's commentaries, especially when they went like this one:

> "I love my great giraffe with a grin.
> She goes to Geneva with a generous gazelle.
> She is gone on gelatin and garlic."

11. There are many plays which the teacher might find advantageous to demonstrate the usage of classified words, especially when the play is used as a basis for discussion about sentence structure. One favorite is "An Adventure On the Planet Grammar" by Kaye M. Howard.

12. Children will enjoy poems which poke fun at grammar such as the following:

The grammar has a rule absurd
Which I would call an outgrown myth.
A preposition is a word
You musn't end a sentence with.

—D. Praley

Certain films help with the understanding of the parts of speech. Some such films are:

"Do Words Ever Fool You?"
(11 minutes—bw—Coronet)
"Grammar: Verbs and Ways We Use Them"
(11 minutes—bs—Young America Films)

13. *Diagramobile:* A study of sentence structure can be dramatized through the use of a diagramobile, which is made from wires or sticks suspended from the ceiling by thread. The subject and the predicate are pasted on cards and form the main crossbar of the diagramobile. From the subject are hung such modifiers as the articles, adjectives, and modifying phrases. Similarly, adverbs and phrases are suspended from the predicate. The more complex the sentence, the more fascinating is the mobile. Added color gives it additional interest—adjectives in red, adverbs in blue, etc. The structure of the mobile appeals to the visual image and helps children remember the proper placement of the parts of speech.

Word Usage

Objective II on page 92 states that each child must acquire necessary communication skills so he may express himself effectively in all media. Three of the skills mentioned in the subheadings which follow are: To learn correct word usage as a social courtesy, to use capitalization and punctuation as a social courtesy, and to use word forms correctly.

Correct word usage carries double meaning here. It means he learns how to communicate freely in the environment where he finds himself. Therefore, he will be taught the dialects and the various levels of usage he finds around him as well as standard English (one level of usage) which will serve him in certain situations much as slang serves him in other situations.

Word usage differs from *grammar* in that in studying word usage we explore the choice we make in using words: the appropriateness of language in context. The adventure described at the opening of this chapter was an exercise in word usage rather than grammar.

One of the reasons for studying the usage of language is to identify the words which communicate as well as the structures in which they appear.

Inasmuch as effective communication is our goal in teaching word usage, many changes have been suggested in recent years to encourage the communication process.

As a result of his work, Pooley[7] recommends that we forget a number of specific items of usage which were formerly taught:

1. Distinctions between shall and will
2. Any reference to the split infinitive
3. Elimination of *like* as a conjunction
4. Objection to the phrase "different than"
5. Objection to "He is one of those boys who *is*"
6. Objection to "the reason . . . is because . . ."
7. Objection to *myself* as a polite substitution for *I*
8. Insistence on the possessive case standing before a gerund

The material which follows has been selected because the children in these classes were motivated to work at improving their own word usage in whatever context they were working.

Primary Grades

The mistakes that children make in word usage center around a few common errors. Teaching directed toward these few errors will remove the necessity of much boring practice.

It is unlikely that every child needs the same instruction in English usage, and the risk of confusing children who already know grammatical structures and correct usage can be diminished if as much individual instruction as possible is given. An evaluation of all written work can take place, and the teacher, with the child, can record his difficulties and mistakes on a 5 × 8 inch card. During the oral expression period in the morning, she may jot down additional notes which show where the child needs help. Children should have access to these cards, so that they can work out their problems with their teachers.

To supplement this individual instruction, much group work can be geared to improving language expression. Many teachers now use a tape recorder and permit children to hear themselves and evaluate their own speech. This is an effective way of letting children hear how they sound.

7. Robert C. Pooley, "Dare Schools Set a Standard in Usage?" *The English Journal* (March 1960), p. 180.

This device can also provide opportunity for critical evaluation among a group with speech defects.

Use of the tape recorder affords the teacher the opportunity to make the distinction between those errors which need to be corrected at the oral level and those which may be corrected at the written level. The teacher quickly learns to use texts for reference when children are able to read them.

Some Ideas: Word Books

1. Some books are written with words which are purposely confusing to make the plot more interesting. These books focus the attention of the children on use of different forms. Some of them are:

Which Witch Is Which by Robert Lawson
Ounce, Dice, Trice by Alistair Reid
Way Beyond Zebra by Dr. Suess
Sparkle and Spin: A Book About Words by Ann and Paul Rand
The First Book of Words: Their Family Histories by Samuel and Beryl Epstein

2. Work out a "proofreading poster" with the children and keep it on display where they may use it for reference.

3. Some books can be used skillfully in teaching word usage. Two such books:

Grammar Can Be Fun by Robert Lawson and Monroe Leaf
Easy in English by Mauree Appelgate

4. Antonyms: Find pictures of opposites (boy-girl) and paste them at the top of a 12 × 18 inch sheet of drawing paper. When children think of a pair of words or find them in reading, they may go and write their words on the sheet.

5. Synonym Golf: Compile a list of eighteen words representing the eighteen holes of golf. Try to find a synonym for each word. The number of letters in the synonym chosen represents your score for the word. Score eight for a word for which you can find no synonym. The lowest score wins.

6. Teakettle: For this game use words that sound alike but have different meanings, such as "write" and "right." One player leaves the room and the rest decide on a double-meaning word. When the player returns, everyone has a chance to use a sentence with the chosen word. But instead of saying that particular word, you substitute "teakettle." For example, "I will teakettle a letter with my teakettle hand."

Word Usage: Intermediate Grades

The point has been made that many problems in written expression arise from the errors that appear in oral speech. An anlysis of some of these errors will show that many of them are due to the patterns of speech mimicked by the child during his growing up. Some are the regional or illiterate level of folksy talk. Others are the peculiar idiosyncrasies of the home or community. For the child, this language communicates as well as the more acceptable forms. Emphasis should not be put on correctness of speech to the degree that the child withdraws from using speech fluently. Rather, he should learn the more acceptable forms of speech just as he should learn two languages, and he will receive help in learning where to apply these acceptable forms.

Certain speech patterns can be altered only at certain age levels as the child matures, and through conditioned responses. Children respond well to suggestions that are made quietly, politely, and with due respect for their feelings. If embarrassment and resentment become associated with suggestion, the value of the instruction is greatly reduced. A child should not be interrupted when he is speaking, and corrections or suggestions for alterations in his speech patterns should be made privately or individually.

Many children become aware of their speech deficiencies when they are allowed to speak on a tape and then to analyze their own voices and speech patterns. One research study showed that significant healthy gains were made in changing speech patterns through the use of the tape recorder. Changes in the writing forms were significantly changed when the speech pattern changed.

Hints for Teaching Word Usage

1. Projection: Using real life experiences. Have children build word concepts by projecting backwards into their own life experiences to recall instances that describe the word concept being developed. For instance, take the word "scary."

There are many episodes in childhood which children remember with quaking knees and pounding hearts. These are the times when they felt fear, *real fear*. Adults feel fright, but to children frightening experiences are called "*SCARY*."

One teacher had the children list experiences which to them were real *scary*.

Their list looked like this:

Times that Were Real SCARY

a. Getting on the school bus the first day of kindergarten.

b. Hearing children crying in the doctor's office before it was *my* turn to go in.
c. Reading about pirates, ghosts, and witches.
d. Seeing a big WARNING sign and not being able to read the rest of the words.
e. Waiting to jump out and say "Boo" to someone and finding that person was waiting to say "Boo" to me.
f. Getting a big kiss from Aunt Bertha in front of my friends.
g. Socking my brother in the back and finding out it wasn't my brother!
h. Doing something you shouldn't be doing like stealing apples from Mr. Brown's tree.
i. Thinking my loose tooth will fall out before I can show someone how loose it is.
j. Holding on to someone's hand that isn't your mother's when you thought it was.
k. Stepping down from something that is higher than you thought it was.
m. Reaching under your bed for your shoes and grabbing something—you don't know what.
n. Stepping on something squishy when you're in your bare feet.
o. Looking in a mirror while you're having a haircut and they're cutting it too short.
p. Having to talk to strange grown-ups.

Children developed other charts of words such as "what is beautiful?" "what is ugly?" and "what is exciting?"

After the lists were completed, the children selected any instance they wished and wrote stories or poems about it.

2. Keep a file of folders and label the tabs with the common mistakes in written word usage, punctuation, and capitalization. In the folders, place sheets torn from workbooks which give help or drill with these problems. Such a file helps develop individualized instruction, because a teacher may explain a common error to a child and afford him practice by sending him to the file to select an appropriate work sheet.

3. Have each individual keep a folder of his own word usage errors. Dittoed sheets listing common errors can be clipped inside the folder. Each child uses his corrected papers to diagnose his mistakes and mark the check sheets.

4. Collect cartoons which help children understand grammar usage or the mechanics of writing.

5. Attention can often be focused on the good use of writing forms, writing mechanics, and word usage by collecting poor samples or mistakes made in newspapers, on television or radio, in magazines and

school papers. Make a bulletin board collection of these poor samples of communication. Call it "Boo-Boos" or "Bloopers." Example:

I am glad to report that my husband who was reported missing is now dead.

6. Focus on effective word usage and the importance of word arrangement can often be demonstrated by reading stories and jokes collected from newspapers, television, and magazines which emphasize misunderstandings due to improper use of words. Many current jokebooks will provide the teacher with such material, such as: Art Linkletter's *Kids Say the Darndest Things*, and Bennett Cerf's *The Life of the Party*, etc. The teacher will need to select carefully those which children will understand. Children will enjoy collecting these excerpts, too.

7. By collecting examples of "levels of usage," help pupils to realize that words can be assembled in many ways and that many levels of usage are possible.

Formal *Teacher*	*Informal* *Mother*	*Slang* *Child*
Do you comprehend my explanation?	Do you understand me?	Dig me?
He is a very annoying child.	He irritates me.	He bugs me.

Be sure to discuss the place where each of these expressions may be acceptably used.

8. Children may set up their own editing committees. (See page 382.)

9. Idioms: Collecting idioms can be a great deal of fun and can lead to an excellent understanding of language and structure.

One day in Mr. Dale's room, Joseph asked what his older brother meant when he said, "Everyone at the party was 'swinging.'" Mr. Dale used this as an opportunity to explain idioms to the children. They began a collection of idioms. The children found it was fun to dramatize these idioms and allow the rest of the class to guess which one they were doing.

It was not long before Joe had the idea that the class should write a play using idioms, and that they should act it out in pantomime with a narrator telling the story.

Since the class was studying Spain at the time, "A Spanish Romance" resulted. This turned out to be a very clever and creative production. A sample from the script follows:

A Spanish Romance

The stage was set simply with a few signs pinned on the rear wall. One said "stairs," one read "door." At the front of the stage, two girls stood holding hands. Each had a sign pinned on her which read "curtain." To one side of the stage sat a boy in a chair. On him was pinned the word "son." A girl stood to the back of the stage holding an old phonograph record on which was printed the word "day.' Another boy labeled "night" sat on the opposite side of the stage. A table of assorted props stood at back stage center.

The announcer entered and read the following script. The play was done completely in pantomime with exaggerated gestures. I have italicized the idioms and placed the action in parentheses so that the reader will better visualize the action.

Narrator: Our little play takes place in the hacienda of Don Joseph in Spain. *The curtains part.* (The two girls labeled "curtain" separate and walk to opposite sides of the stage, waving goodbye to each other)

The sun rises. (The boy labeled "son" stands up) *Day breaks.* (The girl with the record smashes it over the table)

In the distance we hear the sound of horses hoofs. (One boy clomps nut shells on the floor offstage) It is Don Juan, the young lover, coming to see his love. Senorita Rosita. He is a *real swinger.* (Don Juan enters swinging from a rope fastened overhead)

"Where is my beloved!" he asks, "Today is the day we will elope. All night long I have waited while the *hours pass.*" (A group of children, each with a sign reading "hour" pass one by one in front of him across the stage) "Now, today, I have *met my destiny!*" (A boy labeled DESTINY enters. He crosses stage, they shake hands like two people meeting each other) "Hark, I think I hear my beloved coming now!" (Senorita Rosita enters) "Ah, look at her. She is *pretty as a picture.*" (Senorita Rosita picks up a frame from the table and frames her face in it, smiling sweetly) "Come, my love, we *must fly.*" (They both pin on wings and flap their arms) "But wait, what do I hear? Can it be your father, Don Joseph? Has he heard of our plan?"

"Go," said Senorita Rosita, "I shall handle him." So Don Juan *made a B-Line* for the door. (Don Juan takes an envelope out of his pocket, opens it, and takes out a little pack of letter B's cut from cardboard which he proceeds to lay in a line to the sign marked "door." He exits)

Indeed, Don Joseph had heard of the plot of his daughter and Don Juan to escape. He came *Tearing down the stairs.* (Don Joseph enters angrily. He goes to the sign "stairs" on the rear curtain of the stage, rips it down, tears it up, and stamps on it.)

"What is this, what is this?" he cries, "what do I hear? Is it true Rosita? Is that scoundrel here after I forbade him from *setting foot on my property?*" (At the side of the stage, Don Juan holds up a map to the audience labeled PONDEROSA, lays it on the floor, and stamps on it)

"Father," said Rosita, "I will no longer try *to pull the wool over your eyes.*" (She goes to him, reaches under his sombrero, and pulls a piece of sheepskin down over his forehead) "It is true, Don Juan is here and what is more I love him. Today we plan to run away to be married." Don Joseph was enraged. He *ground his teeth* in anger. (Don Joseph goes to the table on which there is a meat grinder. He spits his teeth—chalk—into his hand, puts them into the meat grinder, and grinds them up)

* * *

The play continues to a happy ending with *the sun setting, night falling*, and the *curtains coming together*. Children loved doing this play. The list of idioms grew and grew, and many, many plays and stories came as a result of their fun.

10. Children enjoy creative crossword puzzles. Crossword puzzles are excellent for reviewing definitions. A new twist can be added by suggesting that children make crossword squares in the shapes of an object unique to a particular holiday or season, using the name of the particular holiday as the core of the puzzle as in the crossword puzzle in Figure 93 designed by a fifth grader for Christmas.

Across

2. Pronoun for girl
3. Cake frosting
4. A present
5. Street or Saint (abbr.)
6. By
7. Songs sung at Christmas time
8. Things that ring
9. Father Christmas

Down

1. The best day of the year
10. As far as

Figure 93 *A simple Christmas tree crossword puzzle.*

11. Encourage children to write poems about word usage and the use of words such as the one below:

Words

Sentences, Paragraphs, Novels,
 In one way they're all the same.
They all contain many words,
 From which our language came.

Many people use them.
 Whether funny, harsh or fine.
Able leaders must use them
 To make the people fall in line.

All countries in the world
 Change words to the way they think,
It's very wonderful to realize
 Words make the nation's link.

—Sue O'Shaughnessy
Grade 6

The Mechanics of Composition

Capitalization and Punctuation: Primary Grades

1. An understanding of a need for punctuation may be established by having the teacher read a short story to the children. The story is then written on the board, and the teacher asks the children what they might do to it to make sure a stranger might read it with the intended meaning. Is there some possible way to mark the story so that anyone reading it would get an idea about how it was to be read?

In Miss Peters' third grade class the children knew about periods, so they immediately suggested that periods and capital letters be used to break the story into sentences. One child, who did not know about exclamation points, suggested that they write the loud, excited words with big (capital) letters. Another child suggested that they draw a line under the quotations to show exactly what the speaker said. Because the pitch of the voice goes up with a question mark, one of the children suggested that the word at the end of a question leave the line and go up. A part of their story looked like this:

STOP STOP said the policeman. Where do you think you are going.
But John did not stop. He ran into the store and slammed the door.
HELP he cried.

Miss Peters told the children she thought people would get the idea very well from the way they had marked the story. "Wouldn't it be easier to read," she asked, "if there was a way to mark it that everyone knew about that would tell them how to read it?" The children agreed, so Miss Peters had them get their story books and discover the way in which authors wrote stories so they could be read properly. The children could see the need for a common system of punctuation and applied the punctuation marks to their own story.

2. Miss Weins's second grade wrote a punctuation play. The children cut a large question mark, exclamation point, comma, and period from red poster board. One person was chosen to carry each punctuation mark. There were Mother Question Mark, Father Period, Brother Exclamation Point, and Sister Comma. The object of the play was that each character had to speak in sentences which required his own particular form of punctuation. Here is how one play began.

A Punctuation Play

Announcer: Today boys and girls, we are going to put on a little play. But, before we begin, we would like you to meet the people in the play.

Mother Question Mark: (steps forward) I am mother. You will find me at the end of a sentence. I am curious. I ask many questions. "How are you today?"

Father Period: I am father. I am a little dot and can be found at the end of a sentence too. Here are my children.

Sister Comma: I am not found at the end of a sentence, but in the middle. Sometimes you will find me in more than one place. You have met Mommy, Daddy, and now you will meet Brother.

Brother Exclamation Point: Like Mother and Daddy, I am found at the end of a sentence. Oh boy! Sometimes I get mad and sometimes I get excited!

3. Miss Adams helped her second grade become visually aware of punctuation by having each pupil make a large period on one piece of

paper and an interrogation mark on another. Pupils took turns giving statements or questions. The class responded by holding in the air the proper punctuation mark.

Later, with a slight variation in rules, other punctuation cards were used.

4. Another variation of this activity was a drill Miss Adams created for her primary class for emphasizing the punctuation mark to be used at the end of the sentence. The children drew cards on which there was a period, a comma, or an exclamation point. Then Miss Adams held up a phrase or a card (or spoke it orally) and all the children who had the proper punctuation mark for that particular sentence clapped their hands. Their response was verified by having each hold up his card to see whether he represented the proper punctuation form.

5. Children enjoy poems about punctuation. Read some to focus attention on the punctuation mark being studied. Also, encourage the children to make up their own. Following is a poem created by a first grade about a period:

> Say one idea.
> Then put a dot
> To stop your voice
> On that spot.

Capitalization and Punctuation: Intermediate Grades

Ideas to Try

1. To establish a purpose for punctuation, on the chalkboard write sentences whose meaning is completely changed when different punctuation is added. After a while children will enjoy making up their own sentences. Make a collection like this somewhere in the classroom:

Example: The teacher said the principal was not very good looking.
"The teacher," said the principal, "was not very good looking."
Example: I dont want to eat Grandma!
"I don't want to eat, Grandma!"

2. Distribute sheets of paper with confusing sentences on them, which can be clarified with the addition of punctuation. Examples:

Mary said mother take out the garbage.
"Mary," said mother, "take out the garbage."
Mary said, "Mother, take out the garbage!"
Put the candy down John.
"Put the candy down, John!"

Creating Punctuation Marks

A recent article in a well-known newspaper brought out the fact that our punctuation system was not adequate in terms of modern-day needs. The author felt, for instance, that the use of rhetorical questions called for a punctuation mark not in existence and suggests Figure 94.

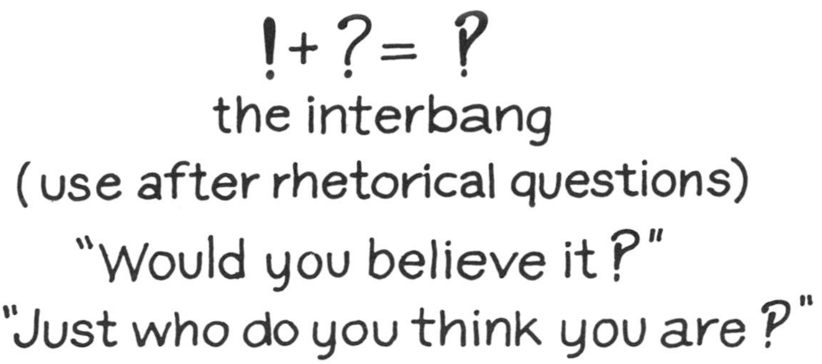

!+?= ‽

the interbang

(use after rhetorical questions)

"Would you believe it‽"

"Just who do you think you are‽"

Figure 94

He calls this the interbang.

Have children construct sentences where the interbang might be appropriately used. Better yet, encourage them to invent punctuation marks that go with sentences which do not seem to have a proper punctuation aid. For instance, what about the stacatto effect found on the Batman television show—could a punctuation mark be invented which shows a gradual build-up in sounds? Perhaps something like this—Wow—. pow=; wham≡; sock≣⁝ boom≣⁝ We could call it the flying exclamation!

Proofreading

Five or so children are chosen to be proofreaders for the written material for a day or a week. These children get name cards to wear on their backs such as Period Pete, Sentence Susie, or Capital Charley. Each child checks a set of papers for any mistakes pertaining to his name and each makes his corrections in a different colored pencil. You change jobs frequently so that each child gets a chance to do some proofreading and becomes aware of the errors made by himself as well as by others.

"Sound" Punctuation

Punctuation is a visual skill that requires concentrated thought process in its use. How much easier it would be to remember where to punctuate if we *talked* punctuation. Children will receive a great deal of pleasure in hearing punctuation in Victor Borge's famous punctuation recording. One sixth grade teacher, who could not seem to help her boys remember about punctuation marks, motivated them to writing stories with complicated punctuation when she challenged them to read the punctuation as Victor Borge reads it.

At another time this teacher asked the children to "show" the punctuation in their stories through dramatization. One group of children worked out the following patterns.

Exclamation Point: One boy stood stiffly with his hands held along his sides. Every time a place for an exclamation mark was read, he jumped straight off the floor and stamped once.

Question Mark: Another boy twisted his body and stamped.

Period: One boy stamped the floor.

Quotation open: Two girls held hands and switched their rear ends to the right.

Quotation closed: They switched back to the left.

Comma: One girl twisted the ball of her right foot on the floor and kicked.

Colon: One boy made two stamps on the floor.

Semicolon: A stamp and a comma (above).

Needless to say, the children became acutely aware of punctuation marks and enjoyed "acting" them out in their stories.

Another teacher to whom I told this story had another creative idea. She brought a box of rhythm instruments into the classroom and her students showed the punctuation marks by using certain musical instruments in proper places. For instance, a period was a clash of cymbals. Other forms worked out by the children were as follows.

Question Mark: A twist of the tambourine followed by a crash on the tambourine with the player's fist.

Exclamation Point: An up-and-down twist of the tambourine followed by a crash.

Comma: A strike on the triangle with a metal bar.

Quotation Marks: A shake of wrist bells.

Colon: Two strikes on the triangle.

Semicolon: A strike on the cymbals followed by a strike on the triangle.

Before this exercise, the children had rarely used punctuation in their stories—particularly not quotation marks and semicolons. However, Miss Harris' remotivation changed all that—their stories began to include pages of conversation. The musical punctuation focused attention on punctuation marks. And even though the technique seems somewhat a violation of what has been said regarding the placement of oral and written skills, it really is not. The "sound" part, in this instance, re-enforces the visual image—it does not substitute for it. Children must know the punctuation well and have a fixed image in their minds before they can "play" it.

Dramatized Punctuation

One group of children in a middle school decided they would review basic punctuation marks for other children in the lower grade class who were still having punctuation problems. They created a punctuation play and went from room to room to present it. Their props consisted of punctuation marks which they had cut out of cardboard and carried. Here is a short excerpt from the play.

Cast

Narrator
The Period
The Comma
The Exclamation Mark
The Question Mark
The Dash
The Colon
The Semicolon
The Quotation Mark

Narrator:

Long ago in Punctuation Land
Lived a very useful band
They were helpful, as you shall see
To make reading easier for you and me.

Today one of them we'll meet
One who lives on Composition Street
"He's the end," his friends all say
He stops sentences and earns his pay.

Period:

I stop all sentences that tell
I end abbreviations well
I'm just a spot and very small
Like a tiny dot on a tiny ball.

Narrator:
And now to meet another guest
Who always tries to do his best.

Comma:
I know you've seen me here and there
I appear on pages everwhere
I separate words, phrases and clauses
And in reading, make the pauses.

Narrator:
Now here's a character who's very jumpy.
He makes your reading and writing bumpy.

Exclamation:
I have many, many dealings
With words that express strong feelings
I also tremble, jump and say
"Oh!" and "Ah!" and "Don't go away!"

Scrambled Punctuation

As the class learns the basic principles of each punctuation mark, they may be printed on strips of tag board and placed on a pocket chart before the room with the particular punctuation mark under study cut from large construction paper and placed over the pocket chart. After a while there will be many principles printed on strips of oaktag for many kinds of punctuation marks. To test the children's knowledge of the principles, scramble them. Place one of the punctuation mark pictures above the pocket chart and have the children place under it all those rules and principles which apply to its use.

Specific Punctuation Marks

1. *Quotation Marks:* Mr. Casey wanted to show his seven year olds the difference between direct and indirect quotations. The thought struck him that he might employ an old comic strip technique and use the little white clouds above the heads of the characters to show direct quotations. Consequently, he drew various characters engaged in interesting activities on transparencies. In each picture he left the cloud above the character's head empty so that any child might suggest what the characters in the pictures were saying.

It was but a step to make the transition from the picture to the paper, showing that without the picture and the cloud, the author must have some way to designate the speaker, and that there is a definite difference in showing *exactly* what one character says in contrast to telling about it, such as the following:

Peanuts said, "Good grief, Charlie Brown, you're a day late. The ball game was yesterday!" and Peanuts told Charlie Brown that he was late and the ball game was yesterday.

* * * *

On a flannel board, write sentences needing quotation marks (use strips of construction paper). Make the necessary marks out of colored paper. Use the strips for initial instruction: games, independent work, or drill.

Have the children write stories restricted to dialogue. One way to start is to write up imaginary telephone calls, the morning greetings, requests to go to a movie or to buy a coveted toy. Soon children will be writing creative dialogue. Here is a dialogue written by a fifth grader.

Just Fine

"Hello, John, how are you?"
"Why, hello Harry, I'm fine. And you?"
"I'm fine, too, John. How's your family?"
"Just fine, Harry, just fine. And yours?"
"Oh, they're fine, John. Just fine. Say what's that policeman doing by my car—oh no, he can't be—he can't be. Officer, what are you putting on my car?"
"Just a fine, sir. Just a fine."

Set up a press conference to help children distinguish between direct and indirect quotations. Let children take turns acting as President, Vice-President, or other figures in the news, while others assume the role of reporters for newspapers and news services.

Holding unrehearsed conferences, the "reporters" take careful and accurate notes. When the study is in this framework, it doesn't take long for boys and girls to learn the difference between the gist of a statement and the statement itself. Combine the role playing with finding examples of official statements and reports about the statement that appear in the daily papers.

Hyphens: When it is time to teach children about dividing words at the ends of lines, turn to a daily newspaper. Newspaper columns are narrow and contain many hyphenated words. Have the children look for these words. Cut out the columns, circle the hyphens with red crayon, and paste them on a chart or place them on a bulletin board. Children may analyze the hyphens and come up with generalizations about hyphenated words, or they may use this experience as a practice period after learning the basic principles about hyphens.

Apostrophes: Apostrophes generally designate the omission of a letter in a word to shorten it, or a possessive. Noticing the missing letter and the substitution of the apostrophe, or noting the apostrophe used as a possessive, is a skill requiring refined visual perception. There are many ways in which teachers can help children focus their vision on the particular part of the word where the apostrophe is used.

1. To designate an omission: Introduce the concept by using the children's natural speech patterns. Write down on the chalkboard those expressions you have heard during the day which contain shortened words with apostrophes.
2. Miss Jones cut several large red apostrophes from construction paper and fastened them to the chalkboard with a curl of masking tape. Children then placed these in their proper places in phrases written on the board. The large red apostrophes could be seen from any place in the room. Miss Jones wrote some phrases on the board each morning and chose some children to place the apostrophes. This became an independent activity which could be done by one or two children and could be checked by Miss Jones from any place in the room.
3. Colored chalk also helps accomplish the objective of establishing the image of the apostrophe in the child's mind.
4. Miss Wagner invented the simple device in Figure 95 which shows how, when a letter is omitted, an apostrophe must take its place.

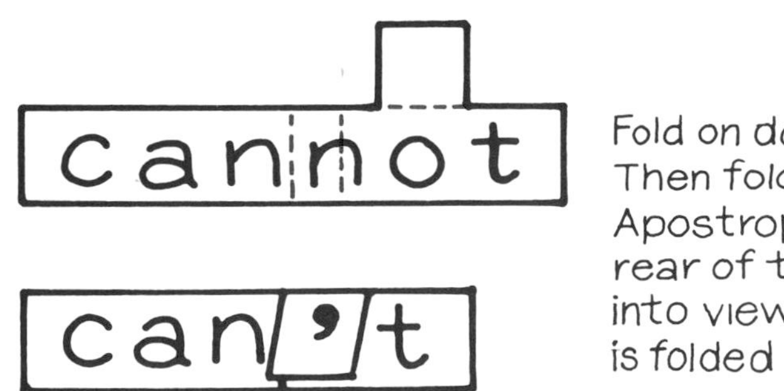

Figure 95 *An apostrophe shows an omission.*

5. Colored felt pens on paper help the children become aware of the apostrophe.
6. A chart on the use of the apostrophe at the front of the room, where apostrophes are put in color, will serve as a good reference for children.
7. On a strip of cardboard, print words that can be combined by the use of the apostrophe. Cut smaller strips of cardboard just large enough to cover the letter that can be omitted. Fasten the strips over the letters

to be omitted with masking tape. With a felt pen, make an apostrophe to replace the letters. Now when the cardboard strip is flipped back, the words show. When flipped over the cardboard, it becomes a contraction.

8. For possessives: The construction paper apostrophes work well here also. The colored chalk and colored felt pens mentioned above will help children visualize apostrophes used in the possessive.

Print phrases on strips of cardboard such as in Figure 96.

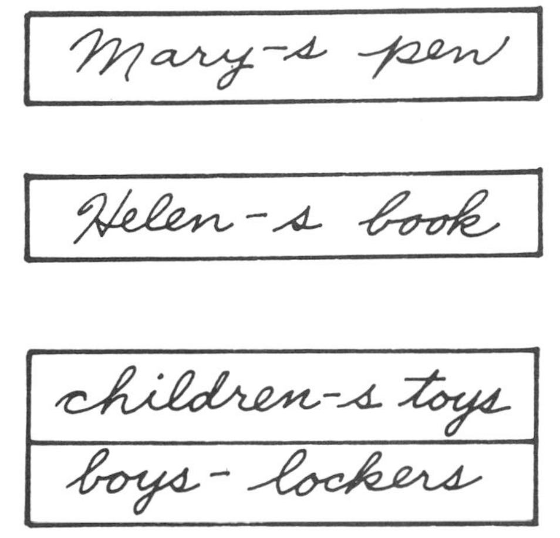

Figure 96 *Visualizing apostrophe possessives.*

Cut a slit in the cardboard where an apostrophe is to be placed. On smaller cardboards make many small apostrophes which fit in the slits. Children can tell where they think the apostrophe belongs and then check by putting it in the slit. This is a "spoonfeeding" technique which makes it almost impossible for a child to get an incorrect visual impression when he is learning about apostrophes. These cards can be set in a pocket chart before the class for individual use.

Make cards of individual nouns and possessive nouns such as in Figure 97.

Cut the letter "s" from the possessive nouns. Make several apostrophes to fit before or after the letter "s." Paste pieces of flannel on all the pieces and play games with them by having the children build singular and plural possessives on the flannel board.

After discovering and using the technique suggested above for checking possessives, children can be asked which words from lists created by themselves can be made possessives. Can these words also be made

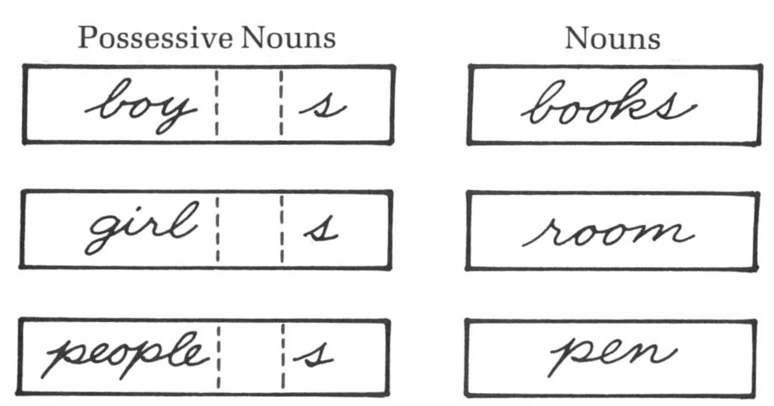

Figure 97 *Possessives, singular and plural.*

plural? The children have then discovered which words in their lists are nouns.

9. One class wrote a letter to Santa in keeping with the season and utilized as many contractions as they could think of. To help develop the concept, the teacher initiated an Apostrophe Scrabble Game. Elbow macaroni was used as an apostrophe. Children had to write as many contractions as they could think of in a ten-minute period. All the letters in the scrabbled words were counted for a score, plus the numbers of macaroni pieces used as apostrophes.

Encourage children to keep individual folders of errors or of papers that have been edited. Date the papers and at least once a month provide a period in which children examine the papers in the folders to analyze their own progress. Which mistakes are they still making and which have they eliminated?

Forms of Written Expression

Sentence Structure: Primary Grades

The first language form to which a child is exposed in writing is generally the simple sentence. Prerequisite to the writing of sentences comes the speaking or telling of stories, poems, and daily events in sentence form. Oral expression periods, such as the Show-and-Tell period described on page 171, help the children to speak using one idea or a related group of ideas in sentences.

As soon as the child is capable of using simple sentences, the teacher takes advantage of this skill and forms first reading experience charts. The short, simple sentences with proper punctuation used on these charts help the child see the correct written form for simple sentences.

Many children attempt to copy reading charts. The teacher can make sure each child uses the correct punctuation for the sentence during these first attempts at copying.

The image of the correct form for a simple sentence is re-enforced when children begin to read in their preprimers and primers. Being exposed to correct form, children reproduce it if they are given careful guidance while making the transition from reading to writing visual images on paper.

As soon as handwriting begins, children should write for a purpose at all times. Even when they can only write a few words, they can write them in sentence form. Many recent workbooks are recognizing the necessity for putting the first words of the child in the context of simple sentences.

The teacher can capitalize very quickly on the few words the child can write by thinking of ways that he can use these few words in simple sentences. She may print a note or a letter on ditto paper for a variety of purposes for the child to take home. All the child does in this instance is to sign his name, but he is seeing sentences and is, at the same time, being introduced to the accepted, correct forms of writing. Samples:

An Invitation Form

Broad Street School
April 4, 1963

Dear Mother and Dad,
We will have a play. It is on Wednesday.
Please come to see it.

Love,
____

A Note Form

Dear Mother,
I need 60 cents for milk.

Love,
____

Sentences can also appear on planning charts, programs, get-well notes to sick classmates, greeting cards, the daily news, science experiments, and in all other written classroom experiences. Very soon children will be using these forms in their own creative writing. Many of the ideas mentioned in Chapter 10 can be used at the early primary level to invite children to write in complete sentence form.

The *question mark* is generally one of the first forms encountered by a child. Often teachers explain the use of the question mark and then use it in:

1. Writing questions on the board for children to answer.
2. Labeling lost and found articles: Am I yours?
3. Labeling science materials: What am I? What can I do?
4. Using surprise items: What is in the box?
5. Writing personal notes to the children which include questions like, "How old are you?"
6. Using questions on charts, such as: "Who are our workers?"
7. Using games: Where is the ball?

Seeing a form used correctly gives the child a correct visual image. When he begins to include questions in his stories, he will use the correct form from the beginning, because he is imitating the form to which he has been exposed.

The *exclamation point* can be introduced early in the child's reading program. Reading charts provide a logical place to introduce it. In exploring punctuation marks (see page 464), the teacher can bring the purpose of exclamation points to the attention of the children. She will find many ways of using it, such as those suggested in the section on reading.

Many first and second graders are able to use complete simple declarative, interrogative, exclamatory, and imperative sentences from the very beginning of their writing attempts, because they are *imitating* the *correct* forms used in their classroom.

Experience with compound and complex sentences is introduced in a parallel manner to the introduction of other sentence forms—in the first readers or storybooks. Once again it is important to find creative ways of keeping the correct forms of the sentences before the children. The continued use of reading charts, designed at this point to fulfill many purposes, will help to give children easy reference material and will keep correct sentence forms before them. Compound and complex sentences can appear in letters, invitations, notes, greeting cards, and on bulletin boards.

In the primary grades, no attempt is made to teach the forms or the nomenclature of sentences, as such, to children. They learn about sentences through continual use of them. Children speak in simple, compound, and complex sentences long before they come to school, so the primary teacher is concerned with helping children have the best start possible in getting their speech forms translated into correct written form.

Ideas for Developing Forms of Written Expression: Primary Grades

1. Collect magazine pictures and mount them. Use each picture for inspiration to write a statement, a question, an exclamation, or a command sentence. If children write on strips of paper, they may display their sentences by tacking them under each picture on the bulletin board.

2. Put a sentence on the board such as:

"The man walked down the road," or
"The boy drew a picture."

Give the children crayon and paper and have them draw as many versions of the sentence as they wish. The sentence is to be copied at the bottom of each drawing. The drawings are stapled together into a small book. All sorts of interpretations will come of the sentences as children translate their experiences into drawings.

3. Ask children to try their hand at writing three-sentence stories. Each story must contain a question, a statement, and an exclamation. This can be used at many grade levels.

From Miss Farrell's second grade came this story:

Run Away

Oh! Oh! Spot ran away. Did you see him go?

From Mr. Brinker's sixth grade came this story:

A Tragedy at Sea

"Help!" Help!" he cried! "Will no one save me?" "I am drowning."

4. Take a small sentence, such as "Mary went." This is a sentence, but not lively.

Add a word or words to tell "when."
Yesterday Mary went.
Add a word to tell "where."
Yesterday Mary went visiting.
Or, "John bought something." Add a word to tell "what."
John bought a pencil.

Add a color word.
John bought a yellow pencil.
Add a word to tell "where," then a word to tell "when."
John bought a yellow pencil today at the book store, etc.

Sentence Structure: Intermediate Grades

In the intermediate grades, sentence sense has been well established if the children have had a sound foundation of experience in the primary grades. A nomenclature regarding sentences should be established so that the children can make a study of sentences in relation to their own creative writing. The words "statement," "question," and "command" can be replaced with declarative, interrogative, exclamatory, and imperative. In the upper grades, such concepts as compound and complex may be used to label sentences, but this should not bė mandatory. Many children like to learn sentence labels and should be encouraged to do so, but the stress should be on the accepted usage.

Ideas for Developing Sentence Skills in the Intermediate Grades

Many of the suggestions given for developing sentence usage in the primary grades can be adapted to use in the intermediate grades, especially for groups of slow-learning children.

1. In the intermediate grades, children should be doing a great deal of creative writing. An analysis of this writing will provide the teacher with the clues to the kinds of sentence structure she needs to teach. Application of the children's learning should come in writing stories, poems, book reports, invitations, letters, puppet shows, dramatizations, roll movie scripts, television and radio scripts, character sketches, social studies reports, science reports, and scripts for shadow plays. Intermediate grade children can begin to learn the basic structure of sentences. Most intermediate grade teachers help the children identify the subject and predicate of a sentence (both the complete and single subject and predicate). Children will enjoy looking for subjects and predicates in the stories they read.

2. Many of the social courtesies of living together can be learned if each classroom teacher has a host and a hostess each week assigned to meet guests to the classroom and make introductions to the teacher and the children. In planning these introductions together, careful attention can be given to sentence structure.

3. Children can also dramatize many social courtesies connected with fifth and sixth grade classroom activities. These dramatizations may

be written and studied for sentence structure after they have been dramatized. Some such instances may be:

a. Helping boys learn how to ask girls for a dance.
b. Showing boys how to serve girls from the refreshment table at classroom parties.
c. Showing children how to introduce their parents to the teacher at the school open house or at a school play.
d. Helping children in making announcements over the school public address system.
e. Preparing for oral reports and radio and television shows.
f. Making announcements to other classrooms (cafeteria menu, coming events, etc.).

4. One film that will help children understand sentence structure is *Making Sense With Sentences* (Coronet).

5. Children can be helped in their creative writing if at times the teacher asks each child to write a paragraph without putting his name on his paper. These paragraphs are then put into an opaque projector and thrown on a screen. As the children analyze each paragraph for sentence structure, they make up a set of basic principles about sentences. This will be very easy to do if the teacher shows the paragraphs by contrasts—first one very good one and then one which is not so good. Should this be too threatening a situation to the children of some classrooms, the teacher may collect specimens from a neighboring teacher.

In Mr. Jackson's fifth grade, after such an experience, the children made this chart.

Sentences

Sentences are important. They make stories and letters interesting. Be careful about building sentences. Here are some things to remember.

a. Use different kinds of sentences to make stories interesting.
b. Try not to tie too many sentences together with "and."
c. Try not to make sentences too short. Use some connecting words like "while," "after," "if," "when," "because," "since," "when," "as."
d. Make sure each sentence is complete. It has a subject and a predicate.
e. Some authors use groups of words like sentences which are not sentences. Sometimes this makes stories more interesting.
f. Sentences are more interesting when good describing words are used.

6. Relay games are fun. Make two teams. One person goes to the board and writes a word. Each person then adds a word until a sentence is complete. The teams try to use all members. The team that uses the whole team and constructs the most sensible sentence gets a point.

7. A Sentence Hunt: The teacher can read some paragraphs from familiar stories. Children number their pages from 1 to ?, and after each paragraph the teacher pauses while the children write down the number of sentences they *heard*. This may be done with supplementary reading materials or material from a textbook so that children may check for themselves and see the sentences in print.

8. To pave the way for learning parts of speech and their use in sentences, make a large chart with four columns. Label each column—"Who Words," "Do Words," "Descriptive Words," "What Words." As the children find simple sentences, they write the appropriate part in the right column. Then discuss and check each entry with the class.

Paragraphing: Ideas

1. Mr. Kaplenoff reports the following activity carried on in his fourth grade which helped children to distinguish between a paragraph and a sentence.

He took this sentence: "He couldn't quite hang onto it." The class wrote, and then read stories using the sentence in one of the paragraphs. Although a complete thought, the sentence meaning was dependent on the context of the paragraph within the scope of the individual story.

2. One film that will help the children in learning about paragraphing is *Building Better Paragraphs* (10 minutes, Coronet).

Outlining

Outlining is largely a way of organizing and classifying a body of material to be used later as a reference for some particular purpose. The basic concepts of outlining begin when kindergarten children group things in order or by topic for any special purpose. After many experiences with organizing and classifying materials, children are ready to outline.

Samples of readiness experiences which prepare children for organizing and classifying are:

1. Putting materials back in their proper place after use in the classroom.
2. Setting up the tables in the room for the mid-morning lunch.
3. Building with blocks and other materials such as Lincoln Logs, Tinkertoys, etc.
4. Planning periods during the school day with the teacher.
5. Matching games (colors, etc.).
6. Presenting roll movies.

7. Planning and taking trips.
8. Planning and having a party.

With these diverse and varied activities as a background, the teacher may pull out many experiences that help children to classify words according to topics, which is an essential understanding in outlining.

Mrs. Henderson made a simple but attractive bulletin board for her second grade by pinning buildings made from big envelopes along a street. There was a grocery store, a gas station, a fruit market, a dairy, a filling station, and a house. The children were then given cards with a word printed on each card. They were told to slip the card into the top of the building where that particular word would be found.

Regardless of the grade level of the children, the ability to classify and organize material in this manner is essential before meaningful outlining can take place. Any teacher may begin to teach outlining with devices such as this.

In a fourth grade classroom, Mr. Eagan felt that his pupils did not have basic concepts of this sort to learn outlining, so he planned a series of experiences for the children to develop them.

Through talking with the children, he learned that some of the girls had kept their doll houses and still played with them on occasion. He also found that some of the boys had received toy forts and toy villages for Christmas gifts. He asked a few children if they could bring these toys to school. Some did. Here is how Mr. Eagan used these toys to teach outlining.

He placed the doll house at the front of the room where all the children could see it. Then he took all the furniture and placed it in a box in the middle of the room. He let Janet tell about the doll house because she had brought it to school. Then he asked the class what it was they had been talking about. He then printed the words "The Doll House" in big letters on the chalkboard.

Next he asked the children if they would name the rooms in the doll house for him. As they named the rooms, he wrote them on the board in this fashion:

The Doll House

I. Rooms in a doll house

A. Living Room	C. Kitchen
1.	1.
2.	2.
3.	3.
4.	4.
5.	5.

B. Master Bedroom	D. Attic
1.	1.
2.	2.
3.	3.
4.	4.
5.	5.

Then Mr. Eagan divided the class into eight groups. Each group was assigned to a room in the doll house. A chairman was to go to the box in the middle of the room and bring back all the furniture that belonged to the room to which his committee was assigned.

After this was done, Mr. Eagan asked one child from each group to go to the chalkboard and list under his topic all the furniture found in that particular room.

Mr. Eagan then asked the children about the miniature dolls Janet had brought to place in the doll house. Janet showed the dolls and Mr. Eagan added Roman numeral II to the chalkboard, followed by this topic: II. Dolls in the Doll House. Mr. Eagan next listed the dolls as the children named them.

The children were then allowed to set up the doll house. After this was done, Mr. Eagan asked the class, "Now, let's look at the chalkboard. What have we done?"

"We've told about my doll house," said Janet.

"Yes," said Mr. Eagan, "but we didn't write a story about it, or a poem about it, or draw a picture. This is a new way of telling about something. It is called outlining. An outline is like a skeleton or frame. It gives us the main parts but we have to fill in the details."

The children then together explored the ways they could use an outline. Someone pointed out that the form they had used in planning trips was really an outline, to which Mr. Eagan agreed.

Their list looked like this:

When We Can Use Outlines

1. In planning trips
2. In planning parties
3. In planning stories and poems
4. For planning our social studies reports
5. For getting an idea about what is coming in our books
6. In taking notes during radio and television programs
7. In doing our science experiments

Then Mr. Eagan helped the children outline a report together. He printed the form of the outline on a chart which he put before the class for reference. He then helped each child make out an outline by giving dittoed sheets to the class, lined and lettered with the correct outline forms. Soon children were outlining material from encyclopedias, almanacs, and supplementary reading materials for their social studies reports. Later Mr. Eagan helped the children learn how to use an outline to study.

Children can classify many kinds of words in preparing for more advanced experiences in outlining. Capitalize on the flowers they bring in. Classify words regarding the *feel* of the flower (soft, silky, satiny, damp), the *looks* of the flower (bright, gay, pretty, droopy, beautiful), the *smell* of the flower (sickish, sweet, fragrant, delightful, etc.).

Another way to provide practice in classification skills is to take roll call by using different topics—when the child's name is called, he must respond with a word in the predetermined category. Some categories might be: names of cars, words in French, types of shoes, names of songs, names of games, words correlated with units, etc.

Poetry Forms: Primary Grades

Most children write their first poems in story form; it is a natural sequence to the instruction they have received in writing stories. In the primary grades, poems generally begin to appear on an individual basis as some children, aware of the concepts of rhyming, make attempts to rhyme their stories. Often these first poems are dictated to the teacher.

The teacher can establish written forms for poetry writing as soon as their children are able to read. Learning poetry forms is a visual skill. Children should see the complete form of a poem as it will appear on a sheet of paper, before they begin to write it. This calls for a sensitivity to the art form or shape of the poem as well as to the wording of it.

There are many acceptable forms for poetry writing. The child must become familiar with many such forms and then be encouraged to choose his own. He must also be informed of the different types of poetry such as free verse, blank verse, and rhyming verse so that he may choose a form which suits his purposes. Often a simple piece of written prose is beautiful enough to be written as free verse. The teacher can be alert to the signals of her children's readiness to write poetry and can capitalize on these signals by using them to introduce poetry forms. A rich background of experiences with poetry will make her instructional task meaningful.

Suggestions for Helping Children to Write Poetry Forms: Primary Grades

1. Put simple poems on reading charts as soon as the children are able to read them. Often simple nursery rhymes that the children know may be used this way. Draw attention to the fact that the beginning lines are capitalized and that a period ends each idea, but that the beginning lines are not always directly under each other as in an experience chart.

2. As soon as a child creates a poem, use it to make a reading chart. Explain that one way people can tell whether the material they are about to read is a poem or a story is by the shape of it on the page. Read the poem that was submitted and print it on a reading chart, using a form different from the straight margins usually used in a reading chart. Note the contrast in form. Accent the shape of the indentations of the beginning lines of poetry by drawing a jagged margin with a brightly colored felt pen.

3. Miss Fleming, a second grade teacher, printed simple poems that her children liked, and poems that they had written, on colored construction paper. She cut out the poems, accenting the pattern of the first lines of the poem by following jagged margins. When mounted on regular tag board, the shape of the poem was easily seen from any place in the classroom and provided an easy reference for the children. One of Miss Fleming's charts looked like Figure 98.

4. Poems with iambic pentameter may be printed on pieces of cardboard in two-line sections and distributed to the children. They then read the poem and assemble it in a pocket chart at the front of the room, thus drawing attention to the alternate indentation of the lines of this type of poetry, and providing the teacher with a method of checking the children's ability to match rhyming lines.

Poetry Forms: Intermediate Grades

The suggestions given for the development of the visual and art form of poetry in the primary grades may be adapted to the instructional program of the intermediate grades. In fact, it will be necessary to develop form consciousness through steps similar to those taken by Miss Fleming if the intermediate grade children have not developed sensitivity to poetry forms.

However, the stress for writing poetry should be on the *content* of the poem and not the form. Much of the instruction for developing poetry forms will be done on an individual basis as the teacher helps each child edit his draft work for final display or publication in the classroom.

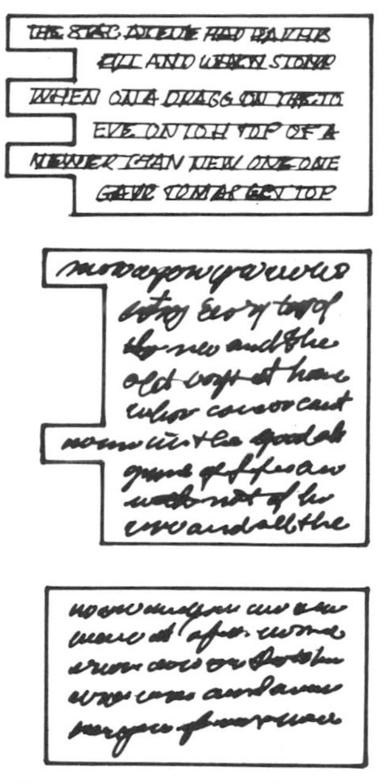

Figure 98 *Poetry forms.*

Forms of Correspondence

Letter writing: The best way to insure the development of a child's ability to write letters is to have him write letters frequently, *and mail them!* One basic purpose in learning language and grammar forms is that it develops skill in an act of social courtesy. It becomes somewhat foolish and irrelevant to practice such forms in isolation from the social situation in which they are to be used.

Miss Raymer's class was working on kites. They had learned science through studying about wind and currents and what it is that makes kites fly. They had studied the history of kites. Mr. Heinlein, the shop teacher, had taught the children the basic structure and construction necessary to build a kite. Each child had made a different kind of kite, and each had painted or decorated his own kite in his own way. At the school picnic, each child flew his kite. Of course there were stories, poems, plays, and reports written about kites. Many of the poems and stories in this volume came from Miss Raymer's sixth grade. Here is Tommy's.

Up, Up and Away

One very windy day last April, I was at Proctor High flying the new kite I had just completed. Suddenly there was a large gust of wind, and up, up and away (not T. W. A.) went my kite, and me right along with it. There I was in space floating around, living on nothing but raindrops and blue cheese from the moon, which isn't much fun.

Finally in July, I heard a thundering sound. I looked around and there was Apollo 11, roaring into space. I maneuvered my kite to the space ship hoping to get close enough to knock on the capsule and hitch a ride home. As I got next to the ship the wind pushed the kite and me away, bumping the capsule. As I was floating away, I overheard Astronaut Armstrong reporting back to Mission Control that they had been struck by a meteor, and up up and away went Apollo 11 to its historical moon trip.

Many months passed, and I was still surviving on my blue cheese and raindrops (falling on my head).

In December Apollo 12 was speeding toward its moon destination, and as before I maneuvered the kite to the ship and knocked, and knocked. Again no one heard me. Then Astronaut Bean told Mission Control that they had been struck by lightning. I don't know how anyone could mistake me for lightning. A meteor yes, but not lightning! Up, up and away went Apollo 12 to its moon landing.

In the months that followed, I made up my mind that I would hitch a ride from the very next Apollo shot.

Thus in April I was ready, really ready! Then up came the Apollo 13! This time my kite maneuvered me to a better position. Once more I tried my luck. I knocked, and no one heard me. I got mad! I knocked so hard my fist went through the service module and made a big hole: But I did manage to attach the kite to the hatch. I overheard Sevigent tell Mission Control that there was a big explosion back in the Service Module.

This cut the Mission short. Soon Apollo 13 was on its return to earth. On the trip home I got a fantastic view of the moon. I froze along with the Astronauts. I was thirsty, and hungry too.

I know you won't believe this. Neither did Nasa, but I can dream can't I?

—Thomas Bucciero
Grade 6

Knowing that I was interested in their work, the children sent me packets of materials, always with a letter from a class spokesman enclosed.

I answered them. I especially enjoyed Tommy's stories and poems so I wrote to him asking him for permission to use his material. He wrote to me, and we corresponded for a while. One of his letters is below:

1289 Mission Place
Utica, New York 13501
May 20, 1970

Dear Dr. Smith,

I've received your letter regarding my story of "Up, Up and Away." I want to thank you for all the wonderful things you've said about the composition.

I appreciate your putting my name under the story, although just including it in your book would have been more than enough.

That letter was shown to former teachers, which made me very happy. It made Miss Raymer, and my former teachers very proud.

You have made me a big shot at home and a celebrity in school, I just hope I could live up to all this.

Thanks for your interest and encouragement.

Sincerely,
Tom Bucciero

Miss Raymer, Tommy's teacher, was taking a course from me so I showed her Tommy's letters. She was astonished that he had done this at home, all on his own initiative without her knowledge. It was an excellent tribute to her good teaching. But it also points up the fact that learning to write effective letters is a matter for direct experiences.

There are so many opportunities for children to write these days, to friends, to pen pals, to visitors to their schools, to relatives located all around the world, to the elderly in nursing homes, to service men, to hospital patients, to children in other schools, and to their parents, that it seems ludicrous to teach letter writing as an irrelevant drill exercise.

The need to write letters arises almost immediately with the child's school experience. For the first time in his life, he is removed from the presence of people with whom he has had close contact. Direct communication with those people is now impossible, and the child will feel a need to communicate in written form if the teacher capitalizes on the situation and helps him develop skills in meeting this need.

Among the most common forms of letter writing which a child needs early in his school experience are:

1. Friendly letters
2. Letters of request
3. Letters of thanks
4. Letters of invitation

Many situations arise in the classroom for which these forms are needed.

Friendly Letters
1. Those situations mentioned above
2. Writing to teachers other than the classroom teacher

Letters of Request
1. Writing to parents for money for supplementary materials or textbooks
2. Writing letters for the teacher for materials to be brought from home (book drives, materials for costumes, props for plays)

3. Writing for permission to take a field trip to a farm, a dairy, or a museum
4. Writing to travel agencies and commercial firms for free materials
5. Writing to authors or consultants
6. Writing letters to the school principal requesting equipment
7. Writing to Santa Claus

Letters of Thanks

1. Writing to thank lay people and commercial enterprises for allowing the class to take a field trip
2. Letters to the principal for new books or materials
3. Letters to the Board of Education for certain granted privileges or gifts to the class
4. Letters of thanks to consultants who visit the class to show the children various materials, films, or filmstrips
5. Letters to another grade thanking them for invitations to assemblies and exhibits
6. Letters to parents and relatives for gifts received at Christmas, holidays, and birthdays
7. Letters to the policeman or another community helper who may have helped the class on a particular trip

Letters of Invitation

1. Invitations to parents to parties, assemblies, exhibits, and class programs
2. Invitations to parents to visit the classroom
3. Invitations to other groups to attend assemblies and exhibits
4. Invitations to the Safety Patrol to accompany the children on a trip
5. Invitations to a policeman or postman to visit the class

Business Letters

At any early age in the child's school experience, he adds another written expression form to his needs—the business letter. Experiences which prompt the use of the business letter are:

1. Writing to commercial companies for free materials
2. Writing to travel agencies for posters
3. Writing to museums, historical societies, and libraries for unusual pieces of information
4. Writing letters of inquiry
5. Writing letters to order classroom supplies
6. Writing to gather material for special reports, such as writing to a college of education to find out how teachers are trained
7. Writing to make arrangements for trips
8. Writing letters for the purpose of sponsoring exhibits

9. Making arrangements for consultants
10. Gathering information for making decisions on bargain prices, quality materials, etc.

As in other forms of written expression, the visual image of the letter form must become clear in the child's mind before he can actually write a letter. Stress should be put on the *shape* of the letter. From the very beginning of instruction, the child should see the complete form of the business and friendly letter. When he is unable to write but can read, letters that are to go home can be run off on a duplicator, with a line drawn in the place where the child is to print his name. As he learns new words, he can write more and more of the letter, but the forms should always be complete each time.

Some newer exercise books introduce written expression forms at an early stage in the child's growth by having him cut printed words from the printed page and paste them in appropriate blanks on the simple but correct letter form. As soon as he is able, the child prints the word in the blank instead of pasting it in. Little by little the printed words are omitted, and only lines remain, drawn so that the child still maintains the pattern of the letter. He now copies his letter from the chalkboard, where he has helped his classmates compose it. Room is left for his own creative endeavors by making certain that he will substitute his own ideas whenever he has them, in place of the ideas used on the chalkboard. Before long each child is writing his own letters on paper, lined by the teacher in a way that aids in the retention of correct form. As soon as the form is fixed in his mind, the child can use his skill on regular lined paper.

The accent in such exercises is placed correctly: upon the visual form of the letter. The child does not write incorrect letter forms, because he does not see them. The instruction that he has been receiving in punctuation and capitalization is applied to letter writing from the beginning.

Many children write their own creative letters at an early age. These letters are often made more creative when they are illustrated or decorated.

In the intermediate grades, the parts of a letter may be studied and a nomenclature for referral developed. This should come only after the child has written many letters in correct form.

Suggestions for Developing the Correct Use of Letter Forms

Use many of the ideas previously mentioned under the development of paragraphing, outlining, and building poetry forms, especially the following:

1. Use a felt pen to outline the shape of a business or friendly letter.
2. Use construction paper cutouts to show form and shape.
3. Use dittoed work sheets (or workbook sheets), lined so that the child keeps correct form in mind.
4. Keep a collection of letters which show various forms.
5. Use a flannel board or pocket chart to construct letters together, arranging in proper form the strips of paper on which the letter has been previously printed.
6. Use colored chalk to emphasize the shape of letters.

Children in the intermediate grades will be able to analyze letters for quality of content, interest value, and correctness of form by using the opaque projector technique used on page 407 to analyze handwriting. From this analysis will come a basic set of principles for letter writing. Through the use of the opaque projector and the overhead projector, children can learn to contrast various letter forms and make lists of the differences between friendly letters and business letters.

As children obtain skill in writing letters of various kinds, more emphasis may be placed on letter content in the intermediate grades. The use of new language skills learned in the analysis of handwriting, punctuation, capitalization, and word usage will be applied to letter writing as well as to stories and reports. Children at this age may enjoy writing imaginary letters such as the following:

- A letter from the bugle boy who was at Valley Forge with General Washington.
- A letter from a colonial girl in New England to her cousin in England.
- A letter written by a boy in the lost colony at Roanoke.
- A letter written by the first astronaut to reach the moon.
- A letter from the first aquanaut to reach the bottom of the ocean.

Children in the intermediate grades will enjoy studying historical letters to see how letter forms have changed over the years. If a museum is nearby, collections of old letters may be available for the children to study. Any fifth grade child would enjoy seeing a letter written by George Washington or Abraham Lincoln. Changes in spelling can also be noted. Encourage children to collect reproductions of historical letters which appear in current publications from time to time.

At all times, remember that the structure and form of the letter are secondary to the content. It is what the child has to say that is most important and the way in which he says it. The ultimate goal in letter writing is, of course, to produce creatively interesting letters that are correctly written, but the mechanics of the writing should be corrected or edited after the child has written a good piece of prose. Repeated editing of the drafts he writes will insure a correct form for the finished product which is to be mailed, or in the case of imaginary letters, posted or published in a school newspaper. Although instruction should be continuous and as individual as possible, exciting letters should take precedence over "correct" ones. The incorrect forms used in letters serve as a diagnosis for the teacher of the kind of instruction small groups of children or individual children need to have repeated after general instruction has been given.

Greeting Cards, Note Cards, and Announcements: Effective human relations are fostered by courteous, considerate communication. This aspect of the communicative process is developed in making children sensitive to the aesthetic value of communication as well as to the practical value. Aesthetic values come from a beautifully written piece of poetry or prose, or from a note or greeting which shows consideration.

Greeting and note cards generally needed as a result of classroom experience include the following:

1. Notes of thanks for a gift
2. Get-well cards sent to a classmate who is hospitalized or ill at home
3. Cards for new children who arrive at the school during the year
4. Season's greetings and holiday cards made by the children
5. Notes of information such as a message from the school nurse to a particular child
6. Notes explaining absences or tardiness
7. Welcome notes to new teachers and principals

Greetings are often given in the form of poems and are printed on greeting cards made by the children.

Announcements may be made by posters or official announcement cards. Children need to study the correct form of announcements so that they may compose announcement cards for classroom use, such as:

1. The announcement of a class tea or dance
2. Graduation announcements
3. Exhibit announcements
4. Special program or assembly announcements
5. Announcements of the opening of a new school or classroom
6. Announcements of weddings of older sisters or brothers
7. Advertising announcements such as the announcement of a bake sale or candy sale to raise funds

As in other written expression forms, the design of the arrangement of words on a greeting or an announcement along with its wording is what makes it an accepted classical form. Techniques suggested in the earlier parts of this chapter for developing form impressions on children are applicable to the teaching of these forms also.

Developing Skills for Self-Study

Alphabetization

This necessary skill for language usage may be developed as soon as children have learned the alphabet. This generally occurs soon after they have learned to read and are beginning to study phonetic sounds.

Alphabetization is a memory and visual skill. Children must remember the *order* of the letters and recognize their *shapes* in order to be able to alphabetize.

The alphabet serves two purposes: that of making words which *do* communicate, and that of providing a system of organizing material—a system known as alphabetization. A knowledge of the sounds of the letters may unlock the pronunciation of a new word; a knowledge of their order will unlock the system by which written material is classified.

Here is how Mrs. Ford made alphabetization meaningful to her second grade:

The children in Mrs. Ford's class learned the alphabet by seeing it placed over the chalkboard on cards, and learned to identify the letters by singing "A, B, C" songs, by playing games and riddles in which various letters were located in sequence, and by writing the letters in proper sequence.

After Mrs. Ford was certain that every child who was able had learned the alphabet, she developed the alphabetizing concept through a series of lessons which included the following activities.

Mrs. Ford introduced the concept by explaining that letters were useful not only to unlock words, but also to organize things. She said she would show them what she meant. Each child was asked to write his last name on a strip of paper, making the capital letter very large so that all could see it when she held it up. Then Mrs. Ford told the children she was going to organize *them* according to the letters of the alphabet. While the children recited the alphabet letter by letter, each child whose name began with that particular letter was asked to come and stand in line. Each child brought his name tag with him in the line. When two or more children responded to a letter, Mrs. Ford arranged them alphabetically in line without any detailed explanation to the children. When the entire class had been arranged alphabetically, Mrs. Ford told them that that was what alphabetization was.

"But," said Mrs. Ford, "it would be really difficult for me to line you all up every time I wanted to find out something about you, so we do it an easier way on paper. Each of you take your name tags and place them one under the other in the pocket chart in the exact same order in which you are now standing. Then take your seats."

Soon the children's names were arranged in alphabetical order before the class. Then Mrs. Ford asked, "Why would I need to have your names in this order. Can any of you guess why?"

After the children had discussed some reasons for this sort of alphabetization, Mrs. Ford showed them her classroom register where the alphabetical lists of boys' and girls' names were kept so that she could mark absences and keep records easily.

The next day the second grade reviewed their alphabet and Mrs. Ford gave each of them a manila folder. She asked them to print their names carefully on the tab, with last names first. As soon as each child had printed his name, Mrs. Ford again had them arrange their cards in a bright-colored apple box she had painted. This class file was to be used to save specimens of the children's work and as a place where children and teacher might swap notes or assignments.

Mrs. Ford then showed the children her own individual file where she kept folders on each child. She took care to point out that her arrangement of the names on the tabs was exactly the same as theirs. The children played games trying to locate each other's names quickly in the apple box file.

On the following day Mrs. Ford brought some manila folders before the class along with several news clippings and pictures. Many of the clippings were those taken down from the bulletin board at various times that were too valuable to discard. Mrs. Ford told the children that she wanted them to think of a way she could arrange this material so she could get at it quickly. Before long the children were able to see that she could make up a topic and place the appropriate pictures and clippings in a folder, and that these folders could be alphabetized as their names had been.

A busy period followed in which the children constructed a class file. Miss Ford held up a picture or an article and the children decided on an overall topic to suit it. Then one child was asked to print the topic on the tab of his manila folder. Soon each child had a topic, and all the clippings and pictures pertaining to his topic were placed in this folder. There followed another session with filing the folders alphabetically in another apple box file.

The next day Mrs. Ford introduced the picture dictionary to the children. They learned to locate material by taking turns in finding answers to questions posed by Mrs. Ford.

On succeeding days Mrs. Ford introduced other purposes for alphabetizing. She introduced the set of encyclopedias in the room, and the children learned how to use the alphabet in locating the correct book in which to find information. The children played many games with the alphabet. Mrs. Ford gave them exercises requiring that they alphabetize simple words.

When Mrs. Ford was certain that the technique of alphabetization was firmly established, she began to give the children experiences in alphabetizing where there were several words beginning with the same initial letter.

In later days these children were introduced to alphabetizing words all of which began with the same letter. This led to an application of new skills such as using the dictionary, the pages of the encyclopedias, the index of a book, the telephone book, the catalogue cards in the library, glossaries, and almanacs.

Each skill was taught and immediately applied to the solution of classroom problems. Children were soon able to alphabetize their own material, to use references to develop their own skills, and to create ways of using alphabetization for their own use.

Alphabetizing can be fun. Mrs. Mans had the children in her first grade make the large printed letters on cards (as they learned them) with flo-pens of various colors. Then the children were to take crayons and make an object or picture from the letter. The phonetic sound of the letter was later introduced when each child was asked to give his object a name beginning with that specific sound. Although the embellishments on the letter *could* detract from its shape (and shape was one of Mrs. Mans's original purposes for using this exercise), it did not because of the bold strokes made by the flo-pen.

Mrs. Osborne, who taught a fourth grade, made a series of nonsense words on large (4 × 8 inch) oaktag, utilizing all beginning consonants and making pairs of beginning consonants (two g's: glap and gopy, etc.). The game was explained to the children. All the cards were distributed so that each child had a card. QUIETLY, the children were to arrange themselves in alphabetical order, holding their cards so that everyone could see. Everyone had to pay attention, and the only talking permitted was in case someone saw something out of alphabetical order. When they were all lined up in a semicircle, they sang the words up and down the scale (fun and good for phonics!). This was so popular that she tried it another time with nonsense words beginning with vowels. The large cards were later used by individuals to practice alphabetizing.

Suggestions for Practicing Alphabetization

Make alphabet cards for the children to arrange in order at their seats.

Encourage children to bring in samples of all the lists they can find where materials are alphabetized. This would include listings in the paper, catalogue lists of books and of children's records, directories, tax lists, inventory lists, etc.

Encourage children to bring last year's telephone directory to school. Write several names on the board and have children practice looking up telephone numbers.

Let children cut out words from old spellers and put them in envelopes. Children may take an envelope and arrange the words in alphabetical order.

Also, a variation is to label envelopes A, B, C, etc. Have the children sort words into the proper envelopes, then later arrange these words, all beginning with the same letter, into alphabetical order.

Note-Taking

The ability to take notes is important in a society that is subjected to much verbalism and produces much printed material. Children will need to know how to take notes for these purposes:

1. To keep records of science experiments
2. To make records from encyclopedias and other reference materials in order to make reports in social studies
3. To report to the class on certain radio and television program assignments
4. To be able to organize material from several resources into one composite report
5. To grasp the main ideas of a speaker's presentation
6. To be able to organize and classify material
7. To be able to glean ideas from textbooks and newspapers

Prerequisite to note-taking are many experiences in classifying and outlining similar to those described on previous pages. Outlining is one form of note-taking, and suggestions for teaching outlining meaningfully and creatively appear on pages 480–483. Other forms of note-taking may be taught to children so that they may master the technique of making authentic and interesting oral and written reports.

Note-taking has its beginnings in the early grades. Here the children learn the value of jotting down ideas for future use.

In a first grade room the children listed the questions they were to ask on a trip to the airport. After the questions were listed, each child copied one question on a 5 × 8 inch card. This was a note to him to remind him of the question for which he was responsible at the airport. When the class returned to the schoolroom, each child wrote the answer on the back of his card. These cards and answers were saved in a file box as a future reference source.

In another first grade the children were asked to copy three words from a list on the board that would tell about the circus, three about a farm, etc.

Experiences such as these are the basis for note-taking. In the primary grades, children can begin to use cards or a notebook to take simple notes: answers to specific questions, records of daily events, plans for coming events, and names of books they have read.

Early in the intermediate grades, note-taking will be very important to children as they collect material for making science and social studies reports. At this point, conditions can be set for developing this skill effectively through a variety of activities.

Activities

1. Show the children notes from which a speech has been made or a manuscript written.

2. Make a list of all the instances in their own classroom where note-taking will be necessary.

3. Make a list of all the possible ways in which notes may be taken (cards, "idiot" cards on television, notebooks, outlines, etc.), and of all the permissible shortcuts used in note-taking (abbreviations, types of shorthand, etc.).

4. Take a question from those the children ask and use it as a demonstration on how to take notes. For example, Tom brought a rock to school. The children asked what kind of rock it was. Mr. Metz, Tom's teacher, used this situation to show the children how to take notes. On the board he wrote this question: What types of rocks are there? Then he wrote the following on a large card.

Kinds of Rocks

Children's Encyclopedia, Volume 13, page 235

I. Igneous
   —once molten, now cooled
   —granite, basalt
II. Metamorphic
   —"changed" rocks
   —slate, marble, micaschist
III. Sedimentary
   —deposits subjected to great heat and pressure
   —shale

Mr. Metz read the children the article from which he had copied his information.

The children then took two other questions from their list of questions on the chalkboard: "What kinds of homes do people live in in China?" and "How are oranges raised?" Mr. Metz divided the class in half. One group of children gathered material from textbooks and encyclopedias to answer question one, and the rest gathered material to answer question two. Group one was called on to read material pertaining to the first question. On the chalkboard, the children made notes with Mr. Metz's guidance. Then question two was handled in the same manner. After the notes were edited, the class took question one and together wrote a report from the notes on the chalkboard. Then they each wrote a report individually from the notes on question two. These reports were shared and suggestions were made for their improvement.

From this experience, Mr. Metz and the children were able to make a chart of suggestions for taking notes.

Suggestions for Taking Notes

a. Always put the reference at the top of your notes.

b. Read the paragraph, page, or article carefully and look for facts to answer your question.

c. Pick out the main ideas from the article or paragraph and write them down as main topics.

d. Add any subtopics which will help you to remember important facts.

e. Group facts under your topics.

f. Record facts accurately.

g. Read your notes over to see if you have all the information you need to make a good report.

h. Work out a plan for note-taking that best suits you.

5. Have all the children take notes to answer one question, using a common textbook as a resource. Make note cards and use an opaque projector to project them on a screen before the class. Evaluate the notes and check them against a chart of suggestions such as those mentioned above.

6. Give children many interesting assignments, other than social studies reports, which will require note-taking. Oral reports can be made from these notes in class.

Examples:

a. Listen to the President's press conference tonight on television and select the five main topics on which he spoke.

b. Watch a certain television program and list the answers to a group of questions prepared by the teacher.

c. Take notes of the main points of an assembly speaker.

d. Make a list of all the things you find on a science field trip and note the places where you find them.

e. Watch a film and select five things suggested to improve your spelling.

f. Observe this filmstrip and make notes of the seven uses of lumber mentioned.

g. Make notes or outlines for debates or panel discussions on such topics as:

It is better to live in the suburbs than in the city.

Children should be allowed to watch television on school nights.

Automobiles should be kept out of cities to lessen the air pollution.

Scripts: Radio, Plays, and Television

In the primary grades, dramatic play is free and planned on the spot. From this spontaneous form of creative play emerges an organized, yet still creative, type of dramatization (Figure 99). Organized dramatization can be used for many purposes in the primary grades (see Chapter 7).

In the intermediate grades, children will want to dramatize rather freely, but they will also want to write plays. They will need to know the correct written forms for scripts, dramatizations, puppet shows, shadow plays, and television shows.

A group of children, for instance, may decide that they want to write a play. They may have written stories before, but not plays. The problem then arises: What is the proper way to write a play? If the ideas for the play have already been suggested, it is wise to get these ideas down on paper or on the board. Then, because it is a new experience for the class, the correct way to write plays can become a group lesson. A search through English books will disclose valuable suggestions for playwriting; the library corner may contain some plays written for children, which may be studied for form. Reading books often have short plays that may be used. Then, from the various forms of material collected, the class reads some plays. They learn how plays are written, the importance of stage directions, lists of characters, scene descriptions, and the like. They list new words like *exit*, *enter*, *upstage*, *downstage*, *climax*, and *plot* on their vocabulary chart. They may write the first scene collectively on the board to apply what they have learned.

After everyone understands how plays are written, the class can divide into committees to write the scenes, reporting to the whole class frequently. A series of good reference charts may result as the play develops. Criteria for a good play may be listed on one to help keep the committees conscious of the factors necessary to make scenes interesting. The scenes need to be outlined from the original plot so that each committee knows exactly what part of the plot it must cover. Then, after each scene is read, evaluated, rewritten, and finally accepted, the play should be typed in proper form so that each child has his own copy. Good reading experiences follow in tryouts for the parts, in chart making for cast of characters, committees, jobs, etc. Written invitations to other classrooms and to parents, posters for advertising, handmade props and scenery will constitute good opportunities for developing oral, written, and creative expression.

Figure 99 *A sixth grade learns about script writing in writing their own script for* The Wizard of Oz.

Teachers often use the writing of scripts as a springboard for teaching predominant types of punctuation such as the colon (used after the name of each character who is speaking), the parentheses (used to set off stage directions), and the semicolon (often used to show sudden changes in thought). As with other forms of written expression, the script has a unique appearance, and children must learn to recognize its design and to have it in mind before they write their own plays.

Book Reports

Forms for book reports have been contrived for teachers. They generally serve two functions: (1) They show the teacher the child's ability to summarize the material read, and (2) they provide an incentive, supposedly, for other children to read the book.

Although the first objective is generally met through the written book report, the form is not relevant to the objective. The second objective is rarely met.

A more creative approach to writing book reports and accomplishing the same objectives would be to present one rule at the beginning of the school year for giving book reports: that no two reports can be given the same way. Children, working alone or in groups, will be challenged by this open-ended learning situation to present book reports in a variety of ways: through dramatization, puppetry, shadow plays, dialogue, games, dancing, choral speaking, scroll movies. There is no limit to the variety of forms that may be created, and all of these would not turn children off as the stereotyped written book report often does.

One alternative to a book report follows: Instead of requiring children to write book reports for presentation on certain days, assign several stories or books and ask that they *compare* them in writing (or orally) before the class. Here is what Ronnie had to say after he had read several short stories. Ronnie has factual information because he knows the stories and can discuss them intelligently.

Summary of Short Stories

Of the short stories our class read most of the class like the stories "The Telltale Heart," "The Last Leaf," "The Doughnuts" and "The Bear in the Black Hat." Almost all the short stories were listed as somebody's favorite. Reading the short stories was fun because we could just read them in our spare time. We read stories about sports, animals, people and even cars. Another good thing was that we had plenty of time to read them.

Many of the short stories we read were very funny. The class liked "The Doughnuts" and "The Bear in the Black Hat." As I read "The Doughnuts" I could just see all those doughnuts piling up and falling out the windows and then that lady trying to find her bracelet. In "The Bear in the Black Hat" I think it would be so funny to see a bear walking around with a hat on.

Two of the short stories stood out in my mind as having an exciting climax. One of these was "The Last Leaf." This story told how a girl was going to die when the last leaf of an ivy vine fell. In the very end you find out that an artist painted the leaf on the wall that the vine was against. In

"The Telltale Heart" the killer kept hearing the heartbeat in his mind until it made him admit to killing the old man in the end.

Most of the animals in these stories had the characteristic of either defending themselves or someone or something else or loyalty to their master. In "Rikki Tikki Tarri" the mongoose defended Teddy. In the story "One Minute Longer" Wolf the dog stayed by his master even though his paws were cut and he was in pain.

I am glad that I read these short stories. I learned something in some of them and I got a whole lot of enjoyment out of reading the funny stories. I wasn't too surprised at how the class reacted to the stories they liked best.

—Ronnie Ashley

Using Reference Materials

A teacher paves the way to discovery by providing children with skills which enable them to find things for themselves. Discovery is an essential element of the creative act. When children are able to use the dictionary, the encyclopedia, almanacs, glossaries, indices, and the school library to satisfy their needs, new worlds, awaiting their discovery, are opened to them.

Reference charts made by the children are often the first stage in the development of the concept that one may go to a specific source (other than the teacher) for help. One of the first sources children use after the reference chart is the picture dictionary. From this usable resource it is but one step to the use of other reference works.

Mr. Garrison was a fourth grade teacher, new to the school. During the first week of school he attempted to launch an Indian unit. He was successful up to the point where he planned to turn the children loose to look up answers to the many questions they had asked. Mr. Garrison had helped the children accumulate many different kinds and levels of material, but when he turned the children loose, chaos resulted. Some careful questioning on his part soon helped Mr. Garrison locate the source of his problem. The children in his fourth grade had never done any "research" before. They had always learned social studies from a textbook. Their lessons had consisted of periods in which the teacher asked questions and the children read until they found the answers and raised their hands as a signal to the teacher that they knew it. Further questioning showed Mr. Garrison that these children did not know how to take notes, outline, organize, and give reports.

Mr. Garrison felt that these were important skills for fourth graders to develop. So he worked out a plan. He knew that the children must be secure and competent if they were to move ahead and become independent in their study skills, so he planned to start with the reading skills they had already acquired and lead them to independent skills of study.

For the next few weeks Mr. Garrison used his language arts periods to teach the children how to take notes, how to outline, and how to use reference materials. Simultaneously with these experiences, he led them to independent and committee study techniques in the following manner.

During the first social studies period following the day of the fiasco, Mr. Garrison explained that he was going to teach the children a new way to study. He moved the furniture in the room into five clusters, making five separate groups. All the children took out the same social studies book that they were in the habit of using. Mr. Garrison then placed one group of questions, which the children had listed, before the class on a chart.

"Today we will work on these questions together," he said. "Let's read the questions together." After the questions were read, Mr. Garrison said, "I have listed the four pages in your books where most of these questions will be answered. Read the four pages I have written on the chart and then see how many questions you can answer."

Mr. Garrison had grouped the children so that his poorer readers were at one table. While the other group were reading, he sat with this group to help them to read. Some of the material he read to them so they would not fall too far behind. When his eyes caught the fact that many children had finished, he asked all the children to stop reading and to look at the questions. The children then answered the questions. Among them they knew all the answers. From the answers they gave, Mr. Garrison helped them to make an outline on the board. Together they wrote a report in three paragraphs from their outline.

Mr. Garrison summarized the day's work by saying, "Today we learned how to read a great deal of material to find several answers. We also learned how outlines help us, and we learned how to make a written report from an outline. Tomorrow we will try something else."

The next day Mr. Garrison held a discussion at the beginning of his social studies period.

"Can you think of a way," he asked, "that we might look up *more* material today than we did yesterday in the same length of time?"

Charlie suggested that different groups might look up different questions, rather than all the children looking up the same questions.

"A good idea," said Mr. Garrison. "Here is what we will do. I will number the groups. Groups 1 and 2 will look up the answers to the questions on this chart. Groups 3, 4, and 5 will look up the answers to the questions on this chart. I have put the page references on the charts, and we will do the same as we did yesterday."

As soon as the children were finished, Mr. Garrison again went through the questions on both charts, made an outline for each, and then selected two capable children from each of the groups to write the report during their work period.

The next day the reports were read and evaluated. Mr. Garrison moved slowly and followed this procedure for three more days. At the end of the week he evaluated the work with the children. He pointed out to them that they had accomplished twice as much work on the last day as they had on the first day. He reminded them that they had been more interested in each other's work and in each other's reports when they had worked and reported on *different* topics. He showed them that they had been learning from each other as well as from him.

The next week Mr. Garrison gradually led the class into working in three groups on the questions on three different charts, then to four groups, and by the end of the week each group was working on a different set of questions and writing a separate outline and report. The classroom was orderly, children were highly involved and highly motivated, and the unit was completed in this manner.

As soon as the children had organized the questions for study for their next unit, Mr. Garrison helped them classify the questions on charts and then asked them to sign up for the chart they would like to work on. The tables in the room were then grouped by committees, and Mr. Garrison said, "During our last unit we worked in groups, but I think now we are ready to work in committees and that is quite different. What is a committee?"

The children discussed the concept of committee and reached this definition, which Mr. Garrison wrote on the chalkboard. "A committee is a group of people that has a definite job to do."

The jobs of the committee were then listed as follows:

1. Each committee has a chairman who:
   a. Assigns jobs to the group
   b. Checks on the group members
   c. Brings together the group work
2. Each committee has a secretary who:
   a. Makes a record of the group work
   b. Writes any reports the group may need
3. Each committee has members who
   a. Do the jobs assigned as well as possible
   b. Go to the chairman for help in finding materials
   c. Keep notes of their readings and give them to the secretary

Mr. Garrison then explained that each committee would work on one chart of questions on which he had printed many references so that they could use their textbooks along with other books. He then appointed the chairman and secretary for each committee and they went to work. Mr. Garrison moved from committee to committee, helping each to get organized.

The children tried working in this manner for two days, each day evaluating their work at the close of the period. On the third day Mr. Garrison said, "Some of you have looked up the answers to almost all of the questions and are ready to make your outlines and write your reports today. Before you do this work today I would like you to think of some interesting ways you can give your report to the rest of the class. It is going to be tiresome if we just read each report. If you can plan an interesting and different way to give it, you can write it so it is suitable for the way you will present it."

The children suggested many ways of giving a report, and with Mr. Garrison's help they wrote these ideas on the chalkboard.

Some Ways We Can Give Reports

1. A TV panel show with questions and answers
2. A dramatization
3. Use charts and graphs
4. Give it with pictures
5. Make it into a roll movie
6. Plan it like a television show such as a newscast or a "You Were There" program
7. Make a tape recording of it
8. Use maps with it

The children met in committees to decide on a way to make their reports. As soon as one committee was ready, the children listed criteria for making a good report. Soon the children were able to organize and carry out committee work with a high degree of efficiency.

In this account of Mr. Garrison's activities, we have seen how one teacher developed the *concepts* and necessary *procedures* for work.

Using the Encyclopedia

This is how Mr. Garrison developed the skill of using reference material simultaneously in his language arts period.

He used the encyclopedia as his main source of reference. He placed a children's encyclopedia on a table before the group in the front of the room. The children had used encyclopedias but mainly on a trial-and-error basis. Mr. Garrison wanted all of them to know and realize the wonders lying between the covers of this set of books.

Mr. Garrison talked about the encyclopedia. He explained to the children that it was the whole record of mankind and all his accomplishments distilled for their use. He told the children how much he used it, and what a help it was to him in his teaching. He informed them that he was going to teach them how to use it so that they could enjoy all of its wonders too. He told them that there were many kinds of encyclopedias printed on all levels, and that he would keep several in the room so that all of them might find one set to read. He then did the following:

1. He asked all the children to write on a slip of paper a word or question they had recently heard that they had wondered about. "Or," he said, "put down a question about something you have been interested in for a long time."
2. Mr. Garrison collected the questions and read them. As he read them, he asked the children to help him group the questions by topics. Mr. Garrison wrote the topics alphabetically across the chalkboard and placed the slips of questions under the appropriate topic.
3. "Now," said Mr. Garrison, "I can find answers to every one of these topics in the encyclopedia. With our dictionaries we learned to look up word meanings. In our encyclopedias we can learn to look up subjects or topics."
4. Drawing on the children's knowledge of alphabetization and the dictionary, Mr. Garrison built these concepts:

a. The encyclopedia, too, is arranged alphabetically.
b. It is arranged by books rather than in one book like the dictionary.
c. It, too, has guide words. Guide letters appear on the front of each book to tell you which book to choose. Guide words appear at the top of the pages to tell you the page on which to find your topic.
d. Encyclopedias must be kept in order so that they are easy to use.

5. Mr. Garrison then passed out the encyclopedias for the children to use by twos. "Let's list what an encyclopedia tells us and what we can find in it," he said. This list resulted.

An Encyclopedia

a. Tells about subjects.
b. Has pictures to help explain the subject.
c. Has page numbers and a one-book index.
d. Explains its abbreviations.
e. Has cross-references.
f. Tells about population, products, etc.
g. Contains charts and graphs.
h. Gives important figures.

Mr. Garrison's use of the encyclopedia on page 504 is an excellent example of a good teaching technique. Children will experience the joy of discovery as soon as they are able to use resource materials to find information to help them in answering their problems. In recent years, the publication of simple picture encyclopedias and picture dictionaries has made it possible for teachers to teach the skills of using reference books as early as the kindergarten and first grade.

Reference work on the elementary level is the basis of research techniques which the child will use throughout his life. Children do not need to know all the answers to the many questions that will cross their minds, but it would be unfortunate if they did not know where to find the answers.

In unit teaching, this simple skill of looking up factual material and reporting on the findings is essential. Children will need to know (a) where they may find answers, and (b) *how* to use the resources which contain their answers. Time must be taken in the child's school years to teach the use of the dictionary, the table of contents, an index, a glossary, an almanac, the encyclopedia, and other children's reference books (such as *The Children's Periodical Guide*, *Information Please*, the telephone books, and various atlases and reader's guides).

A child is motivated to seek information when he is curious or interested in a problem to which no one has a ready answer. He must know (a) where he can go for an answer, (b) how to find the material, (c) how to locate the specific answer, (d) how to take notes on the material, and (e) how to report back to a group (if his motivation came from a group problem).

All through elementary school the teacher should take time to introduce resources available for seeking out materials at each level of the child's development. At the beginning of each unit, children can list available resources in which they may find their answers. The teacher or the school librarian can take time to explain the use of all the textbooks and reference resources available to the children and demonstrate any unique feature in using them. Then the teacher will need to check to be sure that the children have been instructed in how to use the material properly.

Using the Dictionary

In teaching dictionary usage, the teacher should keep several objectives in mind.

1. To give the children resources so that they can develop independent language skills.

2. To teach the arrangement of the alphabet letters.
3. To develop an understanding of the purpose of the dictionary.
4. To learn how to find words in the dictionary quickly and efficiently.
5. To learn how to arrange work alphabetically.
6. To learn what information can be found in the dictionary.
7. To learn the difference between an abridged and an unabridged dictionary.
8. To learn of the many kinds of dictionaries.
9. To make a careful study of the pronunciation of words.
10. To develop an understanding of homonyms, antonyms, and synonyms.

In order for children to be prepared to use the dictionary effectively, they must first be able to alphabetize. Simple picture dictionaries can be effectively used as early as the first grade by children who are interested in words. Often a keen interest in picture dictionaries is the cue for the teacher to begin dictionary work. Many children will look things up in the dictionary on a trial-and-error basis even before they have learned to alphabetize.

Contrary to popular belief, the dictionary is not used by children as a primary means to check spelling. A child must know how to spell a word before he can look it up in a dictionary. At least he must have a substantial visual image of the word in his mind, or the dictionary is of little help to him. Words which are looked up in the dictionary are those whose meaning we question, or for which we need more meaning than our experience produces. The dictionary communicates to children only if it has been carefully chosen so that the definitions in it are within the realm of the children's experience.

Once alphabetization is mastered, children can be encouraged to use the dictionary to help them in their creative work. Inasmuch as phonics are generally introduced in the reading program before the alphabet is learned, the simple dictionary can be used to help children find new words in their reading, or to help them in sounding out unfamiliar words.

Some activities that will encourage children to use the dictionary for each of the above objectives are listed below:

No. I, II, III. See Alphabetization (page 492).

No. IV. To learn how to find words in the dictionary quickly and efficiently: Write the alphabet on the chalkboard. Find the middle letter m and underline it. Divide the alphabet into groups of five letters. Read the letters by groups.

Note which letters come at the beginning of the dictionary, which cluster near the middle, and which fall at the end. Give each child a dictionary and some slips of scrap paper. Have him find the first letter of each of the five groups and insert a slip of paper in it. Note which groups have the most pages and which have fewer pages. Practice opening the dictionary to the approximate place by giving children words to look for. The object is to see whether children can learn to open the dictionary at approximately the correct beginning letters.

Remove the slips of paper and try to open the dictionary to the section where a word which is called by the teacher will be found.

Give the children a dittoed list of words with a string of three boxes drawn after each word. Have them try to open their books to the correct section where the word will be found. If they do it correctly, they give themselves a check in the box. They try all words on the list once; then they add their scores. They try a second and a third time to see if they can improve their scores. Sample list: *apple, man, lotus, zebra, date, kiln.*

Have children make lists of words of their own on the chalkboard, and see how quickly they can find these words in the dictionary. At first use words that begin with different letters. Then use a list in which some words begin with the same letter.

Introduce the use of guide words and explain their use. Almost all companies that publish dictionaries have blown-up master sheets of one page taken from the dictionary. These sheets can be used effectively for group work. Then children can look for guide words in their own dictionaries.

Then have them list words all beginning with the same letter. Using the guide words, have the children find these words as quickly as possible in their dictionaries.

Have children make their own picture dictionaries on the primary level, or word dictionaries on the intermediate level. These dictionaries may be used for one or several purposes, for example, to alphabetize all the spelling words learned during the year; to keep a record of misspelled words; to keep a record of new words which the child encounters in reading or in social studies; to list new vocabulary words that appear on the class vocabulary chart.

Study the thumbed index on the unabridged dictionary or any substitute form on an abridged dictionary. Practice opening the dictionary by using it.

After the children are able to open dictionaries quickly, have them study the pages. (The large page in the front of the room can be used effectively here.) Notice that the words are in dark, heavy print and that all information after each word is in lighter print. Explain some of the uses of the dictionary already discovered.

Have each child make an individual dictionary box. Use the drawer of an ordinary matchbox in which are kept $1 \times 2\frac{1}{2}$ inch cards of oaktag. Children can keep the boxes handy on their desks. When a child needs a word spelled, the teacher writes it on a card, he uses it for his immediate need and files it in the box. Misspelled words from spelling tests are added to these. The child uses his words for further reference as well as for gaining practice in alphabetization.

No. V. To learn how to arrange work alphabetically: See suggestions under Alphabetization, page 492.

No. VI. To learn what information can be found in the dictionary: Find the word *place* in the dictionary by opening to it as quickly as possible. Find the guide words that start with pl and end with plai (according to the dictionary in use). Find out what it means by reading the definition. Notice the markings after it, n. v. Explain what they mean. Notice the pronunciation guide immediately after the word. Find the pronunciation by referring to the key in the front of the book or at the bottom of each page. Explain the use of the key.

Look up the word *placer* on the same page. What additional information is given about this word? (accent mark) Examine other words on the page to see whether any additional information is given.

Now make a chart with the title: Information We Can Find About a Word in the Dictionary. It may look like this:

1. We learn to pronounce the word.
2. We learn the definitions and uses of the word.
3. We learn what part of speech it is.
4. We learn where to accent the word.
5. We learn the correct spelling.
6. We learn how to divide it into syllables.

1. Give children sentences such as: "This is the place where Lincoln was shot," and have them select the definition which best explains the use of the word place.

2. Give children exercises with unfamiliar words to be used as follows:

Example: Inaudible

a. Divide the word into syllables
b. Place main accent
c. Give meanings of word
d. What "guide" words did you use to find this word?

3. Choose a word with several meanings. Set up sentences using this word.

Example: Stalk

a. The plant has a little stalk.
b. The tiger stalks his prey.
c. He stalked haughtily down the street.

4. Dictionary fun—what is it? (develops divergent thinking). Can you tell what the following really are? What is it?

a. A titmouse is not a mouse.
b. A prairie dog is not a dog.
c. A peanut is not actually a nut.
d. Beggar lice do not crawl.

5. Dictionary fun—information (develops convergent thinking skills). Dictionaries tell us many things:

a. How many feet in a mile?
b. How does the python kill its prey?
c. Who were the minutemen?
d. Is the bat a bird or an animal?

6. Give children sentences containing words with different meanings from those they are used to. Ask them to use their dictionaries to see whether the word is properly used, and if so, to take notes on the new meaning of the word.

Examples:

a. The girl had a good *purchase* on the rope.
b. The barnacles will *cleave* to the side of the boat.

7. Make lists of the synonyms for certain words you look up in the dictionary.

8. Give the children lists of words you are sure they do not know, but for which they know synonyms, and ask them to find the pronunciation and meaning and use each in a sentence. Sample list: *heft, swab, abbey, abbot, platypus, Ionic, tartar, zephyr, yokel,* and *chorister.*

Often a few simple rules will help children develop syllabication techniques. The approach to teaching syllables will be more creative if the children discover the rules than it will be if the teacher teaches the rules.

For instance, instruct the children to look up this list of words in their dictionaries:

planning	thinning
running	hopping

Ask them to be detectives and, after they copy these words in syllables as they are presented in the dictionary, to note what these words have in common. From this observation, children will discover the one rule for syllabication: When two consonants come between two vowels, the syllable is formed by dividing these two consonants.

Other "rules" which may be discovered in similar ways are:

1. Each syllable has at least one vowel sound.

2. Compound words made up of two or more words are divided between the words (book-case).

3. If a word has a consonant between two vowels, separate the word so that the consonant is placed with the second vowel (cro-cus).

4. If two like consonants come between two vowels and the consonants are part of the root word, then the word is separated *after* the two like consonants (chill-y, full-y).

5. If two different consonants come between two vowels, the word may be divided so that the two consonants which can be sounded well together go with the next syllable (re-plied, le-thal).

6. If two different consonants come between two vowels, the word may be divided by separating the word between the consonants if they cannot be sounded smoothly together (chap-ter).

No. VII. To learn the difference between an abridged and an unabridged dictionary: Get an abridged and an unabridged dictionary. Look at the tables of contents and compare. Compare other things such as:

size
number of words
information after each word
material in preface and appendix

What is the difference between an abridged and an unabridged dictionary? Make a chart that summarizes these differences.

1. Look up the words "abridged" and "unabridged" in the dictionary to see if your definition was correct.

2. Give the children lists that contain words which will not appear in abridged dictionaries. Divide children in groups and allow half of the groups to look up the words in the unabridged dictionary and the other half in the abridged dictionary. Compare the number of words each group found. Decide why one group found more than the other.

3. Have the children think of the unusual words they know. See which ones are in the abridged and which appear in the unabridged dictionary. Decide why this is so.

4. List the things about abridged and unabridged dictionaries that are alike.

5. Make a list of the places you would find abridged and unabridged dictionaries. Decide why either would be found in any one place.

6. Make lists of the unique contributions of the unabridged dictionary. Example: pages of the flags of states and nations, glossaries of foreign words, pages on weights and measures, etc.

No. VIII. To learn the many kinds of dictionaries. Encourage children to bring in all the dictionaries they can find, from the simplest picture dictionaries to the unabridged dictionary. Discuss each and decide on its purpose. The teacher could bring in special dictionaries to help children develop the concept that there are many dictionaries for many purposes.

1. Make an exhibit of this collection of dictionaries and write other

classes to come to see it. At the exhibit, display other work the class has done with dictionaries.

2. Give the children a list of problems and have them decide which of the dictionaries in the exhibit would supply the most adequate information to solve the problem.

No. IX. To make a careful study of the pronunciation of words: Study the key to pronunciation in the front of the dictionary and at the bottom of each page. Compare two different dictionaries. Are these marks always the same? What must we remember about this then?

1. Give the children a list of unfamiliar words (unfamiliar in sound but familiar in meaning) and have them look up the words. Words such as *forelock, manual, mellow, regatta, spigot, tocsin,* and *cotter* will do. Have them look up the words, find their meanings, and, using the pronunciation key, see if they can say them correctly.

More difficult words can later be introduced, such as *costermonger, corridor, heliotrope, pottage,* and *receipt.*

2. Place lists of words on the board, say them aloud, and have the children divide them into syllables, place the accent mark on them, and check with the dictionary to see whether they are correct. Point out that every syllable has at least one vowel.

3. Have the children make a chart of all the words that are strange to them in their reading and social studies over a period of a few days. Ask them to keep a record of the place they found the word. Then they should look up the words on the list, learn to say them, read their meanings, and finally put the pronunciation and new meaning in the sentence where the word was originally found.

No. X. To develop an understanding of homonyms, antonyms, and synonyms: Inasmuch as definitions deal with synonyms and children study synonyms, antonyms, and homonyms in the early grades, the dictionary may serve as a way of further developing an understanding of the use of these speech forms.

1. Give the children a story with one word repeated many times. Have them substitute synonyms by using the dictionary to find new words. For example:

The Place

There is a wonderful *place* which I like to visit every winter. This *place* is high in the mountains. It is a beautiful *place,* nestled in a little *place* near the water. In the summer this *place* is visited by tourists from many *places.* In the winter, it is a lonely *place.* Old John stays there and old John knows his *place.* He keeps the *place* going and it is then that I like to go there in *place* of the time when people are at the *place.*

Figure 100 *A fourth grade makes a corner mural for the fair. It says:*
A fat lady trying to walk
Elephants hooking on to each others' tails
A big top full of laughter and excitement
Acrobats on a flying trapeze
A lady hanging by her hair
A clown in a "clowning around" act
Popcorn, peanuts and cotton candy
Snow cones and a stomach ache for everyone.

Encourage children to write creative stories such as the one above for their classmates to work on.

2. Make charts of homonyms, words that are pronounced alike. In the early grades, matching cards can be made. One homonym is printed on one card and the other on another card. As children increase their knowledge of homonyms, they will add to the card file. They will have fun matching the cards.

3. Make lists of antonyms on charts and illustrate them.

dull—bright
happy—sad

4. Keep a chart which shows how prefixes sometimes create antonyms.

Examples:

The prefix un makes happy unhappy and interesting uninteresting.
The prefix dis changes illusion to disillusion and able to disable.

5. Apply antonyms to sentences to show how they are opposite.

6. Try to use two homonyms of the same set in the same sentence. Examples:

It is a dull *morning* to wear *mourning.*
There was a *great* deal of discussion over the *grate* in the fireplace.

7. Make up lists of words and have children write antonyms for them.

8. Make lists of words for children to write synonyms.

The School Library

Children should be introduced to the school library soon after they arrive in school. From an early age they should have happy library experiences, rich in discovering new materials and new ideas. There are books to explore; files to use; card catalogues to utilize; posters, films, and charts to take out, and a series of planned library experiences with the children and the school librarian.

The role of the school librarian in such a program cannot be minimized. Her major objective is to *encourage* children to use the library. Proper use of the library and accepted library behavior are important for children to learn. The library should be theirs so that they can explore it on their own and enjoy sharing its books. Well-planned library periods can do much to encourage good library experiences. In planning trips to the library, teacher and children should ask the librarian to sit in so that she knows what each particular class requires and what her role is to be.

If a school library is not available, the need for skillful teaching of library usage is even greater. Lack of a school library is unfortunate in a sense, yet fortunate in another sense. Ideally, the best kind of library is one housed in the same room with the children. All teachers should create a library corner in their rooms; books may be borrowed from state libraries, town libraries, or from the children. Children will often bring a few books a week to school and then share a few more the following week. When many children do this, much joy can be obtained through sharing and through the remotivation which a constantly changing bookshelf affords. Some teachers have utilized a language arts period to have the children write letters to their parents explaining their plight and asking for books for the school. Such book drives often produce much good material.

Summary

Webster defines grammar as a scientific study and classification of the classes, forms, sounds and uses of words in a particular language. For the purpose of teaching grammar, punctuation, capitalization and word usage, classifications of the skills to be taught may well be broken down into spoken and written forms and usage. The written forms of word usage can be considered as the mechanics for producing proper handwritten manuscripts.

The mechanics of handwriting can be taught. They are the tools which free children to be more creative. Knowing the correct use of grammar, of word usage, of language forms and skills for organizing materials gives them a certain psychological security which will make possible the use of the language tools in creative projects and reports.

To the Reader

1. Ask your students (or any group of children if you are a student) to write a report or a story for you. Try to devise a check sheet that will serve as a diagnostic instrument for common grammar problems. Which ones seem to be the greatest problems for the largest number of children in the group? Work out a grouping plan and some techniques which you might use to eliminate some of these problems. Do any of the ideas presented in this chapter help you?
2. Make a collection of appropriate games for teaching grammar or

punctuation or word usage. Create some criterion for choosing these games. Games of this nature are often so complicated that children become so snarled in the process that the purpose of the game is lost. The number one criterion should be that the game *clearly* teaches something.

3. For many exciting, creative ideas for teaching language arts, especially grammar, see these two books listed below in the bibliography at the end of this chapter:

   Easy in English by Mauree Applegate
   and
   New Directions In English by Richard Sanders, ed.

4. Creative teaching was previously described as open-ended teaching, that is, the motivation for learning is presented by the teacher and then the child feels his way to a logical solution to the problem presented in that motivation. Much of language teaching is actually teaching the child to follow predetermined patterns to which he must conform according to accepted social courtesy. Check through the suggestions for teaching in this chapter and classify them under these two headings: (1) creative teaching (open-ended, leading to discovery and invention), and (2) creative ways to teach children to conform.
5. Is it possible to make up a creative test for evaluating language skills? Try it.
6. If you have been following a textbook for the study of the mechanics of written expression, look at the next topic you planned to teach. Abandon the book and: (1) Devise a method by which you can test the children to see which ones already know the material, (2) provide a creative writing incentive for these people to replace the lesson, and (3) create a new, unique way to present the material to the remaining group.

   If you are a student, review an elementary school textbook in English and think through processes 1, 2, and 3 above.
7. Questions for discussion: Do you agree or disagree?
   a. This book suggests that learning is entertainment.
   b. All learning must be fun.
   c. Middle school children should learn how to use microfilm in the library.
   d. The language or resource laboratory can be an excellent idea for meeting individual problems in children.
   e. Punctuation is a kind of international language.
   f. Textbook lessons in grammar are carefully organized in logical

sequence and are, therefore, a superior kind of gimmick for teaching language skills.

g. Children are handicapped in their creative writing if they do not know grammar, punctuation, and capitalization rules.

Selected Bibliography

APPLEGATE, MAUREE. *Easy in English.* New York: Harper and Row, 1963.

———. *Helping Children Write.* New York: Row-Peterson, 1964.

ARMSTRONG, F. A. *Idea-Tracking.* New York: Criterion Books, 1960.

BACH, EMMON. *An Introduction to Transformational Grammars.* New York: Holt, Rinehart and Winston, Inc., 1964.

BRADDOCK, RICHARD, et al. *Research in Written Composition.* Champaign, Illinois: National Council of Teachers of English, 1963.

CHOMSKY, NOAM. *Aspects of the Theory of Syntax.* Cambridge: M. I. T. Press, 1965.

———. *Current Issues in Linguistic Theory.* The Hague, Mouton, 1964.

———. *Topics in the Theory of Generative Grammar.* The Hague, Mouton, 1966.

COBB, STANWOOD. *The Importance of Creativity.* New York: The Scarecrow Press, 1968.

DELANCEY, ROBERT. *Linguistics and Teaching: A Manual of Classroom Practices.* Rochester, New York: State English Council, 1965.

DIXON, ROBERT M. *Linguistic Science and Logic.* The Hague, Mouton, 1963.

EVERTTS, ELDONNA. *What's New in Language Arts: Composition.* Washington, D.C.: American Association of Elementary-Kindergarten-Nursery Educators, NEA Center, 1968.

FRIES, CHARLES CARPENTER. *Linguistics, the Study of Language.* New York: Holt, Rinehart and Winston, 1964.

GLEASON, H. A., JR. *Linguistics and English Grammar.* New York: Holt, Rinehart, and Winston, Inc., 1965.

HAIDER, NORMAN. *Haider's Guide for Structural Linguistics.* Cedar Grove, New Jersey: Phillips-Campbell Publishing Co., 1964.

HOOK, J. N., PAUL H. JACOBS, AND RAYMOND D. CRISP. *What Every English Teacher Should Know.* Champaign, Illinois: National Council of Teachers of English, 1970.

JOOS, MARTIN. *Readings In Linguistics.* Committee on Language Programs of the American Council of Learned Societies, 4th ed. Chicago: University of Chicago Press, 1966.

MACCAMPBELL, JAMES C. (ed.). *Readings in the Language Arts in the Elementary School*, Part VI: "Written Composition," 230–282; "Grammar in Language Teaching," 216–228; "Toward a New Perspective in Grammar," 200–209; "Evaluating Children's Composition," 263–277. Boston: D. C. Heath, 1964.

NEWMAN, HAROLD. "Toward A New Perspective of Grammar and Composition" in James C. MacCampbell (ed.), *Readings in Language Arts in the Elementary School.* Boston: D. C. Heath, 1964, 200–209.

NEWSOME, VERNA L. *Structural Grammar in the Classroom.* Milwaukee: University of Wisconsin, 1962.

PLATTS, MARY E., S. ROSE MARGUERITE, AND ESTHER SHUMAKER. *SPICE: Suggested Activities to Motivate the Teaching of the Language Arts.* Michigan: Educational Service, Inc., 1960.

POWELL, BRIAN. *English Through Poetry Writing.* Itasca, Illinois: F. E. Peacock Publishers, Inc., 1968.

SANDERS, RICHARD (ed.). *New Directions in English.* New York: Harper and Row, 1969.

SHANE, HAROLD GRAY. *Linguistics and the Classroom Teacher.* Washington: Association for Supervision and Curriculum Development, 1967.

SHUY, ROGER W., ALVA L. DAVIS, AND ROBERT F. HOGAN. *Social Dialects and Language Learning.* Champaign, Illinois: National Council of Teachers of English, 1964.

STRICKLAND, RUTH. *The Contribution of Structural Linguistics to the Teaching of Reading, Writing and Grammar.* School of Education, Indiana University: Bureau Educational Studies and Testing, 1963.

STURTEVANT, E. H. *An Introduction to Linguistic Science.* New Haven: Yale University Press, 1947.

TIEDT, IRIS M., AND SIDNEY W. TIEDT. *Contemporary English in the Elementary School.* Englewood Cliffs, New Jersey: Prentice-Hall, Inc., 1967.

———. *Readings On Contemporary English in the Elementary School.* Englewood Cliffs, New Jersey: Prentice-Hall, Inc., 1967.

WAISMANN, FRIEDRICH. *The Principles of Linguistic Philosophy*, R. Harré, (ed.). New York: St. Martin's Press, 1965.

13

Adventures for the Disadvantaged

The following poem was written by an eleven year old after the teacher had shown the class a *Life* magazine cover. It was on the issue labeled "The Negro and the City" and depicted the face of a black boy who was crying bitterly.

In the Slums

A boy sits looking through the window
 into the narrow alley below.
His world is blacker than he is,
 and his tears he cannot outgrow.

The people in his life just exist,
 they do not live.
He is unconscious of the presence.
He doesn't know how to forget or forgive.

His poverty is forced upon him,
 a burden he cannot lift.
He has not eaten in hours or slept in a bed, ever.
His world was handed to him, like a gift.

His tears will never learn his sorrow.
The day cannot dim;
There is no day or night.
Someone help him!

—John

John appears to understand that there is such a classification as "culturally disadvantaged." Also, in his poem, John shows an uncanny ability to empathize with this culturally disadvantaged child. Creative children tend to possess this ability to a strong degree. Perhaps the solutions to the problems of the disadvantaged lie in helping our young children to empathize and understand their problems and feelings as John seems to be able to do. Certainly, understanding is paramount in teaching the disadvantaged.

The adventure at the beginning of Chapter 2, entitled "The Bim Bam Boo" is a lesson that took place in a culturally disadvantaged school. In a class of twenty-four children, the author was working with ten blacks, four Puerto Ricans, two Orientals, and eight Caucasians. All these children came from a low socioeconomic area in an industrial city.

The Disadvantaged Child

Who are disadvantaged children, or, as they are often called, "culturally deprived" or "culturally different"?

They constitute about one-third of the school population, and are probably from families destined to stay in a particular social class for the remainder of their lives because of some unavoidable circumstance.

One prominent misconception about culturally disadvantaged children is they are almost all slow learners. The disadvantaged child's impoverished real and verbal experience, with other deficiencies, impairs his performance on intelligence tests, especially on verbal tests. The vocabulary and concepts of the intelligence test are unfamiliar to these children and their performance cannot be considered accurate.

Studies have shown that these children are slower than normal children due to their inability to conceptualize (and often to read), and the timed I.Q. tests discriminate against them. The I.Q. test, in other words, was not designed to measure the subculture we now identify as the culturally disadvantaged.

Another misconception which stacks the cards against the disadvantaged child is the administration of achievement tests and the consideration given to the scores in reporting the child's progress. The same factors operating against the child in the administration of the intelligence test are present in the use of achievement tests: (a) speed, and (b) the need to conceptualize and see relationships and to draw from experiences which the child has never had. Add to this his deficiencies in language (especially reading), his frustration over his inability to communicate, his failure to understand the abstract skills needed for proper written communication, his lack of motivation, and it is apparent why most culturally disadvantaged children are classified as slow learners whether or not the classification is valid.

Greene and Petty[1] define the disadvantaged child as follows:

> The children who make up this segment are not equipped, for a number of reasons, to survive easily in our traditionally middle-class-oriented educational institutions. They become the dropouts, failing therefore to acquire the kinds of skills and knowledge that are necessary for self-sufficiency in the present economic world. If they are not to become burdens upon the rest of society—on welfare rolls or in mental and correctional institutions, the school, as the most logical instrument of society, must make a particular effort to discover who they are, where they may be found, and the nature of their deficiencies.

Green and Petty identify disadvantaged children as having the following characteristics:

1. They are poor, belonging to the lowest socioeconomic group.
2. Their parents seldom have more than a high school education—usually less—and are employed in semi-skilled or unskilled occupations.
3. They may be of any nationality or race, but they are frequently Negroes, Mexicans, Puerto Ricans, Indians, or second-generation Americans of varied national origins, since these people have limited opportunities for education and/or employment.
4. They are children of migrant workers, inhabitants of city slums, or dwellers in rural and semi-rural areas where few cultural opportunities are present. They may be found in almost any geographical area of the United States, although the greatest numbers are concentrated in large metropolitan areas.

The home environment of all children has a dramatic effect on their language development. This is especially true of the disadvantaged child where the home life differs from that of the teacher or the majority of other children in the class.

The disadvantaged child's environment is lacking in stimulus-producing objects and consequently lacking in words to describe or relate objects and experiences. He has been starved for experiences that can be put into language—and related to other experiences. It is this starvation which needs to be fed when this child comes to school.

Disadvantaged children are known to live in different types of home patterns than suburban children. They do not follow middle class eating, sleeping, and living patterns. Therefore, their concepts of time and space may be undeveloped, or at least they hold different concepts than

1. Harry A. Green and Walter T. Petty, *Developing Language Skills in Elementary Schools*, 3rd ed. (Boston: Allyn and Bacon, 1967), pp. 479–480.

the advantaged child. Disadvantaged children think mostly in the present and the immediate.

Often the disadvantaged children have been abused or "put down" at home. Most of them receive very little individual attention from adults. The result is that many come to school with a poor self-image. This is often shown by unusual shyness or introversion or bravado attempts to cover it up with extreme verbal or physical aggressiveness.

Studies with disadvantaged children show that they do not relate well to adults for a variety of reasons. Often, at home they are ordered about or verbally abused by adults. Many come from homes where the family hierarchy differs from that of other children. Some rarely see their fathers and the mother has become the dominant figure in the home. In some families the authoritative image is shared equally by the mother and father. The type of home from which the child comes makes a great deal of difference as to how he accepts or rejects his teacher.

Because of the manner in which these children are treated at home, they lack self-confidence. They do not feel comfortable or secure in school. They are often afraid or ill at ease, and they tend to manifest their insecurity in unruly behavior.

Their homes offer them little educational stimulii or hope for change. Money is scarce and seldom used for newspapers, books, pads, pencils, crayons, or educational toys. There is no precedent established for obtaining an education and many children come to school looking forward to the time when they can become dropouts.

Deprived children live in cramped quarters, often with inadequate sleeping facilities. They are not fed according to rules of the dietician. They come to school hungry, tired, and bearing handicaps resulting from abuse or neglect.

The principle disadvantages of this group of children are economic poverty and cultural difference. These disadvantages may be found in other groups of children. Both are not always found in *all* disadvantaged children, but they are largely responsible for certain differences in patterns of behavior exhibited by these children which identify them as disadvantaged.

The home environment of disadvantaged children often differs greatly from the home background of the teacher, and she must be sensitive to these differences in order to make certain that her classroom experiences and assignments are realistic. A disadvantaged child, for instance, has little or no place to do "home work." If he had a corner of a table he would be subjected to radio blatting, many people talking, and a continual barrage of noises. He has learned (almost as a technique of survival) to shut out noise. He may frequently shut out the noise of the teacher's voice just as he shuts out noise at home, and by so doing may insult her middle-class sense of "respect to elders."

The problems of disadvantaged children have been emphasized recently because of integration legislation and the mobility of modern time populations. The difficulties with deprived children have often been caused by the inflexibility of the schools and their dogmatic adherence to the old concepts of the traditional schools and its regulated, closed classroom. Problems under these circumstances are often ignored, dismissed, or handled poorly. The democratic concept of providing all children with equal opportunity and an education commensurate with their ability is certainly not fostered. Nor is the creative concept that the individuality of our children is one of our greatest assets. The ability of the schools to readjust curriculum to individuals and to work out organizational plans so individual needs and learning patterns of all children might be honored has resulted in some exciting changes in educational practice. One such plan which opens great promise for the disadvantaged as well as all other children is the open classroom concept of the British Infant School.

In such settings, teachers have looked for the *advantages* of the disadvantaged. In other words, how can these children help other children to learn? Some studies have been conducted on this topic. The results can be of great help to the teacher of the disadvantaged in planning experiences in the classroom.

Disadvantaged children, for instance, have developed a great deal of independence and self-reliance. They do have a wealth of a certain kind of background experiences but these have not been used effectively in the past in furthering their learning. These children are often expert in caring for younger children, and show a great deal of initiative and inventiveness in dealing with problems. They often can cook or prepare food for other members of the family. They have learned a great deal about life and their immediate environment. They know a great deal about cooperation and the value of helping each other. Their attitude towards education is positive although they may not like school.

The major aim in working with disadvantaged children is to provide compensatory education for each child.

Language Problems of the Disadvantaged Child

Impoverished home environments, exposure to specific dialects other than his own, and nonstandard modes of living affect all aspects of the disadvantaged child's language development. He does not arrive at school with the same language patterns as other children. The speech heard at home is almost always a dialect, is meager, and is limited. Busy parents, preoccupied with earning a living and supplying the basic necessities of life are tired, harassed, and disinterested in children's conversation. These children are not read to or talked to fluently. Often, when they are addressed it is with simple directions or demands. Parents have little inclination to engage their children in conversation. Because of their own educational backgrounds, their vocabularies are small and inarticulate.

The disadvantaged child is often left to his own devices. He picks up most of his vocabulary from his peers and rarely has much contact with standard English.

Tiedt and Tiedt[2] identify the needs of the deprived child as follows. The need to develop:

1. Language skills: thinking, listening, speaking, writing, reading (in the order named).
2. Feeling of personal worth; confidence in his ability to succeed.
3. Recognition of school as pleasant and learning as pleasurable.
4. Enthusiasm and interest in environment; wide experimental background.
5. Interest in others and respect for them; ability to work and play with others.

The Problem of Non-Language

Many disadvantaged children seem to withdraw from contact with their teachers. They speak little in school, or not at all. A myth that these children have little or no language at their command needs to be dispelled.

In their book, *Language and Thinking in the Elementary School*, Smith, Goodman, and Meredith[3] make the following statement under the heading, "The Myth of Nonlanguage":

> Lately, a myth has grown up among the general public, and among many teachers and educators as well, that may be called the myth of nonlanguage. Somehow, the belief has developed that children, labeled variously as culturally deprived, culturally disadvantaged, low income, language deprived, or just slum

2. Iris M. Tiedt and Sidney W. Tiedt, *Contemporary English in the Elementary School* (Englewood Cliffs: Prentice-Hall, Inc., 1967), p. 317.
3. E. Brooks Smith, Kenneth S. Goodman, and Robert Meredith, *Language and Thinking in the Elementary School* (New York: Holt, Rinehart and Winston, Inc., 1970), pp. 51–53.

kids are virtually without language. This belief is reinforced for many teachers by their observation of youngsters who are inarticulate and unresponsive in the classroom, who appear not to understand what to the teacher is simple, clear language. But the overwhelming evidence of linguistic research should begin to clear up this myth. All groups of people ever studied have language. All normal children learn the language of their subcultures. The observed lack of language of some children in the classroom, then, is not a real lack of language but is a lack of "appropriate" acceptable language and a lack of "appropriate" acceptable experience to express.

These authors have touched on a very delicate and important problem. The myth of non-language has been perpetuated by teachers who have children in their classrooms with whom they try to communicate in such a way that the teacher's own language and her own set of values serve as a barrier to communication.

All learning, whether with the normal, the retarded, or the culturally disadvantaged, must begin with the child himself. Commercial materials are of great help to the teacher and can save her hours of lesson preparation. Too often, however, the commercial materials become a "filler" or "busy work" to keep children occupied, a substitute for a real, planned curriculum, a poor replacement for real teaching. If a teacher operates by using the vocabulary of the prepared commercial materials, or by imposing her own vocabulary or set of values on the children, she can only compound the problems which these children already bear.

Smith, Goodman, and Meredith also point out that these children are often handicapped by their language simply because it is not the acceptable language of the school. When this is so the child is in a situation where his education will be conducted in another dialect and where the attitude of school personnel often brands his mode of communication as inferior.

The Problem of Dialects

One of the basic facts that has come out of recent linguistic research is that every language changes in time and changes differently in different places.

These regional changes result in dialects: local or provincial forms of language that differ from the standard or literary form. In social dialects, language forms, language structures, and speech sounds constitute much of this difference. When children are transplanted from an environment where they have been "brought up on" a dialect to an environment where standard English is practiced or accepted solely in communicating (such as an average schoolroom), severe handicaps arise in communication unless the teacher is aware of the problems presented by dialect and handles them in such a manner that spontaneous communication continues. Obviously this will call for a great deal of adjustment on the teacher's part in tackling such problems as phonics, word structure, sentence structure, word usage, grammar forms, and forms of oral and written expression.

No one particular dialect should be considered superior to any other. In fact, the so called standard variety of English is but one dialect of English. Stewart[4] points out that the basic language patterns already known by children may be a hindrance in learning standard English rather than a help.

The work of Chomsky[5] has added new dimension to the problem of dialect differentiation. Chomsky states that dialects differ from each other in relatively minor ways and that language is highly resistant to change in time. Dialects differ from each other in some of the phonetic rules used to realized utterances but not in the underlying structure of the system.

Some studies show that it is difficult for children to change their dialect forms under external pressure; the changes that do occur tend to come from within the speaker subconsciously rather than as a result of someone to teach "correct" speech to him. These studies show that adolescents do seem to be better able to accept suggestions of some kinds and to modify their linguistic behavior accordingly.

Some evidence has been obtained which indicates that preference for certain linguistic forms is related to certain age levels and that children "naturally" use the forms in their dialect characteristic of their age level.

Children can change their linguistic habits and modify their dialects with ease, but they apparently cannot do so consciously; much of the modification is the result of unconscious assimilations that occur within peer groups. If the dialect of the peers differs from that of a child's parents, the child tends to reflect the dialect of his peers above that of his parents.

Some students of language feel that standard English should, consequently, be taught to children as a foreign language. McDavid[6] states:

4. William A. Stewart, "Urban Negro Speech: Sociolinguistic Factors Affecting English Teaching" in Shuy, Roger W., Davis, Alva L. and Hogan, Robert I., *Social Dialects and Language Learning* (Champaign, Illinois: National Council of Teachers of English, 1964), pp. 10–18.
5. Naom Chomsky, *Syntactic Structures* (The Hague, Mouton and Company, 1967).
6. Raven I. McDavid, Jr., "Social Dialects: Cause or Symptom of Social Maladjustment" in Shuy, Roger W., Davis, Alva L., and Hogan, Robert I., *Social Dialects and Language Learning* (Champaign, Illinois: National Council of Teachers of English, 1964), p. 7.

We must keep reminding our neighbors that Standard American English has many varieties, all good. We must remind them not to confuse what is regionally and what is socially different . . . A person's dialect is one of his most intimate possessions.

However, opinions differ. Haugen[7] believes that English should not necessarily be taught as a foreign language to deprived children. He urges that we accept the idea that they have learned one dialect of English and they need to learn another. They already know something of the latter. We don't need to make them bidialectal; we only need to change them from passive or unconscious bidialects to active, conscious ones.

Haugen states:[8]

The linguist's task will be that of making a realistic description of the two dialects, of establishing a different analysis of their systematic deviation in sound, grammar, and lexicon; of these the grammar is the hardest and the most important.

Teaching the Culturally Disadvantaged Child

Some obvious facts guide the teacher in working with the culturally disadvantaged child:

1. She must understand that these children are handicapped as far as learning is concerned, and she must come to know each child and his own particular problems, especially his language differences.

2. She must be open-minded and dedicated, or she cannot call herself qualified to teach these children. Being open-minded means that she does not approach them with misconceptions and prejudices. She accepts each child for what he is and is determined to make him feel worthy as an individual. She must become acquainted with the child's subculture and be able to understand and accept it. She must bear no prejudice against race or socioeconomic levels, and must not consider her values as necessarily "best." Although she understands how she acquired her own set of values, she helps these children to develop values of their own without injuring their self-concepts in the process. She cannot prize cleanliness (a middle-class value) over aggressiveness (a lower-class value), but must understand both.

7. Einor Haugen, "Bilingualism and Bidialectalism" in Shuy, et al., *Social Dialects and Language Learning* (Champaign, Illinois: National Council of Teachers of English, 1964), p. 125.

8. Ibid., p. 108.

Being dedicated means that she must be sincerely challenged by her job, *she must enjoy it, and the children must know she enjoys it!* If she does not, they will know it, and communication will not develop.

3. Whereas the teacher of children from ordinary homes will do well to utilize the experiences of her students, the teacher of the culturally disadvantaged will be responsible for more than that; *she must provide all the experiences on which her language program will be built.* She will then progress through the language development sequence in her teaching. But her classroom must abound in all kinds of objects (pets, number boards, typewriters, stuffed toys, toy stores, etc.) and her program must be weighted in favor of direct experiences (trips to the airport, the supermarket, the farm, the factory; science experiments, growing plants, cooking, swimming, painting, sculpting, etc.) and vicarious experiences (films, tape recordings, colored pictures, recordings, etc.)

4. The teacher of the disadvantaged will be skilled at making her own language materials. Understanding that some commercial materials will be of help and will save her a great deal of time, nonetheless she will expend her energies on the making of materials (especially reading materials) which grow out of the oral language experiences of the children, and she will use her time in the careful *selection* of available materials to be certain they will fit in appropriately to the learnings under way. She will also need extensive skills at programming materials.

5. The teacher must show these children love and must give them a great deal of support. The problems of discipline with the culturally disadvantaged differ for obvious reasons from the problems of disciplining the suburban child. Punishment at home is often quick and physical; at school he must learn new skills and new ways of behaving. It is a fact that the best way to eliminate behavior problems is to have an exciting, creative day planned for each child in which he develops a feeling of self-worth.

6. The teacher must change the cultural differences into cultural advantages. In an inner-city school in which I worked, I found a lovely old black grandmother who knew by heart some of the Uncle Remus stories. She told them to my fifth grade as I had never been able to tell them. Another mother, Mrs. Lupinski, came to school at my invitation to show the children how she crocheted doilies, dipped them in cooking sugar, and then shaped them into little baskets while they cooled—a custom she brought with her from Germany. Mr. Clyde, our head custodian, came to our room and told the children about his hobby—coin cleaning. We each cleaned a bright penny on that day.

The mixture of races and ethnic groups provides a potpourri of resources which the teacher must be willing to tap.

7. The teacher of the disadvantaged must be concerned with the total

growth of the child: his intellectual, social, emotional, and physical well-being.

8. The teacher must be willing to work with parents and be responsible for their education to the degree that she can promote the education of each individual child.

9. The teacher must be continually aware of the language problems of the disadvantaged. She will not "impose" her often uncommunicative language on them, but will seek ways to use her own language to develop a communication system. She will not serve as a judge to their language, customs, and expressions, but as a model for helping them. She will endeavor never to make a child ashamed of his speech or of the system of speech he uses with his parents.

10. All this calls for a creative approach to teaching and learning. This volume is rich with experiences developed with culturally disadvantaged children (see p. 28, p. 330, p. 158, and p. 204) and with creative experiences which could be developed with them (see p. 85, p. 173, p. 175, and p. 208).

Teaching Language Arts to the Disadvantaged Child

Oral Expression

Obviously the first step in working with the disadvantaged child is to plan experiences and establish rapport which will give him feelings of security, self-worth, strong motivation to school, trust in people, and a desire to learn. The base for all his formal instruction must stem from a well developed, strong program in oral English. If these children are to develop language skills in using English dialects obviously they must receive instruction at the oral level consistently. Reading and handwriting can wait: listening, thinking, and speaking are basic.

This well developed program in oral expression will not be geared to teaching standard English or "correct" grammar. From the material cited above, we can conclude that the best way to internalize speech patterns and to understand them is to hear and speak them through every day living and that the conditions under which children live together (sense of security, the eagerness to be accepted in peer groups, etc.) play a greater part in the acquisition of speech patterns than formal drill.

The basic adjustments which must be made in applying ideas for teaching oral expression as expressed in Chapter 6 of this book are: (1) these creative ideas and others may be adapted to classrooms of culturally disadvantaged children *if* the techniques are built on experiences within the child's life style; (2) the goals for teaching language must be altered from the ordinary school in that a dialect or dialects must be accepted as standard speech; and (3) standard language patterns become another dialect in the environment: one which is taught through usage by the teacher but not to the exclusion of the neighborhood dialects.

There is no reason why the vocabularies of children in culturally deprived schools cannot be expanded through the use of an experience such as "Sally Flack and the Rabbit," as told on page 143, with the children using as a theme the story of a dog or cat looking for a home instead of a rabbit.

The list of activities for the development of oral expression on page 152 can all be adapted to classrooms with deprived children. All children have *experiences* from which to draw a vocabulary: it is the *type* of experience which differs among schools. Schools can provide new types of experiences for children and help compensate for the limited vocabularies brought from home.

One migrant child's parents came from Florida to a small New York State town to pick apples. The child entered school along with other migrant children but was withdrawn and ill-at-ease. For two weeks she did not speak one word to her teacher. One day another child brought in a snake which he had caught in the orchard. When the children began to talk about snakes Alice suddenly became a fountainhead of information. Her father, it turned out, worked in a snake show in Florida during the winter months. This was the first experience in school where she had felt she had anything to contribute.

The dialect and verbal expressions of disadvantaged children are often beautifully said and worthy of recording. It was Jack, a twelve year old in a slum school who said to me, "It glows with fluorescent beauty" when I showed him how to use the magic chalk and the black light. And on another day he said, "When you turn the light on, the chalk is like burning ribbons." When Bill, a southern black boy, told my class he would "tote a poke" (bring his lunch) to school the children were delighted with the expression and for several days each child in the class went around saying he was going to tote a poke.

Reading

Greene and Petty list the following characteristics as affecting the disadvantaged child's success in learning to read:

1. His habit of inattention, as well as the careless speech of models in the home, will cause him to have difficulty with auditory discrimination skills.

2. His short attention span, along with his orientation toward motoric learning, will cause him to be inattentive and probably easily discouraged.

3. His lack of ability to conceptualize and to relate will cause him to have difficulty in understanding generalizations.

4. The lack of variety of visual stimuli in his environment may give him difficulty with skills of visual discrimination.

These authors emphasize the need for particular attention in the following areas in preparing the primary disadvantaged child for a reading program: (1) vocabulary development, (2) auditory discrimination, (3) word forms and tenses, (4) sentence patterns, (5) perceiving relationships, (6) practice in muscular coordination, and (7) listening activities.

On the middle grade level, these authors advocate: (1) continued vocabulary building, (2) continued experiences through field trips, records, movies, etc., (3) the use of homemade, unique materials such as experience charts, (4) oral usage drills, especially with a tape recorder, (5) provision for wide range of reading abilities through varied, interesting materials, and (6) the continued development of a worthy self image.

All scholars do not agree on a method for teaching reading to the disadvantaged child, especially the disadvantaged child with a dialect.

Linguists have some viewpoints of interest. Wardhaugh[9] states:

> When teachers are confronted with the task of teaching reading to children who speak a nonstandard dialect, they should be aware that the task of modifying a nonstandard dialect is a task of a different kind from that of teaching reading, and the two tasks should be kept strictly apart at all times.
>
> . . . Teachers must recognize that children who speak a nonstandard dialect control a complete phonological system that they can learn to relate to the English spelling system.

Wardhaugh goes on to point out that this relationship may not be the same which holds for standard dialect and that the differences may be minor ones. For instance, some phonemic contrasts may be different and the sounds used to realize the phonemic contrasts may differ . . . The teacher's task is to relate the entire phonological system controlled by the children to the English writing system so that they can understand

9. Ronald Wardhaugh, *Reading: A Linguistic Perspective* (New York: Harcourt, Brace and World, 1969), pp. 125–127.

that English employs an alphabetic writing system which they must master in order to be able to read.

Teachers of reading should build on the fact that the sounds of nonstandard dialects are systematic, that English orthography is for the most part systematic and that the two systems are related.

Wardhaugh states that there is no need to teach children a new dialect to teach them to read. He goes on to say that methods that succeed with speakers of standard dialects can succeed with speakers of nonstandard dialects, provided the teachers realize they are teaching reading, not speaking. They should deliberately exploit the patterns of the nonstandard dialects.

Many educators feel the basic approach to teaching disadvantaged children is to familiarize the child with other forms of dialects (standard language being one such form) at the oral or spoken level and then proceed to teach in the normal language sequence. When such a plan is followed with disadvantaged children, much of the reading material must be made by the teacher insofar as little of the current commercial reading material reflects the experiences or the dialect differences in speaking of the disadvantaged children.

If the teacher will remember that the reading lessons of the disadvantaged must be constructed around their experiences, using to a large degree the words which they are speaking, most of the procedures recounted in the chapter on reading are applicable to the disadvantaged child.

Difficulties will be encountered in phonics training where a cluster of letters sound differently in different dialects. One logical solution is to help the children become aware of the many possible sounds the cluster can produce in different dialects. For instance, one teacher in a first grade found that several southern Negroes pronounced worm as wuhm. Other pronunciations were observed and listed such as *woim* (Brooklyn), *wuhm* (a girl from England), and *worm* (upstate New York). The children enjoyed making charts of words where the same letter combinations (in this case *or*) made different sounds.

Writing Mechanics

The sequence of language development for the culturally disadvantaged child is the same as for any other. Once these children have many words to say they will be able to read them. Then with the image of the words in their minds and with knowledge of word structure and phonics, they are able to write. The teacher will consistently introduce the children to printed words as they dictate stories, newspapers, charts, and aids such as those suggested in Chapter 6. Providing many reasons for writing is an essential step in working with the disadvantaged child, for the usual motivations are not always present. Letters by children to their parents, for instance, are not always possible or accepted by parents of the disadvantaged, but letters of invitation to a school function may be substituted. Experiences in the form of a daily newspaper, class projects such as those described in Chapters 6 and 9, and letters of thanks to people who hosted the class on a trip all make for logical substitutes for these particular children. The chapters on creative writing and grammar provide the teacher with many strategies which will work well with the disadvantaged child.

Summary

Teaching communication arts to culturally disadvantaged children calls for some unique knowledges and skills. Primary among these is a thorough knowledge on the part of the teacher as to why each child is disadvantaged and the identification of his unique problems. A special type of teacher personality is needed to work with disadvantaged children: one who really loves and cares about children, one who is honestly unbiased and can control her prejudices, one who is flexible and can alter her values according to the situation.

The teacher of the disadvantaged must understand dialects and be willing and able to adjust her teaching strategies so she can place the emphasis on the dialect of the child, teaching standard English as another dialect. She will be particularly sensitive to providing many direct and vicarious experiences in school and will exhaust the possibilities for developing vocabulary from each such experience. She will place great emphasis on a planned, deliberate program in oral expression and will then use the children's own vocabulary to invent reading and writing materials which use the new vocabulary words. The teacher of the disadvantaged must be skilled in making her own teaching materials and in adapting commercial materials to individuals in her classroom. She will be able to capitalize on the experiences of the disadvantaged child so his background can be put to use to develop his own self-confidence and his own language.

Dealing effectively with disadvantaged children means prime attention must be given to individual differences, and materials must be created or adapted to individual needs. Truly creative teachers are needed to fill such positions.

To the Reader

1. If you have never visited an inner-city or rural "disadvantaged" school, call for an appointment and plan on a visit. Do not just observe; make plans to talk to people involved in the instruction of children so that you can identify the problems of the inner-city school and see how personnel are attempting to arrive at solutions.
2. Great emphasis has been placed on culturally and educationally deprived schools in urban areas. Several years ago, this author worked on a project for a culturally deprived school in a rural area. Can you imagine what this school was like? List what its problems were.
3. Many students of creative thinking feel that the Montessori method is a noncreative approach to learning, and that Montessori teaches so-called creativity in noncreative ways. Deutsch advocates the use of Montessori methods for the culturally disadvantaged child. How do you justify this; how do you resolve these two diverse viewpoints?
4. The values of disadvantaged children are often very different than the values of the children in the schools to which they are bussed. Migrant children in one school took fruit given to the teacher (left on her desk) because they were hungry and had grown up with the concept that any food left in sight was available to ease their hunger. To the middle class children taking anything from the teacher's desk was stealing. Differences in values such as this constitute the reason why tensions exist in classrooms between peers and teacher. Since the basic need of the disadvantaged child is to feel accepted, wanted, and comfortable in his school environment before any learning can take place, how can the teacher proceed to handle such problems so that mutual understandings and values will be developed other than moralizing (which children resent and which is ineffective)?
5. How might you use the tape recorder to help develop oral standard English in a migrant school with many dialects?
6. Migrant children are often rejected by the community because they come to school in September while their parents pick fruit, and leave to return to pick fruit in Florida in November. Taxpayers feel these transients overpopulate the classrooms, burden the teachers, consume supplies, and yet pay no taxes for these services. List all the complaints against migrants that you can think of and then work out a plan for educating the citizenry to accepting them in the town and school.
7. Although many homes of disadvantaged children are impoverished, they contain television sets. In terms of language development is this beneficial or detrimental? In terms of social values?

Selected Bibliography

BELLACK, ARNO A., et al. *The Language of the Classroom.* New York: Teachers' College Press, 1967.

BLACK, MILLARD H. "Characteristics of the Culturally Disadvantaged Child," *Reading Teacher,* 18 (March 1965), 465–470.

BRYNGELSON, BRYING, AND ELAINE MIDALSON. *Speech Correction Through Listening.* Chicago: Scott, Foresman and Company, 1959.

CARTER, HOMER L. J., AND DOROTHY MCGINNIS. *Diagnosis and Treatment of the Disabled Reader.* New York: The Macmillan Company, 1970.

COHEN, S. ALAN. *Teach Them All to Read: Theory, Methods, and Materials for Teaching the Disadvantaged.* New York: Random House, Inc., 1969.

CORBIN, RICHARD, AND MURIEL CROSBY. *Language Programs for Disadvantaged.* Champaign, Illinois: National Council of Teachers of English, 1965.

DAVIS, ALLISON. *Social Class Influence Upon Learning.* Cambridge, Massachusetts: Harvard University Press, 1962.

DUNN, LLOYD M. *Exceptional Children in the Schools.* New York: Holt, Rinehart and Winston, Inc., 1963.

FRANK, VIRGINIA. *New Curricular Materials and the Teaching of the Disadvantaged* (Project Report/One). Washington, D.C.: The NDEA National Institute for Advanced Study in Teaching Disadvantaged Youth, May 1968.

FRIES, CHARLES C. *Linguistics and Reading.* New York: Holt, Rinehart and Winston, Inc., 1963.

FROST, JOE L., AND GLENN R. HAWKES. *The Disadvantaged Child: Issues and Innovations.* Boston: Houghton Mifflin Company, 1966.

GREEN, WILLIAM D. "Language and the Culturally Different," *English Journal,* 54 (November 1965), 724–733.

KOHL, HERBERT R. *The Open Classroom.* New York: Random House, Inc., 1970.

MILLER, HARRY L. (ed.). *Education for the Disadvantaged.* New York: The Free Press, 1967.

PONDER, EDDIE G. "Understanding the Language of the Culturally Disadvantaged Child," *Elementary English,* 42 (November 1965), 769–774.

WARDHAUGH, RONALD. *Reading: A Linguistic Perspective.* New York: Harcourt, Brace and World, 1969.

WEBSTER, STATEN (ed.). *The Disadvantaged Learner.* San Francisco: Chandler Publishing Company, 1966.

WITTY, PAUL A. (ed.). *The Educationally Retarded and Disadvantaged.* The Sixty-Sixth Yearbook of the National Society for the Study of Education, Part 1. Chicago: University of Chicago Press, 1967.

14

Adventures in Communication

Come to the Fair

Attending a Language Arts Fair was a worthwhile learning adventure. It was an "end-of-the-year" activity in an ungraded middle school, and the children were holding the fair with several purposes in mind.

(1) To review the language facts they had learned during the past year.
(2) To teach some language facts to younger children or to children who had not been exposed to such work.
(3) To show that language can be fun.
(4) To demonstrate how language arts can be integrated with art, music, social studies, science, and mathematics.

The chairs had been removed from the room, and various committees of children had converted the desks into booths around the edge of the large classroom. This was simply done by grouping the desks into the size required for the booth, covering the desks with a bright construction or crepe paper skirt, and then cutting from cardboard (mattress boxes, paper towel boxes, and portable chalkboard packing boxes) a top or a backing to the booth, which also contained a sign telling what activity was taking place. The booths were painted with bright colors and decorated with balloons. Balloons and mobiles were also suspended from the ceiling, providing a festive atmosphere.

Each booth was designed to meet a definite objective: the result of several brainstorming sessions held by the teachers and the class. One was a fishpond. The objective: to show how well the children could use root words to construct larger words. A child was given a pole with a hook on the end. Little boats made of styrofoam floated in large tubs at the rear of the booth. Along the side of a mural of clouds and water which backed the bobbing boats was a list of suffixes and prefixes. If a child "caught" a boat, he discovered that the tiny sail unfolded to give a root word. He then had to make up five words using that root word (he could get help from the prefix and suffix list on the back of the booth). For example, if a child drew the word "law," he could make the words: (1) lawyer, (2) lawless, (3) lawsuit, (4) lawful, and (5) mother-in-law, and win the boat as a prize.

In another booth a "Game of Fortune" was going on. Children were given a set of cards on which they had written sentences. A wheel at the back of the booth was marked around the rim with the punctuation marks. The wheel was spun until it stopped with the pointer showing one punctuation mark, and the contestants had to select from their cards the sentence which needed that particular punctuation mark. Five correct choices entitled the winners to a poker chip. These chips were counted at the close of the fair, and the child having the largest number received a grand prize—a game of anagrams, of course.

At another booth, the children's ability to rhyme words was tested. A child drew an envelope from a box, opened it, and then had to select a rhyming word from the list posted in the booth.

The ability to tell parts of speech was the theme of a booth labeled "How Good Is Your Grammar?" At this booth the children found many words printed individually on cards. Again, a wheel at the rear of the booth on which were printed the names of the parts of speech was spun, and if the pointer showed the word "noun," the first child who could find a noun on one of the cards held it up. If he won three out of five trials, he received a poker chip.

At one end of the fair, tables were set up and decorated for a WORDO game played like BINGO except that the children covered letters (instead of numbers) with transparent disks until they had formed a word on the WORDO card. Prizes were poker chips which counted toward the anagram game.

In another booth, balloons were fastened to cardboards. On each balloon, printed in flo-pen, was a word form such as their, there, to, too, two, waist, waste, etc. A card was held up to a player with a word missing such as "I have seen ______ books." If he then threw a dart and popped the balloon with the word "their," he was awarded a poker chip.

Down the center of the room was an irregular walk made of sheets of newsprint taped to the floor. There was a starting place at which each child entered the maze. He spun a cardboard disk until it rested on a certain number, then he advanced to the third paper. Each paper had certain directions on it, such as, "Tell the tender of the booth what we call a word that is the name of a person, place, or thing," or "Who is the author of Tom Sawyer?" or "Give the tender of the booth a synonym for 'angry,' " etc.

Lively fair music was played on a victrola, and the entire show was run by the children.

I have rarely seen such demonstrations of creative thinking applied to reality! Truly, this was an exciting adventure in creative communication.

Adventures in Communication

This volume has attempted to show that the process of communication, man's one highly developed and unique ability, is a great adventure. It has described, throughout, creative adventures in communication planned by teachers and children. Learning correct and effective means to communicate can be a great adventure, provided that the creative approach to teaching communication skills is used. No subject area in the school curriculum provides more opportunities to foster the development of creativity in both student and teacher than the area of the language arts. Creative teaching of the language arts provides better and quicker ways of learning *correct* skills so that children may exercise social courtesy in their communication. Creative teaching also pays homage to the beauty of language itself and encourages children to manipulate it, mold it, experiment with it, use it, and control it.

Creative use of language means developing metaphor, perhaps one of the most obvious characteristics of creative people. Simply, creative use of language is not just seeing the seashore as sand and water, but seeing it as Andrea, age 12, sees it:

The Seashore

Walking on the seashore at dawn, hearing only the rippling of the almost-still waters or the pounding of the angry surf against the rocks, one finds there is peace enough to pacify even the stormiest of hearts. There is a certain tranquility that makes troubles fly as do the gulls, with their swift, strong strokes, giving a certain beauty that heartens the saddest of lives.

The seashore is a place to rest, a refuge from the pushing, maddening crowds of the city. Here we can air our thoughts freely, with no one but the gulls to bear our secrets away on the wind.

Perhaps this is only an illusion, we feel,—but somehow we know that this is a place for our hearts and our souls, free from the everyday troubles of life.

> As the sunset comes, we realize it will soon be night, and the darkness will close in for another day, leaving us the image of the blue sky and waters with their star reflections. But we are not disappointed, as God leaves us with a beautiful memory and the assurance that today will come again.
>
> —Andrea Forte
> Grade 7

And, to the teacher who teaches language arts through planned adventures in communication, teaching is more than a monotonous, routine repetition of experiences, a dreary routine, a deadly rut. It has been said that a rut is only a grave still open at both ends! Creative teaching can keep that grave from closing in. Creative approaches to language arts teaching can make each year—even each day—an experience to anticipate and enjoy. Through teaching, the creative potential of teachers can become self-realized.

Appendix A

Teacher ______________________ Grade __________ Date ____________

Characteristics of Creative Children

(Most commonly listed in research)

Child *Characteristic*															
1. Sensitive to life experiences															
2. Reacts more fully to emotions															
3. Superior verbal facility															
4. Superior verbal fluency															

5. Superior verbal flexibility															
6. General flexibility															
7. Originality															
8. Prefers perceiving to judging															
9. Self-sufficient															
10. Independent in judgement															
11. More stable															
12. Sense of humor—playfulness															
13. More interested in unconventional roles															
14. More feminine (masc.) in interests															
15. More dominant and self-assertive															
16. Often estranged from peers															
17. More adventurous and resourceful															
18. Great energy—zest—effectiveness															
19. Challenged by disorder															
20. Less susceptible to group pressures															

21. Always baffled by something															
22. Constructive in criticism															
23. Defies conventions of courtesy															
24. Industrious															
25. Introversive															
26. Receptive to ideas of others															
27. Attracted to the mysterious and unknown															
28. Attempts difficult jobs (sometimes too difficult)															
29. Persistent															
30. Self-starter															

Index

D

E

J

K

L

M

T

V

W

Y

Z